ANNOTATED INSTRUCTOR'S EDITION

Fourth Edition

MOSAICS

FOCUSING ON ESSAYS

KIM FLACHMANN
California State University, Bakersfield

Upper Saddle River, New Jersey 07458

Editorial Director: *Leah Jewell*
Editor-in-Chief: *Craig Campanella*
Editorial Assistant: *Deborah Doyle*
Director of Marketing: *Brandy Dawson*
Marketing Manager: *Lindsey Prudhomme*
Marketing Assistant: *Kimberly Caldwell*
VP/Director of Production and Manufacturing: *Barbara Kittle*
Production Liaison: *Maureen Benicasa*
Production Editor: *Karen Berry, Pine Tree Composition, Inc.*
Copyeditor: *Patricia M. Daly*
Text Permission Specialist: *Jane Scelta*
Prepress & Manufacturing Manager: *Nick Sklitsis*
Prepress & Manufacturing Buyer: *Ben Smith*
Creative Design Director: *Leslie Osher*
Interior & Cover Designer: *Kathy Mrozek*
Director, Image Resource Center: *Melinda Patelli*
Manager, Rights and Permissions: *Zina Arabia*
Manager, Visual Research: *Beth Brenzel*
Image Permission Coordinator: *Robert Farrell*
Cover Art: *Photos.com*
Composition: *Pine Tree Composition, Inc.*
Printer/Binder: *The Courier Companies*
Cover Printer: *Phoenix Color Corp.*

This book was set in 11/13 Goudy.
Credits and acknowledgments borrowed from other sources and reproduced, with permission, in this textbook appear on appropriate page within text (or on pages 827–829).

Pearson Education LTD., London
Pearson Education Australia PTY, Limited
Pearson Education Singapore, Pte. Ltd
Pearson Education North Asia Ltd
Pearson Education, Canada, Ltd
Pearson Educación de Mexico, S.A. de C.V.
Pearson Education–Japan
Pearson Education Malaysia, Pte. Ltd
Pearson Education, Upper Saddle River, New Jersey

For
Michael

10 9 8 7 6 5 4 3 2 1

BRIEF CONTENTS

CONTENTS

PART IV The Handbook 509

PREFACE

Experience tells us that students have the best chance of succeeding in college if they learn how to respond productively to the varying academic demands made on them throughout the curriculum. One extremely important part of this process is being able to analyze ideas and think critically about issues in many different subject areas. *Mosaics: Focusing on Essays* is the third in a series of three books that teach the basic skills essential to all good academic writing. This series illustrates how the companion skills of reading and writing are parts of a larger, interrelated process that moves back and forth through the tasks of prereading and reading, prewriting and writing, and revising and editing. In other words, the *Mosaics* series shows how these skills are integrated at every stage of the communication process.

OVERALL GOAL

Ultimately, each book in the *Mosaics* series portrays writing as a way of thinking and processing information. One by one, these books encourage students to discover how the "mosaics" of their own reading and writing processes work together to form a coherent whole. By demonstrating the interrelationship among thinking, reading, and writing on progressively more difficult levels, these books promise to help prepare students for success in college throughout the curriculum.

THE *MOSAICS* SERIES

The *Mosaics* series consists of three books, each with a different emphasis: *Focusing on Sentences in Context*, *Focusing on Paragraphs in Context*, and *Focusing on Essays*. The first book highlights sentence structure, the second book paragraph development, and the third the composition of essays. Part I of each book demonstrates both the reading and writing processes as students are guided toward a reading and writing routine that fits their lifestyle. Each book also asks students to begin writing in the very first chapter and moves from personal to more academic writing. The books differ in the length and level of their reading selections, the complexity of their writing assignments, the degree of difficulty of their revising and editing strategies, and the length and level of their student writing samples.

This entire three-book series is based on the following fundamental assumptions:

- Students build confidence in their ability to read and write by reading and writing.
- Students learn best from discovery and experimentation rather than from instruction and abstract discussions.
- Students need to discover their personal reading and writing processes.
- Students learn both individually and collaboratively.
- Students profit from studying both professional and student writing.
- Students benefit most from assignments that actually integrate thinking, reading, and writing.
- Students learn how to revise by following clear guidelines.
- Students learn grammar and usage rules by editing their own writing.
- Students must be able to transfer their writing skills to all their college courses.
- Students must think critically and analytically to succeed in college.

UNIQUE FEATURES

The goal of any writing text is to produce stronger writers. With *Mosaics*, students encounter many unique and exciting features designed to help them become stronger writers.

With *Mosaics,* students become stronger writers by writing more often and learning from their own writing.

- Early in each chapter of Part II: Writing Effective Essays, students are asked to write their own essay with the **"Preparing to Write Your Own Essay"** and **"Writing Your Own Essay"** boxes. These boxes prompt students to write their own essay early in each chapter so they may learn from it throughout the chapter. (For example, see pages 127, 130, 161, and 164)
- Throughout each chapter in Part II, students learn from their own writing in the **"Your Own Essay"** section. This section walks students through the steps of both revising and editing, using their own work as the guide. (For example, see pages 138 and 171)

- In Part IV: The Handbook, students learn from their own writing in each of the 27 grammar chapters. After each concept, three types of exercises are presented: **Identifying** (in which students simply choose the correct word), **Completing** (in which students fill in a blank), and **Writing Your Own** (for which students draft their own correct sentences). (For example, see pages 533, 535, and 536)
- In the Appendix, *Mosaics* offers **guided worksheets for peer- and self-evaluation.** These worksheets further help students learn from their own writing.

With *Mosaics,* students become stronger writers by becoming stronger readers.

- New Chapters—**Chapter 2: The Reading Process** and **Chapter 3: Reading Critically.** In the Fourth Edition, Kim Flachmann introduces the cyclical nature of the reading and writing process. Part I is now called Reading and Writing: An Overview. (For example, see Table of Contents on page vii.)
- **Reading Critically boxes further integrate reading and writing and teach 10 effective reading strategies.** These boxes occur in Part II, introducing students to reading strategies before they read a professional essay. (For example, see pages 124, 145, 149, 158, 177, and 181)
- **Professional Readings moved into Part II: Reading and Writing Effective Essays.** Each chapter in Part II now both begins and ends with professional essays, further demonstrating the connection between reading and writing for students. There are 28 professional readings in all. (For example, see pages 125, 145, 149, 159, 177, and 182)

Other Unique Features of *Mosaics:*

- It moves students systematically from personal to academic writing.
- It teaches rhetorical modes as patterns of thought.
- It uses both student and professional writing as models.
- It demonstrates all aspects of the writing process throughout student writing.
- It features culturally diverse reading selections that are of high interest to students.
- It includes a complete handbook with exercises.

Students can also become stronger writers with *MyWritingLab,* which comes automatically with every new copy of *Mosaics.*

My*WritingLab* is the first complete learning system that will truly help students become successful writers.

- **A Comprehensive Writing Program:** *MyWritingLab* includes over 9,000 exercises in grammar, writing process, paragraph and essay development, and research.
- **Diagnostic Testing:** *MyWritingLab* includes a comprehensive diagnostic test that thoroughly assesses students' skills in grammar. Based on the diagnostic test results, the students' study plan will reflect the areas where they need help the most and those areas that they have mastered.
- **Recall, Apply, and Write Exercises:** The heart of *MyWritingLab* is the progression of exercises found in each topic. In completing the **Recall, Apply, and Write** exercises, students move from literal comprehension (**Recall**) to critical comprehension (**Apply**) to demonstrating concepts in their own writing (**Write**). This recursive learning process, not available in any other online resource, enables students to master the skills and concepts they need to be successful writers.
- **Grade Book:** All students' work in *MyWritingLab* is captured in the site's Grade Book. Students can track their own progress and instructors can track the progress of their entire class in this flexible and easy-to-use tool.

For more information and to view a demo, go to www.mywritinglab.com!

Instructor Support for *Mosaics:*

- **Annotated Instructor's Edition:** The AIE contains the answers to all the exercises in the text and teaching tips for instructors in the margins (ISBN: 0-13-231968-3).
- **Instructor's Resource Manual with Student Answer Key:** This manual includes sample syllabi, chapter summaries, additional chapter quizzes, and a textbook answer key for instructors who want to give their students access to the text's answers (ISBN: 0-13-231965-7).
- **The Comprehensive Prentice Hall Writing Test Generator:** The best exercises from Prentice Hall's many instructor resources, organized by topic, have been put into a database of over 8,000 writing exercises for quiz and test generation. Comes complete with easy-to-use test-generating software. (ISBN: 0-13-194643-9).

Additional Student Support for *Mosaics:*

College adopters can package any two of these student supplements with *Mosaics*. Please consult your local Prentice Hall representative for the correct package ISBNs. Call 1-800-526-0485, or email us at: English_service@prenhall.com.

Adkins, *The Prentice Hall Grammar Workbook, Second Edition*
250 pages of additional grammar instruction and practice (ISBN: 0-13-194771-0)

Lumpkins, *The Prentice Hall Editing Workbook*
200 pages of grammar instruction and practice, from an editing perspective (ISBN: 0-13-189352-1)

Davis, *Applying English to Your Career*
Summaries and practice of 25 key writing topics, focusing on 7 specific career fields (ISBN: 0-13-192115-0)

Miller, *The Prentice Hall ESL Workbook, Second Edition*
Additional instruction and practice on challenging topics for nonnative speakers (ISBN: 0-13-194759-1)

McGrath, *The Prentice Hall Writer's Journal*
A true writing journal, the spiral bound, 128-page blank book includes access to the Tutor Center (ISBN: 0-13-184900-X)

Levine-Brown, *The Prentice Hall Florida Exit Test Study Guide for Writing*
A workbook specifically designed for the Florida Exit Test (ISBN: 0-13-111652-5)

Nealy, *The Prentice Hall THEA Study Guide for Writing*
A workbook specifically designed for the Texas Higher Education Assessment (ISBN: 0-13-041585-5)

Prentice Hall Pocket Readers. Six different books of about 25 selections each, these pocket readers are perfect for instructors who want more selections for their students. Available in Patterns, Themes, Argument, Literature, Writing Across the Curriculum, and Purposes.

The New American Webster Handy College Dictionary, Third Edition (ISBN: 0-13-032870-7)

The New American Roget's College Thesaurus (ISBN: 0-13-145258-0)

HOW THIS BOOK WORKS

Mosaics: Focusing on Essays teaches students how to read and write critically. For flexibility and easy reference, this book is divided into four parts:

Part I: Reading and Writing: An Overview
Part II: Reading and Writing Effective Essays
Part III: The Research Paper
Part IV: The Handbook

Part I: Reading and Writing: An Overview All seven chapters in Part I demonstrate the cyclical nature of the reading and writing processes. They begin with the logistics of getting ready to read and write and then move systematically through the interlocking stages of the processes by following a student from prereading to rereading and then from prewriting to revising and editing. Part I ends with four review practices that summarize the material and let your students practice what they have learned.

Part II: Reading and Writing Effective Essays Part II, the heart of the instruction in this text, teaches students how to read and write essays by introducing the rhetorical modes as patterns of development. It moves from personal writing to more academic types of writing: describing, narrating, illustrating, analyzing a process, comparing and contrasting, dividing and classifying, defining, analyzing causes and effects, and arguing. Within each chapter, students learn to read critically and write their own essay, study the essay of another student, read professional essays with guidance, and finally revise and edit the essay they wrote earlier in the chapter. Two professional writing samples are now included in each rhetorical mode chapter so students can actually see the features of each strategy at work in different pieces of writing. Each professional essay is preceded by prereading activities that will help students focus on the topic at hand and then is followed by 10 questions that move students from literal to analytical thinking as they consider the essay's content, purpose, audience, and paragraph structure. By following specific guidelines, students learn how to produce a successful essay using each rhetorical mode.

Part III: The Research Paper The next section of this text helps students move from writing effective essays to writing a research paper by systematically illustrating the details of writing a paper with sources. Then it explains the paper through student examples. Part III ends with a series of writing assignments and workshops designed to encourage students to write, revise, and edit a term paper and then reflect on their own writing process.

Part IV: The Handbook Part IV is a complete grammar/usage handbook, including exercises, that covers eight units: Sentences, Verbs, Pronouns, Modifiers, Punctuation, Mechanics, Effective Sentences, and Choosing the Right Word. These categories are coordinated with the Editing Checklist that appears periodically throughout this text. Each chapter starts with five self-test questions so that students can determine their strengths and weaknesses in a specific area. The chapters provide at least three types of practice after each grammar concept, moving the students systematically from identifying grammar concepts to filling in the blanks to writing their own sentences. Each chapter ends with a practical editing workshop that asks students to use the skills they just learned as they work with another student to edit their own writing. Unit pretests and posttests—including practice with single sentences and paragraphs—are offered for each unit at the end of the handbook.

APPENDIXES

The appendixes will help students keep track of their progress in the various skills they are learning in this text. References to these appendixes are interspersed throughout the book so that students know when to use them as they study the concepts in each chapter:

Appendix 1: Critical Thinking Log

Appendix 2: Revising and Editing Peer Evaluation Forms

Appendix 3: Revising and Editing Peer Evaluation Forms for a Research Paper

Appendix 4: Test Yourself Answers

Appendix 5: Editing Quotient Error Chart

Appendix 6: Error Log

Appendix 7: Spelling Log

ACKNOWLEDGMENTS

I want to acknowledge the support, encouragement, and sound advice of several people who have helped me through the development of the *Mosaics* series. First, Prentice Hall has provided guidance and inspiration for this project through the enduring wisdom of Craig Campanella, editor-in-chief; the insight and vision of Marta Tomins and Harriett Prentiss, development editors; Maureen Benicasa, production liaison; Karen Berry, production editor; the foresight and prudence of Leah Jewell, editorial director; the special creative inspiration of Lindsey Prudhomme, marketing manager; Rochelle Diogenes, editor-in-chief of development; the brilliant leadership of Yolanda de Rooy, President of Humanities and Social Sciences; the hard work and patience of Jane Scelta, permissions editor; Patricia M. Daly, copyeditor; and the organization of Deborah Doyle, administrative assistant for developmental English. Also, this book would not be a reality without the insightful persistence of Phil Miller, publisher for modern languages.

I want to give very special thanks to Cheryl Smith, my constant source of inspiration in her role as consultant and adviser for the duration of this project. She was also the author of the margin annotations and the coordinator of the *Mosaics Instructor's Resource Manuals*. I am also grateful to Rebecca Hewett, Valerie Turner, and Li'i Pearl for their discipline and hard work on the *Instructor's Resource Manuals* for each of the books in the series. And I want to thank Laura Peet and Randi Brummett for their expertise and assistance and Tara Polhamus for her technical help.

In addition, I am especially indebted to the following reviewers who have guided me through the development and revision of this book: Lisa Berman, Miami-Dade Community College; Patrick Haas, Glendale Community College; Jeanne Campanelli, American River College; Dianne Gregory, Cape Cod Community College; Clara Wilson-Cook, Southern University at New Orleans; Thomas Beery, Lima Technical College; Jean Petrolle, Columbia College; David Cratty, Cuyahoga Community College; Allison Travis, Butte State College; Suellen Meyer, Meramec Community College; Jill Lahnstein, Cape Fear Community College; Stanley Coberly, West Virginia State University at Parkersville; Jamie Moore, Scottsdale Community College; Nancy Hellner, Mesa Community College; Ruth Hatcher, Washtenaw Community College; Thurmond Whatley, Aiken Technical College; W. David Hall, Columbus State Community College; Marilyn Coffee, Fort Hays State University; Teriann Gaston, University of Texas at Arlington; Peggy Karsten, Ridgewater College; Nancy Hayward, Indiana University of Pennsylvania; Carol Ann Britt, San Antonio College; Maria C. Villar-Smith, Miami-Dade Community College; Jami L. Huntsinger, University of New Mexico at Valencia Campus; P. Berniece Longmore, Essex County College; Lee Herrick, Fresno City College; Elaine Chakonas, North Eastern Illinois University; and Roy Warner, Montana State University.

I also want to express my gratitude to my students, from whom I have learned so much about the writing process, about teaching, and about life itself. Thanks finally to the students who contributed paragraphs and essays to this series: Josh Ellis, Jolene Christie, Mary Minor, Michael Tiede, and Juliana Schweiger.

Finally, I owe a tremendous personal debt to the people who have lived with this project for the last twelve years; they are my closest companions and my best advisers: Michael, Christopher, and Laura Flachmann. To Michael, I owe additional thanks for the valuable support and feedback he has given me through the entire process of creating and revising this series.

Kim Flachmann

Reading and Writing: An Overview

“There is an art of reading, as well as an art of thinking and an art of writing.”

—Isaac D'Israeli

We have learned from experience that reading and writing are so closely related that succeeding in one is directly related to success in the other. So the goal of this part is to help you develop self-confidence as a reader *and* writer. It will give you the basic tools you need to improve your reading and writing. Then, as you move through these seven chapters, you will discover how to adjust these processes to suit your own needs and preferences. As you become more aware of the choices available to you, you will also develop a better understanding of your strengths and weaknesses as a reader and writer. With practice, your personalized reading and writing processes will soon be a routine part of your academic life and will help you confirm your place in the community of college students.

CHAPTER 1

Reading and Writing in College

TEACHING READING AND WRITING IN COLLEGE

Ask your students to bring in a visual representation of them studying. It can be anything—cut-up magazines, something with props, a drawing—that conveys how they feel they look when they study. This exercise can be a real icebreaker if you approach it with a little humor.

TEACHING ON THE WEB

Discussion Topic: Divide students into groups of three or four. Ask the members of each group to think about the recursive steps they go through when they study. Can they map out these steps? Is their study process regulated? Or is it erratic? Have each group report its discussion to the class as a whole.

INSTRUCTOR'S RESOURCE MANUAL

For additional material about teaching reading

Words help us solve problems, discover new ideas, feel better, make people laugh, and understand the world around us. Reading and writing are companion processes for using words. They let us connect with our immediate environment—as we learn from our reading and contribute to society through writing.

WHY LEARN HOW TO READ AND WRITE WELL?

The better you read and write, the more completely you can connect with your environment and the more control you have over your daily routine. Reading and writing well let you understand precisely what issues are important and communicate exactly what you want to say about them. These companion skills actually help you get what you want out of life. So reading and writing well give you power—in a variety of ways.

Reading and Writing as Critical Thinking

Critical thinking is the highest form of mental activity that human beings engage in, and it is a major source of success in college and in life. Thinking critically involves grappling with the ideas, issues, and problems in your immediate environment and in the larger world. It means constantly questioning and analyzing different aspects of life. Since critical thinking is complex, it requires a great deal of concentration and practice. Once you have a sense of how your mind works at this level, you will be able to think critically whenever you want.

Reading and writing are companion activities that engage people in the creation of thought and meaning—either as readers interpreting a text or as writers constructing one. Clear thinking is the pivotal point that joins these two tasks. The traditional rhetorical strategies are presented in this text as ways of processing information that you can use in other academic assignments. We feature one strategy at a time in each chapter so you can understand how it works before you combine it with other strategies. In this way, you will be able to systematically improve your ability to think, read, and write critically.

With some guidance, learning how to read and write according to different rhetorical modes or strategies (such as describing, narrating, or dividing and classifying) can give you the mental workout you need to think critically in much the same way that physical exercise warms you up for various sports. As you move through the chapters in Part II, you will be asked to isolate each rhetorical mode—just as you isolate your abs, thighs, and biceps in a physical workout. Each rhetorical mode offers a slightly different way of seeing the world, processing information, and solving problems. So each rhetorical mode is really a different way of thinking and making sense of the world.

and writing, for journal entries, and for various tests, see the *Instructor's Resource Manual*, Section II, Part I.

Reading and Writing as Discovery

In both reading and writing, we often start out not knowing specifically where we are going. As we read, we are following another person's line of reasoning and discovering our own thoughts and reactions in response to our reading material. Similarly, we often don't actually know the points we want to make until we start writing. As we write, we discover what we think and want to say.

The physical acts of reading and writing help your mind sort through lots of ideas and help you decide exactly what you think and feel on specific topics. Sometimes new ideas will come out of something you have read. Or you might understand an idea better once you start writing about it. Whatever the case, the simple act of reading and writing lead to understanding—of both the subject matter and of your own thought processes.

The more you read and write, the more ideas you generate. This is why your instructor might suggest that you read and/or write if you are stuck on a topic or don't know what to say next. Reading and writing help you discover and express the good ideas that are already in your mind.

Reading and Writing as Necessities

Most important of all, reading and writing are necessary for surviving both in college and on the job. On a daily basis, you have to read and respond to a multitude of documents from endless e-mails to textbooks to professional reports. In addition, you will have to write more in today's electronic age than any previous generation has. Some of your writing will be reports or projects that extend over a long period of time. Other writing tasks will have to be completed immediately, such as responses to e-mail messages. Whatever the terms, reading and writing will be significant parts of your life throughout college and beyond.

The better your reading and writing skills, the better grades you will make in college and the further you will get in your chosen career. Everything you learn about reading and writing in this text applies to all your courses. These strategies will also be helpful on the job, especially when you have to read a dense analysis, write that difficult report, or summarize your accomplishments for a professional evaluation. The same reading and writing guidelines apply to all communication tasks.

PRACTICE 1 Answer the following questions.

1. Why should you learn to read and write?

   Basic reading and writing skills help us solve problems, discover new ideas, feel better, make people laugh, and understand the world around us.

2. Why should you learn to read and write well?

   Reading and writing well let us understand what is going on around us and communicate exactly what we mean. These skills actually help us get what we want out of life.

3. How can reading and writing help you think critically?

   Learning how to read and write according to different rhetorical modes can give us the mental workout we need to think critically just as physical exercise warms us up for various sports.

4. In what ways are reading and writing processes of discovery?

   Both reading and writing help our minds sort through ideas and decide what we think. New ideas can come from reading, and we may understand ideas better once we start writing about them.

5. Why are reading and writing necessary in today's world?

   Reading and writing are necessary for surviving both in college and on the job. You will have to read and write more in today's electronic age than any previous generation has.

THINKING OF YOURSELF AS A READER AND WRITER

Part of this important process is thinking of yourself as both a reader and a writer. You do these tasks every day in a variety of ways. Yet many people don't actually envision themselves as readers and writers. How we use words tends to be the hallmark of our success—no matter what our field. So learning how to read and write critically—at the highest possible level of performance—is a basic requirement for a meaningful, successful life.

Words are a commodity that you use every day and that can help you get what you want out of life. If you want to enter an e-mail conversation at work, you first need to read the words that have already been written. Then you must write your response. Any word choices you put forward reflect on you as a person. They are the grounds on which others judge you.

Whether you read e-mail messages, the newest best-seller novel, or a new agreement you received in the mail, you are a reader. Conversely, if you write a note on the refrigerator, e-mail a friend, write a paper for economics class, or draft a report for your boss, you are a writer. Now that you are in college, you are part of a very special community of readers and writers who are trying to perfect these skills and live your life at a more informed and intellectually stimulating level than your friends not attending college.

As you face more complex reading and writing tasks in college, you need to understand the sequence of activities that make up the reading and writing processes. Learning to use these processes so that the work you produce is the best you are capable of is what this book is all about.

Even though each reader and writer is different, some general principles apply to everyone—students and professionals alike. Before you actually begin to read or write, a wise move is to get your surroundings ready. That involves setting aside a time and place to do your work, gathering supplies, and establishing a routine.

1. **Set aside a special time to read and write, and plan to do nothing else during that time.** The bird's cage can wait to be cleaned until tomorrow, the furniture doesn't have to be dusted today, the garage can be hosed down some other time, and the dirt on your kitchen floor won't turn to concrete overnight. When you first get a reading or writing assignment, a little procrastination is natural. In fact, procrastination can actually work in your favor when you are writing because your mind is working on the task subconsciously. The trick is to know when to quit procrastinating and get down to work so that you meet your deadlines with time to spare.

2. **Find a comfortable place with few distractions.** Joyce Carol Oates, a famous contemporary writer, claims that writing is a very private act that requires lots of patience, time, and space. The same principle applies to reading. First, you need to set up a place to read and/or write that suits your specific needs. It should be a place where you are not distracted or interrupted. Some people work best in a straight-backed chair sitting at a table or desk, while others do their best work sitting cross-legged in bed. The exact place doesn't matter, as long as you can think there.

   Even if you are fortunate enough to have a private study area, you may find that you still want to make some adjustments. You may decide to unplug your phone during your study time. Or you may discover that quiet background music helps you shut out all kinds of noises but doesn't distract you the way talk shows and rock stations would. One student may do her best studying after soaking in a hot tub; another might play jazz when he is getting down to work; and still another may have a Pepsi on one side of his table and a Snicker's bar on the other. Whatever your choices, you need to set up a comfortable working environment.

3. **Gather your supplies before you begin to study.** Don't risk losing your great ideas by not being able to find a pen and paper or a zip disk. Some students keep a yellow tablet and a mechanical pencil by their sides as they study; others write directly in their books. In like manner, with writing, some students draft their essays on paper, and others write directly on their computers. One of the main advantages of writing on a computer is that once you word process your ideas, changing them or moving them around is easy. As a result, you are more likely to make revisions when you work on a computer, and you will therefore turn in a better paper. Whatever equipment you choose, make sure it is ready at the time you have set aside to study.

4. **Establish a personal ritual.** As a member of the community of students, acknowledging your own study habits and rituals is a major part of discovering your reading and writing processes. These rituals begin the minute you are given an assignment. What activities help you get ready to read? Some people exercise, others catch up on e-mail, and still others clean their rooms before they study. What activities prepare you to write? Most people do certain activities when they face reading and writing tasks without even realizing why. But they are preparing their minds for studying. So in the course of validating yourself as a reader and writer, take a moment now to record some of your own preferences and rituals connected with your study time.

PRACTICE 2 Explain the rituals you instinctively follow as you prepare to study. How do you prepare your mind for reading? Where do you write? At what time of day do you produce your best work? Do you like noise? Quiet? What other details describe your study environment? What equipment do you need to read and write? *Answers will vary.*

KEEPING A JOURNAL

The word **journal** refers to a daily log of your thinking. It is a place where you can record ideas, snatches of conversation, dreams, descriptions of people, pictures of places, and thoughts about objects—whatever catches your attention. Keeping a journal to respond to your reading and writing tasks will be very beneficial to your progress as a critical thinker. The more you respond in writing to what you are reading, the more engaged you are in your learning.

A good way to establish the habit of journal writing is to use your journal for answering the questions that accompany the instruction in Parts II and III of this text and the writing exercises in the handbook (Part IV). You should definitely use your journal to respond to your reading in this text, and you can also use it to jot down ideas and plans for essays as they occur to you. In addition, you might want to complete your prewriting activities in your journal. Keeping track of a journal is much easier than finding notes on assorted scraps of paper.

Making a section of your journal private is also a good idea. Sometimes, when you think on paper or let your imagination run free, you don't want to share the results with anyone. Yet those notes can be very important in finding a subject to write about or in developing a topic.

Your journal in college will essentially be a bank of thoughts and topics for you. If used thoughtfully, it can become an incredible resource—a place to both generate and retrieve your ideas. Writing in your journal can help you discover your thoughts and feelings about specific issues as well as let you think through important choices you have to make. So writing can help you solve problems and work your way through various college projects.

If you use a notebook for your journal, choose one that you really like. You might even keep your journal on your computer. However, unless you have a laptop, you won't have your electronic journal with you all the time. The choice is yours (unless your instructor has specific requirements). Just remember that a journal should be a notebook (paper or electronic) you enjoy writing in and carrying with you.

The content of your journal entries depends to a great extent on your instructor's directions. But some basic advice applies to all entries, whether on paper or on a computer.

1. Date your entries, and note the time; you may find it useful to see when your best ideas occur.
2. Record anything that comes to your mind, and follow your thoughts wherever they take you (unless your instructor gives you different directions).
3. Glue or tape anything into your journal that stimulates your thinking, reading, or writing—cartoons, magazine ads, poems, pictures, advice columns, and URLs for useful Web sites.
4. Think of your journal as someone to talk to—a friend who will keep your cherished ideas safe and sound and won't talk back to or argue with you.

PRACTICE 3 Begin your own journal.

1. Buy a notebook that you like, and write in it.
2. Record at least two journal entries on your computer.
3. Which type of journal do you prefer—notebook or computer? Write an entry explaining your preference. *Answers will vary.*

READING AND WRITING IN TANDEM WITH A STUDENT

In the rest of Part I, you will be reading and writing in tandem or along with another student, Beth Olson, who has already completed the assignments you will be doing. In other words, this student will be demonstrating her reading and writing processes as you work on your own. As you consider Beth's words and ideas, concentrate on discovering your own original thoughts as you do each assignment.

PRACTICE 4 Answer the following questions.

1. What does reading and writing in tandem mean in this text?

   It means reading and writing along with another student.

2. How can this approach help you?

   This approach will let you see someone's reading and writing processes at work.

3. Why is it important to discover your own original thoughts for each assignment?

   So that you understand these processes for yourself.

CHAPTER 2

The Reading Process

The reading process, like the writing process, consists of "steps" or "stages" that overlap. But reading, unlike writing, has to occur in a certain order or you will not be able to understand your material. As you write, you might decide to develop a paragraph for your second topic first, then go back to your first topic, and finally write your introduction and conclusion. Reading, however, dictates its own order. To get the most out of the process, you have to start at the beginning and read to the end. What you do during the process, however, is what can raise your level of understanding to the analytical or critical level, which is where you want to be to succeed in college and in life after college. This chapter will introduce you to the entire reading process. But keep in mind that you should adjust the options presented here to your individual preferences.

TEACHING THE READING PROCESS

Ask your students to bring in a visual representation of their reading process. It can be anything—cut-up magazines, something with props, a drawing—that conveys how they go through this process. Be careful not to give students too many ideas so you don't limit the scope of their imaginations. For this exercise, the more vague you are, the more creative students will be.

VISUALIZING THE READING PROCESS

Although we talk about reading in a fairly sequential way, the options you can pursue within the process of reading something from beginning to end can occur and reoccur in any order. The purpose of reading actively (rather than passively) is to make you a critical reader. Once you read critically, your writing will rise to a higher level as well.

Passive readers open a reading assignment, start at the first page, and read to the end without doing any recognizable activities as they read. Active readers are physically working with their reading material from beginning to end—making it their own, trying to understand it on a more sophisticated level, and constantly reacting to it as they read. Identifying your own opinions and thoughts in reference to your reading material is one of the essential parts of the reading process.

As you work with the reading process in this textbook, the following graphic might help you understand how various stages of the process can overlap. The rest of this chapter will explain each of these elements in detail.

TEACHING ON THE WEB

Discussion Topic: Divide students into groups of three or four. Ask the members of each group to think about the recursive steps they go through when researching with a search engine (for example, how many variations do they try in a search?). Have them compare the process of searching for information on the Web to the reading process. How are the two cyclical activities similar? How are they different? Have each group explain its answer.

INSTRUCTOR'S RESOURCE MANUAL
For additional material about teaching the reading process, for journal entries, and for various tests, see the *Instructor's Resource Manual*, Section II, Part I.

The Cycle of Reading

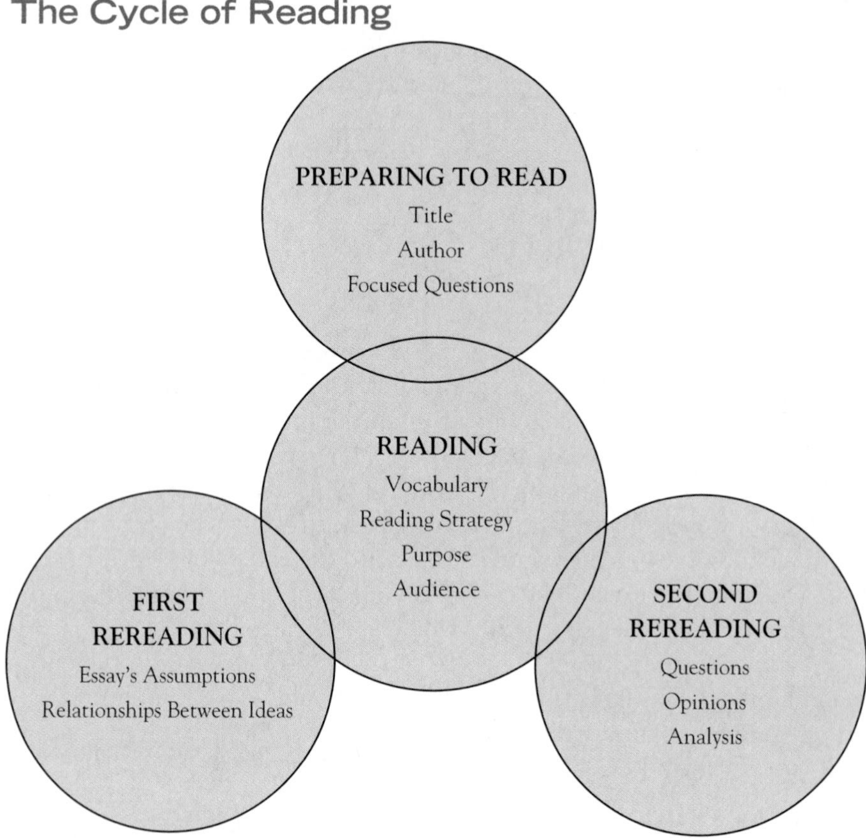

PRACTICE 1 Answer the following questions.

1. List the three elements of prereading.
   Title, author, focused questions
2. List the four elements of reading.
   Vocabulary, reading strategy, purpose, audience
3. List the two elements of the first rereading.
   Essay's assumptions, relationships between ideas
4. List the three elements of the second rereading.
   Questions, opinions, analysis

THE READING PROCESS

The reading process, like the writing process, begins the minute you get a reading assignment. It involves all the activities you do from finding your reading material to reading the entire piece, including trips to the library, text messages, and late-night snacks. Understanding the role these personal choices play in the reading process is just as important as knowing how the formal process works because all these rituals have to work together to help you complete your assignment on or before the assigned deadline. The main parts of the process are discussed in this section.

Preparing to Read

Prereading refers to activities that help you explore your reading material and its general subject so that you can read as efficiently as possible. It includes surveying your assignment and focusing on the task ahead of you. Your mission at this stage is to stimulate your thinking before and during the act of reading.

The most important tasks at this point include looking closely at the title to see if it reveals any clues about the author and his or her attitude, finding out as much as you can about the author (background, profession, biases, etc.), and responding in this text to some preliminary questions that will focus your attention before you read. All of these activities will be demonstrated in Chapter 3 as Beth Olson approaches a reading assignment.

Reading

Once you have previewed your reading material, you can start reading at the beginning of the selection. As you read, you should mark or look up words that you don't understand from the context and annotate your reading material as you move through it. Writing on the material itself will keep you engaged in the process as the tasks become more difficult. You should also try to figure out the author's primary purpose for writing the selection.

Each chapter in Part II of this book will give you a specific reading strategy to master with a particular essay. These strategies can be applied to any reading material and are especially useful in helping you be an active reader. Once you learn different strategies that will improve your reading comprehension, you can choose your favorites to use in other courses.

First Rereading

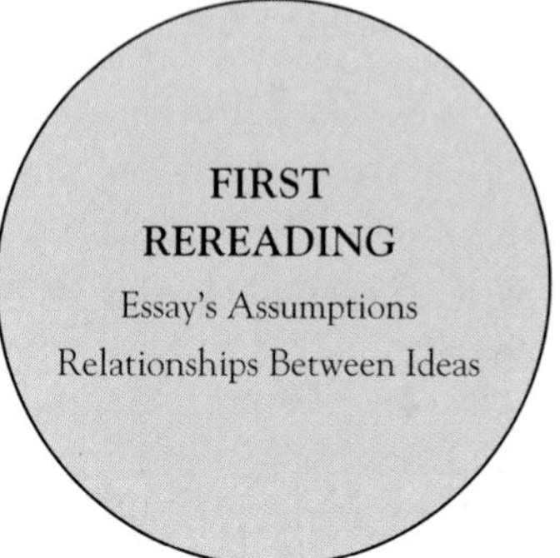

Most students don't want to read their assignments more than once, but the second and third readings are the ones that teach you how to read critically. Only after the first reading can you hope to understand your reading material at a deeper level. This second reading allows you to get to the assumptions that lie behind the words on the page and see relationships between ideas that you didn't notice in the first reading.

With this reading, you are closer to critical reading, but you are not there yet. This reading helps you dig more deeply into what the author is saying and prepares you to go one step further when you read the essay for the third time. Once again, the details of this reading will be demonstrated by Beth Olson in Chapter 3 as she records her reactions to her reading material.

Second Rereading

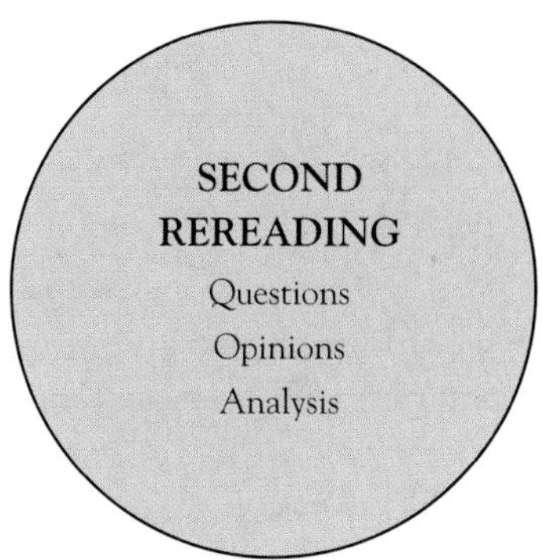

Now read the material one more time slowly and carefully to discover your opinions and analysis of the topic. This critical reading is the highest level of comprehension and should be your goal with each essay that you approach in this book. To achieve this level of understanding, you must actually wrestle with the subject matter—ask questions, make associations of your own, and draw conclusions that capture your personal reaction to the reading material.

This reading requires the most energy on your part because you have to produce the questions and argue with the essay as it moves from point to point. Even though this third reading takes the most energy, it is also the most satisfying because your mind gets to exercise and grapple with ideas on a level that helps you understand both your reading and writing assignments more completely. Ultimately, this level of reading will raise your grades in all subjects.

Once you start reading and you understand where you are headed, these "stages" can occur in any order that you produce them. You may look up a word, argue with an idea in the first paragraph, and go back over a paragraph for a second reading—all in the first few minutes with an essay. Although you may never approach any two reading projects in the same way, the chapters in Part I will help you establish a framework for your personal reading process and guide you toward a comfortable ritual as a reader.

PRACTICE 2 Answer the following questions.

1. When does the reading process start?

   The reading process begins the minute you get a reading assignment.

   ____

   ____

2. Explain "preparing to read" in your own words.

   Prereading helps you explore a reading selection and its general subject matter.

3. Describe your reading environment.

   Answers will vary.

4. What does "reading" consist of?

   Reading includes understanding vocabulary, using a reading strategy that makes you an active reader, and discovering the author's purpose for writing the selection.

5. What does rereading accomplish?

   Rereading lets you understand your reading material at a deeper level and finally be able to argue with and analyze the material.

SAMPLE READING ASSIGNMENT

This first assignment is much like the reading tasks you will be asked to do throughout this book. As you learn some new techniques for reading at a higher level, you will follow the work of student Beth Olson so you can see how she approaches and completes the same assignment. If you work alongside her and mirror her actions, you too will understand the essay analytically and be able to apply it to all your work in college. By the end of Chapter 3, you will have a feel for the entire reading process, which is essential to strengthening your identity as a reader.

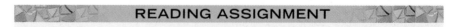

READING ASSIGNMENT

Read the essay in Chapter 3 entitled "I Just Wanna Be Average" by Mike Rose, following the guidelines in that chapter. Do the prereading activities and follow the directions for all three readings. Be aware of your level of understanding as you apply a specific reading strategy to the essay. Also, try to ask more complex questions with each reading.

CHAPTER 3

Reading Critically

Reading critically is the heart and soul of all successful communication. But unfortunately critical reading is not taught at any level. After elementary school, teachers simply assume that students' reading abilities progress with the complexity of their assignments. But we are learning that this assumption is not true. We are living in an age of pictures, X-boxes, cell phones with photo capabilities, and ipods, which has created a culture that does not naturally support reading. Reading requires time and reflection. Only then will the imagination be engaged so that you can read analytically and critically and be productive students and citizens in a very fast-moving world. But since our culture does not naturally promote reading as an activity, you have to work actively as an individual to become a critical reader. Reading critically will positively affect every aspect of your life in and out of college—especially your writing ability. As you read this chapter, record your responses to the exercises in your journal or on a separate piece of paper so that you can refer to them throughout the course.

TEACHING READING CRITICALLY

Reading a book online is quite a different experience than reading it in the traditional way. Ask your students to find a novel that they want to read online. They can start at bibliomania.com. Then they can choose any type of book they want and see what it is like to read online or download the book from the computer.

TEACHING ON THE WEB

Discussion Topic: Divide students into groups of three or four, and have them talk about how the Internet can help them during the prereading stage. What are the advantages of using the Web for prereading? In what ways is the Internet a disadvantage?

PREPARING TO READ

Activities that take place before you actually start reading fall into the general category of **prereading** or **preparing to read.** This is a time when you should get your mind ready to interact with new information so that you can make meaning out of the text. You should also be thinking of using the right side (or the imaginative, creative side) of your brain over the left (more linear, sequential side). This is the part of your brain that thinks up new ideas and sees relationships among old ideas. More specifically, prereading consists of activities that help you do the following tasks:

- Survey and analyze the title
- Find out what you can about the author
- Focus your attention on the subject of the reading selection

INSTRUCTOR'S RESOURCE MANUAL

For additional material about teaching critical reading, for journal entries, and for various tests, see the *Instructor's Resource Manual,* Section II, Part I.

Let's begin by looking at activities that many writers use to stimulate their minds as they approach a reading task. We will be following the thoughts and activities of a student named Beth Olson.

Title: I Just Wanna Be Average

Beth learned that the title of the essay she is about to read is "I Just Wanna Be Average." From the acknowledgments in the back of this book, she discovers that this selection is from a book called *Lives on the Boundary.* This is a surprising title because most people wouldn't admit their desire to be average even if it were true. They would say they want to be better than average. As Beth thinks about this title, she explores the following questions:

What does it mean at face value?
On what assumptions is it based?
Why would someone want to focus on this statement in an essay?

Author: Mike Rose

Beth then finds out the author's name (Mike Rose), but she doesn't know anything about him. So she does a Web search of his name with the intention of trying to learn why he would write an essay on this topic. Here is a biography she found:

> Mike Rose is on the faculty of the UCLA Graduate School of Education and Information Studies, specializing in language and literacy. He has written a number of books and articles on language and literacy and has received awards from the Spencer Foundation, the McDonnell Foundation, and the National Council of Teachers of English. He is the recipient of a Guggenheim Fellowship and is the author of *Lives on the Boundary: The Struggles and Achievements of America's Underprepared* (1989).

One site Beth consulted was www.t3.preservice.org/t0401711/ethical.html. This site and his book jacket told Beth that he is an immigrant who was singled out in school because he couldn't speak English. His experiences in school, in particular, taught him how to fight stereotyping and prejudice. He pushed through oppression and many hardships by continuing to push forward and by taking risks when he didn't know what the outcome would be. His story is one of determination and survival through education.

Focusing Your Attention

In this book, a set of questions will help you focus your attention on the material you are about to read. When you are reading material separate from this book, you should try to generate questions on your own—about the author, about the subject matter, about the title. In this way, you will begin all your reading with an inquiring mind, which is a basic necessity for active rather than passive reading.

Here are some questions to focus your attention on the Mike Rose essay. Writing your thoughts about these questions in a journal is the most beneficial approach to this exercise. Beth wrote her personal reactions to these questions before she started reading the essay.

1. What do you think about tracking, or separating students by ability level, in high school? What are the advantages and disadvantages of this system of teaching? How would it affect your learning? Did your high school track its students?
2. In the essay you are about to read, the writer claims that students use sophisticated defense mechanisms to get through high school. Have you ever used any defenses in school? How did these defenses make you act? Did they help or hinder your learning?

READING

As you approach a reading task, you should plan to read it three times if you want to understand it critically. To get to the deeper levels of meaning, you need to work through literal and interpretive comprehension first. These readings take time and reflection.

As you read, you need to realize that you are making meaning out of a text that someone else has written. To do this, work in partnership with the author and his or her words to make sense of the material. Usually this does not happen in one reading. In like manner, when someone reads your writing, he or she must work with your words on the page to figure out what you are saying and what your words are implying.

Expanding Your Vocabulary

The first task you should undertake in your reading is to get the gist of the selection and look up vocabulary words that you don't understand. In this book, difficult vocabulary is identified and defined for you. You should keep this list handy and add other words to it as you read.

If you want to actually increase your vocabulary and take these words with you into your own speaking and writing, you need to interact with the text and highlight the words, compose your own lists, create index cards—complete some activity that will make the words your own. In this text, a specific task is suggested in each vocabulary section so you can try a few different activities and then choose those that work best for you to use in your reading outside this class.

Here is a list of difficult words you need to know for the first reading of "I Just Wanna Be Average." Beth looked at the words she knew and circled those that were new for her. Then she put each word she wanted to add to her vocabulary on an index card with the definition on the other side. That way she could quiz herself on her new words as she accumulates cards.

vocational: focused on training for a job (paragraph 1)

Horace's Compromise: a novel by Theodore R. Sizer (paragraph 1)

hypotheses: educated guesses (paragraph 1)

disaffected: rebellious, uncooperative (paragraph 1)

skeletal: very basic (paragraph 1)

scuttling: moving quickly (paragraph 1)

somnambulant: walking while asleep (paragraph 2)

wherewithal: ability (paragraph 2)

prowess: strength (paragraph 3)

clique: exclusive social group (paragraph 3)

testament to: proof of (paragraph 3)

dearth: lack (paragraph 3)

much-touted: repeatedly praised (paragraph 4)

salubrious: socially or morally acceptable (paragraph 4)

equivocal: having two or more meanings (paragraph 4)

Argosy: a science-fiction magazine (paragraph 4)

Field and Stream: a hunting and fishing magazine (paragraph 4)

Daily Worker: a Socialist newspaper (paragraph 4)

The Old Man and the Sea: a novel by Ernest Hemingway (paragraph 4)

rough-hewn: unsophisticated, unpolished (paragraph 4)

apocryphal: a story that is not true but is believed by some people anyway (paragraph 4)

ducktail: a hairstyle in which the hair is swept back at the sides to meet in an upturned point at the back (paragraph 5)

parable of the talents: a story from the New Testament (paragraph 5)

restive: restless, fidgety (paragraph 5)

affect: emotion (paragraph 5)

laryngectomize: surgically remove a person's larynx (paragraph 5)

platitudinous: dull, boring, full of unoriginal thoughts (paragraph 5)

melee: battle (paragraph 5)

dissonant: nonconforming, disagreeing (paragraph 6)

elite: privileged individuals (paragraph 6)

constrained: kept within limits (paragraph 6)

liberate: free (paragraph 6)

gray matter: brain (paragraph 7)

diffuse: scatter (paragraph 7)

cultivate: encourage (paragraph 7)

malady: illness (paragraph 7)

Using a Reading Strategy

As you begin to read, you will be prompted to use a reading strategy with each reading assignment. Here are the ten reading strategies we introduce in this book:

Personal Annotations We all naturally make personal associations with our reading material. However, one person's associations are usually quite different from those of someone else. Recording the associations you make with a reading selection lets you "own" the essay, so to speak. It allows you to connect the author's ideas to your own experiences. To perform this strategy, make notes in the margin that relate some of your specific memories to the details in this essay. Be prepared to explain the connection between your notes and the facts in the essay.

TEACHING READING STRATEGIES

Give students a few paragraphs, and have them practice each of the reading strategies. Then have students discuss which strategies they are most comfortable with.

TEACHING ON THE WEB

Discussion Topic: Divide students into groups of three or four, and have them discuss how the Internet has changed the way they read. How much reading do they do in a single day on the Internet? How much reading did they do prior to the Internet? How have reading and the Internet changed their lives?

INSTRUCTOR'S RESOURCE MANUAL

For additional material about teaching critical reading, for journal entries, and for various tests, see the *Instructor's Resource Manual,* Section II, Part I.

Think Aloud As we read and make meaning out of the author's words, we put a string of words together on a literal level, bring in any implications the author suggests, think about how the ideas relate to one another, and keep the process going until the entire essay makes sense. These are focused thoughts that will help you process the author's writing. On another level, however, we also stray from the essay in a wide variety of ways—thinking about chores we need to do, calls we forgot to return, and plans we are looking forward to on the weekend. These are random ideas that are only loosely related to the reading. As you might suspect, focused reading is the most productive, but you can teach yourself to apply even your random ideas toward a better understanding of your reading material. To do this strategy, stop and "think aloud" about what is on your mind throughout the text. Point out places that are confusing to you, connections that you make, specific questions you have, related information you know, and personal experiences you associate with the text. In this way, you are able to hear what your mind does (both focused and random) as you read.

Chunking Reading essays critically means looking closely at the selection to discover how it is structured. To understand how an essay works, circle the main idea or thesis. Then draw horizontal lines throughout the essay to separate the various topics that support the thesis. These lines may or may not coincide with paragraph breaks. Finally, label each "chunk" in the right margin. Be prepared to explain the divisions you made.

Graphic Organizers Students often find that making drawings of the ideas and details in their reading is a much more effective way than outlining to understand the material and see how it works. Graphic organizers, or concept maps, let you literally "draw" the relationship of ideas to one another. Figuring out what framework to use for this exercise is part of the process. You can make up a drawing of your own or do a Web search for "graphic organizers" to see some options. For an essay, show the relationship of the ideas to one another in a graphic form that makes sense to you. Be prepared to explain your drawing.

Peer Teaching Teaching something to your peers is an excellent way to see if you understand it. To practice this technique, the class must first divide an essay into parts. The class members should then get into groups (one for each part of the essay) and choose one of the essay's sections to prepare for the rest of the class. After discovering the main ideas, the details, and their relationship to one another, each group should teach its section to the rest of the class.

Summarizing As you read more difficult essays, the ability to summarize is essential. A summary features the main ideas of a selection in a coherent paragraph. First, identify the main ideas in your reading; then fold them into a paragraph with logical transitions so your sentences flow from one to another. After your write your summary, draft three questions for discussion.

Critical Annotations Forming your own opinions and coming up with new ideas in response to your reading are very important parts of the reading process, but you need to learn how to produce these reactions. As you read an essay, plan to record your notes on a separate piece of paper. First, draw a vertical line down the center of a sheet of paper. Then, as you read, write the author's main ideas on the left and your reactions to those ideas on the right side of the page. Be prepared to explain the connection between your notes and the material in the essay.

Lists Separating related ideas is an important part of understanding an essay. After a first reading, divide a sheet of paper into two parts with a vertical line. Then as you read the essay for a second time, record one set of ideas in the left column and related ideas from the essay on the right. Draw lines from one detail to another (if applicable). Be prepared to explain the connection between your lists and the details in the essay.

Highlighting Reading an argument critically calls for very high-level skills. You need to understand your reading on a literal level, know the difference between opinions and fact, and come up with your own thoughts on the topic by challenging the author's ideas. To do this strategy, highlight facts in one color and the author's opinions in another color. This activity works very well with the next strategy.

Reading with the Author/Against the Author This approach to reading is a very advanced form of reading. It asks you to recognize that you are consciously looking for ideas to agree with and then disagree with. By doing this, you will force yourself to form your own opinions. From the previous highlighting exercise, put an X by any facts or opinions that you do not agree with or want to question in some way. Then record your own thoughts and opinions on a separate sheet of paper. Be prepared to explain any marks you made on the essay.

Beth's Reading Beth read the following essay by Mike Rose. It stimulated her thoughts about learning in general because she believes that the most important part of learning is taking risks. She jotted several personal annotations to herself in the margins as she read.

Yes I agree

1 Students will float to the mark you set. I and the others in the vocational classes were bobbing in pretty shallow water. Vocational education was aimed at increasing the economic opportunities of students who do not do well in our schools. Some serious programs succeed in doing that, and through exceptional teachers—like Mr. Gross in Horace's Compromise—students learn to develop hypotheses and troubleshoot, reason through a problem, and communicate effectively—the true job skills. The vocational track, however, is most often a place for those who are just not making it, a dumping ground for the disaffected. There were a few teachers who worked hard at education; young Brother Slattery, for example, combined a stern voice with weekly quizzes to try to pass along to us a skeletal outline of world history. But mostly the teachers had no idea of how to engage the imaginations of us kids who were scuttling along at the bottom of the pond.

But how does Gross do this?

3 important skills

I know

2 And the teachers would have needed some inventiveness, for none of us was groomed for the classroom. It wasn't just that I didn't know things—didn't know how to simplify algebraic fractions, couldn't identify different kinds of clauses, bungled Spanish translations—but that I had developed various faulty and inadequate ways of doing algebra and making sense of Spanish. Worse yet, the years of defensive tuning out in elementary school had given me a way to escape quickly while seeming at least half alert. During my time in Voc. Ed., I developed further into a mediocre student and a somnambulant problem solver, and that affected the subjects I did have the wherewithal to handle: I detested Shakespeare; I got bored with history. My attention flitted here and there. I fooled around in class and read my books indifferently—the intellectual equivalent of playing with your food. I did what I had to do to get by, and I did it with half a mind.

Why defensive?

3 But I did learn things about people and eventually came into my own socially. I liked the guys in Voc. Ed. Growing up where I did, I understood and admired physical prowess, and there was an abundance of muscle here. There was Dave Snyder, a sprinter and

How did learning about people help Rose?

Max is like this

halfback of true quality. Dave's ability and his quick wit gave him a natural appeal, and he was welcome in any clique, though he always kept a little independent. He enjoyed acting the fool and could care less about studies, but he possessed a certain maturity and never caused the faculty much trouble. It was a testament to his independence that he included me among his friends—I eventually went out for track, but I was no jock. Owing to the Latin alphabet and a dearth of *R*'s and *S*'s, Snyder sat behind Rose, and we started exchanging one-liners and became friends.

4 There was Ted Richard, a much-touted Little League pitcher. He was chunky and had a baby face and came to Our Lady of Mercy as a seasoned street fighter. Ted was quick to laugh, and he had a loud, jolly laugh, but when he got angry he'd smile a little smile, the kind that simply raises the corner of the mouth a quarter of an inch. For those who knew, it was an eerie signal. Those who didn't found themselves in big trouble, for Ted was very quick. He loved to carry on what we would come to call philosophical discussions: What is courage? Does God exist? He also loved words, enjoyed picking up big ones like *salubrious* and *equivocal* and using them in our conversations—laughing at himself as the word hit a chuckhole rolling off his tongue. Ted didn't do all that well in school—baseball and parties and testing the courage he'd speculated about took up his time. His textbooks were *Argosy* and *Field and Stream,* whatever newspapers he'd find on the bus stop—from the *Daily Worker* to pornography—conversations with uncles or hobos or businessmen he'd meet in a coffee shop, *The Old Man and the Sea.* With hindsight, I can see that Ted was developing into one of those rough-hewn intellectuals whose sources are a mix of the learned and the apocryphal, whose discussions are both assured and sad.

like Sam in Intro to Psych

like Sasha in Orientation

5 And then there was Ken Harvey. Ken was good-looking in a puffy way and had a full and oily ducktail and was a car enthusiast. . . . One day in religion class, he said the sentence that turned out to be one of the most memorable of the hundreds of thousands I heard

in those Voc. Ed. years. We were talking about the parable of the talents, about achievement, working hard, doing the best you can do, blah-blah-blah, when the teacher called on the restive Ken Harvey for an opinion. Ken thought about it, but just for a second, and said (with studied, minimal affect), "I just wanna be average." That woke me up. Average?! Who wants to be average? Then the athletes chimed in with the clichés that make you want to laryngectomize them, and the exchange became a platitudinous melee. At the time, I thought Ken's assertion was stupid, and I wrote him off. But his sentence has stayed with me all these years, and I think I am finally coming to understand it.

What a great line, but why not "special"?

English 1A!!

Ken Harvey was gasping for air. School can be a tremendously disorienting place. No matter how bad the school, you're going to encounter notions that don't fit with the assumptions and beliefs that you grew up with—maybe you'll hear these dissonant notions from teachers, maybe from the other students, and maybe you'll read them. You'll also be thrown in with all kinds of kids from all kinds of backgrounds, and that can be unsettling—this is especially true in places of rich ethnic and linguistic mix, like the L.A. basin. You'll see a handful of students far excel you in courses that sound exotic and that are only in the curriculum of the elite: French, physics, trigonometry. And all this is happening while you're trying to shape an identity, your body is changing, and your emotions are running wild. If you're a working-class kid in the vocational track, the options you'll have to deal with this will be constrained in certain ways: You're defined by your school as "slow"; you're placed in a curriculum that isn't designed to liberate you but to occupy you, or, if you're lucky, train you, though the training is for work the society does not esteem; other students are picking up the cues from your school and your curriculum and interacting with you in particular ways. If you're a kid like Ted Richard, you turn your back on all this and let your mind roam where it may. But youngsters like Ted are rare. What Ken and so many others do is protect themselves from such suffocating madness by taking on with a vengeance the 6

I hate this feeling

so true

How?

identity implied in the vocational track. Reject the confusion and frustration by openly defining yourself as the Common Joe. Champion the average. Rely on your own good sense. **** this bullshit. Bullshit, of course, is everything you—and the others—fear is beyond you: books, essays, tests, academic scrambling, complexity, scientific reasoning, philosophical inquiry.

putting down what you don't know or under-stand= a de-fense

The tragedy is that you have to twist the knife in 7
your own gray matter to make this defense work. You'll have to shut down, have to reject intellectual stimuli or diffuse them with sarcasm, have to cultivate stupidity, have to convert boredom from a malady into a way of confronting the world. Keep your vocabulary simple, act stoned when you're not or act more stoned than you are, flaunt ignorance, materialize your dreams. It is a powerful and effective defense—it neutralizes the insult and the frustration of being a vocational kid and, when perfected, it drives teachers up the wall, a delightful secondary effect. But like all strong magic, it exacts a price.

Why a tragedy? Learning goes on hold so this "role" can succeed

Defense = Magic?

What price?

Your Reading Read Mike Rose's essay, and add your own notes to Beth's comments in the margins.

Discovering Purpose and Audience

Finally, at this stage of the reading process, you should determine the writer's purpose and audience. In Beth's case, she learns from the book jacket that Rose set out to write his autobiography, which ended up focusing on his educational experiences. Teachers had a great effect on Rose and his progress as a child trying to survive in American society. His initial audience was probably educators, but now he has a much broader appeal.

FIRST REREADING

Your first rereading must now focus on raising your level of thinking so that you have a deeper understanding of the essay you just finished. Looking again at the essay with an inquiring mind is the heart of this stage.

This book provides questions on progressively more difficult levels to help you accomplish this goal. But without these questions, you need to ask your own questions as you read. Focusing on questions that wonder "why" or "how" something happened will move you to these higher levels. You also want to focus on assumptions that the writer bases his or her points on and the relationship between ideas in an essay. These might be either stated or unstated. As you become a more proficient reader, you will be able to see both with ease.

Beth's First Rereading As Beth read Rose's essay a second time, she saw several relationships that she had not previously seen. She noted these relationships on the essay and then answered the following questions provided in the text. Her answers appear after each question.

Thinking Critically About Content

1. What was vocational education aimed at in Rose's school? Who is this track for?

   Vocational training was aimed at students who were deemed "slow." They were "placed in a curriculum that isn't designed to liberate you but occupy you, or, if you're lucky, train you" (para. 6).

2. What examples from this essay illustrate most clearly what Rose's academic life involved?

   The examples in paragraph 2 illustrate most clearly Rose's academic life. They point out his troubles with academics and his desire to retreat somewhat from the academic world.

3. Rose says the Voc. Ed. students "were bobbing in pretty shallow water" and then refers to them "scuttling along at the bottom of the pond" (paragraph 1). In these examples, he is comparing people trying to swim and stay above water to students on a vocational track in high school. This comparison is called a *metaphor*. Find another comparison like this in paragraph 7.

   Here are two examples: "The tragedy is that you have to twist the knife in your own gray matter to make this defense work" and "But like all strong magic, it exacts a price."

Thinking Critically About Purpose and Audience

4. What do you think Rose's purpose is in this essay? Explain your answer.

   Rose's purpose is to inform readers that teachers who expect mediocre work from students will receive just that. He wants teachers to set the mark higher so that students will reach it.

5. What type of audience do you think would most understand and appreciate this essay?

   Anyone can appreciate this essay, but students who were perceived to be performing at low levels will understand it best.

6. What do you think Ken Harvey meant when he said, "I just wanna be average" (paragraph 5)?

   Harvey probably wanted to go unnoticed. He didn't want to stand out, but at the same time, he didn't want to fail. He was content to live his life somewhere in the middle.

Thinking Critically About Essays

7. Does Rose give you enough examples to understand his learning environment in high school? Explain your answer.

   His examples do paint a picture about his learning environment because they show readers how teachers expected mediocrity from students who were more than willing to provide it.

8. Is this essay unified? Does each of the author's topic sentences support the essay's thesis statement? Explain your answer.

   The topic sentences do support Rose's thesis statement, and the essay is unified. All the paragraphs focus on proving that if teachers don't expect much from their students, they won't get much.

9. What is Rose's thesis in this essay? Where is it located?

   Rose's thesis is the first sentence in the essay: "Students will float to the mark you set."

10. Explain your opinion about tracking students. Is tracking a good idea? Does it help some students? Does it hurt anyone? Can you think of any alternatives to tracking? Respond to these questions in detail.

    I think tracking makes students feel bad. If they are in a low-level class, they know that teachers don't expect much from them. If they're not as strong as Mike Rose, they could be marked by this label beyond school.

Your First Rereading Read "I Just Wanna Be Average" a second time, and take more notes about assumptions and relationships between ideas in the margins as you read. Then, in your journal, generate five "why" or "how" questions about ideas in this essay. Then, exchange questions with a classmate, and answer each other's questions in your journal.

SECOND REREADING

This final reading is the real test of your understanding. It has the potential to raise your grades in all subjects if you complete it for each of your reading assignments. It involves understanding the author's ideas as you also form your own opinions and analyze your thoughts.

To accomplish this reading, you should ask more questions that go beyond the words on the page and then answer them in writing. You should also bring your own opinions to the surface. Write them down as they occur to you. Finally, analyze your thoughts so that you end with some form of self-evaluation.

Beth's Second Rereading Beth took the following notes in her journal as she read Rose's essay for the third time. She asked herself some questions, answered those questions as best she could, recorded her opinions as they occurred to her, and analyzed her thoughts along the way. She covers all of these thought processes in the following journal entry.

Opening yourself up to learning is tough. If you try and don't get it, you feel stupid. I guess that's the advantage of putting up defenses when confronted with something to learn. With a defense, you don't look stupid—you just look cool because you are refusing to try.

I know that feeling. I've dug my heels in before when I thought I wouldn't understand something. And it saved me from embarrassment, but I'm not sure I came out ahead. My feelings were intact/unruffled, but I realized with that behavior I would be stuck in the mud forever. The only way to get ahead is to move forward (even a little bit) and the only way to move is to learn and the only way to learn is to take some risks—risk embarrassment, risk feeling stupid, risk your fragile ego. But defenses are circular. Here's how they work—you get nervous or uncomfortable, you put up a defense of some sort, you save face, and you start all over again. You never learn anything that would help you get out of your rut. You only learn how to save your emotions. That's a form of survival. But I want more.

Your Second Rereading Take notes in your own journal as you read Rose's essay for the third time. Ask yourself more "how" and "why" questions, answer those questions, record your opinions, and analyze your thoughts as they occur.

4 CHAPTER

The Writing Process

TEACHING THE WRITING PROCESS
Ask your students to bring in a visual representation of their writing process. It can be anything—cut-up magazines, something with props, a drawing—that conveys how they go through this process. Be careful not to give students too many ideas so you don't limit the scope of their imaginations. For this exercise, the more vague you are, the more creative students will be.

The writing process consists of identifiable "stages" that overlap in a number of unique ways. No two people write in the same way, so it is important for you to figure out exactly how your writing process works. In other words, you need to know how to arrange these stages to produce the best writing you are capable of. Knowing each of the stages individually will help you organize them in a way that best suits your lifestyle and other obligations in life. This chapter will introduce you to the entire process in the hope that you will tailor it along the way to meet your individual needs.

VISUALIZING THE WRITING PROCESS

Even though we talk about the stages of writing, writing is actually a cyclical process, which means that at any point you may loop in and out of other stages. As you work with the writing process in this textbook, the following graphic might help you understand how various stages of the process can overlap. The rest of this chapter will explain each of these elements in detail.

The Cycle of Writing

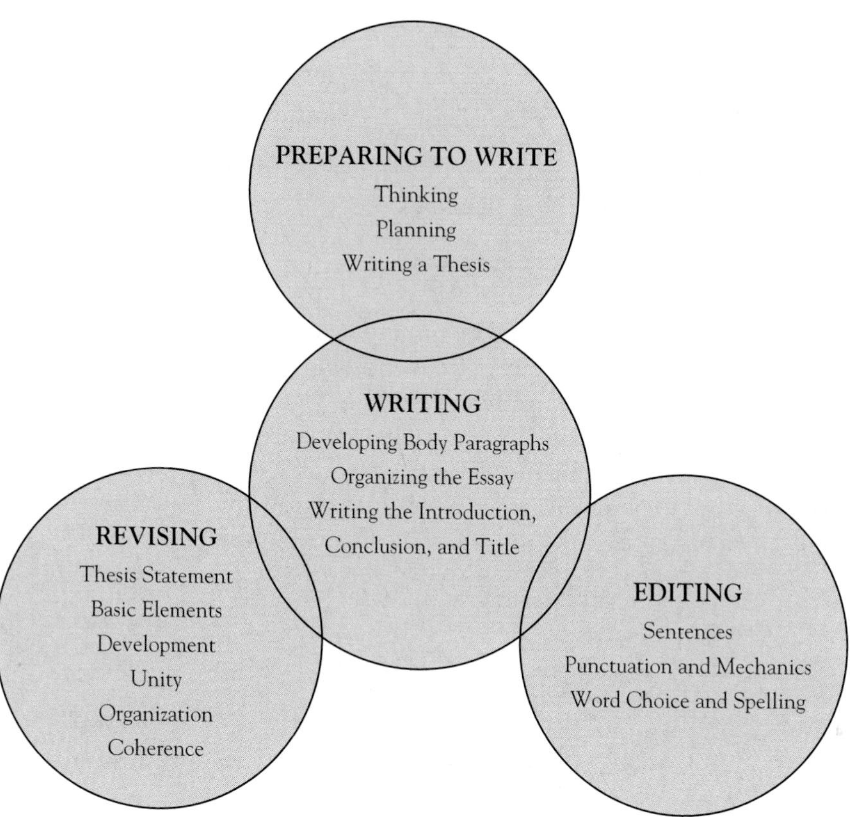

TEACHING ON THE WEB

Discussion Topic: Divide students into groups of three or four. Ask the members of each group to think about the recursive steps they go through when researching with a search engine (for example, how many variations do they try in a search?). Have them compare the process of searching for information on the Web to the writing process. How are the two cyclical activities similar? How are they different? Have each group explain its answer.

INSTRUCTOR'S RESOURCE MANUAL

For additional material about teaching the writing process, for journal entries, and for various tests, see the *Instructor's Resource Manual*, Section II, Part I.

PRACTICE 1 Answer the following questions.

1. List the three elements of prewriting.

   Thinking, planning, writing a thesis statement

2. List the three elements of writing.

   Developing body paragraphs; organizing the essay; writing the introduction, conclusion, and title

3. List the six elements of revising.

   Thesis statement, basic elements, development, unity, organization, coherence

4. List the three elements of editing.

   Sentences, punctuation and mechanics, word choice and spelling

THE WRITING PROCESS

The writing process begins the minute you get a writing assignment. It involves all the activities you do, from choosing a topic to turning in a final draft, including computer searches, text messages, and late-night trips to Starbucks. Understanding these personal choices is just as important as knowing the details of the formal process because all these rituals have to work together to produce a piece of writing on or before the assigned deadline. The main parts of the process are explained in this section.

Preparing to Write

Prewriting refers to activities that help you explore a general subject, generate ideas about it, select a specific topic, establish a purpose, learn as much as possible about your readers, and draft a thesis statement. Chapter 5 will teach you different strategies for accomplishing these goals before you actually begin to write a draft of your essay. Your mission at this stage is to stimulate your thinking before and during the act of writing.

Whenever you generate new material throughout the writing process, you are prewriting. The most common prewriting activities are freewriting, brainstorming, clustering, questioning, and discussing. All of these activities will be demonstrated in Chapter 5 as Beth Olson approaches a writing assignment. The more ideas you generate now and throughout the entire writing process, the more you have to work with as you draft your essay.

Writing

As you try to give your ideas shape, your thesis statement will give your writing focus. This statement or controlling idea, which is already written, should include your purpose for writing or an outline of what you want to accomplish in the essay. This "mission" will help you make important decisions as you begin to actually put your thoughts into essay form. Developing and organizing your ideas will come after you get your thoughts out on paper.

You can start writing after you have some ideas to work with. Writing includes developing some of your ideas further, organizing your thoughts with your purpose in mind, and writing a first draft. To begin writing, you should go back to your notes, journal entries, and other prewriting activities and then mold these ideas into a logical, coherent essay. As you write, you should concentrate on what you are saying and how your ideas fit together.

You might find it easier to add your introduction, conclusion, and title after you compose the body of your essay. Only after you actually generate a draft do you know what you are going to say in an essay. Don't let grammar and spelling distract you from your task at this point. You can correct your grammar and mechanical errors later.

Revising

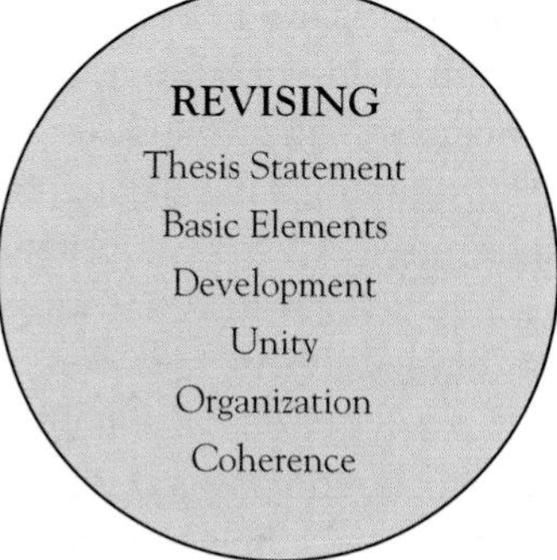

Most people do not want to take the time to revise their writing. But revising always pays off, because it will make your writing stronger. Revising involves rethinking your content and organization so that your words say exactly what you mean. (Editing, the last step, focuses on your grammar, punctuation, mechanics, and spelling.) Your main goal in revising is to make sure that the purpose of your essay is clear to your audience and that your main ideas are supported with adequate details and examples. In addition, you should check that your paper is organized logically and moves smoothly from one idea to the next.

The items listed in the circle above appear on the revising checklist throughout this text. We will explain each one of these elements so that you can use it effectively in the revisions of your own essays. If you go through this list each time you rewrite your essays, you will be creating a better draft with each change you make.

Editing

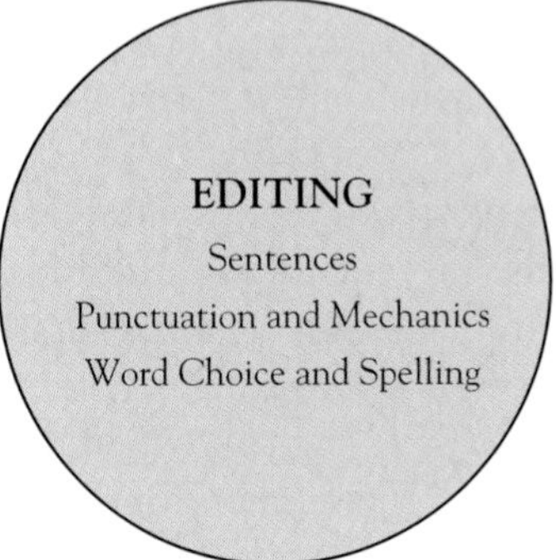

EDITING
Sentences
Punctuation and Mechanics
Word Choice and Spelling

Editing is the final stage of the writing process. After you revise your content, read your writing slowly and carefully to find errors in grammar, punctuation, mechanics, and spelling. Such errors can distract your reader from the message you are trying to convey or can even cause communication to break down. Editing gives you the chance to clean up your draft so that your writing is clear, precise, and effective.

In this text, we have grouped grammar and usage errors into three categories: Sentence errors include fragments and run-together sentences that need to be corrected for clear communication; punctuation and mechanics cover end punctuation (periods, question marks, and exclamation points), internal punctuation (commas, semicolons, colons, apostrophes, quotation marks), capitalization, abbreviations, and numbers; and word choice and spelling ask you to check whether or not you have chosen the right word for what you mean and whether that word is spelled correctly. Checking all these features of your writing will give you the best chance possible to produce an effective essay.

Once you start writing, these "stages" do not necessarily occur in any specific order. You may change a word (revise) in the very first sentence that you write, then think of another detail that you want to add to your opening sentence (prewrite), and next cross out and rewrite a misspelled word (edit)—all in the first two minutes of writing. Although you may never approach any two writing projects in the same way, the chapters in Part I will help you establish a framework for your personal writing process and feel comfortable as a writer working within that framework.

PRACTICE 2 Answer the following questions.

1. When does the writing process start?

   The writing process begins the minute you get a writing assignment.

2. Explain "prewriting" in your own words.

   Prewriting helps you explore a general subject, generate ideas about it, select a specific topic, establish a purpose, learn as much as possible about your readers, and draft a thesis statement.

3. Describe your writing environment.

   Answers will vary.

4. What does "writing" consist of?

   Writing includes developing some of your ideas further, organizing your thoughts with your purpose in mind, and writing a first draft.

5. What is the difference between "revising" and "editing"?

   Revising involves rethinking your content and organization so that your words say exactly what you mean. Editing, the last step, focuses on your grammar, punctuation, mechanics, and spelling.

WRITING ON A COMPUTER

Many people—in school and at work—find that they write most efficiently directly on a computer. This strategy saves them time and energy and helps them meet deadlines. First of all, writing directly on a computer lets you change words and sentences as you go along. It also saves you time since you don't have to write out a draft by hand and then word process it later. When you complete a first draft on a computer, you can move your ideas around without having to rewrite the whole paper. Finally, you can correct your grammar and spelling errors right on the final draft.

To compose on your computer, follow some simple rules so you don't lose your work or make word processing more complex than it is. Here are five essential guidelines for writing on a computer:

1. Give your document a name before you start writing.
2. Save your work often (or set the computer to save at short intervals). This will help you avoid losing your writing in a power failure or other accident.
3. Save your work in two different places—on your hard drive and on a disk. Then if one becomes damaged, you always have the other.
4. Name and number each draft so that you can go back to earlier drafts if you want. For example, you might name and number an assignment this way: Description Essay D1, Description Essay D2, and so forth (D = draft).
5. Print out your work frequently so that you can refer to printed copies as well as electronic copies.

PRACTICE 3 Answer the following questions.

1. What are the advantages of writing directly on a computer?

   Writing directly on a computer lets you change words and sentences as you go along. It also saves you time because you don't have to write out a draft by hand and then type it up later. When you complete a first draft on a computer, you can move your ideas around without having to rewrite your whole paper. Finally, you can correct your grammar and spelling errors right on the final draft.

2. What five guidelines should you remember if you write on a computer?

   1. *Give your document a name before you start writing.*
   2. *Save your work often.*
   3. *Save your work in two different places—on the hard drive and on a disk.*
   4. *Name and number each of your drafts so you can go back to earlier drafts if you want.*
   5. *Print out your work frequently so you can refer to printed as well as electronic copies.*

SAMPLE WRITING ASSIGNMENT

This first writing assignment is much like the writing tasks you will be asked to do throughout this book. You'll be working on this assignment yourself over the next three chapters as you apply what you are learning about the writing process to this task. At the same time, we will follow the work of student Beth Olson so you can see how she approaches and completes the same assignment. By the end of Chapter 7, you will have a feel for the entire writing process, which is essential to strengthening your writing and your identity as a writer.

Write Your Own Essay

We all learn about life in a variety of ways. These lessons help us become who we are. What have you learned over the years? How did you learn these lessons? What experiences have made you the person you are today? Based on a combination of your observations, your reading, and your personal experience, write an essay explaining how you learn best.

CHAPTER 5

Preparing to Write

Activities that take place before you actually start writing your paper fall into the general category of **prewriting** or **preparing to write.** This is a time when you should be generating as many new ideas on a topic as you can, using the right side of your brain over the left. This is the part of your brain that thinks up new ideas and sees relationships among old ideas. More specifically, prewriting consists of activities that help you do the following tasks:

- Explore a subject
- Generate ideas about the subject
- Settle on a specific topic
- Establish a purpose
- Analyze your audience

Let's begin by looking at activities that many writers use to stimulate their minds as they approach a writing task. You will get a chance to try each one. Record your responses to the following exercises in your journal or on a separate piece of paper so that you can refer to them throughout the course.

TEACHING THINKING
Give students a topic, such as "school," "hobbies," "work," or "time with friends," and have them practice each of the thinking strategies. Once students discover which strategy they are most comfortable with, have them use this strategy for future essays.

THINKING

Thinking is always the place to start any writing project. Thinking means exploring your topic and letting your mind run freely over the ideas you generate. We'll demonstrate five activities that students often use to stimulate their best thoughts: freewriting, brainstorming, clustering, questioning, and discussing. You will see how Beth Olson uses each strategy before you have a chance to try out the strategy yourself.

Freewriting

The strategy of freewriting involves writing about anything that comes to your mind. You should write without stopping for five to ten minutes because the act of writing alone will make you think of other ideas. Do not worry about grammar, punctuation, mechanics, or spelling. If you get stuck, repeat an idea or start rhyming words. Just keep writing.

Beth's Freewriting Beth had trouble freewriting, but she got going and then repeated some words to keep herself writing.

> My English teacher wants us to freewrite about whatever comes to our minds, but I can't think of anything to say. It's hard for me to just start writing. I still can't think of anything to say. And it's hard for me to just write. I don't even know what to write about. Everyone in here is writing furiously in their notebooks; I wonder what they're writing about. How many are writing about their girlfriends? their families? their dreams? I wonder what their dreams are. No one could ever guess that one of my dreams is to someday be my own boss in a company that will make enough money for my family to live comfortably. I suppose that's everyone's dream, really, but I don't think many people would think I had enough guts to go out on my own. But I will someday, and it's going to be a great life.

Focused freewriting is the same procedure focused on a specific topic—either one your instructor gives you or one you choose. Apply your guidelines for freewriting to a specific topic. Just write freely about a designated topic so that you find words for your thoughts and impressions.

Beth's Focused Freewriting Beth produced the following focused freewriting in her journal. She is trying to get her mind ready to write her essay about learning.

> People can learn about life from just about everything they do. It seems that every action can result in some sort of lesson. It's like all those fairy tales that have morals at the end of the story. If we keep our eyes open, everything we do can have a moral at the end. We can learn about how to study when we join a study group. We can decide how to treat our boyfriends or girlfriends when we watch our friends. And we can even learn from what's on the tube. I also like asking questions and talking to people about problems I'm

TEACHING ON THE WEB

Discussion Topic: Divide students into groups of three or four, and have them talk about how the Internet can help them generate ideas during the prewriting stage. What are the advantages of using the Web for prewriting in this manner? In what ways is the Internet a disadvantage?

INSTRUCTOR'S RESOURCE MANUAL

For additional material about teaching prewriting, for journal entries, and for various tests, see the *Instructor's Resource Manual*, Section II, Part I.

having. I often get answers that way. Everywhere we look there's something to learn.

Your Freewriting Try a focused freewriting assignment to prepare for the essay you are going to compose by writing in your journal about ways that you learn.

Brainstorming

Like freewriting, brainstorming is based on free association. When you are brainstorming, you let one thought naturally lead to another, generally in the form of a list. You can brainstorm by yourself, with a friend, or with a group. Regardless of the method, list whatever comes into your mind on a topic—ideas, thoughts, examples, facts, anything. As with freewriting, don't worry about grammar, punctuation, mechanics, or spelling.

Beth's Brainstorming Here is Beth's brainstorming on learning about life:

- everyone learns about life through everyday lessons
- from my parents
- from my brothers and sisters
- from friends
- by watching our friends make mistakes
- by listening to others
- by listening to the radio
- by making my own mistakes
- by asking questions
- by listening to music
- by taking risks
- by succeeding and failing
- by reading books or newspapers
- by studying or going to school
- by observing

Your Brainstorming Brainstorm in your journal about how you think you learn.

Clustering

Clustering, like brainstorming, is based on free association, but it also shows how your thoughts are related. To cluster, take a sheet of blank paper, write a key word or phrase in the center of the page, and draw a circle around it. Next, write down and circle any related ideas that come to mind. As you add ideas, draw lines to the thoughts they came from. After two or three minutes, you'll have a map of your ideas that can guide you toward a good essay.

Beth's Cluster Here is Beth's cluster on learning about life:

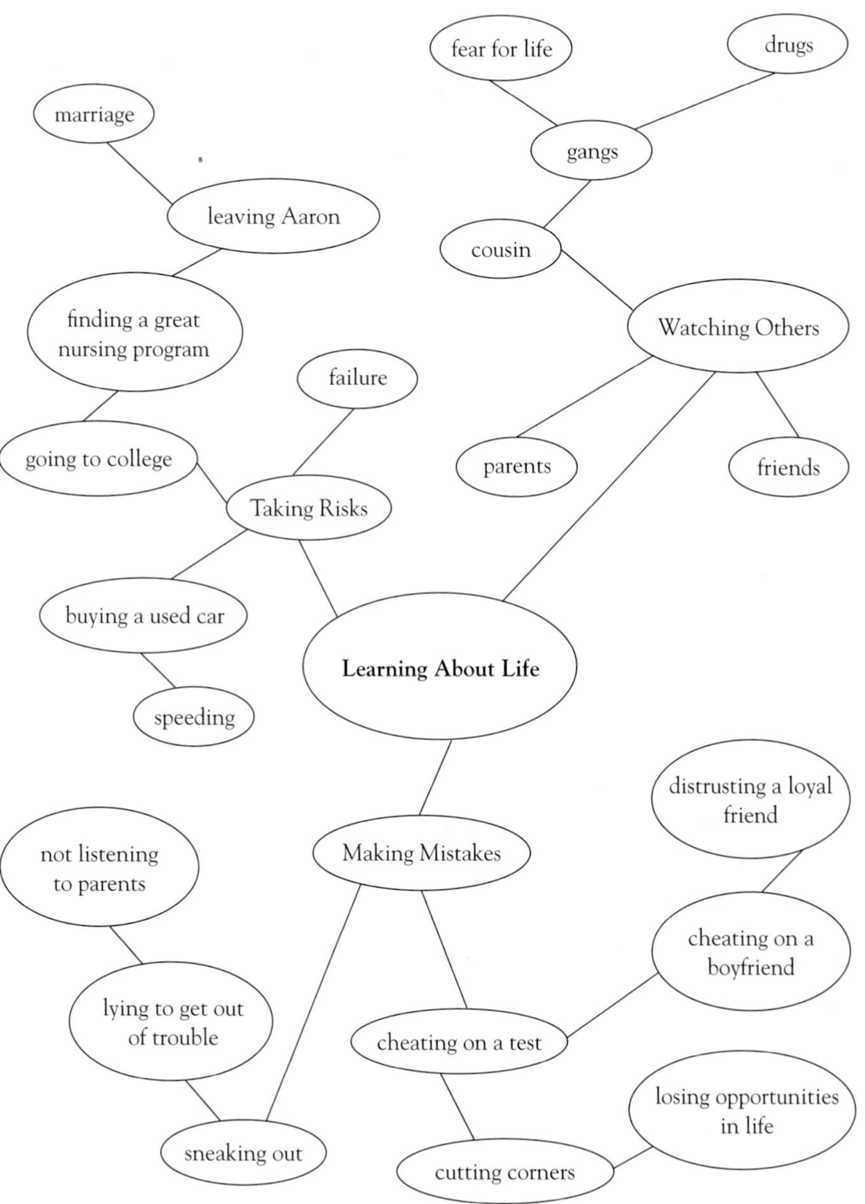

Your Cluster Write "Learning About Life" in the middle of a piece of paper, circle it, and create a cluster of your own associations with this concept.

Questioning

Journalists use the questions known as the "five *W*s and one *H*"—*Who? What? When? Where? Why?* and *How?*—to check that they've covered all the important information in a news story. Other writers use these questions to generate ideas on a writing topic. Ask yourself each question as it relates to a particular topic. Then answer the questions one by one.

Beth's Questions Here is how Beth used questioning to generate ideas on her topic, learning about life:

Who?	everyone I know learns about life
What?	learning about life
When?	all day, every day
Where?	depends on what's being learned
Why?	to better themselves in life, for fun, for a variety of reasons
How?	by paying attention and taking action I guess we can even learn without realizing it.

Your Questions In your journal, answer these six questions about learning in preparation for your essay: Who? What? When? Where? Why? How?

Discussing

Discussing involves talking your ideas out with friends, relatives, classmates, tutors, or anyone who will listen. Often someone else will have a completely new perspective on your topic that will help you come up with even more ideas. Be sure to record your notes from these conversations so that you don't lose the ideas.

Beth's Discussion Here are Beth's notes from a conversation she had with her running partner about how we learn about life.

> When I spoke with my friend Alison, I realized that we all learn about life in just about everything we do. I guess it really depends on how much we want to pay attention. Alison talked about the risks I took when I

decided to leave my hometown and study nursing at my current college. She also reminded me how much I learned from my cousin when she was involved in gangs. And we even reminisced about some of the bad choices I made and what they taught me. We talked about all the ways we learn in life, but realized we learn by watching what other people do, by taking risks throughout our lives, and by actually making mistakes. We figured these were the best ways to learn about life—for us.

Your Discussion Discuss learning about life with someone, and record notes from your conversation in your journal.

PRACTICE 1 Now that you have been introduced to several prewriting strategies, which is your favorite? Why do you like it best? *Answers will vary.*

PRACTICE 2 Using two prewriting strategies on one assignment is often a good idea. What is your second favorite prewriting strategy? Why do you like this strategy? *Answers will vary.*

PLANNING

In this course, you'll be writing essays. Although essays may differ a great deal in design, organization, and content, they share certain identifying features that distinguish them from other types of writing. At the simplest level, how an essay looks on the page tells its audience, "Here's an essay!" An essay usually has a title that names its broad subject. Many longer, more complex essays also have subtitles. When writers move from one topic to another, they indicate this shift by indenting a new paragraph. Most essays have a thesis that is either stated or implied in the introduction, several body paragraphs explaining or supporting that thesis, and a conclusion.

In content, essays are nonfiction, as opposed to short stories, poetry, or drama; that is, they deal with real-life subjects rather than made-up ones. Most essays concentrate on one specific subject and focus on a single purpose. For an essay to be successful, most writers choose methods of development that both suit their purpose and appeal to the audience they hope to inform or persuade. A successful essay gets the reaction from the readers that its author hopes for—whether this response is to appreciate a special scene, identify with someone's grief, or leap into action.

TEACHING PLANNING

Divide your students into three groups, and have them define the term *essay* focusing on one of the following features: subject, purpose, or audience. Then merge the three partial definitions into one coherent definition of the term.

TEACHING ON THE WEB

Discussion Topic: Divide students into groups of three or four and have them discuss the role of e-mail in their lives today: Do their e-mails have purpose? How does e-mail give them a sense of audience? How does Instant Messaging help or hinder their academic writing?

INSTRUCTOR'S RESOURCE MANUAL
For additional material about teaching planning, for journal entries, and for various tests, see the *Instructor's Resource Manual*, Section II, Part I.

If you haven't already discovered it, you will learn in this book that writing an essay takes planning. If you make some decisions about your topic, audience, and purpose before you actually write, the job of writing will be much smoother and less stressful.

- **What is your subject (person, event, object, idea, etc.)?** An essay focuses on a single subject, along with related thoughts and details. In approaching an essay assignment, then, deciding what you are going to write about is very important. Sometimes your topic is given to you, as when your sociology instructor assigns a paper on abused children. But other times, you choose your own subject. In such cases, choosing a subject that interests you is best. You will have more to say, and you will enjoy writing much more if you know something about your topic.
- **What is your purpose?** Your purpose is your reason for writing an essay. Your purpose could be to explore your feelings on a topic (*to do personal writing*), to tell a friend about something funny that happened to you (*to entertain*), to explain something or share information (*to inform*), or to convince others of your position on a controversial issue (*to persuade*). Whatever your purpose, deciding on it in advance makes writing the rest of your essay easier.
- **Who is your audience?** Your audience consists of the people for whom your message is intended. The more you know about your audience, the more likely you are to accomplish your purpose. The audience for your writing in college is usually your instructor, who represents what is called a "general audience"—people with an average amount of knowledge on most subjects. A general audience is a good group to aim for in all your writing unless you are given other directions.

PRACTICE 3 Identify the subject, purpose, and audience of each of the following paragraphs.

1. Schools have been dealing with the issue of bilingual education for many years. The big debate is whether or not students should be allowed to study in their native language in order to learn English. Many people believe that students should be forced to learn in English, even if they don't know the language. Other people believe that this method of teaching will cause students not to learn, but they know bilingual education programs aren't teaching the students. Obviously, a compromise must be reached in order to help the students.

Subject: *Bilingual education*

Purpose: *To inform or persuade*

Audience: *People who teach or people who need or have children who need these programs*

2. The world of computers has reached a point where people can conduct all of their business transactions from the comfort of their homes. Internet companies have made it possible for people to shop and do all of their business online. While most people using these services enjoy the convenience of being able to have a business meeting in their bathrobes, the idea of never having to leave the house worries other computer users. People will be able to do everything from home and won't have to interact with other people face to face. Eventually, the art of human interaction will be lost.

Subject: *Effects of using computers in the home*

Purpose: *To inform*

Audience: *General*

3. Playing sports came naturally to me and also taught me a valuable lesson. I began playing soccer and T-ball when I was five years old and continued playing all different types of sports through high school. I had times when I would get tired of constantly having to be at practice for one sport or another. Having a social life became very difficult because I was always busy with sports or trying to stay caught up in my classes. However, through the years of playing sports, I realized I had learned something that none of the teachers in my classes could ever teach me. I had learned how to deal with people. Competing against people taught me how to play with a team and how to keep calm when something wasn't going my way.

Subject: *Using sports to learn about how to deal with people*

Purpose: *Personal writing or to inform*

Audience: *General*

4. Reading a good book can be a fine substitute for a vacation. Every once in a while, people get the feeling that they need to get away from their normal routine and take a trip. Unfortunately, dropping everything and leaving town is not always possible. In this case, reading a book about somewhere far away can make people believe that they have really left their normal surroundings. People can become so involved in a book that they are completely oblivious to the world around them. Sometimes reading a book is just what people need to get away.

   Subject: *Reading as a form of vacationing*

   Purpose: *To inform*

   Audience: *General*

5. Last summer, my family and I went on a two-day rafting trip. The morning our trip began, we loaded all the camping gear and food into the gear trailer and were on our way. The first day the rapids were Class 2 and 3, which meant that they were moderate rapids and perfect for beginners. Everyone had fun playing in the rapids, swimming, and jumping off the rocks on the side of the river. That night in camp, the entire group was tired from such a full day on the river, so everyone was ready to go to bed early. The rapids the second day were Class 4 because they had large holes and waves and were considered intermediate. I have to admit that the second day was more exciting than the first day. At the end of the trip, everyone was ready to get a good night's sleep but eager to come back and do it all again.

   Subject: *A rafting trip*

   Purpose: *Personal writing or to entertain*

   Audience: *General*

Beth's Plans Beth made the following decisions before beginning to write on learning about life:

> **Subject:** Learning about life
>
> **Purpose:** Informative—to really talk about the different ways of learning
>
> **Audience:** General—anyone from the general population

Your Plans Identify the subject, purpose, and audience of the essay you will write on learning about life.

Subject: ____

Purpose: ____

Audience: ____

WRITING A THESIS STATEMENT

By now, you have a subject (learning about life), and you have used several prewriting techniques with this subject, which means you have generated a number of thoughts that you can use in your essay. You have also decided on a purpose and an audience. Next, you will learn how to write a thesis statement, which you will develop into an essay in the next two chapters. Again, you will be writing alongside Beth Olson as she works through her writing process.

Writing assignments in college are most often broad subjects. To compose a good essay, you need to narrow a broad subject to an idea that you can discuss in a limited number of pages. Your thesis statement is what puts limits on your essay. A **thesis statement** is the controlling idea of an essay. It is the main point that all other sentences relate to. Like a high-powered telescope, your thesis statement zooms in on the specific topic that you will discuss in the body of your essay. The decisions you made earlier in this chapter about subject, purpose, and audience will lead you to your thesis statement.

A thesis statement is usually in the first paragraph of an essay. It works best as the last sentence of the opening paragraph. Ending the introduction with the thesis statement lets the writer use the beginning of the paragraph to capture the reader's interest or give background information.

A thesis statement has two parts—a topic and an opinion you hold on that topic.

Subject	Limited Subject	+	Opinion	=	Thesis Statement
Sports	Playing a team sport		has lots of benefits		Playing a team sport teaches a person self-discipline, cooperation, and leadership.
Anger	Road rage		is very dangerous		Road rage is dangerous because it puts the driver, the victim, and the surrounding cars at risk.

TEACHING WRITING A THESIS STATEMENT

Provide students with thesis statements for many different topics. Make sure you include statements that are too broad ("Sports on TV is an American pastime"), too narrow ("My favorite football player will always be Trent Dilfer"), vague ("Monday Night Football is great"), very specific ("Monday Night Football may be a sports program, but it teaches people about teamwork and sports ethics"), and boring ("My paper will be about Monday Night Football"). Have students discuss the value of each statement and explain why they would or would not use the statement as a thesis statement. This discussion will help students learn how to concentrate their thoughts into one coherent thesis.

Writing	College writing	is similar to writing in the business world	College writing is similar to writing in the business world in three important ways: Both types of writing must be logical, well developed, and clear.

PRACTICE 4 Fill in the blanks in this exercise.

1. A thesis statement is *the controlling idea of an essay. It is the main point that all other sentences relate to.*
2. A thesis statement has two parts, a *topic* and an *opinion you hold on that topic.*
3. Where should you put your thesis? *It works best as the last sentence of the opening paragraph.*

PRACTICE 5 Limit the following subjects that aren't already limited. Then add an opinion to all subjects, and make them into thesis statements. *Answers will vary.*

Subject	Limited Subject	+	Opinion	=	Thesis Statement
1. Friendship	________		______		________
2. Work	Managers		______		________
3. Winning	________		______		________
4. Love	Dating		______		________
5. Winter	________		______		________

When you write a thesis statement, keep the following guidelines in mind:

1. **Your subject should not be too broad or too narrow.** A subject or topic that is too broad would need a book to develop it. One that is too nar-

THESIS STATEMENT CHECK

Here is an exercise for your students to do in pairs.

Writer: Underline your thesis statement (one sentence only).

Peer: Read only your partner's underlined sentence, and answer the following questions.

1. What do you think the topic of the paper is?
2. What is the writer's opinion?
3. On the basis of the underlined sentence, what do you think the paper will be about?

Peer: Discuss the paper (not the thesis) with the writer, and answer the following question: What information needs to be added or dropped from the thesis statement?

Now reverse roles, and do the exercise again.

TEACHING ON THE WEB

Discussion Topic: How can the Internet help students create thesis statements? How else can the Internet help students form opinions?

INSTRUCTOR'S RESOURCE MANUAL

For additonal material about teaching the thesis, for journal entries, and for various tests, see the *Instructor's Resource Manual,* Section II, Part I.

row leaves you nothing to say. A manageable subject is one that you can write about in roughly three body paragraphs. You may find it necessary to limit your subject several times before you arrive at one that will work.

Subject:	Television
Too broad:	Prime-time TV
Still too broad:	Most popular TV shows
Good:	*CSI: Miami*
Too narrow:	William Grissom

2. **State your opinion clearly.** When you give your opinion on the topic, choose your words carefully. Be direct and take a stand. Opinions such as "is interesting," "are not good," "is a problem," or "can teach us a lot" are vague and boring. In fact, if you are specific enough about the opinion you hold, you will be very close to a thesis statement.

Vague opinion:	*CSI: Miami* is fun to watch.
Specific opinion:	*CSI: Miami* teaches us about our legal system.

3. **Do not simply announce your topic.** Make an interesting statement about your topic.

Announcement:	My paper is going to be about *CSI: Miami*. *CSI: Miami* is the topic of this essay.
Statement:	*CSI: Miami* is a TV show that teaches us about our legal system.

4. **Try your thesis statement (TS) as a question.** This does not mean that you should actually express your thesis statement as a question in your essay. Rather, you should try thinking of your thesis statement as a question that you will answer in the rest of your essay. You might want to write out your "TS question" and keep it in front of you as you draft your paper. It will help you keep your focus.

Thesis statement:	The television program *CSI: Miami* teaches us about our legal system.
TS question:	How does *CSI: Miami* teach us about our legal system?

PRACTICE 6 Which of the following are good thesis statements? Mark B for too broad, N for too narrow, MO for missing opinion, and C for complete. Test each thesis statement by turning it into a question.

B 1. Schools have good education programs.

MO 2. In America today, we face the problem of keeping our air clean.

C 3. Vehicles powered by natural gas will cut down on the pollution expelled by automobiles.

B 4. When using a computer, the user should know many things.

MO 5. Human cloning is being studied to determine the scientific and moral consequences of the process.

C 6. Children in America are becoming desensitized to violence because of TV.

N 7. Many people do not eat meat because they cannot stand the thought of eating something that was once alive.

N 8. A lot of people avoid math because they have difficulty with analytical problem solving.

MO 9. Our campus drama department will be performing *Noises Off* this spring.

MO 10. Since the early 1980s, people have been on various health-craze diets and exercise programs.

PRACTICE 7 Complete the following thesis statements. *Answers will vary.*

1. Marriage today ______________________________.
2. ______________ is my favorite class because ______________.
3. Sleeping ______________________________.
4. TV reality shows ______________________________.
5. ______________________ is a role model for college students today.

Beth's Thesis Statement Beth writes a thesis statement by stating her opinion about her subject.

Limited Subject	**Opinion**
I know that I learn	from many things in life.

Your Thesis Statement Write a thesis statement here that can serve as the controlling idea for your essay.

Limited Subject **Opinion**

_______________ ____

Thesis Statement

____

6

CHAPTER

Writing Effectively

Writing is made up of several steps that lead you to your first draft. So far, you have been given a subject (learning about life) and worked with a number of prewriting techniques. You have generated ideas that you can use in your essay and have decided on a purpose and audience. In addition, you have composed a working thesis statement.

At this point, you are ready to write your essay. This chapter deals with the heart of the writing process: developing body paragraphs, organizing your essay, and writing the introduction, conclusion, and title. Once you work through this chapter, you will be more comfortable with these elements of the process and the way they function as part of the whole. Again, you will be writing alongside Beth as she goes through the writing process with you.

As you learned in the first few chapters of this text, all stages of the writing process are part of a recurring cycle that you will mold into a routine to suit your lifestyle. The more you write, the more natural this process will become for you.

DEVELOPING BODY PARAGRAPHS

Now that you have written a thesis statement that comes at the end of your introduction, you are ready to write the body paragraphs of your essay. The body paragraphs explain and support the thesis statement.

TEACHING DEVELOPING BODY PARAGRAPHS

To encourage students to compose directly on a computer, conduct class in a computer lab, and have students practice typing directly into a word-processing program. Show students how to turn off the automatic spell-check and grammar-check so that the red

Support for Your Thesis

What ideas will support the statement you are making in your thesis? This is the question you need to answer at this point. The supporting ideas are what make up the body of your essay. Each body paragraph covers one major idea of your thesis. The body paragraphs consist of a topic sentence and concrete details that support that topic sentence.

PRACTICE 1 For each of the following lists, cross out any ideas that do not support the thesis statement.

1. Thesis: Children are desensitized to violence by television, video games, and comic books.

   Children don't react to the violent acts they see on TV.

   Children do not care when the heroes beat up the villains in comic books.

   ~~Many video games cost too much.~~

   ~~Children often want to be just like the sports figures they watch on TV.~~

   Most children learn very early in life to shoot figures in video games.

2. Thesis: Political campaigns often bring out the worst in candidates.

   ~~Most people are either Republican or Democrat.~~

   Candidates try to find secrets from their opponents' pasts.

   Candidates use the media to help ruin other candidates' reputations.

   ~~Presidential campaigns occur every four years.~~

   Some candidates even resort to name-calling and twisting their opponents' words.

3. Thesis: To qualify for the FBI, applicants must meet certain requirements.

   People interested in joining the FBI must have a college degree.

   FBI applicants must be in great physical shape and have excellent eyesight.

   ~~The events on 9/11 have created a great interest in the CIA.~~

   ~~FBI agents work within the United States, while CIA agents work outside the United States.~~

   FBI applicants must be willing to go through rigorous training and to move anywhere in the United States.

and green underlines don't interfere as students generate ideas. In this way, you are also showing students that they should not focus on revision and editing errors as they write a first draft.

TEACHING ON THE WEB

Discussion Topic: Divide students into groups of three or four, and have them discuss how the Internet has changed the way they view writing. How much writing do they do in a single day on the Internet? How much writing did they do prior to the Internet? How have writing and the Internet changed their lives?

INSTRUCTOR'S RESOURCE MANUAL

For additional material about teaching body paragraphs, for journal entries, and for various tests, see the *Instructor's Resource Manual,* Section II, Part I.

4. Thesis: Starting your own business takes a lot of planning and work.

   Prospective business owners must create a business plan in order to borrow money from a bank.

   ~~Owning your own business is rewarding.~~

   People should research the current trends in the market for the type of business they plan to open.

   ~~Sometimes business owners can get their families to work for free.~~

   People should determine how much money they will spend and how much money they will make so they can project possible earnings.

5. Thesis: To maintain a long-distance relationship, both people must be willing to sacrifice.

   ~~Couples often separate when they go to different universities.~~

   Both parties must be sensitive to the other's needs—even at a distance.

   People have to communicate often with each other, even if it's hard to find the time.

   Both people must put extra effort into the relationship to make it work.

   ~~My parents had a long-distance relationship.~~

PRACTICE 2 For each of the following thesis statements, list three supporting ideas. *Answers will vary.*

1. People should always look for three qualities when searching for a job.

   ____

   ____

   ____

2. Moving away from home for the first time can be hard.

   ____

   ____

   ____

3. Animals can help people live longer.

___

___

___

4. Vacations can often be more strenuous than restful.

___

___

___

5. Studying the right way can make a difference in a test grade.

___

___

___

Essays can be different lengths and often have a varying number of ideas that support their thesis statements. The thesis statement generally determines the length of an essay and the amount of support necessary to make a point. Some statements require very little proof and might need only one body paragraph; others require much more support and might need four or more body paragraphs for a complete explanation. An essay that falls somewhere in the middle has an introduction, three body paragraphs, and a conclusion.

Beth's Supporting Ideas Beth decided on three supporting ideas for her essay, which means she will write three body paragraphs.

Thesis Statement: I know that I learn from many things in life.

Supporting Idea 1: Taking risks

Supporting Idea 2: Watching others

Supporting Idea 3: Making mistakes

Your Supporting Ideas Now list the support you might use for your thesis statement.

Your Thesis Statement: ______________________________

Supporting Idea 1: ______________________________

Supporting Idea 2: ______________________________

Supporting Idea 3: ______________________________

Outlining

At this stage of the writing process, many people benefit from putting their main ideas in the form of a rough, or working, outline. A rough outline can help you plan your essay and let you see the relationship of your ideas to one another. In this way, you can easily identify ideas that don't support your thesis and locate places where you need more information. A rough outline can evolve and become more detailed as your paper develops.

PRACTICE 3 Fill in the following rough outlines. *Answers will vary.*

1. Subject: College life

   Limited Subject: ______________________________

   Thesis Statement: ______________________________

   Topic Sentence: ______________________________

   Topic Sentence: ______________________________

   Topic Sentence: ______________________________

2. Subject: Animal rights

   Limited Subject: ______________________________

   Thesis Statement: ______________________________

   Topic Sentence: ______________________________

   Topic Sentence: ______________________________

   Topic Sentence: ______________________________

3. Subject: Intercollegiate sports

   Limited Subject: ______________________________

   Thesis Statement: ______________________________

Topic Sentence: ______________________________

Topic Sentence: ______________________________

Topic Sentence: ______________________________

4. Subject: Summer jobs

Limited Subject: ______________________________

Thesis Statement: ______________________________

Topic Sentence: ______________________________

Topic Sentence: ______________________________

Topic Sentence: ______________________________

5. Subject: The Internet

Limited Subject: ______________________________

Thesis Statement: ______________________________

Topic Sentence: ______________________________

Topic Sentence: ______________________________

Topic Sentence: ______________________________

Beth's Rough Outline Here is a rough outline of Beth's ideas so far:

Thesis Statement: I know that I learn from many things in life.

A. I learn from taking risks.

B. I learn from watching others.

C. I learn from making mistakes.

Your Rough Outline Now put your ideas in outline form.

Thesis Statement: ______________________________

A. ______________________________

B. ______________________________

C. ______________________________

Topic Sentences

Now you need to state each of your supporting ideas in the form of a topic sentence that will be developed into a body paragraph. The decisions you made in Chapter 5 about subject, purpose, and audience will lead you to your topic sentences. Look back at your prewriting notes and think about which topics will best support your thesis statement. These will be the topics of your body paragraphs. These paragraphs will each include a topic sentence.

The **topic sentence** of a paragraph is its controlling idea. A typical paragraph consists of a topic sentence and details that expand on that topic sentence. A topic sentence performs two important tasks in its paragraph: (1) It supports the essay's thesis statement, and (2) it tells what the paragraph will be about. It functions best as the first or last sentence in its paragraph. Beginning or ending a paragraph with the topic sentence gives direction to the paragraph and provides a kind of road map for the reader.

Like a thesis statement, a topic sentence has two parts—a topic and a statement about that topic. The topic should be limited enough that it can be developed in a paragraph. It should also be focused and not vague or scattered.

Topic	Limited Topic	Statement
Reading	Frequent reading	improves thinking skills.
Lotteries	Winning the lottery	will change a person's life forever.
Children	Having children	is a huge responsibility.
Hate	Hate crimes	are one of life's worst horrors.

PRACTICE 4 Limit the following topics. Then develop them into statements that could be topic sentences. *Answers will vary.*

Topic	Limited Topic	Statement
1. Mondays	____________	____________
2. Hobbies	____________	____________
3. Theme parks	____________	____________
4. Writing	____________	____________
5. Summer	____________	____________

PRACTICE 5 Complete the following topic sentences. Make sure they are general enough to be developed into a paragraph but are not too broad. *Answers will vary.*

1. Work-related injuries ________________________.

2. ________________________ is my favorite television show.

3. Sex education ____________________________________.

4. Stray dogs and cats ________________________________.

5. __________________________ must be looked at on my college campus.

PRACTICE 6 Write topic sentences for the following paragraphs.
Answers may vary.

1. *My mom loves to watch mystery shows on TV.*

   She watches the old ones like *Perry Mason* and can't get enough of the newer ones like *CSI*. But my mom really prefers the not-old and not-new mystery shows like *Matlock* and *Murder, She Wrote*. My mom will watch any of these shows for hours. My dad has a joke that she's watching all these TV shows so she can learn how to get rid of him and get away with it. I think she's just gathering information to write a book similar to these shows she loves to watch.

2. *Learning how to master a new computer program can be difficult.*

   First, you must follow the directions to install it onto your computer. Then you must read the directions to learn what you should do first with the program. It's best to read all the directions first, but most of the time people just go straight to the program and try to navigate their way through it. Once you get a handle on how to work the program, it's best just to play around and use the book only when you have questions. Mastering computer programs can be hard, but once you've done it, you can be sure you'll never forget how to use them.

3. *My sister should have hired a professional consultant to help with her wedding plans.*

   Because she wanted to save money for other parts of her wedding, the consultant was the first expense she cut. Everything went fine until the day of the wedding. My sister didn't get the flowers she ordered, but the ones that were delivered were OK. The cake arrived four hours late, and the reception hall wouldn't let us attach anything to the walls. And just before my sister walked into the church, she discovered that the train on her wedding dress was completely inside out. Luckily, no one but my sister and our family knew of the mishaps, but a consultant would have been worth every penny on the actual day of the wedding.

PRACTICE 7 Supply three topic sentences for each thesis statement.
Answers will vary.

1. Many people enjoy resting on Sundays.

____

____

____

2. Teachers should encourage all students to learn.

____

____

____

3. Computers will enable people to function more efficiently at work, at home, and at play.

____

____

____

4. Planning is the key to a successful vacation.

____

____

____

5. The abilities to think critically, act quickly, and communicate clearly are essential in the business world.

____

____

____

Beth's Topic Sentences Beth writes three topic sentences that she thinks will support her thesis statement.

Thesis Statement: I know that I learn from many things in life.

Topic Sentence: I have discovered that I learn a lot by taking risks.

Topic Sentence I also benefit from watching other people.

Topic Sentence I believe that I learn from making mistakes.

Your Topic Sentences Develop each of the ideas you listed on page 56 into a topic sentence that is directly related to your thesis statement. List your thesis first.

Thesis Statement: ________________________________

Topic Sentence: ________________________________

Topic Sentence: ________________________________

Topic Sentence: ________________________________

Specific Details

Now you are ready to generate the specific details that will make up the bulk of your body paragraphs. Later in this text, you will learn about different methods of developing your ideas, such as describing, comparing and contrasting, and analyzing causes and effects. For now, we are simply going to practice generating concrete supporting details and examples that are directly related to a specific topic. Concrete words refer to anything you can see, hear, touch, smell, or taste, such as *trees*, *boats*, *water*, *friends*, *fire alarm*, and *bread*. They make writing come alive because they help the reader picture what the writer is talking about.

PRACTICE 8 Put a check mark by the details and examples listed that support each topic sentence.

1. Many people are addicted to soap operas.

   __✓__ viewers get caught up in the story

   __✓__ people care about the characters

   _____ soap operas are often springboards for actors wanting more work

   __✓__ people are anxious to see what happens next

   _____ mindless but entertaining TV

   __✓__ viewers often strongly identify with the characters

   _____ CBS has had the number one soap opera for years

2. My parents have reversed the stereotypical roles in their marriage.

    __✓__ my dad decorates the house
    _____ my mom and dad both work
    _____ my sister wants to be just like our mom
    __✓__ my mom mows and takes care of the lawn
    __✓__ my dad cleans the inside of the house
    _____ I hope to marry someone like my mom

3. The members of every generation think they'll understand their kids' music—until they actually hear it.

    __✓__ parents don't appreciate today's rock music
    __✓__ parents who like rock and roll don't understand heavy metal
    __✓__ parents become wary of musicians like Kid Rock and Marilyn Manson
    __✓__ no parents understand new wave or punk music
    _____ Dick Clark has helped all kinds of music get established
    _____ parents have a hard time letting their kids listen to rap music
    _____ Elvis helped put rock and roll on the map

4. Students change their majors often throughout their academic careers.

    _____ general education courses make students learn about a variety of subjects
    __✓__ in college, students discover new interests in subjects they have never been exposed to
    _____ professors bring new subjects to life for many students
    _____ math is difficult for many students
    __✓__ other students often influence a student's decision about a major
    __✓__ the reality of the job market creates changes in majors
    __✓__ academic performance sometimes makes students look for alternative interests

5. The best way to lose weight is through a good diet and exercise.
   - __✓__ snacking all day long can cause a person to eat more than usual
   - _____ people who exercise a lot need enough sleep
   - __✓__ skipping meals is counterproductive for people on diets
   - __✓__ people should exercise at least three times per week
   - __✓__ running is great exercise
   - __✓__ people should eat three sensible meals per day
   - _____ ESPN has many exercise shows

PRACTICE 9 For each of the following topic sentences, list five details or examples to develop them. *Answers will vary.*

1. Everywhere I go, I seem to see someone I know.

   ____

   ____

   ____

   ____

   ____

2. When I was in high school, I enjoyed many different extracurricular activities.

   ____

   ____

   ____

   ____

   ____

3. People are beginning to use their personal computers for many different types of business transactions.

   ____

   ____

____

____

____

4. Friends and family are very important parts of life.

____

____

____

____

____

5. People must be careful when they are swimming.

____

____

____

____

____

Beth's Development To come up with concrete details and examples that would support her topic sentence, Beth uses the brainstorming and focused freewriting techniques she learned in Chapter 5. This is what she wrote:

I have discovered that I learn a lot by taking risks.

- buying a used car
- quitting my new job
- leaving Aaron to come to this school
- driving way too fast
- trying new foods
- changing majors
- procrastinating in school

I also benefit from watching other people.

- moving in with roommates I don't know
- watching my friends make mistakes with their boyfriends

looking at my parents make rules
seeing my cousin ruin her life
watching my brother mess up
observing people around me get involved with drugs
learning about other people's mistakes from my friends

I believe that I learn from making mistakes.

cheating on the test
believing the rumor about my best friend
lying to my parents
not believing my sister
waiting too long to write a paper
watching TV instead of studying

Here is Beth's new freewriting:

> I know I learn a lot by taking risks, watching other people, and making mistakes. I'm sure I learn in other ways too, but these are the ways that seem to give me the most information about life in general.
>
> Taking risks really helps everyone learn in life, but I think this is especially true for me. I mean, right now I'm sitting here in this class thinking about Aaron and how we want to get married someday. But I left my hometown and Aaron to come here for the nursing program. So far everything is great, but I knew it was a risk coming here. But how could I learn if I didn't?
>
> I also learn by watching other people. My parents are great role models, but it's hard to really learn because they are so much older. I mean, they *tell* me not to join a gang, but they're my parents. I learned more about gangs from my cousin than from my parents. Watching my cousin go through her experiences was way better than just listening to my parents. I definitely learn by watching others.
>
> And I definitely learn by making mistakes. And boy do I have tons of those. Most of my mistakes are pretty small, but I still learn from them. I think I learned the most from Mr. Turner, though, when he caught me

> cheating on his test. He talked to me, and that really helped. In fact, I think it's because of him that I started paying attention in class and decided to pursue nursing at this school.
>
> I will always learn about life from these sources. I guess I will always learn about life as long as I keep my eyes open, but these ways seem the most important to me right now.

Your Development Choose at least one of the prewriting strategies that you learned in Chapter 5, and use it to generate more specific details and examples for each of your topic sentences.

ORGANIZING YOUR ESSAY

TEACHING ORGANIZING YOUR ESSAY

Bring to class newspaper articles that you have cut into sections. Divide your students into groups of three or four, and give each group two or three cut-up articles (be sure not to mix up the articles). Have each group try to organize the articles in a logical way. Have students organize at least one of the articles in more than one way. Have each group present one article that can be organized in a couple of different ways and justify the organization in each case.

TEACHING ON THE WEB

Discussion Topic: Web sites must be well organized if people are to find the information they need. In what similar ways do Web sites and essays have to be organized? What types of Web sites

You are moving along quite well in the writing process. You have determined your subject, purpose, and audience, and you have written your thesis statement. You have also written topic sentences for your body paragraphs and thought of details, examples, and facts to develop those topic sentences. You are now ready to organize your ideas. What should come first? What next?

To organize the ideas in your essay, you need to consider the purpose of your essay and the way each body paragraph serves that purpose. Then you should arrange your body paragraphs in a logical manner to achieve that purpose. If your essay's main purpose is informative—to describe the layout of a building, for example—you would probably arrange the details spatially. That is, you might begin with the entrance and move to the other parts of the building as if you were strolling through it. If, however, you want to persuade a reader to buy one type of car over another, you might arrange the essay so that it moves from one extreme to another—for example, from the least important feature of the car to the most important. Once you decide on the order of your paragraphs, you need to organize the details in each paragraph.

Most paragraphs and essays are organized in one of five ways:

1. From general to particular
2. From particular to general
3. Chronologically (by time)
4. Spatially (by physical order)
5. From one extreme to another

Let's look at these methods of organization one by one.

General to Particular

The most common method of organizing an essay or paragraph is from general to particular. This method begins with a general topic and becomes more specific as it progresses. A paragraph organized from general to particular might look like this:

Topic Sentence
  Detail
  Detail
  Detail
  Detail

Here is an example of a paragraph organized from general to particular:

> When I began attending college, I was very nervous because I was afraid I would not do very well in my classes. My first year, I took general education classes that reviewed a lot of the material I learned in high school. There was a lot of studying involved in these classes, but I was able to pass all of them. Soon I decided that my major would be business, so I began taking classes that dealt with business. All of the business classes were harder than the classes I had taken in general education. Just when I thought I would not pass a class, I would do well on a test, which would raise my confidence level again. I worked very hard in every class I took and was able to pass every one. Tomorrow I am graduating with my bachelor's degree in business.

This paragraph moves from the general idea of going to college to the specific notion of taking classes, graduating, and receiving a degree. Notice that it includes such transitions as *when*, *but*, *soon*, and *which*. They show the relationship among the writer's thoughts.

The skeleton of a general-to-particular essay looks like this, although the number of paragraphs and details will vary:

Introduction
  Topic sentence stating the most general point
    Detail
    Detail
    Detail
  Topic sentence stating a more specific supporting point
    Detail
    Detail
    Detail

would use the general-to-particular, particular-to-general, chronological, spatial, or one-extreme-to-another method of organization?

INSTRUCTOR'S RESOURCE MANUAL

For additional material about teaching organizing the essay, for journal entries, and for various tests, see the *Instructor's Resource Manual*, Section II, Part I.

Topic sentence stating the most specific supporting point
Detail
Detail
Detail
Conclusion

An example of an essay organized from general to particular is "The Decorated Body" on page 215. The essay begins by introducing the cultural messages connected with decorating the naked body. The author then explains what various decorations mean in different civilizations, moving to topics that become more and more specific as the essay progresses. You might want to read this selection to see how this method of organization works in a full essay.

PRACTICE 10 Turn to the essay "El Hoyo" on page 145, and find two paragraphs organized from general to specific. *Paragraphs 2, 3, or 4.*

PRACTICE 11 Write a topic sentence for the following group of sentences. Then organize the sentences into a paragraph using general-to-particular order. Add words, phrases, or sentences as necessary to smooth out the paragraph.

Topic Sentence: *Nowadays sports figures are constantly on television.*

3 During these events, not only do you get to watch the athletes play their games, but you get to see former athletes announcing the action play-by-play.

1 Anytime you turn on the TV, there are at least fourteen sporting events happening at one time.

2 You can see anything from basketball to golf to racing to fishing.

5 Let's face it; the likelihood of seeing a sports figure on TV is great.

4 And just when you think you've seen enough of the players, you are flooded with commercials that have athletes selling various products.

Particular to General

When you reverse the first method of organization, you arrange your material from particular to general. In this case, more specific ideas start the essay or paragraph and lead up to a general statement. This type of organization is particularly effective if you suspect that your reader might not agree with the final point you are going to make. With this method, you can lead your reader to your opinion slowly and carefully.

A paragraph organized from particular to general looks like this:

Detail
Detail
Detail
Detail
Topic Sentence

Here is a paragraph of particular-to-general organization.

The water is so crystal clear that I can see every pebble settled on the bottom. A small sandy beach reaches the water's edge and makes a perfect spot to spend the afternoon. Across the water I can see the mountainside covered in the greenest trees imaginable. A log cabin also sits among the trees halfway up the mountain, so peaceful and secluded. The puffy white clouds make the sky appear to be a brighter blue, and the birds seem to enjoy floating on the soft breeze. I could sit all day next to the lake in the valley and just stare at my surroundings.

This paragraph starts with specific details about the area around the lake and ends with a topic sentence. Transitions such as *and*, *across the water*, and *also* move readers through the paragraph.

This is how a particular-to-general essay looks, though the number of details will vary:

Introduction
Topic sentence stating the most specific point
Detail
Detail
Detail
Topic sentence stating a less specific point
Detail
Detail
Detail
Topic sentence stating the most general point
Detail
Detail
Detail
Conclusion

The essay titled "Spanglish Spoken Here" on page 352 is a good example of organization from particular to general. It moves from examples out of the writer's life to his thesis at the end—that work is his therapy. If you read this selection, you will see firsthand how this method of organization works in a complete essay.

PRACTICE 12 Turn to the essay "What Are Friends For?" on page 322, and find two paragraphs that demonstrate particular-to-general organization.
Paragraphs 6 and 12.

PRACTICE 13 Write a topic sentence for the following group of sentences. Then organize the sentences into a paragraph using particular-to-general order. Add words, phrases, or sentences as necessary to smooth out the paragraph.

Topic Sentence: *Pepperoni pizza is my very favorite food.*

6 My mom hopes I'll order something more grown-up, but I never will.
4 My family knew I loved pizza and always let me order one once a week.
1 I have always loved pepperoni, even on sandwiches and in soups.
3 I used to love pizza night when I lived at home.
2 I believe that pizza is the best food ever created.
5 Now when I go home, we just go to an Italian restaurant where I can order pizza.

Chronological Order

When you organize ideas chronologically, you are organizing them according to the passage of time—in other words, in the order in which they occurred. Most of the time, when you tell a story or explain how to do something, you use chronological order: First this happened and then that. Or first you do this, next you do that, and so on.

A paragraph organized chronologically looks like this:

Topic Sentence
  First
  Then
  Next
  Finally

Here is an example of a paragraph organized chronologically:

> Preparing to go snowboarding for the first time can be a lot of fun. First of all, you must get into full gear when you arrive at the mountain. Then you ride a ski lift to the top of the mountain. Once at the top, it is time to buckle your boots into the bindings on the board. The bindings must be tight, but not so tight that they are uncomfortable. Next, you are ready to begin your descent. On the way down the mountain, pay attention to how the board moves when pressure is applied to the toes and heels of the feet. Finally, you need to learn which way to lean in order to turn right and left so you can fly down the mountain. Once you have mastered the basics, you will have fun perfecting your new hobby.

This paragraph is chronological because it explains snowboarding according to a time sequence and uses transitions such as *first of all*, *then*, *next*, and *finally*.

Here is what an essay organized chronologically looks like:

Introduction
- What happened first
  - Detail
  - Detail
  - Detail
- What happened next
  - Detail
  - Detail
  - Detail
- What happened after that
  - Detail
  - Detail
  - Detail

Conclusion

A good example of this method of organization is the essay titled "Black Music in Our Hands" on page 317. It begins with the author explaining the three types of music she sang in the early 1960s. She then explains according to a time sequence all the circumstances that caused her to look at music differently. Reading through this essay will help you understand this method of organization.

PRACTICE 14 Turn to the essay "Writer's Retreat" on page 182, and find two paragraphs that are organized chronologically. *Most paragraphs in this essay are arranged chronologically.*

PRACTICE 15 Write a topic sentence for the following group of sentences. Then organize the sentences into a paragraph using chronological order. Add words, phrases, or sentences as necessary to smooth out the paragraph.

Topic Sentence: *Making a peanut butter and jelly sandwich is easy.*

7 Spread the jelly on top of the peanut butter.
3 Unscrew the lid from a jar of peanut butter and from a jar of jelly.
6 Using the knife again, remove a small amount of jelly from the jar.
2 Place two slices of bread on a plate.
4 Using the knife, remove a small amount of peanut butter from the jar.
8 Place the second slice of bread on top of the slice with the peanut butter and jelly on it.
1 First, remove a butter knife from the drawer.
5 Spread the peanut butter on one slice of bread with the knife.

Spatial Order

Another method of arranging details is by their relationship to each other in space. You might describe the layout of your campus from its front entrance to its back exit or the arrangement of a beautiful garden from one end to the other. Explaining a home page from top to bottom and describing a screened-in porch from inside to outside are also examples of spatial order. Beginning at one point and moving detail by detail around a specific area is the simplest way of organizing by space.

A paragraph organized spatially might look like this:

Topic Sentence
 Here
 There
 Next
 Across
 Beyond

Here is an example of a paragraph organized spatially:

> It was the first football game of the season and her first football game ever as a cheerleader. Standing in front of the huge crowd made the butterflies in her stomach begin to flutter again. In the front row sat a group of her friends cheering her on. Two rows behind them sat her psychology professor. Next to her professor sat a few of her new sorority sisters. As the cheerleader looked across the aisle, she noticed a group of rowdy students screaming and cheering for their team. Beyond the crowd, the tall announcer's booth where all of the press people and the athletic director sat seemed to glare down at her. Any minute the music would begin to blare from that very booth, and she would begin her first half-time dance routine.

This paragraph is arranged spatially because it moves physically around the football stadium, using such words as *in front of*, *behind*, *next to*, and *beyond* as transitions.

Here is what an essay organized spatially looks like:

Introduction
- Here
  - Detail
  - Detail
  - Detail
- There
  - Detail
  - Detail
  - Detail
- Next
  - Detail
  - Detail
  - Detail
- Across
  - Detail
  - Detail
  - Detail
- Beyond
  - Detail

Detail
Detail
Conclusion

An example of this method of organization is the essay titled "Dwellings" on page 149. It moves in spatial order around the vicinity of the author's home. Reading through this essay will help you understand this method of organization.

PRACTICE 16 Turn to the essay "The Sanctuary of School" on page 177, and find two paragraphs that use spatial organization. *Paragraphs 8 and 12.*

PRACTICE 17 Write a topic sentence for the following group of sentences. Then organize the sentences into a paragraph using spatial order. Add words, phrases, or sentences as necessary to smooth out the paragraph.

Topic Sentence: *There are many things to see at the front of the hotel.*

4 The hotel's check-in desk is located on the left side of the lobby.
5 Two little boys are sitting quietly on the couches next to the check-in desk, waiting for their parents to finish checking in.
7 In the center of the lobby are four massive couches arranged in a conversational setting.
6 Directly across from the check-in desk is the activities counter, where people can plan their days.
2 Inside the front door, the guests' attention is immediately drawn to the ceiling.
3 Painted as a sky, the ceiling gives guests the feeling that they have never left the outdoors.
1 Framing the front door are two huge dolphins, each perched in the center of a water fountain.

One Extreme to Another

Sometimes the best way to organize a paragraph is from one extreme to another: from most expensive to least expensive, from most humorous to least humorous, from least frustrating to most frustrating, and so on. Use whatever extremes make sense for your topic. You might explain how to choose a pet by elaborating on the most important qualities of an animal and then considering the least important. For example, an apartment dweller's most important consideration would be the size of the pet and its need for exercise. Least important would be watchdog qualities. To accomplish another purpose, you might reverse this order and begin with the least important quality; this method is good in persuasive writing because you end with your most important idea.

This method of organization has one distinct advantage over the other four approaches: It is the most flexible. When no other method of organization works, you can always arrange details from one extreme to another.

Here is an outline of a paragraph organized from one extreme to another:

Topic Sentence
  Most
  Next most
  Somewhat
  Least

Here is an example of a paragraph that moves from one extreme to another:

> Ever since I was old enough to join Little League teams, I have played a variety of sports. I would have to say that my favorite sport has always been football. Absolutely nothing can top the feeling of running for a touchdown and passing the defensive safety. My next favorite sport would have to be baseball. I used to love to pitch to catchers when we would work as though we were one athlete. My next favorite sport is basketball. As a teenager, I played guard in basketball, but eventually I got bored with the position. My least favorite sport is soccer. No matter how much I trained and ran before soccer season, I always got exhausted during the games—all we did was run up and down the field. Now that I'm in college, I'm grateful for the intramural teams that let me keep playing the sports that I love.

This paragraph moves from most to least preferred sports and is marked by such words as *favorite*, *next favorite*, and *least favorite*.

Here is what an essay organized according to extremes looks like:

Introduction
  Most
    Detail

Detail
Detail
Next most
Detail
Detail
Detail
Somewhat
Detail
Detail
Detail
Least
Detail
Detail
Detail
Conclusion

"What Are Friends For?" on page 322 is a good example of this method of organization. It begins with a discussion of "relative friends" and moves to an explanation of "new friends." The author organizes her essay from least meaningful to most meaningful friends. Reading through this essay will help you understand this strategy.

PRACTICE 18 Turn to the essay "Happiness Is Catching" on page 383, and find two paragraphs that are organized from one extreme to another.
Paragraphs 10 and 11

PRACTICE 19 Write a topic sentence for the following group of sentences. Then write a paragraph arranging the sentences from one extreme to another. Add words, phrases, and sentences as necessary to smooth out the paragraph. Also, label your system of classification (from most to least or from least to most). *Answers will vary.*

Topic Sentence: *New employees who must collect money have a difficult time.*

1 First, they have a hard time asking people for money.
3 Consequently, they allow debtors extra time to pay the bill.
6 But after a few months, the new employee has heard all the sob stories and is immune to their power.
4 That just makes it harder to get the money.

2 This may be because they believe the sob stories they hear, which probably aren't true.

5 Unfortunately, once the date has been extended, we all have to agree to it.

System of Classification: *Chronological*

PRACTICE 20 List the best method of development for paragraphs on the following topics.

1. How to make homemade salsa. *Chronological.*
2. I think I am going to rearrange my dorm room to create more space. *Spatial.*
3. What I will have for dinner tonight. *General to particular.*
4. Today, people question the ethics of capital punishment. *General to particular.*
5. I lift weights for an hour and run five miles every day. *Particular to general.*

PRACTICE 21 Write a topic sentence that introduces the following details in a paragraph. Then arrange the details in logical order, and write a paragraph. *Answers will vary.*

Topic Sentence: *Although sometimes difficult, exercise is an essential part of life.*

exercising three times a week
the advantages of aerobic exercise
exercising with a friend
the difficulty of starting an exercise routine

Beth's Organization Beth decided to organize her essay from one extreme to another—from the most important ways of learning for her to the least important. She first wants to introduce the idea of taking risks, which she believes is very important. Next she will discuss watching others and finally learning from mistakes because she thinks she learns a lot from her own mistakes. She thinks this order might work, so she lists as many concrete details as she can under each main idea.

Here is Beth's working outline at this point:

Thesis Statement: I know that I learn from many things in life.

Taking Risks (*most important*): taking risks and learning from them

Specific Details: finding a good nursing program
leaving my boyfriend back home
going to college

Watching Others (*less important*): learning from watching others

Specific Details: watching my cousin in gangs
living in fear
not in a gang because of her

Making Mistakes (*least important*): making mistakes and learning from those mistakes

Specific Details: cheating on test
talking with Mr. Turner
learning to pay more attention in school for a better future

Concluding Thoughts: people can learn from everything they do

Specific Details: taking risks
watching others
making mistakes

Does the method of organization that Beth has chosen suit her topic? Would any other method of organization work as well?

Your Organization What method of organization will work best for your ideas about learning? Why do you think this method will be best?

TEACHING WRITING THE INTRODUCTION, CONCLUSION, AND TITLE
Divide students into six groups. Provide each group with an extremely dull, short introduction on a topic familiar to them (perhaps a current TV show or an issue in the news). Then assign

WRITING THE INTRODUCTION, CONCLUSION, AND TITLE

By now, you have written your thesis statement and topic sentences for your body paragraphs. You've thought of supporting details, facts, examples, and the most effective way of organizing your thoughts. At the end of this chapter, you will write a complete first draft of your essay. First, though, let's look at three important parts of your essay: the introduction, the conclusion, and the title.

You might have written some of these parts already. Some people write their introduction with their thesis; others write the introduction last.

Some have an idea of how they want to conclude from the time they begin their papers; others write the conclusion last. Some struggle with a title; others write their titles as they generate their drafts. The order in which you write these three parts of an essay depends on your own personal writing process. All that matters is that your papers have a title, an introduction, several body paragraphs, and a conclusion that work together.

each group a different strategy for revising the introduction: (1) furnish vivid descriptions; (2) tell a brief story; (3) give a revealing fact, statistic, or definition; (4) make an interesting comparison; (5) present a dramatic example; and (6) use an exciting quotation. Have the members of each group rewrite the introduction using their assigned technique and read their revisions to the class. Have students vote for the introduction that is the most interesting.

Repeat the same exercise with a very dull conclusion. Have groups (1) summarize main ideas, (2) highlight the most important issue, (3) ask a question that gets the reader to think about something in particular, (4) predict the future, (5) offer a solution to a problem, and (6) call the reader to action.

Finally, provide some very dull titles, and have each group try to come up with catchier versions. You might bring tabloid headlines to help demonstrate how titles can entice people to read an article or essay.

TEACHING ON THE WEB

Discussion Topic: How do Internet advertisers use catchy titles or short introductions to

Introduction

The introduction to your essay—your first paragraph—should both introduce your subject and stimulate your audience's interest. The introduction of an essay captures the readers' interest, gives necessary background information, and presents your thesis statement. This paragraph essentially tells readers what the essay is going to cover without going into detail or discussing specifics.

Writers generally use the introduction to lead up to their thesis statement. As a result, the sentences at the beginning of the introductory paragraph need to grab your readers' attention. Some effective ways of capturing your audience's interest and giving necessary background information are to (1) furnish a vivid description; (2) tell a brief story; (3) give a revealing fact, statistic, or definition; (4) make an interesting comparison; (5) present a dramatic example; and (6) use an exciting quotation.

Also be sure that your introduction gives your readers any information they may need to follow your train of thought. One way to check that your readers have all the necessary background is to apply the five Ws and one H: who, what, when, where, why, and how. Any of this information that is important to your readers' understanding of your thesis statement should go in the introduction. You might also ask a friend to read your first draft and tell you if any background information is missing.

Beth's Introduction and Thesis Beth wrote a first draft of her introduction just to get started. She knew she would have to work with it later, but at least she was able to get some of her ideas down on paper.

> Everyone learns in different ways. Some people learn by watching, some by reading, and others by themselves. The way people learn is a part of who they are. Knowing how we learn can help us understand ourselves better. I know that I learn from many things in life.

lure customers to their Web sites? What would happen if Web sites were dull and uninviting? Would people still read the information? How important are attention-getters to the Web?

INSTRUCTOR'S RESOURCE MANUAL
For additional material about teaching the introduction, conclusion, and title; for journal entries; and for various tests, see the *Instructor's Resource Manual,* Section II, Part I.

Your Introduction Use the guidelines suggested here to capture your readers' interest and, if necessary, give them background information. Write two different introductions for your essay. End each with your thesis statement.

Conclusion

The concluding paragraph is the final paragraph of an essay. It draws your essay to a close, giving readers a sense of closure. That is, readers feel that all the loose ends are wrapped up and the point of the essay is clear. As with introductions, there are many good techniques for writing a conclusion. You might (1) summarize the main ideas, (2) highlight the most important issue, (3) ask a question that gets readers to think about something in particular, (4) predict the future, (5) offer a solution to a problem, or (6) call readers to action. In some cases, you might want to use several of these strategies.

You should avoid two common problems in writing a conclusion. First, do not begin your conclusion with the words "in conclusion," "in summary," or "as you can see." Your conclusion should show—not tell—that you are at the end of your essay. Second, do not introduce a new idea. The main ideas of your essay should be in your body paragraphs. The conclusion is where you finish your essay, leaving your readers with a sense of closure or completeness.

Beth's Conclusion Here is a rough outline of what Beth wants to include in her conclusion. These are the notes that she came up with at this point.

People can learn about life from just about anything.

- made me the person I am
- watching other people
- taking some risks myself
- making mistakes

Your Conclusion Sketch out an outline or write a draft of a possible conclusion for your essay.

Title

A title is a phrase, usually no more than a few words, that gives a hint about the subject, purpose, or focus of what is to follow. For example, the main title chosen for this book, *Mosaics*, reflects a particular view of the writing process—as many bright pieces logically connected to complete a picture. In other words, that title expresses in capsule form this textbook's purpose, which is to guide writers through the process of fitting the separate pieces of their ideas into a single meaningful whole to make an essay. The title of this chapter, however, is a straightforward naming of its contents: "Writing Effectively."

Besides suggesting an essay's purpose, a good title catches an audience's attention or "hooks" readers so that they want to read more. Look at some of the essay titles in the readings in Part II. For example, "Happiness Is Catching: Why Emotions Are Contagious" attracts the readers' attention because they will probably want to find out exactly how happiness is catching. "What Are Friends For?" is a title that will naturally draw in most readers. And "Dawn's Early Light" is intriguing because it brings up so many references in American culture. Do not underline or use quotation marks around your essay titles. Do not put a period at the end of your title, and be sure to capitalize your titles correctly. The first word and last word in a title are always capitalized. Capitalize all other words except articles (*a, an, the*) and short prepositions (such as *in, by, on,* or *from;* see page 520 for a more complete list of prepositions).

Beth's Title Beth has several possible titles for her essay. She doesn't really know which one to use.

Learning About Life

The Way We Learn

Everyone Can Learn

Your Title Write three titles for your essay: (1) one that gives a hint of your subject, (2) one that gives a hint of your purpose, and (3) one that gives a hint of your focus. Make each title as catchy as you can.

Beth's First Draft In Chapters 1 through 5 and again in this chapter, you have watched Beth thinking about, planning, developing, and organizing her essay. It is now time to get a complete first draft down on paper. Here is Beth's first draft.

The Way We Learn

Everyone learns in different ways. Some people learn by watching, some by reading, and others by themselves. The way people learn is a part of who they are. Knowing how we learn can help us understand ourselves better. I know that I learn from many things in life. 1

I have discovered that I learn a lot by taking risks. Being at this college was a risk. I have a boyfriend back 2 home, we want to get married someday. We are hoping for a spring wedding with all of our friends and family. I left my boyfriend to come here. Coming here was a risk to our relationship. But if I am ever going to make it, I have to be willing to take risks.

I also benefit from watching other people. When my 3
cousin became heavily involved with gangs, I watched my cousin live in constant fear. By watching my cousin, I made a conscious decision to be nothing like my cousin. By watching and understanding my cousin's life. I learned to live mine better.

I believe that I learn from making mistakes. When I 4
was in high school, I didn't study for a major science test. So I cheated. My sister cheated once. I was so scared to do it. The teacher caught me. The teacher took the time to talk to me about the mistake I was making. This mistake made me reevaluate my education. I could have laughed off the cheating experience. I decided to slow down and learn from the experience.

People can learn about life from almost anything 5
they do. They just have to be willing to do so. When I take risks, I think about what I will learn. I definitely try to learn as much as I can from watching others. When I make mistakes, I figure out why I made each mistake and how to avoid it a second time.

Your First Draft Now write a complete first draft of your essay on learning.

CHAPTER 7

Revising and Editing

No matter how hard you wish, writing does not end with your first draft. The fun of revising and editing still lies ahead of you. Revising has to do with the development and organization of your ideas, while editing focuses on correctness. Revising is **not** editing. **Revising** means "seeing again," and that is exactly what you should try to do when you revise to improve your writing—see it again from as many different angles as possible. **Editing** involves finding and correcting errors in grammar, punctuation, mechanics, and spelling. You have probably been revising and editing periodically through your entire writing process, but now is the time to perform these tasks systematically before you turn in your paper.

REVISING

More specifically, revising your writing means changing it so that it says exactly what you mean in the most effective way. Revision involves both *content* (what you are trying to say) and *form* (how you deliver your message). Having a friend or tutor read your paper before you revise it is a good idea so that you can see if you are communicating clearly.

Revising content means working with your words until they express your ideas as accurately and completely as possible. Revising form consists of working with the organization of your writing. When you revise, you should look closely at the six basic categories listed in the following checklist. Let's look at these revision strategies one by one.

TEACHING REVISING
Divide students into groups of three or four, and have them exchange papers. Have the first student read his or her paper aloud while the other students listen for and take notes on suggested revisions. When the reader finishes, have each listener explain his or her suggestions; make sure the reader does not talk or try to clarify any points during this interchange. After all suggestions have been relayed, have the next writer read his or her paper, and so on. Allow only 10 minutes per paper.

REVISING CHECKLIST

THESIS STATEMENT

✔ Does the thesis statement contain the essay's controlling idea and an opinion about that idea?

✔ Does the thesis appear as the last sentence of the introduction?

TEACHING ON THE WEB

Discussion Topic: Divide students into groups of three or four, and have them discuss how the Internet can be a tool for revision. What types of Web sites will help students get revising feedback for their papers? How else can the Internet help?

INSTRUCTOR'S RESOURCE MANUAL

For additional material about teaching revising, for journal entries, and for various tests, see the *Instructor's Resource Manual,* Section II, Part I.

BASIC ELEMENTS

✔ Does the title draw in the readers?

✔ Does the introduction capture the readers' attention and build up to the thesis statement effectively?

✔ Does each body paragraph deal with a single topic?

✔ Does the conclusion bring the essay to a close in an interesting way?

DEVELOPMENT

✔ Do the body paragraphs adequately support the thesis statement?

✔ Does each body paragraph have a focused topic sentence?

✔ Does each body paragraph contain specific details that support the topic sentence?

✔ Does each body paragraph include enough details to explain the topic sentence fully?

UNITY

✔ Do the essay's topic sentences relate directly to the thesis statement?

✔ Do the details in each body paragraph support its topic sentence?

ORGANIZATION

✔ Is the essay organized logically?

✔ Is each body paragraph organized logically?

COHERENCE

✔ Are transitions used effectively so that paragraphs move smoothly and logically from one to the next?

✔ Do the sentences move smoothly and logically from one to the next?

THESIS STATEMENT

✔ Does the thesis statement contain the essay's controlling idea and an opinion about that idea?

✔ Does the thesis appear as the last sentence of the introduction?

As you learned in Chapter 5, every successful essay has a thesis statement that states the essay's controlling idea. This sentence gives direction to the rest of the essay. It consists of a limited subject and the writer's position on that subject. Although a thesis statement can appear anywhere in an essay, it is usually the last sentence of the introduction.

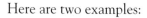

Here are two examples:

Limited Subject	+	**Opinion**	=	**Thesis Statement**
1. Children today		grow up too fast		Children today grow up too fast.
2. Children today		grow up too fast		Children today grow up too fast because of television, advertising, and working parents.

As in the second example, the thesis statement should introduce all the topics in its essay. The first example includes the limited subject and the writer's position on that subject but also needs to introduce its topics.

PRACTICE 1 Review the guidelines for developing a thesis statement in Chapter 5. Then write a thesis statement for each group of topic sentences listed here.

1. Thesis Statement: *Friends are wonderful people with whom you can share activities, good news, and bad times.*

   Everyone needs a friend who likes to do the same things.

   Everyone needs someone to share the good news with.

   Equally important, everyone needs a good listener during bad times.

2. Thesis Statement: *Seeing a movie in a theater is much better than watching one at home.*

   Watching a movie on the big screen of a theater makes the story and characters bigger and more interesting than life.

   The sound system in a movie theater makes me feel that I'm right there in the action.

   The concession stand has all sorts of candy and goodies, and I don't have to clean up my own mess afterward.

3. Thesis Statement: *There are many ways to become upset while driving.*

   Being behind slow drivers can cause people to experience road rage.

Tailgating can cause people to get angry.

People who weave in and out of traffic at extreme speeds make many drivers furious.

4. Thesis Statement: *No matter what, everything about a first date is awkward.*

Asking someone out on a first date can take a lot of courage.

Suggesting places to go or things to do is harder than it sounds.

It seems that there's always one very embarrassing moment on a first date that would never happen on a later date.

5. Thesis Statement: *Skydiving is scary but a lot of fun.*

Signing up for a skydiving class is exciting, and all your friends think you're really cool.

Boarding the plane for your first jump is a strong dose of reality, but not quite like getting up the nerve to actually jump.

Free-falling and landing safely provide a rush that skydivers never forget.

PRACTICE 2 Write thesis statements for the following introductions.

1. *I have great difficulty getting out of bed, which affects my plans for the morning.*

No matter how much I tell myself I am going to get up in the morning and go, I cannot seem to do it. Every night before I go to bed, I lay out my sweats and shoes and set my alarm. In the morning when the alarm rings, I push the snooze button and promise myself that I will get up in 10 minutes. This routine goes on for the next hour until I have to get up in order to make it to work on time. Once again, I have failed to get up and go to the gym, and I have deprived myself of an hour of exercise.

2. *People need to consider many things when buying a new house.*

The most important detail is to determine the number of rooms in the house. A family must consider the needs of the people living in the house and their plans for the near future. Of course, don't forget the backyard. Does the family need a fenced yard for animals or an area for the kids to play? And the family must pay attention to how well the house has been kept up. All of these items are very important details when looking for a new home.

3. *A couple in my neighborhood follows the same routine every day.* ______

______

Every morning, at precisely 8:00, the couple eats breakfast at the corner café. Afterward, they go to the market for fresh fruit or vegetables and run errands. If they have no shopping to do, the couple goes home and does housework or yard work. Every afternoon at 1:00, they sit down to lunch and watch a little television. In the late afternoon, they go for a walk around the lake for a bit of exercise before preparing their dinner. After dinner, they watch the news and play a hand of cards. Soon the sun dips behind the mountain, and the couple retires for the night.

Beth's Revision When Beth looks back at her thesis statement, she realizes it does not completely introduce what she talks about in her essay. Her thesis tells readers only that she learns about life from different things, not that she has three important ways that she learns about life.

Thesis Statement: I know that I learn from many things in life.

She decides to expand her thesis statement so that it more accurately introduces the topics that will follow in her essay:

Revised Thesis Statement: I know that I learn ~~from many things in life~~ best from taking risks, watching others, and making mistakes.

She feels that this thesis statement introduces the notion of learning and the different ways that she has learned.

Your Revision With these guidelines in mind, revise your thesis statement.

Your Revised Thesis Statement: ______

BASIC ELEMENTS

✔ Does the title draw in the readers?

✔ Does the introduction capture the readers' attention and build up to the thesis statement effectively?

✔ Does each body paragraph deal with a single topic?

✔ Does the conclusion bring the essay to a close in an interesting way?

Now that you have written a complete draft of your essay, this is the time to review these basic elements. What changes do you want to make in your title? In your introduction? In your conclusion? Is your thesis statement at the end of your introduction? Do you need to split any body paragraphs? These revision items ask you to check that all the basic elements of the essay are present and are doing the jobs they are supposed to do.

PRACTICE 3 Write an alternative title for "Between Worlds" (page 286). *Answers will vary.*

PRACTICE 4 Write an alternative introduction for "Don't Be Cruel" (page 244). *Answers will vary.*

PRACTICE 5 Write an additional body paragraph for "The Sanctuary of School" (page 177). *Answers will vary.*

PRACTICE 6 Write an alternative conclusion for "Writer's Retreat" (page 182). *Answers will vary.*

Beth's Revision Beth sets out to answer each of these questions one by one. Here are her responses.

✔ Does the title draw in the readers?

No. It's kind of boring.

✔ Does the introduction capture the readers' attention and build up to the thesis statement effectively?

Not really—it's too short; I could use one of the ideas introduced in Chapter 6 to make it more interesting.

✔ Does each body paragraph deal with a single topic?

Yes. So I don't have to break any of them into two or more paragraphs.

✔ Does the conclusion bring the essay to a close in an interesting way?

Sort of. I guess I should look at it again and try to apply some of the material in Chapter 6 to my conclusion.

You saw Beth's first draft at the end of Chapter 6. Here is the second draft of her introduction, conclusion, and title with her changes highlighted.

Introduction

Everyone learns in different ways. Some people learn by watching, **while others learn by doing.** Some **learn** by reading, **while others learn by listening** ~~**and others by themselves**~~. **Some learn best when they work independently, while others do better in groups**. The way people learn is a **major** part of who they are. Knowing how we learn can help us understand ourselves better. I know that I learn best from taking risks, watching others, and making mistakes.

Conclusion

People can learn about life from almost anything they do. They just have to be willing to do so. When I take risks, I think about what I will learn. I definitely try to learn as much as I can from watching others**, which I believe, in the case of my cousin, has already saved my life.** When I make mistakes, I figure out why I made each mistake and how to avoid it a second time. **These three ways of learning are all part of who I am today. I know I'm not finished learning yet. In fact, I don't know if I ever will be.**

Title

~~The Way We Learn~~

The Learning Curve

Your Revision Apply these questions one by one to your essay.

- ☐ Does the title draw in the readers?
- ☐ Does the introduction capture the readers' attention and build up to the thesis statement effectively?
- ☐ Does each body paragraph deal with a single topic?
- ☐ Does the conclusion bring the essay to a close in an interesting way?

DEVELOPMENT

- ✔ Do the body paragraphs adequately support the thesis statement?
- ✔ Does each body paragraph have a focused topic sentence?
- ✔ Does each body paragraph contain specific details that support the topic sentence?
- ✔ Does each body paragraph include enough details to explain the topic sentence fully?

When you develop an essay, you build the body paragraphs. Body paragraphs provide supporting evidence for the thesis statement. They are made up of a clearly focused topic sentence and details that support the topic sentence. Supporting details should be as specific as possible, and you need to provide enough details to support the point you are making in each paragraph.

Specific Details

An important part of developing a good essay is being able to recognize ideas that are more general (for example, *entertainment* and *exercise*) and more specific (the opening scene in *The Green Mile*). Two other essential terms to know in choosing details are *abstract* and *concrete*. Concrete words refer to items you can see, hear, touch, smell, or taste—as opposed to abstract words, which refer to ideas and concepts, such as *entertainment*, *frustration*, and *peacefulness*. Look at the following examples, and notice how each line becomes more detailed.

entertainment (general, abstract)
movies
suspense films
Stephen King films
The Green Mile
opening scene in *The Green Mile* (specific, concrete)

Don't confuse levels of detail with examples. Compare the previous ladder with this one:

sports
team sports
football
college football
UCLA Bruins
Wisconsin Wolverines
University of Texas Longhorns
Florida State Gators

In this ladder, the four college teams are at the same level of detail. One is not more specific than another. So these last four items are just a list of examples.

As a rule, your thesis statement should be the most general statement in your essay. Your topic sentences are more specific than your thesis, and the details in your body paragraphs are the most specific items in the essay. So an outline of these elements looks like this:

Thesis statement (general)
  Topic sentence
    Detail (specific and concrete)
    Detail (specific and concrete)
    Detail (specific and concrete)

PRACTICE 7 Underline the most specific word or phrase in each group.

1. books, library, shelves, page 42, stairs
2. computer, technology, software, power button, online help
3. backyard, swimming pool, Coppertone lotion, pool party
4. drinks, thirst, soda, Dr. Pepper, water in a frosty mug
5. pink candles on a birthday cake, dessert, dinner, sweets, chocolate candy

PRACTICE 8 Fill in each blank with a new level of concrete detail as indicated by the indentions. *Answers will vary.*

1. ______________________

    state lottery

        ____

            ____

2. ______________________

    brother

        ____

            ____

3. boat

        ____

            ____

                ____

4. ______________________

____

____

blue shirt with stripes

5. ______________________

____

Thursday's newspaper

____

Beth's Revision Making your essay more specific involves adding as well as rewriting words, phrases, and whole sentences. Here is one of Beth's body paragraphs with more specific details in bold type in her revision.

First Draft

I have discovered that I learn a lot by taking risks. Being at this college was a risk. I have a boyfriend back home, we want to get married someday. We are hoping for a spring wedding with all of our friends and family. I left my boyfriend to come here. Coming here was a risk to our relationship. But if I am ever going to make it, I have to be willing to take risks.

Revised with Specific Details

I have discovered that I learn a lot by taking risks. **If I didn't take risks, I think I'd never mature.** Being at this college was a risk. I have a boyfriend back home, we want to get married someday. We are hoping for a spring wedding with all of our friends and family. I left my boyfriend to come here. Coming here was a risk to our relationship. **Taking this risk taught me to be responsible and trust my boyfriend back home.** But if I am ever going to ~~make it~~ **reach my potential**, I have to be willing to take risks.

Enough Details

Not only should your details be specific and concrete, but you should furnish enough details to support your topic sentence. No matter how good one detail is, it is not adequate to develop a topic sentence. Without enough details, facts, or reasons, a paragraph can be too short and weak to support a thesis statement. So Beth needs to add more details to her paragraph.

PRACTICE 9 List three details that could support each of the following topic sentences. *Answers will vary.*

1. My favorite pastime is swimming.

   ____

   ____

   ____

2. Eating a balanced diet is an important part of feeling good.

   ____

   ____

   ____

3. A simple gift is often the best.

   ____

   ____

   ____

4. Working for people you like is easy.

   ____

   ____

   ____

5. Spending time outside can change a person's mood.

   ____

   ____

   ____

PRACTICE 10 Develop the following topic sentences with enough specific details. *Answers will vary.*

1. Before taking a test, take a moment to relax.
2. Always discuss major decisions with someone you trust.
3. When interviewing for a job, dress appropriately.
4. My roommate is a real neat freak.
5. When reading a book, think about what you are reading.

Beth's Revision Here is Beth's body paragraph with even more details.

Revised with More Details

I have discovered that I learn a lot by taking risks. If I didn't take risks, I think I'd never mature. Being at this college was a risk. I have a boyfriend back home, we want to get married someday. We are hoping for a spring wedding with all of our friends and family. **But I knew that this school's nursing program was better than the one in my hometown.** I left my boyfriend to come here. Coming here was a risk to our relationship. **Not coming here would have been a risk to my career.** Taking this risk taught me to be responsible and trust my boyfriend back home. **I know that I will take many risks like this throughout my life and that not all of them will work out.** But if I am ever going to reach my potential, I have to be willing to take risks.

Your Revision Add more relevant details to your essay, making your explanations and descriptions as specific as possible. Also make sure all of your body paragraphs have focused topic sentences that support your thesis statement.

UNITY

✔ Do the essay's topic sentences relate directly to the thesis statement?
✔ Do the details in each body paragraph support its topic sentence?

An essay is unified when its topic sentences are all related to the thesis statement and when each body paragraph discusses only one idea.

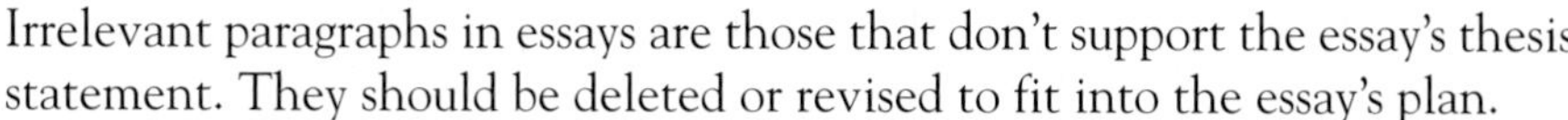

Irrelevant paragraphs in essays are those that don't support the essay's thesis statement. They should be deleted or revised to fit into the essay's plan.

A paragraph's main idea is introduced in its topic sentence. All other sentences in a paragraph should expand on this idea and relate to it in some way. Information that is not about the topic sentence is irrelevant and does not belong in the paragraph.

PRACTICE 11 Cross out the topic sentences that don't support each thesis statement.

1. Thesis: Holidays are fun times in my family.

   My favorite holiday is Thanksgiving.

   July 4th always scares my dogs.

   Chanukah is a time of great celebration in my house.

   ~~My boyfriend doesn't understand my family.~~

2. Thesis: I love working with children.

   Children's games still make me laugh.

   ~~I hate foods that are good for me.~~

   ~~I want a job that pays well.~~

   I have always liked babysitting.

   I have applied to work at the Children's Center on our campus.

3. Thesis: Exercise is essential for good health.

   Exercise keeps our hearts in good shape.

   ~~Exercise is fun.~~

   ~~Exercise is difficult when you are on a tight schedule.~~

   Exercise is necessary for weight control.

   Exercise is good for us emotionally.

4. Thesis: I have learned over the years how to control my anger.

   One way is to count to 10 before I do anything.

   ~~I get angry easily.~~

   Another solution is to take a deep breath before I act.

   The solution I use most often is to take a walk.

5. Thesis: I really like to cook, but I never have the time.

   I am most creative at breakfast.

   The dish I like to make the most is a frittata.

   My class schedule keeps me busy right through dinner.

   ~~My philosophy class is my toughest class.~~

   ~~I don't like spicy foods.~~

PRACTICE 12 Cross out the three irrelevant sentences in the following paragraph.

> I have a very bad habit of waiting until the night before an exam to begin studying, so it is very important for me to have a well-planned and productive cramming session. ~~One time during my junior year of high school, I failed a test.~~ I begin by putting on comfortable clothes so that when I begin to squirm and twist to try and get comfortable, I am able to move around. Next, I get a large glass of milk and several cookies to snack on. ~~Peanut butter cookies have always been my favorite.~~ Once I have my snack, I spread out all my books and study materials on the living room floor. ~~I have a hardwood floor.~~ Finally, I am ready to begin studying for the next few hours.

PRACTICE 13 Cross out the three irrelevant sentences in the following paragraph.

> Most people wonder what it would be like to win the lottery and be able to spend money as they please. ~~The odds are that even the people who buy a lottery ticket every day will never win the lottery.~~ Winning the lottery would change most people's lives drastically. Many people say that they would begin by paying all their debts. ~~There are people in the world who buy so many items on credit that they are constantly trying to get out of debt.~~ Other people say that they would buy a new house or a new car to spoil themselves a little bit. Some people simply say that they would invest the money and use it when they retire so that they can live comfortably. ~~Many elderly people are unable to continue the lifestyles they are accustomed to after retirement.~~

Beth's Revision When Beth reads her paper for unity, she sees that three sentences are off topic. So she deletes them.

In Paragraph 2: ~~We are hoping for a spring wedding with all of our friends and family.~~

In Paragraph 4: ~~My sister cheated once. I was so scared to do it.~~

Your Revision Read your essay carefully, and cross out any irrelevant sentences or paragraphs.

ORGANIZATION

✔ Is the essay organized logically?

✔ Is each body paragraph organized logically?

In Chapter 6, you learned five ways to organize your paragraphs and essays:

1. From general to particular
2. From particular to general
3. Chronologically (by time)
4. Spatially (by physical arrangement)
5. From one extreme to another

The organization that you choose for your essay depends chiefly on your topic and overall purpose. What are you trying to accomplish? In what order should you present your evidence? Is point A the most important? Maybe it should be the last paragraph so you can build up to it.

After you put your paragraphs in order, you are ready to look at the organization of each individual paragraph. It's very likely that your essay will be organized one way (say, from least important to most important) and each of your body paragraphs will have its own method of organization. As you revise, you should check to see that your essay is organized as effectively as possible for what you are trying to accomplish and that your body paragraphs are each arranged logically as well.

PRACTICE 14 Reorganize the following topics so that they are in a logical order. Then label your method of organization. *The order of the items will vary.*

1. east at the mall to the stop light
   west at the grocery store to the flower shop
   north at the flower shop until you get to Anita's
   south at the stop light until you hit the grocery store

Method of Organization: *Spatial*

2. sitcoms
   dramas
   documentaries
   musicals
   awards shows

Method of Organization: *From one extreme to another*

3. community servants
   police badges
   police officers
   police office staff
   police uniforms

Method of Organization: *Either particular to general or general to particular*

Practice 15 Reorganize the following sentences so that they are in a logical order. Then identify your method of organization.

4 Next, I decide what I will have for dinner and begin to cook.
3 Then I change into comfortable clothes.
8 Before I completely wind down, I lay out my clothes for the next day and set my alarm clock.
7 This is always a good time to look at the mail or return phone calls.
5 While I am cooking, I listen to music or turn on the evening news.
2 First, I begin to relax by taking a shower.
1 When I return home in the evenings, I always follow the same routine.
6 After I eat, I do the dishes and sit down in the living room.
9 Finally I watch television or read a book until I fall asleep.

Method of Organization: *Chronological*

PRACTICE 16 Reorganize the following sentences so that they are in a logical order. Then identify your method of organization.

4 Sweatshirts belong next to long-sleeved shirts, so they come next.
2 When I walk in the closet door, all of my T-shirts are hanging directly to my left in the closet.

9 My shoes follow the same pattern on the floor as the clothes on hangers.

3 Next to the T-shirts are my long-sleeved shirts.

8 Starting the summer clothes are the tank-tops, followed by summer dresses.

1 Everything in my closet must be in order, or I will never be able to find anything.

5 All of my sweaters can be found stacked neatly on the shelf just above my long-sleeved sweatshirts.

6 Jackets, of course, go along with sweatshirts, so they are hanging next to the sweatshirts.

10 I have winter shoes immediately as I walk in the door, with sandals for summer toward the back of the closet.

7 After the jackets come the summer clothes.

Method of Organization: *Spatial*

Beth's Revision In Chapter 6, Beth decided that the best way to organize her essay was from one extreme to another (from most to least important). But now she needs to make sure that this is the most effective order for her ideas and that every paragraph is in the right place.

This is the order of the main ideas in her first draft:

Most important:	Taking risks
Next most important:	Watching others
Least important:	Making mistakes

After thinking about this order, Beth realizes that she learns more from making mistakes than from watching others. So she decides to reverse these two topics. She also remembers that she has to revise her thesis statement and her conclusion to reflect this new order.

Revised Thesis Statement:	I know that I learn best from taking risks, **making mistakes, and watching others.**
Revised Conclusion:	People can learn about life from almost anything they do. They just have to be willing to do so. When I take risks, I think about what I will learn. **When I make mistakes, I figure out why I made each mistake and how to avoid it a second time. I definitely try to learn as much as I can from watching others, which I**

> **believe, in the case of my cousin, has already saved my life.** These three ways of learning are all a part of who I am today. I know I'm not finished learning yet. In fact, I don't know if I ever will be.

Also in Chapter 6, Beth organized her three body paragraphs from general to particular. At this point, she checks to see if this is the most effective order for these ideas. She thinks that this order is a good choice for her body paragraphs.

Your Revision Double-check the method of organization you chose in Chapter 6 for your essay. Do you still think this is the most effective order for what you are trying to say? Then check each body paragraph to see that the details are arranged logically.

COHERENCE

✔ Are transitions used effectively so that paragraphs move smoothly and logically from one to the next?

✔ Do the sentences move smoothly and logically from one to the next?

A well-written paragraph is coherent—that is, its parts cohere or stick together. It is smooth, not choppy, and readers move logically from one thought to the next, seeing a clear relationship among the ideas. Here are four different strategies that writers use to help their readers follow their train of thought from one paragraph to the next and within paragraphs: *transitions*, *repeated words*, *synonyms*, and *pronouns*.

Transitions *Transitional words and phrases* provide bridges or links between paragraphs and ideas. They show your readers how your paragraphs or thoughts are related or when you are moving to a new point. Good use of transitions makes your writing smooth rather than choppy.

Choppy: I could have laughed off the cheating experience and the teacher. I decided to slow down and learn from the experience.

Smooth: I could have laughed off the cheating experience and the teacher. **However,** I decided to slow down and learn from the experience.

Transitions have very specific meanings, so you should take care to make logical choices that help you communicate your exact thoughts.

Confusing: I could have laughed off the cheating experience and the teacher. **In addition,** I decided to slow down and learn from the experience.

Here is a list of some common transitional words and phrases that will make your writing more coherent. They are classified by meaning.

Some Common Transitions

Addition:	*again, and, and then, also, besides, finally, first, further, furthermore, in addition, last, likewise, moreover, next, nor, second, third, too*
Comparison:	*in like manner, likewise, similarly*
Contrast:	*after all, and yet, at the same time, but, however, in contrast, nevertheless, on the contrary, on the other hand, otherwise, still, yet*
Emphasis:	*actually, after all, essentially, in any event, indeed, in fact, of course, to tell the truth*
Example:	*for example, for instance, in this case*
Place:	*adjacent to, beyond, here, near, nearby, opposite, there*
Purpose:	*for this purpose, to this end, with this objective*
Result:	*accordingly, as a result, consequently, hence, so, then, therefore, thus*
Summary:	*as I have said, in brief, in other words, in short, in sum, on the whole, that is, to conclude, to sum up, to summarize*
Time:	*after a few days, afterward, at length, (at) other times, immediately, in the meantime, later, meanwhile, now, sometimes, soon, still, then*

See pages 521–522 in the Handbook (Part IV) for more information on transitions.

Sometimes longer phrases provide transitions between paragraphs or main ideas. See if you can find the long transition that Beth adds to the beginning of one of the paragraphs that she moved (pages 106–107). This phrase helps her readers shift gears to a new topic and makes her essay easier to follow.

PRACTICE 17 Fill in the blanks in the following paragraph with logical transitions. *Answers may vary.*

Today, an unlimited amount of information is available through the Internet. *However*, some of this information may not be suitable for younger audiences. Many concerned parents asked for a way to block Internet sites that they did not want their children to view. *Therefore*, a system was developed by which a parent uses a password to choose which Internet sites the household computer will and won't access. *Now*, children who do not know the password cannot access the blocked Internet sites. *Finally*, parents have control over the technology in their homes and feel their children are safe when they use the Internet.

PRACTICE 18 Rewrite the following paragraph, adding at least three transitions to make it more coherent. *Answers will vary.*

In high school, I thought I had everything figured out. I never considered what I would do after graduation. I never made any plans. When I graduated, I was completely lost. I went to see a guidance counselor at the local college. I decided to go to college. I am in college and have made many plans for the future.

Repeated Words *Repeating key words* is another way of binding the ideas of an essay together and guiding readers through the details. A key word is usually a main idea in an essay. You should also know that too much repetition becomes boring.

Effective Repetition: Coming here was a **risk** to our relationship. Not coming here would have been a **risk** to my career.

PRACTICE 19 Underline five effective repeated words or parts of words in the following paragraph.

All my life, I have gone to my grandmother's house near a lake out in farm country during the summer. This year, I'm taking my best friend from college with me. What I like most about summers at the lake is that the weather is so warm that I can swim all day long. I swim near the bridge and see the small fish swimming around the columns. Sometimes I even swim over to the docks where all of the people are loading and unloading their boats. I used to try to swim faster and faster to beat my own record. Now I just go to relax, forget about school, and think about the future.

PRACTICE 20 Underline at least five effective repeated words or parts of words in the following paragraph.

For many people, reading the daily newspaper is their main source of information about the world. The front page usually gives the national news or an international political event that affects the United States. Major world events, such as an earthquake, always make front-page news. On the second page of the first section is the op-ed (opposite editorial) page, where editors and readers give their opinions on current news. The editorial and op-ed pages are among the few places in the newspaper where the writing is not objective, along with book and movie reviews and columnists such as Molly Ivins or Dear Abby. Most newspapers have separate sections for sports, business, entertainment, classified ads, and comics. All in all, a half hour spent with the newspaper over morning coffee keeps a person up-to-date on world affairs and local people, places, and events.

Synonyms *Synonyms* are another way to link your ideas and help you avoid ineffective repetition. Synonyms are words that have identical or similar meanings—*movie/film*, *feeling/emotion*, *fantastic/unbelievable*. They add variety and interest to your writing. A thesaurus, or book of synonyms, can help you choose synonyms for specific words. Be aware, however, that all the words in a thesaurus listing are not interchangeable. *Retreat*, for example, is listed as a synonym for *escape*, but the two words suggest two very different ways of leaving a place. In the following example from Beth's essay, Beth uses *incidents* in place of one of her references to *experiences*.

Boring Repetition: She talked a lot to me about those **experiences.** By watching my cousin go through these horrible **experiences,** I made a conscious decision never to make the bad choices that my cousin made.

Synonym: She talked a lot to me about those **experiences.** By watching my cousin go through these horrible ~~**experiences**~~ **incidents,** I made a conscious decision never to make the bad choices that my cousin made.

PRACTICE 21 Underline four different synonyms for *friend* in the following paragraph.

> My younger brother and his friends were always starting clubs when I was young. The clubhouse and the club name were very important. The pals usually decided on a name first. I think my favorite name that they had was "The Three Amigos," even though it was not very original. Every once in a while, an acquaintance of the boys would be allowed to join the club, and the name would have to be changed. Since the boys always thought that they were such sophisticated companions, they had a sign on the door that read "Associates Only—No Girls Allowed." The boys are all grown now, but I still smile every time I think about all the meetings of "The Three Amigos" that I sat outside of and listened to.

PRACTICE 22 Replace two uses of the word *actor* with two different synonyms in the following paragraph. *Answers will vary.*

> Being an actor seems like a glamorous career choice, but becoming famous is not easy. Many actors start out waiting on tables in restaurants, hoping to be discovered by agents dining there. Other actors go from bit part to bit part in movies and never really earn enough for a living. In the unlikely event that an actor makes it big, he or she suddenly loses all privacy. Still, there are advantages to fame, and most actors adjust quite well to the lifestyle.

Pronouns Finally, you can link your sentences with *pronouns*. Pronouns not only help you avoid needless repetition, but they also keep your writing moving at a fairly fast pace. Personal pronouns (*I, you, he, she, it, we, they*) and indefinite pronouns (*any, some, other, one*) are the ones most commonly used as replacements.

Beth can use a pronoun to get rid of her repetition of the words *my cousin*.

Repetition: When my cousin became heavily involved with gangs and drugs, I watched my cousin live in constant fear.

Revision: When my cousin became heavily involved with gangs and drugs, I watched ~~my cousin~~ **her** live in constant fear.

For more information on pronouns, see pages 7–9 in the Handbook (Part IV).

PRACTICE 23 Underline 10 personal and indefinite pronouns in the following paragraph.

The people down the street have a very large family, which means that there is always something going on in their house. Sometimes when I am at their house, I cannot keep up with everything that is happening. For example, when Sandy answers the phone, she yells that it's for Ryan. Of course, Ryan has to know who it is, and the yelling continues back and forth until Ryan decides to finally pick up the phone. Sometimes when the family members are really busy, they all make dinner individually. Everyone is in the kitchen at one time trying to find something to eat while trying not to step on one another. I'm not sure I could live at the Mitchells' house, but I definitely like visiting.

PRACTICE 24 Add five pronouns where appropriate in the following paragraph.

A few days ago, Brian, Carol, Katie, and I went out to dinner. ~~Brian, Carol, Katie, and I~~ *We* went to a new Italian restaurant on First Street. As soon as ~~Brian, Carol, Katie, and I~~ *we* walked in the door, ~~Brian, Carol, Katie, and I~~ *we* could smell the garlic, basil, and oregano in the rich tomato sauces of pizza, lasagna, and, of course, spaghetti and meatballs. ~~Brian, Carol, Katie, and I~~ *We* couldn't stand it, so ~~Brian, Carol, Katie, and I~~ *we* ordered immediately. The food was even better than it smelled. Before the dinner was over, ~~Brian, Carol, Katie, and I~~ *we* set a date to return.

Beth's Revision When Beth checks her essay for coherence, she thinks her writing could be smoother if she used some of these techniques. So she makes the following revisions that help bind her sentences together and show the specific relationships between her ideas.

Here is Beth's essay with transitions, repeated words, synonyms, and pronouns highlighted. The changes Beth made earlier are underlined.

The Learning Curve

Everyone learns in different ways. Some people learn
by watching, while others learn by doing. Some learn by
reading, and others learn by listening. Some learn best
when they work independently, but others do better in
Transition groups. **In fact, t**~~T~~he way people learn is a major part of
Transition who they are. **So** knowing how we learn can help us
understand ourselves better. I know that I learn best
from taking risks, making mistakes, and watching
others.

Transition **First,** I have discovered that I learn a lot by taking
risks. If I didn't take risks, I think I'd never mature.
Being at this college was a risk. I have a boyfriend back
home, we want to get married someday. But I knew that
this school's nursing program was better than the one in
Transition my hometown~~.~~**, so** I left my boyfriend to come here.
Coming here was a risk to our relationship. **However,** *Transition*
n~~N~~ot coming here would have been a risk to my career.
Taking this risk taught me to be responsible and trust
my boyfriend back home. I know that I will take many
risks like this throughout my life and that not all of
them will work out. But if I am ever going to reach my
potential, I have to be willing to take risks.

Transition **Also,** I believe that I learn from making mistakes.
Transition **For example, w**~~W~~hen I was a sophomore in high school, I
didn't study for a major science test. I knew the test was
important, but I decided to go to a party with my
friends. I really needed the grade, so I cheated. I cut my
notes into small strips of paper that I put in my desk,
but the teacher caught me. Thank goodness ~~**the teacher**~~
Pronoun **he** was a nice person. ~~**The teacher**~~ **He** took the time to *Pronoun*
talk to me about the mistake I was making, not only
Repetition **cheating** for a grade, but **cheating** myself out of the
knowledge that I could have. This mistake made me
Pronoun reevaluate my education. ~~**This mistake**~~ **It** led me into
nursing by making me ~~**reevaluate**~~ **realize** what subjects *Synonym*
I really enjoyed. I could have laughed off the cheating

experience and the teacher. **However,** I decided to slow *Transition* down and learn from the experience.

Transition **In addition to learning from my own actions,** I also benefit from watching other people. **For instance, w**~~W~~hen *Transition* my cousin became heavily involved with gangs and *Pronoun* drugs, I watched ~~my cousin~~ **her** live in constant fear. She was worried that she would end up in jail, overdose on drugs, or become a "plaything" for other gang members. She worked hard to overcome that lifestyle. She talked a lot to me about those experiences. By watching my cousin go through these horrible ~~experiences~~ **incidents,** I *Synonym* made a conscious decision never to make the bad *Pronoun* choices that ~~my cousin~~ **she** made. I had plenty of opportunities to do so. Turning away from this life was difficult, but I did it. By watching and understanding my cousin's life. I learned to live mine better.

Transition **Essentially, p**~~P~~eople can learn about life from almost anything they do. They just have to be willing to do so. *Transition* **Now, w**~~W~~hen I take risks, I think about what I will learn. When I make mistakes, I figure out why I made each mistake and how to avoid it a second time. **Also,** I *Transition* definitely try to learn as much as I can from watching others, which I believe, in the case of my cousin, has already saved my life. These three ways of learning are all part of who I am today. I know I'm not finished learning yet. In fact, I don't know if I ever will be.

Transitions In addition to *however*, Beth added 12 more transitions to her essay. What are they?

In fact, So, First, so, However, Also, For example, [However], In addition to learning from my own actions, For instance, Essentially, Now, Also

List the meaning of five of these transitions:

1. Transition: ____________________ Meaning: ____________________
2. Transition: ____________________ Meaning: ____________________
3. Transition: ____________________ Meaning: ____________________
4. Transition: ____________________ Meaning: ____________________
5. Transition: ____________________ Meaning: ____________________

Repeated Words When Beth checked her essay for repeated key words, she saw that she referred directly to *cheating* twice in the same sentence. She decided this was an effective repetition and chose to keep it in her essay.

Effective Repetition:	He took the time to talk to me about the mistake I was making, not only **cheating** for a grade, but **cheating** myself out of the knowledge that I could have.

Synonyms When Beth looked at her essay again, she found another opportunity to use a synonym to link her ideas more clearly. Besides the addition of *incidents* for *experiences*, what other synonym does Beth use in her revision?

realize for reevaluate

Pronouns Finally, in addition to substituting *her* for *my cousin*, Beth found four more places to use pronouns to bind key parts of her essay together. Where are these places in her essay?

he for the teacher

he for the teacher

It for This mistake

she for my cousin

Your Revision Now it's time to make your essay more coherent.

Transitions Check the transitions in your essay. Do you use enough transitions so that your essay moves smoothly from one paragraph to the next and from one sentence to the next? Do you use your transitions logically?

Repeated Words Look at your essay to see when you might want to repeat a key word. Then revise your essay accordingly.

Synonyms Now look for places in your essay where you might add synonyms to link your sentences. Use a thesaurus (in book or electronic form) if you need help.

Pronouns Finally check your essay for opportunities to use pronouns. Add appropriate pronouns.

Beth's Revised Essay After revising her thesis statement, her development of ideas, and the unity, organization, and coherence of her writing, Beth produced the following revised essay. All of her revisions are highlighted.

~~The Way We Learn~~
The Learning Curve

1 Everyone learns in different ways. Some people learn by watching, **while others learn by doing.** Some **learn** by reading, ~~**while**~~ **and others learn by listening** ~~**and others by themselves**~~. **Some learn best when they work independently,** ~~**while**~~ **but others do better in groups. In fact, t**~~T~~he way people learn is a **major** part of who they are. Knowing how we learn can help us understand ourselves better. I know that I learn ~~**from many things in life**~~ **best from taking risks, making mistakes, and watching others.**

2 **First,** I have discovered that I learn a lot by taking risks. **If I didn't take risks, I think I'd never mature.** Being at this college was a risk. I have a boyfriend back home, we want to get married someday. ~~**We are hoping for a spring wedding with all of our friends and family**~~. **But I knew that this school's nursing program was better than the one in my hometown**~~.~~**, so** I left my boyfriend to come here. Coming here was a risk to our relationship. **However, n**~~N~~**ot coming here would have been a risk to my career. Taking this risk taught me to be responsible and trust my boyfriend back home. I know that I will take many risks like this throughout my life and that not all of them will work out.** But if I am ever going to ~~**make it**~~ **reach my potential**, I have to be willing to take risks.

3 **Also,** I believe that I learn from making mistakes. **For example, w**~~W~~hen I was **a sophomore** in high school, I didn't study for a major science test. **I knew the test was important, but I decided to go to a party with my friends. I really needed the grade, s**~~S~~o I cheated. ~~**My sister cheated once. I was so scared to do it**~~. **I cut my notes into small strips of paper that I put in my desk, but t**~~T~~he teacher caught me. **Thank goodness** ~~**the teacher**~~ **he was a nice**

person. ~~**The teacher**~~ **He** took the time to talk to me about the mistake I was making**, not only cheating for a grade, but cheating myself out of the knowledge that I could have**. This mistake made me reevaluate my education. ~~**This mistake**~~ **It led me into nursing by making me** ~~**reevaluate**~~ **realize what subjects I really enjoyed.** I could have laughed off the cheating experience **and the teacher. However,** I decided to slow down and learn from the experience.

4 **In addition to learning from my own actions,** I also benefit from watching other people. **For instance, w**~~**W**~~hen my cousin became heavily involved with gangs **and drugs**, I watched ~~**my cousin**~~ **her** live in constant fear. ~~**My cousin**~~ **She was worried that she would end up in jail, overdose on drugs, or become a "plaything" for other gang members. She worked hard to overcome that lifestyle. She talked a lot to me about those experiences.** By watching my cousin **go through these horrible** ~~**experiences**~~ **incidents,** I made a conscious decision ~~**to be nothing like my cousin**~~ **never to make the bad choices that** ~~**my cousin**~~ **she made. I had plenty of opportunities to do so. Turning away from this life was difficult, but I did it.** By watching and understanding my cousin's life. I learned to live mine better.

5 **Essentially, p**~~**P**~~eople can learn about life from almost anything they do. They just have to be willing to do so. **Now, w**~~**W**~~hen I take risks, I think about what I will learn. **When I make mistakes, I figure out why I made each mistake and how to avoid it a second time. Also, I definitely try to learn as much as I can from watching others, which I believe, in the case of my cousin, has already saved my life. These three ways of learning are all part of who I am today. I know I'm not finished learning yet. In fact, I don't know if I ever will be.**

Your Revised Essay Now that you have applied all the revision strategies to your own writing, rewrite your revised essay.

TEACHING EDITING
Divide students into six groups, and assign each group a grammar problem (fragments, run-

EDITING

After you have revised your writing, you are ready to edit it. Editing involves finding and correcting errors in grammar, punctuation, mechanics, and spelling. Correct writing is as important to communicating as well-chosen words. Nothing distracts readers from what you are saying more than editing errors. Editing is a two-part job: First, you must locate the errors. Then, you must know how to correct them.

As the checklist here shows, we have divided the editing strategies into three categories: sentences, punctuation and mechanics, and word choice and spelling. This checklist doesn't cover all the grammar and usage problems you may find in your writing, but it focuses on the main errors college students make.

ons, subject-verb agreement, pronouns, punctuation, and spelling). Have students give their papers to the group that they feel will best help their writing. For instance, a student who has comma problems would give the paper to the punctuation group. Have each group look only for its designated grammar problem in each paper and make suggested corrections. If time permits, allow students to submit their papers to more than one group.

EDITING CHECKLIST

SENTENCES

- ✓ Does each sentence have a main subject and verb?
- ✓ Do all subjects and verbs agree?
- ✓ Do all pronouns agree with their nouns?
- ✓ Are modifiers as close as possible to the words they modify?

PUNCTUATION AND MECHANICS

- ✓ Are sentences punctuated correctly?
- ✓ Are words capitalized properly?

WORD CHOICE AND SPELLING

- ✓ Are words used correctly?
- ✓ Are words spelled correctly?

TEACHING ON THE WEB

Discussion Topic: As a class, discuss how the Internet can help with editing. Can students think of any sites that would be useful? How valuable is the Internet for editing? Is it better than having an actual human help with editing?

Finding Your Errors

A major part of editing is proofreading. Proofreading is reading to catch grammar, punctuation, mechanics, and spelling errors. If you do not proofread carefully, you will not catch your errors and make the final changes that will improve your writing.

There are some specific techniques for finding errors. One good method is to read your essay backward, sentence by sentence, starting with the last sentence. Taking sentences out of context lets you concentrate on individual sentences and not get caught up in reading for meaning.

Many students like to keep error logs like the one for grammar, punctuation, and mechanics in Appendix 6 and the one for spelling in Appendix 7. By the second or third paper you write, the logs will show you the types of errors you make most frequently. Then you can proofread your paper for one

INSTRUCTOR'S RESOURCE MANUAL

For additional material about teaching editing, for journal entries, and for various tests, see the *Instructor's Resource Manual*, Section II, Part I.

type of error at a time. For example, if you often write run-on sentences, you should read your paper once just to catch run-ons. Then read it again to find a second type of error, and so on. The error logs can help you reduce the number of errors in your writing. By recording the correction for each error you find, you will eventually learn the corrections.

You can also use the grammar-check or spell-check features on your computer. The grammar-check will point out possible grammar errors and suggest ways to reword sentences, but it is not foolproof. You need to decide if you want to accept or reject the grammar suggestions the computer makes. The spell-check is also not completely reliable because it misses errors. For example, it cannot tell the difference between *there* and *their*. So you should use it cautiously.

Asking a tutor or a friend to read your writing is also a good idea. A fresh pair of eyes may see errors you have missed. When others read your writing, they might want to use the editing symbols on the inside front cover to highlight your errors for you. You can then use the page references on the chart to guide you to the part of this textbook that explains how to correct those errors.

PRACTICE 25 Find your Editing Quotient (EQ) by taking the EQ Test on page 754. This test will help you learn what errors you have the most trouble identifying when you proofread someone's writing.

PRACTICE 26 Score your EQ Test by using the answer key that follows the test. Circle the errors you missed, and chart them in Appendix 5. Do they fall into any clear categories?

Correcting Your Errors

Whenever you find errors, you need to correct them. To guide you through this phase of the writing process, Part IV of this text provides a complete handbook of grammar and usage. As you proofread, apply each question in the Editing Checklist to your essay. If you are not sure whether you have made an error, look up the problem in Part IV. Work with your writing until you can answer yes to every question on the checklist.

PRACTICE 27: Using the Handbook Using the Handbook in Part IV, list the page references for the 15 different types of errors you worked with in Practices 25 and 26. This will help you learn to use the Handbook as a reference guide.

apostrophe page __________

capitalization page __________

comma page __________

comma splice page __________

confused word page __________

dangling modifier page __________

end punctuation page __________

fragment page __________

fused sentence page __________

modifier error page __________

pronoun page __________

pronoun agreement page __________

spelling page __________

subject-verb agreement page __________

verb form page __________

PRACTICE 28: Using the Error Log and Spelling Log Turn to Appendixes 6 and 7, and start an Error Log and a Spelling Log of your own with the errors you didn't identify in Practice 25. For each error, write out the mistake and the rule from the Handbook. Then make the correction. See both appendices for examples. *Answers will vary.*

Beth's Editing When Beth proofreads her paper for grammar, punctuation, mechanics, and spelling, she finds two errors that she looks up in Part IV and corrects. The first error is a comma splice:

> **Comma Splice:** I have a boyfriend back home, we want to get married someday.

Beth realizes that this sentence has too many subjects and verbs without any linking words or end punctuation between them. She looks up "comma splice" on page 548 of Part IV and corrects the error by putting a coordinating conjunction (*and*) between the two clauses.

> **Correction:** I have a boyfriend back home, **and** we want to get married someday.

Beth also finds a sentence that doesn't sound complete—it's not a sentence but a fragment:

Fragment: By watching and understanding my cousin's life.

When she looks up the problem in Part IV (page 538), she learns that a fragment is easily corrected by connecting it to another sentence.

Correction: By watching and understanding my cousin's life~~.~~**,** I learned to live mine better.

Beth's Edited Draft Both of these errors are corrected here in Beth's edited draft.

The Learning Curve

1 Everyone learns in different ways. Some people learn by watching, while others learn by doing. Some learn by reading, and others learn by listening. Some learn best when they work independently, but others do better in groups. In fact, the way people learn is a major part of who they are. Knowing how we learn can help us understand ourselves better. I know that I learn best from taking risks, making mistakes, and watching others.

2 First, I have discovered that I learn a lot by taking risks. If I didn't take risks, I think I'd never mature. Being at this college was a risk. **I have a boyfriend back home, and we want to get married someday.** But I knew that this school's nursing program was better than the one in my hometown, so I left my boyfriend to come here. Coming here was a risk to our relationship. However, not coming here would have been a risk to my career. Taking this risk taught me to be responsible and trust my boyfriend back home. I know that I will take many risks like this throughout my life and that not all of them will work out. But if I am ever going to reach my potential, I have to be willing to take risks.

3 Also, I believe that I learn from making mistakes. For example, when I was a sophomore in high school, I didn't study for a major science test. I knew the test was important, but I decided to go to a party with my friends. I really needed the grade, so I cheated. I cut my notes into small strips of paper that I put in my desk,

but the teacher caught me. Thank goodness he was a nice person. He took the time to talk to me about the mistake I was making, not only cheating for a grade, but cheating myself out of the knowledge that I could have. This mistake made me reevaluate my education. It led me into nursing by making me realize what subjects I really enjoyed. I could have laughed off the cheating experience and the teacher. However, I decided to slow down and learn from the experience.

In addition to learning from my own actions, I also 4
benefit from watching other people. For instance, when my cousin became heavily involved with gangs and drugs, I watched her live in constant fear. She was worried that she would end up in jail, overdose on drugs, or become a "plaything" for other gang members. She worked hard to overcome that lifestyle. She talked a lot to me about those experiences. By watching my cousin go through these horrible incidents, I made a conscious decision never to make the bad choices that she made. I had plenty of opportunities to do so. Turning away from this life was difficult, but I did it. **By watching and understanding my cousin's life~~.~~, I learned to live mine better.**

Essentially, people can learn about life from 5
almost anything they do. They just have to be willing to do so. Now, when I take risks, I think about what I will learn. When I make mistakes, I figure out why I made each mistake and how to avoid it a second time. Also, I definitely try to learn as much as I can from watching others, which I believe, in the case of my cousin, has already saved my life. These three ways of learning are all part of who I am today. I know I'm not finished learning yet. In fact, I don't know if I ever will be.

Your Editing Proofread your essay carefully to find errors, using at least two of the methods described in this chapter. Record your grammar, punctuation, and mechanics errors in the Error Log (Appendix 6) and your spelling errors in the Spelling Log (Appendix 7).

Your Edited Draft Now write a corrected draft of your essay.

Review of the Reading and Writing Processes

Clues for Review

- **The reading process** is a series of tasks that involve prereading, reading, first rereading, and second rereading.

  Prereading: Thinking about the title, the author, and focused questions

  Reading: Focusing on vocabulary, a reading strategy, the author's purpose, the author's audience

  First Rereading: Understanding the essay's assumptions and relationships between ideas

  Second Rereading: Writing questions, forming opinions, analyzing
- **The writing process** is a series of tasks that involve prewriting, writing, revising, and editing. At any time, one activity may loop in and out of another.
- **Prewriting** consists of thinking about and planning your essay.

  Thinking: freewriting, brainstorming, clustering, questioning, discussing

  Planning: Deciding on a subject, purpose, and audience

  Writing a thesis statement: Stating a limited subject and an opinion about that subject
- **Writing** includes developing your ideas; organizing your essay; and writing your introduction, conclusion, and title.

  Developing: Explaining your ideas and adding specific details, examples, facts, and reasons

  Organizing: Arranging ideas from general to particular, particular to general, chronologically, spatially, or from one extreme to another

  Writing your introduction, conclusion, and title: Writing an introduction, conclusion, and title that supports your thesis
- **Revising** means "seeing again" and improving all aspects of an essay's organization and development.

  Thesis statement

  Basic elements

  Development

Unity
Organization
Coherence

- **Editing** involves proofreading and correcting your grammar, punctuation, mechanics, and spelling errors.

REVIEW PRACTICE 1 Answer the following questions.

1. What are the four main parts of the reading process?

   Prereading, reading, first rereading, and second rereading

2. What are the four main parts of the writing process?

   Prewriting, writing, revising, and editing

3. What is your favorite reading strategy? Why is it your favorite?

   Answers will vary.

4. What is your favorite prewriting activity? Why is it your favorite?

   Answers will vary.

5. What personal rituals do you go through when you read?

   Answers will vary.

6. What personal rituals do you go through as you write?

   Answers will vary.

7. Where do you usually do your academic reading? Why do you choose this place?

   Answers will vary.

8. Where do you usually do your academic writing? Do you write your first draft on a computer? What time of day do you do your best writing?

   Answers will vary.

9. What is a thesis statement?

   The controlling idea of an essay

10. What is the difference between topic sentences and details?

    Topic sentences relate directly to the thesis statement of an essay.

    Details support their topic sentences.

11. What are the five main methods of organization?

    General to particular, particular to general, chronological, spatial, and from one extreme to another

12. Do you usually ask a tutor or friend to look at your draft before you revise it?

    Answers will vary.

13. What is the difference between revising and editing?

    Revising deals with development and organization; editing deals with grammar, punctuation, mechanics, and spelling.

14. Draw a picture or graphic version of your own reading process. What happens first, second, third, and so on from the time you get a reading assignment? Don't use any words in your picture. *Answers will vary.*

15. Draw a picture or graphic version of your own writing process. What happens first, second, third, and so on from the time you get a writing assignment? Don't use any words in your picture. *Answers will vary.*

REVIEW PRACTICE 2 Write a thesis statement for five of the following topics. Then develop one thesis statement into a first draft of an essay. *Answers will vary.*

1. My best friend
2. Politics
3. My best adventure
4. Animals
5. In the middle of the night
6. My family
7. My future career
8. The best car
9. Parents should never
10. Sports

REVIEW PRACTICE 3 Revise the essay you wrote for Review Practice 2, using the checklist on pages 83–84. *Answers will vary.*

REVIEW PRACTICE 4 Edit the essay you wrote for Review Practice 2, using the checklist on page 111. *Answers will vary.*

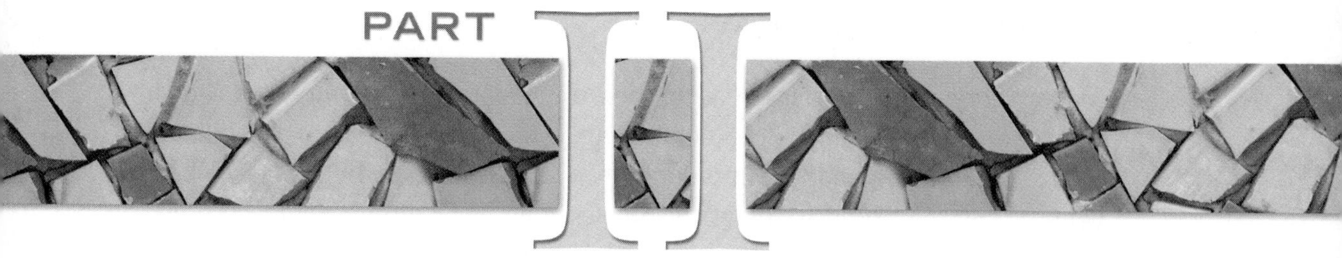

Reading and Writing Effective Essays

"We do not write in order to be understood; we write in order to understand."

—CECIL DAY LEWIS

In Part I of *Mosaics,* you learned about the various parts of the reading and writing processes. You discovered that you have to work with the author of an essay to create meaning when you read and with your potential reader to produce meaning when you write. Part II of *Mosaics* focuses on nine different ways of thinking or processing information, called rhetorical modes. In this part, you will concentrate on one mode at a time so you can understand in detail how a particular strategy actually works. In reality, however, although an essay may emphasize one mode, several rhetorical strategies function together to communicate a message.

Each chapter in Part II begins with an explanation of a rhetorical strategy and then provides specific guidelines for using that strategy in reading and writing. First, the chapter features the rhetorical strategy in a reading selection with specific guidelines for approaching this type of reading critically. Next, after furnishing specific guidelines for writing this type of essay, the chapter guides you through two writing samples to help you understand how this particular rhetorical strategy actually works: (1) a student essay and (2) your own essay. Students can usually see patterns in other students' writing more easily than they can in their own essays, so you will work with someone else's writing before composing your own essay in a particular mode. Finally, the chapter introduces two essays written by professional writers. The questions framing these selections will help you process the content of the essays critically so you will ultimately be prepared to write a well-thought-out essay of your own at the end of each chapter.

CHAPTER 8

Describing

"When you show, you get out of the readers' way and let them come right at the experience itself."

—DONALD MURRAY

Description is an essential part of your life every day. Your friends might want to know what kind of car you just bought; your parents may ask what your new friend is like; your supervisor might need a description of the project you just finished. You constantly need to describe people, places, objects, and activities for different audiences if you want to communicate clearly and effectively.

In addition, you frequently use description when writing. Actually, description is a major part of our writing in our personal lives, in college, and at work:

- You describe your new leather jacket in an e-mail message to a friend.
- You describe the damage to your car in an insurance report.
- A student describes a cell and its parts on a biology exam.
- A nurse describes the appearance of a wound in a patient report.
- A landscape contractor describes a design for a rock garden.

Description creates a picture in words to help a reader visualize something a writer has seen, heard, or done. It helps the reader understand or share a sensory experience by *showing* rather than *telling*. Description is one of our primary forms of self-expression.

At times, description is used as an end in itself. That is, you write a description for the sole purpose of telling what something looks, sounds, feels, tastes, or smells like. For instance, you might use pure description to tell a friend about your new apartment. More often, though, description is used to help accomplish another purpose—to explain a problem, to analyze the

TEACHING DESCRIPTION

Divide students into five groups, and assign each group one sense—seeing, hearing, touching, smelling, or tasting.

Provide each group with a word that is not usually associated with its sense. For example, have students describe the smell of a desk, the taste of rain, the sight of "irritation," the sound of autumn, or the feel of sour (opposite of sweet). Make sure the groups don't know each other's words. Have each group describe its word using only sensory details assigned to its group. For example, the group that is describing the smell of a closet can use only words associated with smell—not sight.

Have one person from each group describe the group's word to the other groups to see if the other groups can guess the word. This exercise will compel students to see the power of description by focusing on only one sense in an unusual way.

causes and effects of an event, or to persuade your readers to change their thinking or take some specific action.

TEACHING TIPS

The following eight teaching tips are based on Howard Gardner's multiple intelligences:

Verbal/Linguistic

Have students write a short but extremely detailed account of the last vacation they took. How many sensory words can they use to describe one aspect of the trip?

Musical/Rhythmic

Have students listen to a pastoral piece of music, such as Mendelssohn's *Song Without Words* or Vivaldi's *Spring* from *Four Seasons*. Then have them list the sights, sounds, smells, tastes, and textures that the music conjures up.

Logical/Mathematical

Have students list in chronological order all the sensory details they experience from the moment they arrive home for the day to the moment they go to sleep.

Visual/Spatial

Have students draw a scene that includes all five senses; it might be a busy city street corner, a country fair, or some other location. Which senses are predominant in the scene?

READING AND WRITING A DESCRIPTION ESSAY

If you learn how to read a description essay critically, these skills will naturally transfer to your writing. But you need to be conscious of the process you use to understand your reading so you can use this strategy just as effectively in your writing. Reading and writing critically in any mode are demanding, but they are necessary tools for succeeding in college and in life beyond college. Like two halves of a circle, these two processes complement each other and enhance your ability to perform many other tasks in all facets of life.

Reading a Description Essay

Writing about the dust storms of the 1930s, Margaret Bourke-White describes in the following essay their various trails of destruction. In what ways has nature played a role in your life? What is this role? Is it a positive or negative one? What recent natural events have dramatically changed our entire country? What natural events have affected the world?

READING CRITICALLY

We all naturally make personal associations with our reading material. However, one person's associations are usually quite different from those of someone else. Recording the associations you make with a reading selection lets you "own" the essay, so to speak. It allows you to connect the author's ideas to your own experiences. As you read the following essay, make at least five notes in the margin that relate some of your specific memories of nature to the details in this essay. Be prepared to explain the connection between your notes and the facts in the essay.

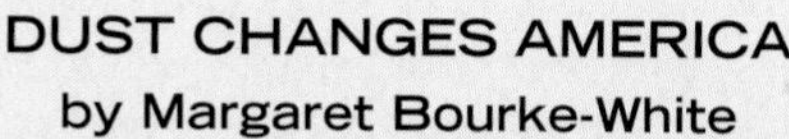

DUST CHANGES AMERICA

by Margaret Bourke-White

1 Vitamin K they call it—the dust which sifts under the door sills, and stings in the eyes, and seasons every spoonful of food. The dust storms have distinct personalities, rising in formation like rolling clouds, creeping up silently like formless fog, approaching violently like a tornado. Where has it come from? It provides topics of endless speculation. Red, it is the topsoil from Oklahoma; brown, it is the fertile earth of western Kansas; the good grazing land of Texas and New Mexico sweeps by as a murky yellow haze. Or, tracing it locally, "My uncle will be along pretty soon," they say; "I just saw his farm go by."

2 The town dwellers stack their linen in trunks, stuff wet cloths along the window sills, estimate the tons of sand in the darkened air above them, paste cloth masks on their faces with adhesive tape, and try to joke about Vitamin K. But on the farms and ranches there is an attitude of despair.

3 By coincidence I was in the same parts of the country where last year I photographed the drought. As short a time as eight months ago there was an attitude of false optimism. "Things will get better," the farmers would say. "We're not as hard hit as other states. The government will help out. This can't go on." But this year there is an atmosphere of utter hopelessness—nothing to do: no use digging out your chicken coops and pigpens after the last "duster" because the next one will be coming along soon; no use trying to keep the house clean; no use fighting off that foreclosure any longer; no use even hoping to give your cattle anything to chew on when their food crops have literally blown out of the ground.

4 It was my job to avoid dust storms, since I was commissioned by an airplane company to take photographs of their course from the air, but frequently the dust storms caught up with us, and as we were grounded anyway, I started to photograph them. Thus I saw five dust-storm states from the air and from the ground.

5 In the last several years, there have been droughts and sand storms and dusters, but they have been localized, and always one state could borrow from another. But this year the scourge assumes tremendous proportions. Dust storms are bringing distress and death to 300,000 square miles; they are blowing over all of Kansas, all of Nebraska and Wyoming, strips of the Dakotas, about half of Colorado, sections of Iowa and Missouri, the greater part of Oklahoma, and the northern panhandle of Texas, extending into the eastern parts of New Mexico.

Bodily/Kinesthetic

Suggest that students bicycle for a few miles, run through a park, play tennis, or do some other activity to see if they experience a heightened awareness of sensory details when they are active versus inactive. What senses do they experience differently?

Intrapersonal

Ask students to close themselves in their rooms and think about the most peaceful place they would like to visit. What sensory details do they think they would find most satisfying about this special place? What sensory details would make them think of this place when they are not there?

Interpersonal

Put students in groups of five to discuss a childhood vacation they took. What sensory details do they remember from the experience? Can they still see, hear, feel, smell, or taste any of the trip?

Naturalist

Suggest that students walk on a beach, kayak in a lake, roller-blade down a walkway, or otherwise move through nature and watch for vivid sensory details. What sounds are loudest? What sights are brightest? What smells are strongest? What tastes or textures are most obvious?

INSTRUCTOR'S RESOURCE MANUAL

For additional material about teaching description; for journal entries; and for multiple-choice, short-answer, and paragraph tests, see the *Instructor's Resource Manual,* Section II, Part II.

6 Last year, I saw farmers harvesting the Russian thistle. Never before had they thought of feeding thistles to cattle. But this prickly fodder became precious for food. This year even the Russian thistles are dying out and the still humbler soap weed becomes as vital to the farmer as the fields of golden grain he tended in the past. Last year's thistle-fed cattle dwindled to skin and bone. This year's herds on their diet of soap weed develop roughened hides, ugly growths around the mouth, and lusterless eyes.

7 Years of the farmers' and ranchers' lives have gone into the building up of their herds. Their herds were like their families to them. When AAA [American Agricultural Association] officials spotted cows and steers for shooting during the cattle-killing days of last summer, the farmers felt as though their own children were facing the bullets. Kansas, a Republican state, has no love for the AAA. This year, winds whistled over land made barren by the drought and the crop-conservation program. When Wallace [Henry Agard Wallace, Secretary of Agriculture under Franklin D. Roosevelt] removed the ban on the planting of spring wheat, he was greeted by cheers. But the wheat has been blown completely out of the ground. Nothing is left but soap weed, or the expensive cotton-seed cake, and after that—bankruptcy.

8 The storm comes in a terrifying way. Yellow clouds roll. The wind blows such a gale that it is all my helper can do to hold my camera to the ground. The sand whips into my lens. I repeatedly wipe it away trying to snatch an exposure before it becomes completely coated again. The light becomes yellower, the wind colder. Soon there is no photographic light, and we hurry for shelter to the nearest farmhouse.

9 Three men and a woman are seated around a dust-caked lamp, on their faces grotesque masks of wet cloth. The children have been put to bed with towels tucked over their heads. My host greets us: "It takes grit to live in this country." They are telling stories: A bachelor harnessed the sandblast which ripped through the keyhole by holding his pots and pans in it until they were spick and span. A pilot flying over Amarillo got caught in a sand storm. His motor clogged; he took to his parachute. It took him six hours to shovel his way back to earth. And when a man from the next county was struck by a drop of water, he fainted, and it took two buckets of sand to revive him.

10 The migrations of the farmer have begun. In many of the worst-hit counties, 80 percent of the families are on relief. In the open farm country, one crop failure follows another. After perhaps three successive crop failures, the farmer can't stand it any longer. He moves in with relatives and hopes for a job in Arizona or Illinois or some neighboring state where he knows he is not needed. Perhaps he gets a job as a cotton picker, and off he goes with his family, to be turned adrift again after a brief working period.

We passed them on the road, all their household goods piled on wagons, one lucky family on a truck—lucky, because they had been able to keep their truck when the mortgage was foreclosed. All they owned in the world was packed on it; the children sat on a pile of bureaus topped with mattresses, and the sides of the truck were strapped up with bed springs. The entire family looked like a Ku Klux Klan meeting, their faces done up in masks to protect them from the whirling sand. 11

Near Hays, Kansas, a little boy started home from school and never arrived there. The neighbors looked for him till ten at night, and all next day a band of two hundred people searched. At twilight they found him, only a quarter of a mile from home, his body nearly covered with silt. He had strangled to death. The man who got lost in his own ten-acre truck garden and wandered around choking and sniffling for eight hours before he found his house considered himself lucky to escape with his life. The police and sheriffs are kept constantly busy with calls from anxious parents whose children are lost, and the toll is mounting of people who become marooned and die in the storms. 12

But the real tragedy is the plight of the cattle. In a rising sand storm, cattle quickly become blinded. They run around in circles until they fall and breathe so much dust that they die. Autopsies show their lungs caked with dust and mud. Farmers dread the birth of calves during a storm. The newborn animals will die within twenty-four hours. 13

And this same dust that coats the lungs and threatens death to cattle and men alike, that ruins the stock of the storekeeper lying unsold on his shelves, that creeps into the gear shifts of automobiles, that sifts through the refrigerator into the butter, that makes housekeeping, and gradually life itself, unbearable, this swirling drifting dust is changing the agricultural map of the United States. It piles ever higher on the floors and beds of a steadily increasing number of deserted farmhouses. A half-buried plowshare, a wheat binder ruffled over with sand, the skeleton of a horse near a dirt-filled water hole are stark evidence of the meager life, the wasted savings, the years of toil that the farmer is leaving behind him. 14

Preparing to Write Your Own Description Essay

What are some memorable experiences you have had with nature (for example, a snowstorm, a sunny day, a drought, a tornado, a sunset, a thunderstorm)? Why do you remember these experiences? Do any of them form a single impression when you think about them? Use one or more of the prewriting techniques you learned in Chapter 2 to generate as many thoughts as possible about these memories.

Writing a Description Essay

Describing is a very natural process that is based on good observing. But some people describe items more vividly than others. When they describe an experience, you feel as though you were there too. We can all improve our ability to describe by following a few simple guidelines:

1. **Decide on a dominant impression—the feeling or mood you want to communicate.** How do you want your readers to feel after reading your description? Good about the characters in the scene? Angry at the situation? Satisfied with the outcome? Choosing a dominant impression gives your description focus and unity. You can't possibly write down everything you observe about a person, place, incident, or object. The result would be a long, confusing—and probably boring—list. But if you first decide on a dominant impression for your description, you can then choose the details that will best convey that impression.

   The dominant impression Bourke-White conveys is a feeling of frustration and despair at the thought of the destruction that nature can bring. This dominant impression gives her essay focus and helps her choose the details that will best communicate this feeling.

2. **Decide how much of your description should be objective (factual) and how much should be subjective (personal reactions).** An objective description is like a dictionary definition—accurate and without emotion. Scientific and technical writing are objective. If, for example, you are describing a piece of equipment used in a chemistry experiment or the packaging needed to ship a computer, you would be objective. Subjective description, in contrast, tries to produce a specific emotional response in the reader. It focuses on feelings rather than facts and tries to activate as many senses as possible. An advertisement describing a Caribbean cruise might be very subjective, as might a restaurant or movie review. Most descriptive writing has a combination of objective and subjective elements. The degree to which you emphasize one over the other depends on your purpose and your audience.

   Bourke-White's essay demonstrates a good balance of objective and subjective writing. She presents the facts about the dust storms and the ways the midwesterners deal with the dust—putting linen in trunks, stuffing wet cloths in window sills, using masks on their faces, and so on. Then she mixes these facts with subjective stories about families who are suffering, children who never make it home from school, and cattle who are like family to their owners. This combination of objective and subjective elements makes the essay realistic and powerful at the same time.

3. **Draw on your five senses to write a good description.** Although observing is at the heart of good description, limiting yourself to what you see is a mistake. Good description relies on all five senses: seeing, hearing, touching, smelling, and tasting. If you use all your senses to relay your description, your readers will be able to see, hear, touch, smell, and taste what you are describing as if they were there with you participating in the same experience.

   Look again at Bourke-White's description. She draws on sight throughout the essay but especially in paragraph 8 when she describes her attempts at taking pictures. She refers to our sense of touch when she talks about the dust stinging the eyes (paragraph 1) and the cloth masks on people's faces (paragraph 2). She relies on taste when she mentions the dust seasoning the food (paragraph 1) and the cattle eating thistles (paragraph 6). Her description of the wind whistling over the barren land (paragraph 7) appeals to our sense of hearing. Her entire essay is vivid because of all the specific sensory details she furnishes.

4. **When you describe, try to show rather than tell your readers what you want them to know.** Your ultimate goal in writing a descriptive essay is to give your readers an experience as close to yours as possible. Therefore, do not simply tell your readers what you saw or experienced; show them. Use your writing skills to re-create the event so that your readers can see, hear, feel, smell, taste, and understand as if they were there. For example, you can tell someone you bought a "terrific new car." But if you say you bought a "beautiful, new blue Mustang with a gray interior, custom wheels, and an awesome stereo," you're *showing* your readers why you are so excited about your purchase.

   If Bourke-White had simply stated her dominant impression (that dust storms bring frustration and despair to the Midwest) with no examples or details to support her statement, she would only be *telling* her readers how she felt. Instead, she *shows* them. Her sensory details demonstrate her main point.

5. **Organize your description so that your readers can easily follow it.** Most descriptions are organized from general to particular (from main idea to details), from particular to general (from details to main idea), or spatially (from top to bottom or left to right). Because the organization of your essay often depends on your point of view, you should choose a specific perspective from which to write your description. If your description jumps around your house, referring to a picture on the wall in your bedroom, then to the refrigerator in the kitchen, and next to the quilt on your bed, your readers are likely to become confused and

disoriented. They will not be able to follow you. If, however, you move from room to room in a logical way, your audience will be able to stay with you. In fact, your vision will become their vision.

Bourke-White organizes her essay from one extreme to another—in this case, from least to most tragic. She starts by describing the inconveniences of the dust storms on a personal level—the dirty houses, the piles of dust in the fields, the health problems. Then she moves on to the more serious issues of death on 300,000 square miles of land. The essay ends with references to farms collapsing financially, children dying from the dust, and whole families being displaced. The author leaves us at the end of her essay with a sense of loss and hopelessness that reflects the feelings of the farmers in the Midwest during a drought.

Writing Your Own Description Essay

What direct encounters have you had with nature? What are some of the details of these encounters? Was your general impression good or bad? Write an essay describing one of these encounters. Describe your experience through the senses, following the guidelines for writing a description essay. Remember to show rather than tell your readers about your memory. Begin by reviewing your prewriting notes. Then choose your dominant impression, and put it into a thesis statement.

A STUDENT'S DESCRIPTION ESSAY

In an essay about a fond memory, a student named Abby Reed reminisces about her grandfather. As you read this draft, ask yourself what dominant impression Abby is trying to communicate to her readers.

Grandma's House

1 My grandma lives in the country, near a large, blue lake and a small, green forest. I look forward to visiting her house. I think of my grandpa when I'm there.

2 Whenever I walk into my grandma's house, I always go directly to my grandpa's favorite room—the den. I am immediately reminded of my grandpa in this room. My grandma has a soft, brown sofa and a brown leather

loveseat in this small, dark room, but all I see is the old, worn chair that was my grandpa's. The chair was re-covered in an itchy tweed fabric. I used to pretend to be asleep in his chair so my grandpa would gently lift me from the coarse fabric and place me on his lap. I would lie there even though I wasn't sleeping and enjoy the warmth of his body. I remember the times I sat on his sturdy lap in that chair while he read One Fish, Two Fish, Red Fish, Blue Fish or The Cat in the Hat in his deep voice.

Now when I sit in his chair, I look on the mantle and see an old Air 3
Force picture of my grandpa and three of his Air Force buddies. They are all dressed in informal flight clothes and are standing in front of a World War II airplane. Next to this picture is a single portrait of my grandpa when he was 70. This picture represents the way I still see him in my mind. His gray hair is thin, his face has light brown sun spots on it that show his years of working outdoors. His gentle, light blue eyes sparkle in a way that usually meant he was up to something mischievous. But most of all. I love looking at his smile. The right side of his mouth always turned slightly downward, but it is a smile that I would give anything to see in person just one more time.

I also love to play with the pipe stand that sits on the table next to my 4
grandpa's chair. I like the worn feeling of the pipe. It once was rough with ridges but is now smooth from use. When I quietly pick up his pipe and smell the sweet tobacco that was once housed in its shell, I think of all the times I knew my grandpa were near me because of this same aroma.

I have wonderful memories of my grandpa. When I go to my grandma's 5
house, I can sit in my grandpa's old chair in my grandpa's favorite room and reminisce about all the times I felt safe when my grandpa was near. I will always treasure this one tiny room, with its smells from the past and its picture of my grandpa smiling.

Discovering How the Essay Works

1. This essay creates a certain mood. What is the dominant impression that Abby creates?

   She feels happy and content when she thinks of her grandfather.

2. Is this description primarily subjective or objective? Explain your answer.

   It is subjective because most of the details she mentions are not facts but personal memories of her grandfather.

3. In this particular essay, the student writer describes her subjects mainly through the sense of sight, with a few references to hearing, touching, and smelling. Find at least one example of each of these senses in this essay. *Answers will vary. Here are some possibilities.*

   Seeing: *blue lake; an old Air Force picture; light brown sun spots*

   Hearing: *he read; deep voice; quietly pick up his pipe*

   Touching: *soft, brown sofa; itchy tweed fabric; sturdy lap; coarse fabric*

   Smelling: *sweet tobacco; this same aroma; smells from the past*

4. Abby works hard in this essay to *show* rather than *tell* us what she sees in the house. List three details that go beyond telling to *show* us what she observes?

   Answers will vary.

   ______

   ______

5. How does Abby organize her essay? List the topics of each of her body paragraphs, and then identify her method of organization.

   going to the den

   sitting in her grandpa's chair

   touching the pipe

   Method of organization: *Spatial*

REVISING AND EDITING OPTIONS

Consider varying your approach to revising and editing. You could teach these skills in a class discussion, in small groups, or in pairs.

Revising and Editing the Student Essay

This essay is Abby's first draft, which now needs to be revised and edited. First, apply the Revising Checklist on page 133 to the content of Abby's draft. When you are satisfied that her ideas are fully developed and well organized, use the Editing Checklist on page 136 to correct her grammar and mechanics errors. Do the tasks, and answer the questions after each checklist. Then write your suggested changes directly on Abby's draft.

REVISING CHECKLIST

REVISING STRATEGIES

This chapter focuses on the following revising elements:

Thesis statement
Basic elements

THESIS STATEMENT

✔ Does the thesis statement contain the essay's controlling idea and an opinion about that idea?

✔ Does the thesis appear as the last sentence of the introduction?

BASIC ELEMENTS

✔ Does the title draw in the readers?

✔ Does the introduction capture the readers' attention and build up to the thesis statement effectively?

✔ Does each body paragraph deal with a single topic?

✔ Does the conclusion bring the essay to a close in an interesting way?

DEVELOPMENT

✔ Do the body paragraphs adequately support the thesis statement?

✔ Does each body paragraph have a focused topic sentence?

✔ Does each body paragraph contain *specific* details that support the topic sentence?

✔ Does each body paragraph include *enough* details to explain the topic sentence fully?

UNITY

✔ Do the essay's topic sentences relate directly to the thesis statement?

✔ Do the details in each body paragraph support its topic sentence?

ORGANIZATION

✔ Is the essay organized logically?

✔ Is each body paragraph organized logically?

COHERENCE

✔ Are transitions used effectively so that paragraphs move smoothly and logically from one to the next?

✔ Do the sentences move smoothly and logically from one to the next?

Thesis Statement

1. Put brackets around the last sentence in Abby's introduction. Does it contain her dominant impression?

   No

2. Rewrite Abby's thesis statement if necessary so that it states her dominant impression as clearly as possible.

   Here is one possibility: I love my grandma's house because I can go to my grandpa's favorite room and remember him in detail.

Basic Elements

1. Give Abby's essay an alternate title.

   Answers will vary.

2. Rewrite Abby's introduction so that it captures the readers' attention and builds up to the thesis statement at the end of the paragraph.

   Answers will vary.

3. Does each of Abby's body paragraphs deal with only one topic?

   Yes

4. Rewrite Abby's conclusion using at least one suggestion from Part I.

   Answers will vary.

Development

1. Write out Abby's thesis statement (revised, if necessary), and list her three topic sentences below it. *Thesis may vary.*

   Thesis statement: *I love my grandma's house because I can go to my grandpa's favorite room and remember him in detail.*

Topic 1: *Whenever I walk into my grandma's house, I always go directly to my grandpa's favorite room—the den.*

Topic 2: *Now when I sit in his chair, I look on the mantle and see an old Air Force picture of my grandpa and three of his Air Force buddies.*

Topic 3: *I also love to play with the pipe stand that sits on the table next to my grandpa's chair.*

2. Do Abby's topics adequately support her thesis statement?
   Yes
3. Does each body paragraph have a focused topic sentence?
   Yes
4. Does the essay draw on all five senses?
   There is no tasting in the essay.
5. Add at least one detail to Abby's essay that refers to a new sense. Label the detail you are adding. *Answers will vary.*

   Sense: ____________ Detail: ____________
6. In what way does Abby's essay *show* rather than *tell* her readers about her memories of her grandfather?
   She uses many sensory details to make an image of her grandfather for readers. They can almost see and feel him.

Unity

1. Read each of Abby's topic sentences with her thesis statement (revised, if necessary) in mind. Do they go together?
   Answers will vary.
2. Revise her topic sentences if necessary so they are directly related.
3. Drop or rewrite any of the sentences in her body paragraphs that are not directly related to their topic sentences*All sentences are directly related to their topic sentences.*

Organization

1. Read Abby's essay again to see if all the paragraphs are arranged logically.

2. Move any paragraphs that are out of order. *All paragraphs are arranged logically.*
3. Look closely at Abby's body paragraphs to see if all her sentences are arranged logically within paragraphs.
4. Move any sentences that are out of order. *All sentences are in order.*

Coherence

For a list of transitions, see page 101.

1. Circle five transitions Abby uses. *Answers will vary.*
2. Explain how two of these make Abby's essay easier to read.

   Answers will vary.

Now rewrite Abby's essay with your revisions.

EDITING STRATEGIES
This chapter focuses on the following editing problems:
Fragments
Run-together sentences
Subject-verb agreement

EDITING CHECKLIST

SENTENCES

✓ Does each sentence have a main subject and verb?
✓ Do all subjects and verbs agree?
✓ Do all pronouns agree with their nouns?
✓ Are modifiers as close as possible to the words they modify?

PUNCTUATION AND MECHANICS

✓ Are sentences punctuated correctly?
✓ Are words capitalized properly?

WORD CHOICE AND SPELLING

✓ Are words used correctly?
✓ Are words spelled correctly?

Sentences

Subjects and Verbs

For help with subjects and verbs, see Chapter 25.

1. Underline the subjects once and verbs twice in paragraphs 3 and 4 of your revision of Abby's essay. Remember that sentences can have more than one subject-verb set.
2. Does each of the sentences have at least one subject and verb that can stand alone?

   No

3. Did you find and correct Abby's fragment? If not, find and correct it now. *Paragraph 3, sentence 7*

For help with fragments, see Chapter 26.

4. Did you find and correct Abby's run-together sentence? If not, find and correct it now. *Paragraph 3, sentence 5*

For help with run-togethers, see Chapter 27.

Subject-Verb Agreement

1. Read aloud the subjects and verbs you underlined in your revision of Abby's essay.

For help with subject-verb agreement, see Chapter 30.

2. Did you find and correct the subject and verb that do not agree? *Paragraph 4, sentence 4*

Pronoun Agreement

1. Find any pronouns in your revision of Abby's essay that do not agree with their nouns. *All pronouns agree with their nouns.*
2. Correct any pronouns that do not agree with their nouns.

For help with pronoun agreement, see Chapter 34.

Modifiers

1. Find any modifiers in your revision of Abby's essay that are not as close as possible to the words they modify. *There are no modifier errors.*
2. Rewrite sentences if necessary so that modifiers are as close as possible to the words they modify.

For help with modifier errors, see Chapter 37.

Punctuation and Mechanics

Punctuation

1. Read your revision of Abby's essay for any errors in punctuation.
2. Find the fragment and the run-together sentence you revised, and make sure they are punctuated correctly.

For help with punctuation, see Chapters 38–42.

Mechanics

1. Read your revision of Abby's essay for any errors in capitalization. *There are no capitalization errors.*
2. Be sure to check Abby's capitalization in the fragment and run-together sentence you revised.

For help with capitalization, see Chapter 43.

Word Choice and Spelling

Word Choice

1. Find any words used incorrectly in your revision of Abby's essay. *All words are used correctly.*
2. Correct any errors you find.

For help with confused words, see Chapter 49.

For help with spelling, see Chapter 50.

Spelling

1. Use spell-check and a dictionary to check the spelling in your revision of Abby's essay. *All words are spelled correctly.*
2. Correct any misspelled words.

Now rewrite Abby's essay again with your editing corrections.

YOUR OWN DESCRIPTION ESSAY

Returning to the description you wrote earlier in this chapter, you are now ready to revise and edit your own writing. Remember that revision involves reworking the content and organization of your essay while editing asks you to check your grammar and usage. Work first with the content, making sure your thoughts are fully developed and organized effectively before you correct your grammar and usage errors. At this stage, you should repeat these processes over and over until you feel you have a draft that says exactly what you want it to say.

WRITING CRITICALLY

As you begin to rework your essay, use the same technique you did in your reading. Just as you made personal associations with your reading to help you understand what the author was saying, expand your own writing with personal associations and sensory details that will help your readers understand your experience as if they were there.

CLASS ACTIVITY
Put a sentence on the board that *tells* readers information, and have the students, as a class, offer suggestions to change it to *show* readers that information. For example, change "The boat went down the river" to "The red and white paddleboat gently glided down the murky Guadalupe River."

Revising and Editing Your Own Essay

The checklists here will help you apply what you have learned in this chapter to your essay.

REVISING CHECKLIST

THESIS STATEMENT

☐ Does the thesis statement contain the essay's controlling idea and an opinion about that idea?
☐ Does the thesis appear as the last sentence of the introduction?

BASIC ELEMENTS

☐ Does the title draw in the readers?
☐ Does the introduction capture the readers' attention and build up to the thesis statement effectively?

- ☐ Does each body paragraph deal with a single topic?
- ☐ Does the conclusion bring the essay to a close in an interesting way?

DEVELOPMENT

- ☐ Do the body paragraphs adequately support the thesis statement?
- ☐ Does each body paragraph have a focused topic sentence?
- ☐ Does each body paragraph contain *specific* details that support the topic sentence?
- ☐ Does each body paragraph include *enough* details to explain the topic sentence fully?

UNITY

- ☐ Do the essay's topic sentences relate directly to the thesis statement?
- ☐ Do the details in each body paragraph support its topic sentence?

ORGANIZATION

- ☐ Is the essay organized logically?
- ☐ Is each body paragraph organized logically?

COHERENCE

- ☐ Are transitions used effectively so that paragraphs move smoothly and logically from one to the next?
- ☐ Do the sentences move smoothly and logically from one to the next?

Thesis Statement

1. What dominant impression are you trying to communicate in your essay?

   ____

2. Put brackets around the last sentence in your introduction. Does it contain your dominant impression?

   ____

3. Rewrite your thesis statement if necessary so that it states your dominant impression as clearly as possible.

Basic Elements

1. Give your essay a title if it doesn't have one.

   ____

2. Does your introduction capture your readers' attention and build up to your thesis statement at the end of the paragraph?

   ____

3. Does each of your body paragraphs deal with only one topic?

____

4. Does your conclusion follow some of the suggestions offered in Part I?

____

Development

1. Write out your thesis statement (revised, if necessary), and list your topic sentences below it.

   Thesis statement: ____________________________________

   Topic 1: ____________________________________

   Topic 2: ____________________________________

   Topic 3: ____________________________________

2. Do your topics adequately support your thesis statement?

____

3. Does each body paragraph have a focused topic sentence?

____

4. Does your essay draw on all five senses?

____

5. Record three details from your essay that draw on three different senses. Label each example with the sense it refers to.

Detail	**Sense**
____________________	____________________
____________________	____________________
____________________	____________________

6. Add at least one new detail to your essay.

7. Does your essay *show* rather than *tell* readers what they need to know? Give three examples.

____

____

____

Unity

1. Read each of your topic sentences with your thesis statement in mind. Do they go together?

    ____

2. Revise your topic sentences if necessary so they are directly related.
3. Drop or rewrite any of the sentences in your body paragraphs that are not directly related to their topic sentences.

Organization

1. Read your essay again to see if all the paragraphs are arranged logically.
2. Refer to your answers to the development questions. Then identify your method of organization.

    ____

3. Is the order you chose for your paragraphs the most effective approach to your topic?

    ____

4. Move any paragraphs that are out of order.
5. Look closely at your body paragraphs to see if all the sentences are arranged logically within paragraphs.
6. Move any sentences that are out of order.

Coherence

1. Circle five transitions you use.
2. Explain how two of these make your essay easier to read.

    ____

    ____

For a list of transitions, see page 101.

Now rewrite your essay with your revisions.

EDITING CHECKLIST

SENTENCES

☐ Does each sentence have a main subject and verb?

☐ Do all subjects and verbs agree?

- ☐ Do all pronouns agree with their nouns?
- ☐ Are modifiers as close as possible to the words they modify?

PUNCTUATION AND MECHANICS

- ☐ Are sentences punctuated correctly?
- ☐ Are words capitalized properly?

WORD CHOICE AND SPELLING

- ☐ Are words used correctly?
- ☐ Are words spelled correctly?

Sentences

Subjects and Verbs

For help with subjects and verbs, see Chapter 25.

1. Underline the subjects once and verbs twice in a paragraph of your revised essay. Remember that sentences can have more than one subject-verb set.
2. Does each of your sentences have at least one subject and verb that can stand alone?

For help with fragments, see Chapter 26.

For help with run-togethers, see Chapter 27.

3. Correct any fragments you have written.
4. Correct any run-together sentences you have written.

Subject-Verb Agreement

For help with subject-verb agreement, see Chapter 30.

1. Read aloud the subjects and verbs you underlined in your revised essay.
2. Correct any subjects and verbs that do not agree.

Pronoun Agreement

For help with pronoun agreement, see Chapter 34.

1. Find any pronouns in your revised essay that do not agree with their nouns.
2. Correct any pronouns that do not agree with their nouns.

Modifiers

For help with modifier errors, see Chapter 37.

1. Find any modifiers in your revised essay that are not as close as possible to the words they modify.
2. Rewrite sentences if necessary so that your modifiers are as close as possible to the words they modify.

Punctuation and Mechanics

Punctuation

For help with punctuation, see Chapters 38–42.

1. Read your revised essay for any errors in punctuation.

2. Make sure any fragments and run-together sentences you revised are punctuated correctly.

Mechanics

1. Read your revised essay for any errors in capitalization.
2. Be sure to check your capitalization in any fragments or run-together sentences you revised.

For help with capitalization, see Chapter 43.

Word Choice and Spelling

Word Choice

1. Find any words used incorrectly in your revised essay.
2. Correct any errors you find.

For help with confused words, see Chapter 49.

Spelling

1. Use spell-check and a dictionary to check your spelling.
2. Correct any misspelled words.

For help with spelling, see Chapter 50.

Now rewrite your essay again with your editing corrections.

PRACTICING DESCRIPTION: FROM READING TO WRITING

Reading Workshop

Here are two essays that demonstrate good descriptive writing: "El Hoyo" by Mario Suarez describes a small town near Tucson and its citizens, and "Dwellings" by Linda Hogan focuses on the habitats of different animals. As you read, notice how the writers pull you into each experience through sensory details.

EL HOYO
by Mario Suarez

Focusing Your Attention

1. Think of a place from your childhood that had special meaning for you as you were growing up. Where was this place? Why was it special?
2. In the essay you are about to read, the writer recounts the many sights, sounds, smells, textures, and tastes that he connects with the place where he grew up. What sights, sounds, smells, textures, and tastes do you remember about the city, town, or farm where you grew up? Can you describe the place where you grew up for someone who has never been there?

SUMMARY

Through sensory details, Suarez describes a small town near Tucson.

READABILITY

(Flesch–Kincaid grade level)
8.9

INSTRUCTOR'S RESOURCE MANUAL
For additional teaching strategies, for journal entries, for vocabulary and reading quizzes, and for more writing assignments, see the *Instructor's Resource Manual,* Section II, Part II.

Expanding Your Vocabulary

The following words are important to your understanding of this essay. Highlight them throughout the essay before you begin to read. Then refer to this list as you get to these words in the essay.

Tucson: city in southeastern Arizona (paragraph 1)

chicanos: Mexican Americans (paragraph 1)

padre: father, priest (paragraph 1)

paisanos: countrymen (paragraph 1)

bicker: quarrel (paragraph 1)

adobe: sun-dried brick (paragraph 1)

chavalos: small boys (paragraph 1)

inundated: flooded (paragraph 1)

Octavio Perea's Mexican Hour: Spanish radio program (paragraph 2)

"Smoke in the Eyes": song (paragraph 2)

solace: comfort (paragraph 2)

benevolent: kind (paragraph 2)

solicited: asked, begged (paragraph 2)

señora: married woman (paragraph 2)

chicanas: Mexican American females (paragraph 2)

Baja California: peninsula along the western coast of Mexico (paragraph 2)

boleros: music for Spanish dances (paragraph 3)

comadres: gossiping women (paragraph 3)

bloodwell: family ancestry (paragraph 3)

conquistador: a Spanish conqueror (paragraph 3)

capirotada: Mexican bread pudding (paragraph 4)

panocha: corn (paragraph 4)

Sermeños: family name (paragraph 4)

READING CRITICALLY

As you learned at the beginning of this chapter, practice making connections with your reading by writing personal associations in the margins of this essay. Jot down anything that comes to mind. These notes will put your individual stamp on the essay with a set of memories that only you can recall. They will also help you understand the essay on an analytical level. Share your notes with one of your classmates.

EL HOYO
by Mario Suarez

From the center of downtown Tucson, the ground slopes gently away to Main Street, drops a few feet, and then rolls to the banks of the Santa Cruz River. Here lies the section of the city known as El Hoyo. Why it is called El Hoyo is not very clear. In no sense is it a hole as its name would imply; it is simply the river's immediate valley. Its inhabitants are chicanos who raise hell on Saturday night and listen to Padre Estanislao on Sunday morning. While the term *chicano* is the short way of saying Mexicano, it is not restricted to the paisanos who came from old Mexico with the territory or the last famine to work for the railroad, labor, sing, and go on relief. Chicano is the easy way of referring to everybody. Pablo Gutíerrez married the Chinese grocer's daughter and now runs a meat department; his sons are chicanos. So are the sons of Killer Jones who threw a fight in Harlem and fled to El Hoyo to marry Cristina Mendez. And so are all of them. However, it is doubtful that all these spiritual sons of Mexico live in El Hoyo because they love each other—many fight and bicker constantly. It is doubtful they live in El Hoyo because of its scenic beauty—it is everything but beautiful. Its houses are simple affairs of unplastered adobe, wood, and abandoned car parts. Its narrow streets are mostly clearings which have, in time, acquired names. Except for some tall trees which nobody has ever cared to identify, nurse, or destroy, the main things known to grow in the general area are weeds, garbage piles, dark-eyed chavalos, and dogs. And it is doubtful that the chicanos live in El Hoyo because it is safe—many times the Santa Cruz has risen and inundated the area. 1

In other respects, living in El Hoyo has its advantages. If one is born with a weakness for acquiring bills, El Hoyo is where the collectors are less likely to find you. If one has acquired the habit of listening to Octavio Perea's Mexican Hour in the wee hours of the morning with the radio on at full blast, El Hoyo is 2

ANSWERS TO QUESTIONS

Thinking Critically About Content

1. According to Suarez, *el hoyo*

means "a hole" (para. 1).

2. Answers will vary. Here are some possibilities.

seeing
- "unplastered adobe, wood, and abandoned car parts" (para. 1)
- "body resembling a patchwork quilt" (para. 3)
- "his hair is straight and his face beardless" (para. 3)

hearing
- "many fight and bicker constantly" (para. 1)
- "radio on at full blast" (para. 2)
- "babbling comadres and shrieking children" (para. 3)

touching
- "metal plate for a skull" (para. 3)
- "hard bread" (para. 4)

smelling or tasting
- "pots of beans and trays of tortillas" (para. 2)
- "cooked with peanuts, raisins, onions, cheese, and panocha" (para. 4)

3. People live in El Hoyo to be in a small community where people care about one another and to "remain chicanos" (para. 4).

where you are less likely to be reported to the authorities. Besides, Perea is very popular and sooner or later to everyone "Smoke in the Eyes" is dedicated between the pinto beans and white flour commercials. If one, for any reason whatever, comes on an extended period of hard times, where, if not in El Hoyo, are the neighbors more willing to offer solace? When Teofila Malacara's house burned to the ground with all her belongings and two children, a benevolent gentleman carried through the gesture that made tolerable her burden. He made a list of five hundred names and solicited from each a dollar. At the end of a month, he turned over to the tearful but grateful señora one hundred dollars in cold cash and then accompanied her on a short vacation. When the new manager of a local store decided that no more chicanas were to work behind the counters, it was the chicanos of El Hoyo who, on taking their individually small but collectively great buying power elsewhere, drove the manager out and the girls returned to their jobs. When the Mexican Army was en route to Baja, California, and the chicanos found out that the enlisted men ate only at infrequent intervals, it was El Hoyo's chicanos who crusaded across town with pots of beans and trays of tortillas to meet the train. When someone gets married, celebrating is not restricted to the immediate friends of the couple. Everybody is invited. Anything calls for a celebration, and a celebration calls for anything. On Memorial Day there are no less than half a dozen good fights at the Riverside Dance Hall. On Mexican Independence Day, more than one flag is sworn allegiance to amid cheers for the queen.

3 And El Hoyo is something more. It is this something more which brought Felipe Sanchez back from the wars after having killed a score of Vietnamese with his body resembling a patchwork quilt to marry Julia Armijo. It brought Joe Zepeda, a gunner, . . . back to compose boleros. He has a metal plate for a skull. Perhaps El Hoyo is proof that those people exist, and perhaps exist best, who have as yet failed to observe the more popular modes of human conduct. Perhaps the humble appearance of El Hoyo justifies the indifferent shrug of those made aware of its existence. Perhaps El Hoyo's simplicity motivates an occasional chicano to move away from its narrow streets, babbling comadres, and shrieking children to deny the bloodwell from which he springs and to claim the blood of a conquistador while his hair is straight and his face beardless. Yet El Hoyo is not an outpost of a few families against the world. It fights for no causes except those which soothe its immediate angers. It laughs and cries with the same amount of passion in times of plenty and of want.

4 Perhaps El Hoyo, its inhabitants, and its essence can best be explained by telling a bit about a dish called capirotada. Its origin is uncertain. But, according to the time and the circumstance, it is made of old, new, or hard

bread. It is softened with water and then cooked with peanuts, raisins, onions, cheese, and panocha. It is fired with sherry wine. Then it is served hot, cold, or just "on the weather" as they say in El Hoyo. The Sermeños like it one way, the Garcias another, and the Ortegas still another. While it might differ greatly from one home to another; nevertheless, it is still capirotada. And so it is with El Hoyo's chicanos. While being divided from within and from without, like the capirotada, they remain chicanos.

Thinking Critically About Content

1. What does *el hoyo* mean, according to the author?
2. List two details from this essay for each of the five senses: seeing, hearing, touching, smelling, and tasting. How do these details show rather than tell the readers the writer's impressions of El Hoyo?
3. What is the main reason people choose to live in El Hoyo?

Thinking Critically About Purpose and Audience

4. What dominant impression does the writer create in this description? Explain your answer in detail.
5. Do you think readers who have never been to this place can appreciate and enjoy this essay? Why or why not?
6. What details about El Hoyo are most interesting to you? Why do you find them interesting?

Thinking Critically About Essays

7. If an essay is unified, all of its paragraphs are related to one central idea. Based on this explanation, is this essay unified? Explain your answer.
8. How does Suarez organize his ideas and observations in this essay? (Refer to pages 66–78 for information on organization.) Make a rough outline of the essay.
9. Suarez ends his essay with an analogy that compares El Hoyo to a dish called *capirotada*. Is this an effective end for his essay? Why or why not?
10. Describe as fully as possible the inner feelings of the narrator from inside El Hoyo on a typical day.

Thinking Critically About Purpose and Audience

4. The dominant impression is a sense of community. He creates this by explaining all the ways the people help each other in El Hoyo.
5. Anyone can appreciate this essay because of Suarez's vivid descriptions.
6. Answers will vary.

Thinking Critically About Essays

7. The essay is unified because all the paragraphs describe different aspects of El Hoyo.
8. Suarez organizes his ideas from least to most important.
   paragraph 1: background of town
   paragraph 2: description of people
   paragraph 3: feeling of community
   paragraph 4: comparison to *capirotada*
9. The comparison in paragraph 4 is effective because it refers to the discussion of *chicano* in paragraph 1 and shows readers why chicanos like to live in the town.
10. The narrator feels at peace in El Hoyo. Beyond this, answers will vary.

DWELLINGS
by Linda Hogan

SUMMARY
Hogan shows readers habitats of various people and animals and explains why each dwelling is suitable for its residents.

READABILITY
(Flesch–Kincaid grade level)
8.5

INSTRUCTOR'S RESOURCE MANUAL
For additional teaching strategies, for journal entries, for vocabulary and reading quizzes, and for more writing assignments, see the *Instructor's Resource Manual,* Section II, Part II.

Focusing Your Attention

1. Think about the place you currently live. Does it serve your purposes? In what ways?
2. The essay you are about to read describes different habitats that suit different animals and humans. If you could move to a new "dwelling," where would you go? Why?

Expanding Your Vocabulary

The following words are important to your understanding of this essay. Highlight them throughout the essay before you begin to read. Then refer to this list as you get to these words in the essay.

eroded: worn down (paragraph 1)

Anasazi: Indian tribe (paragraph 1)

excavations: caves, holes in the earth (paragraph 1)

beetle: jut, project (paragraph 1)

catacombs: tunnels, hollowed-out passageways, burial places (paragraph 2)

droning: monotonous (paragraph 3)

sanctuary: safe place (paragraph 6)

troglodite: caveman (paragraph 7)

utopia: ideal place (paragraph 7)

felled: cut down (paragraph 8)

spired: rising like a church steeple (paragraph 9)

fledglings: baby birds just learning to fly (paragraph 9)

arid: dry (paragraph 10)

pellets: animal droppings (paragraph 13)

fetal: newborn (paragraph 13)

downy: soft (paragraph 14)

rafter: roof beam (paragraph 14)

Zia Pueblo: an Indian village (paragraph 15)

shards: broken pieces (paragraph 15)

sage: an herb (paragraph 16)

READING CRITICALLY

As you did with the previous essay, write any personal associations you make with this essay in the margins as you read. This process will give you some good insights into the author's approach to her topic and into her methods of developing her ideas. Write down anything at all that occurs to you. Then share your notes with one of your classmates.

DWELLINGS

by Linda Hogan

Not far from where I live is a hill that was cut into by the moving water of a creek. Eroded this way, all that's left of it is a broken wall of earth that contains old roots and pebbles woven together and exposed. Seen from a distance, it is only a rise of raw earth. But up close it is something wonderful, a small cliff dwelling that looks almost as intricate and well made as those the Anasazi left behind when they vanished mysteriously centuries ago. This hill is a place that could be the starry skies at night turned inward into the thousand round holes where solitary bees have lived and died. It is a hill of tunneling rooms. At the mouths of some of the excavations, half-circles of clay beetle out like awnings shading a doorway. It is earth that was turned to clay in the mouths of the bees and spit out as they mined deeper into their dwelling places. 1

This place is where the bees reside at an angle safe from rain. It faces the southern sun. It is a warm and intelligent architecture of memory, learned by whatever memory lives in the blood. Many of the holes still contain gold husks of dead bees, their faces dry and gone, their flat eyes gazing out from death's land toward the other uninhabited half of the hill that is across the creek from the catacombs. 2

The first time I found the residence of the bees, it was dusty summer. The sun was hot, and land was the dry color of rust. Now and then a car rumbled along the dirt road, and dust rose up behind it before settling back down on older dust. In the silence, the bees made a soft droning hum. They were alive then and working the hill, going out and returning with pollen, in and out through the holes, back and forth between daylight and the cooler, darker regions of the inner earth. They were flying an invisible map through 3 air, a map charted by landmarks, the slant of light, and a circling story they told one another about the direction of food held inside the center of yellow flowers.

4 Sitting in the hot sun, watching the small bees fly in and out around the hill, hearing the summer birds, the light breeze, I felt right in the world. I belonged there. I thought of my own dwelling places, those real and those imagined. Once I lived in a town called Manitou, which means "Great Spirit," where hot mineral springwater gurgled beneath the streets and rose into open wells. I felt safe there. With the underground movement of water and heat a constant reminder of other life, of what lives beneath us, it seemed to be the center of the world.

5 A few years after that, I wanted silence. My daydreams were full of places I longed to be, shelters and solitudes. I wanted a room apart from others, a hidden cabin to rest in. I wanted to be in a redwood forest with trees so tall the owls called out in the daytime. I daydreamed of living in a vapor cave a few hours away from here. Underground, warm, and moist, I thought it would be the perfect world for staying out of cold winter, for escaping the noise of living.

6 And how often I've wanted to escape to a wilderness where a human hand has not been in everything. But those were only dreams of peace, of comfort, of a nest inside stone or woods, a sanctuary where a dream or life wouldn't be invaded.

7 Years ago, in the next canyon west of here, there was a man who followed one of those dreams and moved into a cave that could only be reached by climbing down a rope. For years he lived there in comfort, like a troglodite. The inner weather was stable, never too hot, too cold, too wet, or too dry. But then he felt lonely. His utopia needed a woman. He went to town until he found a wife. For a while after the marriage, his wife climbed down the rope along with him, but before long she didn't want the mice scurrying about in the cave or the untidy bats that wanted to hang from the stones of the ceiling. So they built a door. Because of the closed entryway, the temperature changed. They had to put in heat. Then the inner moisture of earth warped the door, so they had to have air-conditioning, and after that the earth wanted to go about life in its own way, and it didn't give in to the people.

8 In other days and places, people paid more attention to the strong-headed will of earth. Once homes were built of wood that had been felled from a single region in a forest. That way, it was thought, the house would hold together more harmoniously, and the family of walls would not fall or lend themselves to the unhappiness or arguments of the inhabitants.

9 An Italian immigrant to Chicago, Aldo Piacenzi, built birdhouses that were dwellings of harmony and peace. They were the incredible spired shapes of cathedrals in Italy. They housed not only the birds, but also his memories, his own past. He painted them the watery blue of his Mediterranean, the wild rose of flowers in a summer field. Inside them was straw and the droppings of lives that laid eggs, fledglings who grew there. What places to inhabit, the bright and sunny birdhouses in dreary alleyways of the city.

10 One beautiful afternoon, cool and moist, with the kind of yellow light that falls on earth in these arid regions, I waited for barn swallows to return from their daily work of food gathering. Inside the tunnel where they live, hundreds of swallows had mixed their saliva with mud and clay, much like the solitary bees, and formed nests that were perfect as a potter's bowl. At five in the evening, they returned all at once, a dark, flying shadow. Despite their enormous numbers and the crowding together of nests, they didn't pause for even a moment before entering the nests, nor did they crowd one another. Instantly they vanished into the nests. The tunnel went silent. It held no outward signs of life.

11 But I knew they were there, filled with the fire of living. And what a marriage of elements was in those nests. Not only mud's earth and water, the fire of sun and dry air, but even the elements contained one another. The bodies of prophets and crazy men were broken down in that soil.

12 I've noticed often how, when a house is abandoned, it begins to sag. Without a tenant, it has no need to go on. If it were a person, we'd say it is depressed or lonely. The roof settles in, the paint cracks, the walls and floorboards warp and slope downward in their own natural ways, telling us that life must stay in everything as the world whirls and tilts and moves through boundless space.

13 One summer day, cleaning up after long-eared owls where I work at a rehabilitation facility for birds of prey, I was raking the gravel floor of a flight cage. Down on the ground, something looked like it was moving. I bent over to look into the pile of bones and pellets I'd just raked together. There, close to the ground, were two fetal mice. They were new to the planet, pink and hairless. They were so tenderly young. Their faces had swollen blue-veined eyes. They were nestled in a mound of feathers, soft as velvet, each one curled up smaller than an infant's ear, listening to the first sounds of earth. But the ants were biting them. They turned in agony, unable to pull away, not yet having the arms or legs to move, but feeling, twisting away from the pain of the bites. I was horrified to see them bitten out of life that way. I dipped them in water, as if to take away the sting, and let the ants fall in the bucket.

Answers to Questions

Thinking Critically About Content

1. Answers will vary. Here are some possibilities.

Bees:

Their dwelling shows the intricacies of a place of a busy insect.

Humans:

Their dwellings are never perfect and show how they constantly ruin nature to accommodate their needs. The dwellings reflect human egos.

Birds:

Quiet dwellings with many birds show the community nature of the animal.

Mice:

They live in other species' habitats, showing their adaptable nature.

2. Answers will vary. Here are some possibilities.

seeing

"old roots and pebbles woven together and exposed" (para. 1)

"half-circles of clay beetle out like awnings shading a doorway" (para. 1)

"fine gray globes the wasps have woven together, the white

cocoons of spiders in a corner, the downward tunneling anthills" (para. 14)

hearing

"moving water of a creek" (para. 1)

"soft droning hum" (para. 3)

"hearing the summer birds" (para. 4)

touching

"faces the southern sun" (para. 2)

"cooler, darker regions of the inner earth" (para. 3)

"light breeze" (para. 4)

tasting

"turned to clay in the mouths of bees" (para. 1)

"mixed their saliva with mud and clay" (para. 10)

"wild grapes would soon ripen on the vines" (para. 17)

smelling

No smelling descriptions are in the essay.

3. Hogan is referring to her environment that seems to be perfect as "the center of the world." Because nothing is wrong there, everything else must revolve around it.

Thinking Critically About Purpose and Audience

4. The dominant impression is that

Then I held the tiny mice in the palm of my hand. Some of the ants were drowning in the water. I was trading one life for another, exchanging the lives of the ants for those of mice, but I hated their suffering, and hated even more that they had not yet grown to a life, and already they inhabited the miserable world of pain. Death and life feed each other. I know that.

14 Inside these rooms where birds are healed, there are other lives besides those of mice. There are fine gray globes the wasps have woven together, the white cocoons of spiders in a corner, the downward tunneling anthills. All these dwellings are inside one small walled space, but I think most about the mice. Sometimes the downy nests fall out of the walls where their mothers have placed them out of the way of their enemies. They are so well made and soft, woven mostly from the chest feathers of birds. Sometimes the leg of a small quail holds the nest together like a slender cornerstone with dry, bent claws. The mice have adapted to life in the presence of their enemies, adapted to living in the thin wall between beak and beak, claw and claw. They move their nests often, as if a new rafter or wall will protect them from the inevitable fate of all our returns home to the deeper, wider nests of earth that houses us all.

15 One August at Zia Pueblo during the corn dance, I noticed tourists picking up shards of all the old pottery that had been made and broken there. The residents of Zia know not to take the bowls and pots left behind by the older ones. They know that the fragments of those earlier lives need to be smoothed back to earth, but younger nations, travelers from continents across the world who have come to inhabit this land, have little of their own to grow on. The pieces of earth that were formed into bowls, even on their way home to dust, provide the new people a lifeline to an unknown land, help them remember that they live in the old nest of earth.

16 It was in early February, during the mating season of the great horned owl. It was dusk, and I hiked up the back of a mountain to where I'd heard the owls a year before. I wanted to hear them again, the voices so tender, so deep, like a memory of comfort. I was halfway up the trail when I found a soft, round nest. It had fallen from one of the bare-branched trees. It was a delicate nest, woven together of feathers, sage, and strands of wild grass. Holding it in my hand in the rosy twilight, I noticed that a blue thread was entwined with the other gatherings there. I pulled at the thread a little, and then I recognized it. It was a thread from one of my skirts. It was blue cotton. It was the unmistakable color and shape of a pattern I knew. I liked it, that a thread of my life was in an abandoned nest, one that had held eggs and new life. I took the nest home. At home, I held it to the light and looked more

closely. There, to my surprise, nestled into the gray-green sage, was a gnarl of black hair. It was also unmistakable. It was my daughter's hair, cleaned from a brush and picked up out in the sun beneath the maple tree or the pit cherry where the birds eat from the overladen, fertile branches until only the seeds remain on the trees.

17 I didn't know what kind of nest it was or who had lived there. It didn't matter. I thought of the remnants of our lives carried up the hill that way and turned into shelter. That night, resting inside the walls of our home, the world outside weighed so heavily against the thin wood of the house. The sloped roof was the only thing between us and the universe. Everything outside of our wooden boundaries seemed so large. Filled with the night's citizens, it all came alive. The world opened in the thickets of the dark. The wild grapes would soon ripen on the vines. The burrowing ones were emerging. Horned owls sat in treetops. Mice scurried here and there. Skunks, fox, the slow and holy porcupine, all were passing by this way. The young of the solitary bees were feeding on the pollen in the dark. The whole world was a nest on its humble tilt, in the maze of the universe, holding us.

Thinking Critically About Content

1. How do the dwellings Hogan describes suit their inhabitants? Refer to two specific dwellings to answer this question.
2. Find at least one detail for each of the five senses: seeing, hearing, touching, smelling, and tasting. Does Hogan draw on any one sense more than the others?
3. In paragraph 4, what is Hogan referring to as "the center of the world"? Explain your answer.

Thinking Critically About Purpose and Audience

4. What dominant impression does Hogan create in this essay?
5. Who do you think Hogan's primary audience is?
6. Explain your understanding of this essay's title.

Thinking Critically About Essays

7. Each section of Hogan's essay is about a different dwelling. Is each section unified? Look at the topic sentence of paragraph 7. Do all the sentences in this paragraph relate to its topic sentence? Explain your answer.
8. If a paragraph is coherent, it is considered logical and easy to read. Often, well-chosen transitions help a writer achieve coherence. (Refer

being able to adapt is essential in nature.

5. Hogan's primary audience is general readers.
6. The title refers to the different habitats used by the various people and animals described in the essay.

Thinking Critically About Essays

7. The topic sentence of paragraph 7 is "Years ago, in the next canyon west of here, there was a man who followed one of those dreams and moved into a cave that could only be reached by climbing down a rope." The paragraph is unified because all sentences after this refer to his life in the cave.
8. Transitions in paragraph 13 include "One summer day," "Down on the ground," "There," "But," and "Then." The transitions help the paragraph read smoothly by giving the readers indications of shifts in focus or time and showing changes in emphasis.
9. Hogan's conclusion is effective because Hogan is showing how the earth itself is a dwelling for all of its creatures. The

conclusion ties the essay together because she is referring to the biggest dwelling of all, the one that encompasses all other dwellings.

10. Answers will vary.

to page 101 for a list of transitions.) Underline the words, phrases, and clauses Hogan uses as transitions in paragraph 13. How do these transitions help this paragraph read smoothly? Explain your answer.

9. Look at Hogan's conclusion. Is it effective for this essay? How does the last sentence ("The whole world was a nest on its humble tilt, in the maze of the universe, holding us") tie the whole essay together?

10. Describe in detail what you think the secret to a perfect dwelling is. Before you begin to write, you might want to review the writing process in Part I.

TEACHING ON THE WEB

Discussion Topic: The Internet has become indispensable in today's society. Put students in groups of three or four, and have them discuss whether or not they think people are growing out of touch with their senses because they spend so much time on the Internet instead of experiencing life firsthand. Have one person from each group report the group's conclusions to the class.

TEACHING ON THE WEB

Links: Have students link to world-renowned museums and view famous pieces of art. How do some of these masterpieces convey the five senses?

Possible sites:

Tate Britain, London, www.tate.org.uk/britain

Guggenheim Museum, Venice, www.guggenheim-venice.it

Smithsonian American Art Museum, Washington, D.C., www.nmaa.si.edu

Writing Workshop

This final section gives you opportunities to apply what you have learned in this chapter to another writing assignment. This time, we provide very little prompting beyond a summary of the guidelines for writing a description essay. This section will let you demonstrate that you can go through the entire writing process on your own with only occasional feedback from your peers. Loop back into the chapter as necessary when you have questions so that this process becomes as automatic to you as possible before you move on to new material. Then pause at the end of the chapter to reflect briefly on what you have learned.

Guidelines for Writing a Description Essay

1. Decide on a dominant impression—the feeling or mood you want to communicate.
2. Decide how much of your description should be objective (factual) and how much should be subjective (personal reactions).
3. Draw on your five senses to write a good description.
4. When you describe, try to *show* rather than *tell* your readers what you want them to know.
5. Organize your description so that your readers can easily follow it.

Writing About Your Reading

1. In the first descriptive essay, Mario Suarez draws on impressions from all the senses to describe this *barrio*. Think of a place that is very important to you, a place that is a part of your life now or that was a part of your life in the past. Write a description of that place, drawing on as many of the senses as possible—seeing, hearing, touching, smelling, and tasting—so that your reader can experience it the way you did.

2. How well suited to you is the place where you live now? Write a description of the features of your house or apartment that make it most suitable or unsuitable for you.
3. What do you think are the most important features of a good description? Why are they important? What effect do they have on you?

TEACHING ON THE WEB

Research: Have students search various Web sites to find one that incorporates all five senses. How difficult was it to find this site? How are all the senses represented?

Writing About Your World

1. Place yourself in the scene above, and describe it in as much detail as possible. Imagine that you can see, hear, touch, smell, and taste everything in this picture. What are your sensations? How do you feel? Before you begin to write, decide on the dominant impression you want to convey. Then choose your details carefully.
2. Describe for your classmates a class environment that is ideal for you. What kind of classroom atmosphere makes you thrive? What should the people in your class understand about you as a student? What kind of instructor brings out the best in you? Why?
3. A national travel magazine is asking for honest descriptions (positive or negative) of places people have visited. The magazine is offering $100 to the writers of the essays chosen for publication. You may decide to write about a place with a marvelous beach or about an absolutely awful hotel. In either case, remember to begin with the dominant impression you want to create.
4. Create your own description assignment (with the help of your instructor), and write a response to it.

Revising

Small Group Activity (5–10 minutes per writer) Working in groups of three or four, read your description essays to each other. Those listening should record their reactions on a copy of the Peer Evaluation Form in Appendix 2A. After your group goes through this process, give your evaluation forms to the appropriate writers so that each writer has two or three peer comment sheets for revising.

Paired Activity (5 minutes per writer) Using the completed Peer Evaluation Forms, work in pairs to decide what you should revise in your essay. If time allows, rewrite some of your sentences, and have your partner look at them.

Individual Activity Rewrite your paper, using the revising feedback you received from other students.

Editing

Paired Activity (5–10 minutes per writer) Swap papers with a classmate, and use the editing portion of your Peer Evaluation Form to identify as many grammar, punctuation, mechanics, and spelling errors as you can. If time allows, correct some of your errors, and have your partner look at them. Record your grammar, punctuation, and mechanics errors in the Error Log (Appendix 6) and your spelling errors in the Spelling Log (Appendix 7).

Individual Activity Rewrite your paper again, using the editing feedback you received from other students.

Reflecting on Your Writing When you have completed your own essay, answer these six questions.

1. What was most difficult about this assignment?
2. What was easiest?
3. What did you learn about description by completing this assignment?
4. What do you think are the strengths of your description? Place a wavy line by the parts of your essay that you feel are very good.
5. What are the weaknesses, if any, of your paper? Place an X by the parts of your essay you would like help with. Write any questions you have in the margin.
6. What did you learn from this assignment about your own writing process—about preparing to write, about writing the first draft, about revising, and about editing?

CHAPTER 9

Narrating

"I try to remember times in my life, incidents in which there was the dominating theme of cruelty or kindness or generosity or envy or happiness or glee. Then I select one."

—MAYA ANGELOU

Because we are constantly telling other people about various events in our lives, we all know how to use narration. Think of how many times a day you tell someone about an event that happened to you: your accident on the way to school; the conversation you had at the bus stop yesterday; your strange experience at the restaurant last night. Narrating is an essential part of all of our lives. In fact, stories can teach us how to live our lives.

Narration also plays an important role in our writing. Think about how many times we tell a story when we write—in our personal lives, in classes, and at work:

- You tell a friend in an e-mail about how you met the person you're now dating.
- On a history exam, a student summarizes the chain of events that led to the United States' entry into World War II.
- A student summarizes a short story in an English class.
- An emergency medical technician gives an account of her 911 calls for the day.
- A supervisor writes a report explaining an employee's accident on the job.

Narration, or storytelling, is an interesting way of getting someone's attention by sharing thoughts or experiences. Like description, narration is sometimes used as an end in itself (for example, when you tell a friend a joke or the plot of a movie). But very often it's used in conjunction with explaining or persuading. You might start a term paper analyzing drug abuse, for example, with a brief story of one addict's life, or a lawyer might seek a not-guilty verdict by telling the jury about the hardships his or her client

TEACHING NARRATION

Write an introduction that could lead to an unusual story line (such as "Ballerina leaves company to join Navy SEALS"). At the beginning of class, read the introduction aloud to all your students. Give the introduction to a student, and have him or her add a line or two to begin an essay. Then have the student pass the paper to the next student.

The next student should read only the lines written by the student before him or her and then add a line or two to the essay. Students should not read the entire essay, just the last lines that were written. This should continue until every student has contributed to the essay.

After class, type the essay and add natural

suffered as a child. Basically, people use storytelling to help focus their readers' or listeners' attention.

paragraph breaks and a conclusion, if necessary. Hand out copies of the essay to the class next time you meet. Use whatever disorganized connections or lucky coincidences that were written to discuss how to write an effective narrative essay.

TEACHING TIPS

The following eight teaching tips are based on Howard Gardner's multiple intelligences:

Verbal/Linguistic

Have students sit in a small circle and remember any jokes they heard, read, or saw. How does the joke use elements of narration? Have the group choose the joke that is the best.

Musical/Rhythmic

Have students find a current country song that tells a story. How does this story affect the way they view the song? How important is narration to the genre of country music?

Logical/Mathematical

Have students make a flowchart that displays the action or plot of their favorite movie. Have them explain how the flowchart represents the story.

Visual/Spatial

Have students draw a scene from their favorite book and present it to their classmates.

READING AND WRITING A NARRATION ESSAY

Learning how to read narration essays critically gives you insight into the writing process in this particular rhetorical mode. Narration represents a way of thinking that you need to master so that you can use it in both your reading and writing. Approaching narration critically helps you raise your level of communication and function more successfully in college and in life. In this chapter, you will see how the processes of reading and writing complement each other to form a whole. If you learn how to work with the author of a narration essay to understand how he or she makes meaning, your insights will transfer naturally to your writing so that you will also be improving your writing ability.

Reading a Narration Essay

Jane Maher, who teaches college in New York City, wrote the following autobiographical essay to help her come to terms with the loss of her father. Can you think of an event that taught you something important about life? What was the event? What did you learn?

READING CRITICALLY

As we read and make meaning out of an author's words, we put a string of words together on a literal level, bring in any implications the author suggests, think about how the ideas relate to one another, and keep the process going until the entire essay makes sense. These are focused thoughts that will help you process the author's writing. On another level, however, we also stray from the essay in a wide variety of ways—thinking about chores we need to do, calls we forgot to return, and plans we are looking forward to on the weekend. These are random ideas that are only loosely related to the reading. As you might suspect, focused reading is the most productive, but you can teach yourself to even apply your random ideas toward a better understanding of your reading material. As you read this selection, stop and "think aloud" about what is on your mind throughout the text. Point out places that are confusing to you, connections that you make, specific questions you have, related information you know, and personal experiences you associate with the text. In this way, you are letting others hear what your mind does (both focused and random) as you read.

GIRL
by Jane Maher

1 I don't remember exactly when I began to be offended when my father called me, or other girls or women, "girl." I guess he always did it; at least I don't remember him ever not doing it. He'd often use it as a term of affection: "How's my girl today?" But just as often, he'd use it carelessly or callously, the way some men use the expression "sweetie." "Listen girl," my father would say, "I make the rules around here."

2 Women, girls, were perceived by my father as less than men: less important, less intelligent, less capable, less in need of education or direction. In fact, for a long period of my life, I was so indoctrinated by my father's views, and by society's confirmation of those views, that I agreed with him.

3 But as I grew older, the term "girl" began to hurt me and make me angry. As my father became aware of my strong and growing aversion to the word, he'd use it even more often. "What's the matter," he'd ask. "You don't like it anymore when your old man calls you girl? You're my daughter; I'll call you whatever I want." Or he'd ask my mother, pretending I wasn't in the room, "What kind of daughter did you raise that she wants to become a man? Is she ashamed to be a girl?" The word took on stronger and stronger connotations for me as I began to realize how permanently, and adversely, my father's attitudes had affected my life. I had been sent to an all-girls commercial high school. "Listen, girl," my father declared, "as long as you know typing and stenography, you'll never starve." College was not mentioned very much in our house. I was one of three daughters. If one of us had a date, my father would tell my mother to remind us "what can happen to a girl if she's not careful." When I got married, I heard my father joking with my uncle: "One down, two to go." We were objects to be dispensed with, burdens of no conceivable use to him.

4 This does not mean that he did not love us or care for us; for my entire childhood, he worked two jobs so that he could afford to send us away to the country every summer. But it was the terms upon which he loved and cared for us which were so distressing to me. Nor did I always get angry when he used the term. When my first daughter was born, he arrived at the hospital carrying a silver dollar he had saved in his collection for many years as a gift for her. "Now I've got four of you girls instead of three," he said, knowing that I knew at this special time he was only teasing and did not intend to hurt me.

5 I saw less and less of my father after I moved to Connecticut in 1980. He and my mother kept their house in Brooklyn but spent most of the winter

Bodily/Kinesthetic
Have students act out (through monologues, dance, and other performing arts) one scene from their favorite movie. What role does narration play in this presentation?

Intrapersonal
Have students evaluate the latest episode they saw of their favorite TV show. Did it follow the guidelines of narration? What aspects of the story did they find most enjoyable? Why?

Interpersonal
Have students choose their favorite hero from a popular movie. Have them act out a scene from the movie to see if other students can guess who the hero might be.

Naturalist
Have students go outdoors to a park, lake, ocean, or mountain. Have them imagine what could have happened on this spot 100 years ago. What story did they envision while reflecting on this place?

INSTRUCTOR'S RESOURCE MANUAL
For additional material about teaching narration; for journal entries; and for multiple-choice, short-answer, and paragraph tests, see the *Instructor's Resource Manual*, Section II, Part II.

months in Florida. Sometimes when I called on the phone, I could tell how happy he was to hear my voice. "Hey, girl, is that husband of yours taking as good care of you as I did?" But other times, over Thanksgiving dinner or while opening Christmas presents, he'd use the term as he had when I was young. "Girl, get me a little more coffee will you?" Or when I enrolled my daughter in an expensive private school: "Why spend money you don't have to, girl? She's just going to get married the way you did." I'd keep my countenance at those times; I had grown wise to my father—I wouldn't give him the satisfaction of showing my anger. That's not to say he didn't keep trying: "So now you like it when your old man calls you girl, huh? You're finally getting wise to the fact that men aren't so bad to have around when you need something."

6 And I suspected that secretly he was proud of me. Soon after I got married, I returned to college, part-time, in the evening, and graduated magna cum laude. By then, both of my daughters were in school, so I earned my master's degree from Columbia University, again part-time. It was my father who picked up my daughters from the school bus stop on the day I took my comprehensive exam. When I began to teach part time at a local community college, my father asked my mother, again pretending I wasn't in the room, "if there was a girl around here who thought her father was going to start calling her Professor."

7 My father had always had a heart condition, exacerbated by twenty-two years as a New York City fireman, two packs of cigarettes a day, and my mother's delicious Italian cooking. When he suddenly became seriously ill, my mother got him home from Florida and into a hospital in Brooklyn in less than 24 hours. But it still wasn't soon enough. My father died before they could perform a triple bypass and before I got to say goodbye to him.

8 I had left Connecticut at nine in the morning, intending to wait out the surgery with my mother and to be with my father when he awoke. Instead, when I arrived at the hospital, one of my sisters and my mother were in a small, curtained-off section of the intensive care unit being told by a busy, preoccupied young resident that my father had experienced very little discomfort before he died. It sounded too pat, too familiar, too convenient to me. I was overcome with the fear that my father had been alone that entire morning, that no one in that overcrowded municipal hospital had even known that he was dead until they arrived to prepare him for surgery.

9 They left us alone to say goodbye to him, but I was so concerned over my mother's anguish that I didn't take the time I should have to kiss him or even to touch his forehead. A nurse came in and suggested, gently, that it was time to leave. She was right, of course; another moment and my mother would have collapsed.

I thanked the nurse and asked her, nonchalantly, if she knew exactly 10
when my father had died, secretly convinced that she didn't have an answer, that he had been alone all morning. "I didn't see him this morning," she replied, "but I'll get the nurse who did."

A young, pretty nurse appeared several minutes later. "My shift is over," 11
she said, "but I was waiting around to see the family."

"Was he in pain?" my mother asked. 12

"No, not at all. He even teased me a bit. I remember his exact words. 13
'Go take care of the patients who need you, girl,' he said. 'I'm perfectly fine.' "

I wasn't exactly fine, but I have never felt more comforted in my life 14
than when I heard that word.

Preparing to Write Your Own Narration Essay

We have all learned important lessons from various events in our lives. Over time, we find that some lessons are more worthwhile than others. What events in your life have taught you important lessons? What lessons did you learn? Use one or more of the prewriting techniques you learned in Chapter 2 to gather your thoughts on these events.

Writing a Narration Essay

Narrating involves telling a story about an experience—one of yours or someone else's. When you write a narrative essay, you focus on a particular event and make a specific point about it. You should provide enough detail so that readers can understand as completely as possible what your experience was like. Here are some guidelines to help you make your narrative interesting.

1. **Make sure your essay has a point.** The most important feature of a narrative essay is that it makes a point. Simply recording your story step by step is a boring exercise for both writer and reader. Writing an account of your walk to class in the morning might not be particularly interesting. But the walk becomes interesting when something important or significant happens on the way. An event is significant if it helps both writer and reader understand something about themselves, about other people, or about the world we live in. If you can complete one of the following sentences, you will produce a focused narrative:

   This essay shows that . . .

   This essay teaches us that . . .

In Jane Maher's essay, the narrator focuses on the pain she felt, growing up, when her father referred to her as a "girl." She thought the term was degrading until she understood, after he died, that it was really a term of endearment. Maher is able to communicate the process of growing up through her experience with this one word. Her essay teaches us that the relationship between words and emotions is complex.

2. **Use the five Ws and one *H* to construct your story.** The five *W*s and one *H* are the six questions—*Who? What? When? Where? Why?* and *How?*—that journalists use to make sure they cover all the basic information when they write a news story. These questions can help you come up with details and ideas for a well-developed narrative essay. You should make sure that your essay answers each of these questions in detail.

   When you look at Maher's narrative again, you can see that she covered the answers to all these questions:

   Who was involved? Maher, her father, her mother, and the nurses

   What was the central problem? Maher was offended by her father's use of the word "girl."

   When did this story take place? As Maher was growing up

   Where were they? At home

   Why was Maher offended? Because she thought the word "girl" was degrading to her as a person and to other females

   How did the author learn from this event? She finally understood that her father's use of "girl" wasn't as offensive as she thought it was.

   Since Maher covers all these basic details, the reader can appreciate her full story and understand its significance.

3. **Develop your narrative with vivid details.** Your readers will be able to imagine the events in your narrative essay if you provide them with specific details. In fact, the more specific your details, the more vivid your essay will become. These details should develop the ideas you generated with the six journalistic questions. At the same time, you should omit any irrelevant details that don't support your thesis statement.

   Look again at Maher's essay. In this narrative, the author provides many vivid details about the narrator: She is a girl whose father thinks girls are less important than boys; he calls her "girl"; this term starts to bother the narrator as she is growing up; she gets married and moves to Connecticut; she has two daughters; she gets her master's degree at Columbia University and starts teaching at a local community college;

and her father dies of a heart attack. The amount of detail in Maher's essay helps us participate in her narrative.

4. **Build excitement in your narrative with careful pacing.** To be most effective, narration should prolong the exciting parts of a story and shorten the routine facts that simply move the reader from one episode to another. If you were robbed on your way to work, for example, a good narrative describing the incident would concentrate on the traumatic event itself rather than on such boring details as what you had for breakfast or what clothes you were wearing. One writer might say, "I was robbed this morning." A better writer would draw out the exciting parts: "As I was walking to work around 7:30 this morning, a huge, angry-looking man ran up to me, thrust a gun into my stomach, and demanded my money, my new wristwatch, my credit cards, and my pants—leaving me broke and embarrassed." The details themselves tell the story.

   Maher reveals the details in her story through some of her father's quotations that bothered her: "Listen girl, I make the rules around here"; "Listen girl, as long as you know typing and stenography, you'll never starve." She feels frustrated and belittled by her father, even as an adult: "Hey, girl, is that husband of yours taking as good care of you as I did?" Finally, she works through the hurtfulness when her father dies. At this point, Maher draws out the search for the nurse who could tell her if her father died alone. The pacing of her story holds our interest throughout the essay.

5. **Organize your narration so that your readers can easily follow it.** Most narrative essays follow a series of actions through time, so they are organized chronologically, or according to a time sequence. Once you choose the details you will use, you should arrange them so that your story has a clear beginning, middle, and end. If you add clear, logical transitions, such as *then, next, at this point,* and *suddenly,* you will guide your readers smoothly through your essay from one event to the next.

   Jane Maher organizes her narrative chronologically. It moves through time from her childhood to going to high school to getting married and having a baby as her father raises her, retires, and grows old. In other words, the two main characters—Maher and her father—move through normal life events. Because it follows a logical time sequence and does not jump around, Maher's narrative is easy to follow. She guides her readers through her essay with such transitions as "in fact," "as I grew older," "when," "sometimes," and "soon."

Writing Your Own Narration Essay

Choose one of the events from your prewriting notes that taught you an important lesson in life, and write a narration essay explaining this incident and the lesson you learned. Follow the guidelines in this chapter to develop your essay.

A STUDENT'S NARRATION ESSAY

In an essay about a dramatic incident, student writer Tommy Poulos tells a story that taught him an important lesson in life. Here is his first draft. As you read this paragraph, try to figure out what Tommy's main point is.

"My Brother"

1 My family and I lead a fairly quiet life. My parents go to work, and my brother and I go to school. We never make headlines with sports events or science fairs. We essentially live a normal American life out of the spotlight. It was quite a shock, then, when a lot of attention was focused on our family.

2 My brother, Wayne, was driving on a highway that is nicknamed "The Death Loop." It got its name because it's a two-lane highway that loops around the city, and many people have died because of drivers who take too many chances and cause head-on collisions. One afternoon, Wayne saw a woman's car wrecked into a guardrail with her passenger side of the car completely smashed in. The driver's side was mangled, and my brother could tell the woman inside was in trouble. Wayne didn't think twice about running up to help them. She was badly injured, but my brother knew not to move her!

3 The woman had not been wearing her seat belt. Her car was too old to have an airbag. She had obviously hit her head because she had blood gushing from a gaping wound in her forehead. She was conscious, so my brother sat with her, trying to keep her calm and awake. He kept asking her questions like if she had any children? Two other cars stopped, and my brother remembers telling one man to call 911. Wayne stayed with the woman until the paramedics arrived.

4 Wayne left the scene after giving a statement to the police. Later, he heard from the local newspapers and news stations that his heroic actions had saved the woman. In these stories, the woman's husband said he believed his wife was still alive because she had a guardian angel keeping her awake. Even the paramedics said Wayne probably kept her alive. By keeping

her awake. In public, Wayne acts very humble, but in private, he is loving the attention.

Now my brother is the local hero. Our house used to be quiet, but since 5
Wayne's act of heroism, it's become Grand Central Station. Everyone wants to talk to Wayne. I'm happy for him. But most of all, I'm glad Wayne realizes the importance of seat belts. He used to be macho and say seat belts were too uncomfortable to wear. Now he won't leave the driveway until everyone has buckled their seat belts. Perhaps the woman will save Wayne's life as well.

Discovering How the Essay Works

1. All the details in Tommy's essay lead to one main point. What is that point?

   His brother became a hero and learned an important lesson.

2. Tommy covers all the journalistic questions in his essay. Record at least one detail he uses for each question: *Answers may vary.*

   Who? *Wayne*

   What? *Wayne saved a woman's life.*

   When? *One afternoon*

   Where? *"The Death Loop"*

   Why? *She was injured.*

   How? *By staying with her and keeping her awake*

3. In your opinion, which two details of Tommy's are most vivid? What makes them so vivid?

   Answers will vary.

4. How does Tommy pace his essay to build excitement?

   He spreads out important details. For example, the driver wasn't wearing a seat belt, and the woman might have died if she didn't stay awake. Then, right at the end, Tommy tells us that his brother didn't wear a seat belt until this incident.

5. How does Tommy organize his essay? List the topic of each of his body paragraphs; then identify his method of organization.

   Paragraph 2: *Wayne found an injured motorist.*

   Paragraph 3: *Wayne helped the badly injured woman.*

   Paragraph 4: *Wayne was considered a hero by the media.*

   Method of organization: *Chronological*

REVISING AND EDITING OPTIONS
Consider varying your approach to revising and editing. You could teach these skills in a class discussion, in small groups, or in pairs.

Revising and Editing the Student Essay

This essay is Tommy's first draft, which now needs to be revised and edited. First, apply the following Revising Checklist to the content of Tommy's draft. When you are satisfied that his ideas are fully developed and well organized, use the Editing Checklist on page 169 to correct his grammar and mechanics errors. Do the tasks, and answer the questions after each checklist. Then write your suggested changes directly on Tommy's draft.

REVISING STRATEGIES
This chapter focuses on the following revising elements:
Thesis statement
Basic elements
Development

 **REVISING CHECKLIST** 

THESIS STATEMENT

✔ Does the thesis statement contain the essay's controlling idea and an opinion about that idea?

✔ Does the thesis appear as the last sentence of the introduction?

BASIC ELEMENTS

✔ Does the title draw in the readers?

✔ Does the introduction capture the readers' attention and build up to the thesis statement effectively?

✔ Does each body paragraph deal with a single topic?

✔ Does the conclusion bring the essay to a close in an interesting way?

DEVELOPMENT

✔ Do the body paragraphs adequately support the thesis statement?

✔ Does each body paragraph have a focused topic sentence?

✔ Does each body paragraph contain *specific* details that support the topic sentence?

✔ Does each body paragraph include *enough* details to explain the topic sentence fully?

UNITY

✔ Do the essay's topic sentences relate directly to the thesis statement?

✔ Do the details in each body paragraph support its topic sentence?

ORGANIZATION

✔ Is the essay organized logically?

✔ Is each body paragraph organized logically?

COHERENCE

✔ Are transitions used effectively so that paragraphs move smoothly and logically from one to the next?

✔ Do the sentences move smoothly and logically from one to the next?

Thesis Statement

1. Put brackets around the last sentence in Tommy's introduction. Does it contain his main point? Does it express his opinion about that point?

   No

2. Rewrite Tommy's thesis statement if necessary so that it states his main point and an opinion about that main point.

   Here is one possibility: It was quite a shock, then, when my brother suddenly became the town hero and a lot of attention was focused on our family.

Basic Elements

1. Give Tommy's essay an alternate title. Also drop the quotation marks, since original titles should not be in quotation marks.

   Answers will vary.

2. Rewrite Tommy's introduction so that it captures the readers' attention and builds up to the thesis statement at the end of the paragraph.

   Answers will vary.

3. Does each of Tommy's body paragraphs deal with only one topic?
   Yes

4. Rewrite Tommy's conclusion using at least one suggestion from Part I.
   Answers will vary.

Development

1. Write out Tommy's thesis statement (revised, if necessary), and list his three topic sentences below it. *Thesis may vary.*

   Thesis statement: *It was quite a shock, then, when my brother suddenly became the town hero and a lot of attention was focused on our family.*

   Topic 1: *My brother, Wayne, was driving on a highway that is nicknamed "The Death Loop."*

   Topic 2: *The woman had not been wearing her seat belt.*

   Topic 3: *Wayne left the scene after giving a statement to the police.*

2. Do Tommy's topics adequately support his thesis statement?
   Yes

3. Does each body paragraph have a focused topic sentence?
   Yes

4. Add more specific information to two of Tommy's supporting details.
5. Add two new details to Tommy's essay that support his main idea.

Unity

1. Read each of Tommy's topic sentences with his thesis statement (revised, if necessary) in mind. Do they go together?
   Answers will vary.

2. Revise his topic sentences if necessary so they are directly related.
3. Drop or rewrite any of the sentences in his body paragraphs that are not directly related to their topic sentences. *All sentences are directly related to their topic sentences.*

Organization

1. Read Tommy's essay again to see if all the paragraphs are arranged chronologically.
2. Move any paragraphs that are out of order. *All paragraphs are in order.*
3. Look closely at Tommy's body paragraphs to see if all his sentences are arranged logically within paragraphs.
4. Move any sentences that are out of order. *All sentences are in order.*

Coherence

1. Circle five words or phrases Tommy repeats. *Answers will vary.*
2. Explain how two of these words or phrases make Tommy's essay easier to read.

____

____

Now rewrite Tommy's essay with your revisions.

EDITING CHECKLIST

SENTENCES

✔ Does each sentence have a main subject and verb?

✔ Do all subjects and verbs agree?

✔ Do all pronouns agree with their nouns?

✔ Are modifiers as close as possible to the words they modify?

PUNCTUATION AND MECHANICS

✔ Are sentences punctuated correctly?

✔ Are words capitalized properly?

WORD CHOICE AND SPELLING

✔ Are words used correctly?

✔ Are words spelled correctly?

EDITING STRATEGIES

This chapter focuses on the following editing problems:

Fragments

Pronoun agreement

End punctuation

Sentences

Subjects and Verbs

1. Underline the subjects once and verbs twice in paragraph 4 of your revision of Tommy's essay. Remember that sentences can have more than one subject-verb set.

For help with subjects and verbs, see Chapter 25.

2. Does each of the sentences have at least one subject and verb that can stand alone?

   No

For help with fragments, see Chapter 26.

3. Did you find and correct Tommy's fragment? If not, find and correct it now. *Paragraph 4, sentence 5*

Subject-Verb Agreement

For help with subject-verb agreement, see Chapter 30.

1. Read aloud the subjects and verbs you underlined in your revision of Tommy's essay.
2. Correct any subjects and verbs that do not agree with each other. *All subjects and verbs agree.*

Pronoun Agreement

For help with pronoun agreement, see Chapter 34.

1. Find any pronouns in your revision of Tommy's essay that do not agree with their nouns.
2. Did you find and correct the two pronouns that do not agree with their nouns? If not, find and correct them now. *Paragraph 2, sentence 5; paragraph 5, sentence 7*

Modifiers

For help with modifier errors, see Chapter 37.

1. Find any modifiers in your revision of Tommy's essay that are not as close as possible to the words they modify. *There are no modifier errors.*
2. Rewrite sentences if necessary so that modifiers are as close as possible to the words they modify.

Punctuation and Mechanics

Punctuation

For help with punctuation, see Chapters 38–42.

1. Read your revision of Tommy's essay for any errors in punctuation.
2. Find the fragment you revised, and make sure it is punctuated correctly.
3. Did you find and correct Tommy's two other punctuation errors? *Paragraph 2, sentence 6; paragraph 3, sentence 4*

Mechanics

For help with capitalization, see Chapter 43.

1. Read your revision of Tommy's essay for any errors in capitalization. *There are no capitalization errors.*
2. Be sure to check Tommy's capitalization in the fragment you revised.

Word Choice and Spelling

Word Choice

For help with confused words, see Chapter 49.

1. Find any words used incorrectly in your revision of Tommy's essay. *All words are used correctly.*
2. Correct any errors you find.

Spelling

1. Use spell-check and a dictionary to check the spelling in your revision of Tommy's essay. *All words are spelled correctly.*
2. Correct any misspelled words.

For help with spelling, see Chapter 50.

Now rewrite Tommy's essay again with your editing corrections.

YOUR OWN NARRATION ESSAY

Returning to the narration you wrote earlier in this chapter, you are now ready to revise and edit your own writing. Remember that revision involves moving ideas around and developing them as fully as you can for your readers while editing is the process of finding and correcting grammar and usage errors. When you get your ideas where you want them, then you should proofread and correct your grammar and usage errors. At this stage, you should repeat these processes until your essay achieves the purpose you set for it.

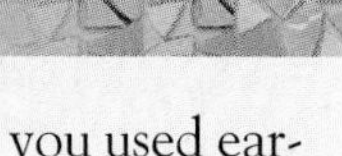

WRITING CRITICALLY

As you begin your revision, apply the reading strategy that you used earlier to your writing. Read your essay aloud, and interrupt your reading regularly to talk about the focused or random thoughts going on in your head. Add to your essay any new material from your "think aloud" that you believe your readers will need to help them more fully understand your logic. Fill out your thoughts, and move them around until they communicate your full message to your readers.

Revising and Editing Your Own Essay

The checklists here will help you apply what you have learned in this chapter to your essay.

CLASS ACTIVITY

Provide students with an essay that is missing part of the five *W*s and one *H* and has few descriptive details. In groups of three or four, have the students fill in the gaps to make the story more vivid and interesting.

REVISING CHECKLIST

THESIS STATEMENT

- ☐ Does the thesis statement contain the essay's controlling idea and an opinion about that idea?
- ☐ Does the thesis appear as the last sentence of the introduction?

BASIC ELEMENTS

- ☐ Does the title draw in the readers?
- ☐ Does the introduction capture the readers' attention and build up to the thesis statement effectively?
- ☐ Does each body paragraph deal with a single topic?
- ☐ Does the conclusion bring the essay to a close in an interesting way?

DEVELOPMENT

- ☐ Do the body paragraphs adequately support the thesis statement?
- ☐ Does each body paragraph have a focused topic sentence?
- ☐ Does each body paragraph contain *specific* details that support the topic sentence?
- ☐ Does each body paragraph include *enough* details to explain the topic sentence fully?

UNITY

- ☐ Do the essay's topic sentences relate directly to the thesis statement?
- ☐ Do the details in each body paragraph support its topic sentence?

ORGANIZATION

- ☐ Is the essay organized logically?
- ☐ Is each body paragraph organized logically?

COHERENCE

- ☐ Are transitions used effectively so that paragraphs move smoothly and logically from one to the next?
- ☐ Do the sentences move smoothly and logically from one to the next?

Thesis Statement

1. What is the main point of your essay?

   ____

2. What is your opinion about the main point?

   ____

3. Put brackets around the last sentence in your introduction. Does it contain your main point and your opinion about that point?

   ____

4. Rewrite your thesis statement if necessary so that it states your main point and your opinion.

Basic Elements

1. Give your essay a title if it doesn't have one.

    ___

2. Does your introduction capture your readers' attention and build up to your thesis statement at the end of the paragraph?

    ___

3. Does each of your body paragraphs deal with only one topic?

    ___

4. Does your conclusion follow some of the suggestions offered in Part I?

    ___

Development

1. Write out your thesis statement (revised, if necessary), and list your topic sentences below it.

    Thesis statement: ___

    Topic 1: ___

    Topic 2: ___

    Topic 3: ___

2. Do your topics adequately support your thesis statement?

    ___

3. Does each body paragraph have a focused topic sentence?

    ___

4. Record at least one detail you use in response to each journalistic question.

    Who? ___

    What? ___

    When? ___

    Where? ___

Why? ______________________________

How? ______________________________

5. Add at least two new details to your essay that support your main idea.

Unity

1. Read each of your topic sentences with your thesis statement in mind. Do they go together?

   ____

2. Revise your topic sentences if necessary so they are directly related.
3. Drop or rewrite any of the sentences in your body paragraphs that are not directly related to their topic sentences.

Organization

1. Read your essay again to see if all the paragraphs are arranged logically.
2. Refer to your answers to the development questions. Then identify your method of organization:

   ____

3. Is the order you chose for your paragraphs the most effective approach to your topic?

   ____

4. Move any paragraphs that are out of order.
5. Look closely at your body paragraphs to see if all the sentences are arranged logically within paragraphs.
6. Move any sentences that are out of order.

Coherence

1. Circle five words or phrases you repeat.
2. Explain how two of these make your essay easier to read.

   ____

   ____

Now rewrite your essay with your revisions.

EDITING CHECKLIST

SENTENCES

- ☐ Does each sentence have a main subject and verb?
- ☐ Do all subjects and verbs agree?

☐ Do all pronouns agree with their nouns?

☐ Are modifiers as close as possible to the words they modify?

PUNCTUATION AND MECHANICS

☐ Are sentences punctuated correctly?

☐ Are words capitalized properly?

WORD CHOICE AND SPELLING

☐ Are words used correctly?

☐ Are words spelled correctly?

Sentences

Subjects and Verbs

1. Underline the subjects once and verbs twice in a paragraph of your revised essay. Remember that sentences can have more than one subject-verb set.

2. Does each of your sentences have at least one subject and verb that can stand alone?

    ____

3. Correct any fragments you have written.

4. Correct any run-together sentences you have written.

For help with subjects and verbs, see Chapter 25.

For help with fragments, see Chapter 26.

For help with run-togethers, see Chapter 27.

Subject-Verb Agreement

1. Read aloud the subjects and verbs you underlined in your revised essay.

2. Correct any subjects and verbs that do not agree.

For help with subject-verb agreement, see Chapter 30.

Pronoun Agreement

1. Find any pronouns in your revised essay that do not agree with their nouns.

2. Correct any pronouns that do not agree with their nouns.

For help with pronoun agreement, see Chapter 34.

Modifiers

1. Find any modifiers in your revised essay that are not as close as possible to the words they modify.

2. Rewrite sentences if necessary so that your modifiers are as close as possible to the words they modify.

For help with modifier errors, see Chapter 37.

Punctuation and Mechanics

Punctuation

For help with punctuation, see Chapters 38–42.

1. Read your revised essay for any errors in punctuation.
2. Make sure any fragments and run-together sentences you revised are punctuated correctly.

Mechanics

For help with capitalization, see Chapter 43.

1. Read your revised essay for any errors in capitalization.
2. Be sure to check your capitalization in any fragments or run-together sentences you revised.

Word Choice and Spelling

Word Choice

For help with confused words, see Chapter 49.

1. Find any words used incorrectly in your revised essay.
2. Correct any errors you find.

Spelling

For help with spelling, see Chapter 50.

1. Use spell-check and a dictionary to check your spelling.
2. Correct any misspelled words.

Now rewrite your essay again with your editing corrections.

PRACTICING NARRATION: FROM READING TO WRITING

Reading Workshop

Here are two essays that illustrate good narrative writing: "The Sanctuary of School," in which Lynda Barry tells a story about using her school as an escape from her home life, and "Writer's Retreat" by Stan Higgins, which talks about his life as a writer in prison. As you read, notice how the writers cover the journalistic questions and use vivid descriptive details to pull you into their narratives, making the main point of the essays all the more meaningful.

THE SANCTUARY OF SCHOOL

by Lynda Barry

Focusing Your Attention

1. Can you recall a time in your life when you felt particularly lonely or afraid? Write down as many facts, impressions, and memories as you can recall about that period of your life.

2. In the essay you are about to read, the writer describes a person who had a lasting impact on her. Do you think you have ever had such an important impact on someone that he or she would write an essay about you? Have you had such an impact on more than one person? Who are these people? What would they say about you in their recollections?

Expanding Your Vocabulary

The following words are important to your understanding of this essay. Start a vocabulary log of your own by recording any words you don't understand as you read. When you finish reading the essay, write down what you think the words mean. Then check your definitions in the dictionary.

sanctuary: safe place (title)

nondescript: not distinctive (paragraph 7)

monkey bars: playground equipment (paragraph 8)

breezeway: covered passage between two buildings (paragraph 13)

SUMMARY

Barry explains why her school was a sanctuary in her life and recalls one morning when she particularly needed the safety within its walls.

READABILITY

(Flesch–Kincaid grade level)
8.9

INSTRUCTOR'S RESOURCE MANUAL

For additional teaching strategies, for journal entries, for vocabulary and reading quizzes, and for more writing assignments, see the *Instructor's Resource Manual*, Section II, Part II.

READING CRITICALLY

As you learned at the beginning of this chapter, "think aloud" as you read. Interject personal references and focused ideas into your oral reading of the essay. The clearer you make your connections, the more deeply you will understand the essay. Read the essay at least two times. Discuss with a classmate the types of ideas you had as you read (focused or random). Which one of you did more focused reading?

THE SANCTUARY OF SCHOOL
by Lynda Barry

I was 7 years old the first time I snuck out of the house in the dark. It was winter, and my parents had been fighting all night. They were short on money and long on relatives who kept "temporarily" moving into our house because they had nowhere else to go. 1

My brother and I were used to giving up our bedroom. We slept on the couch, something we actually liked because it put us that much closer to the light of our lives, our television. 2

3 At night when everyone was asleep, we lay on our pillows watching it with the sound off. We watched Steve Allen's mouth moving. We watched Johnny Carson's mouth moving. We watched movies filled with gangsters shooting machine guns into packed rooms, dying soldiers hurling a last grenade, and beautiful women crying at windows. Then the sign-off finally came, and we tried to sleep.

4 The morning I snuck out, I woke up filled with a panic about needing to get to school. The sun wasn't quite up yet, but my anxiety was so fierce that I just got dressed, walked quietly across the kitchen, and let myself out the back door.

5 It was quiet outside. Stars were still out. Nothing moved, and no one was in the street. It was as if someone had turned the sound off on the world.

6 I walked the alley, breaking thin ice over the puddles with my shoes. I didn't know why I was walking to school in the dark. I didn't think about it. All I knew was the feeling of panic, like the panic that strikes kids when they realize they are lost.

7 That feeling eased the moment I turned the corner and saw the dark outline of my school at the top of the hill. My school was made up of about 15 nondescript portable classrooms set down on a fenced concrete lot in a rundown Seattle neighborhood, but it had the most beautiful view of the Cascade Mountains. You could see them from anywhere on the playfield, and you could see them from the windows of my classroom—Room 2.

8 I walked over to the monkey bars and hooked my arms around the cold metal. I stood for a long time just looking across Rainier Valley. The sky was beginning to whiten, and I could hear a few birds.

9 In a perfect world, my absence at home would not have gone unnoticed. I would have had two parents in a panic to locate me, instead of two parents in a panic to locate an answer to the hard question of survival during a deep financial and emotional crisis.

10 But in an overcrowded and unhappy home, it's incredibly easy for any child to slip away. The high levels of frustration, depression, and anger in my house made my brother and me invisible. We were children with the sound turned off. And for us, as for the steadily increasing number of neglected children in this country, the only place where we could count on being noticed was at school.

11 "Hey there, young lady. Did you forget to go home last night?" It was Mr. Gunderson, our janitor, whom we all loved. He was nice and he was funny and he was old with white hair, thick glasses, and an unbelievable number of keys. I could hear them jingling as he walked across the playfield. I felt incredibly happy to see him.

He let me push his wheeled garbage can between the different portables as he unlocked each room. He let me turn on the lights and raise the window shades, and I saw my school slowly come to life. I saw Mrs. Holman, our school secretary, walk into the office without her orange lipstick on yet. She waved. 12

I saw the fifth-grade teacher, Mr. Cunningham, walking under the breezeway eating a hard roll. He waved. 13

And I saw my teacher, Mrs. Claire LeSane, walking toward us in a red coat and calling my name in a very happy and surprised way, and suddenly my throat got tight and my eyes stung and I ran toward her crying. It was something that surprised both of us. 14

It's only thinking about it now, 28 years later, that I realize I was crying from relief. I was with my teacher, and in a while I was going to sit at my desk, with my crayons and pencils and books and classmates all around me, and for the next six hours I was going to enjoy a thoroughly secure, warm, and stable world. It was a world I absolutely relied on. Without it, I don't know where I would have gone that morning. 15

Mrs. LeSane asked me what was wrong, and when I said, "Nothing," she seemingly left it at that. But she asked me if I would carry her purse for her, an honor above all honors, and she asked if I wanted to come into Room 2 early and paint. 16

She believed in the natural healing power of painting and drawing for troubled children. In the back of her room there was always a drawing table and an easel with plenty of supplies, and sometimes during the day she would come up to you for what seemed like no good reason and quietly ask if you wanted to go to the back table and "make some pictures for Mrs. LeSane." We all had a chance at it—to sit apart from the class for a while to paint, draw, and silently work out impossible problems on 11 × 17 sheets of newsprint. 17

Drawing came to mean everything to me. At the back table in Room 2, I learned to build myself a life preserver that I could carry into my home. . . . 18

By the time the bell rang that morning, I had finished my drawing, and Mrs. LeSane pinned it up on the special bulletin board she reserved for drawings from the back table. It was the same picture I always drew—a sun in the corner of a blue sky over a nice house with flowers all around it. 19

Thinking Critically About Content

1. Notice how the writer describes herself and her brother as "children with the sound turned off" (paragraph 10) and their environment "as if

ANSWERS TO QUESTIONS

Thinking Critically About Content

1. It is an effective image because it painfully shows that Barry had no voice, that she was neglected and ignored as a child.
2. The warm and vivid details Barry uses to describe the school show that she thought of the school as a wonderful, warm, safe place to be. The descriptions she provides of her home life show that she felt awful when she was there.
3. Answers will vary.

Thinking Critically About Purpose and Audience

4. Barry's purpose was to inform readers about a particularly difficult time in her life. She wanted to show how the school helped her become who she is today.
5. Anyone can appreciate this essay, but readers who have similar home lives will probably understand it best.
6. She probably excludes this information because she

doesn't want to put the focus on her parents, and ultimately, their problems don't excuse their behavior.

Thinking Critically About Essays

7. The writer believes that her school is a safe retreat from the rest of the world.
8. Her details are arranged chronologically, which is effective for this essay.
9. The title describes her feelings for the school, which is her sanctuary away from a disturbing home life.
10. If written by Barry's parents, this essay would probably discuss the selfish nature of an ungrateful child. Beyond this, answers will vary.

someone had turned the sound off on the world" (paragraph 5). Is this an effective image? Why? What effect does it have on you? What does it tell you about Lynda Barry's childhood?

2. Why do you think the writer used warm and vivid details to describe the arrival of school employees (paragraphs 11 through 16)? What effect does this description have on you, compared with the description of her home life?
3. Did this essay make you compare your own childhood to Lynda Barry's?

Thinking Critically About Purpose and Audience

4. What do you think Barry's purpose is in writing this narrative essay? Explain your answer.
5. What readers do you think would most understand and appreciate this recollection?
6. In your opinion, why doesn't the writer tell us more about her parents' problems?

Thinking Critically About Essays

7. Describe in a complete sentence the writer's point of view in this essay.
8. How does Barry organize the details in this essay? Is this an effective order?
9. Explain Barry's title for this essay.
10. Explain in detail how this essay would be different if it were written by Lynda Barry's parents.

WRITER'S RETREAT
by Stan Higgins

SUMMARY

Higgins, an inmate in prison, ironically talks about his writing getaway, where he attempts to write amid numerous interruptions.

Focusing Your Attention

1. Can you remember a time in your life when you were frustrated trying to meet a goal you set for yourself? Write down as many facts, impressions, and memories as you can about this feeling.
2. In the essay you are about to read, the writer describes a person who is trying to write in prison. What do you think is his motivation? Have you ever wanted to do something so much you would even do it in prison? Explain your answer.

Expanding Your Vocabulary

The following words are important to your understanding of this essay. Start a vocabulary log of your own by recording any words you don't understand as you read. When you finish reading the essay, write down what you think the words mean. Then check your definitions in the dictionary.

within a pole vault: a few yards away (paragraph 1)

the Muse: inspiration (paragraph 2)

staccato: consisting of short, sharp sounds (paragraph 2)

ransacked: torn apart (paragraph 3)

confiscated: taken away (paragraph 3)

contraband: prohibited items (paragraph 3)

lock down: lock all prisoners in their cells (paragraph 4)

Bugler: brand of tobacco (paragraph 7)

mud: coffee (paragraph 16)

tier: row of prison cells (paragraph 23)

persevere: continue (paragraph 30)

tantamount: equal (paragraph 32)

misdemeanors: minor crimes (paragraph 32)

subsides: decreases (paragraph 34)

nebulous: vague, uncertain (paragraph 34)

girth: size (paragraph 41)

obscenities: offensive comments (paragraph 42)

READABILITY
(Flesch–Kincaid grade level)
9.8

INSTRUCTOR'S RESOURCE MANUAL
For additional teaching strategies, for journal entries, for vocabulary and reading quizzes, and for more writing assignments, see the *Instructor's Resource Manual*, Section II, Part II.

READING CRITICALLY

As you did with the previous essay, "think aloud" as you read this essay by Stan Higgins. This process will give you some good insights into the author's approach to his topic. Write down any new ideas that you discover. As you continue to read critically, you will deepen your understanding of this essay. Read the essay at least two times. Discuss with a classmate the types of ideas you had as you read (focused or random). Which one of you did more focused reading?

WRITER'S RETREAT
by Stan Higgins

1 Sandwiched between mountain snow and desert sand, hidden by sandstone walls 150 years old within a pole vault of the Arkansas River, it just doesn't get any better than this writer's retreat I call home. I write from a Colorado prison cell.

2 During the day I wash dishes, clean tables, and mop floors. They call it Vocational Training. And today, as every day at three P.M., I return to my cozy, bathroom-size suite and drag out my tiny portable. We've all night, just the two of us, my blue typewriter that has been my steady cell-mate for six years, through seven facilities across two states, and I. Today's goal is three pages. I blow dust from the cover and clean the keys. The Muse calls. *Tack-tack. Tack. Tack-tack-tack.* My typewriter sings its staccato song as I search for a fertile word or idea, some harmonious junction of thought and paper. Locked in solitary combat with my machine, nothing exists outside my cell, or so I pretend. I type a line. My door opens. Two blue-uniformed guards stand there grinning. "Guess what?" one says. "Your number came up."

3 Somehow I know he doesn't mean the Lottery. One begins searching my cell. The other pats me down as I leave. I return twenty minutes later to find my house ransacked, my bed torn up, papers scattered, pencils and pens strewn about, socks, shorts, and typewriter piled in a heap on the floor. Taped to the shelf above my desk is a slip of yellow paper with a fancily scrawled list of books, magazines, and other confiscated contraband. I can't help but question their appreciation for the written word.

4 I put my house back in order. We lock down, and the guards count us. After ten minutes the Count is cleared. My hands tremble. I can't write, not now. It's time for the ultimate challenge to a prisoner's courage . . . Chow!

5 Buoyed at having survived another meal, I return to my cell and begin anew. *Tack-tack-tack.*

6 "Hey, Bro," a green-uniformed inmate named O'Neil hollers from my doorway. "Think I can get a pinch of tobacco?"

7 This, too, is part of the territory. I pause to hand him a can of Bugler. My attention returns to writing as I study the list of disjointed, unrelated words I have accumulated, but I see out of the corner of my eye that I still have company.

8 "Think I can get a rolling paper?" O'Neil asks as he pops the lid off the can.

With a deep breath, I fish him a pack of papers from my pocket and hand them over. He fumbles with the paper as I reread my typed words. 9

"Think you could roll it for me, Bro?" 10

"What else, O'Neil?" I say whisking the paper and tobacco from his hands and rolling him a quick, crooked cigarette. He asks for a light as I usher him to the door. 11

Tack-tack-tack-tack, I resume. Just more words. I pinch my lips and study the nearly blank sheet of paper. *Write what you know,* memories of books past suggest. What do I know? Steel and concrete, jingling keys, and slamming doors. *Tack-tack-tack. Tack-tack.* 12

"M-m-Mr. Higgins?" another prisoner interrupts. It's a skinny kid in oversize greens, and his voice squeaks. "W-would you maybe have a dictionary I could, you know, sorta read, please?" He hesitates at the door in his stiff, fresh-out-of-the-package uniform that reminds me of pajamas, eyeing my bookshelf from a safe distance until I stand. I pull a *Webster's New Collegiate Dictionary* from my shelf above the desk and sit down again as he thumbs through it. He clears his throat. "Uh, excuse me, how do you spell *the?*" 13

"With two *r*'s instead of one," I tell him, shooing him away with the back of my hand. 14

Tack-tack. Tack-tack, tack-tack-tack, tack. Bones of steel, concrete skin, I type, and a soul as slippery as time. 15

Digger B. struts into my house. "Ya got a cup a mud I can get or what?" He pushes his empty cup in front of me, and as I fill it, he peers over my shoulder. "So what ya doin'?" 16

"Trying to write about trying to write." 17

"Man," he says and slurps coffee from his cup. "Whyn't ya write about somethin' interestin', know what I mean? Murder, war, sex, ya know—interestin'!" 18

I love encouragement. He wanders out. 19

I stare at my typewriter. I wait a few minutes. Nothing. My fingers creep back into place. *Tack-tack-tack.* 20

"Got a weed?" asks a gruff voice. It's Thunder. Six-foot-six and almost as wide, 300 pounds of beard and tattoo, he slides sideways into my cell. I quickly roll him a cigarette and light it. 21

"Anything else, Mr. Thunder?" 22

"Heared you typing clean down the tier," he grumbles. "What you doing?" 23

"Typing. Trying to type. Trying to write, I guess." 24

25 "You ain't writing 'bout me, are you?" He stares at me with eyes like rocks.

26 "No, sir, Mr. Thunder," I assure him, pointing to my almost blank paper. "Check it out."

27 He squints at it. "Don't like people writing 'bout me 'hind my back."

28 "I wouldn't do that, Mr. Thunder."

29 "Just so you ain't. 'At's all I care." He turns and sidles out the doorway. Thunder is unpredictable. Thunder hears voices. Thunder caught a guy in the shower once and stabbed him 53 times with a sharpened Number 2 pencil; he thought the man was talking about him. All in all, I figure it's not a bad idea to get along with Mr. Thunder.

30 The sun is setting. I've completed three sentences. My goal of three pages for the day is becoming as gray as my cell. At this rate I'm confident I can finish an 800-word article by my 2006 discharge date. *Persevere!* I get up and flip on the light.

31 Back to my typewriter; back on track. *Tack-tack-tack. Tack-tack, tack-tackity-tack.* I'm into it finally, my head is there, I'm on the verge of something . . . when Thunder stops at my door and pokes his woolly head in. "You sure you ain't writing things 'bout me?"

32 In prison, opening a can of tobacco, a bag of potato chips, or brewing a pot of coffee—like trying to type—is tantamount to throwing a side of beef into shark-infested waters. But these are minor distractions . . . misdemeanors. Prison overcrowding being what it is, Colorado officials have on several occasions sent inmates to faraway places for temporary storage. Two years ago guards came to my door with a green duffel bag and ordered me to pack up. I surveyed my four-year accumulation of books, magazines, and notes that converted my six-by-ten-foot cell into a private classroom. Each book and magazine, then highlighted for frequent reference, had been a hard-collected treasure. There were works-in-progress scattered on my desk. "Now!" a guard encouraged. "You're going to Washington state. If your stuff don't all fit . . . ," he reassured me with a glint in his eye and a broad sweep of his arm, ". . . you don't need it!" A year later, I was returned to sender. Back in Colorado, I set up housekeeping, mailed out another batch of address changes.

33 An aluminum trash can falls to the floor from an upper tier, perhaps with a little help. I try to type. The cell block explodes in cheering and clapping. Pop cans rain from above. I hesitate at the keyboard. It might be boredom; it might be a fight or a stabbing. It might be a riot. Then again, it might be they just discovered what was for breakfast tomorrow.

It is dark outside. The noise subsides. I sit for a few minutes blissfully alone, rescuing my thoughts, pondering my last sentence, imagining some nebulous, faraway, fairy tale future where everything is happily-ever-after. I imagine a steak dinner, the meat still sizzling, its pink and brown juice puddling the plate beneath a twice-baked potato and fresh asparagus, steam rising. . . . 34

"You ain't writing 'bout me!?" Thunder startles me. This time I didn't hear or see him fill my doorway. 35

"No, sir," I tell him, cigarette smoke replacing the scent of steak. "Not one word, Mr. Thunder." 36

He scratches his beard and stares. He steps in and looks over my shoulder. When he speaks again, after some moments, his voice is uncharacteristically soft and plaintive. "Not one word?" 37

I shake my head. 38

"Ain't I good enough to be in your stories?" 39

For a minute I think he is about to cry. I tell him I'll write something about him if he likes. He reaches across the desk for the can of Bugler, rolls a cigarette, pats me on the back, and leaves. 40

I sigh into the typewriter keys and look up in time to see a couple of guards making the rounds, parading their girth like badges of authority, jingling keys. "Attention on the Block! Attention on the Block!" blares the loudspeaker. "Five minutes to Count! Lock up now!" 41

Inmates shout obscenities, but they are just pretending. They filter off to their cells. Visions of solitude dance in my head. Alone! Just me and my typewriter! Now I'll get something done. But maybe I am pretending also. Maybe we are all just pretending. 42

I get up and stretch, close my door, return to my desk, and wait. 43

"Count!" the loudspeaker squawks. "Count!" 44

Doors slam shut. Suddenly it is quiet. I pause to savor the silence. A plastic Salvation Army cup rests next to my typewriter, its contents cold, thick, and dark, but it is the best cup I've had all day. For a moment I think I hear crickets, distant, anonymous traffic, dogs barking, the hum of street lights. 45

Ticktickticktick . . . complains my clock, its face turned away, hiding time. 46

This is it. I'm either going to write, or I'm not. I remove a three-by-five-inch wire-bound notebook: musings for the day, observations carried with me through the day. Flipped open and set on the desk beside my typewriter, it reminds me that place can also be irrelevant. I turn a page and begin typing. 47

ANSWERS TO QUESTIONS

Thinking Critically About Content

1. Higgins's "writer's retreat" is a tiny jail cell that is repeatedly being invaded by inmates and authorities.
2. Higgins is explaining how difficult writing from a prison cell is.
3. Higgins tries to keep the amount of time people take away from him to a minimum. The interruptions have become a part of his writing process because he was forced to make them so. Now he uses the interruptions as a form of prewriting; he jots down his "musings for the day" in the hope that they will inspire him (para. 47).

Tack-tack, tack-tack, tack-tackity-tack. Tack-tack. What is it like to write from a prison cell? I write. *Tack-tack.*

48 The glare of a flashlight hits me in the eyes. There is a pounding at my door. A guard is aiming his light in my face. "What're ya doing this time of night?" he asks.

49 I take a deep breath and count to ten before answering. Writing from prison, I tell myself, just ain't what it used to be. Maybe it never was. I count to twenty.

50 "Baking a cake," I finally answer.

51 He grins. "Yeah? Is it fun?"

52 "I don't know," I say. "I'll tell you when it's done."

Thinking Critically About Purpose and Audience

4. The main point of the essay is that writing is very important to this author. It's the only freedom he has.
5. Higgins's primary audience is general readers.
6. He was frustrated because he wanted to write three pages, but with the constant interruptions, he was unable to do so.

Thinking Critically About Essays

7. Higgins's point of view is that writing can be therapeutic. Although his point of view doesn't change, he certainly demonstrates how difficult getting to the therapeutic stage can be.
8. Answers will vary.
9. It is an effective ending because it shows the absurdity of the disruptions he faces. It also alludes to the fact that he is creating something that has many "ingredients."
10. Answers will vary.

Thinking Critically About Content

1. What characterizes this "writer's retreat"?
2. What is Higgins writing about on his typewriter?
3. How does Higgins deal with all the interruptions? In what ways are these incidents part of his writing process?

Thinking Critically About Purpose and Audience

4. Explain your understanding of the writer's main point in this essay.
5. Who do you think Higgins's primary audience is?
6. Why was Higgins frustrated trying to meet his goal of three pages of writing for the day?

Thinking Critically About Essays

7. Describe Higgins's point of view in this essay. Does it change throughout the essay? If so, in what ways?
8. Higgins uses many details to illustrate his frustration as he tries to write. Which details communicate his frustration most clearly to you?
9. Higgins talks about baking a cake in his conclusion. Is this an effective ending? Why or why not?
10. Tell this same story from Mr. Thunder's perspective.

Writing Workshop

This final section gives you opportunities to apply what you have learned in this chapter to another writing assignment. This time, we provide very little prompting beyond a summary of the guidelines for writing a narration essay. This section will let you demonstrate that you can go through the entire writing process on your own with only occasional feedback from your peers. Loop back into the chapter as necessary when you have questions so that this process becomes as automatic to you as possible before you move on to new material. Then pause at the end of the chapter to reflect briefly on what you have learned.

Guidelines for Writing a Narration Essay

1. Make sure your essay has a point.
2. Use the five *W*s and one *H* to construct your story.
3. Develop your narrative with vivid details.
4. Build excitement in your narrative with careful pacing.
5. Organize your narration so that your readers can easily follow it.

Writing About Your Reading

1. In "The Sanctuary of School," Lynda Barry recalls the way her school and her teachers provided a sanctuary, a place where she could escape from the problems of home. Write an essay in which you recall a place, a person, or an event that made you feel safe, secure, and welcome.
2. We all deal with frustration in different ways. Explain the coping strategies you have observed in friends and relatives. Do they work? Are they effective? Write a narrative essay focusing on various coping strategies that you have seen in action.
3. What do you think are the most important features of a good story? Why are they important? What effect do they have on you?

Writing About Your World

TEACHING ON THE WEB

Discussion Topic: Divide your students into groups of three or four, and have them discuss how narration is a large part of the Internet. Where do students think narration is most valuable on the Internet? In how many ways do they think narration can be used?

TEACHING ON THE WEB

Links: Find famous authors' Web pages, and discover what they say about writing a narration or story.

Possible sites:

James Patterson, www.jamespatterson.com

Danielle Steel, www.daniellesteel.com

Sandra Cisneros, www.sandracisneros.com

TEACHING ON THE WEB

Research: Have students search online for Web sites that teach how to write novels or short stories for future publication. What advice do these Web sites give that will help students learn more about narration?

1. Place yourself in the scene pictured on page 187, and write a narrative about what is happening. How did you get here? Why are you here? Where are you going from here? Be sure to decide on a main point before you begin to write.
2. Your old high school has asked you, as a graduate, to submit an essay to the newsletter recalling a job or volunteer experience that you enjoyed. The editors want to inform current high school students about options for volunteer and paid work. Your purpose is to tell your story in enough interesting detail so that you convince the current high school students that the job you had is worth looking into.
3. Your college class is putting together a collection of essays that explain how classmates decided to go to their college. What happened first? When did you decide? What helped you decide? What activities or people influenced your decision the most? Tell your story in vivid detail.
4. Create your own narration assignment (with the help of your instructor), and write a response to it.

Revising

Small Group Activity (5–10 minutes per writer) Working in groups of three or four, read your narration essays to each other. Those listening should record their reactions on a copy of the Peer Evaluation Form in Appendix 2B. After your group goes through this process, give your evaluation forms to the appropriate writers so that each writer has two peer comment sheets for revising.

Paired Activity (5 minutes per writer) Using the completed Peer Evaluation Forms, work in pairs to decide what you should revise in your essay. If time allows, rewrite some of your sentences, and have your partner look at them.

Individual Activity Rewrite your paper, using the revising feedback you received from other students.

Editing

Paired Activity (5–10 minutes per writer) Swap papers with a classmate, and use the editing portion of your Peer Evaluation Form to identify as many grammar, punctuation, mechanics, and spelling errors as you can. If time allows, correct some of your errors, and have your partner look at them. Record your grammar, punctuation, and mechanics errors in the Error Log (Appendix 6) and your spelling errors in the Spelling Log (Appendix 7).

Individual Activity Rewrite your paper again, using the editing feedback you received from other students.

Reflecting on Your Writing When you have completed your own essay, answer these six questions.

1. What was most difficult about this assignment?
2. What was easiest?
3. What did you learn about narration by completing this assignment?
4. What do you think are the strengths of your narration? Place a wavy line by the parts of your essay that you feel are very good.
5. What are the weaknesses, if any, of your paper? Place an X by the parts of your essay you would like help with. Write any questions you have in the margin.
6. What did you learn from this assignment about your own writing process—about preparing to write, about writing the first draft, about revising, and about editing?

Illustrating

❝When I began to write, I found it was the best way to make sense out of my life.❞

—John Cheever

TEACHING ILLUSTRATION

Provide students with a concept like "generation gaps," and ask them to find as many examples of the concept in the media as possible—both where it is present and where it is not. They can look on billboards, in magazines, in movies, on TV, and so on.

Have students make a list of where they find examples and where examples are conspicuously missing. Which types of media show the most examples? Which show the least? Why do your students think this is so?

Giving examples to make a point is a natural part of communication. For example, if you are trying to demonstrate how much time you waste, you can cite the fact that you talk on the phone about two hours every day. Or to tell your friends how much fun you are having, you might say, "College is great because no one tells me what to do or when to go to bed. I am completely on my own." The message is in the examples you choose.

We also use examples every day to make various points in our writing. Think about the following situations that take place in our personal lives, at school, and at work.

- In a letter to your parents, you tell them how hard you are studying in college by giving them examples of your weekend study schedule.
- A student gives examples of gestures, facial expressions, and posture in a paper on nonverbal communication for a psychology course.
- A student answers a sociology exam question by giving examples to show how children are integrated into society.
- A human resource director of a large company writes a memo on sexual harassment in the workplace, including examples of inappropriate behavior.
- The owner of a catering business writes a brochure listing examples of dinners available in different price ranges.

An example is an **illustration** of the point you want to make. Well-chosen examples, then, are the building blocks of an illustration essay. You draw examples from your experience, your observations, and your reading. They help you show rather than tell what you mean, usually by supplying concrete details (what you see, hear, touch, smell, or taste) to support abstract ideas (such as faith, hope, understanding, and love), by providing specifics ("I like chocolate") to explain generalizations ("I like sweets"), and by giving definite references ("Turn left at the second stoplight") to clarify vague statements ("Turn left in a few blocks").

Not only do examples help you make your point, but they also add interest to your writing. Would you like to read an essay stating that being a server in a restaurant is a lot harder than it looks? Or would you be more interested in reading an essay describing what it is like serving too many tables, carrying heavy trays, taking the wrong order to a table, and dealing with rude customers? The first statement tells, but vivid examples show your readers the point you want to make.

READING AND WRITING AN ILLUSTRATION ESSAY

Reading and writing are actually two halves of a whole process. For example, if you can see how a writer is accomplishing his or her purpose in a particular rhetorical mode, you will be more likely to use that same strategy effectively in your own writing. Being able to use these strategies critically or analytically is especially important for success in college and in life beyond college. This section will guide you to higher levels of thinking as you learn to use illustration.

Reading an Illustration Essay

In her essay "Hold the Mayonnaise," Julia Alvarez uses examples to explain the difficulties involved in blending two cultures—American and Latino—in a stepfamily. Have you ever visited a foreign country? What was it like to be in a different culture? Have you ever been part of a group that blended two or more cultures? What did you learn?

READING CRITICALLY

Reading illustration essays critically means looking closely at the selection to discover its purpose and then analyzing each example the author uses to prove his or her point. To understand how this essay works, circle the main idea or thesis. Then draw horizontal lines throughout the essay to separate the various examples Alvarez uses to support her thesis. These lines may or may not coincide with paragraph breaks. Finally, label each example in the right margin. Be prepared to explain the divisions you make.

TEACHING TIPS

The following eight teaching tips are based on Howard Gardner's multiple intelligences:

Verbal/Linguistic

Have students create lists of every example they can think of on a topic of their choice (such as teen pregnancy, air pollution, or aerobic exercise). How many can they come up with?

Musical/Rhythmic

Choose a word such as *rejection* or *love*, and have students find examples of the term in at least three different pieces of music.

Logical/Mathematical

Provide students with a list of examples on at least two different topics. Have students sort the examples into categories to determine which specifics go with which topic. Include examples that don't fit either topic.

Visual/Spatial
Provide each student with an art book, and assign a topic such as "peace." Then have students find examples from many different artistic time periods that portray the topic.

Bodily/Kinesthetic
Divide students into groups of three, and send them on a pseudo scavenger hunt around your campus to find examples of items that relate to athletics. The students should list the items and their locations. The group that brings back the longest list wins.

Intrapersonal
Have students reflect on times when they realized that they think best when they are alone. What examples can help them show that this is true?

Interpersonal
Have a small group of students think of a current issue affecting your city or state. How does the group think the issue should be resolved? Have the students provide as many examples as possible to help illustrate their views.

Naturalist
Have students recall times they have spent outdoors and determine how they feel about being out in nature. Have them provide numerous examples that illustrate why they feel the way they do.

HOLD THE MAYONNAISE

by Julia Alvarez

1 "If I die first and Papi ever gets remarried," Mami used to tease when we were kids, "don't you accept a new woman in my house. Make her life impossible, you hear?" My sisters and I nodded obediently and a filial shudder would go through us. We were Catholics, so, of course, the only kind of remarriage we could imagine had to involve our mother's death.

2 We were also Dominicans, recently arrived in Jamaica, Queens, in the early '60s, before waves of other Latin Americans began arriving. So, when we imagined whom exactly my father might possibly ever think of remarrying, only American women came to mind. It would be bad enough having a *madrastra,* but a "stepmother. . . ."

3 All I could think of was that she would make me eat mayonnaise, a food which I identified with the United States and which I detested. Mami understood, of course, that I wasn't used to that kind of food. Even a *madrastra,* accustomed to our rice and beans and *tostones* and *pollo frito,* would understand. But an American stepmother would think it was normal to put mayonnaise on food, and if she were at all strict and a little mean, which all stepmothers, of course, were, she would make me eat potato salad and such. I had plenty of my own reasons to make a potential stepmother's life impossible. When I nodded obediently with my sisters, I was imagining not just something foreign in our house, but in our refrigerator.

4 So it's strange now, almost 35 years later, to find myself a Latina stepmother of my husband's two tall, strapping, blond, mayonnaise-eating daughters. To be honest, neither of them is a real aficionado of the condiment, but it's a fair thing to add to a bowl of tuna fish or diced potatoes. Their American food, I think of it, and when they head to their mother's or off to school, I push the jar back in the refrigerator behind their chocolate pudding and several open cans of Diet Coke.

5 What I can't push as successfully out of sight are my own immigrant childhood fears of having a *gringa* stepmother with foreign tastes in our house. Except now, I am the foreign stepmother in a *gringa* household. I've wondered what my husband's two daughters think of this stranger in their family. It must be doubly strange for them that I am from another culture.

6 Of course, there are mitigating circumstances—my husband's two daughters were teenagers when we married, older, more mature, able to understand differences. They had also traveled when they were children with

their father, an eye doctor, who worked on short-term international projects with various eye foundations. But still, it's one thing to visit a foreign country, another altogether to find it brought home—a real bear plopped down in a Goldilocks house.

Sometimes, it's a whole extended family of bears. My warm, loud Latino family came up for the wedding: my *tía* from Santo Domingo; three dramatic, enthusiastic sisters and their families; my papi, with a thick accent I could tell the girls found it hard to understand; and my mami, who had her eye trained on my soon-to-be stepdaughters for any sign that they were about to make my life impossible. "How are they behaving themselves?" she asked me, as if they were 7 and 3, not 19 and 16. "They're wonderful girls," I replied, already feeling protective of them. 7

I looked around for the girls in the meadow in front of the house we were building, where we were holding the outdoor wedding ceremony and party. The oldest hung out with a group of her own friends. The younger one whizzed in briefly for the ceremony, then left again before the congratulations started up. There was not much mixing with me and mine. What was there for them to celebrate on a day so full of confusion and effort? 8

On my side, being the newcomer in someone else's territory is a role I'm used to. I can tap into that struggling English speaker, that skinny, dark-haired, olive-skinned girl in a sixth grade of mostly blond and blue-eyed giants. Those tall, freckled boys would push me around in the playground. "Go back to where you came from!" "*No comprendo!*" I'd reply, though of course there was no misunderstanding the fierce looks on their faces. 9

Even now, my first response to a scowl is that old pulling away. (My husband calls it "checking out.") I remember times early on in the marriage when the girls would be with us, and I'd get out of school and drive around doing errands, killing time, until my husband, their father, would be leaving work. I am not proud of my fears, but I understand—as the lingo goes—where they come from. 10

And I understand, more than I'd like to sometimes, my stepdaughters' pain. But with me, they need never fear that I'll usurp a mother's place. No one has ever come up and held their faces and then addressed me, "They look just like you." If anything, strangers to the remarriage are probably playing Mr. Potato Head in their minds, trying to figure out how my foreign features and my husband's fair Nebraskan features got put together into these two tall, blond girls. "My husband's daughters," I kept introducing them. 11

Once, when one of them visited my class and I introduced her as such, two students asked me why. "I'd be so hurt if my stepmom introduced me 12

Instructor's Resource Manual

For additional material about teaching illustration; for journal entries; and for multiple-choice, short-answer, and paragraph tests, see the *Instructor's Resource Manual*, Section II, Part II.

that way," the young man said. That night I told my stepdaughter what my students had said. She scowled at me and agreed. "It's so weird how you call me Papa's daughter. Like you don't want to be related to me or something."

13 "I didn't want to presume," I explained. "So it's O.K. if I call you my stepdaughter?"

14 "That's what I am," she said. Relieved, I took it for a teensy inch of acceptance. The takings are small in this stepworld, I've discovered—sort of like being a minority. It feels as if all the goodies have gone somewhere else.

15 Day to day, I guess I follow my papi's advice. When we first came, he would talk to his children about how to make it in our new country. "Just do your work and put in your heart, and they will accept you!" In this age of remaining true to your roots, of keeping your Spanish, of fighting from inside your culture, that assimilationist approach is highly suspect. My Latino students—who don't want to be called Hispanics anymore—would ditch me as faculty adviser if I came up with that play-nice message.

16 But in a stepfamily where everyone is starting a new life together, it isn't bad advice. Like a potluck supper, an American concept my mami never took to. ("Why invite people to your house and then ask them to bring the food?") You put what you've got together with what everyone else brought and see what comes out of the pot. The luck part is if everyone brings something you like—no potato salad, no deviled eggs, no little party sandwiches with you know what in them.

Preparing to Write Your Own Illustration Essay

When did you last try something new in your life? Was it difficult? Did you plan this new experience, or did it just happen? Do you like new experiences, or do you prefer keeping your life routine? Use one or more of the prewriting strategies you learned in Chapter 2 to recall several times you tried something new, planned or not. Then think about the positive and negative aspects of trying new experiences. What value do they have in your life? What are the disadvantages of trying new experiences?

Writing an Illustration Essay

In the art world, a good illustrator is someone who makes an image or an idea come alive with the perfect drawing. The same principle applies in writing: Someone who uses illustrations, or examples, effectively makes an essay or other piece of writing come alive. Moreover, in college, most essay exam questions are based on illustration—finding the best examples to support your main point. Here are some guidelines to help you use examples effectively:

1. **State your main point and your opinion about that point in the last sentence of your introduction.** Write a thesis statement that clearly and plainly states the main idea of your essay, and place it at the end of your introduction. This is the controlling idea of your essay and should consist of a limited subject and your opinion about that subject. You will explain this main point through the examples you furnish in the following body paragraphs.

   In the sample essay, Alvarez's introduction is two paragraphs long. She expresses her main point in the last sentence of the second paragraph: "It would be bad enough having a *madrastra*, but a 'stepmother.' " She introduces this idea as the focus of her essay, including her opinion ("bad enough"), and then explains it with examples. Through her examples, the author is talking about her new family as much as her fears as a child.

2. **Choose examples that are relevant to your point.** In an illustration essay, examples serve as the writer's explanation. Well-chosen examples are an essay's building blocks. They help you prove your point and must directly support the point you are trying to make. Examples that are not relevant are distracting, causing readers to lose their train of thought. Your readers will appreciate the point you are making not because you tell them what to think but because you show them with relevant examples what you are trying to say. Keep in mind, too, that the more specific your examples are, the more likely your readers are to agree with your point.

   Finding relevant examples is a fairly easy task. The best examples often come from your own experience and observation. You can also draw examples from your reading—books, newspapers, magazines. In addition, as technology advances, more and more information is available online, making the Internet a good place to find examples for an illustration essay.

   In Alvarez's essay, all of her examples focus on how difficult the role of stepmother is. Since Alvarez's point has to do with merging two cultures in a stepfamily, her examples refer to either her Dominican experience or her stepdaughters' American experience. Alvarez uses her dislike of mayonnaise to help her illustrate some of the differences people have to deal with when they combine cultures. These focused examples make her essay coherent and unified.

3. **Choose examples that your readers can identify with.** To do this, you need to know as much as possible about your audience. Once you know who your readers are, you can tailor your examples to them. In this way, your readers are most likely to follow your line of reasoning. Suppose, for instance, that you want your parents to finance an off-campus apartment for you. You are not likely to make your point by citing examples of European universities that do not provide any student housing, because this is not an example that American parents can identify with. You need to furnish examples that address your specific situation.

   Alvarez's essay was first published in the *New York Times*, so she chose examples that a diverse group of educated people would relate to. She knew that many of these readers would also be parents, so they would understand the issue of merging families and cultures. In that way, she could keep the attention of her readers for her entire essay and get them to sympathize with her particular point of view.

4. **Use a sufficient number of examples to make your point.** Nobody has a set formula for determining the perfect number of examples, because that depends on the point you are trying to make. Sometimes several short examples will make your point best. Or perhaps three or four fairly detailed examples—each in its own body paragraph—work best. At other times the most effective way to develop an essay is with a single extended example. Usually, however, three or four examples are sufficient. If you are in doubt whether to add another example or more vivid details, you should probably do so. Most students err on the side of using too few examples or not adding enough detail to their examples.

   Alvarez opens her essay with a fairly extended example (three paragraphs) to show her dislike of mayonnaise and stepmothers. Later, in paragraph 7, she provides four short examples—all in one sentence—of how her stepdaughters might find her Dominican family difficult to be around. In paragraphs 9 and 11 through 14, Alvarez develops her examples in single paragraphs. She also tries to put herself in her stepdaughters' place. Overall, she gives enough examples from many perspectives so that we understand the complexity and importance of the point she is making. These different types of examples give her essay variety and make it interesting.

5. **Organize your examples to make your point in the clearest, strongest way.** When you have gathered enough relevant examples, you are ready to organize them into an essay. Most illustration essays are organized from general to particular (from a general statement—the thesis—to specific examples that support the general statement) or chronologically (according to a time sequence).

The examples themselves must also be organized within their paragraphs in some logical way—chronologically, spatially, or by extremes. Which example should come first? Second? Last? The simple act of arranging examples can help you and your reader make sense of an experience or idea. Use basic logic to guide you to different patterns.

Alvarez opens her essay with a childhood memory (fearing a stepmother), moves to present time (she's now a stepmother), and then looks back at episodes in her life and her stepdaughters' lives that show how blending two cultures can be difficult. For every point she makes, she provides an example. Overall, her organization is chronological, though someone else might have arranged these examples a different way.

Writing Your Own Illustration Essay

Based on the prewriting that you did earlier, write an essay about three new experiences you have had. Which were planned? Which were unplanned? Did they affect you in positive ways? In negative ways? Or were the outcomes mixed? What did you learn from these experiences? Draft a thesis statement. Then write a first draft of your essay, including an introduction and a conclusion. Use well-organized examples in your body paragraphs to support your thesis statement.

A STUDENT'S ILLUSTRATION ESSAY

In the following essay, student writer Taleah Trainor uses examples to explain her relationship with Murphy's Law. As you read this draft of her essay, try to find Taleah's main point.

Murphy's Law

Murphy's Law: If something can go wrong, it will. I have always been familiar with the concept of this law, but never from actual experience. It was not until the summer before my first year in college that different events taught me about Murphy's Law. 1

The first event was when my father informed me that on our family trip to Washington, D.C. we would be using my car. Since I had made previous plans I was not bubbling with enthusiasm. I had 14 "fun-filled" days in D.C. 2

And to top it all off, on the way home from D.C., my car decided to have a breakdown between two Louisiana towns. Louisiana has a really long stretch of highway that driver's hate. People feel like they're on it forever. Luckily, my father had AAA, our delay was short.

3 This particular instance had familiarized me with Murphy's Law, and for the remainder of the summer, I began to notice it every time I turned around. At first it was little things like catching the flu just hours before a date. After a while, it turned into bigger hassles, like getting flat tires on the way to job interviews. I prayed my luck would take a turn for the better rather then the worse.

4 Murphy showed up again on August 29, when I left my hometown to travel to my new school. Having to entrust my 397-mile journey to an old AAA map, I pictured getting sidetracked onto an out-of-the-way farm road leading me to an uncharted town. But I did not get lost until arriving at the infamous "traffic circle" in my new home town. Realizing my highway map was of know use in town, I frantically looked around and happened to catch a glimpse of the "I ❤ Bulldogs" bumper sticker plastered on the car in front of me. I said to myself, "Now how many cars could have that sticker?" I convinced myself that I was in luck and that the car in front of me was headed toward campus. I decided to follow it. After arriving in a gruesome alley, which accurately resembled the pictures I had seen of a Third World country, I came to the conclusion the car was not headed toward campus but probably to the local chicken fights. Pulling in to the nearest Texaco station, directions were given to me. Three service stations later, their I was, at my new dorm on campus. Once again, I knew that Murphy's Law had decided to play with me.

5 I realized Murphy's Law was becoming a permanent part of my life. If something in my life could possibly go wrong, Murphy would be there to make sure of it. I had finally come to the conclusion that Murphy, and I would be friends for life—unless, of course, something went wrong.

Discovering How the Essay Works

1. What main idea do you think Taleah is trying to communicate in this essay?

   Murphy's Law is going to haunt her forever.

   Does her thesis communicate this main idea?

   It could be stronger.

2. How is each of Taleah's examples related to her main point? List three examples she furnishes, and explain how they are related to her thesis statement. *Answers will vary.*

3. Knowing that this essay was written for her college writing class, do you think Taleah's audience could identify with these examples? Explain your answer. *Answers will vary.*

4. Does Taleah include enough examples to make her point? Explain your answer. *Yes, except in paragraph 3.*

5. How are the examples in Taleah's essay arranged? List some of her examples in the order they appear; then identify her method of organization. *Answers may vary.*

going to D.C., having to change plans	*flat tires before job interviews*
car breakdown between two Louisiana towns	*getting lost in new town*
getting flu before a date	*ending up in a strange alley*

Method of organization: *chronological*

Revising and Editing the Student Essay

This essay is Taleah's first draft, which now needs to be revised and edited. First, apply the following Revising Checklist to the content of Taleah's draft. When you are satisfied that her ideas are fully developed and well organized, use the Editing Checklist on page 203 to correct her grammar and mechanics errors. Do the tasks, and answer the questions after each checklist. Then write your suggested changes directly on Taleah's draft.

REVISING AND EDITING OPTIONS

Consider varying your approach to revising and editing. You could teach these skills in a class discussion, in small groups, or in pairs.

REVISING STRATEGIES

This chapter focuses on the following revising elements:

Thesis statement
Basic elements
Development
Unity

REVISING CHECKLIST 

THESIS STATEMENT

✔ Does the thesis statement contain the essay's controlling idea and an opinion about that idea?

✔ Does the thesis appear as the last sentence of the introduction?

BASIC ELEMENTS

- ✔ Does the title draw in the readers?
- ✔ Does the introduction capture the readers' attention and build up to the thesis statement effectively?
- ✔ Does each body paragraph deal with a single topic?
- ✔ Does the conclusion bring the essay to a close in an interesting way?

DEVELOPMENT

- ✔ Do the body paragraphs adequately support the thesis statement?
- ✔ Does each body paragraph have a focused topic sentence?
- ✔ Does each body paragraph contain *specific* details that support the topic sentence?
- ✔ Does each body paragraph include *enough* details to explain the topic sentence fully?

UNITY

- ✔ Do the essay's topic sentences relate directly to the thesis statement?
- ✔ Do the details in each body paragraph support its topic sentence?

ORGANIZATION

- ✔ Is the essay organized logically?
- ✔ Is each body paragraph organized logically?

COHERENCE

- ✔ Are transitions used effectively so that paragraphs move smoothly and logically from one to the next?
- ✔ Do the sentences move smoothly and logically from one to the next?

Thesis Statement

1. Put brackets around the last sentence in Taleah's introduction. Does it introduce her main point? Does it include her opinion about that point?

   It could be a little stronger.

2. Rewrite Taleah's thesis statement if necessary so that it states her main point and her opinion about that point.

   Here is one possibility: It wasn't until my first year in college that I realized Murphy's Law would constantly disrupt my life.

Basic Elements

1. Give Taleah's essay an alternate title.

   Answers will vary.

2. Rewrite Taleah's introduction so that it captures the readers' attention and builds up to the thesis statement at the end of the paragraph.

   Answers will vary.

3. Does each of Taleah's body paragraphs deal with only one topic?

   Yes

4. Rewrite Taleah's conclusion using at least one suggestion from Part I.

   Answers will vary.

Development

1. Write out Taleah's thesis statement (revised, if necessary), and list her three topic sentences below it. *Thesis may vary.*

   Thesis statement: *It wasn't until my first year in college that I realized that Murphy's Law would constantly disrupt my life.*

   Topic 1: *The first event was when my father informed me that on our family trip to Washington, D.C. we would be using my car.*

   Topic 2: *This particular instance had familiarized me with Murphy's Law, and for the remainder of the summer, I began to notice it every time I turned around.*

Topic 3: *Murphy showed up again on August 29, when I left my hometown to travel to my new school.*

2. Do Taleah's topics adequately support her thesis statement?

   Yes

3. Does each body paragraph have a focused topic sentence?

   Yes

4. Are Taleah's examples specific?

   Answers will vary.

   Add another more specific detail to one of the examples in her essay.

5. Does she offer enough examples to make her point?

   Answers will vary.

   Add at least one new example to strengthen Taleah's essay.

Unity

1. Read each of Taleah's topic sentences with her thesis statement (revised, if necessary) in mind. Do they go together?

   Answers will vary.

2. Revise her topic sentences if necessary so they are directly related.
3. Drop or rewrite the two sentences in paragraph 2 that are not directly related to their topic sentence. *Sentences 5 and 6*

Organization

1. Read Taleah's essay again to see if all the paragraphs are arranged logically.
2. Move any paragraphs that are out of order. *All paragraphs are in order.*
3. Look closely at Taleah's body paragraphs to see if all her sentences are arranged logically within paragraphs.
4. Move any sentences that are out of order. *All sentences are in order.*

Coherence

1. Circle five transitions, repetitions, synonyms, or pronouns Taleah uses.
2. Explain how two of these make Taleah's essay easier to read.

Answers will vary.

____

For a list of transitions, see page 101.

For a list of pronouns, see pages 7–8.

Now rewrite Taleah's essay with your revisions.

EDITING CHECKLIST

SENTENCES

✔ Does each sentence have a main subject and verb?

✔ Do all subjects and verbs agree?

✔ Do all pronouns agree with their nouns?

✔ Are modifiers as close as possible to the words they modify?

PUNCTUATION AND MECHANICS

✔ Are sentences punctuated correctly?

✔ Are words capitalized properly?

WORD CHOICE AND SPELLING

✔ Are words used correctly?

✔ Are words spelled correctly?

EDITING STRATEGIES

This chapter focuses on the following editing problems:

Run-togethers

Modifier errors

Commas

Confused words

Sentences

Subjects and Verbs

1. Underline the subjects once and verbs twice in paragraph 2 of your revision of Taleah's essay. Remember that sentences can have more than one subject-verb set.
2. Does each of Taleah's sentences have at least one subject and verb that can stand alone?

   No

3. Did you find and correct Taleah's run-together sentence? If not, find and correct it now. *Paragraph 2, sentence 7*

For help with subjects and verbs, see Chapter 25.

For help with run-togethers, see Chapter 27.

Subject-Verb Agreement

For help with subject-verb agreement, see Chapter 30.

1. Read aloud the subjects and verbs you underlined in your revision of Taleah's essay.
2. Correct any subjects and verbs that do not agree. *All subjects and verbs agree.*

Pronoun Agreement

For help with pronoun agreement, see Chapter 34.

1. Find any pronouns in your revision of Taleah's essay that do not agree with their nouns. *All pronouns agree with their nouns.*
2. Correct any pronouns that do not agree with their nouns.

Modifiers

For help with modifier errors, see Chapter 37.

1. Find any modifiers in your revision of Taleah's essay that are not as close as possible to the words they modify.
2. Did you find and correct her dangling modifier? If not, find and correct it now. *Paragraph 4, sentence 9*

Punctuation and Mechanics

Punctuation

For help with punctuation, see Chapters 38–42.

1. Read your revision of Taleah's essay for any errors in punctuation.
2. Find the run-together sentence you revised, and make sure it is punctuated correctly.
3. Did you find and correct Taleah's two comma errors? *Paragraph 2, sentence 2; paragraph 5, sentence 3*

Mechanics

For help with capitalization, see Chapter 43.

1. Read your revision of Taleah's essay for any errors in capitalization.
2. Be sure to check Taleah's capitalization in the run-together sentence you revised.

Word Choice and Spelling

Word Choice

For help with confused words, see Chapter 49.

1. Find any words used incorrectly in your revision of Taleah's essay.
2. Did you find and correct the three confused words in Taleah's essay? If not, find and correct them now. *then/than (paragraph 3), know/no (paragraph 4), their/there (paragraph 4)*

Spelling

For help with spelling, see Chapter 50.

1. Use spell-check and a dictionary to check the spelling in your revision of Taleah's essay. *All words are spelled correctly.*
2. Correct any misspelled words.

Now rewrite Taleah's essay again with your editing corrections.

YOUR OWN ILLUSTRATION ESSAY

Returning to the illustration you wrote earlier in this chapter, you are now going to revise and edit your own writing. Remember that to revise you should focus on your development and organization while editing requires you to check your grammar and usage. Consider your content, especially your development and organization, before you correct your grammar and usage errors. As you rework your composition, you should repeat these processes until your essay achieves the purpose you intended.

READING CRITICALLY

Apply the reading strategy you learned earlier to your own essay. Circle your thesis or main idea; then draw horizontal lines between the examples you use to support your main idea. As you label these examples in the margin, decide whether they are the best choices to prove your point. Should you change any of them? Should you explain any of them further?

Revising and Editing Your Own Essay

The checklists here will help you apply what you learned in this chapter to your own essay.

CLASS ACTIVITY

Write a topic on the board, and have students provide examples that support the topic. Have class members fill the board with many ideas and then determine which examples would work best if they were going to write an illustration essay.

REVISING CHECKLIST

THESIS STATEMENT

☐ Does the thesis statement contain the essay's controlling idea and an opinion about that idea?

☐ Does the thesis appear as the last sentence of the introduction?

BASIC ELEMENTS

☐ Does the title draw in the readers?

☐ Does the introduction capture the readers' attention and build up to the thesis statement effectively?

☐ Does each body paragraph deal with a single topic?

☐ Does the conclusion bring the essay to a close in an interesting way?

DEVELOPMENT

☐ Do the body paragraphs adequately support the thesis statement?

☐ Does each body paragraph have a focused topic sentence?

☐ Does each body paragraph contain specific details that support the topic sentence?

- ☐ Does each body paragraph include enough details to explain the topic sentence fully?

UNITY

- ☐ Do the essay's topic sentences relate directly to the thesis statement?
- ☐ Do the details in each body paragraph support its topic sentence?

ORGANIZATION

- ☐ Is the essay organized logically?
- ☐ Is each body paragraph organized logically?

COHERENCE

- ☐ Are transitions used effectively so that paragraphs move smoothly and logically from one to the next?
- ☐ Do the sentences move smoothly and logically from one to the next?

Thesis Statement

1. What is the main point you are trying to convey in your essay?

____

____

2. What is your opinion about that main point?

____

____

____

3. Put brackets around the last sentence in your introduction. Does it convey your main point and your opinion about that point?

____

____

____

4. Rewrite your thesis statement if necessary so that it states your main point and your opinion.

Basic Elements

1. Give your essay a title if it doesn't have one.

 ____

2. Does your introduction capture your readers' attention and build up to your thesis statement at the end of the paragraph?

 ____

3. Does each of your body paragraphs deal with only one topic?

 ____

4. Does your conclusion follow some of the suggestions offered in Part I?

 ____

Development

1. Write out your thesis statement (revised, if necessary), and list your topic sentences below it.

 Thesis statement: _______________

 Topic 1: _______________

 Topic 2: _______________

 Topic 3: _______________

2. Do your topics adequately support your thesis statement?

 ____

3. Does each body paragraph have a focused topic sentence?

 ____

4. Are your examples specific?

 ____

 Add another more specific detail to an example in your essay.

5. Do you give enough examples to make your point?

____

Add at least one new example to your essay.

6. Can your readers identify with your examples?

____

Unity

1. Read each of your topic sentences with your thesis statement in mind. Do they go together?

____

2. Revise your topic sentences if necessary so they are directly related.
3. Drop or rewrite any of the sentences in your body paragraphs that are not directly related to their topic sentences.

Organization

1. Read your essay again to see if all the paragraphs are arranged logically.
2. Refer to your answers to the development questions. Then identify your method of organization.

____

3. Is the order you chose for your paragraphs the most effective approach to your topic?

____

4. Move any paragraphs that are out of order.
5. Look closely at your body paragraphs to see if all the sentences are arranged logically within paragraphs.
6. Move any sentences that are out of order.

Coherence

For a list of transitions, see page 101.

For a list of pronouns, see pages 7–8.

1. Circle five transitions, repetitions, synonyms, or pronouns you use.
2. Explain how two of these make your essay easier to read.

____

____

Now rewrite your essay with your revisions.

EDITING CHECKLIST

SENTENCES

- ☐ Does each sentence have a main subject and verb?
- ☐ Do all subjects and verbs agree?
- ☐ Do all pronouns agree with their nouns?
- ☐ Are modifiers as close as possible to the words they modify?

PUNCTUATION AND MECHANICS

- ☐ Are sentences punctuated correctly?
- ☐ Are words capitalized properly?

WORD CHOICE AND SPELLING

- ☐ Are words used correctly?
- ☐ Are words spelled correctly?

Sentences

Subjects and Verbs

1. Underline the subjects once and verbs twice in a paragraph of your revised essay. Remember that sentences can have more than one subject-verb set.
2. Does each of your sentences have at least one subject and verb that can stand alone?

   ____

3. Correct any fragments you have written.
4. Correct any run-together sentences you have written.

For help with subjects and verbs, see Chapter 25.

For help with fragments, see Chapter 26.

For help with run-togethers, see Chapter 27.

Subject-Verb Agreement

1. Read aloud the subjects and verbs you underlined in your revised essay.
2. Correct any subjects and verbs that do not agree.

For help with subject-verb agreement, see Chapter 30.

Pronoun Agreement

1. Find any pronouns in your revised essay that do not agree with their nouns.
2. Correct any pronouns that do not agree with their nouns.

For help with pronoun agreement, see Chapter 34.

Modifiers

For help with modifier errors, see Chapter 37.

1. Find any modifiers in your revised essay that are not as close as possible to the words they modify.
2. Rewrite sentences if necessary so that your modifiers are as close as possible to the words they modify.

Punctuation and Mechanics

Punctuation

For help with punctuation, see Chapters 38–42.

1. Read your revised essay for any errors in punctuation.
2. Make sure any fragments and run-together sentences you revised are punctuated correctly.

Mechanics

For help with capitalization, see Chapter 43.

1. Read your revised essay for any errors in capitalization.
2. Be sure to check your capitalization in any fragments or run-together sentences you revised.

Word Choice and Spelling

Word Choice

For help with confused words, see Chapter 49.

1. Find any words used incorrectly in your revised essay.
2. Correct any errors you find.

Spelling

For help with spelling, see Chapter 50.

1. Use spell-check and a dictionary to check your spelling.
2. Correct any misspelled words.

Now rewrite your essay again with your editing corrections.

PRACTICING ILLUSTRATION: FROM READING TO WRITING

Reading Workshop

Here are two essays that use examples to make their point: "Dawn's Early Light" by Richard Rodriguez gives examples from his experience to show how immigrants in the United States have changed us, and "The Decorated Body" by France Borel uses examples to talk about the importance of altering our physical appearance. As you read, notice how the writers use examples to support and advance their ideas.

DAWN'S EARLY LIGHT
by Richard Rodriguez

Focusing Your Attention

1. What are your current opinions on border control in the United States? Who should be allowed to be an American? What guidelines do you suggest we use in deciding who can become Americans?
2. The essay you are about to read considers our current problems in the United States with immigration. What role do immigrants play in our country's economy? In our social structure? In our workplace?

Expanding Your Vocabulary

The following words are important to your understanding of this essay. Organize this list into two columns—words you know and words you don't know. Which of the words you don't know can you guess from their sentences?

amnesty: an official pardon (paragraph 1)
feckless: unthinking and irresponsible (paragraph 5)
stamina: the ability to sustain prolonged effort (paragraph 9)
undermine: weaken (paragraph 11)
exalted: praised highly (paragraph 11)
Trabajo: work (paragraph 11)
Señor: Sir (paragraph 11)
Barato: cheap (paragraph 11)

SUMMARY
Rodriguez uses examples to demonstrate how the addition of immigrants has changed the way Americans think about themselves.

READABILITY
(Flesch–Kincaid grade level)
8.9

INSTRUCTOR'S RESOURCE MANUAL
For additional teaching strategies, for journal entries, for vocabulary and reading quizzes, and for more writing assignments, see the *Instructor's Resource Manual*, Section II, Part II.

READING CRITICALLY

As you learned earlier, circle the thesis of the following essay, and then separate each example with horizontal lines. Share your marks with a classmate, and justify each of your decisions.

DAWN'S EARLY LIGHT
by Richard Rodriguez

We see them lined up on American streets at dawn's early light. Depending on our point of view, we call them "illegal" or "undocumented." The 1 question preoccupying us now as a nation, from the White House on down, is "them"—what to do with them? Grant them amnesty? Send them all back? Make them guest workers?

2 But I wonder about us. How they have changed us, even while we have paid them cheaply to wash our restaurant dishes and to pick our apples and to sit with a dying grandparent. For much of the 20th century, we employed Mexicans when it suited us.

3 For example, during the war, we needed Mexicans to harvest our crops. Slowly, mutual dependence was established. A rumor of dollars spread through Mexican villages, and Americans grew accustomed to cheap laboring hands.

4 Now they come, children following the footsteps of parents and grandparents, often at the risk of death or injury. We say about them that they are disrespectful of American laws. But for every illegal worker employed today in America, there is an employer—one unequally disrespectful of American law. Mexicans reveal our hypocrisy to ourselves. They, in their relentless movement back and forth, are forcing us to see America within the Americas.

5 Long before diplomats and politicians spoke of NAFTA or feckless college students headed to Cancun for spring break, Mexican peasants saw the Americas whole. They—in Peruvian villages, they know when apples are being picked in the Yakima Valley. Brazilian teenagers know when fishing companies are hiring in Alaska. They—they know all about us.

6 But now they are forcing us to acquire a working knowledge of them. Because of them, Spanish is, unofficially, the second language of the United States, apparent on signs all over the city. Though we are the employers dispensing dollars at the end of the day or short-changing them or threatening to call the police if they complain, they leave us with an odd sense of powerlessness, for we are not in control of the movements of peoples across the borders.

7 We are not in control because the movement of peoples across the earth is an aspect of tragedy, of circumstances—drought, plague, civil war, poverty. Peasants all over the world are in movement, violating borders.

8 Even President Bush, in announcing his sympathetic proposals for how to deal with them, assumed the given: They are here. We pay them as little as we can, of course, which is how the undocumented undercut America's working class, white and black. We say about them, sometimes, that "the illegals work very hard, work harder for less than we can get Americans to work."

9 On a carefree weekend, we might suddenly see "them" on the horizon working amidst rows of dusty green. They force us to wonder if we have the courage of such labor or the stamina. Sometimes, Americans will compare these people to their own great-grandparents.

Answers to Questions

Thinking Critically About Content

1. Rodriguez refers to illegal or undocumented people from Mexico as "them."
2. Rodriguez says that Mexicans are disrespectful of American laws because they are employed illegally. Any example of illegal employment would support this answer.
3. They force us to acknowledge that the United States is part of a larger group of Americans, including North, Central, and South America, and isn't just restricted to our United States of America.

Thinking Critically About Purpose and Audience

4. Rodriguez wants to make Americans re-

The difference, people say, is that these Mexicans and central Americans are illegally here, whereas our ancestors came here legally. Consider the familiar images of those ships headed for Ellis Island, which have become commonplace in American legend. We picture those immigrants enthralled to the Goddess of Liberty and the freedom she represents. 10

Today's undocumented workers do not speak of the Federalist Papers or of Thomas Jefferson. They want only a job. They undermine the romanticism we harbor about earlier generations and about ourselves. They, today's illegal immigrants, may lead us to wonder whether for our ancestors America was not simply an exalted vision, but also partook of tragedy: A loaf of stale bread. A backbreaking job. A terrible loneliness. "Trabajo? Cheap, Señor, cheap. Roof? Digging? Barato, si, barato." I'm Richard Rodriguez. 11

Thinking Critically About Content

1. Based on Richard Rodriguez's essay, describe "them" in your own words.
2. In what ways are Mexicans "disrespectful of American laws" (paragraph 4)? Give an example from Rodriguez's essay to support your answer.
3. In what ways do immigrants force us "to see America within the Americas" (paragraph 4)?

Thinking Critically About Purpose and Audience

4. What do you think Rodriguez's purpose is in this essay? Explain your answer.
5. What type of audience do you think would most understand and appreciate this essay?
6. What do you think Rodriguez's title means?

Thinking Critically About Essays

7. Does Rodriguez give you enough examples to understand his learning environment in high school? Explain your answer.
8. Is this essay unified? Does each of the author's topic sentences support the essay's thesis statement? Explain your answer.
9. What is Rodriguez's thesis in this essay? Where is it located?
10. Explain your opinion on immigration today. What are the problems? How can we solve these problems? Respond to these questions in detail.

think their views about immigration.

5. Immigrants and families of immigrants would best understand this essay.
6. "Dawn's Early Light" is a lyric from our National Anthem. It forces us to rethink our views of patriotism and citizenship.

Thinking Critically About Essays

7. Answers will vary.
8. The essay is unified because each of its topics further explains the thesis statement. Then the topics are supported with examples. Here is a rough outline of the essay:
   The presence of Mexicans
   How Mexicans have changed us in the United States
   Jobs
   Disrespect
   The Americas
   Control of our borders
   Cheap labor
   Reevaluation of our courage
   Role of illegal workers
9. The thesis is the following statement: "For much of the twentieth century, we employed Mexicans when it suited us." It comes at the end of the first paragraph.
10. Answers will vary.

THE DECORATED BODY
by France Borel

SUMMARY
Borel discusses the importance human beings place on decorating our bodies by citing examples from hair color and makeup to tattoos and piercings.

READABILITY
(Flesch–Kincaid grade level)
12.2

INSTRUCTOR'S RESOURCE MANUAL
For additional teaching strategies, for journal entries, for vocabulary and reading quizzes, and for more writing assignments, see the *Instructor's Resource Manual*, Section II, Part II.

Focusing Your Attention

1. In what ways have you changed your natural appearance—hair color, makeup, tattoos, piercings, and the like? Why do you make these alternations? What messages do they send to others?
2. The essay you are about to read deals with the ways we decorate our bodies. These methods vary according to someone's culture. Why do you think people change their appearance in the United States? What physical decorations are appealing to you? Which are unappealing? Why do you think you have these various reactions?

Expanding Your Vocabulary

The following words are important to your understanding of this essay. Organize this list into two columns—words you know and words you don't know. Which of the words you don't know can you guess from their sentences?

unfathomably: impossible to measure (paragraph 1)

artiface: device used to trick people (paragraph 2)

millennia: thousands of years (paragraph 3)

prevalent: widespread (paragraph 3)

aesthetically: concerned with appearances (paragraph 4)

amorous: pertaining to love (paragraph 4)

scarification: scarring of the skin (paragraph 6)

pretexts: false justifications (paragraph 8)

malleable: easily influenced (paragraph 9)

eludes: evades or escapes from (paragraph 12)

homogenous: of the same kind (paragraph 12)

tacit: implied (paragraph 12)

adhere: stick to (paragraph 13)

READING CRITICALLY

Once again, circle the thesis of the following essay, and draw horizontal lines in the essay to show the different examples the author has chosen to support his thesis. Compare your marks with those of a classmate, and justify your decisions to each other.

THE DECORATED BODY
by France Borel

"Nothing goes as deep as dress nor as far as the skin; ornaments have the dimensions of the world."

—Michel Serres, *The Five Senses*

Human nakedness, according to social custom, is unacceptable, unbearable, and dangerous. From the moment of birth, society takes charge, managing, dressing, forming, and deforming the child—sometimes even with a certain degree of violence. Aside from the most elementary caretaking concerns—the very diversity of which shows how subjective the motivation is—an unfathomably deep and universal tendency pushes families, clans, and tribes to rapidly modify a person's physical appearance. 1

One's genuine physical makeup, one's given anatomy, is always felt to be unacceptable. Flesh, in its raw state, seems both intolerable and threatening. In its naked state, body and skin have no possible existence. The organism is acceptable only when it is transformed, covered with signs. The body only speaks if it is dressed in artifice. 2

For millennia, in the four quarters of the globe, mothers have molded the shape of their newborn babies' skulls to give them silhouettes conforming to prevalent criteria of beauty. In the nineteenth century, western children were tightly swaddled to keep their limbs straight. In the so-called primitive world, children were scarred or tattooed at a very early age in rituals which were repeated at all the most important steps of their lives. At a very young age, children were fitted with belts, necklaces, or bracelets; their lips, ears, or noses were pierced or stretched. 3

Some cultures have designed sophisticated appliances to alter physical structure and appearance. American Indian cradleboards crushed the skull to flatten it; the Mangbetus of Africa wrapped knotted rope made of bark around the child's head to elongate it into a sugar-loaf shape, which was 4 considered to be aesthetically pleasing. The feet of very young Chinese girls were bound and spliced, intentionally and irreversibly deforming them, because this was seen to guarantee the girls' eventual amorous and matrimonial success.[1]

5 Claude Lévi-Strauss said about the Caduveo of Brazil: "In order to be a man, one had to be painted; whoever remained in a natural state was no different from the beasts."[2] In Polynesia, unless a girl was tattooed, she would not find a husband. An unornamented hand could not cook, nor dip into the communal food bowl. Pink lips were despicable and ugly. Anyone who refused the test of the tattoo was seen to be marginal and suspect.

6 Among the Tivs of Nigeria, women called attention to their legs by means of elaborate scarification and the use of pearl leg bands; the best decorated calves were known for miles around. Tribal incisions behind the ears of Chad men rendered the skin "as smooth and stretched as that of a drum." The women would laugh at any man lacking these incisions, and they would never accept him as a husband. Men would subject themselves willingly to this custom, hoping for scars deep enough to leave marks on their skulls after death.

7 At the beginning of the eighteenth century, Father Laurent de Lucques noted that any young girl of the Congo who was not able to bear the pain of scarification and who cried so loudly that the operation had to be stopped was considered "good for nothing."[3] That is why, before marriage, men would check to see if the pattern traced on the belly of their intended bride was beautiful and well-detailed.

8 The fact that such motivations and pretexts depend on aesthetic, erotic, hygienic, or even medical considerations has no influence on the result, which is always in the direction of transforming the appearance of the body. Such a transformation is wished for, whether or not it is effective.

9 The body is a supple, malleable, and transformable prime material, a kind of modeling clay, easily molded by social will and wish. Human skin is an ideal subject for inscription, a surface for all sorts of marks which make it possible to differentiate the human from the animal. The physical body offers itself willingly for tattooing or scarring so that, visibly and recognizably, it becomes a social entity.

10 The absolutely naked body is considered as brutish, reduced to the level of nature where no distinction is made between man and beast. The decorated body, on the other hand, dressed (if even only in a belt), tattooed, or mutilated, publicly exhibits humanity and membership in an established group. As Theophile Gautier said, "The ideal disturbs even the roughest nature, and the taste for ornamentation distinguishes the intelligent being from

the beast more exactly than anything else. Indeed, dogs have never dreamed of putting on earrings."

So, it is by their categorical refusal of nakedness that human beings are distinguished from nature. The "mark makes unremarkable"—it creates an interval between what is biologically and brutally given in the animal realm and what is won in the cultural realm. The body is tamed continuously; social custom demands, at any price—including pain, constraint, or discomfort—that wildness be abandoned. 11

Each civilization chooses—through a network of elective relationships which are difficult to determine—which areas of the body deserve transformation. These areas are as difficult to define and as shifting as those of eroticism or modesty. An individual alone eludes bodily modifications; they are the expression of a homogeneous collectivity which, at a chosen moment, comes to a tacit agreement to attack one or another part of the anatomy. 12

Whatever the choices, options, or differences may be, that which remains constant is the transformation of appearance. In spite of our contemporary western belief that the body is perfect as it is, we are constantly changing it: clothing it in musculature, suntan, or makeup; dying its head hair or pulling out its bodily hair. The seemingly most innocent gestures for taking care of the body very often hide a persistent and disguised tendency to make it adhere to the strictest of norms, reclothing it in a veil of civilization. The total nudity offered at birth does not exist in any region of the world. Man puts his stamp on man. The body is not a product of nature, but of culture. 13

Notes

1. Of course, there are also many different sexual mutilations, including excisions and circumcisions, which we will not go into at this time as they constitute a whole study in themselves.
2. C. Lévi-Strauss, *Tristes Tropiques* (Paris: Plon, 1955), p. 214.
3. J. Cuvelier, *Relations sur le Congo du Père Laurent de Lucques* (Brussels: Institut royal colonial belge, 1953), p. 144.

Thinking Critically About Content

1. What does Borel mean when he says, "The body only speaks if it is dressed in artifice" (paragraph 2)?

ANSWERS TO QUESTIONS

Thinking Critically About Content

1. An unadorned body delivers no message.
2. People alter their bodies to portray particular aspects of their personalities, often to be more attractive to the opposite sex.
3. Body altering both creates a social group of humans (as it makes us different from animals) and different social groups within humans.

Thinking Critically About Purpose and Audience

4. Borel wrote the essay to explain why body decorating is so popular.
5. Both students and parents might be interested in this essay.
6. Answers will vary.

Thinking Critically About Essays

7. Here is Borel's thesis: "Aside from the most elementary caretaking concerns—

the very diversity of which shows how subjective the motivation is—an unfathomably deep and universal tendency pushes families, clans, and tribes to rapidly modify a person's physical appearance." This sentence comes at the end of the first paragraph.

8. The first part of the essay discusses why people decorate their bodies; the second part focuses on how.
9. It summarizes his main point about body alterations as social reactions.
10. Answers will vary.

TEACHING ON THE WEB
Discussion Topic: Divide students into groups of three or four, and have them discuss the many ways in which the Internet can help them search for a career or find a job. Have them list specific examples and then share them with the other groups.

TEACHING ON THE WEB
Links: Find Web sites that use examples. How does this mode help Internet users understand the purpose of the Web site?

2. According to Borel, what are the primary reasons people make changes in their appearance? Do you notice any common thread in these reasons?
3. In what ways is tattooing "a social entity" (paragraph 9)?

Thinking Critically About Purpose and Audience

4. What do you think France Borel's purpose is in this essay?
5. Do you think all students would be interested in this essay? What other groups would find this essay interesting? Why?
6. Do you think this essay might change someone's opinion about body decorations? Explain your answer.

Thinking Critically About Essays

7. What is the thesis of this essay?
8. Why do you think Borel divides this essay into two parts? What is the main idea of each part? Is this an effective way to break up this essay? Explain your answer.
9. In what way does the last sentence serve as a summary for the essay?
10. Were your views on any forms of body decoration changed as a result of reading this essay? If so, in what way? Explain your answer in detail.

Writing Workshop

This final section gives you opportunities to apply what you have learned in this chapter to another writing assignment. This time, we provide very little prompting beyond a summary of the guidelines for writing an illustration essay. This section will let you demonstrate that you can go through the entire writing process on your own with only occasional feedback from your peers. Loop back into the chapter as necessary when you have questions so that this process becomes as automatic to you as possible before you move on to new material. Then pause at the end of the chapter to reflect briefly on what you have learned.

Guidelines for Writing an Illustration Essay

1. State your main point in the last sentence of your introduction.
2. Choose examples that are relevant to your point.
3. Choose examples that your readers can identify with.
4. Use a sufficient number of examples to make your point.
5. Organize your examples to make your point in the clearest, strongest way.

Writing About Your Reading

1. Contemporary American society can't make up its mind about illegal immigrants. In some cases, Americans want to allow illegal immigrants to stay in the country; in other instances, Americans say that illegal immigrants should return to their home countries. How do you think this feud will be resolved? Give examples to explain your reasoning.
2. What are some of the differences between the generations regarding body decorations? What do you think accounts for these differences? Give examples to support your claims.
3. What do you think writers should consider first when choosing examples in an essay? How should the examples be related to the thesis statement? Why are these criteria important when working with examples?

Possible sites:

Sample Résumés, www.sampleresumes.com

Executed for Example, www.clarkehome58.freeserve.co.uk

Timothy's JavaScript Examples, www.essex1.com/people/timothy/js-index.htm

TEACHING ON THE WEB

Research: Give your students a controversial topic to research on the Web (for example, funding for stem cell research or the value of affirmative action), and have them find as many Web sites as possible that advocate either side of the issue. How do these Web sites collectively show students the usefulness of illustration?

Writing About Your World

1. Identify some common themes in this collage. Then come up with a thesis statement that explains the message of the collage. Write an essay to support your thesis that is developed with relevant examples from the picture and from your own experience to support your thesis statement.
2. Share with your classmates your opinion on a national issue, such as capital punishment, abortion, or gun laws. Use examples in your body paragraphs to support your main point.
3. Why do you think Americans are interested in exercise and weight loss? What actions illustrate this attitude? Use examples or illustrations to

explain your observations on the current interest in health and weight among Americans.

4. Create your own illustration assignment (with the help of your instructor), and write a response to it.

Revising

Small Group Activity (5–10 minutes per writer) Working in groups of three or four, read your illustration essays to each other. Those listening should record their reactions on a copy of the Peer Evaluation Form in Appendix 2C. After your group goes through this process, give your evaluation forms to the appropriate writers so that each writer has two or three peer comment sheets for revising.

Paired Activity (5 minutes per writer) Using the completed Peer Evaluation Forms, work in pairs to decide what you should revise in your essay. If time allows, rewrite some of your sentences, and have your partner look at them.

Individual Activity Rewrite your paper, using the revising feedback you received from other students.

Editing

Paired Activity (5–10 minutes per writer) Swap papers with a classmate, and use the editing portion of your Peer Evaluation Form to identify as many grammar, punctuation, mechanics, and spelling errors as you can. If time allows, correct some of your errors, and have your partner look at them. Record your grammar, punctuation, and mechanics errors in the Error Log (Appendix 6) and your spelling errors in the Spelling Log (Appendix 7).

Individual Activity Rewrite your paper again, using the editing feedback you received from other students.

Reflecting on Your Writing When you have completed your own essay, answer these six questions.

1. What was most difficult about this assignment?
2. What was easiest?
3. What did you learn about illustration by completing this assignment?
4. What do you think are the strengths of your illustration? Place a wavy line by the parts of your essay that you feel are very good.

5. What are the weaknesses, if any, of your paper? Place an X by the parts of your essay you would like help with. Write any questions you have in the margin.
6. What did you learn from this assignment about your own writing process—about preparing to write, about writing the first draft, about revising, and about editing?

CHAPTER

Analyzing a Process

"I see but one rule: to be clear."

—STENDHAL

TEACHING PROCESS ANALYSIS

Divide students into pairs. Using one circle, one triangle, one square, and one rectangle, have students draw an abstract picture. They should not let their partners see what they have drawn.

Once the pictures are drawn, have one student explain to the partner, step by step, how to draw the picture the student drew. Since the partners can't see the drawings, they can only use the instructions provided by the speaker. Once they have drawn their partners' pictures, have the students reverse roles.

When the students have all drawn their partners' pictures, have them show each other what they actually drew. How many students came close to drawing the correct picture? Use this exercise

Process analysis satisfies our natural desire for basic information—how to be more assertive, how to invest in the stock market, how to eat more healthfully, or how to help your child do a better job in school.

Process analysis writing, more than other types of writing, helps you understand the world around you and improve yourself—in your personal life, in college, and in the workplace. Consider the following situations:

- People who are coming to visit you from out of town e-mail you for directions to your house.
- A student needs to write a paper on how to improve employee morale for a course in business management.
- A student needs to explain how to be a good listener for the midterm exam in speech communication.
- The owner of an apartment building posts a notice in the laundry room explaining how to operate the new washers and dryers.
- The manager of a shoe store has to write a memo reminding employees about the correct procedure for taking returns.

Process analysis is a form of explaining. Process analysis essays fall into one of two main types—giving directions or giving information. The first type, giving directions, tells *how to do something*, such as how to write a research paper or change the oil in your car. The second type, giving information, analyzes *how something works*, such as satellite TV or a bread machine, or *how something happened*, such as how the Soviet Union broke into separate nations. In each case, the explanation starts at the beginning and moves step by step, usually in chronological order, to the end result. Process analysis can be about something mental (how to solve a math problem) or something physical (how to pitch a tent).

to show the importance of providing accurate directions when writing a process analysis.

READING AND WRITING A PROCESS ANALYSIS ESSAY

If you learn how to approach each rhetorical mode critically, these skills will transfer to your other college work. In fact, reading and writing are two parts of the same process. Reading process analysis essays critically involves understanding the steps of a process or sequence of an event and then going further to evaluate the steps or sequence. Are these steps the best way to create the final product or carry out the event? Would the results have been different with another approach? Dealing with this type of inquiry in both reading and writing will raise your level of thinking in all that you do.

Reading a Process Analysis Essay

In "Dare to Change Your Job and Your Life in 7 Steps," Carole Kanchler explains how to take the right risks in order to change jobs and improve your life. This essay demonstrates the first type of process analysis—how to do something. Have you ever held a job that you intensely disliked? Were you able to quit? Why or why not? Do you know what career you want to follow? What steps are you taking to prepare for it?

READING CRITICALLY

Recently, students are finding that making drawings of the ideas and details in their readings is a much more effective way to understand them and see how they work than outlining. Graphic organizers, or concept maps, let you literally "draw" the relationship of ideas to one another. Figuring out what framework to use for this exercise is part of the process. You can make up a drawing of your own or do a Web search for "graphic organizers" to see some options. After you read the following essay, show the relationship of the ideas to one another in a graphic form that makes sense to you. Be prepared to explain your drawing.

TEACHING TIPS

The following eight teaching tips are based on Howard Gardner's multiple intelligences:

Verbal/Linguistic

Have students take a difficult how-to document that you supply (for example, directions for assembling a bicycle), and put it into words that make the process easy to understand.

Musical/Rhythmic

Have students explain the steps of a musical process, such as playing the guitar, using a metronome, or singing a song. How will the music sound if even one step is left out?

Logical/Mathematical

Have students list the steps people need to take for logging on to the Internet. Have one person read the list while another demonstrates it. What would happen if one small step were left out?

Visual/Spatial

Have students watch a documentary to determine how something happened. How well did the documentary account for everything that occurred? Were there any gaps in the film?

Bodily/Kinesthetic

Put students in pairs, and blindfold one of the two in each pair. Have the blindfolded student tell the other student how to do an activity while the other student follows the directions. Make sure students know that if, for instance, the blindfolded student gives the direction to walk through a doorway without saying to open the door, the other student cannot progress beyond the closed door. When the instructions are complete, have the blindfolded students guess where they are.

Intrapersonal

Have students think of the process they typically go through before they write a paper. Does this ritual ever change? What steps may be different from assignment to assignment?

Interpersonal

Divide students into small groups of three or four. Have them list the steps to a process that all students would most likely know (for example, ordering a pizza or making a sandwich), but have them omit some seemingly insignificant steps. See if the other groups can find the omissions.

Naturalist

Have students explain the steps for an outdoor

DARE TO CHANGE YOUR JOB AND YOUR LIFE IN 7 STEPS

by Carole Kanchler

1 Small, dark-haired, attractive, and warm, Melissa belies her 44 years. In a sharp gray suit and becoming blouse, she projects a professional yet approachable image. She is now director of training and development for a large retail outlet—and loves it.

2 "I feel good about myself," she says, "and at the end of the day, I have lots of energy left over." Melissa feels content because she believes she is doing something worthwhile. Her new position gives her life meaning and purpose. But getting there wasn't easy.

3 First a flight attendant, then a high school English teacher, then a manager in a retail store, Melissa stumbled about from what was for her one dead-end job to another. How did she finally find a meaningful, fulfilling, well-paid career? And how did she do what so many of us fail to do—dare to change?

4 A career change can take months or even years of soul-searching—10 months in Melissa's case. You need to know the steps, how to master the troublesome feelings that accompany change, where the possible dangers lie, and how to maximize your gains while minimizing your losses. While creating a life worth living isn't easy, Melissa and millions of others have shown that anything is possible.

5 In interviews and surveys with more than 30,000 people over the past 25 years, I have identified seven steps that are key to a successful career and life shift.

1. Become AWARE of Negative Feelings

6 Your body and mind may be sending you messages about your job satisfaction. The messages may be physical—lingering colds, flu, or headaches—or verbal—"23 minutes till lunch!" or "One more day till Friday!"

7 Perhaps you've been working for several years in your job, and it appears to be going well. You've had steady promotions, praise from superiors, and admiration from colleagues. Then one day you get a queasy feeling that something is lacking. But what? You run the film of your life in reverse but you can't figure it out. These feelings may persist for months or even years, depending on your ability to tolerate them, but, sooner or later, you have to admit you have a problem.

2. DEFINE the Problem

8 A good written definition of your problem can help to put you on the road toward change.

9 First, ask yourself, "What's making me feel this way? What is it about my situation that is unpleasant? Does this job help me reach my goals?" If not, why?

10 Next, describe any barriers that may be blocking you from making a move—perhaps fear of change; fear of losing a secure income, pension or other benefits; fear that the change will interfere with your relationships; or fear that you'll lose power or status.

11 Fear is the result of conditioning, and because it is learned, it can be unlearned. Reprogram your old attitudes and beliefs with new ones by learning and practicing specific ways to overcome the fears blocking your path toward change. Think of FEAR as an acronym for "False Expectations Appear Real." Don't spend time worrying about what might happen. Focus on the now.

3. Listen to AMBIVALENCE

12 Milton, a rehabilitation counselor, was approached by a prospective partner to start an executive recruitment agency. For weeks before making the move, he went straight to bed immediately after dinner and pulled the sheets up over his head. He tried to make light of this behavior, but he had undertaken many risks before and had never felt this way about them.

13 His underlying fears were prophetic. He later discovered that the hard-sell, aggressive style required for executive recruiting was not for him. The difference in basic values between Milton and his partner proved such a handicap that, within five months, the two parted ways.

14 The decision to change can provoke mixed feelings. A certain amount of ambivalence is natural. Inner emotional preparation—weighing losses as well as gains, fears as well as hopes—is a necessary prerequisite for successful risk taking.

15 But if the prospect of undertaking a change is so great that your stomach is churning, you can't sleep, you have constant headaches. or you feel you're developing an ulcer, your body, in its wisdom, is telling you to forgo the risk.

4. PREPARE for Risk

16 The key to avoiding potential potholes is to set tentative career goals before you explore new roads. Goals force you to focus on what you really want. Years from now, as you review your life, what would you regret not having done?

adventure, such as making a campfire, preparing a fish for cooking, or getting into a canoe. What is the consequence if one step is missing?

INSTRUCTOR'S RESOURCE MANUAL

For additional material about teaching process analysis; for journal entries; and for multiple-choice, short-answer, and paragraph tests, see the *Instructor's Resource Manual*, Section II, Part II.

17 Fantasize about the ultimate goal, your shining star. If you could do anything in the world, what would it be? Write all of your ideas or fantasies in a notebook. Include everything you want to do, be, and have. The sky is the limit. Once you know what you want, you'll be more willing to take the risks necessary to achieve it.

18 Choosing a satisfying career and lifestyle also requires a basic understanding of yourself. A variety of exercises can help. To identify your strengths, for example, list some of the successes you've had—say, substituting for your son's soccer coach. Next to each success, identify what gave you the positive feelings. Did you contribute to the team's first win of the season?

19 Also list the skills and abilities you used to bring about that success. Were you well organized and adept at working with parents? Finally, decide how your interests, needs, accomplishments, and other personal strengths add up. What pattern do they form?

20 Self-exploration is just part of the process. You also need to take a careful look at your current situation, as well as the available alternatives. Some popular reference tools, available at your local library, can help. Check out the *Occupational Handbook,* the *Dictionary of Occupational Titles,* and the *Encyclopedia of Careers and Work Issues.* The Internet also offers excellent sites for exploring general occupational fields, job descriptions, and educational opportunities.

5. NARROW Your Options

21 Successful career management hinges on finding a position that's compatible with your personal qualities and goals. Do you have the necessary intelligence and skills to do the work? Can you afford the training required for the job? Might your shortcomings—health, vision, size, or strength, for example—pose a problem?

22 To help narrow your options, draw a series of vertical and horizontal lines so that your paper is divided into squares. Across the top of the page, list the most important elements of your ideal job: income, responsibility, public image, creativity, challenge, and so on (one in each square). Down the left side of the page, list each occupational option you're considering.

23 Next, for each alternative, place a −1 in the appropriate box if that job option doesn't satisfy the criterion listed at the top of the page. If the criterion is met, but not as much as you'd like, record a 0. If the criterion is well met, record a +1. Add the points for each job option and place them in a column labeled "total" at the far right. The job with the highest score meets the greatest number of criteria that you have deemed important.

6. Take ACTION

Once you've determined your occupational goal, take steps to realize it. You'll need a well-planned campaign to market yourself for the job, establish your own business, or return to school. 24

Stay focused on your goals, and believe you will achieve them. View failures along the way as learning experiences—detours that might offer an unexpected dividend. 25

7. EVALUATE the Decision

When you have worked hard at making a decision, take the time not just to enjoy the outcome, but to evaluate it. Ask yourself 26

- Do I feel good about the move?
- What other gains did I derive from the move? What did I lose?
- What factors contributed to the success of my move?
- If I could do it all over again, what would I do differently?
- Who was most helpful in the process? Who let me down?

Evaluation is a continuous process. Assess your needs, goals, and job satisfaction periodically to determine if your developing personality fits your position and lifestyle. Don't wait for a crisis to clear your vision. 27

There really is no substitute for risk as a way to grow. Knowing you have honestly faced the painful struggle and accepted the trade-offs, and yet proceeded in spite of them, is extremely gratifying. 28

Melissa learned that the tremendous investment of energy a successful job search demands is exactly what enables people to look back and say, "Win, lose, or draw, I gave it my everything." Being able to say with satisfaction that you risked for a dream may be the biggest prize of all. 29

To remain fulfilled, however, you'll need to risk again and again until you've created a life in which you feel comfortable being yourself, without apology or pretense—a life in which you can continue to have choices. 30

Preparing to Write Your Own Process Analysis Essay

Think of some advice you would like to give to a friend or classmate—for example, how to survive your first year of college, how to find the partner of your dreams, how to buy a used car, or how to find good daycare for your child. Use one or more of the prewriting strategies you learned in Chapter 2 to generate ideas about advice you have for others.

Writing a Process Analysis Essay

Both types of process analysis call for careful step-by-step thinking, but especially the first—how to do something. If you leave out even one detail, you may confuse your reader or even endanger someone's life. If, for example, you forget to tell a patient who is coming to a doctor's office for some tests that she shouldn't eat after midnight and she has breakfast, the test results will not be accurate, and a serious medical condition might go unnoticed.

Good process analysis of the second type—how something works or how something happened—can help your reader see a product or an event in a totally new light. Someone looking at a product that is already assembled or at a completed event has no way of knowing how it got to the final stage without an explanation. Good process analysis gives the reader a new way of "seeing" something. The following guidelines will help you write clear and complete process analysis essays.

1. **State in the thesis statement what the reader should be able to do or understand by the end of the essay.** Stating the end result at the beginning, in the thesis statement, gives your readers a road map for what follows. The thesis statement in a process essay should also state the number of steps or stages in the process. For example, someone giving directions might start by saying, "It's easy to get to the library from here with just four turns." Even if a process involves many separate steps, you should divide the list into a few manageable groups: "Most experts agree that there are four stages in overcoming an addiction." Stating the end result and the number of steps or stages in the thesis statement helps the reader follow your explanation. These statements set up the tasks.

   Carole Kanchler's thesis statement, which appears in paragraph 5 at the end of her introduction, tells her readers exactly what they will be able to do by the end of her article: make "a successful career and life shift." She also tells them how many steps are involved—seven. In this way, she gives a very clear road map for reading her essay.

2. **Know your audience.** In a process analysis essay, more than in others, the success of your essay depends on how well you know your audience. Knowing your audience helps you decide how much detail to include, how many examples to add, and which terms to define. Also keep in mind that your readers won't be able to ask you questions, so if they can't follow your explanation, they will become confused and frustrated. Whoever your audience is, explaining clearly is essential.

   Kanchler's essay was first published in *Psychology Today*, which is read mostly by educated adults. The author's audience seems to be working adults of any age who are unhappy in their jobs. Kanchler addresses them in a very businesslike way; she doesn't talk down. Knowing that being unhappy in a job is very depressing, she strives for an upbeat "you can do it" tone.

3. **Explain the process clearly in the body of your essay.** By the end of a how-to essay, the reader should be able to perform the activity. By the end of a how-something-works essay, the reader should understand what is going on behind the scenes, and by the end of a how-something-happened essay, the reader should understand more about a specific event.

   In writing the body paragraphs of a process essay, pay special attention to transitions. Use transitions such as *first, next, then, after that,* and *finally* to guide your readers through the process from beginning to end.

   Since Kanchler's process has seven parts, she numbers each step. This is a good idea if a process is complicated. If you are writing about a process with only three or four steps, you can use transitions to indicate to your readers where you are in the process.

4. **Organize your material logically.** Most process analysis essays are organized chronologically or according to a time sequence. The explanation starts at one point and progresses through time to the final point. If a process is complicated, figure out the most logical organization for the process you are explaining. For instance, playing the guitar involves pressing the strings with the fingers of one hand and strumming with the other hand. You might therefore explain each part of the process separately and then explain how the hands work together to make music.

   Kanchler's essay is organized chronologically. She moves from recognizing the problem to taking action and then to evaluating the action. To help readers follow along smoothly, she numbers the steps and uses transitions such as *first, next,* and *then.*

5. **End your essay by considering the process as a whole.** Don't just stop after you have explained the last step of a process. Instead, in the conclusion, look at the process as a whole. There are many ways to do this. You might state why knowing about this process is important: Knowing how to perform CPR (cardiopulmonary resuscitation) can save a life; knowing how your car runs might save you money in repair bills. Or you might review your introduction, summarize the steps of the process, call for action, or end with a fitting quotation. Whatever your method, leave your reader feeling that your essay has reached a natural close.

   Kanchler concludes by returning to her introduction. She brings back Melissa, the person from the opening example, to emphasize the rewards of taking risks. She ends her essay by saying that a satisfying life requires taking risks again and again.

Writing Your Own Process Analysis Essay

Look at the prewriting you did earlier on the topic of giving advice to a friend or classmate. If your directions involve many steps, divide them into three groups. Come up with a thesis statement that states the end result of the process and tells how many steps or stages are involved. Then write the first draft of your essay by following the guidelines for writing a process analysis essay. Make sure you have an introduction and a conclusion.

A STUDENT'S PROCESS ANALYSIS ESSAY

A student writer named Emily Bliss wrote the following essay about procrastination. See if you can follow her steps as you read her first draft.

You Too Can Procrastinate

1 My name is Emily, and I am a procrastinator. But I have discovered over the years that procrastination is not all bad. Especially when I have to write. At my college, the English instructors requires rough drafts. I have somehow mastered the art of procrastinating but still meeting deadlines with my papers. So I have perfected a successful plan for procrastinating that I now want to share with the world.

2 You will know the dreaded day you have to write has arrived when you wake up with a start. This day is different from the rest. You actually have to do something about your paper today. But whatever you do, resist the temptation to sit down and write early in the day by following two more steps. First (step 1), to avoid sitting down to write, you can clean, take a bike ride, do the laundry, rearrange the furniture, dust the light bulbs, and so on. But don't write. Then (step 2), when you finally think you are ready to start writing, call a friend. Talk about anything but your paper for about 15 or 20 minutes. This final delay is what creates the tension that a real procrastinator needs to do his or her best work.

3 Whether you want to or not, you will naturally think about the assignment from the moment you get it. If you have two weeks or two months, you will spend most quiet moments haunted by your paper topic. No matter what you do, your paper topic will be bouncing around in your head giving you

headaches, making you worry, wanting attention. But that's OK. Don't give in and write. Ignore it until the day before it is due.

At this point, your third step is to prepare your immediate environment for work. You need to get ready for serious business. Sharpen your pencils, and lay them in a row. Get out the white paper if you can't think on yellow, or get out the yellow paper if you can't think on white. Go to the kitchen for snacks. Whether or not you actually drink or eat these item's is irrelevant—as long as they are by your side. You can't be distracted if you don't have them next to you. My stomach growls really loudly when I'm hungry. Some sort of bread usually takes away the hunger pangs. Step 4 is to sit back in your chair and stare at the computer while you think long and hard about your paper. Fifth, brainstorm, list, or cluster your ideas on the colored paper of your choice. Sixth, put all your procrastination strategies aside. Its finally time to write. 4

If you follow these six simple steps, you too can become a master procrastinator. You can perform your very own procrastinating ritual and still get your first draft in on time. If you go through the same ritual every time you write. You can perfect it and get your own system for writing essays down to a science. The trick is just to make sure you start writing before you has to join Procrastinators Anonymous. 5

Discovering How the Essay Works

1. What should the reader be able to do by the end of this essay?

   Procrastinate and still meet deadlines

2. Who do you think Emily's audience is? Does she meet their needs?

   Her audience is students who might have to write papers. Her advice might be helpful to them.

3. Do you understand how to procrastinate and still meet your deadlines? If so, list the six steps of this process.

   Step 1: *Do chores to avoid writing.*

   Step 2: *Call a friend.*

   Step 3: *Prepare your environment for writing.*

   Step 4: *Think about your paper while you stare at your computer.*

Step 5: *Brainstorm, list, or cluster.*

Step 6: *Write.*

If you do not understand, what else do you need to know?

Answers will vary.

4. Are the details in the essay organized logically? Is this order effective for what the author is trying to say? Why or why not?

Paragraph 3 is out of order, but the rest of the essay is organized chronologically. It is effective because the writer clearly outlines the steps of the process.

5. Does the essay conclude by considering the process as a whole? Explain your answer.

Emily concludes by reminding students that procrastination is really prewriting. Her reference to "Procrastinators Anonymous" refers to her introduction and brings her essay to a clever end.

REVISING AND EDITING OPTIONS
Consider varying your approach to revising and editing. You could teach these skills in a class discussion, in small groups, or in pairs.

REVISING STRATEGIES
This chapter focuses on the following revising elements:
Thesis statement
Basic elements
Development
Unity
Organization

Revising and Editing the Student Essay

This essay is Emily's first draft, which now needs to be revised and edited. First, apply the following Revising Checklist to the content of Emily's draft. When you are satisfied that her ideas are fully developed and well organized, use the Editing Checklist on page 236 to correct her grammar and mechanics errors. Do the tasks, and answer the questions after each checklist. Then write your suggested changes directly on Emily's draft.

REVISING CHECKLIST

THESIS STATEMENT

✔ Does the thesis statement contain the essay's controlling idea?

✔ Does the thesis appear as the last sentence of the introduction?

BASIC ELEMENTS

✔ Does the title draw in the readers?

✔ Does the introduction capture the readers' attention and build up to the thesis statement effectively?

✔ Does each body paragraph deal with a single topic?

✔ Does the conclusion bring the essay to a close in an interesting way?

DEVELOPMENT

✔ Do the body paragraphs adequately support the thesis statement?

✔ Does each body paragraph have a focused topic sentence?

✔ Does each body paragraph contain *specific* details that support the topic sentence?

✔ Does each body paragraph include *enough* details to explain the topic sentence fully?

UNITY

✔ Do the essay's topic sentences relate directly to the thesis statement?

✔ Do the details in each body paragraph support its topic sentence?

ORGANIZATION

✔ Is the essay organized logically?

✔ Is each body paragraph organized logically?

COHERENCE

✔ Are transitions used effectively so that paragraphs move smoothly and logically from one to the next?

✔ Do the sentences move smoothly and logically from one to the next?

Thesis Statement

1. Put brackets around the last sentence in Emily's introduction. Does it state her purpose?

   Yes, but it is incomplete.

2. Rewrite Emily's thesis statement if necessary so that it introduces her process and states her purpose.

   Here is one possibility: So I have perfected a successful plan of six easy steps for procrastination that I now want to share with the world.

Basic Elements

1. Give Emily's essay an alternate title.

   Answers will vary.

2. Rewrite Emily's introduction so that it captures the readers' attention and builds up to the thesis statement at the end of the introduction.

   Answers will vary.

3. Does each of Emily's body paragraphs deal with only one topic?

   Yes

4. Rewrite Emily's conclusion using at least one suggestion from Part I.

   Answers will vary.

Development

1. Write out Emily's thesis statement (revised, if necessary), and list her three topic sentences below it. *Thesis may vary.*

   Thesis statement: *So I have perfected a successful plan of six easy steps for procrastination that I now want to share with the world.*

   Topic 1: *You will know the dreaded day you have to write has arrived when you wake up with a start.*

   Topic 2: *Whether you want to or not, you will naturally think about the assignment from the moment you get it.*

Topic 3: *At this point, your third step is to prepare your immediate environment for work.*

2. Do Emily's topics adequately support her thesis statement?

   Yes

3. Do Emily's details in the essay explain the process step by step?

   Yes

4. Where do you need more information?

   She could provide more examples for steps 4, 5, and 6.

5. Add at least two new details to make the steps clearer. *Answers will vary.*

Unity

1. Read each of Emily's topic sentences with her thesis statement (revised, if necessary) in mind. Do they go together?

   Answers will vary.

2. Revise her topic sentences if necessary so they are directly related.
3. Drop or rewrite the two sentences in paragraph 4 that are not directly related to their topic sentence. *Sentences 8 and 9*

Organization

1. Read Emily's essay again to see if all the paragraphs are arranged logically. Look at your list of steps in response to question 3 after Emily's essay.
2. Reverse the two paragraphs that are out of order. *Reverse paragraphs 2 and 3.*
3. Look closely at Emily's body paragraphs to see if all her sentences are arranged logically within paragraphs.
4. Move any sentences that are out of order. *All sentences are in order.*

For a list of transitions, see page 101.

Coherence

1. Circle five transitions Emily uses.

2. Explain how two of these make Emily's essay easier to read.

Answers will vary.

Now rewrite Emily's essay with your revisions.

EDITING STRATEGIES
This chapter focuses on the following editing problems:
Fragments
Subject-verb agreement
Apostrophes (contractions)

EDITING CHECKLIST

SENTENCES

✓ Does each sentence have a main subject and verb?
✓ Do all subjects and verbs agree?
✓ Do all pronouns agree with their nouns?
✓ Are modifiers as close as possible to the words they modify?

PUNCTUATION AND MECHANICS

✓ Are sentences punctuated correctly?
✓ Are words capitalized properly?

WORD CHOICE AND SPELLING

✓ Are words used correctly?
✓ Are words spelled correctly?

Sentences

Subjects and Verbs

For help with subjects and verbs, see Chapter 25.

1. Underline the subjects once and verbs twice in paragraphs 1 and 5 of your revision of Emily's essay. Remember that sentences can have more than one subject-verb set.
2. Does each of the sentences have at least one subject and verb that can stand alone?

   No

For help with fragments, see Chapter 26.

3. Did you find and correct Emily's two fragments? If not, find and correct them now. *Paragraph 1, sentence 3; paragraph 5, sentence 3*

Subject-Verb Agreement

For help with subject-verb agreement, see Chapter 30.

1. Read aloud the subjects and verbs you underlined in your revision of Emily's essay.

2. Did you find and correct the two subjects and verbs that do not agree? If not, find and correct them now. *Paragraph 1, sentence 4; paragraph 5, sentence 5*

Pronoun Agreement

1. Find any pronouns in your revision of Emily's essay that do not agree with their nouns. *All pronouns agree with their nouns.*
2. Correct any pronouns that do not agree with their nouns.

For help with pronoun agreement, see Chapter 34.

Modifiers

1. Find any modifiers in your revision of Emily's essay that are not as close as possible to the words they modify. *There are no modifier errors.*
2. Rewrite sentences if necessary so that modifiers are as close as possible to the words they modify.

For help with modifier errors, see Chapter 37.

Punctuation and Mechanics

Punctuation

1. Read your revision of Emily's essay for any errors in punctuation.
2. Find the two fragments you revised, and make sure they are punctuated correctly.
3. Did you find and correct Emily's two apostrophe errors? If not, find and correct them now. *Paragraph 4, sentences 6 and 13*

For help with punctuation, see Chapters 38–42.

Mechanics

1. Read your revision of Emily's essay for any errors in capitalization.
2. Be sure to check Emily's capitalization in the fragments you revised.

For help with capitalization, see Chapter 43.

Word Choice and Spelling

Word Choice

1. Find any words used incorrectly in your revision of Emily's essay. *All words are used correctly.*
2. Correct any errors you find.

For help with confused words, see Chapter 49.

Spelling

1. Use spell-check or a dictionary to check the spelling in your revision of Emily's essay. *All words are spelled correctly.*
2. Correct any misspelled words.

For help with spelling, see Chapter 50.

Now rewrite Emily's essay again with your editing corrections.

YOUR OWN PROCESS ANALYSIS ESSAY

Returning to the process analysis you wrote earlier in this chapter, you are now going to revise and edit your own writing. Remember that revision comes before editing and requires you to work with the content and organization of your essay while editing asks you to check your grammar and usage. The more you repeat these processes, the better draft you will write. Make sure your essay fulfills its stated purpose.

WRITING CRITICALLY

As you set out to revise and edit your essay, apply the strategy you learned for critical reading to your writing. Draw a picture of the relationship of your ideas to one another. In this way, you can check for logic and organization and make any changes that you think are necessary at this time. Then, you can turn to grammar and usage.

CLASS ACTIVITY

Put on the board or overhead projector a how-to paragraph that is filled with jargon or technical terms. Ask the class to determine what is wrong with the paragraph. Remind students to consider their audience and to be sure that their words are clear; for example, they should be careful not to tell a new employee to "do a JE to compensate for the credit balance in the AR" if the employee has no accounting experience.

Revising and Editing Your Own Essay

The checklists here will help you apply what you have learned in this chapter to your writing.

REVISING CHECKLIST

THESIS STATEMENT

- ☐ Does the thesis statement contain the essay's controlling idea?
- ☐ Does the thesis appear as the last sentence of the introduction?

BASIC ELEMENTS

- ☐ Does the title draw in the readers?
- ☐ Does the introduction capture the readers' attention and build up to the thesis statement effectively?
- ☐ Does each body paragraph deal with a single topic?
- ☐ Does the conclusion bring the essay to a close in an interesting way?

DEVELOPMENT

- ☐ Do the body paragraphs adequately support the thesis statement?
- ☐ Does each body paragraph have a focused topic sentence?
- ☐ Does each body paragraph contain *specific* details that support the topic sentence?

- ☐ Does each body paragraph include *enough* details to explain the topic sentence fully?

UNITY

- ☐ Do the essay's topic sentences relate directly to the thesis statement?
- ☐ Do the details in each body paragraph support its topic sentence?

ORGANIZATION

- ☐ Is the essay organized logically?
- ☐ Is each body paragraph organized logically?

COHERENCE

- ☐ Are transitions used effectively so that paragraphs move smoothly and logically from one to the next?
- ☐ Do the sentences move smoothly and logically from one to the next?

Thesis Statement

1. What is your purpose in the essay?

   ____

2. Put brackets around the last sentence in your introduction. Does it state your purpose?

   ____

3. Revise your thesis statement if necessary so that it states your purpose and introduces your topics.

Basic Elements

1. Give your essay a title if it doesn't have one.

   ____

2. Does your introduction capture your readers' attention and build up to your thesis statement at the end of the paragraph?

   ____

3. Does each of your paragraphs deal with only one topic?

   ____

4. Does your conclusion follow some of the suggestions offered in Part I?

____

Development

1. Write out your thesis statement (revised, if necessary), and list your topic sentences below it.

   Thesis statement: ________________________________

   Topic 1: ________________________________

   Topic 2: ________________________________

   Topic 3: ________________________________

2. Do your topics adequately support your thesis statement?

____

3. Does each body paragraph have a focused topic sentence?

____

4. Do the details in your essay explain the process step by step?

____

5. Where do you need more information?

____

6. Add at least two new details to make the steps clearer.

Unity

1. Read each of your topic sentences with your thesis statement in mind. Do they go together?

____

2. Revise your topic sentences if necessary so they are directly related.
3. Drop or rewrite any of the sentences in your body paragraphs that are not directly related to their topic sentences.

Organization

1. List the steps in your essay to make sure your process analysis is in chronological order.
2. Move any steps or paragraphs that are out of order.
3. What word clues help your readers move logically through your essay?

   ____

4. Look closely at your body paragraphs to see if all the sentences are arranged logically within paragraphs.
5. Move any sentences that are out of order.

Coherence

1. Circle five transitions you use.
2. Explain how two of these make your essay easier to read.

   ____

   ____

For a list of transitions, see page 101.

Now rewrite your essay with your revisions.

EDITING CHECKLIST

SENTENCES

- ☐ Does each sentence have a main subject and verb?
- ☐ Do all subjects and verbs agree?
- ☐ Do all pronouns agree with their nouns?
- ☐ Are modifiers as close as possible to the words they modify?

PUNCTUATION AND MECHANICS

- ☐ Are sentences punctuated correctly?
- ☐ Are words capitalized properly?

WORD CHOICE AND SPELLING

- ☐ Are words used correctly?
- ☐ Are words spelled correctly?

Sentences

Subjects and Verbs

For help with subjects and verbs, see Chapter 25.

1. Underline your subjects once and verbs twice in a paragraph of your revised essay. Remember that sentences can have more than one subject-verb set.
2. Does each of your sentences have at least one subject and verb that can stand alone?

____

For help with fragments, see Chapter 26.

For help with run-togethers, see Chapter 27.

3. Correct any fragments you have written.
4. Correct any run-together sentences you have written.

Subject-Verb Agreement

For help with subject-verb agreement, see Chapter 30.

1. Read aloud the subjects and verbs you underlined in your revised essay.
2. Correct any subjects and verbs that do not agree.

Pronoun Agreement

For help with pronoun agreement, see Chapter 34.

1. Find any pronouns in your revised essay that do not agree with their nouns.
2. Correct any pronouns that do not agree with their nouns.

Modifiers

For help with modifier errors, see Chapter 37.

1. Find any modifiers in your revised essay that are not as close as possible to the words they modify.
2. Rewrite sentences if necessary so that your modifiers are as close as possible to the words they modify.

Punctuation and Mechanics

Punctuation

For help with punctuation, see Chapters 38–42.

1. Read your revised essay for any errors in punctuation.
2. Make sure any fragments and run-together sentences you revised are punctuated correctly.

Mechanics

For help with capitalization, see Chapter 43.

1. Read your revised essay for any errors in capitalization.
2. Be sure to check your capitalization in any fragments or run-together sentences you revised.

Word Choice and Spelling

Word Choice

1. Find any words used incorrectly in your revised essay.
2. Correct any errors you find.

For help with confused words, see Chapter 49.

Spelling

1. Use spell-check or a dictionary to check your spelling.
2. Correct any misspelled words.

For help with spelling, see Chapter 50.

Now rewrite your essay again with your editing corrections.

PRACTICING PROCESS ANALYSIS: FROM READING TO WRITING

Reading Workshop

Here are two essays that illustrate good process analysis writing: "Don't Be Cruel" by Dr. Roger Flax explains how to criticize people without humiliating them, and "Why We Have a Moon" by David Levy explains the role of the moon in relation to the earth. As you read, notice how the writers explain every step of the process carefully and completely.

DON'T BE CRUEL

by Roger Flax

Focusing Your Attention

1. Think of a time when you had to explain to someone how to do something. Was it an easy or a difficult task? Did the person understand you? Was the person able to follow your directions?
2. In the process analysis essay you are about to read, the writer tells us how to criticize other people effectively. Have you ever wanted to tell someone about something he or she did wrong without ruining the relationship? What did you do to solve the problem?

Expanding Your Vocabulary

The following words are important to your understanding of this essay. As you read, circle any words you don't know beyond this list. Then break

SUMMARY
Flax provides a step-by-step process of reprimanding employees while simultaneously motivating them to perform better.

READABILITY
(Flesch–Kincaid grade level)
10.6

INSTRUCTOR'S RESOURCE MANUAL
For additional teaching strategies, for journal

entries, for vocabulary and reading quizzes, and for more writing assignments, see the *Instructor's Resource Manual*, Section II, Part II.

into groups, and help each other figure out the meanings of these unknown words.

coronary: heart attack (paragraph 1)

mercilessly: cruelly (paragraph 1)

reprimands: expressions of disapproval (paragraph 4)

manager-subordinate scenarios: boss-employee situations (paragraph 4)

Project Management Work Teams: groups of individuals who work together in the workforce to improve their management style (paragraph 7)

rapport: sense of trust (paragraph 10)

repercussions: results or effects (paragraph 14)

malice: desire to cause harm or suffering (paragraph 16)

facilitate: guide (paragraph 20)

implementation: the act of putting something into practice (paragraph 21)

misconstrues: misunderstands (paragraph 21)

stroke: flatter, compliment (paragraph 22)

perennial: constant (paragraph 29)

belittle: say negative things about a person (paragraph 31)

READING CRITICALLY

As you learned at the beginning of this chapter, practice drawing graphic organizers for the ideas in this essay. Exchange "pictures" with someone in your class, and write a brief statement of what your classmate's drawing communicates to you.

DON'T BE CRUEL

by Roger Flax

1 Picture this scenario: Seymour Axshun (we'll call him), a terrific manager who has been a loyal employee for several years, messes up on an assignment. He misses a deadline on a proposal and that three-day delay costs

the company $9,100. Seymour's boss, Sy Kottick, has a near coronary over the incident, lashes out at Seymour, and criticizes him mercilessly. In front of four of Seymour's co-workers, Kottick shouts, "Axshun, how many times do I have to tell you to be more efficient with your planning? You blew it, and your mistake will cost us almost $10,000. I don't know what it takes to drill into your head that you must meet deadlines. It's disgusting, and I'm fed up. If you treated the money as if it were your own, you wouldn't be so careless."

"Incidentally, Seymour, on another issue, don't you think you should come to work dressed a bit more professionally? That suit you wore yesterday was a bit outdated, especially since we had our big client, Meyer Fivis, here. And one more thing, while we're at it Seymour. . . ." 2

Seymour shrinks from humiliation. He wishes he could push a button and disappear. He looks around him and sees four embarrassed colleagues. His boss storms out of the room and slams the door. 3

This thoughtless, but real-life, managerial scenario happens every minute of every day, in every city of every state. People insensitively and ruthlessly come down on others with reprimands and criticisms that leave permanent scars. And it happens not only in manager-subordinate scenarios, but in parent-child relationships, teacher-student interfaces, sports coach–player affairs, and friendships. 4

It's called *unconstructive, unmotivational criticism* or, in better words, *relationship breaking.* 5

Put yourself in Seymour Axshun's shoes. Would you ever want to work for that jerk again? And if you did, how dedicated would you really be? How motivated would you be to make him look good? 6

The two most critical assets of companies are people and time. Valuable people are hard to replace, and time is irreplaceable. With the evolution of Project Management Work Teams in companies throughout the world, it's absolutely imperative that team leaders and managers master the art of giving constructive, tactful, motivational criticism. After all, if the goal of the project group is to work as a team to attain a goal, unconstructive criticism can destroy the group quickly. *Motivation magic,* as I call it, can only enhance the team. 7

You shouldn't be a robot when giving constructive criticism, but there is a human-relations approach that does work. Here's a several-step process to follow the next time you have to reprimand another person, but truly want to motivate that person and enhance the relationship. 8

1. *Always begin constructive criticism with a positive statement.* Open with an energizing comment that builds up the person's esteem and sincerely expresses your approval and support on a specific item. For 9

example, in the Seymour Axshun incident, why not begin with, "Seymour, you've done an outstanding job in the Quality Improvement Program, and the results are quickly having an impact on our operation. Many people have commented to me about your great work."

10 2. *Never follow that complimentary opening remark with "but" or "however."* Those words immediately eliminate the good feeling and rapport initiated by the compliment. The person will quickly surmise that the opening statement was merely lip service—a manipulative tool geared to set up the reprimand or criticism. It's very natural, and even habitual, to say "but" or "however" after you open with a positive statement, but it will destroy the initial goodwill created and result in perceived insincerity.

11 3. *Use the acronym PEN to plan and verbalize the actual criticism.*

P—Problem. State the problem that exists. Be concise and to the point. Remember: Don't begin expressing the problem with "but" or "however."

E—Example. Give an example or two that clearly supports the problem or reason for criticism. Get your facts straight, and keep them brief. The lengthier the criticism is, the more painful it becomes.

N—Negative Impact. Let the person know what negative effects have resulted from the problem or action. It's important to do some planning before the criticism session. Think through your PEN before giving it. It will come across more concisely, smoothly, and convincingly.

12 4. *Avoid using the word "you" when giving the actual criticism.* This is definitely the most important rule to remember. Discipline yourself to criticize the object or the problem, not the person. Don't let yourself say "you"—it's accusatory, threatening and puts the criticism on a personal, emotional, confrontational level.

13 Example: "Seymour, you've done an outstanding job in the Quality Improvement Program, and the results are quickly having an impact on our operation. There's one situation that could be improved upon, and that is meeting deadlines. On one occasion this month, a deadline was missed by three days, and that has cost our company several thousand dollars. The negative effects not only include a large dollar loss, but a potential loss in credibility for future dealings."

Now go back and read the opening example—the confrontational, 14
insensitive way of criticizing. Notice in the second example that the criticizer avoided the word "you" (except for the opening praise) and dealt with the problem, not the person. You need to practice this technique over and over again. Don't just use it at work, but also use it with your spouse, children, friends, relatives—everyone. It goes a long way in relationship building and effective human relations, and it reduces the enormous repercussions that can occur from giving cutthroat criticism.

Of course, it's okay to use "you" when you're praising the person or 15
engaging in a subsequent dialogue after the initial criticism has been communicated. However, the word "you" should be avoided when the actual bad news is being stated.

If husbands and wives disciplined themselves to avoid the word 16
"you" during potential emotional outbursts, they wouldn't build up years of frustration and marital malice. If coaches stopped publicly criticizing their players and saying "you" every time the players made a mistake, there'd be many more motivated athletes exploiting and reaching their fullest potential.

5. *Ask for feedback.* After "PEN-ning" people, find out what their feel- 17
ings or opinions are on the matter. Let them talk. Let them express their emotions, and don't interrupt. If they're looking to save a little face, go ahead and let them. Lose the battle, but win the war. Open the window of communication, and let the air flow in.

6. *Actively listen to their response.* Instead of just gazing at them as they 18
speak, be an active, nonverbal listener. Show facial expressions, nod, react with sounds, such as "hmmm," "oh, I see," or "really." Show a genuine, caring interest.

When someone has a problem, active listening helps reduce the 19
pain. That's what psychologists do every day. The client reveals painful experiences to the psychologist, and the psychologist uses active listening techniques to show support, concern, and empathy. It's also a technique used by successful sales pros who strive to develop relationships with customers.

7. *Discuss the situation in a low-key manner.* Your two-way communica- 20
tion, although unstructured, should remain focused on the problem. Facilitate the discussion to an agreed-upon action or solution. Clearly state what you want the person to do, if it's not clear, and make sure

you obtain a mutual understanding. Don't dominate the communication. If the other person raises his or her voice, keep yours down. That will keep the discussion less emotional and more low-key.

21 8. *Mutually agree upon an action or next step.* It's always better this way. Forcing a person to do something usually produces substantially less long-term growth and relationship building. Both parties should agree upon an action, set a date for its implementation, and end with a handshake. Try getting the person to verbalize what the action steps will be, thereby ensuring that both people are in sync. You'd be surprised how many times the criticized person misconstrues the next action step.

22 9. *End with a positive.* Now that the hard work is completed (and nobody likes giving criticism), go back and stroke the person a bit. Remind him or her that you greatly appreciate the person's effort and dedication and are very supportive of his or her performance. Make sure that no negative feelings exist, and if they do, probe and uncover them. You want to assure the person that this is a very correctable problem and that, in the big picture, you're a very satisfied manager.

23 Example: "Seymour, remember, I am extremely pleased with your performance. You are a valuable asset to our department."

24 A few musts to keep in mind when giving constructive, motivational criticism:

25 First, *always do it in private.* Nobody is proud of reprimands, so do it when you're alone with the person. It's humiliating when done in public.

26 Second, *limit the criticism session to one act.* If you bring up things from the past, you're turning the knife and potentially destroying the relationship. You should communicate criticism within a day or two of the occurrence; otherwise, drop it. Some people bring up events that occurred six months or even six years ago. That's a no-no.

27 Third, *criticize face-to-face, never over the phone.* You never know how the person is reacting. If you're criticizing over the phone, the other person might be dying inside, and you'll never know it. Even if it's timely to do it over the phone, hold it in. Set up an immediate meeting with the person.

28 Finally, *don't dig it in.* Statements such as "you see," "I told you so," or "you don't listen" are worthless. They might make you feel good, but they ruin relationships.

ANSWERS TO QUESTIONS

Thinking Critically About Content

1. "Motivation magic" is a way of offering constructive criticism while motivating employees so that they can all work better as a team.
2. The main steps are as follows:
   Always begin constructive criticism with a positive statement.
   Never follow that complimentary opening remark with *but* or *however.*
   Use the acronym PEN to plan and verbalize the actual criticism.
   Avoid using the word *you* when giving the actual criticism.
   Ask for feedback.
   Actively listen to people's responses.
   Discuss the situation in a low-key manner.
   Mutually agree on an action or a next step.
   End with a positive.

29 A great example of how *not* to criticize can be seen during a sports event—basketball, baseball, or football. How many times does a basketball coach yell at his point guard for missing the play and use the accusatory "you" over and over again? The coach raises his voice in frustration and does it in front of teammates and fans. The player feels abused, his confidence is shaken, and his motivation is drained from within. It's no wonder certain professional coaches go from team to team but continue to lose year after year. They might know the sport, but they know little about human motivation. A little motivational psychology would go a long way for these perennial losers.

30 How do you tie all these points together the next time you must criticize a person? Remember: The goal of motivational criticism should be to leave the person feeling helped, not hurt. So, the next time you're about to criticize a person, think it through before you do. Be tactful, firm, empathetic, and concise.

31 After all, you have to be little to belittle. You hold the key to motivational magic.

Thinking Critically About Content

1. What does Dr. Roger Flax mean by "motivation magic" (paragraph 7)?
2. What are the nine main steps of Flax's method?
3. What does Flax say the main goal of motivational criticism is?

Thinking Critically About Purpose and Audience

4. What do you think Flax's purpose is in this essay?
5. Do you think that only businesspeople can benefit from this essay? Why? Explain your answer.
6. Which piece of Flax's advice do you find most useful for your own life?

Thinking Critically About Essays

7. Describe in a complete sentence Flax's point of view in his last paragraph.
8. How does Flax organize this essay? Write a rough outline to show his method of organization.
9. Choose a paragraph from his essay, and explain how it is developed.
10. Explain in detail whether or not you agree with Flax when he says that using "you" to criticize people makes them feel like they are being attacked.

3. The goal is "to leave the person feeling helped, not hurt" (para. 30).

Thinking Critically About Purpose and Audience

4. Flax wants to inform readers how to reprimand employees while motivating them at the same time. He is probably hoping to alter some employer behavior through this essay.
5. Anyone can benefit from this essay because people make mistakes every day, and not just in business situations. Readers can take this advice and use it in personal situations.
6. Answers will vary.

Thinking Critically About Essays

7. Flax thinks that ridiculing others is an act of small-minded people and believes that everyone has the potential to criticize and motivate at the same time.
8. Flax organizes his essay in the order in which the steps should occur (chronologically); see the answer to question 2.
9. Answers will vary.
10. Answers will vary.

WHY WE HAVE A MOON
by David Levy

SUMMARY

In this essay, Levy explains the process the moon went through in its formation and the role it plays now.

READABILITY

(Flesch–Kincaid grade level)
9.3

INSTRUCTOR'S RESOURCE MANUAL

For additional teaching strategies, for journal entries, for vocabulary and reading quizzes, and for more writing assignments, see the *Instructor's Resource Manual,* Section II, Part II.

Focusing Your Attention

1. Astronomy is the study of planets and stars. What interests you about the world of astronomy?
2. In the essay you are about to read, the writer explains his research on how the moon was formed and what its role is in relation to the earth. Have you ever been interested enough in something that you took the time to look into its origins or related facts?

Expanding Your Vocabulary

The following words are important to your understanding of this essay. As you read, circle any words you don't know beyond this list. Then break into groups, and help each other figure out the meanings of these unknown words.

orbit: the path of a planet, moon, or satellite (paragraph 3)

gravitational pull: the pull of a planet on an object near its surface (paragraph 3)

supercolossal: extremely large (paragraph 3)

plummeted: fell (paragraph 4)

devastation: severe damage (paragraph 4)

promontory: a piece of land that juts out into the sea (paragraph 7)

mottled: spotted (paragraph 11 and 12)

exhalations: letting air out (paragraph 12)

meteors, comets, asteroids: bodies of rock and air in space (paragraph 13)

imminent: about to happen (paragraph 16)

carbon: a chemical element (paragraph 17)

hydrogen, nitrogen, oxygen: gases in the earth's atmosphere (paragraph 17)

READING CRITICALLY

As you did with the previous essay, draw a graphic organizer for the ideas in the following essay. Make the drawing so accurate that someone could look at the drawing and understand the basic concepts in the essay. Compare your drawing with someone in your class, and write a brief statement about the reading from the graphic organizer.

WHY WE HAVE A MOON

by David Levy

I remember the beautiful clear sky the day my granddaughter, then 14 months old, first fell under its spell. She called it the "oon." Soon, I knew, she'd be asking, "How did the Moon get there? Did people really walk on it? Will *I* someday?"—the same questions asked by Moonwatchers of all ages. So, how *did* the Moon get there? 1

About 4.5 billion years ago, the Earth had a bad day. The Sun was shining on our young world, which had no oceans yet and no life, but a surface filled with erupting volcanoes. The sky was awash with stars, though not the ones we see now. But the familiar planets were there—Venus, Jupiter, Saturn, Mars—and another planet the size of Mars but much closer. 2

Had we been alive back then, we would have noticed this other planet looping again and again around the Sun in an odd orbit that brought it very close to Earth, then farther away. On this day, that odd planet, approaching us again, became brighter than ever before, filling the sky and getting bigger by the minute, its gravitational pull now so great that rocks began to stretch and rumble. Then, with unimaginable energy and deafening noise, it sideswiped the Earth, bounced off and, seconds later, tore right back into our planet with a supercolossal force. 3

That Mars-size world broke apart, and huge chunks of Earth's crust flew off into space. Two rings of debris, their particles much larger than those in the fine-grained rings of Saturn, grew and circled the Earth. For many days, pieces of the inner ring plummeted down again, adding to the Earth's devastation. Pieces of the outer ring slowly gathered together around its largest chunks. In just a year, those pieces formed a large new world, a world that we can still see. That world we call the Moon. 4

5 So goes the prevailing theory, developed in the 1970s. In its earliest days, our Moon was probably no more than 10,000 miles away. The Earth spun around faster then, in a 10-hour day. But over time, the Moon slowly veered away from Earth, its gravity forever slowing Earth's rotation. By the time of the dinosaurs, more than 4 billion years after the Moon's formation, a day was about 22 hours long. With our day now at 24 hours, the Moon, still inching away at approximately 3 feet every century, is about 240,000 miles away. But even at this distance, it has a powerful influence on the Earth's waters.

The Moon and the Tides

6 We have tides on Earth because of the gravitational pull of the Moon (and the Sun, especially when the two are in alignment) across the diameter of the Earth. If you've ever been to an ocean beach, you have felt the Moon's whisper as its gravity brings the water in, then out, twice each day. One day in Nova Scotia, I felt the Moon roar.

7 At the eastern end of Canada's Bay of Fundy, a flow of water equal to the combined currents of all the rivers on Earth thunders through the Minas Channel into the Minas Basin twice a day for six hours. To see this marvelous sight, I traveled to a remote Nova Scotia promontory called Cape Split. I arrived as the incoming tidal flow was at its maximum.

8 A first-quarter Moon hung in the sky as a *million million* gallons of water poured into the Minas Basin. I found it incredible that the Moon, from a distance of 240,000 miles, was responsible for the tremendous noise in the channel below. After a few hours, the flow slowed, then stopped. For a half hour or so, the water was still. Then the huge basin began to empty, flowing *in reverse* like a movie running backward, the noise rising once again. Such is the power of the Moon's gravity.

9 The shape of the land makes the tides stronger. In midocean, the daily tidal bulge is about a yard. But at Minas Basin, it's 45 feet—the largest tidal flow on the planet—owing to the peculiar geography of the Gulf of Maine, the Bay of Fundy, the Minas Channel and basin. It's like a child playing in a bathtub, pushing the water to the front, then letting it flow back. A rhythm builds. If the child lifts up slightly each time, the water sloshes toward one end. Eventually, the water rides up the side of the tub and spills out. The child's movement is "in sync" with the natural motion of the water in the tub. The water's increased momentum, plus the confining shape of the tub, results in more force on the water—just as the Moon's gravity, aided by the shape of the land, strengthens the force of the Fundy tides.

The Moon Is a Mirror

When we look at the Moon, we see on its uneven surface a record of billions of years of bashing. The Moon's face is trying to tell us something about Earth's own past. If the Moon has been hit so often, the Earth, being a much bigger target, must have been struck even more often. 10

The first thing you notice about the Moon is its uneven, mottled surface. With binoculars, the unevenness appears more pronounced, with clear evidence of dark and bright spots. What are they? 11

To the ancient Greeks, the Moon's "spots" were exhalations from the Earth that rose all the way to the Moon. By the 1500s, it was common to compare the Moon to green cheese—not because of its mysterious color but because "green cheese" meant round, uncut cheese with a mottled surface. As recently as 1960, most scientists believed craters were the result of volcanic forces beneath the Moon's surface. 12

That was before Gene Shoemaker appeared on the scene. A young geologist, he was studying craters formed by underground nuclear testing near Las Vegas in the late 1950s. He noted that these craters, formed by far greater heat and pressure than a volcano could produce, resembled some of the great natural craters on Earth. Perhaps the latter—as well as the craters on the Moon—had resulted from impacts by meteors, comets or asteroids, whose energy would have been closer to that of an atomic bomb. 13

By 1960, Shoemaker had proved that a 1.2-mile-wide crater near Flagstaff, Arizona, was the result of the crash of an asteroid some 50,000 years ago. By studying detailed photographs of craters on the Moon, plus images taken by the *Ranger* and *Surveyor* spacecraft, Shoemaker established that the Moon's surface was a story of impacts over billions of years. 14

In 1972, the astronaut Harrison Schmidt went to the Moon on *Apollo 17* and confirmed Shoemaker's theory live on television. "Gene defined what the characteristics of the Moon's surface layer would be," Schmidt told me. 15

But the Moon's surface revealed a far more important story—that of the solar system's violent past, when the planets, including Earth, were bombarded by comets and meteors. On March 25, 1993, Shoemaker, his wife, Carol, and I discovered that a collision in the solar system was imminent. And 16 months later, as the world watched, comet Shoemaker-Levy 9 slammed into Jupiter at 37 miles per second—the equivalent of going from New York to Los Angeles *in 70 seconds.* 16

The spectacle of these comets hitting Jupiter was a replay of an ancient scenario in which comets—comprised of carbon, hydrogen, nitrogen, and 17

Answers to Questions

Thinking Critically About Content

1. David Levy's personal stories include his granddaughter's reference to the moon (para. 1), the author's trip to Cape Split (paragraphs 7–9), and his discovery of the forthcoming collision in the solar system in 1993 (para. 16). These stories make the essay personal and accessible to a general audience.
2. The steps in the moon's formation were (1) a planet hits and bounces off the earth, (2) debris from the earth flies into space, (3) pieces of debris start to circle the earth, and (4) within a year, the moon forms from this debris.
3. The tides are caused by the gravitational pull of the moon.

Thinking Critically About Purpose and Audience

4. The purpose of this essay is to explain in terms anyone can understand how the moon was formed.
5. Answers will vary.
6. Levy relates scientific information to everyday occurrences in four other instances: comparing spots on the moon to "exhalations" (para. 12); comparing the moon to green cheese (para. 12); comparing the impacts of meteors, comets, and asteroids to the force of an atomic bomb (para. 13); and comparing the vibration of the moon to a huge bell after "being clanged" (para. 21).

Thinking Critically About Essays

7. Answers will vary.
8. He probably introduces current research to show that scientists are still studying the moon today.
9. The three main parts of Levy's essay are (1) how the moon was formed, (2) the moon and the tides, and (3) the moon as a mirror of the past. This order is actually

oxygen—crashed into Earth, starting a slow process that eventually led to the earliest life here.

18 Is the Moon still being bombarded today? On July 10, 1941, Walter Haas, one of the world's most experienced observers, saw a speck of light move across Gassendi, a large lunar crater. Did Haas see a meteorite striking the Moon at enormous speed? Smaller particles did hit the Moon on Nov. 17, 1999, during the Leonid meteor shower.

19 If small objects still hit the Moon, can large ones? In 1178, some monks near Canterbury, England, reported a terrifying experience on a night of a crescent Moon: "Suddenly," the account reads, "the upper horn split in two. From the division, a flaming torch sprang up, spewing out, over a considerable distance, fire, hot coals, and sparks."

20 Could they have seen a major impact on the Moon? Conceivably, a 20-mile crater on the Moon's far side, called Giordano Bruno, was caused by a large impact. We may never know the answer, but there's a clue.

21 In the 1970s, the McDonald Observatory in Texas, bouncing laser beams off the Moon, found that it "sways" by a few yards about every three years. Like a huge bell vibrating after being clanged, the Moon is acting as if it had been struck by a large object within the last 1000 years. Perhaps, someday, my granddaughter, caught by the Moon's wondrous pull, will walk there as others once did and find an answer.

Thinking Critically About Content

1. Writers often use personal stories to get the readers' attention or understanding. Where does Levy use stories in this essay? What effect do they have?
2. What were the steps in the moon's formation 4.5 billion years ago?
3. According to Levy, what is the relationship between the moon and the oceans?

Thinking Critically About Purpose and Audience

4. What do you think the purpose of this essay is?
5. How do you think a general audience would respond to the author's description of the moon as a mirror of the earth's past?
6. Levy often relates scientific information to everyday occurrences—like comparing the motion of the tides to a child playing in the bathtub (paragraph 9). Find one other example of this technique. How do you respond to this strategy as a reader?

chronological, starting with the formation of the moon and progressing to research on the moon today.

10. For an audience of scientists, the essay would include many more scientific references. Beyond this, answers will vary.

Thinking Critically About Essays

7. Describe in a complete sentence the writer's point of view.
8. Why do you think Levy introduces current research on the moon in the last section of his essay?
9. What are the three main parts of Levy's essay? Why do you think he put these topics in this order?
10. If Levy were writing this essay for a publication to be read only by scientists, how might it be different? How might it be the same? Rewrite the introduction or the conclusion for an audience of scientists.

Writing Workshop

This final section gives you opportunities to apply what you have learned in this chapter to another writing assignment. This time, we provide very little prompting beyond a summary of the guidelines for writing a process analysis essay. This section will let you demonstrate that you can go through the entire writing process on your own with only occasional feedback from your peers. Loop back into the chapter as necessary when you have questions so that this process becomes as automatic to you as possible before you move on to new material. Then pause at the end of the chapter to reflect briefly on what you have learned.

TEACHING ON THE WEB

Discussion Topic: Divide students into groups of three or four, and have them discuss the many ways in which process analysis can be found on the Internet. How can process analysis on the Net help them in their daily lives?

Guidelines for Writing a Process Analysis Essay

1. State in the thesis statement what the reader should be able to do or understand by the end of the essay.
2. Know your audience.
3. Explain the process clearly in the body of your essay.
4. Organize your material logically.
5. End your essay by considering the process as a whole.

TEACHING ON THE WEB

Links: Have students find links to Web sites that sell videos about historical events. What three titles in each category sound most interesting to them?

Possible sites:

A&E, www.aetv.com

History Channel, www.historychannel.com

Discovery Channel, www.discovery.com

Writing About Your Reading

1. In the first essay, Flax talks about motivating people by criticizing without using the word *you*. Are you usually aware of your word choice as you talk? How can careful use of words help you get what you want in life? Explain a process that involved getting something you wanted by using words carefully.

TEACHING ON THE WEB

Research: Have students find Web sites

that explain how something happened. Have them determine whether all the steps are given or if any were left out. Then ask them to explain how important each step is to the process analysis they found.

2. Think of something in life that you want to study as much as Levy wants to study the moon and stars. Then discuss your plans for achieving your goals in this area of study.
3. Which type of process analysis do you find most interesting—the how-to essays or the background explanations? Explain your answer.

Writing About Your World

1. Place yourself in a scene similar to the one above, and write a process analysis essay explaining something that you find as interesting as this person finds this activity. Be sure to cover all steps or stages of the process you are discussing.
2. Choose an appliance or a piece of equipment that you understand well, and write a process analysis essay explaining how it works. Don't identify the item in your essay. Then see if the class members can guess what device you are talking about.
3. Research the history of your college or university, and write an essay explaining its background to prospective students. Be sure to give a focus to your study and decide on a purpose before you begin writing.
4. Write your own process analysis assignment (with the help of your instructor), and write a response to it.

Revising

Small Group Activity (5–10 minutes per writer) In groups of three or four, read your process analysis essays to each other. Those listening should record their reactions on a copy of the Peer Evaluation Form in Appendix 2D. After your group goes through this process, give your evaluation forms to the appropriate writers so that each writer has two or three peer comment sheets for revising.

Paired Activity (5 minutes per writer) Using the completed Peer Evaluation Forms, work in pairs to decide what you should revise in your essay. If time allows, rewrite some of your sentences, and have your partner look at them.

Individual Activity Rewrite your paper, using the revising feedback you received from other students.

Editing

Paired Activity (5–10 minutes per writer) Swap papers with a classmate, and use the editing portion of your Peer Evaluation Form to identify as many grammar, punctuation, mechanics, and spelling errors as you can. If time allows, correct some of your errors, and have your partner look at them. Record your grammar, punctuation, and mechanics errors in the Error Log (Appendix 6) and your spelling errors in the Spelling Log (Appendix 7).

Individual Activity Rewrite your paper again, using the editing feedback you received from other students.

Reflecting on Your Writing When you have completed your own essay, answer these six questions.

1. What was most difficult about this assignment?
2. What was easiest?
3. What did you learn about process analysis by completing this assignment?
4. What do you think are the strengths of your process analysis? Place a wavy line by the parts of your essay that you feel are very good.
5. What are the weaknesses, if any, of your paper? Place an X by the parts of your essay you would like help with. Write any questions you have in the margin.
6. What did you learn from this assignment about your own writing process—about preparing to write, about writing the first draft, about revising, and about editing?

CHAPTER

Comparing and Contrasting

"The difference between the right word and the almost-right word is really a large matter—'tis the difference between the lightning-bug and the lightning."

—MARK TWAIN

TEACHING COMPARISON AND CONTRAST
Bring a portable CD player to class, and play songs that have been recorded by more than one artist. (Possible pairs include George Michael's "Faith" and Limp Bizkit's "Faith," Dolly Parton's "I Will Always Love You" and Whitney Houston's "I Will Always Love You," and Freddy Mercury and David Bowie's "Under Pressure" and Vanilla Ice's "Ice Ice Baby.")
Tell students to find the five most obvious similarities or differences. Then have students find the ten most subtle similarities or differences. As students find similarities and differences, write them on the board.
When students have found as many similari-

Comparison and contrast are at the heart of our democratic society. Our competitive natures encourage us to compare our lives to those of others so we can try to better ourselves. Even if we simply attempt to improve on our "personal best," comparison and contrast keep us striving for more. In school, we learn about different writers, different cultures, different musical instruments, and different political platforms by comparing them to one another. And every day we make decisions based on comparisons of one sort or another—which clothes we should wear, which person we should date, which apartment we should rent, which job we should take. Comparisons help us establish a frame of reference and figure out where we fit into the larger world around us.

On another level, comparison and contrast are also part of our writing. They play an important role in our personal lives, in our college courses, and in the workplace, as in the following situations:

- Someone looking for a new car does comparison shopping on the Internet.
- A student doing a report in a nursing course compares and contrasts traditional and alternative approaches to medical care.
- A student compares and contrasts two Native American cultures for an exam in anthropology.
- An insurance agent prepares a report for a client that compares and contrasts several different insurance policies.
- A travel agent compares and contrasts two travel packages for a client.

Comparison and contrast help us understand one subject by putting it next to another. When we *compare*, we look for similarities, and when we *contrast*, we look for differences. Nearly always, however, comparison and contrast are part of the same process. For this reason, we often use the word *compare* to refer to both techniques.

READING AND WRITING A COMPARISON/CONTRAST ESSAY

Looking closely at how a comparison/contrast essay works will improve your reading comprehension and transfer over time to your writing. Like two parts of a circle, the reading and writing processes function together and, as you learn how they operate, will serve you well in your college courses and in life. Reading and writing critically will help you succeed in all your life ventures.

Reading a Comparison/Contrast Essay

In the essay "Thrills and Chills," Eric Minton compares and contrasts roller coasters and haunted houses to show how amusement parks play on our deepest fears. Do you like being scared? Do you like roller coasters and haunted houses? Are they a means of escape for you?

READING CRITICALLY

Teaching something to your peers is an excellent way to see if you understand it. To practice this technique, the class must first divide the following essay into four or five parts. The class members should then get into four or five groups and choose one of the sections to prepare for the rest of the class. After discovering the main ideas, the details, and their relationship to one another, each group should teach its section to the rest of the class. This strategy is called "reciprocal teaching."

THRILLS AND CHILLS

by Eric Minton

1 In Orlando, Florida, David Clevinger stands in a back corridor of *Terror on Church Street* and listens expectantly as customers make their way through the haunted house's passages. Suddenly screams erupt, sending

ties and differences as possible, have a class discussion about how relatively easy it is to do this exercise because everyone can hear the similarities and differences, even though some took longer to spot than others. Then discuss the correlation to writing: When writing comparison/contrast essays, students should be sure to look for what is obvious and what is not so obvious and then compare and contrast in a logical manner.

TEACHING TIPS

The following eight teaching tips are based on Howard Gardner's multiple intelligences:

Verbal/Linguistic

Write a few sentences with similar meanings but with variations in key words. For example, write the following three sentences:

My uninspired brother lies around the house not doing much.

My silly brother is wasting his life away by sitting around the house watching TV.

My stupid brother sits on his butt watching *Jerry Springer* reruns for hours.

Have students compare and contrast the different meanings of the sentences. Do they each have the same connotations? Could they all be said about the same person under similar circumstances? What type of person is most likely to speak each sentence?

Musical/Rhythmic

Have students compare different songs or pieces of music that were recorded by the same artist. How are the songs the same? How are they different? What characteristics does the artist keep in his or her music?

Logical/Mathematical

Provide students with Picasso prints that depict many of his unique stylistic traits. Have students compare and contrast the unusual features in the prints. Which print do they prefer? Why?

Visual/Spatial

Have students visit a museum (in person or online) to look at the various art periods. Have them compare and contrast the artwork in different periods to determine their favorite era. What made them choose this time period?

Bodily/Kinesthetic

Have students row a boat for five miles and then row an indoor machine for five miles. How are these two relatively identical forms of exercise similar and different?

Intrapersonal

Have students keep a journal for three days

Clevinger, the attraction's artistic director and operations manager, into gales of glee. "I love that sound," he chortles. So does Dave Focke. Watching shrieking riders hurtle through the drops of *The Beast,* the massive wooden coaster at Paramount's Kings Island near Cincinnati, Ohio, Focke beams with pride. "Guests come off breathless, hearts pounding, scared out of their wits," exults Focke, the park's vice president of construction and maintenance, "and wanting to get in line to go again!"

2 Call them shockmeisters, terror tacticians, spookologists, and booologists. The small band of designers who create the roller coasters and haunted houses that are amusement parks' premier attractions are master manipulators of our deepest fears. They get us to walk through pitch black hallways and step into cutaway coaster cars that dangle our arms and legs. They exploit our most closely held vulnerabilities—and make us like it.

3 For designers, primarily engineers for coasters and theatrical artists for haunted houses, turning fear into fun depends on illusion. No matter how precarious a roller coaster or alarming a haunted house may appear, it must be totally safe. "We always try to make them look and feel more dangerous than they really are," says Michael Boodley, president of Great Coasters International, Inc., of Santa Cruz, California.

4 Though the experience offered by roller coasters and haunted houses diverges dramatically—it's the difference between pushing a wagon over a steep hill versus telling campfire ghost stories—the attractions are constructed of common elements. Both draw on all our senses, both rely on surprise for their shocks and both quote heavily from the movies (Coasters replicate action-adventure perils, à la *Indiana Jones* and *Star Wars,* and haunted houses feature quasi-Frankensteins and *Friday the 13th* Jasons).

5 But the biggest common denominator is that the two feed on the same basic fear: loss of control. Once a coaster takes off, passengers can do nothing but sit, or on some rides stand, and scream. "The closest thing to compare it to is driving with an idiot," observes Boodley. Lynton Harris, director of *Madison Scare Garden,* an annual fright fest in New York City, also uses an auto analogy for haunted houses. "It's a hundred degrees outside, and you'd expect to get in a car and have air conditioning, and all of a sudden the heater gets turned on," he says. "Then the doors lock. Cocky as you are, you realize you're not in charge."

6 With roller coasters, the psychological games start before customers even get into the train. Boodley purposely makes his wooden coasters as diabolical looking as possible. "It's kind of like a black widow spider web," he explains. "It's a very, very pretty thing, but when the black widow gets

you. . . ." Queueing customers at *Outer Limits: Flights of Fear,* one of 12 coasters at Kings Island, are treated to dim lights, alien noises, and a video of a space station in the grip of a mysterious force. "Even after having ridden that ride probably close to a hundred times, I sit there anticipating the start, and my palms still sweat," says *Outer Limits* designer Jim Seay, president of Premier Rides of Millersville, Maryland.

7 Whether the traditional chain-driven wooden or steel clackers or the newer linear induction motor (LIM) rides that harness electromagnetic force to blast off trains, all roller coasters play on two related—and universal—terrors: fear of heights and fear of falling. "The loops and elements, they come and go, but the coaster always has to have the big drop," says Focke of Kings Island.

8 Traditional coasters provide an excruciatingly slow buildup to the plunge. "There's a lot of self-abuse on that chain lift," says Boodley. "Your own mind puts you in a state of paralysis." (Wooden coasters also creak, rumble, and clickity-clack naturally as they flex, but riders get a queasy feeling that the structure is about to collapse. "That's probably one of the funniest things we as designers get to appreciate," says Boodley.) LIMs, on the other hand, rocket you into terror with trains that go from 0 to 60 mph in under four seconds. The big drops are actually shorter on LIMs, but the sense of speed sets hearts pounding.

9 Most coasters travel below 70 miles an hour, slower than many people drive, but designers heighten the sense of speed and danger with close flybys of terrain, buildings, people, even other trains. At Busch Gardens Tampa Bay, *Montu* dives riders into five trenches, one of which emerges through the patio of an ersatz Egyptian temple. "Not knowing exactly where the bottom is or where you come out is important," says Mark Rose, the park's vice president of design and engineering. "If you could see the whole thing, then you could kind of play it out in your mind." Some coasters, like *Outer Limits* and Disney World's *Space Mountain,* intensify the fear and suspense by keeping passengers in the dark for the entire ride.

10 Upping the vulnerability quotient even further is a recent innovation: inverted coasters which suspend riders below the track and carve away as much of the train as possible. "There is less fiberglass, less coach around you, so your feet are just hanging out there," notes Rose. During one stretch of track on *Montu,* passengers' soles skim just 24 inches above the ground. Riders also get dangled over a pit of live Nile crocodiles.

11 A coaster's effects, though, are not all illusory. Passengers pull close to 4 positive G's on some plummets. They turn upside down on loops and rotate

on a computer and for three days in a binder. Then ask if the choice of medium had any effect on their journal entries. Which medium did students prefer? Why?

Interpersonal

Have students watch the movie version of a book they have read. Have them compare and contrast the two to determine which one they prefer.

Naturalist

Have students think of their two favorite outdoor sports. If they had to choose one over the other, which one would they choose and why?

INSTRUCTOR'S RESOURCE MANUAL

For additional material about teaching comparison and contrast; for journal entries; and for multiple-choice, short-answer, and paragraph tests, see the *Instructor's Resource Manual*, Section II, Part II.

head over heels through corkscrews. They literally feel the wind in their hair and, on a LIM coaster launch, the air in their eyes. Human bodies don't commonly experience such acrobatic maneuvers, and that in itself is psychologically disorienting. "Anytime you put riders in a situation they're not used to, there's an element of the unknown," declares Boodley. "And for 80% of people, fear is the unknown."

12 The biggest unknown of all is death, and creators of haunted houses are masters at exploiting our fear of dying, especially in a gruesome manner. To unnerve guests, designers depend on two elements. The first is setting a spooky mood with sights, sounds, smells, and "feels"—"all the things that make you uneasy," says Drew Edward Hunter, co-chairman of the International Association of Haunted Attractions and design director of haunted attractions at Sally Corporation of Jacksonville, Florida. "Then you have the second part, the attack, the out-and-out scare. I don't think you can have one without the other."

13 For the "creep-out" effect, haunts are always dark; skeletons, skulls, fog, ticking clocks, and screaming ghouls abound. "On my sets, I try to capture a claustrophobic feeling," says *Terror on Church Street*'s Clevinger. "I bring my ceilings low, the walls close." To further emphasize the sense of enclosure, he hangs tree branches, Spanish moss, rags, and spider webs.

14 Just the suggestion of something loathsome will give customers the screaming meemies. "Do the sounds of insects, and people scratch their heads all the way through," says John Denley, president and owner of Boneyard Productions of Salem, Massachusetts. Run a soundtrack that whispers of rats, turn on ankle-aimed air hoses, and professional football players tap dance. A strong whiff of formaldehyde, and you have the scent of death, "no matter what country you're in," says Clevinger.

15 The second part of the equation is the scare, which, say spookologists, is really a "startle." "All scares are primarily based on two things," instructs Edward Marks, president of Jets Productions of Chatsworth, California. "One, it's there and does something you don't expect it to do, or two, it's not there and it appears."

16 In *Terror on Church Street,* customers come upon Hannibal Lecter, the cannibal psychiatrist of *Silence of the Lambs.* He yells and lunges against his cell's bars, drawing yelps from viewers. The cries quickly subside into nervous tittering. As guests make their way around the bars, Lecter follows along inside. Then, just when viewers feel safest, Lecter opens the cage door and steps out. "The guys who were taunting him usually scream the loudest," observes Clevinger.

In the second type of gag, designers have people or objects suddenly emerge from in front, beside, above, or below patrons. A surefire gag—and the simplest of all—is dropping a spider on a person's head. "We call that a $2 scare," says Harris of *Madison Scare Garden.* "It's the best value-for-money scare we've ever used." 17

Another never-fail gotcha goes by the generic term "UV Dot Man." Guests enter a dark room with ultraviolet dots on the wall (variations would be skeletons or geometric patterns). A black-masked actor wearing a black body-suit, likewise bearing UV dots, stands against the wall and jumps out. "You are actually looking at him before he leaps out at you," Marks says. "It works every time, and it's so simple." (Another certain scare that designers hate, but feel compelled to use, is the hockey-masked goon waving a whirring chain-saw. Customers complain if a haunted house doesn't have one.) 18

For designers, combining the two types of gags may be the most satisfying scare of all. In his favorite trick, Denley once draped sheets over padding, topped them with masked and wigged heads, and attached the forms to the caging on oscillating fans. He plugged the fans into a power strip but left the cords clearly visible. These "monsters" started moving in unison when people entered the room. After the initial surprise, guests noticed the power strip and began mocking the amateurish setup. Suddenly, the middle white-sheeted monster—actually a man with one of the plugged-in extension cords tied to his leg—leaped out. 19

"It was hilarious," recalls a chuckling Denley, who is also known as Professor Nightmare. "We had a woman hyperventilate. We had people wet themselves. They thought they knew the gag—and, bam! we hit them with something totally different." Guests losing control of their bladders is considered a badge of honor among haunt producers. "We call it yellow control," Clevinger says. Getting an entire group to cower on the ground is another measure of success. 20

While the live actors who sometimes assume roles in haunted productions are forbidden to touch patrons, they are encouraged to invade their personal space. "Everybody's got this wonderful circle around them," says Denley, who likes to have actors suddenly appear as close to a person as possible, then disappear. "We want to leave you thinking, 'What was that?'" 21

Designers also like to pick their victims. "We call it 'slicing the group,'" says Marks at Jets Productions. "We actually can single out a person from 20 people. A guy and girl clinging together—I can slice them apart with the right scare." A trained actor watches their body language, whether they tighten up, stare him down, or avert their eyes. 22

23 Male customers are a favorite target. "We try to take the guys who are hecklers and make examples of them," observes Denley. "If you nail them, the rest of the group will follow." Men also pose a special challenge. "Guys are harder to read than women," Denley explains. "They don't do body language as much. Women are more animated, more intent on being scared. Guys play it cool." Designers usually get them with strikes from above or below, but they're careful. Men sometimes lash out with their fists.

24 "The scariest things come from your mind," sums up Edward Hunter. "With the right setup, the right imagination, the right story, your mind creates things we couldn't possibly show you." "No matter how good the makeup or the costume, nothing is more effective than your imagination," echoes Denley. One proof: guests at *Terror on Church Street* scream loud and long when, at a particular point, they catch a glimpse of lurking monsters. The fiends: themselves, reflected in strategically placed mirrors.

Preparing to Write Your Own Comparison/Contrast Essay

Think of several ways you escape or relieve stress. What do you like about these methods of relaxation? Use one or more of the prewriting strategies you learned in Chapter 2 to generate ideas about these forms of relaxation. Why do they work for you?

Writing a Comparison/Contrast Essay

To write a comparison/contrast essay, you should consider two items that have something in common, such as cats and dogs (both are family pets) or cars and motorcycles (both are means of transportation). A discussion of cats and motorcycles, for example, would not be very interesting or useful because the two do not have common features. This is the basic rule underlying the following guidelines for writing a good comparison/contrast essay.

1. **Decide what point you want to make with your comparison, and state it in your thesis statement.** A comparison/contrast essay is usually written for one of two purposes: to examine the subjects separately or to show the superiority of one over the other. This purpose should be made clear in your thesis statement.

   In the sample essay, Minton's main idea is that the experience of roller coasters and of haunted houses plays in a similar manner on people's deepest fears. Minton makes the purpose of his essay clear in his thesis statement at the end of paragraph 2: "They exploit our most closely held vulnerabilities—and make us like it." This thesis promises to examine its subjects separately. If, however, this essay was going to show the superiority of one of its subjects over the other, its thesis statement might read something like this: "Although roller coasters and haunted houses both draw on our deepest fears, roller coasters are far more popular." In either case, readers would be interested in reading further to find out why they are attracted to roller coasters and haunted houses.

2. **Choose items to compare and contrast that will make your point most effectively.** Usually, the subjects you plan to compare and contrast have many similarities and differences. Your task, then, is to look over the ideas you generated in prewriting and choose the best points for making your comparison clearly and strongly.

   In his essay, Minton compares his subjects—roller coasters and haunted houses—on four points:

   Point 1: They draw on all five senses.

   Point 2: They rely on surprise.

   Point 3: They refer to movies.

   Point 4: They feed on loss of control.

3. **Use as many specific details and examples as possible to expand your comparison.** The most common way of developing a comparison/contrast essay is to use description and example. Generate as many details and examples as you can for each of your subjects. Try to think of both obvious and not-so-obvious points of comparison.

   In "Thrills and Chills," Minton relies heavily on description and examples. First, he describes both of these attractions with equal attention to detail throughout the essay. You can look at almost any body paragraph (paragraphs 6 to 23) in Minton's essay and find an example with vivid description. When he finally gets down to the common elements that make both of these subjects appeal to people who like to be scared, Minton makes his details more and more specific. Here is an example of his varying level of detail:

   haunted houses

   fear of death

   spooky mood

low ceilings

close walls

sound of insects

smell of formaldehyde

the attack

unexpected action

jumping from cage

unexpected appearance

spider

"UV Dot Man"

These specific examples draw the readers into the essay.

4. **Develop your comparison in a balanced way.** Having selected the points on which you will compare your two subjects, you are ready to develop the comparison in your body paragraphs. You should make sure, however, that your treatment of each subject is balanced. That means, first, you cover the same topics for each subject. In other words, you should give equal coverage to both subjects, no matter what your conclusion is. In addition, you should spend the same amount of time on each point. If you describe one of your subjects in detail, you should also describe the other. In like manner, you should provide a similar number of examples for both subjects. In this way, your readers will feel that you have been fair to both subjects and that you are not presenting a biased discussion that favors one subject over the other.

   Minton covers all four of his points for both of his subjects and spends approximately the same amount of time developing both subjects. In discussing the ways that roller coasters make us feel out of control, for example, he names specific roller coasters and describes the way they build fear and suspense. Then he names specific haunted house attractions and describes how they "creep out" and scare people.

5. **Organize your essay subject by subject or point by point—or combine the two approaches.** When you are ready to write, you have three choices for organizing a comparison/contrast essay: (1) subject by subject (AAA, BBB), (2) point by point (AB, AB, AB), or (3) a combination of the two.

   In the subject arrangement, you say everything you have to say about the first subject, A, before you move on to talk about the second subject, B. In a point-by-point arrangement, both subjects are compared on point 1; then both are compared on point 2; and so on through all the points.

To choose which method of organization would be most effective, just use your common sense. If the subjects themselves are the most interesting part of your essay, use the subject pattern. But if you want single characteristics to stand out, use the point-by-point pattern.

Minton's essay is organized point by point. He spends most of his time on point 4 for both subjects. Here is what Minton's organization looks like:

Point 1: They draw on all five senses.

A. Roller coasters
B. Haunted houses

Point 2: They rely on surprise.

A. Roller coasters
B. Haunted houses

Point 3: They refer to movies.

A. Roller coasters
B. Haunted houses

Point 4: They feed on loss of control.

A. Roller coasters
    i. Fear of heights
    ii. Fear of falling
B. Haunted houses
    i. Spooky mood
    ii. The scare

Writing Your Own Comparison/Contrast Essay

Write an essay comparing and contrasting two methods of escape, based on the ideas you generated in your prewriting activities. How are they alike? How are they different? Decide what point you want to make before you start writing. Then spend some time choosing and organizing your topics and deciding on your method of organization (subject by subject, point by point, or a combination of the two). Form a clear thesis statement, and follow the guidelines for writing a comparison/contrast essay.

A STUDENT'S COMPARISON/ CONTRAST ESSAY

Let's look at a student's management of a comparison/contrast essay. This next essay, called "The Truth About Cats and Dogs," was written by a student named Maria Castillo. See if you can identify her main point as you read this draft of her essay.

The Truth About Cats and Dogs

1 The majority of people in the world will say that dogs are man's best friends and that cats were put on this earth to aggravate dogs. Some people are closet cat lovers, meaning he or she is afraid to tell family and friends that they actually like cats. Others will proudly state, "I hate cats, except for yours." People who resist cats do so because they believe they are; aloof, self-centered, and dull. People prefer dogs because they are friendly, protective, and playful. However, cats exhibit these same qualities and deserve the same respect as dogs.

2 Dogs have always been considered to be friendly, but cats can also fit this description. Dogs stay by their owners' sides and live to make their masters happy. They are the first to greet their family at the front door, they want nothing more than to be praised by their owners. Yet cats are much the same way. They, too, will be at the front door when their family gets home and are always excited to see them. They usually sit near their owners just to be by their sides. And despite what some people believe, a cat does come when they're called. Birds do not sit with their owners unless they are trained. Cats are very friendly to their owners.

3 As much as dogs love to play, so do cats. Most dogs love to play with chew toys, searching for the hidden-squeaker treasure. They often parade around with their "kill" until their masters notice their triumph. Some owners will awaken to find that their dogs have strewn all their toys all over the house. Dogs love the toys they know are theirs. However, so do cats. Cats will make a toy out of anything that will slide across a tile floor, whether it's a hair clip, a milk jug ring, a toy mouse, or a spool of thread. They can amuse themselves for hours. If the toy-of-the-day gets trapped under the refrigerator, cats will whine and wait for their owner to get the toy. Cats just love to play.

4 Even though dogs are great defenders, cats have been known to protect the family as well. Dogs bark or growl whenever they want to alert their owners to possible danger. They stand at the door and wait for their owners to

check for danger. If they see their owner being attacked, they will attack the enemy. Most people think cats would just stand by and watch, but this simply isn't true. Cats also alert their owners of danger by growling or standing to stiff attention. They, too, stand near the door waiting for their owner to react. Cats have been known to bite people who harm their loved ones. Cats can be excellent watch animals.

5 Dogs and cats are a lot alike. People say cats are very different from dogs, but this is not the case. The truth is, most people love to hate cats. It's now an old American pastime. But it's time for all cat lovers to unite and prove that it can be a cat-eat-cat world too.

Discovering How the Essay Works

1. What is Maria's main point in this essay?

   That cats are great animals, just like dogs

2. What exactly is Maria comparing or contrasting in this essay? List her points under the subjects below.

Dogs	Cats
Dogs are friendly.	*Cats are just as friendly.*
Dogs love to play with toys.	*Cats love to play with anything that will move.*
Dogs signal danger by barking and growling.	*Cats signal danger by growling or stiffening.*

3. Does Maria use as many specific details and examples as possible? List three of her specific references.

   Answers will vary.

4. Does Maria develop her comparison in a balanced way? Explain your answer.

   Yes. Maria compares the same three points for both dogs and cats, and she provides many examples of both subjects for each topic.

5. How does Maria organize her essay: subject by subject, point by point, or a combination of the two?

   The essay is organized point by point.

REVISING AND EDITING OPTIONS
Consider varying your approach to revising and editing. You could teach these skills in a class discussion, in small groups, or in pairs.

Revising and Editing the Student Essay

This essay is Maria's first draft, which now needs to be revised and edited. First, apply the following Revising Checklist to the content of Maria's draft. When you are satisfied that her ideas are fully developed and well organized, use the Editing Checklist on page 274 to correct her grammatical and mechanical errors. Do the tasks, and answer the questions after each checklist. Then write your suggested changes directly on Maria's draft.

REVISING STRATEGIES
This chapter focuses on the following revising elements:
Thesis statement
Basic elements
Development
Unity
Organization
Coherence

REVISING CHECKLIST

✔ Does the thesis statement contain the essay's controlling idea?
✔ Does the thesis appear as the last sentence of the introduction?

BASIC ELEMENTS

✔ Does the title draw in the readers?
✔ Does the introduction capture the readers' attention and build up to the thesis statement effectively?
✔ Does each body paragraph deal with a single topic?
✔ Does the conclusion bring the essay to a close in an interesting way?

DEVELOPMENT

✔ Do the body paragraphs adequately support the thesis statement?
✔ Does each body paragraph have a focused topic sentence?
✔ Does each body paragraph contain *specific* details that support the topic sentence?
✔ Does each body paragraph include *enough* details to explain the topic sentence fully?

UNITY

✔ Do the essay's topic sentences relate directly to the thesis statement?
✔ Do the details in each body paragraph support its topic sentence?

ORGANIZATION

✔ Is the essay organized logically?

✔ Is each body paragraph organized logically?

COHERENCE

✔ Are transitions used effectively so that paragraphs move smoothly and logically from one to the next?

✔ Do the sentences move smoothly and logically from one to the next?

Thesis Statement

1. Put brackets around the last sentence in Maria's introduction. Does it contain her main point?

   No

2. Rewrite Maria's thesis statement if necessary so that it states her main point and introduces her topics.

   Here is one possibility: People prefer dogs because they are friendly, protective, and playful; however, cats exhibit these same qualities and deserve the same respect as dogs.

Basic Elements

1. Give Maria's essay an alternate title.

   Answers will vary.

2. Rewrite Maria's introduction so that it captures readers' attention and builds up to the thesis statement at the end of the paragraph.

   Answers will vary.

3. Does each of Maria's body paragraphs deal with only one topic?

   Yes

4. Rewrite Maria's conclusion using at least one suggestion from Part I.

   Answers will vary.

Development

1. Write out Maria's thesis statement (revised, if necessary), and list her three topic sentences below it. *Thesis may vary.*

   Thesis statement: *People prefer dogs because they are friendly, protective, and playful; however, cats exhibit these same qualities and deserve the same respect as dogs.*

   Topic 1: *Dogs have always been considered to be friendly, but cats can also fit this description.*

   Topic 2: *As much as dogs love to play, so do cats.*

   Topic 3: *Even though dogs are great defenders, cats have been known to protect the family as well.*

2. Do Maria's topic sentences adequately support her thesis statement?

   Yes

3. Does each body paragraph have a focused topic sentence?

   Yes

4. Do Maria's details adequately characterize both cats and dogs?

   Yes

5. Where do you need more information?

   Answers will vary.

6. Make two of Maria's details more specific. *Answers will vary.*
7. Add at least two new details to make her comparison clearer. *Answers will vary.*

Unity

1. Read each of Maria's topic sentences with her thesis statement (revised, if necessary) in mind. Do they go together? *Answers will vary.*
2. Revise her topic sentences if necessary so they are directly related.
3. Drop or rewrite the sentence in paragraph 2 that is not directly related to its topic sentence. *Sentence 8*

Organization

1. Read Maria's essay again to see if all the paragraphs are arranged logically.
2. Reverse the two paragraphs that are out of order. *Reverse paragraphs 3 and 4 to match thesis.*
3. Look closely at Maria's body paragraphs to see if all her sentences are arranged logically within paragraphs.
4. Move any sentences that are out of order. *All sentences are in order.*

Coherence

1. Add two transitions to Maria's essay. *Answers will vary.*
2. Circle five synonyms that Maria uses. *Answers will vary.*
3. Explain how two of these make Maria's essay easier to read.

Answers will vary.
____
____
____

For the list of transitions, see page 101.

Now rewrite Maria's essay with your revisions.

EDITING STRATEGIES

This chapter focuses on the following editing problems:

Run-togethers

Pronoun agreement

Semicolons

EDITING CHECKLIST

SENTENCES

✔ Does each sentence have a main subject and verb?

✔ Do all subjects and verbs agree?

✔ Do all pronouns agree with their nouns?

✔ Are modifiers as close as possible to the words they modify?

PUNCTUATION AND MECHANICS

✔ Are sentences punctuated correctly?

✔ Are words capitalized properly?

WORD CHOICE AND SPELLING

✔ Are words used correctly?

✔ Are words spelled correctly?

Sentences

Subjects and Verbs

For help with subjects and verbs, see Chapter 25.

1. Underline Maria's subjects once and verbs twice in paragraph 2 of your revision of Maria's essay. Remember that sentences can have more than one subject-verb set.
2. Does each of Maria's sentences have at least one subject and verb that can stand alone?

   Yes

For help with run-togethers, see Chapter 27.

3. Did you find and correct Maria's run-together sentence? If not, find and correct it now. *Paragraph 2, sentence 3*

Subject-Verb Agreement

For help with subject-verb agreement, see Chapter 30.

1. Read aloud the subjects and verbs you underlined in your revision of Maria's essay.
2. Correct any subjects and verbs that do not agree. *All subjects and verbs agree.*

Pronoun Agreement

For help with pronoun agreement, see Chapter 34.

1. Find any pronouns in your revision of Maria's essay that do not agree with their nouns.

2. Did you find and correct the two pronouns that do not agree with their nouns? *Paragraph 1, sentence 2; paragraph 2, sentence 7*

Modifiers

1. Find any modifiers in your revision of Maria's essay that are not as close as possible to the words they modify. *There are no modifier errors.*
2. Rewrite sentences if necessary so modifiers are as close as possible to the words they modify.

For help with modifier errors, see Chapter 37

Punctuation and Mechanics

Punctuation

1. Read your revision of Maria's essay for any errors in punctuation.
2. Find the run-together sentence you revised, and make sure it is punctuated correctly.
3. Did you find and correct Maria's semicolon error? If not, find and correct it now. *Paragraph 1, sentence 4*

For help with punctuation, see Chapters 38–42.

Mechanics

1. Read your revision of Maria's essay for any errors in capitalization.
2. Be sure to check Maria's capitalization in the run-together sentence you revised.

For help with capitalization, see Chapter 43.

Word Choice and Spelling

Word Choice

1. Find any words used incorrectly in your revision of Maria's essay. *All words are used correctly.*
2. Correct any errors you find.

For help with confused words, see Chapter 49.

Spelling

1. Use spell-check and a dictionary to check the spelling in your revision of Maria's essay. *All words are spelled correctly.*
2. Correct any misspelled words.

For help with spelling, see Chapter 50.

Now rewrite Maria's essay again with your editing corrections.

YOUR OWN COMPARISON/ CONTRAST ESSAY

Returning to the comparison/contrast essay you wrote earlier in this chapter, you are now ready to revise and edit your own writing. Remember that revision involves reworking the development and organization of your essay while editing asks you to check your grammar and usage. Keep revising and editing until your essay fulfills its intended purpose. Work first with the essay's content and then with the grammar and usage.

WRITING CRITICALLY

As you approach the writing task, apply the reading technique you learned to your writing. Divide yourselves into groups of three or four, and work on one essay at a time. Divide each essay into parts, and "teach" it to each other. Point out gaps and problems as you move from person to person.

CLASS ACTIVITY

Ask students to think of every *instance* they compared or contrasted in the past week. Write their examples on the board, trying to fill all available space. Prompt them when necessary. After the board is relatively full, point out that they compare and contrast instinctively, so transferring this process into writing will not be difficult.

Revising and Editing Your Own Essay

The checklists here will help you apply what you have learned in this chapter to your essay.

 **REVISING CHECKLIST** 

THESIS STATEMENT

☐ Does the thesis statement contain the essay's controlling idea?
☐ Does the thesis appear as the last sentence of the introduction?

BASIC ELEMENTS

☐ Does the title draw in the readers?
☐ Does the introduction capture the readers' attention and build up to the thesis statement effectively?
☐ Does each body paragraph deal with a single topic?
☐ Does the conclusion bring the essay to a close in an interesting way?

DEVELOPMENT

☐ Do the body paragraphs adequately support the thesis statement?
☐ Does each body paragraph have a focused topic sentence?
☐ Does each body paragraph contain *specific* details that support the topic sentence?
☐ Does each body paragraph include *enough* details to explain the topic sentence fully?

UNITY

- ☐ Do the essay's topic sentences relate directly to the thesis statement?
- ☐ Do the details in each body paragraph support its topic sentence?

ORGANIZATION

- ☐ Is the essay organized logically?
- ☐ Is each body paragraph organized logically?

COHERENCE

- ☐ Are transitions used effectively so that paragraphs move smoothly and logically from one to the next?
- ☐ Do the sentences move smoothly and logically from one to the next?

Thesis Statement

1. What main point are you trying to make in your essay?

   ____

2. Put brackets around the last sentence in your introduction. Does it contain your main point?

   ____

3. Rewrite your thesis statement if necessary so that it states your main point and introduces your topics.

Basic Elements

1. Give your essay a title if it doesn't have one.

   ____

2. Does your introduction capture your readers' attention and build up to your thesis statement at the end of the paragraph?

   ____

3. Does each of your body paragraphs deal with only one topic?

   ____

4. Does your conclusion follow some of the suggestions offered in Part I?

____

Development

1. Write out your thesis statement (revised, if necessary), and list your topic sentences below it.

   Thesis statement: _______________________________

   Topic 1: _______________________________

   Topic 2: _______________________________

   Topic 3: _______________________________

2. Do your topics adequately support your thesis statement?

____

3. Does each body paragraph have a focused topic sentence?

____

4. Do you cover the same characteristics of both topics?

____

5. Where do your readers need more information?

____

6. Make two of your details more specific.
7. Add at least two new details to make your comparison clearer.

Unity

1. Read each of your topic sentences with your thesis statement in mind. Do they go together?

____

2. Revise your topic sentences if necessary so they are directly related.

3. Drop or rewrite any of the sentences in your body paragraphs that are not directly related to their topic sentences.

Organization

1. Read your essay again to see if all the paragraphs are arranged logically.
2. How is your essay organized: subject by subject, point by point, or a combination of the two?

    ____

3. Is the order you chose for your paragraphs the most effective approach to your subject?

    ____

4. Move any paragraphs that are out of order.
5. Look closely at your body paragraphs to see if all the sentences are arranged logically within paragraphs.
6. Move any sentences that are out of order.

Coherence

1. Add two transitions to your essay.
2. Circle five synonyms you use.
3. Explain how two of these make your essay easier to read.

    ____

    ____

For a list of transitions, see page 101.

Now rewrite your essay with your revisions.

EDITING CHECKLIST

SENTENCES

- ☐ Does each sentence have a main subject and verb?
- ☐ Do all subjects and verbs agree?
- ☐ Do all pronouns agree with their nouns?
- ☐ Are modifiers as close as possible to the words they modify?

PUNCTUATION AND MECHANICS

- ☐ Are sentences punctuated correctly?
- ☐ Are words capitalized properly?

WORD CHOICE AND SPELLING

- ☐ Are words used correctly?
- ☐ Are words spelled correctly?

Sentences

Subjects and Verbs

For help with subjects and verbs, see Chapter 25.

1. Underline the subjects once and verbs twice in a paragraph of your revised essay. Remember that sentences can have more than one subject-verb set.
2. Does each of your sentences have at least one subject and verb that can stand alone?

   ____

For help with fragments, see Chapter 26.

For help with run-togethers, see Chapter 27.

3. Correct any fragments you have written.
4. Correct any run-together sentences you have written.

Subject-Verb Agreement

For help with subject-verb agreement, see Chapter 30.

1. Read aloud the subjects and verbs you underlined in your revised essay.
2. Correct any subjects and verbs that do not agree.

Pronoun Agreement

For help with pronoun agreement, see Chapter 34.

1. Find any pronouns in your revised essay that do not agree with their nouns.
2. Correct any pronouns that do not agree with their nouns.

Modifiers

For help with modifier errors, see Chapter 37.

1. Find any modifiers in your revised essay that are not as close as possible to the words they modify.
2. Rewrite sentences if necessary so that your modifiers are as close as possible to the words they modify.

Punctuation and Mechanics

Punctuation

1. Read your revised essay for any errors in punctuation.
2. Make sure any fragments and run-together sentences you revised are punctuated correctly.

For help with punctuation, see Chapters 38–42.

Mechanics

1. Read your revised essay for any errors in capitalization.
2. Be sure to check your capitalization in any fragments or run-together sentences you revised.

For help with capitalization, see Chapter 43.

Word Choice and Spelling

Word Choice

1. Find any words used incorrectly in your revised essay.
2. Correct any errors you find.

For help with confused words, see Chapter 49.

Spelling

1. Use spell-check and a dictionary to check your spelling.
2. Correct any misspelled words.

For help with spelling, see Chapter 50.

Now rewrite your essay again with your editing corrections.

PRACTICING COMPARISON AND CONTRAST: FROM READING TO WRITING

Reading Workshop

Here are two essays that illustrate good comparison/contrast writing: "American Space, Chinese Place" by Yi-Fu Tuan compares the concept of space in two different cultures, and "Between Worlds" by Tony Cohan compares and contrasts a writer's life in two separate locations. As you read, notice how the writers make their points through well-thought-out, detailed comparisons and contrasts.

AMERICAN SPACE, CHINESE PLACE
by Yi-Fu Tuan

SUMMARY
In this essay, Tuan compares the concept of space in the Chinese and American cultures.

READABILITY
(Flesch–Kincaid grade level)
9.5

INSTRUCTOR'S RESOURCE MANUAL
For additional teaching strategies, for journal entries, for vocabulary and reading quizzes, and for more writing assignments, see the *Instructor's Resource Manual*, Section II, Part II.

Focusing Your Attention

1. Are you aware of how most Americans respond to space in our culture? Do you generally like open spaces or closed spaces?
2. The essay you are about to read compares our concept of space with that of the Chinese. Do you know any culture that thinks differently than we do about space? What are the differences? The similarities? What is the source of these differences and similarities?

Expanding Your Vocabulary

The following words are important to your understanding of this essay. Start a vocabulary log of your own by recording any words you don't understand as you read. When you finish reading the essay, write down what you think the words mean. Then check your definitions in the dictionary.

exurbia: prosperous areas beyond the suburbs (paragraph 1)

vistas: pleasant views (paragraph 1)

ambiance: the atmosphere of a place (paragraph 2)

terrestrial: relating to the earth (paragraph 2)

wanderlust: a strong desire to travel (paragraph 3)

pecuniary: relating to money (paragraph 3)

nostalgia: sentimental longing for the past (paragraph 4)

beckons: encourages someone to approach (paragraph 5)

READING CRITICALLY

As you learned at the beginning of this chapter, practice reciprocal teaching by dividing the following essay up into logical pieces and teaching it to each other. This time, get into five small groups (one for each paragraph), and study the paragraph as deeply as you can in the time allowed. Then teach it to the rest of the class.

AMERICAN SPACE, CHINESE PLACE
by Yi-Fu Tuan

Americans have a sense of space, not of place. Go to an American home in exurbia, and almost the first thing you do is drift toward the picture window. How curious that the first compliment you pay your host inside his house is to say how lovely it is outside his house! He is pleased that you should admire his vistas. The distant horizon is not merely a line separating earth from sky, it is a symbol of the future. The American is not rooted in his place, however lovely: his eyes are drawn by the expanding space to a point on the horizon, which is his future. By contrast, consider the traditional Chinese home. Blank walls enclose it. 1

Step behind the spirit wall and you are in a courtyard with perhaps a miniature garden around the corner. Once inside the private compound, you are wrapped in an ambiance of calm beauty, an ordered world of . . . buildings, pavement, rock, and decorative vegetation. But you have no distant view: nowhere does space open out before you. Raw nature in such a home is experienced only as weather, and the only open space is the sky above. The Chinese is rooted in his place. When he has to leave, it is not for the promised land on the terrestrial horizon, but for another world altogether along the vertical, religious axis of his imagination. 2

The Chinese tie to place is deeply felt. Wanderlust is an alien sentiment. The Taoist classic Tao Te Ching captures the ideal of rootedness in place with these words: "Though there may be another country in the neighborhood so close that they are within sight of each other and the crowing of cocks and barking of dogs in one place can be heard in the other, yet there is no traffic between them; and throughout their lives the two peoples have nothing to do with each other." In theory if not in practice, farmers have ranked high in Chinese society. The reason is not only that they are engaged in the "root" industry of producing food but that, unlike pecuniary merchants, they are tied to the land and do not abandon their country when it is in danger. 3

Nostalgia is a recurrent theme in Chinese poetry. An American reader of translated Chinese poems will be taken aback—even put off—by the frequency as well as the sentimentality of the lament for home. To understand the strength of this sentiment, we need to know that the Chinese desire for 4

ANSWERS TO QUESTIONS

Thinking Critically About Content

1. Americans are drawn to the open outdoors while the Chinese are more focused on the indoors.
2. It is an area beyond the suburbs.
3. The Chinese prefer to stay where they are rather than wander like Americans do.

Thinking Critically About Purpose and Audience

4. He is comparing and contrasting the

American and Chinese values of home.

5. His primary audience is Americans.
6. Space is a means by which we judge success as it is reflected in mobility and accomplishment.

Thinking Critically About Essays

7. The thesis appears at the end of the first paragraph: "The American is not rooted in his place, however lovely: his eyes are drawn by the expanding space to a point on the horizon, which is his future. By contrast, consider the traditional Chinese home. Blank walls enclose it." The window example leads up to it.
8. Yes, the topic sentences (the first two sentences) in paragraph 5 set up the controlling idea of the paragraph—the "rootlessness" of the Americans and the "rootedness" of the Chinese, and then the rest of the paragraph explain these claims.
9. Tuan gets his point across very effectively.
10. Answers will vary.

stability and rootedness in place is prompted by the constant threat of war, exile, and the natural disasters of flood and drought.

5 Forcible removal makes the Chinese keenly aware of their loss. By contrast, Americans move, for the most part, voluntarily. Their nostalgia for home town is really longing for childhood to which they cannot return: in the meantime the future beckons and the future is "out there" in open space. When we criticize American rootlessness we tend to forget that it is a result of ideals we admire, namely, social mobility and optimism about the future. When we admire Chinese rootedness, we forget that the word "place" means both location in space and position in society: to be tied to place is also to be bound to one's station in life, with little hope of betterment. Space symbolizes hope, place, achievement, and stability.

Thinking Critically About Content

1. What are the main differences between American homes and Chinese homes? Where is the focus in both of these settings?
2. What is "exurbia" (paragraph 1)?
3. In what ways are the Chinese rooted in their places?

Thinking Critically About Purpose and Audience

4. Why do you think Tuan wrote this essay?
5. Who do you think is his main audience?
6. How could space symbolize "hope, place, achievement, and stability" (paragraph 5)? How are all these notions related?

Thinking Critically About Essays

7. What is Tuan's thesis statement? How does he lead up to this thesis?
8. Explain how the topic sentence works in paragraph 5. Does it supply the controlling idea for the entire paragraph?
9. This is one of the shortest essays in this collection. Does Tuan get his point across effectively in this essay or does he need more paragraphs? Explain your answer.
10. Do you agree or disagree with his general conclusions about the Chinese and American concepts of space? Write a detailed response to some of Tuan's observations.

BETWEEN WORLDS
by Tony Cohan

Focusing Your Attention

1. Do you ever feel like you live in two or more different worlds? What are they?
2. In the essay you are about to read, the author compares and contrasts the "worlds" of San Miguel de Allende in Mexico and Los Angeles from a writer's point of view. What similarities and differences do you imagine that Cohan discovered?

Expanding Your Vocabulary

The following words are important to your understanding of this essay. Start a vocabulary log of your own by recording any words you don't understand as you read. When you finish reading the essay, write down what you think the words mean. Then check your definitions in the dictionary.

entwine: weave (paragraph 1)

revelatory: revealing (paragraph 1)

mired: buried (paragraph 1)

recession: decline (paragraph 1)

unkempt: messy, untidy (paragraph 4)

***la frontera*:** border (paragraph 5)

calibrations: adjustments (paragraph 6)

referent: point of reference (paragraph 7)

jargon: specialized language (paragraph 7)

deciphering: figuring out (paragraph 7)

***corrido*:** run (paragraph 8)

Proustian: emotional (paragraph 8)

feigned: pretend (paragraph 9)

reticent: uncommunicative, silent (paragraph 9)

xenophobic: afraid of strangers or foreigners (paragraph 9)

primordial: primitive (paragraph 9)

SUMMARY

In this essay, Cohan compares life in San Miguel de Allende, Mexico, and Los Angeles from a writer's point of view and finds that they are two necessary parts of his life.

READABILITY

(Flesch–Kincaid grade level)
8.2

INSTRUCTOR'S RESOURCE MANUAL

For additional teaching strategies, for journal entries, for vocabulary and reading quizzes, and for more writing assignments, see the *Instructor's Resource Manual*, Section II, Part II.

brujos: wizards (paragraph 9)

audibility: hearing (paragraph 10)

near-monastic: almost monk-like (paragraph 13)

muster: create (paragraph 13)

sabor: flavor (paragraph 13)

ambiente: atmosphere (paragraph 13)

celebratory: festive (paragraph 14)

norteño bands: bands from northern Mexico (paragraph 14)

patina: shine (paragraph 14)

conditional: tentative (paragraph 14)

corrugated: with parallel ridges (paragraph 17)

lumpen detritus: accumulated debris (paragraph 17)

READING CRITICALLY

As you did in the previous essay, teach the following essay to each other in class. This time, the class might divide into two large groups and then break again into two smaller groups (one for California and one for Mexico). Each large group should work on both cultures but should eventually compare notes with the culture in the other large group. This is an excellent way to make sure you understand all the details in a complex essay.

BETWEEN WORLDS

by Tony Cohan

1 Our fourth year in Mexico. We live between worlds these days, frequent flyers. The Mexican cycles of seasons and holidays entwine us deeper in town and country. Friends come and go, fall in love, split up; babies are born. Our life in San Miguel de Allende remains the intimate sum of our days—sensual, revelatory, engaged. Mexico, still mired in post-earthquake recession, muddles through somehow. New friends emerge: Arnaud, a

Haitian poet in exile who has awakened me to Caribbean culture; a Chilean painter and his wife; a Mexican professor.

Our world widens southward. The sprawling lands below the Rio Grande, a mere blip on CNN or ABC, remain to us norteamericanos, after all these centuries, the New World. Often after a flight from California we remain in Mexico City to explore, see new friends, venture out into other regions—Oaxaca, Guerrero, Yucatán, Chiapas—before returning to San Miguel, the heart's abode. 2

Still we feel unsettled at times, uneasily poised between cultures: losing a foothold in the old country, still on tourist visas in the new one. Masako's art bursts with imagery found here. Slowly Mexico takes root in my work, too: yet the language I hear and speak every day is not the one I write in. Gore Vidal, in an introduction to Paul Bowles's collected short stories, touches on the problem: "Great American writers are supposed not only to live in the greatest country in the world . . . but to write about that greatest of all human themes: the American Experience." A novelist friend I work with in PEN, the international writers group, says only half jokingly, "Careful you don't become a *desaparecido,* a disappeared person, yourself." 3

Sometimes I do fear liking Mexico too much, getting lost in it. One day I saw a scraggly, unkempt gringo on the Mexico City metro around my age with bad teeth and a bad haircut, tangled in another land, beyond return. He reminded me of Russians I'd seen in China, poor and disheveled, hunched atop bundles in train stations—the ones who'd stayed on too long. 4

On plane trips back to California, I gaze down at the Sea of Cortez: tidal blue stripes graduating from pale agate to turquoise to aquamarine. Salty inlets and rust basins, green algal meadows. Violet badlands etched with tiny straight-line roads, barren as Mars. We cross *la frontera,* that invisible, charged border, and belly down over L.A.'s carpet of light. From the back of a taxi running up the 405, the city spreads away before us, a bobbing, firefly-infested lake. 5

We stay on friends' couches, house-sit, sublet. We see people necessary to the work we do, thumbing our Rolodexes, trying to make the days count. Observing age's effects upon our parents, we make careful calibrations between desire and duty. Sometimes we talk of buying another place in L.A. just to have an anchor in the home country, but we can't summon the interest. We hurry through our tasks so we can leave all the sooner. 6

Old friends are busy climbing up, clinging to, falling off career ladders. The conversation is the same one we checked out on six months earlier, different only in detail, with television and movies the referent, not live 7 experience or books. I'm losing the jargon, the codes, the names of things. In conversations I blank on celebrities' names, hip expressions. Car alarms go off like crazy toys. Helicopters throb overhead, spotlighting evil. The nightly news imbues pedestrian acts with hysterical urgency. Few people walk for pleasure. There's little time to talk, and seldom of important things. It's easier to get some tasks done, as long as you don't need another human: I spend hours deciphering new telephone message menus, wading through oceans of calling options, waiting on hold. Arnaud, my Haitian poet friend in San Miguel, refers to revisiting his beloved Haiti as *the exile of return.*

8 Mexico in memory can be flat, flavorless, a postcard—like trying to remember sex or a good meal. It lives in the senses, not the mind, collapsing all abstractions into the brimming moment. Yet hearing a *corrido* on the radio or Spanish spoken in an L.A. market can unleash a near-overwhelming, Proustian effect, bringing tears. Now I understand better the mariachis' howling laments of memory and loss.

9 In California we don't talk much about Mexico. We've grown tired of the blank stares, the feigned interest, the allusions to Tijuana and the border towns, the beaches of Cabo or Cancún. Now I know why Mina and Paul used to be so reticent. In glossy, xenophobic, dollar-grubbing late-eighties U.S.A., Mexico is buzzless: a torpid blank somewhere south. Mexico, grail to generations of artists, site of primordial revelation—Mayan temples, *brujos,* muralists, hallucinatory mushrooms—has fallen off the map. This whorled, ornate neighbor civilization, secretly and essentially entwined with ours, is invisible, its people among us silent, nameless wraiths who clip lawns and clear tables.

10 In a West Hollywood eatery, we sit with friends, poking at endive salad, designer pizza. A plate glass window offers a view of the foothills behind the Strip. A Sade tape teases the threshold of lyric audibility. Noticing the nine-dollar taco on the menu, we glance at each other.

11 "Yes, but what do you *do* there?" one friend asks.

12 How to describe a trip to the Tuesday market? A four-hour dinner with Carlos, Elenita, Arnaud, and Colette in our patio by the Quebrada bridge? Waking up to the bells' sweet clangor? Hurrying along the cobbles in the rain, ducking under archways? How to describe Friday lunches at El Caribe or checking out Thomas More's *Utopia* at the little bilingual library and actually reading it through? It's as if we have a secret life, in a secret place.

13 I used to like L.A.: the cool speed, the indifference to history, the near-monastic life of house, car, house. It freed the mind to run along some ever widening horizon line. Flatness, the absence of affect: not a bad place for a writer. There's no world out there so you invent one. I can't muster that ap-

preciation any longer. I want taste, smell, *sabor, ambiente.* I want the human shape to my days.

14 In another sense, though, Mexico has redeemed L.A. to me. I've discovered a buried city there—a Latino L.A., warm and celebratory, where Spanish traces an invisible heart line deeper than place. In the course of my days, I may encounter a man or woman hailing from Guanajuato or Jalisco or Oaxaca, and matters of truth and fullness of heart may pass between us, and much laughter: riches invisible to most of my other friends. I can trace Los Lobos riffs back to *norteño* bands that come through our part of Mexico: Los Tigres del Norte, Los Bukis. California street names and foods reveal their origins. Suddenly the century-old Anglo patina looks flimsy, conditional.

15 Sometimes I get energy off the displacement, the dislocation, the back-and-forth. Each country seems the antidote to the other's ills. "In Rio, dreaming of New England/In New England, dreaming of Rio," the poet Elizabeth Bishop wrote.

16 Sometimes it feels like the two countries, through me, dream each other.

17 Invariably our L.A. trips end with a visit to the storage bin in Glendale. We introduce the seven-digit code, pass through the security gates, inch down aisles of identical metal containers and cinder-block structures. We remove the lock, raise the corrugated door, and consider the lumpen detritus of our former life.

18 We shut the door, lock it, drive off.

19 Finally, our lists checked off, we head back to Mexico. At journey's end, the Flecha Amarilla bus pulls into the dusty turnaround at the foot of San Miguel. We step out into darkness, as on that first night four years ago. The street dogs, the boys who want a coin to help with the baggage, the waiting taxi driver—those shades that so alarmed us then—appear to us now as town greeters, familiars. Wending up unlit streets once mysterious but intimate now from walking them, we make small talk with the taxi driver. "*Si,*" he says. "*Un poco frio.*" A little chilly. At Calle Quebrada we drag our bags down the dark stairwell, brush past a pair of young lovers. We open the door. The dusky smell of the last mesquite fire we'd built hits us. Our luggage slumps to the stone floor, our hands unclench. We're back.

Thinking Critically About Content

1. What do you think is Cohan's main point in this essay?
2. Why does Cohan call San Miguel "the heart's abode" (paragraph 2)?
3. In what ways is Cohan "poised between cultures" (paragraph 3)

Answers to Questions

Thinking Critically About Content

1. Cohan's main point is that his two homes (San Miguel and Los Angeles) complement each other in his role as a person and as a writer.
2. Cohan probably calls San Miguel "the heart's abode" because that's the place he likes the best.
3. He goes back and forth between Mexico and California with commitments in both places.

Thinking Critically About Purpose and Audience

4. Cohan probably wrote this essay to try to explain, if only to himself, what his feelings are about each of his residences.
5. Any readers would enjoy this essay, especially those who have lived in two different countries or who bring another culture to the place where they now live.
6. Answers will vary.

Thinking Critically About Essays

7. Answers will vary. There are points of comparison in

almost every paragraph.

8. Most of the paragraphs discuss both San Miguel and Los Angeles in reference to the topic of the paragraph. If a paragraph deals with only one of these locations in relation to a topic, the next paragraph usually deals with that topic and the other location.

9. Answers will vary.

10. Answers will vary.

Thinking Critically About Purpose and Audience

4. Why do you think Cohan wrote this essay?
5. Who would be most interested in this essay?
6. How does this essay make you feel about your home town?

Thinking Critically About Essays

7. Name four points of comparison and four points of contrast in this essay.
8. How are most of the paragraphs in this essay organized? Use one paragraph to explain your answer.
9. Is Cohan's title effective? Explain your answer.
10. Write a short fable about a similarity or difference between two cities you know.

TEACHING ON THE WEB

Discussion Topic: Divide students into groups of three or four. Ask them to compare and contrast a single search engine (like google.com) with one that surveys multiple search engines (like dogpile.com). In what circumstances is one better than the other? What are the advantages of both?

TEACHING ON THE WEB

Links: Provide students with a topic, and have them link to three Web sites that deal with that topic. How are these sites similar in their treatment of the topic? How are they different?

Writing Workshop

This final section gives you opportunities to apply what you have learned in this chapter to another writing assignment. This time, we provide very little prompting beyond a summary of the guidelines for writing a comparison/contrast essay. This section will let you demonstrate that you can go through the entire writing process on your own with only occasional feedback from your peers. Loop back into the chapter as necessary when you have questions so that this process becomes as automatic to you as possible before you move on to new material. Then pause at the end of the chapter to reflect briefly on what you have learned.

Guidelines for Writing a Comparison/Contrast Essay

1. Decide what point you want to make with your comparison, and state it in your thesis statement.
2. Choose items to compare and contrast that will make your point most effectively.
3. Use as many specific details and examples as possible to expand your comparison.
4. Develop your comparison in a balanced way.
5. Organize your essay subject by subject or point by point—or combine the two approaches.

Writing About Your Reading

1. In the first essay, Yi-Fu Tuan talks about the changes he sees in two countries' concept of space. But even in a single culture, we often think in different ways about space. Some people like to be physically close to others; some touch people while they talk; and others keep their distance at all times. Compare and contrast your personal notion of space with that of another person. What is the same between you two? What is different?
2. Expand the fable you wrote in response to question 10 after Tony Cohan's essay by adding more characters and more points.
3. What process do you have to go through to come up with an interesting comparison or contrast? How is it different from the process you go through for other rhetorical modes?

Possible sites for the topic "education":
U.S. Department of Education, www.ed.gov
Chronicle of Higher Education, http://chronicle.merit.com
American Council on Education, www.acenet.edu

TEACHING ON THE WEB
Research: Have students find Web sites that sell the same types of products. How are these sites similar? How are they different? Which product would students buy based on the Web sites? How did comparison and contrast help them come to this decision?

Writing About Your World

1. Compare and contrast the two buildings in the picture above. What details in both buildings are different? What are the same? What is the overall message you get from these two buildings? Look at both the obvious and the not-so-obvious.
2. Choose a job being advertised in your local newspaper's classified section, and write a cover letter to the employer comparing yourself to your

probable competition. What are your best qualifications compared to others who might be applying for this job? What are your weaknesses in comparison to them? Why would you be the best candidate for the job?

3. Discuss the similarities and differences between two cities that you know well. How are they the same? How are they different? What do you think accounts for these similarities and differences? When you write your essay, consider whether a subject-by-subject or a point-by-point organization would be more effective.
4. Create your own comparison/contrast assignment (with the help of your instructor), and write a response to it.

Revising

Small Group Activity (5–10 minutes per writer)
Working in groups of three or four, read your comparison/contrast essays to each other. Those listening should record their reactions on a copy of the Peer Evaluation Form in Appendix 2E. After your group goes through this process, give your evaluation forms to the appropriate writers so that each writer has two or three peer comment sheets for revising.

Paired Activity (5 minutes per writer) Using the completed Peer Evaluation Forms, work in pairs to decide what you should revise in your essay. If time allows, rewrite some of your sentences, and have your partner look at them.

Individual Activity Rewrite your paper, using the revising feedback you received from other students.

Editing

Paired Activity (5–10 minutes per writer) Swap papers with a classmate, and use the editing portion of your Peer Evaluation Form to identify as many grammar, punctuation, mechanics, and spelling errors as you can. If time allows, correct some of your errors, and have your partner look at them. Record your grammar, punctuation, and mechanics errors in the Error Log (Appendix 6) and your spelling errors in the Spelling Log (Appendix 7).

Individual Activity Rewrite your paper again, using the editing feedback you received from other students.

Reflecting on Your Writing When you have completed your own essay, answer these six questions.

1. What was most difficult about this assignment?
2. What was easiest?
3. What did you learn about comparison and contrast by completing this assignment?
4. What do you think are the strengths of your comparison/contrast essay? Place a wavy line by the parts of your essay that you feel are very good.
5. What are the weaknesses, if any, of your paper? Place an X by the parts of your essay you would like help with. Write any questions you have in the margin.
6. What did you learn from this assignment about your own writing process—about preparing to write, about writing the first draft, about revising, and about editing?

13

CHAPTER

Dividing and Classifying

"Words are the copies of your ideas."

—HUGH BLAIR

TEACHING DIVISION AND CLASSIFICATION Bring the word game Outburst to class. Divide your students into groups of four or five, and have them play a few rounds of the game. (You might want to modify the game to suit your classroom.) One of the goals is for students to think of many divisions of one category, but you might want to alter the rules and have them work backward—trying to guess the classification from all the categories—to show them how both division and classification work. Consider giving prizes to the students who win in their groups.

Not only is this game fun, but it also provides students with a grasp of the difference between division and classification. It also shows how these strategies work together.

Division and classification ensure that we have a certain amount of order in our lives. In fact, we constantly use these two processes to navigate through our days. Thanks to classification, you know where to find the milk in the grocery store and the chapter on World War II in your history textbook. Also, when you choose a major and a career, you use division and classification to make your choice. Division and classification are such a natural part of everyday life that we often don't even know we are using them.

In addition, we regularly use division and classification when we write. Actually, division and classification are a vital part of our written communication every day—in our personal lives, in college courses, and in the workplace:

- You divide your expenses into categories to create a budget.
- A student explains three types of bacteria on a biology exam.
- A student writes a report on types of hazardous materials for a science course.
- A personal banker prepares a flyer about the types of savings accounts that are available.
- The manager of a music store suggests to the home office a new system for arranging CDs.

Like comparison and contrast, division and classification are really two parts of the same process. **Division** is sorting—dividing something into its basic parts, such as a home into rooms. Division moves from a single, large category (home) to many smaller subcategories (kitchen, bath, living room, and so forth). **Classification,** grouping items together, moves in the opposite direction, from many subgroups to a single, large category. For example, all the pieces of furniture in a home can be classified as living room furniture or bedroom furniture. Division and classification help us organize information so that we can make sense of our complex world. Dividing large categories into smaller ones (division) and grouping many items into larger categories (classification) both help us put a lot of information into useful groups.

READING AND WRITING A DIVISION/ CLASSIFICATION ESSAY

Learning how to read division/classification essays critically will help you become a better writer. As you see how an essay is constructed and how a thesis is developed in this mode, you will be able to apply what you discover to your own writing. Reading and writing in any mode are demanding, but they are both necessary for success in college and in life. Like two halves of a circle, these two processes complement each other and enhance your ability to perform many other tasks.

Reading a Division/Classification Essay

Here is a sample division/classification essay by Fran Lebowitz called "The Sound of Music: Enough Already." It classifies the types of music Lebowitz dislikes the most. What are some of your dislikes? Are these also your biggest pet peeves? Why do you dislike these things or behaviors?

READING CRITICALLY

As you read more difficult essays, the ability to summarize is essential. A summary features the main ideas of a selection in a coherent paragraph. First, you identify the main ideas in your reading; then you fold them into a paragraph with logical transitions so your sentences flow from one to another. Write a summary of the following selection, and then draft three questions for discussion that come from your summary.

TEACHING TIPS

The following eight teaching tips are based on Howard Gardner's list of multiple intelligences:

Verbal/Linguistic

Provide students with four very limited categories, and ask them to determine how many classifications the categories can fall into. For example, show students how "small, eight-week-old golden retriever puppy" might fall into the classifications "family," "children," "friend," "playmate," "responsibility," and so on.

Musical/Rhythmic

Have students divide "popular music" into categories and subcategories. How can these categories help someone understand the music of today?

Logical/Mathematical

Provide students with an abundance of related words that can be divided into three levels. Then have students diagram the main classification and the divisions that can stem from this category. For example, use "*fun*" as one level; *sports, leisure,* and *vacation* as a second level; and *soccer, softball, racquetball, reading, watching TV, sunbathing, family trips, spring break,* and *weekend getaways* as a third level.

Visual/Spatial

Bring several books to class. Have students divide the books into logical categories. How many categories can students generate? How many books fit into more than one category?

Bodily/Kinesthetic

Blindfold students one at a time, and ask them to identify the categories of objects you place in their hands. For example, you might have a dog bone, a leash, a chew toy, and a piece of rawhide for the students to identify as "dog supplies."

Intrapersonal

Have students classify their routine activities. If "family," "friends," and "work" are classifications they use, have them further divide their daily activities to determine how they spend their time.

Interpersonal

Have students classify the types of friends they have had in their lives. How many categories do their friends fall into?

THE SOUND OF MUSIC: ENOUGH ALREADY

by Fran Lebowitz

1 First off, I want to say that as far as I am concerned, in instances where I have not personally and deliberately sought it out, the only difference between music and Muzak is the spelling. Pablo Casals practicing across the hall with the door open—being trapped in an elevator, the ceiling of which is broadcasting "Parsley, Sage, Rosemary, and Thyme"—it's all the same to me. Harsh words? Perhaps. But then again these are not gentle times we live in. And they are being made no more gentle by this incessant melody that was once real life.

2 There was a time when music knew its place. No longer. Possibly this is not music's fault. It may be that music fell in with a bad crowd and lost its sense of common decency. I am willing to consider this. I am willing even to try and help. I would like to do my bit to set music straight in order that it might shape up and leave the mainstream of society. The first thing that music must understand is that there are two kinds of music—good music and bad music. Good music is music that I want to hear. Bad music is music that I don't want to hear.

3 So that music might more clearly see the error of its ways, I offer the following. If you are music and you recognize yourself on this list, you are bad music.

1. Music in Other People's Clock Radios

4 There are times when I find myself spending the night in the home of another. Frequently the other is in a more reasonable line of work than I and must arise at a specific hour. Ofttimes the other, unbeknownst to me, manipulates an appliance in such a way that I am awakened by Stevie Wonder. On such occasions I announce that, if I wished to be awakened by Stevie Wonder, I would sleep with Stevie Wonder. I do not, however, wish to be awakened by Stevie Wonder and that is why God invented alarm clocks. Sometimes the other realizes that I am right. Sometimes the other does not. And that is why God invented many others.

2. Music Residing in the Hold Buttons of Other People's Business Telephones

5 I do not under any circumstances enjoy hold buttons. But I am a woman of reason. I can accept reality. I can face the facts. What I cannot face is the

music. Just as there are two kinds of music—good and bad—so there are two kinds of hold buttons—good and bad. Good hold buttons are hold buttons that hold one silently. Bad hold buttons are hold buttons that hold one musically. When I hold, I want to hold silently. That is the way it was meant to be, for that is what God was talking about when he said, "Forever hold your peace." He would have added, "and quiet," but he thought you were smarter.

Naturalist
Have students find as many types of plants and flowers as possible on your campus. How many varieties are there? Can they be classified or divided into other groups?

3. Music in the Streets

6 The past few years have seen a steady increase in the number of people playing music in the streets. The past few years have also seen a steady increase in the number of malignant diseases. Are these two facts related? One wonders. But even if they are not—and, as I have pointed out, one cannot be sure—music in the streets has definitely taken its toll. For it is at the very least disorienting. When one is walking down Fifth Avenue, one does not expect to hear a string quartet playing a Strauss waltz. What one expects to hear while walking down Fifth Avenue is traffic. When one does indeed hear a string quartet playing a Strauss waltz while one is walking down Fifth Avenue, one is apt to become confused and imagine that one is not walking down Fifth Avenue at all but rather that one has somehow wound up in Old Vienna. Should one imagine that one is in Old Vienna, one is likely to become upset when one realizes that in Old Vienna there is no sale at Charles Jourdan. And that is why when I walk down Fifth Avenue I want to hear traffic.

Instructor's Resource Manual
For additional material about teaching division and classification; for journal entries; and for multiple-choice, short-answer, and paragraph tests, see the *Instructor's Resource Manual*, Section II, Part II.

4. Music in the Movies

7 I'm not talking about musicals. Musicals are movies that warn you by saying, "Lots of music here. Take it or leave it." I'm talking about regular movies that extend no such courtesy but allow unsuspecting people to come to see them and then assault them with a barrage of unasked-for tunes. There are two major offenders in this category: black movies and movies set in the fifties. Both types of movies are afflicted with the same misconception. They don't know that movies are supposed to be movies. They think that movies are supposed to be records with pictures. They have failed to understand that if God had wanted records to have pictures, he would not have invented television.

5. Music in Public Places Such as Restaurants, Supermarkets, Hotel Lobbies, Airports, Etc.

8 When I am in any of the above-mentioned places, I am not there to hear music. I am there for whatever reason is appropriate to the respective place. I am no more interested in hearing "Mack the Knife" while waiting for the shuttle to Boston than someone sitting ringside at the Sands Hotel is

interested in being forced to choose between sixteen varieties of cottage cheese. If God had meant for everything to happen at once, he would not have invented desk calendars.

Epilogue

9 Some people talk to themselves. Some people sing to themselves. Is one group better than the other? Did not God create all people equal? Yes, God created all people equal. Only to some he gave the ability to make up their own words.

Preparing to Write Your Own Division/Classification Essay

Everyone has pet peeves. What are yours? How did you develop these pet peeves? Do your pet peeves form any particular patterns? Use one or more of the prewriting strategies that you learned in Chapter 2 to explore this topic.

Writing a Division/Classification Essay

To write a division/classification essay, keep in mind that the same items can be divided and classified in many different ways. Your friends probably don't all organize their closets the way you do, and no two kitchens are organized exactly alike. The United States can be divided many different ways—into 50 states, four regions (Northeast, Midwest, South, and Pacific), and six time zones (Eastern, Central, Mountain, Pacific, Alaska, and Hawaii). Similarly, in writing you can divide and classify a topic in different ways. Whatever your method of dividing or classifying, use the following guidelines to help you write an effective division/classification essay.

1. **Decide on your purpose for writing, and make it part of your thesis statement.** Dividing and classifying in themselves are not particularly interesting. But they are very useful techniques if you are trying to make a specific point. That point, or purpose, should be in your thesis statement. Look at these two examples:

   A. There are three types of dangerous drivers on the road today.
   B. Being aware of three types of dangerous drivers on the road today could save your life.

   Both thesis statements name a category—dangerous drivers—but only thesis statement B gives the reader a good reason to keep reading: Knowing the three types could save your life.

In our sample essay, Lebowitz uses division and classification to make fun of the types of music she dislikes. She divides all music into good music and bad music. Then she breaks bad music into five categories. She captures the humor of her essay in her thesis at the end of paragraph 3: "If you are music and you recognize yourself on this list, you are bad music."

2. **Divide your topic into categories that don't overlap.** Since most subjects can be classified in different ways, your next task in writing a division/classification essay is to decide on what basis you will divide your subject into categories. First, gather information to come up with a list of all the possible topics. Second, decide on what basis you will put these topics into categories. Next, make sure some of your topics don't fall into two categories. Your categories should be separate enough that your topics fall into one category only. Also, don't add a category at the last minute to accommodate a topic. Keep adjusting your categories until they work with your thesis.

   In the sample essay, the author uses a combination of division and classification to make her point. First, she divides all music into good and bad. Then she classifies bad music into five categories: (1) music in other people's clock radios, (2) music in the hold buttons of other people's business telephones, (3) music in the streets, (4) music in the movies, and (5) music in public places such as restaurants, supermarkets, hotel lobbies, and airports. She might have tried to classify bad music in other ways, such as public and private; indoor, outdoor, and a combination of the two; or personal, business related, and involving other people. But none of these options would be effective. The first two groupings are too general to supply the detailed information that Lebowitz's categories give us. The third set of categories would force the author to classify many topics, like music in the movies and music in public places, in two categories, which would be confusing. Lebowitz's more specific categories are all about the same size and are very effective in sending her humorous message.

3. **Clearly explain each category.** With division, you are trying to show what differences break the items into separate groups or types. With classification, you let the similarities in the items help you set up categories that make sense. In either case, you need to explain each category fully and provide enough details to help your readers see your subject in a new way. To do this, use vivid description and carefully chosen examples. Comparison and contrast (Chapter 12) are also useful techniques because when you classify items, you are looking at how they are alike (comparison) and how they are different (contrast).

Lebowitz uses comparison and contrast to place her ideas into categories. Then she describes each category and provides detailed examples, such as Stevie Wonder, a Strauss waltz, and "Mack the Knife," to fill out her descriptions. As a result, she explains each of her categories fully and clearly.

4. **Organize your categories logically.** Your method of organization should make sense and be easy for readers to follow. Most often, this means organizing from one extreme to another. For example, you might organize your types from most obvious to least obvious. Or you might move from least important to most important, from least humorous to most humorous, from largest to smallest—or the other way around. In every case, though, try to end with the category that is most memorable.

   Fran Lebowitz's essay is arranged from one extreme to another—from personal to public. The categories move from clock radios to business phones to music in the streets to music in movies to music in public places. Each category gets farther from the personal realm, which helps Lebowitz prove that bad music is everywhere.

5. **Use transitions to move your readers through your essay.** Transitions will help your readers move from one category to another and follow your train of thought. They will also keep your essay from sounding choppy or boring.

   Since Lebowitz gives her categories headings, she doesn't need to use transitions to move from one category to another. But she does use transitions within her paragraphs. Here are some effective transitions from Lebowitz's essay: "first off" (paragraph 1), "there was a time when" (paragraph 2), "frequently" (paragraph 4), "on such occasions" (paragraph 4), "but" (paragraph 5), and "when" (paragraphs 6 and 8). These words and phrases serve as traffic signals that guide Lebowitz's readers through her essay.

Writing Your Own Division/Classification Essay

Write an essay explaining your various pet peeves. How did these pet peeves start? Why do you have them? Begin by reviewing your prewriting notes. Next, divide your subject into distinct categories, organize your categories, and write a clear thesis statement. Then, by following the guidelines for writing a division/classification paper, develop your essay with specific examples that explain each category.

A STUDENT'S DIVISION/ CLASSIFICATION ESSAY

Sergio Mendola, a student writer, uses division and classification in an essay about neighbors. Called "Won't You Be My Neighbor?" it divides and classifies neighbors into specific categories to prove a point. See if you can identify his main point as you read this draft of his essay.

Won't You Be My Neighbor?

Neighborhoods can be strange places. Every one is different, but they are all made up of the same ingredient—neighbors. In today's world, though, most people don't know there neighbors. It's not like the '50s. When people knew what their neighbors were doing. But in every neighborhood today, you can find at least one Mystery Neighbor, one Perfect Cleaver Family, and one Good Neighbor Family. 1

The first type of neighbor everyone has is the Perfect Cleaver Family. This family has the perfect parents and the perfect children. They are the June and Ward Cleavers of today. They have 2.5 perfect children. Although these children get in their share of minor trouble, the children never repeat the same mistake after the parents express their disappointment. And then, to avoid future disappointments, the children always keep their parents' values in mind before making decisions. Eddie Haskell left a lot to be desired. I don't know what his values are. The Cleaver-type children later become heart surgeons or police chiefs in order to help the world around them. These neighbors are the role models for everyone else. 2

Then there is the Mystery Neighbor. The Mystery Neighbor remains aloof, and the only way the other neighbors know someone lives at the Mystery House is because the newspaper disappears sometime during the day and the lawn somehow gets mowed every week. Every once in a while, a car will sit in the driveway, but no one knows for sure if the car belongs to the people who own the house. Neighborhood children make up stories about the Mystery Neighbor, which are based on nothing and compete with the best urban legends. The Mystery Neighbor is usually a workaholic or a traveling salesperson, but this doesn't stop the neighbors from wondering. 3

The best type of neighbor in any neighborhood is the Good Neighbor Family. Made up of very reliable people. This family is always reaching out to other neighbors. Whenever something goes wrong, someone from the Good Neighbor Family is the first person at the doorstep to lend a helping hand. 4

These neighbors will water the plants and feed the animals for people on vacation who always want to help others. They create the kinds of friendships that continue even when one family moves away. Sometimes the parents might try to "fix up" their boy and girl children so that the families relationship can be legally cemented for life. The Good Neighbor Family is one that everyone hopes to encounter at least once in a lifetime.

5 This mixture of neighbors makes up a very good neighborhood. It creates a neighborhood that functions smoothly and thoughtfully. And even though people don't no their neighbors like they used to 50 years ago, they will probably find at least three different types of neighbors if they look hard enough: the Perfect Cleaver Family, the Mystery Neighbor, and the Good Neighbor Family. It would be sad to be missing any one of them.

Discovering How the Essay Works

1. This essay doesn't simply classify neighbors for their own sake. It has a broader message. What is Sergio's general purpose in this essay?

   To explain that every neighborhood has the same three basic types of neighbors that make a neighborhood interesting.

2. Does Sergio divide his subject into categories that don't overlap?

   He makes sure that he has three distinct categories, and he develops each one separately.

3. Does Sergio adequately clarify each of his categories? Explain your answer.

   Sergio clearly explains each category by providing examples that illustrate the different types of neighbors.

4. How does Sergio organize his categories? Is this the most logical order for this purpose? Explain your answer.

   He moves from least to most desirable neighbor. It is effective and logical, although the body paragraphs are out of order.

5. What transitions does Sergio use to move his essay along smoothly?

The first type

Then

The best type of neighbor

Revising and Editing the Student Essay

This essay is Sergio's first draft, which now needs to be revised and edited. First, apply the following Revising Checklist to the content of Sergio's draft. When you are satisfied that his ideas are fully developed and well organized, use the Editing Checklist on pages 306–307 to correct his grammar and mechanics errors. Do the tasks, and answer the questions after each checklist. Then write your suggested changes directly on Sergio's draft.

REVISING AND EDITING OPTIONS
Consider varying your approach to revising and editing. You could teach these skills in a class discussion, in small groups, or in pairs.

REVISING CHECKLIST

REVISING STRATEGIES
This chapter focuses on the following revising elements:

Basic elements
Development
Unity
Organization
Coherence

THESIS STATEMENT

✔ Does the thesis statement contain the essay's controlling idea?

✔ Does the thesis appear as the last sentence of the introduction?

BASIC ELEMENTS

✔ Does the title draw in the readers?

✔ Does the introduction capture the readers' attention and build up to the thesis statement effectively?

✔ Does each body paragraph deal with a single topic?

✔ Does the conclusion bring the essay to a close in an interesting way?

DEVELOPMENT

✔ Do the body paragraphs adequately support the thesis statement?

✔ Does each body paragraph have a focused topic sentence?

✔ Does each body paragraph contain *specific* details that support the topic sentence?

✔ Does each body paragraph include *enough* details to explain the topic sentence fully?

UNITY

✔ Do the essay's topic sentences relate directly to the thesis statement?

✔ Do the details in each body paragraph support its topic sentence?

ORGANIZATION

✔ Is the essay organized logically?

✔ Is each body paragraph organized logically?

COHERENCE

✔ Are transitions used effectively so that paragraphs move smoothly and logically from one to the next?

✔ Do the sentences move smoothly and logically from one to the next?

Thesis Statement

1. Put brackets around the last sentence in Sergio's introduction. Does it introduce his purpose?

   Yes

2. Rewrite Sergio's thesis statement if necessary so that it states his purpose and introduces his topics.

   His thesis states his purpose and introduces his topics.

Basic Elements

1. Give Sergio's essay an alternate title.

   Answers will vary.

2. Rewrite Sergio's introduction so that it captures the readers' attention and builds up to the thesis statement at the end of the paragraph.

   Answers will vary.

3. Does each of Sergio's body paragraphs deal with only one topic?

   Yes

4. Rewrite Sergio's conclusion using at least one suggestion from Part I.

   Answers will vary.

Development

1. Write out Sergio's thesis statement (revised, if necessary), and list his three topic sentences below it.

   Thesis statement: *But in every neighborhood today, you can find at least one Mystery Neighbor, one Perfect Cleaver Family, and one Good Neighbor Family.*

   Topic 1: *The first type of neighbor everyone has is the Perfect Cleaver Family.*

   Topic 2: *Then there is the Mystery Neighbor.*

   Topic 3: *The best type of neighbor in any neighborhood is the Good Neighbor Family.*

2. Do Sergio's topics adequately support his thesis statement?

   Yes

3. Does each body paragraph have a focused topic sentence?

   Yes

4. Do Sergio's details adequately explain his categories?

   Yes, but he could use more detail.

5. Where do you need more information?

   Answers will vary.

6. Make two of Sergio's details more specific. *Answers will vary.*
7. Add two new details to make his essay clearer. *Answers will vary.*

Unity

1. Read each of Sergio's topic sentences with his thesis statement (revised, if necessary) in mind. Do they go together?

   Yes

2. Revise his topic sentences if necessary so they are directly related.
3. Drop or rewrite the two sentences in paragraph 2 that are not directly related to their topic sentences. *Sentences 7 and 8*

Organization

1. Read Sergio's essay again to see if all the paragraphs are arranged logically.
2. Reverse the two paragraphs that are out of order. *Reverse paragraphs 2 and 3.*
3. Look closely at Sergio's body paragraphs to see if all his sentences are arranged logically within paragraphs.
4. Move any sentences that are out of order. *All sentences are in order.*

Coherence

For a list of transitions, see page 101.

For a list of pronouns, see pages 7–8.

1. Add two transitions to Sergio's essay.
2. Circle five transitions, repetitions, synonyms, or pronouns Sergio uses.
3. Explain how two of these make Sergio's essay easier to read.

   ____

   ____

Now rewrite Sergio's essay with your revisions.

EDITING STRATEGIES
This chapter focuses on the following editing problems:
Fragments
Modifier errors

EDITING CHECKLIST

SENTENCES

✓ Does each sentence have a main subject and verb?

✓ Do all subjects and verbs agree?

✓ Do all pronouns agree with their nouns?

✓ Are modifiers as close as possible to the words they modify?

Apostrophes (possession)
Confused words

PUNCTUATION AND MECHANICS

✓ Are sentences punctuated correctly?

✓ Are words capitalized properly?

WORD CHOICE AND SPELLING

✓ Are words used correctly?

✓ Are words spelled correctly?

Sentences

Subjects and Verbs

1. Underline the subjects once and verbs twice in paragraphs 1 and 4 of your revision of Sergio's essay. Remember that sentences can have more than one subject-verb set.

For help with subjects and verbs, see Chapter 25.

2. Does each of the sentences have at least one subject and verb that can stand alone?

   No

3. Did you find and correct Sergio's two fragments? If not, find and correct them now. *Paragraph 1, sentence 5; paragraph 4, sentence 2*

For help with fragments, see Chapter 26.

Subject-Verb Agreement

1. Read aloud the subjects and verbs you underlined in your revision of Sergio's essay.
2. Correct any subjects and verbs that do not agree. *All subjects and verbs agree.*

For help with subject-verb agreement, see Chapter 30.

Pronoun Agreement

1. Find any pronouns in your revision of Sergio's essay that do not agree with their nouns. *All pronouns agree with their nouns.*
2. Correct any pronouns that do not agree with their nouns.

For help with pronoun agreement, see Chapter 34.

Modifiers

1. Find any modifiers in your revision of Sergio's essay that are not as close as possible to the words they modify.
2. Did you find and correct Sergio's modifier error? If not, find and correct it now. *Paragraph 4, sentence 5*

For help with modifier errors, see Chapter 37.

Punctuation and Mechanics

Punctuation

For help with punctuation, see Chapters 38–42.

1. Read your revision of Sergio's essay for any errors in punctuation.
2. Find the two fragments you revised, and make sure they are punctuated correctly.
3. Did you find and correct the missing apostrophe in Sergio's essay? *Paragraph 4, sentence 7*

Mechanics

For help with capitalization, see Chapter 43.

1. Read your revision of Sergio's essay for any errors in capitalization.
2. Be sure to check Sergio's capitalization in the fragments you revised.

Word Choice and Spelling

Word Choice

For help with confused words, see Chapter 49.

1. Find any words used incorrectly in your revision of Sergio's essay. *there/their (paragraph 1, sentence 3); too/to (paragraph 4, sentence 4); know/no (paragraph 5, sentence 3)*
2. Did you find and correct his three confused words? If not, find and correct them now.

Spelling

For help with spelling, see Chapter 50.

1. Use spell-check and a dictionary to check the spelling in your revision of Sergio's essay. *All words are spelled correctly.*
2. Correct any misspelled words.

Now rewrite Sergio's essay again with your editing corrections.

YOUR OWN DIVISION/CLASSIFICATION ESSAY

Returning to the division/classification essay you wrote earlier in this chapter, you are now ready to revise and edit your own writing. Remember that revision involves reworking the content and organization of your essay while editing asks you to check your grammar and usage. At this stage, you should repeat these processes until you feel you have a draft that says exactly what you want it to say.

WRITING CRITICALLY

Now write a summary of your own essay. See if all your main ideas are clear and easy to identify. Make sure the connections between the ideas in your summary are logical and understandable. Are these connections also clear in your essay itself? Change any elements of your essay that will make your main ideas clearer and more logical to your readers.

Revising and Editing Your Own Essay

The checklists here will help you apply what you have learned in this chapter to your essay.

CLASS ACTIVITY

Take some of the categories that students created for the "Write Your Own Division/Classification Essay" at the beginning of this chapter, and show how the categories were divided from the classification "pet peeves" and how, when reversed, the divisions create the same main classification.

REVISING CHECKLIST

THESIS STATEMENT

- ☐ Does the thesis statement contain the essay's controlling idea?
- ☐ Does the thesis appear as the last sentence of the introduction?

BASIC ELEMENTS

- ☐ Does the title draw in the readers?
- ☐ Does the introduction capture the readers' attention and build up to the thesis statement effectively?
- ☐ Does each body paragraph deal with a single topic?
- ☐ Does the conclusion bring the essay to a close in an interesting way?

DEVELOPMENT

- ☐ Do the body paragraphs adequately support the thesis statement?
- ☐ Does each body paragraph have a focused topic sentence?
- ☐ Does each body paragraph contain *specific* details that support the topic sentence?
- ☐ Does each body paragraph include *enough* details to explain the topic sentence fully?

UNITY

- ☐ Do the essay's topic sentences relate directly to the thesis statement?
- ☐ Do the details in each body paragraph support its topic sentence?

ORGANIZATION

- ☐ Is the essay organized logically?
- ☐ Is each body paragraph organized logically?

COHERENCE

- ☐ Are transitions used effectively so that paragraphs move smoothly and logically from one to the next?
- ☐ Do the sentences move smoothly and logically from one to the next?

Thesis Statement

1. What is the purpose or general message you want to send to your readers?

   ____

2. Put brackets around the last sentence in your introduction. Does it explain your purpose?

   ____

3. Rewrite your thesis statement if necessary so that it states your purpose and introduces your topics.

Basic Elements

1. Give your essay a title if it doesn't have one.

   ____

2. Does your introduction capture your readers' attention and build up to your thesis statement at the end of the paragraph?

   ____

3. Does each of your body paragraphs deal with only one topic?

   ____

4. Does your conclusion follow some of the suggestions offered in Part I?

   ____

Development

1. Write out your thesis statement (revised, if necessary), and list your topic sentences below it.

   Thesis statement: ______________________________

   Topic 1: ______________________________

   Topic 2: ______________________________

   Topic 3: ______________________________

2. Do your topics adequately support your thesis statement?

   ____

3. Does each body paragraph have a focused topic sentence?

   ____

4. Do your details adequately explain your categories?

   ____

5. Where do you need more information?

   ____

6. Make two of your details more specific.
7. Add at least two new details to make your essay clearer.

Unity

1. Read each of your topic sentences with your thesis statement in mind. Do they go together?

   ____

2. Revise your topic sentences if necessary so they are directly related.
3. Drop or rewrite any of the sentences in your body paragraphs that are not directly related to their topic sentences.

Organization

1. Read your essay again to see if all the paragraphs are arranged logically.
2. Refer to your answers to the development questions. Then identify your method of organization.

 ____

3. Is the order you chose for your paragraphs the most effective approach to your topic?

 ____

4. Move any paragraphs that are out of order.
5. Look closely at your body paragraphs to see if all the sentences are arranged logically within paragraphs.
6. Move any sentences that are out of order.

Coherence

For a list of transitions, see page 101.

For a list of pronouns, see pages 7–8.

1. Add two transitions to your essay.
2. Circle five transitions, repetitions, synonyms, or pronouns you use.
3. Explain how two of them make your paragraphs easier to read.

 ____

 ____

Now rewrite your essay with your revisions.

EDITING CHECKLIST

SENTENCES

- ☐ Does each sentence have a main subject and verb?
- ☐ Do all subjects and verbs agree?
- ☐ Do all pronouns agree with their nouns?
- ☐ Are modifiers as close as possible to the words they modify?

PUNCTUATION AND MECHANICS

- ☐ Are sentences punctuated correctly?

☐ Are words capitalized properly?

WORD CHOICE AND SPELLING

☐ Are words used correctly?

☐ Are words spelled correctly?

Sentences

Subjects and Verbs

1. Underline the subjects once and verbs twice in a paragraph of your revised essay. Remember that sentences can have more than one subject-verb set.
2. Does each of your sentences have at least one subject and verb that can stand alone?

For help with subjects and verbs, see Chapter 25.

____

3. Correct any fragments you have written.
4. Correct any run-together sentences you have written.

For help with fragments, see Chapter 26.

For help with run-togethers, see Chapter 27.

Subject-Verb Agreement

1. Read aloud the subjects and verbs you underlined in your revised essay.
2. Correct any subjects and verbs that do not agree.

For help with subject-verb agreement, see Chapter 30.

Pronoun Agreement

1. Find any pronouns in your revised essay that do not agree with their nouns.
2. Correct any pronouns that do not agree with their nouns.

For help with pronoun agreement, see Chapter 34.

Modifiers

1. Find any modifiers in your revised essay that are not as close as possible to the words they modify.
2. Rewrite sentences if necessary so your modifiers are as close as possible to the words they modify.

For help with modifier errors, see Chapter 37.

Punctuation and Mechanics

Punctuation

For help with punctuation, see Chapters 38–42.

1. Read your revised essay for any errors in punctuation.
2. Make sure any fragments and run-together sentences you revised are punctuated correctly.

Mechanics

For help with capitalization, see Chapter 43.

1. Read your revised essay for any errors in capitalization.
2. Be sure to check your capitalization in any fragments or run-together sentences you revised.

Word Choice and Spelling

Word Choice

For help with confused words, see Chapter 49.

1. Find any words used incorrectly in your revised essay.
2. Correct any errors you find.

Spelling

For help with spelling, see Chapter 50.

1. Use spell-check and a dictionary to check your spelling.
2. Correct any misspelled words.

Now rewrite your essay again with your editing corrections.

PRACTICING DIVISION/CLASSIFICATION: FROM READING TO WRITING

Reading Workshop

Here are two essays that illustrate good division and classification writing: "Black Music in Our Hands" by Bernice Reagon categorizes different kinds of music she has encountered, while "What Are Friends For?" by Marion Winik discusses different types of friends. As you read, notice how the authors' categories support the points they are making.

BLACK MUSIC IN OUR HANDS

by Bernice Reagon

SUMMARY

In this essay, Reagon explains the different types of music she has encountered that have "helped to shape my present-day use of music" (paragraph 15).

READABILITY

(Flesch–Kincaid grade level)
10.3

INSTRUCTOR'S RESOURCE MANUAL

For additional teaching strategies, for journal entries, for vocabulary and reading quizzes, and for more writing assignments, see the *Instructor's Resource Manual*, Section II, Part II.

Focusing Your Attention

1. What are some of your main interests in life? Have any of these interests been part of your life for a long time? How have they changed over time?
2. In the essay you are about to read, the writer divides and classifies music from a number of different perspectives. What role does music play in your life? Has it always played this role? How has it changed in your life over the years?

Expanding Your Vocabulary

The following words are important to your understanding of this essay. Organize this list into two columns—words you know and words you don't know. Which of the words you don't know can you guess from their sentences?

Albany State: college in Albany, Georgia (paragraph 1)

contralto soloist: a woman singer with a very low voice (paragraph 1)

arias: songs in an opera (paragraph 1)

lieder: traditional German songs (paragraph 1)

Nathaniel Dett: 1882–1943, American composer and pianist (paragraph 1)

William Dawson: 1899–1990, African American composer (paragraph 1)

unaccompanied: without musical instruments (paragraph 2)

ornate: complex (paragraph 2)

congregational responses: singing by the people in the pews in reply to someone at the front of the church (paragraph 2)

Civil Rights Movement: push for equal rights for African Americans in the 1950s and 1960s (paragraph 5)

integrative: uniting (paragraph 5)

Albany Movement: a movement started in Albany, Georgia, and led by Reverend Martin Luther King Jr. that hoped to gain more freedom for African Americans but ended in racial violence (paragraph 8)

Freedom Singers: African Americans who sang about civic rights during the Civil Rights Movement (paragraph 12)

Georgia Sea Island Singers: international performing artists who sing about African American culture (paragraph 13)

Newport Festival: summer music festival held in Newport, Rhode Island (paragraph 13)

repertoire: collection of songs that an artist is able to perform (paragraph 13)

casings: coverings (paragraph 16)

sit-in: an act of protest in which demonstrators sit down and refuse to leave the premises (paragraph 17)

Wallace: George Wallace, 1919–1998, the segregationist governor of Alabama (paragraph 17)

Freedom Rides: rides taken by civil rights activists to ensure that public facilities had been desegregated (paragraph 17)

ensemble: a group of musicians who perform together (paragraph 17)

Thelonious Monk: 1917–1982, composer and pianist who created a new type of jazz known as bebop (paragraph 18)

Charlie Mingus: 1922–1979, jazz performer on bass and piano, hailed as a composer and a poet (paragraph 18)

SNCC: Student Nonviolent Coordinating Committee, a group of black and white students that promoted peace between races (paragraph 18)

Coltrane: John Coltrane, 1926–1967, jazz saxophonist who also played the flute (paragraph 18)

Charlie Parker: 1920–1955, a bebop jazz artist who played the alto saxophone (paragraph 18)

Coleman Hawkins: 1901–1969, known as the father of the jazz tenor saxophone (paragraph 18)

compost: mixture (paragraph 20)

READING CRITICALLY

As you learned at the beginning of this chapter, practice your summary skills on the following essay. Then work with someone in the class, and write a single paragraph that represents both of your summaries.

BLACK MUSIC IN OUR HANDS

by Bernice Reagon

In the early 1960s, I was in college at Albany State. My major interests were music and biology. In music I was a contralto soloist with the choir, studying Italian arias and German lieder. The black music I sang was of three types: (1) Spirituals sung by the college choir. These were arranged by such people as Nathaniel Dett and William Dawson and had major injections of European musical harmony and composition. (2) Rhythm 'n' Blues, music done by and for Blacks in social settings. This included the music of bands at proms, juke boxes, and football game songs. (3) Church music; gospel was a major part of Black church music by the time I was in college. I was a soloist with the gospel choir. 1

Prior to the gospel choir, introduced in my church when I was twelve, was many years' experience with unaccompanied music—Black choral singing, hymns, lined out by strong song leaders with full, powerful, richly ornate congregational responses. These hymns were offset by upbeat, clapping call-and-response songs. 2

I saw people in church sing and pray until they shouted. I knew *that* music was part of a cultural expression that was powerful enough to take people from their conscious selves to a place where the physical and intellectual were being worked in harmony with the spirit. I enjoyed and needed that experience. The music of the church was an integral part of the cultural world into which I was born. 3

Outside of church, I saw music as good, powerful sounds you made or listened to. Rhythm and blues—you danced to; music of the college choir—you clapped after the number was finished. 4

The Civil Rights Movement changed my view of music. It was after my first march. I began to sing a song and in the course of singing changed the song so that it made sense for that particular moment. Although I was not consciously aware of it, this was one of my earliest experiences with how my music was supposed to *function*. This music was to be integrative of and consistent with everything I was doing at that time; it was to be tied to activities that went beyond artistic affairs such as concerts, dances, and church meetings. 5

The next level of awareness came while in jail. I had grown up in a rural area outside the city limits, riding a bus to public school or driving to college. My life had been a pretty consistent, balanced blend of church, school, 6 and proper upbringing. I was aware of a Black educated class that taught me in high school and college of taxi cabs I never rode in and of people who used buses I never boarded. I went to school with their children.

7 In jail with me were all these people. All ages. In my section were women from about thirteen to eighty years old. Ministers' wives and teachers and teachers' wives who had only nodded at me or clapped at a concert or spoken to my mother. A few people from my classes. A large number of people who rode segregated city buses. One or two women who had been drinking along the two-block stretch of Little Harlem as the march went by. Very quickly, clashes arose: around age, who would have authority, what was proper behavior?

8 The Albany Movement was already a singing movement, and we took the songs to jail. There the songs I had sung because they made me feel good or because they said what I thought about a specific issue did something. I would start a song, and everybody would join in. After the song, the differences among us would not be as great. Somehow, making a song required an expression of that which was common to us all. The songs did not feel like the same songs I had sung in college. This music was like an instrument, like holding a tool in your hand.

9 I found that although I was younger than many of the women in my section of the jail, I was asked to take on leadership roles. First as a song leader and then in most other matters concerning the group, especially in discussions or when speaking with prison officials.

10 I fell in love with that kind of music. I saw that to define music as something you listen to, something that pleases you, is very different from defining it as an instrument with which you can drive a point. In both instances, you can have the same song. But using it as an instrument makes it a different kind of music.

11 The next level of awareness occurred during the first mass meeting after my release from jail. I was asked to lead the song that I had changed after the first march. When I opened my mouth and began to sing, there was a force and power within myself I had never heard before. Somehow this music—music I could use as an instrument to do things with, music that was mine to shape and change so that it made the statement I needed to make—released a kind of power and required a level of concentrated energy I did not know I had. I liked the feeling.

12 For several years, I worked with the Movement eventually doing Civil Rights songs with the Freedom Singers. The Freedom Singers used the songs, interspersed with narrative, to convey the story of the Civil Rights

Movement's struggles. The songs were more powerful than spoken conversation. They became a major way of making people who were not on the scene feel the intensity of what was happening in the South. Hopefully, they would move the people to take a stand, to organize support groups or participate in various projects.

The Georgia Sea Island Singers, whom I first heard at the Newport Festival, were a major link. Bessie Jones, coming from within twenty miles of Albany, Georgia, had a repertoire and song-leading style I recognized from the churches I had grown up in. She, along with John Davis, would talk about songs that Black people had sung as slaves and what those songs meant in terms of their struggle to be free. The songs did not sound like the spirituals I had sung in college choirs; they sounded like the songs I had grown up with in church. There I had been told the songs had to do with worship of Jesus Christ. 13

The next few years I spent focusing on three components: (1) the music I had found in the Civil Rights Movement; (2) songs of the Georgia Sea Island Singers and other traditional groups and the ways in which those songs were linked to the struggles of Black peoples at earlier times; (3) songs of the church that now sounded like those traditional songs and came close to having, for many people, the same kind of freeing power. 14

There was another experience that helped to shape my present-day use of music. After getting out of jail, the mother of the church my father pastored was at the mass meeting. She prayed, a prayer I had heard hundreds of times. I had focused on its sound, tune, rhythm, chant, whether the moans came at the proper pace and intensity. That morning I heard every word that she said. She did not have to change one word of the prayer she had been praying for much of her Christian life for me to know she was addressing the issues we were facing at that moment. More than her personal prayer, it felt like an analysis of the Albany, Georgia, Black community. 15

My collection, study, and creation of Black music has been, to a large extent, about freeing the sounds and the words and the messages from casings in which they have been put, about hearing clearly what the music has to say about Black people and their struggle. 16

When I first began to search, I looked for what was then being called folk music, rather than for other Black forms, such as jazz, rhythm and blues, or gospel. It slowly dawned on me that during the Movement we had used all those forms. When we were relaxing in the office, we made up songs using popular rhythm and blues tunes; songs based in rhythm and blues also came out of jails, especially from the sit-in movement and the march to 17

ANSWERS TO QUESTIONS

Thinking Critically About Content

1. She divides her categories into music she encountered in college, in jail, and after jail.
2. In college, she focused on spiritual music, rhythm 'n' blues, and church music; in jail, she created music to persuade people; and after jail, she discovered the Freedom Singers, prayer music, and jazz.

3. Reagon is referring to the history of the black people; in order to tell their tales in songs, they must first remember what they have endured.

Thinking Critically About Purpose and Audience

4. Reagon probably wants to educate readers on the evolution of some black music, but she is also informing people of her journey through her appreciation of music.
5. She is describing through narration her journey toward musical discovery (personal) and is showing readers the struggles of blacks and the difficulties they overcame through song (social).
6. Reagon's main audience is general but probably not black people. She is trying to educate those who are unaware of her music.

Thinking Critically About Essays

7. The topic sentence, "The Civil Rights Movement changed my view of music," supplies the controlling idea for paragraph 5 because the following sentences explain this idea.
8. Answers will vary.

Selma, Alabama. "Oh Wallace, You Never Can Jail Us All" is an example from Selma. "You Better Leave Segregation Alone" came out of the Nashville Freedom Rides and was based on a bit by Little Willie John, "You Better Leave My Kitten Alone." Gospel choirs became the major musical vehicle in the urban center of Birmingham, with the choir led by Carlton Reese. There was also a gospel choir in the Chicago work, as well as an instrumental ensemble led by Ben Branch.

18 Jazz had not been a strong part of my musical life. I began to hear it as I traveled north. Thelonious Monk and Charlie Mingus played on the first SNCC benefit at Carnegie Hall. I heard of and then heard Coltrane. Then I began to pick up the pieces that had been laid by Charlie Parker and Coleman Hawkins and whole lifetimes of music. This music had no words. But, it had power, intensity, and movement under various degrees of pressure; it had vocal texture and color. I could feel that the music knew how it felt to be Black and Angry. Black and Down, Black and Loved, Black and Fighting.

19 I now believe that Black music exists in every place where Black people run, every corner where they live, every level on which they struggle. We have been here a long while, in many situations. It takes all that we have created to sing our song. I believe that Black musicians/artists have a responsibility to be conscious of their world and to let their consciousness be heard in their songs.

20 And we need it all—blues, gospel, ballads, children's games, dance, rhythms, jazz, lovesongs, topical songs—doing what it has always done. We need Black music that functions in relation to the people and community who provide the nurturing compost that makes its creation and continuation possible.

Thinking Critically About Content

1. Reagon divides and classifies music into at least three different categories. What are these categories?
2. What are the main differences in these categories?
3. What does Reagon mean when she says, "It takes all that we have created to sing our song" (paragraph 19)?

Thinking Critically About Purpose and Audience

4. What do you think Reagon's purpose is in this essay?
5. What makes this purpose both personal and social?
6. Who do you think is Reagon's main audience?

Thinking Critically About Essays

7. Explain how the topic sentence works in paragraph 5. Does it supply the controlling idea for the entire paragraph?
8. Choose a paragraph from this essay, and explain whether or not it is unified. Be as specific as possible.
9. What do you think "in our hands" means in the title of this essay?
10. What role does music play in your life? Divide and classify its role in your life over the years.

9. Reagon uses "in our hands" in her title because she is showing how the music that is available to us (in our hands) can be used for situations that can help change society.
10. Answers will vary.

WHAT ARE FRIENDS FOR?

by Marion Winik

Focusing Your Attention

1. Who do you rely on to talk out your problems? To confide in? To tell secrets to? How do these people fit into your life? How do you fit into theirs?
2. In the essay you are about to read, the author divides and classifies the types of friends people generally have. What do you think these types are?

SUMMARY

In this essay, Winik humorously divides "friends" into nine different categories.

READABILITY

(Flesch–Kincaid grade level)
9.8

Expanding Your Vocabulary

The following words are important to your understanding of this essay. Organize this list into two columns—words you know and words you don't know. Which of the words you don't know can you guess from their sentences?

half-slip: undergarment worn by women (paragraph 1)

innumerable: too many to count (paragraph 2)

Aquarena Springs: a theme park in San Marcos, Texas, that is now a preservation and education center (paragraph 2)

infallible: unfailing (paragraph 6)

indispensable: absolutely necessary (paragraph 8)

wistful: nostalgic (paragraph 10)

INSTRUCTOR'S RESOURCE MANUAL

For additional teaching strategies, for journal entries, for vocabulary and reading quizzes, and for more writing assignments, see the *Instructor's Resource Manual*, Section II, Part II.

ill-conceived: poorly planned (paragraph 10)

inopportune: inconvenient (paragraph 11)

tonic: boost (paragraph 14)

READING CRITICALLY

Once again, write a summary of the following essay, and exchange it with another person in your class. Then combine your two summaries into one summary that accurately represents the main ideas in this essay.

WHAT ARE FRIENDS FOR?

by Marion Winik

1 I was thinking about how everybody can't be everything to each other, but some people can be something to each other, thank God, from the ones whose shoulders you cry on to the ones whose half-slips you borrow to the nameless ones you chat with in the grocery line.

2 Buddies, for example, are the workhorses of the friendship world, the people out there on the front lines, defending you from loneliness and boredom. They call you up, they listen to your complaints, they celebrate your successes and curse your misfortunes, and you do the same for them in return. They hold out through innumerable crises before concluding that the person you're dating is no good, and even then understand if you ignore their good counsel. They accompany you to a movie with subtitles or to see the diving pig at Aquarena Springs. They feed your cat when you are out of town and pick you up from the airport when you get back. They come over to help you decide what to wear on a date. Even if it is with that creep.

3 What about family members? Most of them are people you just got stuck with, and though you love them, you may not have very much in common. But there is that rare exception, the Relative Friend. It is your cousin, your brother, maybe even your aunt. The two of you share the same views of the other family members. Meg never should have divorced Martin. He was the best thing that ever happened to her. You can confirm each other's memories of things that happened a long time ago. Don't you remember when Uncle

Hank and Daddy had that awful fight in the middle of Thanksgiving dinner? Grandma always hated Grandpa's stamp collection; she probably left the windows open during the hurricane on purpose.

While so many family relationships are tinged with guilt and obligation, 4
a relationship with a Relative Friend is relatively worry-free. You don't even have to hide your vices from this delightful person. When you slip out Aunt Joan's back door for a cigarette, she is already there.

Then there is that special guy at work. Like all the other people at the 5
job site, at first he's just part of the scenery. But gradually he starts to stand out from the crowd. Your friendship is cemented by jokes about co-workers and thoughtful favors around the office. Did you see Ryan's hair? Want half my bagel? Soon you know the names of his turtles, what he did last Friday night, exactly which model CD player he wants for his birthday. His handwriting is as familiar to you as your own.

Though you invite each other to parties, you somehow don't quite fit 6
into each other's outside lives. For this reason, the friendship may not survive a job change. Company gossip, once an infallible source of entertainment, soon awkwardly accentuates the distance between you. But wait. Like School Friends, Work Friends share certain memories which acquire a nostalgic glow after about a decade.

A Faraway Friend is someone you grew up with or went to school with or 7
lived in the same town as until one of you moved away. Without a Faraway Friend, you would never get any mail addressed in handwriting. A Faraway Friend calls late at night, invites you to her wedding, always says she is coming to visit but rarely shows up. An actual visit from a Faraway Friend is a cause for celebration and binges of all kinds. Cigarettes, Chips Ahoy, bottles of tequila.

Faraway Friends go through phases of intense communication, then 8
may be out of touch for many months. Either way, the connection is always there. A conversation with your Faraway Friend always helps to put your life in perspective: When you feel you've hit a dead end, come to a confusing fork in the road, or gotten lost in some crackerbox subdivision of your life, the advice of the Faraway Friend—who has the big picture, who is so well acquainted with the route that brought you to this place—is indispensable.

Another useful function of the Faraway Friend is to help you remember 9
things from a long time ago, like the name of your seventh-grade history teacher, what was in that really good stir-fry, or exactly what happened that night on the boat with the guys from Florida.

10 Ah, the Former Friend. A sad thing. At best a wistful memory, at worst a dangerous enemy who is in possession of many of your deepest secrets. But what was it that drove you apart? A misunderstanding, a betrayed confidence, an unrepaid loan, an ill-conceived flirtation. A poor choice of spouse can do in a friendship just like that. Going into business together can be a serious mistake. Time, money, distance, cult religions: all noted friendship killers. You quit doing drugs, you're not such good friends with your dealer anymore.

11 And lest we forget, there are the Friends You Love to Hate. They call at inopportune times. They say stupid things. They butt in, they boss you around, they embarrass you in public. They invite themselves over. They take advantage. You've done the best you can, but they need professional help. On top of all this, they love you to death and are convinced they're your best friend on the planet.

12 So why do you continue to be involved with these people? Why do you tolerate them? On the contrary, the real question is, What would you do without them? Without Friends You Love to Hate, there would be nothing to talk about with your other friends. Their problems and their irritating stunts provide a reliable source of conversation for everyone they know. What's more, Friends You Love to Hate make you feel good about yourself, since you are obviously in so much better shape than they are. No matter what these people do, you will never get rid of them. As much as they need you, you need them too.

13 At the other end of the spectrum are Hero Friends. These people are better than the rest of us; that's all there is to it. Their career is something you wanted to be when you grew up—painter, forest ranger, tireless doer of good. They have beautiful homes filled with special handmade things presented to them by villagers in the remote areas they have visited in their extensive travels. Yet they are modest. They never gossip. They are always helping others, especially those who have suffered a death in the family or an illness. You would think people like this would just make you sick, but somehow they don't.

14 A New Friend is a tonic unlike any other. Say you meet her at a party. In your bowling league. At a Japanese conversation class, perhaps. Wherever, whenever, there's that spark of recognition. The first time you talk, you can't believe how much you have in common. Suddenly, your life story is interesting again, your insights fresh, your opinion valued. Your various shortcomings are as yet completely invisible.

15 It's almost like falling in love.

ANSWERS TO QUESTIONS

Thinking Critically About Content

1. Winik introduces nine categories of friends: Buddies, Relative Friends, Work Friends, School Friends, Faraway Friends, Former Friends, Friends You Love to Hate, Hero Friends, and New Friends.
2. She creates the categories on the basis that different kinds of friends serve different purposes in people's lives.
3. New Friends are like a tonic because they spark life into both people. Everything is new and exciting; New Friends are like energy pills.

Thinking Critically About Purpose and Audience

4. Winik wrote this essay to entertain her readers.
5. Anyone would be interested in this essay.

Thinking Critically About Content

1. How many types of friends does Winik introduce? What are they?
2. On what basis does Winik create these categories?
3. In what ways is a new friend "a tonic" (paragraph 14)?

Thinking Critically About Purpose and Audience

4. Why do you think Winik wrote this essay?
5. Who would be most interested in this essay?
6. How does this essay make you feel about the role of friends in your life?

Thinking Critically About Essays

7. How does Winik organize her essay? Why do you think she puts her categories in this order?
8. How does the author develop each category? Use one paragraph to explain your answer.
9. Explain Winik's title.
10. Write a detailed description of one of your friends. Why is this person a friend of yours?

6. Answers will vary.

Thinking Critically About Essays

7. Winik organizes her essay from least to most exciting. In this way, she can hold her readers' attention throughout the essay.
8. She develops her categories by first defining the type of friend and then providing examples. Beyond this, answers will vary.
9. This essay is Winik's answer to the question in her title, "What are friends for?"
10. Answers will vary.

Writing Workshop

This final section gives you opportunities to apply what you have learned in this chapter to another writing assignment. This time, we provide very little prompting beyond a summary of the guidelines for writing a division/classification essay. This section will let you demonstrate that you can go through the entire writing process on your own with only occasional feedback from your peers. Loop back into the chapter as necessary when you have questions so that this process becomes as automatic to you as possible before you move on to new material. Then pause at the end of the chapter to reflect briefly on what you have learned.

TEACHING ON THE WEB

Discussion Topic: Bring in printouts from a Web site that shows the various links people go through as they navigate around the site. Divide students into groups of three or four, and have them discuss how the Web site divides the links by categories. What are these categories? Have students discuss the different ways that the Web site uses division and classification.

Guidelines for Writing a Division/Classification Essay

1. Decide on your purpose for writing, and make it part of your thesis statement.
2. Divide your topic into categories that don't overlap.
3. Clearly explain each category.
4. Organize your categories logically.
5. Use transitions to move your readers through your essay.

TEACHING ON THE WEB

Research: Have students go to educational or government Web sites to determine how these sites use division and classification. Then have students do the same with a commercial Web site. Do these Web sites use division and classification differently? If so, in what ways? How do division and classification help sell the products on a commercial site?

TEACHING ON THE WEB

Links: Provide students with a topic, and have them link to Web sites that will divide the topic into categories. What are the different divisions that Web sites make? Which Web site is easiest to follow?

Possible sites for the topic "movies":

DreamWorks SKG Fansite, www.dreamworks. com

Walt Disney Pictures, www.disney.com/DisneyPictures

Paramount Pictures, www.paramount.com

Writing About Your Reading

1. In the first essay, Reagon talks about the changing role of music in her life. Divide and classify one of your interests over the years.
2. Divide and classify your friends into meaningful categories, and write an essay explaining your classification system.
3. What process do you have to go through to come up with an interesting comparison or contrast? How is it different from the process you go through for other rhetorical modes?

Writing About Your World

1. Looking at the picture above, think of the types of activities college students do in their spare time. Classify these activities into a few categories, and explain their advantages and disadvantages.
2. What are some rituals that you follow in your own life? Do these rituals serve a purpose in your life? Use division and classification to explain three rituals that you follow.
3. We all dream about trips we'd like to take. Sometimes we get to take one of these trips. Others have to remain dreams. What are your ideal trips? Discuss the types of trips you would like to take. What categories do they fall into? Why do you dream about these types of travel?
4. Create your own division/classification assignment (with the help of your instructor), and write a response to it.

Revising

Small Group Activity (5–10 minutes per writer) Working in groups of three or four, read your division/classification essays to each other.

Those listening should record their reactions on a copy of the Peer Evaluation Form in Appendix 2F. After your group goes through this process, give your evaluation forms to the appropriate writers so that each writer has two or three peer comment sheets for revising.

Paired Activity (5 minutes per writer) Using the completed Peer Evaluation Forms, work in pairs to decide what you should revise in your essay. If time allows, rewrite some of your sentences, and have your partner look at them.

Individual Activity Rewrite your paper, using the revising feedback you received from other students.

Editing

Paired Activity (5–10 minutes per writer) Swap papers with a classmate, and use the editing portion of your Peer Evaluation Form to identify as many grammar, punctuation, mechanics, and spelling errors as you can. If time allows, correct some of your errors, and have your partner look at them. Record your grammar, punctuation, and mechanics errors in the Error Log (Appendix 6) and your spelling errors in the Spelling Log (Appendix 7).

Individual Activity Rewrite your paper again, using the editing feedback you received from other students.

Reflecting on Your Writing When you have completed your own essay, answer these six questions.

1. What was most difficult about this assignment?
2. What was easiest?
3. What did you learn about division and classification by completing this assignment?
4. What do you think are the strengths of your division/classification essay? Place a wavy line by the parts of your essay that you feel are very good.
5. What are the weaknesses, if any, of your paper? Place an X by the parts of your essay you would like help with. Write any questions you have in the margin.
6. What did you learn from this assignment about your own writing process—about preparing to write, about writing the first draft, about revising, and about editing?

CHAPTER 14

Defining

"Writers, most of all, need to define their tasks . . . their themes, their objectives."

— HENRY SEIDAL CANBY

TEACHING DEFINITION

Divide students into groups of four or five, and give each group five abstract words that the other groups don't see (for example, *abandonment, freedom, ethnicity, boredom,* and *hope*). Have the groups define each of their words using three sentences: one using synonyms, one using negation, and one using categories. Make sure students do not use the actual word in the definition.

After each group has defined its words, have a spokesperson for each group read the definitions. As soon as another group knows the word being defined, its members should shout out the answer. Limit guessing time to three minutes. The group that guesses the most definitions correctly wins.

All communication depends on our understanding of a common set of definitions. If we did not work from a set of shared definitions, we would not be able to carry on coherent conversations, write clear letters, or understand any form of media.

It's no surprise, then, that we regularly use definitions in writing as well—in our personal lives, in college courses, and in the workplace:

- You e-mail a friend to tell him or her about the equipment at the fitness center you just joined.
- A student has to define melody, harmony, and rhythm on a music appreciation quiz.
- A student begins a report for a criminal justice course with a definition of criminal law and civil law.
- A financial planner prepares a summary sheet defining the basic financial terms a client should know.
- The manager of a sporting goods shop writes a classified ad for an opening on the staff.

Definition is the process of explaining what a word, an object, or an idea is. A good definition focuses on what is special about a word or an idea and what sets it apart from similar words or concepts. Definitions help us understand basic concrete terms (*cell phone, large fries, midterm exams*), discuss events in our lives (*baseball game, graduation, dentist appointment*), and grasp complex ideas (*friendship, courage, success*). Definitions are the build-

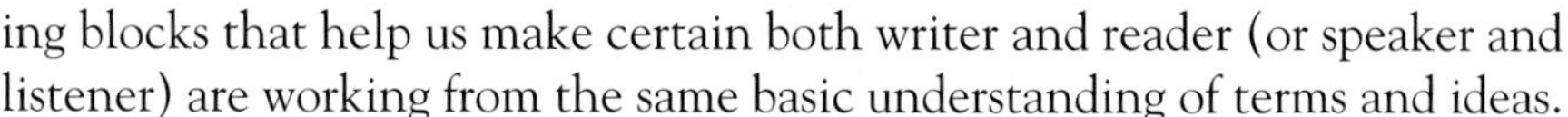

ing blocks that help us make certain both writer and reader (or speaker and listener) are working from the same basic understanding of terms and ideas.

Definitions vary greatly. They can be as short as one word (a "hog" is a motorcycle) or as long as an essay or even a book. Words or ideas that require such extended definitions are usually abstract, complex, and controversial. Think, for example, how difficult it might be to define an abstract idea like *equality* compared to concrete words such as *dog* or *cat*.

READING AND WRITING A DEFINITION ESSAY

Reading definition essays critically will help you write effective definition essays. You will find that the two processes of reading and writing work together to help you deal with information on a relatively high level. Like two halves of the same circle, these two skills will enhance your ability to perform a variety of other tasks in many other aspects of life.

Reading a Definition Essay

In the following essay, Lars Eighner writes an extended definition of the fine art of "Dumpster diving" or living out of Dumpsters, the big containers designed to be raised and emptied into a garbage truck. Have you ever witnessed someone Dumpster diving? Have you yourself ever found something in the trash that you took home? How would you feel if you lost your home and with it your sense of security?

READING CRITICALLY

Forming your own opinions and coming up with new ideas in response to your reading are very important parts of the reading process, but you need to learn how to produce these reactions. As you read the following essay, record your notes on a separate piece of paper. First, draw a vertical line down the center of a sheet of paper. Then, as you read, write the author's main ideas on the left and your reactions to those ideas on the right side of the page. Be prepared to explain the connection between your notes and the material in the essay.

TEACHING TIPS

The following eight teaching tips are based on Howard Gardner's list of multiple intelligences:

Verbal/Linguistic

Provide students with a list of words and a list of definitions, and have them try to match the words with their definitions. Don't let students use a dictionary until after they have guessed.

Musical/Rhythmic

Have students listen to a song in a language they don't speak. Based solely on the music, what do they think the song is about?

Logical/Mathematical

Provide students with a list of words that sound like they would have one definition but actually have another (such as *noisome,* which sounds like it should have something to do with noise but actually means "foul-smelling" or "unwholesome"). What are the oddest words students can find?

Visual/Spatial
Think of four words. Find five synonyms for each of the four words. Paste the words on a poster board, and have students find the words that belong together.

Bodily/Kinesthetic
Give students a stack of cards that have both words and definitions. Have students play charades to try to guess the definitions of the words. Be sure to provide words that can be acted out (such as "firefighter" or "family").

Intrapersonal
Provide students with the words *loud* and *soft*, and ask them to make lists of synonyms for each. How many words on their lists are positive words? How many are negative? Which list has more positive words? Why do students think this is the case?

Interpersonal
Put students into groups of three or four. Have each student think of an object he or she loves to use or look at and then give a one-sentence definition of the object without actually naming it. Can the members of the group determine what this object is?

Naturalist
Have students recall one of their favorite outdoor activities and

DUMPSTER DIVING
by Lars Eighner

1 I began Dumpster diving about a year before I became homeless. I prefer the term *scavenging.* I have heard people, evidently meaning to be polite, use the word *foraging,* but I prefer to reserve that word for gathering nuts and berries and such, which I also do, according to the season and opportunity.

2 I like the frankness of the word *scavenging.* I live from the refuse of others. I am a scavenger. I think it a sound and honorable niche, although if I could I would naturally prefer to live the comfortable consumer life, perhaps—and only perhaps—as a slightly less wasteful consumer owing to what I have learned as a scavenger.

3 Except for jeans, all my clothes come from Dumpsters. Boom boxes, candles, bedding, toilet paper, medicine, books, a typewriter, a virgin male love doll, coins sometimes amounting to many dollars—all came from Dumpsters. And, yes, I eat from Dumpsters, too.

4 There is a predictable series of stages that a person goes through in learning to scavenge. At first the new scavenger is filled with disgust and self-loathing. He is ashamed of being seen.

5 This stage passes with experience. The scavenger finds a pair of running shoes that fit and look and smell brand-new. He finds a pocket calculator in perfect working order. He finds pristine ice cream, still frozen, more than he can eat or keep. He begins to understand: People do throw away perfectly good stuff, a lot of perfectly good stuff.

6 At this stage he may become lost and never recover. All the Dumpster divers I have known come to the point of trying to acquire everything they touch. Why not take it, they reason; it is all free. This is, of course, hopeless, and most divers come to realize that they must restrict themselves to items of relatively immediate utility.

7 The finding of objects is becoming something of an urban art. Even respectable, employed people will sometimes find something tempting sticking out of a Dumpster or standing beside one. Quite a number of people, not all of them of the bohemian type, are willing to brag that they found this or that piece in the trash.

8 But eating from Dumpsters is the thing that separates the dilettanti from the professionals. Eating safely involves three principles: using the senses and common sense to evaluate the condition of the found materials;

knowing the Dumpsters of a given area and checking them regularly; and seeking always to answer the question Why was this discarded?

Yet perfectly good food can be found in Dumpsters. Canned goods, for 9
example, turn up fairly often in the Dumpsters I frequent. I also have few qualms about dry foods such as crackers, cookies, cereal, chips, and pasta if they are free of visible contaminants and still dry and crisp. Raw fruits and vegetables with intact skins seem perfectly safe to me, excluding, of course, the obviously rotten. Many are discarded for minor imperfections that can be pared away.

A typical discard is a half jar of peanut butter—though non-organic 10
peanut butter does not require refrigeration and is unlikely to spoil in any reasonable time. One of my favorite finds is yogurt—often discarded, still sealed, when the expiration date has passed—because it will keep for several days, even in warm weather.

No matter how careful I am, I still get dysentery at least once a month, 11
oftener in warm weather. I do not want to paint too romantic a picture. Dumpster diving has serious drawbacks as a way of life.

I find from the experience of scavenging two rather deep lessons. The 12
first is to take what I can use and let the rest go. I have come to think that there is no value in the abstract. A thing I cannot use or make useful, perhaps by trading, has no value, however fine or rare it may be.

The second lesson is the transience of material being. I do not suppose 13
that ideas are immortal, but certainly they are longer-lived than material objects.

The things I find in Dumpsters, the love letters and rag dolls of so many 14
lives, remind me of this lesson. Now I hardly pick up a thing without envisioning the time I will cast it away. This, I think, is a healthy state of mind. Almost everything I have now has already been cast out at least once, proving that what I own is valueless to someone.

I find that my desire to grab for the gaudy bauble has been largely 15
sated. I think this is an attitude I share with the very wealthy—we both know there is plenty more where whatever we have came from. Between us are the rat-race millions who have confounded their selves with the objects they grasp and who nightly scavenge the cable channels for they know not what.

I am sorry for them. 16

provide a definition of it that would make other students want to try it. Which part of the students' definition most entices others to try the activity?

INSTRUCTOR'S RESOURCE MANUAL

For additional material about teaching definition; for journal entries; and for multiple-choice, short-answer, and paragraph tests, see the *Instructor's Resource Manual*, Section II, Part II.

Preparing to Write Your Own Definition Essay

What do you think of when you hear the word *security?* What associations do you make with this word? What examples does it bring to mind? Use one or more of the prewriting strategies you learned in Chapter 2 to generate ideas for writing an extended definition of *security*.

Writing a Definition Essay

Clear definitions give writer and reader a mutual starting point on the road to successful communication. Sometimes a short summary and an example are all the definition that's needed. But in the case of abstract and complex words or ideas, a writer may use several approaches to a definition. Use the following guidelines to help you write an extended definition essay.

1. **Choose your word or idea carefully, and give a working definition of it in your thesis statement.** First, you need to choose a word or idea that can be defined and explained from several angles, or you will end up with a short, lifeless essay. At the same time, you need to give your readers a working definition right at the start. Put that brief, basic definition in your thesis statement so that readers have a mental hook on which to hang the definitions and explanations in the rest of your essay. Also include the purpose of your essay in your thesis statement.

   At the start of his essay, Eighner defines *Dumpster diving* as "scavenging," explaining "I live from the refuse of others." This simple, direct definition—given at the beginning—guides readers through the rest of the essay.

2. **Decide how you want to define your term: by synonym, by negation, or by category.** These are the three common ways to develop a definition.

   When you define by using a *synonym*, you furnish readers with a similar word or a short explanation with synonyms. Eighner uses a synonym right at the beginning of his essay. "Dumpster diving" is an informal term that is used by city people to refer to taking garbage out of trash bins. Apartment houses and office buildings often use Dumpsters to hold garbage until it is taken to the dump. Because *Dumpster* is not a term that everyone knows and because the meaning of the expression "Dumpster diving" is not immediately obvious, Eighner provides the synonym "scavenging," which most people understand.

   When you define a word by *negation*, you say what the term is not. That is, you define a term by contrasting it with something else. Eighner uses definition by negation twice in his essay. First, he states that "scavenging" is not "foraging," meaning that it is not gathering nuts and berries. He also says that life as a scavenger is not a comfortable consumer life. The rest of his essay explains his life as a scavenger.

Defining a term by *category* is a more formal type of definition, as in a dictionary. Defining by category has two parts: the class or general category that the word belongs to and the way the word is different from other words in that group. For example, *heart* might be defined as "the organ that pumps blood through the body." The general category is *organ*, and it is different from other organs (brain, lungs, stomach, liver, and so on) because it pumps blood. Eighner doesn't use this type of definition directly. He does, however, suggest that scavenging falls into the category of *lifestyle* in paragraph 2 when he compares his life as a scavenger to the life of a consumer.

3. **Develop your definition with examples.** Nearly every definition can be improved by adding examples. Well-chosen examples show your definition in action. Definitions can be *objective*—strictly factual, as in a dictionary definition—or *subjective*—combined with personal opinions. A definition essay is usually more subjective than objective because you are providing your personal opinions about a word or concept. You are explaining to your readers your own meaning, which is what makes your essay interesting. If your readers wanted an objective definition, they could go to a dictionary.

   Eighner uses examples throughout his essay to expand on his definition. Paragraph 3 consists entirely of examples of things he has found in Dumpsters. Later he gives examples of the kinds of food he finds, including canned goods, cookies and crackers, raw fruits and vegetables, peanut butter, and yogurt. These examples help Eighner strike a balance in his definition between objective (factual) and subjective (personal) references. From these and Eighner's other examples, we get a very clear idea of how a person could live by Dumpster diving.

4. **Use other rhetorical strategies, such as description, comparison, or process analysis, to support your definition.** When you write a definition essay, you want to look at your word or idea in many different ways. The other techniques you have learned for developing body paragraphs can help you expand your definition even further. Perhaps a description, a short narrative, or a comparison will make your definition come alive.

   In addition to examples, Eighner uses process analysis, classification, and cause and effect to expand his definition. He uses process analysis to explain the four stages that new Dumpster divers go through—how something happens. His three rules for eating safely are also process analysis—how to do something. He draws on classification to name the types of foods he finds and then gives examples of each category. At the end of his essay, he uses cause and effect when he explains that Dumpster diving (the cause) has taught him two lessons (the effects): that only items you can use are valuable and that material objects don't last.

5. **Organize your essay in a logical way.** Because a definition essay can be developed through several strategies and techniques, there is no set pattern of organization. So you need to figure out the most logical way to explain your word or idea. You might move from particular to general or from general to particular. Or you might arrange your ideas from one extreme to the other, such as from most important to least important, least dramatic to most dramatic, or most familiar to least familiar. In some cases, you might organize your definition chronologically or spatially. Or you might organize part of your essay one way and the rest another way. What's important is that you move in some logical way from one point to another so that your readers can follow your train of thought.

   Eighner organizes his essay chronologically. He says he started Dumpster diving about a year before he became homeless. Now he is homeless and lives by Dumpster diving. He defines the term in two ways (synonym and negation) and gives examples of what he finds. Then he switches to a general-to-particular organization in paragraphs 7 to 11, explaining how someone learns to dive in general and then to actually dive for food in particular. The last five paragraphs conclude the essay.

Writing Your Own Definition Essay

If you have a roof over your head, food to eat, and money in your pocket, you have a sense of security. Write an essay defining *security*. Begin by reviewing your prewriting notes. Then decide how you are going to approach your subject. Next, write your essay, starting with a clear thesis statement and then following the preceding guidelines.

A STUDENT'S DEFINITION ESSAY

In the following essay, titled "True Friends," a student named Francine Feinstein defines *friendship*. See if you can identify her main point as you read this draft of her essay.

True Friends

Many people throw the term "friend" around loosely. They think they 1
have friends at work, friends at school, and friends from the Internet. But is all these people really friends? The word "friend" seems to be used today to refer to anyone from long-term to short-term relationships. However, a true friend is someone who will always be there in times of need, who will always be the best company, and who will always listen and give advice.

Without any questions asked, a good friend will always be there in times 2
of need. No matter how bad a problem is, a true friend will be the person who sits up nights and take days off work just to sit with a friend. If someone is in trouble with a difficult paper a friend will help brainstorm to figure out the problem. If someone is sick, a friend will be the first one at the door with chicken soup and will baby-sit the kids until the sick person feel better. I hate the feeling of being sick. If someone is stranded across town with a broken-down car, a friend will drop everything to make a rescue and drive the person wherever he or she needs to go. Not everyone has a friend like this a true friend will always be the first one there, no matter what.

Most of all, a true friend is also someone who will listen and give reliable 3
advice. Some people will listen to problems and then give the advice that they think will work best for them, but that advice isn't necessarily best for their friend. Other people will listen but then interject personal stories that relate to the problem but don't solve it. But a true friend listens to a problem and gives suggestions to help a friend figure out the best solution for himself or herself. In other words, a true friend knows how to listen and help a person solve problems.

In addition, a friend is someone who is always great company, because 4
friends have so much in common with each other. Imagine working out together, grabbing a sandwich, and then spending the evening just talking—about life, about good times, about bad times, about classes at school. Right now my classes are really hard. At the end of the day, friends might rent their favorite DVD and make some fresh popcorn. Sometimes they even seem to be on the same biological clock, getting tired and waking up at the same time. Friends can always be themselves around each other.

The word "friend" may be misused in the English language, but at least 5
we can agree on what true friends are. True friends are hard to find. But once you find them, they will always be there, listen to you and be the best people to spend time with. No wonder true friends are so rare!

Discovering How the Essay Works

1. What is this essay defining?

   The meaning of a true friend

2. Does this author define mainly by synonym, by negation, or by category in her essay? Explain your answer.

   She relies mainly on category. She starts with a broad definition of "friend" and then talks about how a true friend differs from other friends.

3. List three specific examples that Francine uses to develop her definition.

   Answers will vary.

   Are her examples more objective or subjective?

   Subjective

4. What other techniques does Francine use to develop her definition?

   Paragraph 2 uses examples, paragraph 3 uses comparison and contrast, and paragraph 4 uses narration.

5. How does Francine organize the examples in her essay?

   From least to most important

   Explain your answer.

   She begins by discussing how friends will always be there in times of need, moves to how friends always give great advice, and finishes with how friends are fun to be with. But paragraph 3 is out of place.

REVISING AND EDITING OPTIONS
Consider varying your approach to revising

Revising and Editing the Student Essay

This essay is Francine's first draft, which now needs to be revised and edited. First, apply the following Revising Checklist to the content of

Francine's draft. When you are satisfied that her ideas are fully developed and well organized, use the Editing Checklist on page 340 to correct her grammar and mechanics errors. Do the tasks, and answer the questions after each checklist. Then write your suggested changes directly on Francine's draft.

and editing. You could teach these skills in a class discussion, in small groups, or in pairs.

REVISING CHECKLIST

THESIS STATEMENT

✔ Does the thesis statement contain the essay's controlling idea?

✔ Does the thesis appear as the last sentence of the introduction?

BASIC ELEMENTS

✔ Does the title draw in the readers?

✔ Does the introduction capture the readers' attention and build up to the thesis statement effectively?

✔ Does each body paragraph deal with a single topic?

✔ Does the conclusion bring the essay to a close in an interesting way?

DEVELOPMENT

✔ Do the body paragraphs adequately support the thesis statement?

✔ Does each body paragraph have a focused topic sentence?

✔ Does each body paragraph contain *specific* details that support the topic sentence?

✔ Does each body paragraph include *enough* details to explain the topic sentence fully?

UNITY

✔ Do the essay's topic sentences relate directly to the thesis statement?

✔ Do the details in each body paragraph support its topic sentence?

ORGANIZATION

✔ Is the essay organized logically?

✔ Is each body paragraph organized logically?

COHERENCE

✔ Are transitions used effectively so that paragraphs move smoothly and logically from one to the next?

✔ Do the sentences move smoothly and logically from one to the next?

REVISING STRATEGIES

This chapter focuses on the following revising elements:

Development
Unity
Organization
Coherence

Thesis Statement

1. Put brackets around the last sentence in Francine's introduction. Does it state her purpose?

   Yes

2. Rewrite Francine's thesis statement if necessary so that it states her purpose and introduces her topics.

   Her thesis states her purpose and introduces her topics.

Basic Elements

1. Give the writer's essay an alternate title.

   Answers will vary.

2. Rewrite Francine's introduction so that it captures the readers' attention and builds up to the thesis statement at the end of the paragraph.

   Answers will vary.

3. Does each of Francine's body paragraphs deal with only one topic?

   Yes

4. Rewrite Francine's conclusion using at least one suggestion from Part I.

   Answers will vary.

Development

1. Write out Francine's thesis statement (revised, if necessary), and list her three topic sentences below it.

Thesis statement: *However, a true friend is someone who will always be there in times of need, who will always be the best company, and who will always listen and give advice.*

Topic 1: *Without any questions asked, a good friend will always be there in times of need.*

Topic 2: *Most of all, a true friend is also someone who will listen and give reliable advice.*

Topic 3: *In addition, a friend is someone who is always great company, because friends have so much in common with each other.*

2. Do Francine's topic sentences adequately support her thesis statement?

   Yes

3. Does each body paragraph have a focused topic sentence?

   Yes

4. Do the examples in the essay help define "friend"?

   They do, but many more could be added.

5. Where do you need more information?

   Answers will vary.

6. Make two of Francine's details more specific. *Answers will vary.*
7. Add at least two new details to make her essay clearer. *Answers will vary.*

Unity

1. Read each of Francine's topic sentences with her thesis statement in mind. Do they go together?

   Answers will vary.

2. Revise her topic sentences if necessary so they are directly related.
3. Drop or rewrite the sentences in paragraph 2 and in paragraph 4 that are not directly related to their topic sentence. *Paragraph 2, sentence 5; paragraph 4, sentence 3*

Organization

1. Read Francine's essay again to see if all the paragraphs are arranged logically.
2. Reverse the two paragraphs that are out of order. *Reverse paragraphs 3 and 4.*
3. Look closely at Francine's body paragraphs to see if all her sentences are arranged logically within paragraphs.
4. Move any sentences that are out of order. *All sentences are in order.*

Coherence

1. Add two transitions to Francine's essay. *Answers will vary.*
2. Circle five transitions Francine uses.
3. Explain how two of these make Francine's essay easier to read.

Answers will vary. ______________________________

____

For a list of transitions, see page 101.

Now rewrite Francine's essay with your revisions.

EDITING STRATEGIES
This chapter focuses on the following editing problems:
Run-togethers
Subject-verb agreement
Commas

EDITING CHECKLIST

SENTENCES

- ✔ Does each sentence have a main subject and verb?
- ✔ Do all subjects and verbs agree?
- ✔ Do all pronouns agree with their nouns?
- ✔ Are modifiers as close as possible to the words they modify?

PUNCTUATION AND MECHANICS

- ✔ Are sentences punctuated correctly?
- ✔ Are words capitalized properly?

WORD CHOICE AND SPELLING

- ✔ Are words used correctly?
- ✔ Are words spelled correctly?

Sentences

Subjects and Verbs

1. Underline the subjects once and verbs twice in paragraphs 1 and 2 of your revision of Francine's essay. Remember that sentences can have more than one subject-verb set.

For help with subjects and verbs, see Chapter 25.

2. Does each of the sentences have at least one subject and verb that can stand alone?

   Yes

3. Did you find and correct Francine's run-together sentence? If not, find and correct it now. *Paragraph 2, sentence 7*

For help with run-togethers, see Chapter 27.

Subject-Verb Agreement

1. Read aloud the subjects and verbs you underlined in your revision of Francine's essay.

For help with subject-verb agreement, see Chapter 30.

2. Did you find and correct the three subjects and verbs that do not agree? *Paragraph 1, sentence 3; paragraph 2, sentence 2; paragraph 2, sentence 4*

Pronoun Agreement

1. Find any pronouns in your revision of Francine's essay that do not agree with their nouns. *All pronouns agree with their nouns.*

For help with pronoun agreement, see Chapter 34.

2. Correct any pronouns that do not agree with their nouns.

Modifiers

1. Find any modifiers in your revision of Francine's essay that are not as close as possible to the words they modify.

For help with modifier errors, see Chapter 37.

2. Rewrite sentences if necessary so that modifiers are as close as possible to the words they modify. *There are no modifier errors.*

Punctuation and Mechanics

Punctuation

1. Read your revision of Francine's essay for any errors in punctuation.

For help with punctuation, see Chapters 38–42.

2. Find the run-together sentence you revised, and make sure it is punctuated correctly.
3. Did you find and correct the two comma errors in Francine's essay? *Paragraph 2, sentence 3; paragraph 5, sentence 3*

Mechanics

For help with capitalization, see Chapter 43.

1. Read your revision of Francine's essay for any errors in capitalization.
2. Be sure to check Francine's capitalization in the run-together sentence you revised.

Word Choice and Spelling

Word Choice

For help with confused words, see Chapter 49.

1. Find any words used incorrectly in your revision of Francine's essay.
   All words are used correctly.
2. Correct any errors you find.

Spelling

For help with spelling, see Chapter 50.

1. Use spell-check and a dictionary to check the spelling in your revision of Francine's essay. *All words are spelled correctly.*
2. Correct any misspelled words.

Now rewrite Francine's essay with your editing corrections.

YOUR OWN DEFINITION ESSAY

Returning to the definition you wrote earlier in this chapter, you are now ready to revise and edit your own writing. Remember that revision involves reworking the content and organization of your essay while editing asks you to check your grammar and usage. Work first with the content, making sure your thoughts are fully developed and organized effectively before you turn to your grammar and usage errors. Repeating these processes again and again will ensure that you are producing the best draft possible.

WRITING CRITICALLY

As you begin to rework your essay, use the same technique you did in your reading. Just as you identified the author's ideas and recorded your reactions to them to help you understand what the essay was saying, record the ideas from your own writing on the left side of a piece of paper and your reactions to them on the right. Expand your essay with any new ideas that surface from this exercise.

Revising and Editing Your Own Essay

The checklists here will help you apply what you have learned in this chapter to your essay.

CLASS ACTIVITY

Put a few words on the board (such as *vacation, Ford Ranger,*

 **REVISING CHECKLIST** 

THESIS STATEMENT

- ☐ Does the thesis statement contain the essay's controlling idea?
- ☐ Does the thesis appear as the last sentence of the introduction?

BASIC ELEMENTS

- ☐ Does the title draw in the readers?
- ☐ Does the introduction capture the readers' attention and build up to the thesis statement effectively?
- ☐ Does each body paragraph deal with a single topic?
- ☐ Does the conclusion bring the essay to a close in an interesting way?

DEVELOPMENT

- ☐ Do the body paragraphs adequately support the thesis statement?
- ☐ Does each body paragraph have a focused topic sentence?
- ☐ Does each body paragraph contain *specific* details that support the topic sentence?
- ☐ Does each body paragraph include *enough* details to explain the topic sentence fully?

UNITY

- ☐ Do the essay's topic sentences relate directly to the thesis statement?
- ☐ Do the details in each body paragraph support its topic sentence?

ORGANIZATION

- ☐ Is the essay organized logically?
- ☐ Is each body paragraph organized logically?

COHERENCE

- ☐ Are transitions used effectively so that paragraphs move smoothly and logically from one to the next?
- ☐ Do the sentences move smoothly and logically from one to the next?

friendship, and *peace*), and have the class provide definitions for each by using all three defining strategies: synonym, negation, and category. Which one do students think is most effective?

Thesis Statement

1. What are you defining?

____

2. What is the purpose of your definition essay?

____

3. Put brackets around the last sentence in your introduction. Does it state your purpose?

____

4. Rewrite your thesis statement if necessary so that it states your purpose and introduces your topics.

Basic Elements

1. Give your essay a title if it doesn't have one.

____

2. Does your introduction capture your readers' attention and build up to your thesis statement at the end of the paragraph?

____

3. Does each of your body paragraphs deal with only one topic?

____

4. Does your conclusion follow some of the suggestions offered in Part I?

____

Development

1. Write out your thesis statement (revised, if necessary), and list your topic sentences below it.

   Thesis statement: ______________________________

   Topic 1: ______________________________

   Topic 2: ______________________________

   Topic 3: ______________________________

2. Do your topics adequately support your thesis statement?

____

3. Does each body paragraph have a focused topic sentence?

____

4. Do the examples in the essay help develop your definition?

____

5. Where do you need more information?

____

6. Make two of your details more specific.
7. Add at least two new details to make your definition clearer.

Unity

1. Read each of your topic sentences with your thesis statement in mind. Do they go together?

____

2. Revise your topic sentences if necessary so they are directly related.
3. Drop or rewrite any of the sentences in your body paragraphs that are not directly related to their topic sentences.

Organization

1. Read your essay again to see if all the paragraphs are arranged logically.
2. Refer to your answers to the development questions. Then identify your method of organization:

____

3. Is the order you chose for your paragraphs the most effective approach to your topic?

____

4. Move any paragraphs that are out of order.
5. Look closely at your body paragraphs to see if all the sentences are arranged logically within paragraphs.
6. Move any sentences that are out of order.

Coherence

For a list of transitions, see page 101.

1. Add two transitions to your essay.
2. Circle five transitions you use.
3. Explain how two of them make your essay easier to read.

____

____

Now rewrite your essay with your revisions.

EDITING CHECKLIST

SENTENCES

- ☐ Does each sentence have a main subject and verb?
- ☐ Do all subjects and verbs agree?
- ☐ Do all pronouns agree with their nouns?
- ☐ Are modifiers as close as possible to the words they modify?

PUNCTUATION AND MECHANICS

- ☐ Are sentences punctuated correctly?
- ☐ Are words capitalized properly?

WORD CHOICE AND SPELLING

- ☐ Are words used correctly?
- ☐ Are words spelled correctly?

Sentences

Subjects and Verbs

For help with subjects and verbs, see Chapter 25.

1. Underline the subjects once and verbs twice in a paragraph of your revised essay. Remember that sentences can have more than one subject-verb set.
2. Does each of your sentences have at least one subject and verb that can stand alone?

____

For help with fragments, see Chapter 26.

For help with run-togethers, see Chapter 27.

3. Correct any fragments you have written.
4. Correct any run-together sentences you have written.

Subject-Verb Agreement

1. Read aloud the subjects and verbs you underlined in your revised essay.
2. Correct any subjects and verbs that do not agree.

For help with subject-verb agreement, see Chapter 30.

Pronoun Agreement

1. Find any pronouns in your revised essay that do not agree with their nouns.
2. Correct any pronouns that do not agree with their nouns.

For help with pronoun agreement, see Chapter 34.

Modifiers

1. Find any modifiers in your revised essay that are not as close as possible to the words they modify.
2. Rewrite sentences if necessary so that your modifiers are as close as possible to the words they modify.

For help with modifier errors, see Chapter 37.

Punctuation and Mechanics

Punctuation

1. Read your revised essay for any errors in punctuation.
2. Make sure any fragments and run-together sentences you revised are punctuated correctly.

For help with punctuation, see Chapters 38–42.

Mechanics

1. Read your revised essay for any errors in capitalization.
2. Be sure to check your capitalization in any fragments or run-together sentences you revised.

For help with capitalization, see Chapter 43.

Word Choice and Spelling

Word Choice

1. Find any words used incorrectly in your revised essay.
2. Correct any errors you find.

For help with confused words, see Chapter 49.

Spelling

1. Use spell-check and a dictionary to check your spelling.
2. Correct any misspelled words.

For help with spelling, see Chapter 50.

Now rewrite your essay again with your editing corrections.

PRACTICING DEFINITION: FROM READING TO WRITING

Reading Workshop

Here are two good definition essays: "What Is Intelligence, Anyway?" by Isaac Asimov defines intelligence with a humorous touch, and "Spanglish Spoken Here" by Janice Castro explains how English and Spanish words and phrases are combined in many American communities on a daily basis. As you read, notice how the writers make their points through well-chosen examples and details.

WHAT IS INTELLIGENCE, ANYWAY?

by Isaac Asimov

SUMMARY

Based on personal experiences from his everyday life, Asimov defines *intelligence* in this essay.

READABILITY

(Flesch–Kincaid grade level)
8.2

INSTRUCTOR'S RESOURCE MANUAL

For additional teaching strategies, for journal entries, for vocabulary and reading quizzes, and for more writing assignments, see the *Instructor's Resource Manual*, Section II, Part II.

Focusing Your Attention

1. Do you ever feel smart in some subjects and not so smart in others? What do you think is the reason for these differences?
2. The essay you are about to read uses examples to explain different types of intelligence we all have. Do you think people can be intelligent in one area and not in another? How could this happen? Do you think these "intelligences" could be altered?

Expanding Your Vocabulary

The following words are important to your understanding of this essay. Highlight them throughout the essay before you begin to read. Then refer to this list as you get to these words in the essay.

aptitude: natural ability (paragraph 1)

KP: kitchen police or workers in the military (paragraph 1)

complacent: smug and satisfied (paragraph 2)

bents: angles (paragraph 2)

oracles: people with great wisdom (paragraph 3)

academician: someone connected to education (paragraph 4)

intricate: complicated or detailed (paragraph 4)

foist: impose something unnecessary (paragraph 4)

arbiter: person who settles a dispute (paragraph 4)

raucously: harshly or loudly (paragraph 6)

READING CRITICALLY

As you learned at the beginning of this chapter, practice generating your reactions to your reading by recording the author's ideas on the left side of a piece of paper and your own reactions on the right. These notes will also help you understand the essay on an analytical level. Share your notes with someone in the class.

WHAT IS INTELLIGENCE, ANYWAY?

by Isaac Asimov

What is intelligence, anyway? When I was in the Army, I received a kind of aptitude test that all soldiers took and, against a normal of 100, scored 160. No one at the base had ever seen a figure like that, and for two hours they made a big fuss over me. (It didn't mean anything. The next day I was still a buck private with KP as my highest duty.) 1

All of my life I've been registering scores like that, so that I have the complacent feeling that I'm highly intelligent, and I expect other people think so too. Actually, though, don't such scores simply mean that I am very good at answering the type of academic questions that are considered worthy of answers by the people who make up the intelligence tests, people with intellectual bents similar to mine? 2

For instance, I had an auto repairman once, who, on these intelligence tests, could not possibly have scored more than 80, by my estimate. I always took it for granted that I was far more intelligent than he was. Yet, when anything went wrong with my car, I hastened to him with it, watched him anxiously as he explored its vitals, and listened to his pronouncements as though they were divine oracles—and he always fixed my car. 3

Well, then, suppose my auto repairman devised questions for an intelligence test. Or suppose a carpenter did, or a farmer, or, indeed, almost anyone but an academician. By every one of those tests, I'd prove myself a moron. And I'd be a moron too. In a world where I could not use my academic training and my verbal talents but had to do something intricate or hard, working with my hands, I would do poorly. My intelligence, then, is not absolute but is a function of the society I live in and of the fact that a small subsection of that society has managed to foist itself on the rest as an arbiter of such matters. 4

5 Consider my auto repairman, again. He had a habit of telling me jokes whenever he saw me. One time he raised his head from under the automobile hood to say, "Doc, a deaf-and-dumb guy went into a hardware store to ask for some nails. He put two fingers together on the counter and made hammering motions with the other hand. The clerk brought him a hammer. He shook his head and pointed to the two fingers he was hammering. The clerk brought him nails. He picked out the sizes he wanted and left. Well, doc, the next guy who came in was a blind man. He wanted scissors. How do you suppose he asked for them?"

6 Indulgently, I lifted my right hand and made scissoring motions with my first two fingers. Whereupon my auto repairman laughed raucously and said, "Why, you dumb jerk, he used his *voice* and asked for them." Then he said, smugly, "I've been trying that on all my customers today." "Did you catch many?" I asked. "Quite a few," he said, "but I knew for sure I'd catch you." "Why is that?" I asked. "Because you're so goddamned educated, doc, I knew you couldn't be very smart."

7 And I have an uneasy feeling he had something there.

Thinking Critically About Content

1. What is the main idea of this essay?
2. What does Asimov mean when he says his intelligence "is not absolute but is a function of the society I live in" (paragraph 4)?
3. Think of a synonym for "smart" in paragraph 6. What is Asimov implying about intelligence in this paragraph.

Thinking Critically About Purpose and Audience

4. What do you think Asimov's purpose is in this essay?
5. Who do you think is his primary audience?
6. What would Asimov's audience say education and intelligence have in common?

Thinking Critically About Essays

7. How does Asimov use examples in this definition essay?
8. What would Asimov say is his actual definition of *intelligence?*
9. Does this essay imply there are different types of intelligence? Explain your answer with details from the essay.
10. Write a paragraph defining *intelligence* from the auto repairman's point of view.

Answers to Questions

Thinking Critically About Content

1. Asimov claims in this essay that there are different types of intelligence.
2. Asimov means that his intelligence is a product of his environment.
3. Asimov could be comparing wisdom and intelligence in paragraph 6.

Thinking Critically About Purpose and Audience

4. His purpose is to introduce the idea of different intelligences.
5. His main audience is the general reader.
6. Asimov would say there are different types of both education and intelligence. Also, they are both products of society.

Thinking Critically About Essays

7. He uses the example of the auto repairman to further his point.
8. Asimov would define intelligence as that which is useful to you in your daily life.
9. Yes. Examples will vary.
10. Answers will vary.

SPANGLISH SPOKEN HERE

by Janice Castro

Focusing Your Attention

1. Have you ever made up words? What were the sources of these creations?
2. The essay you are about to read discusses the various ways we have combined English and Spanish in the United States over the years. Do you live in an area that draws from more than one language? What signs of multiple languages do you see in your immediate environment?

Expanding Your Vocabulary

The following words are important to your understanding of this essay. Highlight them throughout the essay before you begin to read. Then refer to this list as you get to these words in the essay.

bemused: confused or bewildered (paragraph 1)

linguistic currency: valued language (paragraph 2)

syntax: the arrangement of words into sentences (paragraph 3)

languorous: enjoyable inactivity (paragraph 5)

hybrids: things made from a combination of two other things (paragraph 6)

gaffes: embarrassing blunders (paragraph 10)

luxuriant: rich or thick (paragraph 10)

SUMMARY

Castro defines *Spanglish* by giving real-world examples of this hybrid language.

READABILITY

(Flesch–Kincaid grade level)
11.7

INSTRUCTOR'S RESOURCE MANUAL

For additional teaching strategies, for journal entries, for vocabulary and reading quizzes, and for more writing assignments, see the *Instructor's Resource Manual*, Section II, Part II.

READING CRITICALLY

Once again, practice generating your reactions to your reading by recording the author's ideas on the left side of a piece of paper and your own reactions on the right. This activity will help you understand this essay at a deeper level than reading without annotating it. Share your notes with someone in the class.

SPANGLISH SPOKEN HERE
by Janice Castro

1 In Manhattan a first-grader greets her visiting grandparents, happily exclaiming, "Come here, sientate!" Her bemused grandfather, who does not speak Spanish, nevertheless knows she is asking him to sit down. A Miami personnel officer understands what a job applicant means when he says, "Quiero un part time." Nor do drivers miss a beat reading a billboard alongside a Los Angeles street advertising CERVEZA-SIX-PACK!

2 This free-form blend of Spanish and English, known as Spanglish, is common linguistic currency wherever concentrations of Hispanic Americans are found in the U.S. In Los Angeles, where 55% of the city's 3 million inhabitants speak Spanish, Spanglish is as much a part of daily life as sunglasses. Unlike the broken-English efforts of earlier immigrants from Europe, Asia, and other regions, Spanglish has become a widely accepted conversational mode used casually—even playfully—by Spanish-speaking immigrants and native-born Americans alike.

3 Consisting of one part Hispanicized English, one part Americanized Spanish, and more than a little fractured syntax, Spanglish is a bit like a Robin Williams comedy routine: a crackling line of cross-cultural patter straight from the melting pot. Often it enters Anglo homes and families through the children, who pick it up at school or at play with their young Hispanic contemporaries. In other cases, it comes from watching TV; many an Anglo child watching *Sesame Street* has learned *uno dos tres* almost as quickly as *one two three.*

4 Spanglish takes a variety of forms, from the Southern California Anglos who bid farewell with the utterly silly "*hasta la* bye-bye" to the Cuban American drivers in Miami who *parquean their carros.* Some Spanglish sentences are mostly Spanish, with a quick detour for an English word or two. A Latino friend may cut short a conversation by glancing at his watch and excusing himself with the explanation that he must "*ir al supermarket.*"

5 Many of the English words transplanted in this way are simply handier than their Spanish counterparts. No matter how distasteful the subject, for example, it is still easier to say "income tax" than *impuesto sobre la renta.* At the same time, many Spanish-speaking immigrants have adopted such terms as VCR, microwave, and dishwasher for what they view as largely American phenomena. Still other English words convey a cultural context that is not implicit in the Spanish. A friend who invites you to *lonche* most

likely has in mind the brisk American custom of "doing lunch" rather than the languorous afternoon break traditionally implied by *almuerzo.*

Mainstream Americans exposed to similar hybrids of German, Chinese, or Hindi might be mystified. But even Anglos who speak little or no Spanish are somewhat familiar with Spanglish. Living among them, for one thing, are 19 million Hispanics. In addition, more American high school and university students sign up for Spanish than for any other foreign language. 6

Only in the past ten years, though, has Spanglish begun to turn into a national slang. Its popularity has grown with the explosive increases in U.S. immigration from Latin American countries. English has increasingly collided with Spanish in retail stores, offices and classrooms, in pop music and on street corners. Anglos whose ancestors picked up such Spanish words as *rancho, bronco, tornado,* and *incommunicado,* for instance, now freely use such Spanish words as *gracias, bueno, amigo,* and *por favor.* 7

Among Latinos, Spanglish conversations often flow easily from Spanish into several sentences of English and back. 8

Spanglish is a sort of code for Latinos: the speakers know Spanish, but their hybrid language reflects the American culture in which they live. Many lean to shorter, clipped phrases in place of the longer, more graceful expressions their parents used. Says Leonel de la Cuesta, an assistant professor of modern languages at Florida International University in Miami: "In the U.S., time is money, and that is showing up in Spanglish as an economy of language." Conversational examples: *taipiar* (type) and *winshi-wiper* (windshield wiper) replace *escribir a maquina* and *limpiaparabrisas.* 9

Major advertisers, eager to tap the estimated $134 billion in spending power wielded by Spanish-speaking Americans, have ventured into Spanglish to promote their products. In some cases, attempts to sprinkle Spanish through commercials have produced embarrassing gaffes. A Braniff airlines ad that sought to tell Spanish-speaking audiences they could settle back *en* (in) luxuriant *cuero* (leather) seats, for example, inadvertently said they could fly without clothes (*encuero*). A fractured translation of the Miller Lite slogan told readers the beer was "Filling, and less delicious." Similar blunders are often made by Anglos trying to impress Spanish-speaking pals. But if Latinos are amused by mangled Spanglish, they also recognize these goofs as a sort of friendly acceptance. As they might put it, *no problema.* 10

Thinking Critically About Content

1. Write a definition of *Spanglish* in your own words.
2. How does Spanglish usually enter Anglo homes?

ANSWERS TO QUESTIONS

Thinking Critically About Content

1. *Spanglish* is a mix of Spanish and English.
2. It enters most homes through the children, who pick it up from other children or from television.
3. Exposure to Spanish caused the flux of Spanglish.

Thinking Critically About Purpose and Audience

4. The author's purpose is to educate people about the prevalence of Spanglish in America—with both immigrants and native-born Americans.

5. Her primary audience is Americans.
6. The audience probably acknowledges its widespread use in society after reading this essay.

Thinking Critically About Essays

7. Here are two other examples: "Spanglish is as much a part of daily life as sunglasses" (para. 2) and "a crackling line of cross-cultural patter straight from the melting pot" (para. 3).
8. Answers will vary.
9. Answers will vary.
10. Answers will vary.

TEACHING ON THE WEB

Discussion Topic: Have students as a class discuss how definition is used on the Internet. In what ways can students find uses of definition other than simply defining words? What else is defined on the Internet?

TEACHING ON THE WEB

Links: Provide students with a complex term, and have them link to Web sites that define the term. How does each of the sites use definition? Which site defines the term most clearly?

3. What does Castro think is the main reason this hybrid language started to catch on in American society?

Thinking Critically About Purpose and Audience

4. Why do you think Castro wrote this essay?
5. Who do you think is her primary audience?
6. What do you suspect the primary audience for this essay thinks of Spanglish and its use in society today?

Thinking Critically About Essays

7. Castro uses a few comparisons to make her point about language. One is "linguistic currency," an implied comparison equating language use with money. Find one other comparison in this essay.
8. Give some examples from your own experience of words and/or phrases from different languages. Are these examples common where you live?
9. In your opinion, is the last sentence of the essay effective: "As they might put it, *no problema*"?
10. Choose one paragraph, and write a paragraph analyzing its mood and tone.

Writing Workshop

This final section gives you opportunities to apply what you have learned in this chapter to another writing assignment. This time, we provide very little prompting beyond a summary of the guidelines for writing a definition essay. This section will let you demonstrate that you can go through the entire writing process on your own with only occasional feedback from your peers. Loop back into the chapter as necessary when you have questions so that this process becomes as automatic to you as possible before you move on to new material. Then pause at the end of the chapter to reflect briefly on what you have learned.

Guidelines for Writing a Definition Essay

1. Choose your word or idea carefully, and give a working definition of it in your thesis statement.
2. Decide how you want to define your term: by synonym, by negation, or by category.
3. Develop your definition with examples.
4. Use other rhetorical strategies, such as description, comparison, or process analysis, to support your definition.
5. Organize your essay in a logical way.

Writing About Your Reading

1. In the first essay, Isaac Asimov defines *intelligence*. Write your own definition of another state of mind, such as *joy*, *fear*, *loneliness*, or *stress*.
2. Using Castro's method of development through example, define for your class a made-up word of your own.
3. Now that you have studied different approaches to the process of definition, what makes a definition effective or useful for you? Apply what you have studied about definition to your answer.

Possible sites for the topic "pathology":

World Wide Web Pathology Case Review, www.kumc.edu/pathology/casesearch.html

University of Pittsburgh, Department of Pathology, www.path.upmc.edu/cases.html

Armed Forces Institute of Pathology, www.afip.org

TEACHING ON THE WEB

Research: Provide students with an abstract concept like "justice" or "harmony," and have them search Web sites for a definition of these terms. Which Web site has the best definition? Why, in the context of the overall Web site, do they think this is so?

Writing About Your World

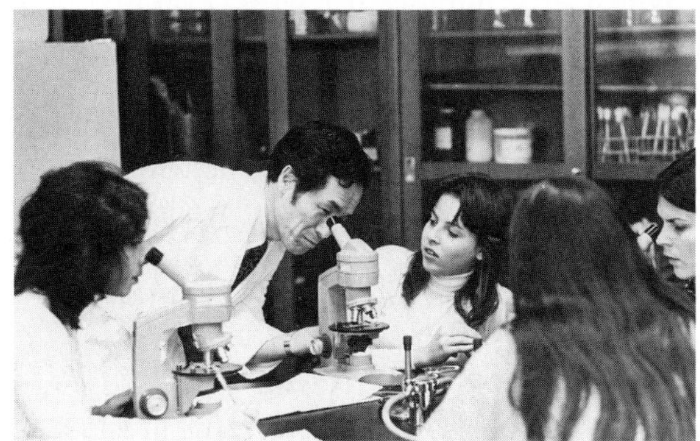

1. What does education mean to you? Define *education* as portrayed in this picture.
2. The concept of "family" has undergone a number of changes over the past few years. How would you define this term in our current society?
3. Define one of the following abstract terms: *fear, love, inferiority, wonder, pride, self-control, discipline, anger, freedom, violence, assertiveness, courtesy, kindness*.
4. Create your own definition assignment (with the help of your instructor), and write a response to it.

Revising

Small Group Activity (5–10 minutes per writer) Working in groups of three or four, read your definition essays to each other. The listeners should record their reactions on a copy of the Peer Evaluation Form in Appendix 2G. After your group goes through this process, give your evaluation forms to the appropriate writers so that each writer has two or three peer comment sheets for revising.

Paired Activity (5 minutes per writer) Using the completed Peer Evaluation Forms, work in pairs to decide what you should revise in your essay. If time allows, rewrite some of your sentences, and have your partner look at them.

Individual Activity Rewrite your paper, using the revising feedback you received from other students.

Editing

Paired Activity (5–10 minutes per writer) Swap papers with a classmate, and use the editing portion of your Peer Evaluation Form to identify as many grammar, punctuation, mechanics, and spelling errors as you can. If time allows, correct some of your errors, and have your partner look at them. Record your grammar, punctuation, and mechanics errors in the Error Log (Appendix 6) and your spelling errors in the Spelling Log (Appendix 7).

Individual Activity Rewrite your paper again, using the editing feedback you received from other students.

Reflecting on Your Writing When you have completed your own essay, answer these six questions.

1. What was most difficult about this assignment?
2. What was easiest?
3. What did you learn about definition by completing this assignment?
4. What do you think are the strengths of your definition essay? Place a wavy line by the parts of your essay that you feel are very good.
5. What are the weaknesses, if any, of your paper? Place an X by the parts of your essay you would like help with. Write any questions you have in the margin.
6. What did you learn from this assignment about your own writing process—about preparing to write, about writing the first draft, about revising, and about editing?

CHAPTER 15

Analyzing Causes and Effects

“The act of writing is one of the most powerful problem-solving tools humans have at their disposal.”

—TOBY FULWILER

We are born with a natural curiosity. Wanting to know why things happen is one of our earliest, most basic instincts: Daddy, why is the sky blue? Closely related to this desire to understand *why* is our interest in *what* will happen as a result of some particular action: If I stay outside much longer, will I get a bad sunburn? But thinking about causes and effects is not only part of human nature but also an advanced mental process and the basis for most decisions we make. When faced with a decision, we naturally consider it from different perspectives. If we choose option A, what will happen? What if we choose B—or C? In other words, we look at the possible results—the effects—of the choices and then make up our minds.

Analyzing causes and effects is also an essential part of our writing lives. We use cause-and-effect writing in our personal lives, in college, and in the marketplace:

- A volunteer for a mayor's campaign designs a poster telling how a vote for this candidate will benefit the city.
- A student discusses the causes of schizophrenia in a paper for a psychology course.
- A student explains the effects of the Civil Rights Act of 1964 on a history exam.
- A sales representative writes a report to her manager explaining why she didn't meet her sales projections.
- The owner of a florist shop writes a letter of complaint to one of his suppliers about the negative effect of late deliveries on sales.

TEACHING CAUSE AND EFFECT

Show the first part of a movie, just enough for students to understand what the movie is about and what effects will occur based on the causes they saw. Be sure to show them a film that has a shocking and unexpected ending, based on the portion of the movie students saw (for example, *Along Came a Spider* with Morgan Freeman and Monica Potter). Ask them what they think will happen in the movie and what causes and effects will occur.

Then show students enough of the end of the film that they can see the twist and understand the plot. How close were the students' predictions? Knowing now what happens in the end of the movie, what causes and effects do the students think happened in between the portions of the movie they saw?

Analyzing causes and effects requires the ability to look for connections between two or more items or events and to analyze the reasons for those connections. As the name implies, this writing strategy is composed of two parts: cause and effect. To understand **causes,** we look in the past for reasons why something happened. To discover **effects,** we look to the future for possible results of an action. In other words, we break a situation into parts so we can look at the relationships between these parts and then reach conclusions that are logical and useful.

TEACHING TIPS

The following eight teaching tips are based on Howard Gardner's list of multiple intelligences:

Verbal/Linguistic

Have students select an ad and look for all the causes and effects associated with its message. What hints in the ad help a reader know when either a cause or an effect is being referred to? What parts of the ad, if removed, weaken the cause/effect relationships?

Musical/Rhythmic

Listen to an old song that you had an emotional connection with years ago. What feelings does this song arouse? What causes this song to have such an effect on you?

Logical/Mathematical

Have students diagram the causes and effects associated with a typical job. For example,

Cause	Effect
Work hard and efficiently	Raise or promotion

READING AND WRITING A CAUSE/EFFECT ESSAY

Learning how to read cause/effect essays critically will improve your writing. Understanding how a reading selection actually works (in both form and content) will show you how to develop your own writing assignments. Reading and writing critically in any mode are demanding, but they are necessary for success in college and in life beyond college. Like two parts of a whole, these two processes work together to increase your ability to perform other tasks in all facets of life.

Reading a Cause/Effect Essay

In "Why Do Schools Flunk Biology?" Lynnell Hancock makes the point that education in the United States is stuck in the nineteenth century. She deals with both the causes and the effects of students' ability to learn. What do you think of our educational system on the high school level? What do you think of your local high schools?

READING CRITICALLY

Separating causes from effects is an important part of understanding a cause/effect essay. After a first reading, divide a sheet of paper into two parts with a vertical line. Then as you read the essay for a second time, record the causes in the left column and the results on the right. Draw lines from each cause to its related effect (if applicable). Be prepared to explain the connection between your lists and the details in the essay.

WHY DO SCHOOLS FLUNK BIOLOGY?

by Lynnell Hancock

1 Biology is a staple at most American high schools. Yet when it comes to the biology of the students themselves—how their brains develop and retain knowledge—school officials would rather not pay attention to the lessons. Can first graders handle French? What time should school start? Should music be cut? Biologists have some important evidence to offer. Not only are they ignored, but their findings are often turned upside down.

2 Force of habit rules the hallways and classrooms. Neither brain science nor education research has been able to free the majority of America's schools from their 19th-century roots. If more administrators were tuned in to brain research, scientists argue, not only would schedules change, but subjects such as foreign language and geometry would be offered to much younger children. Music and gym would be daily requirements. Lectures, worksheets, and rote memorization would be replaced by hands-on materials, drama, and project work. And teachers would pay greater attention to children's emotional connections to subjects. "We do more education research than anyone else in the world," says Frank Vellutino, a professor of educational psychology at State University of New York at Albany, "and we ignore more as well."

3 Plato once said that music "is a more potent instrument than any other for education." Now scientists know why. Music, they believe, trains the brain for higher forms of thinking. Researchers at the University of California, Irvine, studied the power of music by observing two groups of preschoolers. One group took piano lessons and sang daily in chorus. The other did not. After eight months the musical 3-year-olds were expert puzzle-masters, scoring 80 percent higher than their playmates did in spatial intelligence—the ability to visualize the world accurately.

4 This skill later translates into complex math and engineering skills. "Early music training can enhance a child's ability to reason," says Irvine physicist Gordon Shaw. Yet music education is often the first "frill" to be cut when school budgets shrink. Schools on average have only one music teacher for every 500 children, according to the National Commission on Music Education.

5 Then there's gym—another expendable hour by most school standards. Only 36 percent of school children today are required to participate in daily

Goof off miss work a lot	Probation or loss of job

Visual/Spatial

Bring in several pictures (without any words) that depict cause/effect relationships. For example, you might bring in pictures of a fire, firefighters trying to control the fire, wind carrying the fire farther, a neighborhood close to the destruction, families trying to leave the area on congested streets, and a family looking at where its home used to stand. Then ask students to put the pictures into a logical order. Finally, have them justify and explain the order.

Bodily/Kinesthetic

Have students play *Kerplunk* (available at most toy stores), a game that tests people's ability to understand critical thinking skills. But before students remove a stick from the tube in the game, have them state what they think the effects of removing the stick will be (for example, "This will not cause the marbles to fall, but it will cause them to fall on the next move"). If they miscalculate, have them state the reasons the marbles fell.

Intrapersonal

Have students think about times when they tried to study or work but were distracted. What were the causes of the distraction? What effects did these causes produce? How would students make sure these distractions don't occur again?

Interpersonal

Have a group of students go to a fitness center and look closely at some of the machines. Then have students try to figure out what (causes) makes the machines work (effects).

Naturalist

Have students film a video or take pictures that show the influence of nature on humans. Then have them explain the causes and effects of nature on humans from their collection of pictures.

INSTRUCTOR'S RESOURCE MANUAL

For additional material about teaching cause and effect; for journal entries; and for multiple-choice, short-answer, and paragraph tests, see the *Instructor's Resource Manual*, Section II, Part II.

physical education. Yet researchers now know that exercise is good not only for the heart. It also juices up the brain, feeding it nutrients in the form of glucose and increasing nerve connections—all of which make it easier for kids of all ages to learn. Neuroscientist William Greenough confirmed this by watching rats at his University of Illinois at Urbana–Champaign lab. One group did nothing. A second exercised on an automatic treadmill. A third was set loose in a Barnum & Bailey obstacle course requiring the rats to perform acrobatic feats. These "supersmart" rats grew "an enormous amount of gray matter" compared with their sedentary partners, says Greenough. Of course, children don't ordinarily run such gantlets; still, Greenough believes, the results are significant. Numerous studies, he says, show that children who exercise regularly do better in school.

6 The implication for schools goes beyond simple exercise. Children also need to be more physically active in the classroom, not sitting quietly in their seats memorizing subtraction tables. Knowledge is retained longer if children connect not only aurally but emotionally and physically to the material, says University of Oregon education professor Robert Sylwester in *A Celebration of Neurons.*

7 Good teachers know that lecturing on the American Revolution is far less effective than acting out a battle. Angles and dimensions are better understood if children chuck their work sheets and build a complex model to scale. The smell of the glue enters memory through one sensory system, the touch of the wood blocks another, the sight of the finished model still another. The brain then creates a multidimensional mental model of the experience—one easier to retrieve. "Explaining a smell," says Sylwester, "is not as good as actually smelling it."

8 Scientists argue that children are capable of far more at younger ages than schools generally realize. People obviously continue learning their whole lives, but the optimum "windows of opportunity for learning" last until about the age of 10 or 12, says Harry Chugani of Wayne State University's Children's Hospital of Michigan. Chugani determined this by measuring the brain's consumption of its chief energy source, glucose. (The more glucose it uses, the more active the brain.) Children's brains, he observes, gobble up glucose at twice the adult rate from the age of 4 to puberty. So young brains are as primed as they'll ever be to process new information. Complex subjects such as trigonometry or foreign language shouldn't wait for puberty to be introduced. In fact, Chugani says, it's far easier for an elementary-school child to hear and process a second language—and even speak it without an accent. Yet most U.S. districts wait until junior high to introduce Spanish or French—after the "windows" are closed.

9 Reform could begin at the beginning. Many sleep researchers now believe that most teens' biological clocks are set later than those of their fellow humans. But high school starts at 7:30 a.m., usually to accommodate bus schedules. The result can be wasted class time for whole groups of kids. Making matters worse, many kids have trouble readjusting their natural sleep rhythm. Dr. Richard Allen of Johns Hopkins University found that teens went to sleep at the same time whether they had to be at school by 7:30 a.m. or 9:30 a.m. The later-to-rise teens not only get more sleep, he says; they also get better grades. The obvious solution would be to start school later when kids hit puberty. But at school, there's what's obvious, and then there's tradition.

10 Why is this body of research rarely used in most American classrooms? Not many administrators or school-board members know it exists, says Linda Darling-Hammond, professor of education at Columbia University's Teachers College. In most states, neither teachers nor administrators are required to know much about how children learn in order to be certified. What's worse, she says, decisions to cut music or gym are often made by noneducators, whose concerns are more often monetary than educational. "Our school system was invented in the late 1800s, and little has changed," she says. "Can you imagine if the medical profession ran this way?"

Preparing to Write Your Own Cause/Effect Essay

What can be improved in our educational system at the high school level? What do you want to change? What would be the possible results of these changes? What do you want to keep the same? Use one or more of the prewriting techniques you learned in Chapter 2 to generate ideas on this subject.

Writing a Cause/Effect Essay

When you write a cause/effect essay, your purpose is to give your readers some insight into the causes and effects of an event or a situation. Cause/effect writing is based on your ability to analyze. Good cause/effect essays follow a few simple guidelines.

1. **Write a thesis statement that tells what you are analyzing.** Cause/effect thinking requires that you look for connections between two or more situations. That is, you want to discover what caused an incident

or what its results might be. Then you can focus on the causes (what made something else happen) or the effects (the results), or some combination of the two.

In her essay, Hancock puts her thesis statement at the end of her first paragraph: "Not only are they [the biology lessons] ignored, but their findings are often turned upside down." She goes on to say that if school administrators paid attention to research (the cause), we would see many changes (the effects), which she names. The rest of the essay examines each effect in detail.

2. **Choose facts, details, and reasons to support your thesis statement.** Cause/effect essays are usually written to prove a specific point. As a result, your body paragraphs should consist mainly of facts, details, and reasons—not opinions. Your reader should be able to check what you are saying, and any opinions that you include should be based on clear evidence.

   Since Hancock sets out to prove that American education ignores research, she must name specific research studies that help her prove her point. She breaks her subject into five areas: music, gym, teaching methods, curriculum (subjects studied), and school hours. She then cites evidence in each area. For example, in the area of music, she describes research at the University of California, Irvine; for gym, she discusses rat studies from the University of Illinois; for curriculum, she describes research done at Wayne State University's Children's Hospital.

   Hancock also quotes many experts, such as Frank Vellutino, a professor of educational psychology at State University of New York at Albany (paragraph 2), and gives statistics from the National Commission on Music Education (paragraph 4). A reader could check every one of Hancock's research studies, quotations, statistics, and observations (such as when most high schools begin classes in the morning). By providing facts and reasons rather than opinions in her body paragraphs, Hancock proves her point—that American education is not paying attention to current research about learning.

3. **Do not mistake coincidence for cause or effect.** If you get up every morning at 5:30, just before the sun rises, you cannot conclude that the sun rises *because* you get up. The relationship between these two events is coincidence. Confusing coincidence with cause and effect is faulty reasoning—reasoning that is not logical. To avoid this kind of faulty reasoning, you can look deeper into the issues connected with your subject. The more you search for real causes and effects, the less likely you will be thrown off by coincidence.

Hancock does not seem to mistake coincidence for cause or effect in any part of her essay. If, however, she had said that ignoring research on how teens learn has resulted in fewer students studying foreign languages today compared to 40 years ago, her reasoning would be faulty. She has no evidence to prove that the research about how students learn and the decline in students taking foreign languages in high school are related. It's only a coincidence that the research has been ignored and that fewer students study foreign languages today.

4. **Search for the real causes and effects connected with your subject.** Just as you wouldn't stop reading halfway through a good murder mystery, you shouldn't stop too early in your analysis of causes and effects. Keep digging. The first reasons or results that you uncover are often not the real reasons or results. Suppose that a character in a mystery dies by slipping in the shower. You should try to find out what caused the fall. A good detective who keeps digging might find that someone administered a drug overdose, which caused her to fall in the shower. In other words, you are looking for the most basic cause or effect.

   Hancock shows us through the large amount of evidence she presents that she has searched hard to discover the real causes and effects of education's lagging behind the times. She names two causes—administrators ignore research and noneducators make decisions about education—and gives the effects of ignoring research in five areas of education.

5. **Organize your essay so that your readers can easily follow your analysis.** Though it may be difficult to think through the causes and effects of a situation, organizing this type of essay is usually straightforward. Your thesis statement tells what you are going to analyze. Then your body paragraphs discuss the main causes or main effects in the order they occurred, from one extreme to another, from general to particular, or from particular to general. You might, for example, use chronological order to show how one effect led to another and then to a third. Or you might move from the most important cause or effect to the least important. Your goal in a cause/effect essay is to get your readers to agree with you and see a certain issue or situation the way you do. To accomplish this purpose, your readers need to be able to follow what you are saying.

   Hancock discusses five effects of ignoring research on how students learn, moving from particular to general. First, she deals with the two subjects that school boards cut for budget reasons, music and gym. From these specific classes she moves to more general concerns—teaching methods and curriculum. Finally, she discusses high school hours, the most general topic of all. In other words, she organizes her essay from specific to general, moving from specific classes to the general logistics of the school day.

Writing Your Own Cause/Effect Essay

Write an essay analyzing one of the changes you think is necessary in our high school educational system. What caused the current problem as you see it? Why is this change necessary? What will be the results of this change? Review your prewriting notes first. Then draft a thesis statement, and write your analysis, following the preceding guidelines for writing a cause/effect essay.

A STUDENT'S CAUSE/EFFECT ESSAY

Jefferson Wright, the student writer of the following essay, titled "The Budget Crisis," explores the problems of budget cuts at his college. Can you find the points in this draft of his essay when he deals with causes? When does he focus on effects?

The Budget Crisis

1 The local college has a budget crisis. Now, when a staff person quits their job or retires, no one is hired to replace that person. This wouldn't be of great concern to most students, except now the lack of money is starting to affect the campus grounds. The college no longer has the money to replace some of the maintenance and facilities crew, which means the campus grounds, classrooms, and offices are no longer well maintained.

2 A campus that used to be beautiful has turned into a wasteland because of the neglect in keeping up its grounds. The small maintenance crew simply cannot handle the workload necessary to maintain the campus. The flower beds in front of the buildings have not been weeded, so now it has more weeds than flowers. Trash that is thrown around the campus has not been picked up. Around every doorway are cigarette butts ground into the concrete. People shouldn't smoke anyway. It's not a great habit. There are old newspapers and candy wrappers caught on grass that has not been mowed in over two weeks, making the grounds look like the aftermath of a concert.

Trash cans are overflowing with garbage and have colonies of flies circling them. The outside of the campus just looks unkempt and uncared for.

However, the campus grounds are not all that is ugly. The classroom buildings are also neglected. Everything inside is as messy as outside. The floors that used to shine are now covered with a sticky gray film. There are spills on the floors by all the soft drink machines. The bulletin boards are never cleaned off, so people just put new flyers over three or four layers of old flyers. On warm days, a strange smell overwhelms the classrooms, which the students have named "the biohazard." Restrooms are in desperate need of attention. And would probably fail any government check. The campus is really disgusting. 3

But the students aren't the only people suffering; the teachers are feeling the effects also. Their offices have ants crawling from various cracks in the walls. The dust in their offices is two inches thick. Spiders have woven cobwebs high in the windows and corners of the offices. Making both teachers and students wonder exactly where the insects hide during the day. Many light bulbs are broken near the offices, and the fluorescent bulbs flicker as if it is dancing to an unheard rhythm. The offices are as bad as the rest of the campus. 4

The condition of the campus can hardly be blamed on the maintenance crew. They are constantly working and trying to keep up with the workload. The problem lies in the fact that by the time they finish one job, two or more weeks pass by before they can get back to that job. There just isn't enough money to hire the necessary personnel to cover the demands of the job. The college should put money into hiring more maintenance personnel before students transfer to other colleges because of the condition of this one. Why can't the college just spend the necessary money to make the campus beautiful again. 5

Discovering How the Essay Works

1. What is Jefferson analyzing in this essay?

   He is examining how the budget crisis is affecting his college campus.

2. Do Jefferson's facts, details, and reasons support his thesis statement? Explain your answer.

   They are all directly related to his thesis statement.

3. Does Jefferson confuse any coincidences with causes and effects? Explain your answer.

   He does not confuse coincidences with causes and effects.

4. Do you feel that Jefferson gets to the real problems connected with his college's budget crisis? Explain your answer.

   Yes, because he shows how the budget crisis affects the hiring of personnel, which affects the campus grounds, classrooms, and offices.

5. How does Jefferson organize the topics in his essay?

   From farthest to closest

REVISING AND EDITING OPTIONS
Consider varying your approach to revising and editing. You could teach these skills in a class discussion, in small groups, or in pairs.

Revising and Editing the Student Essay

This essay is Jefferson's first draft, which now needs to be revised and edited. First, apply the following Revising Checklist to the content of Jefferson's draft. When you are satisfied that his ideas are fully developed and well organized, use the Editing Checklist on page 370 to correct his grammar and mechanics errors. Do the tasks, and answer the questions after each checklist. Then write your suggested changes directly on Jefferson's draft.

REVISING STRATEGIES
This chapter focuses on the following revising elements:
Unity
Organization
Coherence

REVISING CHECKLIST

THESIS STATEMENT

✔ Does the thesis statement contain the essay's controlling idea?

✔ Does the thesis appear as the last sentence of the introduction?

BASIC ELEMENTS

✔ Does the title draw in the readers?

✔ Does the introduction capture the readers' attention and build up to the thesis statement effectively?

✔ Does each body paragraph deal with a single topic?

✔ Does the conclusion bring the essay to a close in an interesting way?

DEVELOPMENT

✔ Do the body paragraphs adequately support the thesis statement?

✔ Does each body paragraph have a focused topic sentence?

✔ Does each body paragraph contain *specific* details that support the topic sentence?

✔ Does each body paragraph include *enough* details to explain the topic sentence fully?

UNITY

✔ Do the essay's topic sentences relate directly to the thesis statement?

✔ Do the details in each body paragraph support its topic sentence?

ORGANIZATION

✔ Is the essay organized logically?

✔ Is each body paragraph organized logically?

COHERENCE

✔ Are transitions used effectively so that paragraphs move smoothly and logically from one to the next?

✔ Do the sentences move smoothly and logically from one to the next?

Thesis Statement

1. Put brackets around the last sentence in Jefferson's introduction. What does it say he is analyzing?

   The effect of the budget crisis on the campus grounds, classrooms, and offices

2. Rewrite Jefferson's thesis statement if necessary so that it states his purpose and introduces all his topics.

   Answers will vary.

Basic Elements

1. Give Jefferson's essay an alternate title.

   Answers will vary.

2. Rewrite Jefferson's introduction so that it captures the readers' attention and builds up to the thesis statement at the end of the paragraph.

   Answers will vary.

3. Does each of Jefferson's body paragraphs deal with only one topic?

   Yes

4. Rewrite Jefferson's conclusion using at least one suggestion from Part I.

   Answers will vary.

Development

1. Write out Jefferson's thesis statement (revised, if necessary), and list his topic sentences below it.

   Thesis statement: *The college no longer has the money to replace some of the maintenance and facilities crew, which means the campus grounds, classrooms, and offices are no longer well maintained.*

   Topic 1: *A campus that used to be beautiful has turned into a wasteland because of the neglect in keeping up its grounds.*

   Topic 2: *However, the campus grounds are not all that is ugly.*

   Topic 3: *But the students aren't the only people suffering; the teachers are feeling the effects also.*

2. Do the topics adequately develop the essay's thesis statement?

   Yes

3. Does each body paragraph have a focused topic sentence?

   Yes

4. Does Jefferson get to the *real* causes and effects in his essay?

   He does examine the real causes and effects.

5. Where do you need more information?

   Answers will vary.

6. Make two of Jefferson's details more specific.
7. Add at least two new details to make his essay clearer.

Unity

1. Read each of Jefferson's topic sentences with his thesis statement. Do they go together?

   Answers will vary.

2. Revise his topic sentences if necessary so they are directly related.
3. Drop or rewrite the two sentences in paragraph 2 that are not directly related to their topic sentence. *Sentences 6 and 7*

Organization

1. Read Jefferson's essay again to see if all the paragraphs are arranged logically.
2. Move any paragraphs that are out of order. *All paragraphs are arranged logically.*
3. Do you think his method of organization is the most effective one for his purpose? Explain your answer.

   It is the most effective because it moves the crisis from outside to the office space that affects people personally.

4. Look closely at Jefferson's body paragraphs to see if all his sentences are arranged logically within paragraphs.
5. Move the sentence in paragraph 2 that is out of order. *Move sentence 9 after sentence 4.*

Coherence

For a list of transitions, see page 101.

For a list of pronouns, see pages 7–8.

1. Add two transitions to Jefferson's essay.
2. Circle five pronouns Jefferson uses.
3. Explain how two of these make Jefferson's essay easier to read.

Answers will vary.

Now rewrite Jefferson's essay with your revisions.

EDITING STRATEGIES
This chapter focuses on the following editing problems:
Fragments
Pronoun agreement
End punctuation

 **EDITING CHECKLIST** 

SENTENCES

✔ Does each sentence have a main subject and verb?
✔ Do all subjects and verbs agree?
✔ Do all pronouns agree with their nouns?
✔ Are modifiers as close as possible to the words they modify?

PUNCTUATION AND MECHANICS

✔ Are sentences punctuated correctly?
✔ Are words capitalized properly?

WORD CHOICE AND SPELLING

✔ Are words used correctly?
✔ Are words spelled correctly?

Sentences

Subjects and Verbs

For help with subjects and verbs, see Chapter 25.

1. Underline the subjects once and verbs twice in paragraphs 3 and 4 of your revision of Jefferson's essay. Remember that sentences can have more than one subject-verb set.

2. Does each of the sentences have at least one subject and verb that can stand alone?

   No

3. Did you find and correct Jefferson's two fragments? If not, find and correct them now. *Paragraph 3, sentence 9; paragraph 4, sentence 5*

For help with fragments, see Chapter 26.

Subject-Verb Agreement

1. Read aloud the subjects and verbs you underlined in your revision of Jefferson's essay.
2. Correct any subjects and verbs that do not agree. *All subjects and verbs agree.*

For help with subject-verb agreement, see Chapter 30.

Pronoun Agreement

1. Find any pronouns in your revision of Jefferson's essay that do not agree with their nouns.
2. Did you find and correct the three pronoun agreement errors in Jefferson's essay? If not, find and correct them now. *Paragraph 1, sentence 2; paragraph 2, sentence 3; paragraph 4, sentence 6*

For help with pronoun agreement, see Chapter 34.

Modifiers

1. Find any modifiers in your revision of Jefferson's essay that are not as close as possible to the words they modify. *There are no modifier errors.*
2. Rewrite sentences if necessary so that modifiers are as close as possible to the words they modify.

For help with modifier errors, see Chapter 37.

Punctuation and Mechanics

Punctuation

1. Read your revision of Jefferson's essay for any errors in punctuation.
2. Find the two fragments you revised, and make sure they are punctuated correctly.
3. Did you find and correct Jefferson's two errors in end punctuation? If not, find and correct them now. *Paragraph 3, sentence 10; paragraph 5, sentence 6*

For help with punctuation, see Chapters 38–42.

Mechanics

1. Read your revision of Jefferson's essay for any errors in capitalization.
2. Be sure to check Jefferson's capitalization in the fragments you revised.

For help with capitalization, see Chapter 43.

Word Choice and Spelling

Word Choice

For help with confused words, see Chapter 49.

1. Find any words used incorrectly in your revision of Jefferson's essay. *All words are used correctly.*
2. Correct any errors you find.

Spelling

For help with spelling, see Chapter 50.

1. Use spell-check and a dictionary to check the spelling in your revision of Jefferson's essay. *All words are spelled correctly.*
2. Correct any misspelled words.

Now rewrite Jefferson's essay again with your editing corrections.

YOUR OWN CAUSE/EFFECT ESSAY

Returning to the cause/effect essay you wrote earlier in this chapter, you are now ready to revise and edit your own writing. Remember that revision involves reworking the content and organization of your essay while editing asks you to check your grammar and usage. Work first with the content, making sure your thoughts are fully developed and organized effectively before you correct your grammar and usage errors. The more times you repeat these processes, the better your draft will be.

WRITING CRITICALLY

As you begin to rework your essay, use the same technique you did in your reading. List the causes and effects that you discuss in your essay in two columns. Then draw lines from causes to related effects, making sure the relationship between these items is clear to your readers. Revise any connections that are unclear.

CLASS ACTIVITY
Find a published cause/effect essay that also incorporates many

Revising and Editing Your Own Essay

The checklists here will help you apply what you have learned in this chapter to your essay.

REVISING CHECKLIST

THESIS STATEMENT

- ☐ Does the thesis statement contain the essay's controlling idea?
- ☐ Does the thesis appear as the last sentence of the introduction?

BASIC ELEMENTS

- ☐ Does the title draw in the readers?
- ☐ Does the introduction capture the readers' attention and build up to the thesis statement effectively?
- ☐ Does each body paragraph deal with a single topic?
- ☐ Does the conclusion bring the essay to a close in an interesting way?

DEVELOPMENT

- ☐ Do the body paragraphs adequately support the thesis statement?
- ☐ Does each body paragraph have a focused topic sentence?
- ☐ Does each body paragraph contain *specific* details that support the topic sentence?
- ☐ Does each body paragraph include *enough* details to explain the topic sentence fully?

UNITY

- ☐ Do the essay's topic sentences relate directly to the thesis statement?
- ☐ Do the details in each body paragraph support its topic sentence?

ORGANIZATION

- ☐ Is the essay organized logically?
- ☐ Is each body paragraph organized logically?

COHERENCE

- ☐ Are transitions used effectively so that paragraphs move smoothly and logically from one to the next?
- ☐ Do the sentences move smoothly and logically from one to the next?

of the other modes. Have the students identify the instances of the other modes, and then ask them how they think these other modes help establish the cause and effect relationships in the essay as a whole.

Thesis Statement

1. What are you analyzing?

____

2. Put brackets around the last sentence in your introduction. What do you say you are analyzing in this sentence?

____

3. Rewrite your thesis statement if necessary so that it states your purpose and introduces your topics.

Basic Elements

1. Give your essay a title if it doesn't have one.

____

2. Does your introduction capture your readers' attention and build up to your thesis statement at the end of the paragraph?

____

3. Does each of your body paragraphs deal with only one topic?

____

4. Does your conclusion follow some of the suggestions offered in Part I?

____

Development

1. Write out your thesis statement (revised, if necessary), and list your topic sentences below it.

   Thesis statement: _______________

   Topic 1: _______________

   Topic 2: _______________

   Topic 3: _______________

2. Do your topics adequately support your thesis statement?

____

3. Does each body paragraph have a focused topic sentence?

____

4. Do you get to the *real* causes and effects in your essay?

____

5. Where do you need more information?

____

6. Make two of your details more specific.
7. Add at least two new details to make your cause/effect clearer.

Unity

1. Read each of your topic sentences with your thesis statement in mind. Do they go together?

____

2. Revise your topic sentences if necessary so they are directly related.
3. Drop or rewrite any of the sentences in your body paragraphs that are not directly related to their topic sentences.

Organization

1. Read your essay again to see if all the paragraphs are arranged logically.
2. Refer to your answers to the development questions. Then identify your method of organization:

____

3. Move any paragraphs that are out of order.
4. Look closely at your body paragraphs to see if all the sentences are arranged logically within paragraphs.
5. Move any sentences that are out of order.

Coherence

1. Add two transitions to your essay.
2. Circle five pronouns you use.

For a list of transitions, see page 101.

For a list of pronouns, see pages 7–8.

3. Explain how two of these make your essay easier to read.

____

____

Now rewrite your essay with your revisions.

EDITING CHECKLIST

SENTENCES

- ☐ Does each sentence have a main subject and verb?
- ☐ Do all subjects and verbs agree?
- ☐ Do all pronouns agree with their nouns?
- ☐ Are modifiers as close as possible to the words they modify?

PUNCTUATION AND MECHANICS

- ☐ Are sentences punctuated correctly?
- ☐ Are words capitalized properly?

WORD CHOICE AND SPELLING

- ☐ Are words used correctly?
- ☐ Are words spelled correctly?

Sentences

Subjects and Verbs

For help with subjects and verbs, see Chapter 25.

1. Underline the subjects once and verbs twice in a paragraph of your revised essay. Remember that sentences can have more than one subject-verb set.
2. Does each of your sentences have at least one subject and verb that can stand alone?

____

For help with fragments, see Chapter 26.

For help with run-togethers, see Chapter 27.

3. Correct any fragments you have written.
4. Correct any run-together sentences you have written.

Subject-Verb Agreement

1. Read aloud the subjects and verbs you underlined in your revised essay.
2. Correct any subjects and verbs that do not agree.

For help with subject-verb agreement, see Chapter 30.

Pronoun Agreement

1. Find any pronouns in your revised essay that do not agree with their nouns.
2. Correct any pronouns that do not agree with their nouns.

For help with pronoun agreement, see Chapter 34.

Modifiers

1. Find any modifiers in your revised essay that are not as close as possible to the words they modify.
2. Rewrite sentences if necessary so that your modifiers are as close as possible to the words they modify.

For help with modifier errors, see Chapter 37.

Punctuation and Mechanics

Punctuation

1. Read your revised essay for any errors in punctuation.
2. Make sure any fragments and run-together sentences you revised are punctuated correctly.

For help with punctuation, see Chapters 38–42.

Mechanics

1. Read your revised essay for any errors in capitalization.
2. Be sure to check your capitalization in any fragments or run-together sentences you revised.

For help with capitalization, see Chapter 43.

Word Choice and Spelling

Word Choice

1. Find any words used incorrectly in your revised essay.
2. Correct any errors you find.

For help with confused words, see Chapter 49.

Spelling

1. Use spell-check and a dictionary to check your spelling.
2. Correct any misspelled words.

For help with spelling, see Chapter 50.

Now rewrite your essay again with your editing corrections.

PRACTICING CAUSE/EFFECT: FROM READING TO WRITING

Reading Workshop

The two essays in this chapter show cause and effect at work: The first essay, "Shedding the Weight of My Dad's Obsession" by Linda Lee Andujar, deals with the lifelong burden of an insensitive father; the second essay, "Happiness Is Catching: Why Emotions Are Contagious" by Stacey Colino, analyzes the role of moods in our daily lives. As you read, notice how the writers make their points through well-thought-out, detailed reasoning.

SHEDDING THE WEIGHT OF MY DAD'S OBSESSION
by Linda Lee Andujar

SUMMARY
An overweight woman describes how her unsympathetic father exacerbated her childhood weight problem and how her father's past obsession with her weight affects her life today.

READABILITY
(Flesch–Kincaid grade level)
6.5

INSTRUCTOR'S RESOURCE MANUAL
For additional teaching strategies, for journal entries, for vocabulary and reading quizzes, and for more writing assignments, see the *Instructor's Resource Manual*, Section II, Part II.

Focusing Your Attention

1. Do you have a personal problem that plagues you consistently? What is this problem?
2. The essay you are about to read explains how the author finally shed an emotional burden she carried since her childhood. How do you deal with emotional problems? Where did you learn your "survival skills"? What do you do to find security and safety when you are upset about something?

Expanding Your Vocabulary

The following words are important to your understanding of this essay. As you read, circle any words you don't know beyond this list. Then break into groups, and help each other figure out the meanings of these unknown words.

Bluebird: entry-level organization for future Girl Scouts (paragraph 1)

clambered: climbed awkwardly (paragraph 4)

timber: quality of life (paragraph 5)

authoritarian regimens: strict regulations (paragraph 5)

incarceration: imprisonment (paragraph 7)

skirmish: battle (paragraph 8)

amphetamines: stimulants that lessen appetite (paragraph 9)

diuretics: drugs that increase the production of urine (paragraph 9)

metabolism: bodily process that changes food into energy (paragraph 11)

READING CRITICALLY

As you learned at the beginning of this chapter, practice recognizing causes and effects by listing them in the following essay. Put them in two columns on a separate sheet of paper. These lists will help you understand the essay on an analytical level. Compare your notes with someone in the class.

SHEDDING THE WEIGHT OF MY DAD'S OBSESSION

by Linda Lee Andujar

Instead of selling the Camp Fire candy, I ate it. Eight boxes of it. Each Bluebird in our fourth-grade troop was assigned 12 boxes of chocolate candy to sell for a dollar a box. I sold four boxes to my family and then ran out of ideas for selling the rest. 1

As the days passed and the stack of candy remained in a corner of my room, the temptation to eat it overwhelmed my conscience. Two months after we'd been given the goodies, the troop leader announced that the drive was over and we were to bring in our sales money, along with any unsold candy, to the next Tuesday meeting. I rushed home in a panic and counted $4 in my sales money envelope and 12 boxes of candy gone. 2

I thought of the piggy bank filled with silver dollars that my father kept on a shelf in his closet. It was a collection that he added to but never spent. I tried to push this financial resource out of my mind, but Tuesday was approaching, and I still had no money. 3

By Monday afternoon I had no choice. I tiptoed into my parents' bedroom, pulled the vanity chair from Mother's dressing table and carried it to the walk-in closet. There was the piggy bank smiling down at me from the high shelf. After stacking boxes on the chair, I reached up and laid hands on the bank. When I had counted out eight silver dollars, I returned the pig to its place and clambered down. For days I felt bad about my theft, but what I felt even guiltier about was eating all those treats. 4

5 Throughout my childhood, my parents weighed me every day, and Daddy posted the numbers on my bedroom door. He never called me fat, but I came to learn every synonym. He discussed every health aspect of obesity endlessly. The daily tone and timber of our household was affected by Dad's increasingly authoritarian regimens.

6 I remember one Friday night, months after the candy caper. I heard the garage door rumble shut, and I knew that Daddy was home. He came in the back door, kissed Mother and asked what my weight was for the day. Mother admitted that I was still a pound over the goal he had set. "Get a pillow and a book, Linda," he said.

7 He firmly ushered me to the bathroom, then shut and locked the door behind me. As the door was closing, I caught a glimpse of Mother and my sister looking on as though they were witnessing an execution. For the next two days, the only time I was allowed out was for meals. It was late Sunday evening when I was finally released from my cell, supposedly taught a lesson by my incarceration.

8 The bathroom episode was one skirmish in a long war that had begun when, unlike my older sister, I failed to shed the "baby fat" many children are born with. Although I was cheerful, affectionate, and good-natured, none of these qualities interested my father. He had one slender child—he meant to have two. It was simply a matter of my self-discipline.

9 My slightly chubby figure had become a target for my physician father's frustration as he struggled to establish his medical practice. Dad told me constantly that if I was a pound overweight, I would be teased at school and nobody would like me. I stayed away from the other kids, fearing harsh words that never came. When I was 16, Daddy came up with the ultimate punishment: any day that I weighed more than 118 pounds (the weight my father had deemed ideal for my 5-foot, 4-inch frame) I'd have to pay him. In an attempt to shield me from this latest tactic, my exhausted, loving mother secretly took me to an internist friend of the family who prescribed what he described as "diet pills"—amphetamines and diuretics. Although the pills caused unpleasant side effects like light-headedness, taking them landed me a slim figure and, two years later, an engineer husband.

10 I quit the hated amphetamines at 27 and accepted my divorce as a result of my weight gain. I became a single, working mother devoted to raising my son and daughter. Over time, I realized that people liked my smile and my laugh and, contrary to my father's predictions, didn't shun me because of my size.

11 Many years ago, at my annual physical, I mentioned to my doctor that I couldn't eat the same quantity of food that normal people eat without getting

ANSWERS TO QUESTIONS

Thinking Critically About Content

1. Andujar is analyzing how her father's obsession with her weight affected her childhood and how her childhood affects her life as an adult.
2. The fundamental cause of Andujar's weight problem is a slow metabolism, and the effect is that she cannot eat the same amount of food as "normal people" without gaining weight.
3. Andujar is upset that her father could not see past the extra weight she carried to the wonderful girl behind it.

Thinking Critically About Purpose and Audience

4. Andujar's purpose is to inform readers of her experiences being overweight so

bigger. He kindly reassured me that people do indeed have different metabolisms, some more efficient than others. This discussion ultimately helped me to accept my size and shed the emotional burden carried over from my childhood.

My sister and her husband have a daughter who was pudgy as a child. 12
They asked me what they should do about her weight "problem." My reply, "Don't make it an issue. Let her find her own weight level." To their great credit, they did.

Thinking Critically About Content

1. What is Andujar analyzing in this essay?
2. The author is very honest and open about the causes and effects of her weight problem. What is the most fundamental cause and the ultimate effect?
3. What does Andujar seem upset about when she says, "Although I was cheerful, affectionate, and good-natured, none of these qualities interested my father" (paragraph 8)?

Thinking Critically About Purpose and Audience

4. What do you think Andujar's purpose is in this essay?
5. Who do you think is her primary audience?
6. Explain the essay's title.

Thinking Critically About Essays

7. Andujar opens her essay with the story about the Camp Fire candy. Do you think this is an effective beginning? Explain your answer.
8. Paragraph 5 gives us a hint of what the real problem is in Andujar's life. How does the writer organize her details in that paragraph?
9. What is the topic sentence of paragraph 9? Do all the sentences in that paragraph support this topic sentence? Explain your answer.
10. Write a paragraph about the role of a particular relative in your life. Are you very emotionally attached to this person? How did you become so close?

that others can learn from them.

5. Andujar's primary audience is people who are overweight or those who treat overweight people badly.
6. Andujar is no longer carrying the extra burden of her father's obsession with her weight and is finally content with her weight as it is.

Thinking Critically About Essays

7. Answers will vary.
8. The paragraph is organized from one extreme to another (from least to most harmful).
9. The topic sentence, "My slightly chubby figure had become a target for my physician father's frustration as he struggled to establish his medical practice," sets the tone for Andujar to be harassed by her father. The remaining sentences support this idea by showing how Andujar's father incessantly agonized over her weight to the point that she took drugs to become thin.
10. Answers will vary.

HAPPINESS IS CATCHING: WHY EMOTIONS ARE CONTAGIOUS

by Stacey Colino

SUMMARY
Colino explains how people "catch" moods from other people.

READABILITY
(Flesch–Kincaid grade level)
11.4

INSTRUCTOR'S RESOURCE MANUAL
For additional teaching strategies, for journal entries, for vocabulary and reading quizzes, and for more writing assignments, see the *Instructor's Resource Manual,* Section II, Part II.

Focusing Your Attention

1. Are you easily influenced by other people's moods? How do you know this?
2. In the essay you are about to read, Stacey Colino explains how we "catch" the feelings of others. Think of someone who generally makes you happy and someone who usually makes you sad. What is the difference between these two people? How do they each approach life? How do they each relate to you?

Expanding Your Vocabulary

The following words are important to your understanding of this essay. As you read, circle any words you don't know beyond this list. Then break into groups, and help each other figure out the meanings of these unknown words.

elation: joy, happiness (paragraph 1)

euphoria: extreme happiness (paragraph 1)

inoculate against: become immune to, resist (paragraph 1)

milliseconds: thousandths of a second (paragraph 2)

synchronize: coordinate (paragraph 2)

extroverts: outgoing people (paragraph 4)

engulfed: completely surrounded, overwhelmed (paragraph 5)

introverts: shy, quiet people (paragraph 5)

susceptible to: easily influenced by (paragraph 8)

mimicry: copying (paragraph 9)

READING CRITICALLY

As you did with the previous essay, list the causes and effects in the following essay on a separate sheet of paper. Then draw lines from specific causes to the related effects. This process will give you some good insights into the author's approach to her topic and her methods of developing her ideas. Compare your notes with those of one of your classmate's.

HAPPINESS IS CATCHING: WHY EMOTIONS ARE CONTAGIOUS

by Stacey Colino

Researchers have found that emotions, both good and bad, are nearly as contagious as colds and flus. You can catch elation, euphoria, sadness, and more from friends, family, colleagues, even strangers. And once you understand how to protect yourself, you can inoculate yourself against the bad. 1

Mood "infection" happens in milliseconds, says Elaine Hatfield, Ph.D., a professor of psychology at the University of Hawaii in Honolulu and coauthor of *Emotional Contagion* (Cambridge University Press, 1994). And it stems from a primitive instinct: During conversation, we naturally tend to mimic and synchronize our facial expressions, movements, and speech rhythms to match the other person's. "Through this, we come to feel what the person is feeling," explains Dr. Hatfield. In other words, it puts us in touch with their feelings and affects our behavior. 2

Not surprisingly, spouses are especially likely to catch each other's moods, but so are parents, children, and good friends. In fact, a recent study at the University of Texas Medical Branch at Galveston found that depression was highly contagious among college roommates. "The same thing can occur with a spouse or co-worker, where one person is moderately depressed," says study author Thomas E. Joiner Jr., Ph.D., assistant professor of psychiatry and behavioral sciences. 3

Dr. Hatfield's research shows that extroverts and emotionally expressive people tend to transmit their feelings more powerfully. There's also a breed of people who, consciously or not, may want or need you to feel what they feel; they're the ones who live by the adage "misery loves company." They manipulate other people's moods—perhaps without even realizing it—to gain the upper hand or to feel better about themselves. "They express emotion to get a response—perhaps attention or sympathy," says Ross Buck, Ph.D., professor of communication sciences and psychology at the University of Connecticut. 4

On the other hand, some personality types are more likely to be engulfed by others' moods. Introverts are vulnerable because they're easily aroused. So are highly sensitive individuals who react physically to emotionally charged situations—their hearts flutter before giving a speech, for example. 5

6 If anyone knows how quickly moods spread, it's Ginny Graves, 33, a San Francisco writer. Last year, when she was pregnant with her first child, her mood took a nosedive every time she saw a particular friend.

7 "Basically nothing good was going on in her life—she didn't like her job, and she was obsessed with her weight," recalls Ginny. "I tried to bolster her up, but whenever I talked to her, I'd feel tense and tired." Afterward, Ginny was left with a case of the moody blues that lingered a day or so.

8 Indeed, there's some evidence that women may be particularly susceptible to catching moods, perhaps because we're better able to read other people's emotions and body language, according to psychologist Judith Hall, Ph.D., professor of psychology at Northeastern University in Boston.

9 Since women perceive facial expressions so readily, we may be more likely to mimic them—and wind up sharing the feeling. Just how mimicry leads to catching a mood is not known, notes John T. Cacioppo, Ph.D., professor of psychology at Ohio State University and coauthor of *Emotional Contagion.* One theory holds that when you frown or smile, the muscular movements in your face alter blood flow to the brain, which in turn affects mood; another theory maintains that the sensations associated with specific facial expressions trigger emotional memories—and hence the feelings—linked with those particular expressions.

10 With any luck, we catch the happy moods—infectious laughter at a dinner party or a colleague's enthusiasm for a project, for instance. Some psychologists suspect, however, that negative emotions—especially depression and anxiety—may be the most infectious of all. "For women, stress and depression are like emotional germs—they jump from one person to the next," notes Ellen McGrath, Ph.D., a psychologist in Laguna Beach, California, and author of *When Feeling Bad Is Good* (Bantam, 1994).

11 Being susceptible to other people's moods does make for a rich emotional life. But let's face it: When you catch a happy mood, you don't want to change it. Downbeat emotions are harder to deal with. And who wants her life to be ruled by other people's bad moods?

12 Fortunately, there are ways to protect yourself from unpleasant emotions, while letting yourself catch the good ones. For starters, pay attention to how you feel around different people, suggests Dr. McGrath. Then label your emotions—noting, for example, whether you feel optimistic around your best friend or gloomy after seeing your aunt. Then ask yourself if you're feeling what you do because you actually feel that way or because you've caught a mood from the other person. Just recognizing that an emotion belongs to someone else, not you, can be enough to short-circuit its transmission.

ANSWERS TO QUESTIONS

Thinking Critically About Content

1. Colino is analyzing how people begin to feel the way others feel; they catch the moods of those around them. The title prepares readers for this concept.
2. Answers may vary.
   Causes
   Other people
   Contagious nature of moods
   Effects
   Specific feelings
   Specific behaviors

Once you know how people affect you, you can be more selective about whom you spend time with. Instead of going on an all-day outing with family members who bring you down, for instance, try spending shorter periods of time with them. Another solution is to give yourself a time-out: It could be as simple as a restroom break during an intense dinner. 13

Putting up emotional barriers is not the answer, though. If the channels are open, both positive and negative influences flow in. Shutting out the bad precludes you from catching joyful moods, too. Instead, it's better to monitor the floodgates—and to come to your own rescue when you feel yourself catching other people's negativity. And if you get swept up in another person's excitement, sit back and enjoy the ride. 14

Thinking Critically About Content

1. What is Colino analyzing in this essay? How does her title help focus her analysis?
2. Name two causes and two effects of people's moods.
3. How does Colino suggest that you can protect yourself from unpleasant emotions?

Thinking Critically About Purpose and Audience

4. Why do you think Colino wrote this essay?
5. Considering that this essay was originally published in a magazine called *Family Circle*, who do you think Colino's intended audience is? Explain your answer.
6. Are you susceptible to other people's moods? Why or why not?

Thinking Critically About Essays

7. The author of this essay quotes many authorities in the field of psychology. Are these quotations convincing to you? Explain your answer.
8. Which of Colino's paragraphs deal primarily with causes? Which with effects? Do you think this is a good balance? Explain your answer.
9. Find five transitions in Colino's essay that work well, and explain why they are effective.
10. Discuss the emotional climate in the place where you live. Are you able to separate your emotions from those of the people you live with? Are you affected by the emotions of roommates, friends, family? How might you manage emotional swings after reading this essay?

3. We can protect ourselves from unpleasant emotions by paying attention to how we feel around certain people and by recognizing when we are feeling low because of someone else's bad mood.

Thinking Critically About Purpose and Audience

4. Colino probably wrote this essay to warn readers not to let other people's moods affect us.
5. Colino's primary intended audience is probably women. *Family Circle* is read primarily by women, and Colino even mentions in her essay that moods are caught more easily by women.
6. Answers will vary.

Thinking Critically About Essays

7. The quotations are convincing because they are spoken by reputable people who have studied mood behavior.
8. Colino deals mostly with causes (paragraphs 1–4, 8–10, 12–14) and integrates a discussion of effects at important points throughout the essay (paragraphs 5–7 and 11).
9. Answers will vary.
10. Answers will vary.

Writing Workshop

This final section gives you opportunities to apply what you have learned in this chapter to another writing assignment. This time, we provide very little prompting beyond a summary of the guidelines for writing a cause/effect essay. This section will let you demonstrate that you can go through the entire writing process on your own with only occasional feedback from your peers. Loop back into the chapter as necessary when you have questions so that this process becomes as automatic to you as possible before you move on to new material. Then pause at the end of the chapter to reflect briefly on what you have learned.

TEACHING ON THE WEB
Discussion Topic: Divide students into groups of three or four, and have them discuss the effects of the Internet on college life today. In what other ways does the Internet affect a student's life? Which effects are negative, and which are positive?

TEACHING ON THE WEB
Links: Think of a recent disaster in the United States, and have students link to news Web sites to see how the news agencies reported the story. How does each use cause and effect differently to recount what happened?
Possible sites:
CNN, www.cnn.com
Newsweek, www.newsweek.com
The New York Times, www.nytimes.com

TEACHING ON THE WEB
Research: Have students find a Web site that explains a recent scientific discovery. What is the discovery, and how will it affect the world? What causes made this discovery possible?

Guidelines for Writing a Cause/Effect Essay

1. Write a thesis statement that tells what you are analyzing.
2. Choose facts, details, and reasons to support your thesis statement.
3. Do not mistake coincidence for cause or effect.
4. Search for the real causes and effects connected with your subject.
5. Organize your essay so that your readers can easily follow your analysis.

Writing About Your Reading

1. Are you currently dealing with any personal dilemmas? What are they? Does one bother you more than the others? Write an essay analyzing the causes and effects of this particular dilemma.
2. In "Happiness Is Catching," Stacey Colino talks about how contagious moods are. Do you think you might have been responsible for giving a good or bad mood to someone? What were the circumstances? How did someone "catch" your mood? Write an essay analyzing the causes and effects of the situation.
3. How would looking closely at causes and effects help you live a better life? How would the process of discovering causes and effects help you think through your decisions and problems more logically? Explain your answer.

Writing About Your World

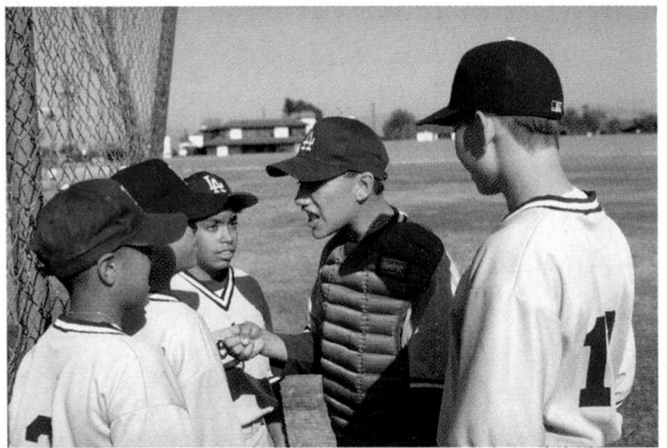

1. Explain how the scene above got started. What caused this reaction? Why did it happen? What were the results of the actions pictured here? Write an essay focusing on either the causes or the effects of this scene.
2. We all deal with change differently, but it is generally difficult to accept change in our lives. Think of a significant change in your life, and write about its causes and effects. What was the incident? What were the circumstances connected with the incident?
3. Write an essay that analyzes a current social problem—homelessness, drugs, environmental concerns—including the reasons for its existence.
4. Create your own cause/effect assignment (with the help of your instructor), and write a response to it.

Revising

Small Group Activity (5–10 minutes per writer) Working in groups of three or four, read your cause/effect essays to each other. Those listening should record their reactions on a copy of the Peer Evaluation Form in Appendix 2H. After your group goes through this process, give your evaluation forms to the appropriate writers so that each writer has two or three peer comment sheets for revising.

Paired Activity (5 minutes per writer) Using the completed Peer Evaluation Forms, work in pairs to decide what you should revise in your essay. If time allows, rewrite some of your sentences, and have your partner look at them.

Individual Activity Rewrite your paper, using the revising feedback you received from other students.

Editing

Paired Activity (5–10 minutes per writer) Swap papers with a classmate, and use the editing portion of your Peer Evaluation Form to identify as many grammar, punctuation, mechanics, and spelling errors as you can. If time allows, correct some of your errors, and have your partner look at them. Record your grammar, punctuation, and mechanics errors in the Error Log (Appendix 6) and your spelling errors in the Spelling Log (Appendix 7).

Individual Activity Rewrite your paper again, using the editing feedback you received from other students.

Reflecting on Your Writing When you have completed your own essay, answer these six questions.

1. What was most difficult about this assignment?
2. What was easiest?
3. What did you learn about cause and effect by completing this assignment?
4. What do you think are the strengths of your cause/effect essay? Place a wavy line by the parts of your essay that you feel are very good.
5. What are the weaknesses, if any, of your paper? Place an X by the parts of your essay you would like help with. Write any questions you have in the margin.
6. What did you learn from this assignment about your own writing process—about preparing to write, about writing the first draft, about revising, and about editing?

CHAPTER 16

Arguing

"Those who do not know their opponent's arguments do not completely understand their own."

—DAVID BENDER

Argument may be our most important form of communication because it helps us get what we want in life. The main reason people argue is to persuade someone of something. When you want to get a certain job, sell your car, or borrow some money, you need to present your request clearly and convincingly. On the flip side, others try to persuade you to do things all the time: Politicians make speeches trying to persuade you to vote for them; your friends try to persuade you to go to a movie when you know you should study for an exam; TV commercials, magazine ads, and billboards everywhere try to persuade you to buy this cereal or that car.

As you might suspect, your ability to argue in writing is also important in life. In fact, writing arguments is fundamental to your success on a personal level, in college courses, and in the workplace:

- The chairperson for your college reunion sends a letter with clear reasons why everyone should attend this year.
- A student writes an essay in a freshman composition course arguing for or against the death penalty.
- A student writes a paper in a sociology course arguing that laws against hate crimes need to be stronger.
- A sales representative writes a letter arguing that customers should order supplies from him rather than from his competitor.
- A restaurant owner writes an advertisement to persuade people to eat at her restaurant.

The purpose of **arguing** is to persuade someone to take a certain action or to think or feel a specific way. You can use either logical arguments

TEACHING ARGUMENT

From different magazines, bring in various advertisements that are subtle in their message (for example, showing a rumpled bed to promote a certain alcohol or a basketball game to sell cigarettes). Ask students how the advertisers are using argument to convince consumers to buy their products. What is actually for sale? Who is the intended audience? Will the advertisement convince people to purchase the products even though the advertisement doesn't explicitly say "Buy this product"?

If possible, bring in advertisements from fifty years ago that are advertising the same types of products, and ask students how the focus of the argument has changed over the years. How has the intended audience changed? What elements from the old advertisements would not work on consumers today?

(based on facts and reasoning) or emotional arguments (based on vivid description and details) to achieve your purpose.

Some of the most important laws affecting people's lives in the United States are the result of arguments made to the Supreme Court. Lawyers argue such issues as gun control, abortion, immigrants' rights, and drunk driving. If, for instance, lawmakers are trying to get stricter jail sentences for drunk driving, they might rely heavily on facts and statistics (logical evidence). But then they might add an emotional element by describing the mangled bike, the bloodstained clothes, and the grief in the faces of the parents of a 12-year-old girl killed by a drunk driver as she rode her bike home from school. Such an appeal to feelings would create a much stronger argument than statistics alone.

The better you become at arguing—in both thinking and writing—the more you will get what you want out of life (and out of college). Arguing effectively means getting the pay raises you hope for, the refund you deserve, and the grades you've worked hard for. Argumentation is a powerful tool.

TEACHING TIPS

The following eight teaching tips are based on Howard Gardner's list of multiple intelligences:

Verbal/Linguistic

Have students prepare a list of words and phrases that can help their communication in an argument essay. How can choosing the right word strengthen or weaken an argument? What are some words and phrases that can weaken arguments?

Musical/Rhythmic

Have students create a rap song that tries to persuade people that either rap music has value in our society or rap music should be banned from the airwaves. At what audi-

READING AND WRITING AN ARGUMENT ESSAY

Reading arguments critically will help you write arguments critically, which are both necessary skills for success in college and in life beyond college. Like two halves of a whole, these processes work together to create a coherent approach to important tasks. Reading and writing arguments effectively calls for high-level thought processes that will ensure your success in all that you do.

Reading an Argument Essay

The following argument, "Racial Profiling Is Unjust" by Bob Herbert, tries to persuade its readers that law-enforcement agents should not take action based on race alone. It uses a combination of logic and emotion to achieve its purpose. Have you ever been stopped by the police because of your appearance? If you have, what was your reaction? If you haven't, what do you think your reaction would be?

READING CRITICALLY

Reading an argument critically calls for very high-level skills. You need to understand your reading on a literal level, know the difference between opinions and fact, and come up with your own opinions on the topic by challenging the author's ideas. As you read the following essay for the first time, highlight facts in one color and the author's opinions in another color. Then, put an X by any facts or opinions that you do not agree with or want to question in some way. Be prepared to explain any marks you made on the essay.

RACIAL PROFILING IS UNJUST

by Bob Herbert

1 An anti-loitering law that allowed the Chicago police to arrest more than 42,000 people from 1992 to 1995 was declared unconstitutional in June of 1999 by the Supreme Court.

2 [Supreme Court justice] Antonin Scalia howled in dissent, which should tell you something. The law was an abomination, just like the practice in New York of stopping and frisking black and Hispanic people by the tens of thousands for no good reason and just like the practice of pulling over and harassing perfectly innocent black and Hispanic motorists on streets and highways in many parts of the country.

The Faces of Ethnic Profiling

3 Ethnic profiling by law-enforcement authorities in the United States comes in many forms, and all of them are disgusting.

4 In the summer of 1998, sadistic members of the State Police in Oklahoma spent more than two hours humiliating Rossano Gerald, a 37-year-old Army sergeant, and his 12-year-old son, Greg.

5 Sergeant Gerald was pulled over and interrogated. He was ordered out of his car and handcuffed. The troopers asked if he had any guns. They asked permission to search the car, and when he refused they searched it anyway. They separated Greg from his father and locked him in a police vehicle. They interrogated him. They brought drug-sniffing dogs to the scene. They dismantled parts of the car. When they finally tired of the madness,

ence should this song be aimed?

Logical/Mathematical

Provide students with a short argumentative speech. Have students identify key arguments and explain why they are organized as they are. Have them change the order of the argumentative points and explain why the new order either strengthens or weakens the argument.

Visual/Spatial

Provide students with a short argumentative essay, and have them make a rough outline of the essay. Does knowing the blueprint of the argument make the essay more or less persuasive?

Bodily/Kinesthetic

Have students, without using words, try to persuade a friend on campus to do something for them, such as carry their books or cross the street. Then ask students to explain how difficult it was to persuade people with only their facial expressions and actions.

Intrapersonal

Have students find an article that they believe presents a very convincing argument. What makes the argument so persuasive? How can other students learn from this essay?

Interpersonal
Have students openly debate a current federal issue. Have them try to persuade others to believe their opinions and join the opposing side of the issue. How heated does the debate become? How many people altered their beliefs? What caused them to do so?

Naturalist
Have students think of an outdoor activity that they like but that others think is ridiculous or absurd. Have students try to persuade someone who thinks the activity is ridiculous to try it. Can the other person be swayed?

INSTRUCTOR'S RESOURCE MANUAL
For additional material about teaching arguing; for journal entries; and for multiple-choice, short-answer, and paragraph tests, see the *Instructor's Resource Manual*, Section II, Part II.

they told Sergeant Gerald he was free to go. No arrest was made. Greg, of course, was petrified. When the ordeal ended he wept uncontrollably.

6 Why did this happen? Greg and Sergeant Gerald were guilty of America's original sin. They were born black.

Profiling Targets the Innocent

7 In New York, profiling was not only perpetuated but elevated to astonishing new heights during the regime of [New York City mayor] Rudolph Giuliani. Here, the targets are mostly pedestrians, not motorists. Young black and Hispanic males (and in some cases females) are stopped, frisked, and harassed in breathtaking numbers.

8 By the Police Department's own count, more than 45,000 people were stopped and frisked by members of the Street Crimes Unit in 1997 and 1998. But the total number of arrests made by the unit over those two years was less than 10,000. And it is widely believed that the number of people stopped during that period was far higher than the 45,000 reported by the cops. The true number likely was in the hundreds of thousands.

9 Ira Glasser, executive director of the American Civil Liberties Union [ACLU], noted that two things characterize the New York City stops: "Virtually everybody is innocent, and virtually everybody is not white."

10 Mayor Giuliani, like most public officials, will not acknowledge that his police officers are targeting people by race. "The stops are driven by the descriptions of the person who committed the crime," Mr. Giuliani said.

11 Spare me. The vast majority of these stops are in no way connected to the commission of a specific crime, and the mayor knows it. They are arbitrary and unconscionable intrusions on the rights of New Yorkers who are supposed to be protected, not humiliated, by the police.

Profiling Is Extensive

12 Most Americans have no idea of the extent of the race-based profiling that is carried out by law-enforcement officials and the demoralizing effect it has on its victims. The ACLU, in a report called "Driving While Black: Racial Profiling on Our Nation's Highways," said, "No [people] of color [are] safe from this treatment anywhere, regardless of their obedience to the law, their age, the type of car they drive, or their station in life."

13 The Chicago law that resulted in more than 42,000 arrests over three years was aimed at curbing gang activity. It was clearly unconstitutional. It made it a crime for anyone in the presence of suspected gang members to "remain in any one place with no apparent purpose" after being told by the police to move on.

Why should one's purpose for being in a public place have to be apparent? As a reporter for *The New York Times,* I might be in the presence of a suspected gang member. What business is that of the police? And how could that possibly be a legitimate basis for an arrest? 14

The suit challenging the law was brought by the Chicago office of the ACLU. A spokesman for the group noted that the "vast majority" of the people arrested under the law were African-American or Hispanic. What a surprise. 15

Preparing to Write Your Own Argument Essay

Choose a controversial issue on your campus or in the news that is important to you, and use one or more of the prewriting techniques that you learned in Chapter 2 to generate ideas on the issue. Consult your campus or local newspaper for ideas if you want. What is the exact issue? Why is it important? Why do people care about it? How do you think the issue should be resolved?

Writing an Argument Essay

When you write an argument essay, choose a subject that matters to you. If you have strong feelings, you will find it much easier to gather evidence and convince your readers of your point of view. Keep in mind, however, that your readers might feel just as strongly about the opposite side of the issue. The following guidelines will help you write a good argument essay.

1. **State your opinion on your topic in your thesis statement.** To write a thesis statement for an argument essay, you must take a stand for or against an action or an idea. In other words, your thesis statement should be debatable—a statement that can be argued or challenged and will not be met with agreement by everyone who reads it. Your thesis statement should introduce your subject and state your opinion about that subject.

   Bob Herbert's thesis is in his third paragraph: "Ethnic profiling by law-enforcement authorities in the United States comes in many forms, and all of them are disgusting." This is a debatable thesis. Some other statements on the topic of ethnic profiling would not be good thesis statements.

   Not debatable: Ethnic profiling by law-enforcement authorities in the United States often involves African Americans and Hispanics.

Not debatable: Some law-enforcement agencies have strict rules regarding ethnic profiling.

Herbert sets up his essay with some facts about anti-loitering laws and a reference to the practice in New York of stopping and frisking blacks and Hispanics. This background information leads up to his thesis statement.

2. **Find out as much as you can about your audience before you write.** Knowing your readers' background and feelings on your topic will help you choose the best supporting evidence and examples. Suppose that you want to convince people in two different age groups to quit smoking. You might tell the group of teenagers that cigarettes make their breath rancid, their teeth yellow, and their clothes smell bad. But with a group of adults, you might discuss the horrifying statistics on lung and heart disease associated with long-term smoking.

   Herbert's essay was first published in *The New York Times*, which addresses a fairly educated audience. The original readers probably thought a lot like he does on this issue. So he chooses his support as if he is talking to people who agree with him.

3. **Choose evidence that supports your thesis statement.** Evidence is probably the most important factor in writing an argument essay. Without solid evidence, your essay is nothing more than opinion; with it, your essay can be powerful and persuasive. If you supply convincing evidence, your readers will not only understand your position but perhaps agree with it.

   Evidence can consist of facts, statistics, statements from authorities, and examples or personal stories. Examples and personal stories can be based on your own observations, experiences, and reading, but your opinions are not evidence. You can also develop your ideas with the writing strategies you've learned in Chapters 8 through 16. Comparison/contrast, definition, and cause/effect can be particularly useful in building an argument. Use any combination of evidence and writing strategies that will help you support your thesis statement.

   In his essay, Herbert uses several different types of evidence. Here are some examples:

   Facts

   An anti-loitering law was declared unconstitutional in June 1999 (paragraph 1)

   Sergeant Rossano Gerald was stopped by the Oklahoma police in the summer of 1998 (paragraph 4)

Statistics

Chicago police arrested over 42,000 people from 1992 to 1995 for loitering (paragraph 1)

In New York, more than 45,000 people were stopped and frisked by the Street Crimes Unit in 1997 and 1998 (paragraph 8)

Only 10,000 arrests were made in New York in 1997 and 1998 (paragraph 8)

Statements from Authorities

Quotation by Ira Glasser, ACLU director (paragraph 9)

Quotation by Mayor Giuliani (paragraph 10)

ACLU report (paragraph 12)

Examples and Personal Stories

Story about Sergeant Gerald and his son (paragraphs 4–6)

4. **Anticipate opposing points of view.** In addition to stating and supporting your position, anticipating and responding to opposing views is important. Presenting only your side of the argument leaves half the story untold—the opposition's half. If you admit that there are opposing arguments and answer them, you will move your reader more in your direction.

   In paragraph 10, Herbert acknowledges a statement made by Mayor Giuliani as his opposition. Giuliani flatly denies the claims against his police force. "The stops are driven by the descriptions of the person who committed the crime." Acknowledging this statement raises Herbert's credibility and then lets him counter Giuliani's claim, which he does in the next paragraph.

5. **Find some common ground.** Pointing out common ground between you and your opponent is also an effective strategy. *Common ground* refers to points of agreement between two opposing positions. For example, one person might be in favor of gun control and another strongly opposed. But they might find common ground—agreement—in the need to keep guns out of teenagers' hands. Locating some common ground is possible in almost every situation. When you state in your essay that you agree with your opponent on certain points, your reader sees you as a fair person.

   Herbert assumes that most of his readers know that ethnic profiling by law-enforcement agencies is going on around the country. His job, then, is to prove the extent and unfairness of it.

6. **Maintain a reasonable tone.** Just as you probably wouldn't win an argument by shouting or making nasty or sarcastic comments, don't expect

your readers to respond well to such tactics. Keep the "voice" of your essay calm and sensible. Your readers will be much more open to what you have to say if they think you are a reasonable person.

Herbert maintains a reasonable tone throughout his essay. Even when he quotes some unbelievable statistics, as in paragraphs 1 and 8, or uses an occasional harsh word ("abomination" in paragraph 2 or "disgusting" in paragraph 3), he keeps his voice under control and therefore earns the respect of his readers.

7. **Organize your essay so that it presents your position as effectively as possible.** By the end of your essay, you want your audience to agree with you. So you want to organize your essay in such a way that your readers can easily follow it. The number of your paragraphs may vary, depending on the nature of your assignment, but the following outline shows the order in which the features of an argument essay are most effective:

Outline

Introduction
- Background information
- Introduction of subject
- Statement of your opinion

Body Paragraphs
- Common ground
- Lots of evidence (logical and emotional)
- Opposing point of view
- Response to opposing point of view

Conclusion
- Restatement of your position
- Call for action or agreement

The arrangement of your evidence in an argument essay depends to a great extent on your readers' opinions. Most arguments will be organized from general to particular, from particular to general, or from one extreme to another. When you know that your readers already agree with you, arranging your details from general to particular or from most to least important is usually most effective. With this order, you are building on your readers' agreement and loyalty as you explain your thinking on the subject.

If you suspect that your audience does not agree with you, reverse the organization of your evidence and arrange it from particular to general or from least to most important. In this way, you can take your readers step by step through your reasoning in an attempt to get them to agree with you.

Bob Herbert's essay follows the general outline just presented. Here is a skeleton outline of his essay.

Introduction

Background statistics and facts about anti-loitering laws and stopping and frisking

Body Paragraphs

The Faces of Ethnic Profiling

Subject introduced:	racial profiling
Statement of opinion:	racial profiling is disgusting
Evidence—example:	Sergeant Gerald's story

Profiling Targets the Innocent

Evidence—fact:	blacks and Hispanics stopped in New York
Evidence—statistics:	more than 45,000 people stopped, less than 10,000 arrested
Evidence—statements from authorities:	Ira Glasser, ACLU director
Opposing point of view:	Mayor Giuliani
Response to opposition:	Herbert's opinion

Conclusion: Profiling Is Extensive

Restatement of problem:	extent of race-based profiling
Evidence—statements from authorities:	quotation from ACLU report
Evidence—statistics:	over 42,000 arrests in Chicago in three years
Herbert's opinion	
Evidence—fact:	ACLU lawsuit
Herbert's final comment	

Writing Your Own Argument Essay

Write an essay that presents your opinion on the controversial issue you considered in your prewriting. Begin with a debatable thesis statement. Then follow the guidelines for writing an argument essay. As you write your essay, be sure you support your opinions with reasons. If a newspaper article inspired this assignment, attach it to your paper before you turn it in.

A STUDENT'S ARGUMENT ESSAY

Melinda Jackson, the student writer of the following essay, titled "A Call for Policies on Drinking," argues that drinking on college campuses is a serious problem. See if you can identify her main point and supporting evidence as you read this draft of her essay.

A Call for Policies on Drinking

1 College and drinking, drinking and college—most students believe the two go hand in hand. If asked, they would say that drinking in college is just a part of life, and it is not a major concern. However, when we examine drinking in college more closely, we see it is a serious problem that people on all levels are not facing. Drinking on college campuses is a bigger problem than parents and administrators realize, and something needs to be done about it—now.

2 No one would ever realistically believe that college students will never drink. In fact, most students, parents, and administrators are in favor of students taking a break and having fun. Studying during every available minute, parents and administrators realize the strain students are under. And they know that students will probably drink. What they don't understand is the trap students can fall into.

3 Jerry, a college student, explained how he got involved with alcohol and how it soon took over his life. Jerry went to a different fraternity party every weekend night, where his main goal was to get as drunk as possible. What he didn't know was that he was confrontational when he drank and that people didn't want to be around him. He didn't know his limit, so he often exceeded it. He usually passed out on someone's couch after drinking. In the morning he would wake up and find the next party. Jerry is just one of many students on every U.S. college campus.

4 Whereas most people think drinking occurs just during parties, it actually occurs for many students on a daily basis. Students like Jerry begin by drinking on weekends then they all too easily start drinking every day. They begin to need alcohol in order to feel normal. Once they fall into this pattern, several other serious problems can occur. Not only are they missing classes and falling behind in their coarses, but they are also endangering their lives. Drinking becomes the most important aspect in their lives. But it's not just the drinker who's life is effected. Drinkers disrupt their roommates, who are either distracted from their studying or awakened from their sleep. When the

roommate complains about being disturbed. The drinker gets angry. And so the pattern repeats itself again and again.

According to our dean of students, students who drink often take risks that endanger their lives and the lives of others. The most obvious risk involves a drinker who gets behind the wheel of a car. Drinkers also tend to get into more fights, because they mistakenly believe they are invincible. In this case, they risk harming the people they fight with and themselves, because they are in no condition to defend themselves. Everyone on the road is a potential victim of the drinker. Drinkers are also likely to have unprotected sex. This could lead to unwanted pregnancies, sexually transmitted diseases, or even AIDS. With the widespread drinking that occurs on college campuses, these consequences are very likely to occur to a student who drinks. 5

Drinking is a major problem on college campuses, but like every other controversial issue, some people say it has been given too much publicity by overzealous worriers. They believe that the college knows light drinking occurs and that the administration has control of the students who drink. They believe that kids will be kids, students will drink no matter what. These people say that letting students have fun is what's important. But to adopt this attitude is possibly placing someone's life in danger. If even one person is in danger from a drunken student. Then the college must take action. 6

Drinking in college is definitely going to happen, but there are measures that can be taken to prevent serious harm to students who do decide to drink. Campuses could have alcohol awareness programs and give students easy access to condoms. Campuses could set up a response team that would pick up any student who was incapable of driving. They could require all sororities and fraternities to confiscate keys before anyone is given a drink to ensure that a person who has been drinking won't drive. They can offer literature on organizations that can help students who become addicted to alcohol. Its time for students, parents, and administrators to see the problem before them and take steps to fix it before it's too late. 7

Discovering How the Essay Works

1A. What is Melinda's thesis statement?

Drinking on college campuses is a bigger problem than parents and administrators realize, and something needs to be done about it—now.

1B. Does it state her opinion clearly? Explain your answer.

It lets the reader know she thinks drinking on college campuses is a bigger problem than parents and administrators realize.

1C. Is it debatable? (Does it have more than one side?)

Yes, people can certainly argue that drinking is not a problem on college campuses.

2. Who do you think Melinda is addressing in this essay? How did you come to this conclusion?

   She is addressing parents, administrators, and students. She states her audience.

3. What evidence does the author use to support her thesis statement? Find an example of each type of evidence in her essay.

   Facts: *Students are drinking in college.*

   Statistics: *No statistics provided.*

   Statements from authorities: *Statement from the dean of students*

   Examples and personal stories: *Jerry's story is one example.*

4. Does Melinda anticipate an opposing point of view? Explain your answer.

   In paragraph 6, Melinda acknowledges her opponents.

5. Did Melinda find some common ground with her readers? Explain your answer.

   In paragraph 2, she says her readers know that most students drink at some time during their college years.

6. Does Melinda maintain a reasonable tone? Explain your answer.

   Yes. Beyond this, answers will vary.

7. How does Melinda organize the topics in her essay: general to particular, particular to general, or from one extreme to another?

   From general to particular

Revising and Editing the Student Essay

This essay is Melinda's first draft, which now needs to be revised and edited. First, apply the following Revising Checklist to the content of Melinda's draft. When you are satisfied that her ideas are fully developed and well organized, use the Editing Checklist on page 406 to correct her grammar and mechanics errors. Do the tasks, and answer the questions after each checklist. Then write your suggested changes directly on Melinda's draft.

REVISING AND EDITING OPTIONS

Consider varying your approach to revising and editing. You could teach these skills in a class discussion, in small groups, or in pairs.

 **REVISING CHECKLIST** 

REVISING STRATEGIES

This chapter focuses on the following revising elements:

Organization

Coherence

THESIS STATEMENT

✔ Does the thesis statement contain the essay's controlling idea?

✔ Does the thesis appear as the last sentence of the introduction?

BASIC ELEMENTS

✔ Does the title draw in the readers?

✔ Does the introduction capture the readers' attention and build up to the thesis statement effectively?

✔ Does each body paragraph deal with a single topic?

✔ Does the conclusion bring the essay to a close in an interesting way?

DEVELOPMENT

✔ Do the body paragraphs adequately support the thesis statement?

✔ Does each body paragraph have a focused topic sentence?

✔ Does each body paragraph contain *specific* details that support the topic sentence?

✔ Does each body paragraph include *enough* details to explain the topic sentence fully?

UNITY

✔ Do the essay's topic sentences relate directly to the thesis statement?

✔ Do the details in each body paragraph support its topic sentence?

ORGANIZATION

✔ Is the essay organized logically?

✔ Is each body paragraph organized logically?

COHERENCE

✔ Are transitions used effectively so that paragraphs move smoothly and logically from one to the next?

✔ Do the sentences move smoothly and logically from one to the next?

Thesis Statement

1. Put brackets around the last sentence in Melinda's introduction. Does it contain her opinion?

   Yes
   ____

   Is it debatable?

   Yes
   ____

2. Rewrite Melinda's thesis statement if necessary so that it states her opinion and is debatable.

   Answers will vary.
   ____

Basic Elements

1. Give Melinda's essay an alternate title.

   Answers will vary.
   ____

2. Rewrite Melinda's introduction so that it captures the readers' attention and builds up to the thesis statement at the end of the paragraph.

   Answers will vary.
   ____

   ____

   ____

3. Does each of Melinda's body paragraphs deal with only one topic?

   Yes

4. Rewrite Melinda's conclusion using at least one suggestion from Part I.

   Answers will vary.

Development

1. Write out Melinda's thesis statement (revised, if necessary), and list her topic sentences below it.

   Thesis statement: *Drinking on college campuses is a bigger problem than parents and administrators realize, and something needs to be done about it—now.*

   Topic 1: *No one would ever realistically believe that college students will never drink.*

   Topic 2: *Jerry, a college student, explained how he got involved with alcohol and how it soon took over his life.*

   Topic 3: *Whereas most people think drinking occurs just during parties, it actually occurs for many students on a daily basis.*

   Topic 4: *According to our dean of students, students who drink often take risks that endanger their lives and the lives of others.*

   Topic 5: *Drinking is a major problem on college campuses, but like every other controversial issue, some people say it has been given too much publicity by overzealous worriers.*

2. Do Melinda's topics adequately support her thesis statement?

   Yes

3. Does each body paragraph have a focused topic sentence?

   Yes

4. Does her evidence support her topic sentences?

   Yes

5. What type of evidence does Melinda provide in each body paragraph?

   Paragraph 2: *Facts*

   Paragraph 3: *Example*

   Paragraph 4: *Fact, examples*

   Paragraph 5: *Facts, statement from authority, examples*

   Paragraph 6: *Facts*

   What type of evidence does she use the most? *Facts*

6. Is this a good choice for what she is trying to argue?

   Yes, because she is showing the scope of the problem.

7. Where do you need more information?

   Answers will vary.

Unity

1. Read each of Melinda's topic sentences with her thesis statement in mind. Do they go together?

   Yes

2. Revise her topic sentences if necessary so they are directly related.
3. Drop or rewrite any sentences in her body paragraphs that are not directly related to their topic sentences. *All sentences are directly related to their topic sentences.*

Organization

1. Outline Melinda's essay to see if all her ideas are arranged logically.

____

____

____

____

____

____

____

____

2. Do you think her method of organization is the most effective one for her purpose? Explain your answer.

It is logical because it moves from general to particular, from the problem to the solution.

3. Move any paragraphs that are out of order. *All paragraphs are in order.*
4. Look closely at Melinda's body paragraphs to see if all her sentences are arranged logically within paragraphs.
5. Move any sentences that are out of order. *In paragraph 5, put sentence 5 before sentence 3.*

Coherence

1. Add two transitions to Melinda's essay.
2. Circle five transitions, repetitions, synonyms, or pronouns Melinda uses.
3. Explain how two of these make Melinda's essay easier to read.

Answers will vary.

____

____

For a list of transitions, see page 101.

For a list of pronouns, see pages 7–8.

Now rewrite Melinda's essay with your revisions.

EDITING STRATEGIES
This chapter focuses on the following editing problems:
Fragments
Run-togethers
Modifier errors
Confused words

 **EDITING CHECKLIST** 

SENTENCES

✓ Does each sentence have a main subject and verb?

✓ Do all subjects and verbs agree?

✓ Do all pronouns agree with their nouns?

✓ Are modifiers as close as possible to the words they modify?

PUNCTUATION AND MECHANICS

✓ Are sentences punctuated correctly?

✓ Are words capitalized properly?

WORD CHOICE AND SPELLING

✓ Are words used correctly?

✓ Are words spelled correctly?

Sentences

Subjects and Verbs

For help with subjects and verbs, see Chapter 25.

1. Underline the subjects once and verbs twice in paragraphs 4 and 6 of your revision of Melinda's essay. Remember that sentences can have more than one subject-verb set.
2. Does each of Melinda's sentences have at least one subject and verb that can stand alone?

   No

For help with fragments and run-togethers, see Chapters 26 and 27.

3. Did you find and correct Melinda's two fragments and two run-together sentences? If not, find and correct them now. *Fragments: paragraph 4, sentence 9; paragraph 6, sentence 6. Run-ons: paragraph 4, sentence 2; paragraph 6, sentence 3*

Subject-Verb Agreement

For help with subject-verb agreement, see Chapter 30.

1. Read aloud the subjects and verbs you underlined in your revision of Melinda's essay.
2. Correct any subjects and verbs that do not agree. *All subjects and verbs agree.*

Pronoun Agreement

For help with pronoun agreement, see Chapter 34.

1. Find any pronouns in your revision of Melinda's essay that do not agree with their nouns. *All pronouns agree with their nouns.*
2. Correct any pronouns that do not agree with their nouns.

Modifiers

1. Find any modifiers in your revision of Melinda's essay that are not as close as possible to the words they modify.
2. Did you find and correct Melinda's two modifier errors? If not, find and correct them now. *Paragraph 2, sentence 3; paragraph 3, sentence 5*

For help with modifier errors, see Chapter 37.

Punctuation and Mechanics

Punctuation

1. Read your revision of Melinda's essay for any errors in punctuation.
2. Find the two fragments and two run-together sentences you revised, and make sure they are punctuated correctly.

For help with punctuation, see Chapters 38–42.

Mechanics

1. Read your revision of Melinda's essay for any errors in capitalization.
2. Be sure to check Melinda's capitalization in the fragments and run-together sentences you revised.

For help with capitalization, see Chapter 43.

Word Choice and Spelling

Word Choice

1. Find any words used incorrectly in your revision of Melinda's essay.
2. Did you find and correct the four words Melinda uses incorrectly? If not, find and correct them now. *coarses/courses (paragraph 4, sentence 5); who's/whose (paragraph 4, sentence 7); effected/affected (paragraph 4, sentence 7); Its/It's (paragraph 7, sentence 6)*

For help with confused words, see Chapter 49.

Spelling

1. Use spell-check and a dictionary to check the spelling in your revision of Melinda's essay. *All words are spelled correctly.*
2. Correct any misspelled words.

For help with spelling, see Chapter 50.

Now rewrite Melinda's essay again with your editing corrections.

YOUR OWN ARGUMENT ESSAY

Returning to the argument you wrote earlier in this chapter, you are now ready to revise and edit your own writing. Remember that revision involves reworking the development and organization of your essay while editing asks you to check your grammar and usage. Work first with the content, making sure your thoughts are fully developed and organized effectively before you consider your grammar and usage errors. Repeating the revising and editing processes several times will ensure that you have written the best paper you can write.

WRITING CRITICALLY

As you begin to rework your essay, use the same technique you did in your reading. Highlight your own opinions and facts in two different colors to demonstrate that you see the difference between the two. Then check to see that you support each of your main ideas with enough details to make your point.

CLASS ACTIVITY
Write some argument statements on the board that begin with "I believe," "I think," and "In my opinion." Demonstrate to students how these types of personal statements can weaken rather than strengthen arguments.

Revising and Editing Your Own Essay

The checklists here will help you apply what you have learned in this chapter to your essay.

REVISING CHECKLIST

THESIS STATEMENT

- ☐ Does the thesis statement contain the essay's controlling idea?
- ☐ Does the thesis appear as the last sentence of the introduction?

BASIC ELEMENTS

- ☐ Does the title draw in the readers?
- ☐ Does the introduction capture the readers' attention and build up to the thesis statement effectively?
- ☐ Does each body paragraph deal with a single topic?
- ☐ Does the conclusion bring the essay to a close in an interesting way?

DEVELOPMENT

- ☐ Do the body paragraphs adequately support the thesis statement?
- ☐ Does each body paragraph have a focused topic sentence?
- ☐ Does each body paragraph contain *specific* details that support the topic sentence?
- ☐ Does each body paragraph include *enough* details to explain the topic sentence fully?

UNITY

- ☐ Do the essay's topic sentences relate directly to the thesis statement?
- ☐ Do the details in each body paragraph support its topic sentence?

ORGANIZATION

- ☐ Is the essay organized logically?
- ☐ Is each body paragraph organized logically?

COHERENCE

- ☐ Are transitions used effectively so that paragraphs move smoothly and logically from one to the next?
- ☐ Do the sentences move smoothly and logically from one to the next?

Thesis Statement

1. What is the subject of your essay?

   ____

2. Put brackets around the last sentence in your introduction. Does it contain your opinion?

   ____

   Is it debatable?

   ____

3. Rewrite your thesis statement if necessary so that it states your opinion and is debatable.

Basic Elements

1. Give your essay a title if it doesn't have one.

   ____

2. Does your introduction capture your readers' attention and build up to your thesis statement at the end of the paragraph?

   ____

3. Does each of your body paragraphs deal with only one topic?

____

4. Does your conclusion follow some of the suggestions offered in Part I?

____

Development

1. Write out your thesis statement (revised, if necessary), and list your topic sentences below it.

   Thesis statement:

   Topic 1: ______________________________

   Topic 2: ______________________________

   Topic 3: ______________________________

   Topic 4: ______________________________

   Topic 5: ______________________________

2. Do your topics adequately support your thesis statement?

____

3. Does each body paragraph have a focused topic sentence?

____

4. Does your evidence support your topic sentences? List and label at least one type of evidence you use for each of your topics.

   Topic 1: Evidence: ______________________________

   Type: ______________________________

   Topic 2: Evidence: ______________________________

   Type: ______________________________

Topic 3: Evidence: ______________________________

Type: ______________________________

Topic 4: Evidence: ______________________________

Type: ______________________________

Topic 5: Evidence: ______________________________

Type: ______________________________

What type of evidence do you use the most?

____

Is this a good choice for what you are trying to argue?

____

5. Where do you need more information?

____

Unity

1. Read each of your topic sentences with your thesis statement in mind. Do they go together?

   ____

2. Revise your topic sentences if necessary so they are directly related.
3. Drop or rewrite any of the sentences in your body paragraphs that are not directly related to their topic sentences.

Organization

1. Outline your essay to see if all the paragraphs are arranged logically.
2. Do you think your method of organization is the most effective one for your purpose? Explain your answer.
3. Move any paragraphs that are out of order.

4. Look closely at your body paragraphs to see if all the sentences are arranged logically within paragraphs.
5. Move any sentences or ideas that are out of order.

Coherence

For a list of transitions, see page 101.

For a list of pronouns, see pages 7–8.

1. Add two transitions to your essay.
2. Circle five transitions, repetitions, synonyms, or pronouns you use.
3. Explain how two of these make your essay easier to read.

____

____

Now rewrite your essay with your revisions.

EDITING CHECKLIST

SENTENCES

☐ Does each sentence have a main subject and verb?
☐ Do all subjects and verbs agree?
☐ Do all pronouns agree with their nouns?
☐ Are modifiers as close as possible to the words they modify?

PUNCTUATION AND MECHANICS

☐ Are sentences punctuated correctly?
☐ Are words capitalized properly?

WORD CHOICE AND SPELLING

☐ Are words used correctly?
☐ Are words spelled correctly?

Sentences

Subjects and Verbs

For help with subjects and verbs, see Chapter 25.

1. Underline the subjects once and verbs twice in a paragraph of your revised essay. Remember that sentences can have more than one subject-verb set.

2. Does each of your sentences have at least one subject and verb that can stand alone?

____

3. Correct any fragments you have written.
4. Correct any run-together sentences you have written.

For help with fragments, see Chapter 26.

For help with run-togethers, see Chapter 27.

Subject-Verb Agreement

1. Read aloud the subjects and verbs you underlined in your revised essay.
2. Correct any subjects and verbs that do not agree.

For help with subject-verb agreement, see Chapter 30.

Pronoun Agreement

1. Find any pronouns in your revised essay that do not agree with their nouns.
2. Correct any pronouns that do not agree with their nouns.

For help with pronoun agreement, see Chapter 34.

Modifiers

1. Find any modifiers in your revised essay that are not as close as possible to the words they modify.
2. Rewrite sentences if necessary so that your modifiers are as close as possible to the words they modify.

For help with modifier errors, see Chapter 37.

Punctuation and Mechanics

Punctuation

1. Read your revised essay for any errors in punctuation.
2. Make sure any fragments and run-together sentences you revised are punctuated correctly.

For help with punctuation, see Chapters 38–42.

Mechanics

1. Read your revised essay for any errors in capitalization.
2. Be sure to check your capitalization in any fragments or run-together sentences you revised.

For help with capitalization, see Chapter 43.

Word Choice and Spelling

Word Choice

For help with confused words, see Chapter 49.

1. Find any words used incorrectly in your revised essay.
2. Correct any errors you find.

Spelling

For help with spelling, see Chapter 50.

1. Use spell-check and a dictionary to check your spelling.
2. Correct any misspelled words.

Now rewrite your essay again with your editing corrections.

PRACTICING ARGUMENT: FROM READING TO WRITING

Reading Workshop

Here are three examples of good argument essays: "We are Training Our Kids to Kill" by Dave Grossman, which tries to persuade readers that our children are conditioned to kill from the violence they are exposed to through TV, movies, and video games; and two essays on loitering and gang violence—"Anti-Loitering Laws Can Reduce Gang Violence" by Richard Willard and "Anti-Loitering Laws Are Ineffective and Biased" by David Cole. As you read, notice how the writers make their claims through well-thought-out, detailed reasoning.

WE ARE TRAINING OUR KIDS TO KILL

by Dave Grossman

SUMMARY
In this essay, retired colonel Dave Grossman exposes some of the dire consequences of treating violence in various forms of the media as entertainment. Most serious of these is that we are training our children to kill.

Focusing Your Attention

1. At what age or in what situation do you think children can handle violence in the media?
2. In the essay you are about to read, the writer discusses the dangers connected with violence on TV for children. What do you think some of these issues are?

Expanding Your Vocabulary

The following words are important to your understanding of this essay. To help you add them to your vocabulary, write out a synonym and an example from your own experience for each new word.

averted (para. 4): avoided

phenomenally (para. 6): amazingly

Draconian (para. 7): harsh

indiscriminately (para. 8): casually

pervasively (para. 9): universally

anomaly (para. 15): an exception from the normal

desensitized (para. 22): numbed

epidemiological (para. 25): referring to childhood behaviors

variable (para. 25): element being compared

bayonet (para. 28): stab

dismay (para. 32): fear, dread

benign (para. 34): good

READABILITY
(Flesch–Kincaid grade level)
12.0

INSTRUCTOR'S RESOURCE MANUAL
For additional teaching strategies, for journal entries, for vocabulary and reading quizzes, and for more writing assignments, see the *Instructor's Resource Manual*, Section II, Part II.

READING CRITICALLY

As you learned at the beginning of this chapter, practice recognizing the facts and opinions in the following essay by highlighting them in two different colors. Then put an X by any points that you disagree with or want to challenge. These notes will give you insights into the topic and guide you to a deeper level of understanding. Compare your notes with someone else's in the class.

WE ARE TRAINING OUR KIDS TO KILL
by Dave Grossman

I am from Jonesboro, Arkansas. I travel the world training medical, law 1
enforcement, and U.S. military personnel about the realities of warfare. I try to make those who carry deadly force keenly aware of the magnitude of

killing. Too many law enforcement and military personnel act like "cowboys," never stopping to think about who they are and what they are called to do. I hope I am able to give them a reality check.

2 So here I am, a world traveler and an expert in the field of "killology," when the (then) largest school massacre in American history happens in my hometown of Jonesboro, Arkansas. That was the March 24, 1998, schoolyard shooting deaths of four girls and a teacher. Ten others were injured, and two boys, ages 11 and 13, were jailed, charged with murder.

Virus of Violence

3 To understand the why behind Littleton, Jonesboro, Springfield, Pearl, and Paducah, and all the other outbreaks of this "virus of violence," we need to first understand the magnitude of the problem. The per capita murder rate doubled in this country between 1957—when the FBI started keeping track of the data—and 1992. A fuller picture of the problem, however, is indicated by the rate at which people are attempting to kill one another—the aggravated assault rate. That rate in America has gone from around 60 per 100,000 in 1957 to over 440 per 100,000 in 2002. As bad as this is, it would be much worse were it not for two major factors.

4 The first is the increased imprisonment of violent offenders. The prison population in America nearly quintupled between 1975 and 2002. According to criminologist John A. DiIulio, "dozens of credible empirical analyses . . . leave no doubt that the increased use of prisons averted millions of serious crimes." If it were not for our tremendous imprisonment rate (the highest of any industrialized nation), the aggravated assault rate and the murder rate would undoubtedly be even higher.

5 The second factor keeping the murder rate from being even worse is medical technology. According to the U.S. Army Medical Service Corps, a wound that would have killed nine out of ten soldiers in World War II, nine out of ten could have survived in Vietnam. Thus, by a very conservative estimate, if we still had a 1940-level medical technology today, our murder rate would be ten times higher than it is. The murder rate has been held down by the development of sophisticated lifesaving skills and techniques, such as helicopter medevacs, 911 operators, paramedics, CPR, trauma centers, and medicines.

6 Today, both our assault rate and murder rate are at phenomenally high levels. Both are increasing worldwide. In Canada, according to their Center for Justice, per capita assaults increased almost fivefold between 1964 and 2002, attempted murder increased nearly sevenfold, and murders doubled. Similar trends can be seen in other countries in the per capita violent crime rates reported to Interpol between 1977 and 2002. In Australia and New

Zealand, the assault rate increased approximately fourfold, and the murder rate nearly doubled in both nations. The assault rate tripled in Sweden and approximately doubled in Belgium, Denmark, England and Wales, France, Hungary, the Netherlands, and Scotland. Meanwhile, all these nations had an associated (but smaller) increase in murder.

This virus of violence is occurring worldwide. The explanation for it has to be some new factor that is occurring in all of these countries. There are many factors involved, and none should be discounted: for example, the prevalence of guns in our society. But violence is rising in many nations with Draconian gun laws. And though we should never downplay child abuse, poverty, or racism, there is only one new variable present in each of these countries that bears the exact same fruit: media violence presented as entertainment for children. 7

Killing is Unnatural

Before retiring from the military, I spent almost a quarter of a century as an army infantry officer and a psychologist, learning and studying how to enable people to kill. Believe me, we are very good at it. But it does not come naturally; you have to be taught to kill. And just as the army is conditioning people to kill, we are indiscriminately doing the same thing to our children, but without the safeguards. 8

After the Jonesboro killings, the head of the American Academy of Pediatrics Task Force on Juvenile Violence came to town and said that children don't naturally kill. It is a learned skill. And they learn it from abuse and violence in the home and, most pervasively, from violence as entertainment in television, the movies, and interactive video games. 9

Killing requires training because there is a built-in aversion to killing one's own kind. I can best illustrate this fact by drawing on my own military research into the act of killing. 10

We all know how hard it is to have a discussion with a frightened or angry human being. Vasoconstriction, the narrowing of the blood vessels, has literally closed down the forebrain—that great gob of gray matter that makes one a human being and distinguishes one from a dog. When those neurons close down, the midbrain takes over and your thought processes and reflexes are indistinguishable from your dog's. If you've worked with animals, you have some understanding of what happens to frightened human beings on the battlefield. The battlefield and violent crime are in the realm of midbrain responses. 11

Within the midbrain there is a powerful, God-given resistance to killing your own kind. Every species, with a few exceptions, has a hard-wired resistance to killing its own kind in territorial and mating battles. When animals 12 with antlers and horns fight one another, they head-butt in a nonfatal fashion. But when they fight any other species, they go to the side to gut and gore. Piranhas will turn their fangs on anything, but they fight one another with flicks of the tail. Rattlesnakes will bite anything, but they wrestle one another. Almost every species has this hard-wired resistance to killing its own kind.

13 When we human beings are overwhelmed with anger and fear, we slam head-on into that midbrain resistance that generally prevents us from killing. Only sociopaths—who by definition don't have that resistance—lack this innate violence immune system.

14 Throughout all human history, when humans have fought each other, there has been a lot of posturing. Adversaries make loud noises and puff themselves up, trying to daunt the enemy. There is a lot of fleeing and submission. Ancient battles were nothing more than great shoving matches. It was not until one side turned and ran that most of the killing happened, and most of that was stabbing people in the back. All of the ancient military historians report that the vast majority of killing happened in pursuit when one side was fleeing.

15 In more modern times, the average firing rate was incredibly low in Civil War battles. British author Paddy Griffith demonstrates in his book *The Battle Tactics of the Civil War* that the killing potential of the average Civil War regiment was anywhere from five hundred to a thousand men per minute. The actual killing rate was only one or two men per minute per regiment. At the Battle of Gettysburg, of the 27,000 muskets picked up from the dead and dying after the battle, 90 percent were loaded. This is an anomaly, because it took 90 percent of their time to load muskets and only 5 percent to fire. But even more amazing, of the thousands of loaded muskets, only half had multiple loads in the barrel—one had 23 loads in the barrel.

16 In reality, the average man would load his musket and bring it to his shoulder, but he could not bring himself to kill. He would be brave, he would stand shoulder to shoulder, he would do what he was trained to do; but at the moment of truth, he could not bring himself to pull the trigger. And so he lowered the weapon and loaded it again. Of those who did fire, only a tiny percentage fired to hit. The vast majority fired over the enemy's head.

17 During World War II, U.S. Army Brig. Gen. S. L. A. Marshall had a team of researchers study what soldiers did in battle. For the first time in history, they asked individual soldiers what they did in battle. They discovered that only 15 to 20 percent of the individual riflemen could bring themselves to fire at an exposed enemy soldier.

That is the reality of the battlefield. Only a small percentage of soldiers are able and willing to participate. Men are willing to die. They are willing to sacrifice themselves for their nation; but they are not willing to kill. It is a phenomenal insight into human nature; but when the military became aware of that, they systematically went about the process of trying to fix this "problem." From the military perspective, a 15 percent firing rate among riflemen is like a 15 percent literacy rate among librarians. And fix it the military did. By the Korean War, around 55 percent of the soldiers were willing to fire to kill. And by Vietnam, the rate rose to over 90 percent. 18

The method in this madness: desensitization. 19

How the military increases the killing rate of soldiers in combat is instructive because our culture today is doing the same thing to our children. The training methods militaries use are brutalization, classical conditioning, operant conditioning, and role modeling. I will explain each of these in the military context and show how these same factors are contributing to the phenomenal increase of violence in our culture. 20

Brutalization and desensitization are what happens at boot camp. From the moment you step off the bus, you are physically and verbally abused: countless push-ups, endless hours at attention or running with heavy loads, while carefully trained professionals take turns screaming at you. Your head is shaved; you are herded together naked and dressed alike, losing all individuality. This brutalization is designed to break down your existing mores and norms and force you to accept a new set of values that embraces destruction, violence, and death as a way of life. In the end, you are desensitized to violence and accept it as a normal and essential survival skill in your brutal new world. 21

Something very similar to this desensitization toward violence is happening to our children through violence in the media—but instead of 18-year-olds, it begins at the age of 18 months when a child is first able to discern what is happening on television. At that age, a child can watch something happening on television and mimic that action. But it isn't until children are six or seven years old that the part of the brain kicks in that lets them understand where information comes from. Even though young children have some understanding of what it means to pretend, they are developmentally unable to distinguish clearly between fantasy and reality. 22

When young children see somebody shot, stabbed, raped, brutalized, degraded, or murdered on TV, to them it is as though it were actually happening. To have a child of three, four, or five watch a "splatter" movie, learning to relate to a character for the first 90 minutes and then in the last 23

30 minutes watch helplessly as that new friend is hunted and brutally murdered, is the moral and psychological equivalent of introducing your child to a friend, letting her play with that friend, and then butchering that friend in front of your child's eyes. And this happens to our children hundreds upon hundreds of times.

24 Sure, they are told, "Hey, it's all for fun. Look, this isn't real; it's just TV." And they nod their little heads and say OK. But they can't tell the difference. Can you remember a point in your life or in your children's lives when dreams, reality, and television were all jumbled together? That's what it is like to be at that level of psychological development. That's what the media are doing to them.

25 The *Journal of the American Medical Association* published the definitive epidemiological study on the impact of TV violence. The research demonstrated what happened in numerous nations after television made its appearance as compared to nations and regions without TV. The two nations or regions being compared are demographically and ethnically identical; only one variable is different: the presence of television. In every nation, region, or city with television, there is an immediate explosion of violence on the playground, and within 15 years there is a doubling of the murder rate. Why 15 years? That is how long it takes for the brutalization of a three- to five-year-old to reach the "prime crime age." That is how long it takes for you to reap what you have sown when you brutalize and desensitize a three-year-old.

26 Today the data linking violence in the media to violence in society are superior to those linking cancer and tobacco. Hundreds of sound scientific studies demonstrate the social impact of brutalization by the media. The *Journal of the American Medical Association* concluded that "the introduction of television in the 1950s caused a subsequent doubling of the homicide rate, i.e., long-term childhood exposure to television is a causal factor behind approximately one half of the homicides committed in the United States, or approximately 10,000 homicides annually." The article went on to say that "if, hypothetically, television technology had never been developed, there would today be 10,000 fewer homicides each year in the United States, 70,000 fewer rapes, and 700,000 fewer injurious assaults" (June 10, 1992).

Classical Conditioning

27 Classical conditioning is like the famous case of Pavlov's dogs they teach in Psychology 101. The dogs learned to associate the ringing of the bell with food, and once conditioned, the dogs could not hear the bell without salivating.

The Japanese were masters at using classical conditioning with their soldiers. Early in World War II, Chinese prisoners were placed in a ditch on their knees with their hands bound behind them. And one by one, a select few Japanese soldiers would go into the ditch and bayonet "their" prisoner to death. This is a horrific way to kill another human being. Up on the bank, countless other young soldiers would cheer them on in their violence. Comparatively few soldiers actually killed in these situations, but by making the others watch and cheer, the Japanese were able to use these kinds of atrocities to classically condition a very large audience to associate pleasure with human death and suffering. Immediately afterwards, the soldiers who had been spectators were treated to sake, to the best meal they had in months, and to so-called comfort girls. The result? They learned to associate committing violent acts with pleasure. 28

The Japanese found these kinds of techniques to be extraordinarily effective at quickly enabling very large numbers of soldiers to commit atrocities in the years to come. Operant conditioning (which we will look at shortly) teaches you to kill, but classical conditioning is a subtle but powerful mechanism that teaches you to like it. 29

This technique is so morally reprehensible that there are very few examples of it in modern U.S. military training, but there are some clear-cut examples of it being done by the media to our children. What is happening to our children is the reverse of the aversion therapy portrayed in the movie *A Clockwork Orange.* In *A Clockwork Orange,* a brutal sociopath, a mass murderer, is strapped to a chair and forced to watch violent movies while he is injected with a drug that nauseates him. So he sits and gags and retches as he watches the movies. After hundreds of repetitions of this, he associates violence with nausea. And it limits his ability to be violent. 30

We are doing the exact opposite: Our children watch vivid pictures of human suffering and death, and they learn to associate it with their favorite soft drink and candy bar or their girlfriend's perfume. 31

After the Jonesboro shootings, one of the high-school teachers told me how her students reacted when she told them about the shootings at the middle school. "They laughed," she told me with dismay. A similar reaction happens all the time in movie theaters when there is bloody violence. The young people laugh and cheer and keep right on eating popcorn and drinking pop. We have raised a generation of barbarians who have learned to associate violence with pleasure, like the Romans cheering and snacking as the Christians were slaughtered in the Colosseum. 32

The result is a phenomenon that functions much like AIDS, a phenomenon I call AVIDS—Acquired Violence Immune Deficiency Syndrome. AIDS 33 has never killed anybody. It destroys your immune system, and then other diseases that shouldn't kill you become fatal. Television violence by itself does not kill you. It destroys your violence immune system and conditions you to derive pleasure from violence. And once you are at close range with another human being and it's time for you to pull that trigger, Acquired Violence Immune Deficiency Syndrome can destroy your midbrain resistance.

Operant Conditioning

34 The third method the military uses is operant conditioning, a very powerful repetitive procedure of stimulus-response, stimulus-response. A benign example is the use of flight simulators to train pilots. An airline pilot in training sits in front of a flight simulator for endless hours; when a particular warning light goes on, he is taught to react in a certain way. When another warning light goes on, a different reaction is required. Stimulus-response, stimulus-response, stimulus-response. One day the pilot is actually flying a jumbo jet; the plane is going down, and 300 people are screaming behind him. He is wetting his seat cushion, and he is scared out of his wits; but he does the right thing. Why? Because he has been conditioned to respond reflexively to this particular crisis.

35 When people are frightened or angry, they will do what they have been conditioned to do. In fire drills, children learn to file out of the school in orderly fashion. One day there is a real fire, and they are frightened out of their wits; but they do exactly what they have been conditioned to do, and it saves their lives.

36 The military and law enforcement community have made killing a conditioned response. This has substantially raised the firing rate on the modern battlefield. Whereas infantry training in World War II used bull's-eye targets, now soldiers learn to fire at realistic, man-shaped silhouettes that pop into their field of view. That is the stimulus. The trainees have only a split second to engage the target. The conditioned response is to shoot the target, and then it drops. Stimulus-response, stimulus-response, stimulus-response—soldiers or police officers experience hundreds of repetitions. Later, when soldiers are on the battlefield or a police officer is walking a beat and somebody pops up with a gun, they will shoot reflexively and shoot to kill. We know that 75 to 80 percent of the shooting on the modern battlefield is the result of this kind of stimulus-response training.

37 Now, if you're a little troubled by that, how much more should we be troubled by the fact that every time a child plays an interactive point-and-shoot video game, he is learning the exact same conditioned reflex and motor skills?

38 I was an expert witness in a murder case in South Carolina offering mitigation for a kid who was facing the death penalty. I tried to explain to the jury that interactive video games had conditioned him to shoot a gun to kill. He had spent hundreds of dollars on video games learning to point and shoot, point and shoot. One day he and his buddy decided it would be fun to rob the local convenience store. They walked in, and he pointed a snub-nosed .38 pistol at the clerk's head. The clerk turned to look at him, and the defendant shot reflexively from about six feet. The bullet hit the clerk right between the eyes—which is a pretty remarkable shot with that weapon at that range—and killed this father of two. Afterward, we asked the boy what happened and why he did it. It clearly was not part of the plan to kill the guy—it was being videotaped from six different directions. He said, "I don't know. It was a mistake. It wasn't supposed to happen."

39 In the military and law-enforcement worlds, the right option is often not to shoot. But you never, ever put your money in that video machine with the intention of not shooting. There is always some stimulus that sets you off. And when he was excited, and his heart rate went up, and vasoconstriction closed his forebrain down, this young man did exactly what he was conditioned to do: he reflexively pulled the trigger, shooting accurately just like all those times he played video games.

40 This process is extraordinarily powerful and frightening. The result is ever more "homemade" sociopaths who kill reflexively. Our children are learning how to kill and learning to like the idea of killing; and then we have the audacity to say, "Oh my goodness, what's wrong?"

41 One of the boys involved in the Jonesboro shootings (and they are just boys) had a fair amount of experience shooting real guns. The other one, to the best of our knowledge, had almost no experience shooting. Between them, those two boys fired 27 shots from a range of over 100 yards, and they hit 15 people. That's pretty remarkable shooting. We run into these situations often—kids who have never picked up a gun in their lives pick up a real gun and are incredibly accurate. Why? Video games.

Thinking Critically About Content

1. According to Grossman, what is the "virus of violence" (paragraph 3)?
2. What three methods does the military use to train its soldiers to kill?
3. What does Grossman mean when he claims that the media are presenting violence "as entertainment for children"?

Answers to Questions

Thinking Critically About Content

1. The "virus of violence" is the spreading of violence throughout the nation and, in fact, throughout the world.
2. The military uses desensitization, classical conditioning, and operant conditioning.
3. He is referring to the fact that TV shows, movies, and video games all make violence interesting and appealing to children.

Thinking Critically About Purpose and Audience

4. Grossman's purpose in this essay is to communicate to parents and others that violent TV shows, movies, and video games are training our children to kill.
5. Parents and educators will most likely be interested in Grossman's ideas. Beyond this point, answers to this question will vary.
6. Answers to this question will vary.

Thinking Critically About Essays

7. Grossman believes that the violence masquerading as "entertainment"

that our children are exposed to through TV, movies, and video games is teaching them to kill.

8. He is trying to show the extent and seriousness of the problem of violence in children.
9. The title of this essay is straightforward—stating Grossman's opinion that American society, including parents, the media, and others, is collectively showing our kids how to kill.
10. Answers will vary.

Thinking Critically About Purpose and Audience

4. What do you think Grossman's purpose is in this essay?
5. Who do you think would be most interested in this essay?
6. What effect do you think this essay would have on parents?

Thinking Critically About Essays

7. Describe in a complete sentence the writer's argument.
8. Why does Grossman cite statistics to explain the "virus of violence" that concerns him?
9. Explain the title of this essay.
10. This essay discusses the sensitive issues related to children and violence in the media and then ends abruptly. Add a paragraph to the essay making some concrete suggestions for solving the problem the author poses.

ARGUING A POSITION

Focusing Your Attention

1. If you were asked to take a position for or against a topic of great importance to you or to society, what are some of the topics you would consider?
2. In the two essays that you will be reading, one writer claims that if we control loitering, we can control gang activity. The other writer claims loitering is not related to gang activity. Before you read these essays, try to predict some of the arguments each author will make.

READING CRITICALLY

Once again, highlight the facts and opinions in both of the following essays, put an X by ideas you disagree with, and form your own opinions about the issue of loitering and gang violence. Be prepared to defend your thoughts with details from the essays and examples from your own experience.

ANTI-LOITERING LAWS CAN REDUCE GANG VIOLENCE
by Richard Willard

Expanding Your Vocabulary

The following words are important to your understanding of this essay. To help you add them to your vocabulary, write out a synonym and an example from your own experience for each new word.

anti-loitering: forbidding people to hang around in a public place without an obvious reason (title)

innovative: clever, original (paragraph 1)

curfew: time by which individuals must be off the public streets (paragraph 1)

statutes: laws (paragraph 1)

court injunctions: orders issued by the courts (paragraph 1)

deterrence: avoidance (paragraph 1)

sanctions: punishments (paragraph 1)

constrained: limited (paragraph 1)

discretion: personal judgment (paragraph 1)

gang-loitering ordinances: laws against gangs hanging around public places without reason (paragraph 2)

implemented: used, enforced (paragraph 2)

pervasiveness: extent (paragraph 2)

engenders: produces, causes (paragraph 3)

panhandling: begging for money (paragraph 5)

vending: the selling of merchandise (paragraph 5)

commons: open public areas such as parks and squares (paragraph 6)

prevalent: widespread (paragraph 7)

skewed: distorted (paragraph 7)

augment: increase (paragraph 10)

condemnation: blame (paragraph 10)

suppression: control (paragraph 11)

abatement: decrease (paragraph 11)

SUMMARY

In this essay, Willard argues that anti-loitering laws are an effective means for reducing gang violence.

READABILITY

(Flesch–Kincaid grade level)
15.8

INSTRUCTOR'S RESOURCE MANUAL

For additional teaching strategies, for journal entries, for vocabulary and reading quizzes, and for more writing assignments, see the *Instructor's Resource Manual*, Section II, Part II.

ANTI-LOITERING LAWS CAN REDUCE GANG VIOLENCE

by Richard Willard

1 Chicago is not alone in seeking to resist the devastating effects of gang violence. Having witnessed the failure of more traditional policing methods, many other threatened localities—from Los Angeles to Washington, D.C.—have reacted by passing a variety of innovative laws, which range from curfew measures to anti-loitering statutes to court injunctions against specific gang members. All of these measures emphasize prevention and deterrence strategies over increased criminal sanctions. In order to meet the particular challenges of increased gang violence, communities have also strongly supported constrained expansions of police discretion to help communities reassert their own law-abiding norms.

2 Residents of high-crime communities are much more likely to support gang-loitering ordinances, curfews, and other order-maintenance policies, which they perceive to be appropriately moderate yet effective devices for reducing crime. Communities have implemented these policies in various ways, tailored to their particular needs and depending on the pervasiveness of the problem.

Maintaining Order

3 Just as community disorder engenders increasing disorder and crime, reinforcement of [existing] community law-abiding norms engenders increasing social order and prevents more serious crime. Modern policing theory has undergone a "quiet revolution" to learn that, in cooperation with community efforts, enforcing community public order norms is one of the most effective means of combating all levels of crime. By focusing on order maintenance and prevention, advocating a more visible presence in policed areas, and basing its legitimacy on the consent of policed populations, police can most effectively prevent the occurrence of more serious crime.

4 New York City's experience confirms this. Today, that city has much less crime than it did five years ago. From 1993 to 1996, the murder rate dropped by 40 percent, robberies dropped by 30 percent, and burglary dropped by more than 25 percent, more than double the national average.

5 These drops are not the result of increased police resources, but rather more effectively applied resources. While New York has not increased its law enforcement expenditures substantially more than other cities, since 1993 the city began to focus intensively on "public order" offenses, including van-

dalism, aggressive panhandling, public drunkenness, unlicensed vending, public urination, and prostitution. This focus on order maintenance is credited for much of the crime reduction.

Anti-loitering ordinances implement community-driven order maintenance policing citywide—appropriate to the extreme pervasiveness of Chicago's gang problem—but on a neighborhood scale. Preservation of neighborhood commons is essential to ensuring healthy and vital cities. 6

Ineffective Strategies

Gang loitering works to increase disorder. Order-maintenance policing strikes a reasonable intermediate balance between harsh criminal penalties and inaction. Conventional suppression strategies are ineffective in gang-threatened communities. Where gang activity is prevalent, individuals are more likely to act in an aggressive manner in order to conform to gang norms of behavior. When numerous youths act according to these skewed norms, more are likely to turn to crime: Widespread adoption of aggressive mannerisms sends skewed signals about public attitudes toward gang membership and creates barriers to mainstream law-abiding society, which strongly disfavors aggression. 7

Accordingly, policies that "raise the price" of gang activity can sometimes function at cross-purposes. If juveniles value willingness to break the law, delinquency may be seen as "status-enhancing." As penalties grow more severe, lawbreaking gives increasing status. More severe punishments may also provoke unintended racist accusation, if community minorities view harsher penalties as unfairly applied to their particular groups. Thus, any strategy dependent on harsh penalties may in fact be "at war with itself." 8

Why Anti-Loitering Laws Work

Strategies that instead attack public signals to juveniles' peers about the value of gang criminality are more effective. Gang anti-loitering laws do this, for example, by "authorizing police to disperse known gang members when they congregate in public places" or by "directly prohibiting individuals from displaying gang allegiance through distinctive gestures or clothing." By preventing gangs from flaunting their authority, such laws establish community authority while combating the perception that gangs have high status. As that perception weakens, so does the pressure to join gangs that youths might otherwise perceive. 9

Such strategies also positively influence law-abiding adults. Gang-loitering laws augment law-abiders' confidence so that they can oppose 10 gangs. When public deterrence predominates, individuals are much less likely to perceive that criminality is widespread and much more likely to see private precautions as worthwhile. When the community as a whole is again able to express its condemnation, gang influence quickly wanes.

11 The most successful anti-gang programs combine effective gang suppression programs with targeted community aid efforts: increased social services, job placement, and crisis intervention. Civil gang abatement, together with other government and community-based efforts, has reduced crime and visibly improved the neighborhood's quality of life.

12 Chicago has also implemented alternative community aid programs. Since 1992, for example, the Gang Violence Reduction Project has targeted Little Village to serve as a model gang violence reduction program.

13 The program coordinates increased levels of social services—the carrot—in conjunction with focused suppression strategies—the stick. The result has been a lower level of serious gang violence among the targeted gangs than among comparable gangs in the area. The project also noted improvement in residents' perceptions of gang crime and police effectiveness in dealing with it. Chicago's anti-loitering ordinance is the necessary "stick" of an effective gang violence reduction equation.

ANTI-LOITERING LAWS ARE INEFFECTIVE AND BIASED
by David Cole

SUMMARY
Cole argues that anti-loitering laws are backfiring on the police because (1) they do not deter gang violence and (2) people are losing respect for law agencies.

READABILITY
(Flesch–Kincaid grade level)
13.6

INSTRUCTOR'S RESOURCE MANUAL
For additional teaching strategies, for journal entries, for vocabulary

Expanding Your Vocabulary

The following words are important to your understanding of this essay. To help you add them to your vocabulary, write out a synonym and an example from your own experience for each new word.

anti-loitering: forbidding people to hang around in a public place without an obvious reason (title)

starkly: boldly (paragraph 1)

ordinance: law (paragraph 1)

due process: the requirement that laws treat all individuals fairly (paragraph 1)

discretion: personal judgment (paragraph 3)

empirical: theoretical (paragraph 4)

aldermen: members of the town council or governing board (paragraph 4)

apartheid regime: political system in which people of different races were separated (paragraph 4)

disparities: differences (paragraph 4)

invalidated: canceled (paragraph 5)

unfettered: free, unlimited (paragraph 6)

mores: moral attitudes (paragraph 6)

strictures: restraints and limits (paragraph 6)

discriminatory: biased, unfair (paragraph 6)

legitimacy: acceptance as lawful (paragraph 6)

cynicism: doubt, distrust (paragraph 6)

alienation: sense of not belonging (paragraph 6)

Kerner Commission: task force established by President Lyndon Johnson to investigate the causes of race riots (paragraph 7)

street sweeps: stopping and searching everyone on the street as if they are guilty of a crime (paragraph 7)

antithetical: opposing (paragraph 7)

carte blanche: complete freedom (paragraph 7)

impeding: blocking, obstructing (paragraph 7)

ANTI-LOITERING LAWS ARE INEFFECTIVE AND BIASED

by David Cole

Do "quality of life" policing and "community" policing, the law enforcement watchwords of the nineties, require the abandonment or dilution of civil rights and civil liberties? On December 9, 1998, the Supreme Court heard arguments in a case that starkly poses that question. At issue is a sweeping Chicago ordinance that makes it a crime for gang members or anyone associated with them merely to stand in public "with no apparent purpose." Chicago calls the offense "gang loitering," but it might more candidly 1

and reading quizzes, and for more writing assignments, see the *Instructor's Resource Manual*, Section II, Part II.

ANSWERS TO QUESTIONS

Thinking Critically About Content

1. *Willard:*
   reasons
   Anti-loitering laws can help disperse gangs.
   Community resources will give gang members a place to go.
   evidence
   New York City's crime rate has decreased.
   Focusing on minor infractions helps lower the crime rate.
   Community-based efforts have reduced crime.
   statistics
   From 1993 to 1996, the murder rate in New York dropped by 40 percent, robberies by 30 percent, and burglary by 25 percent.

Cole:
reasons
Anti-loitering laws cause mistrust.
Anti-loitering laws focus on minorities.
evidence
Crime rates have dropped everywhere, not just in states with anti-loitering laws.
Communities mistrust the motives of the police and therefore avoid the police.
statistics
45,000 citizens in Chicago were arrested over a three-year period.

2. Willard states that Chicago has attacked loitering on such a scale that gang violence has been reduced. Cole uses Chicago throughout most of his essay to prove that anti-loitering laws cause many arrests but do not deter crime in any way.
3. Answers will vary.

Thinking Critically About Purpose and Audience

4. Willard wants to maintain anti-loitering laws; Cole wants to abolish them.
5. People who are affected by gangs in any way would be most interested in these essays.
6. Answers will vary.

be termed "standing while black." Sixty-six of the more than 45,000 Chicago citizens arrested for this offense in the three years that the law was on the books challenged its constitutionality, and in 1997 the Illinois Supreme Court unanimously ruled that it violated due process.

2 But the Supreme Court agreed to review that decision, and lined up in defense of the ordinance is not only the city of Chicago but also the United States, the attorneys general of thirty-one states, the National District Attorneys Association, the International Association of Chiefs of Police, the U.S. Conference of Mayors, and, perhaps most interesting, a pair of otherwise liberal University of Chicago law professors representing several Chicago neighborhood groups.

Disputing the Arguments for Loitering Laws

3 The ordinance's advocates argue that it played a critical role in making Chicago's high-crime neighborhoods safe and therefore served the interests of the minority poor who live there. They suggest that strict constitutional standards need to be loosened in order to give police the discretion to engage in the day-to-day encounters of "quality of life" or "community" policing. Most astounding, they argue that criminal laws no longer must be clear in places where minority groups have a voice in the political process and can protect themselves. These arguments resonate with one commonly heard these days, particularly but not exclusively in [former] Mayor Rudolph Giuliani's New York City—namely, that heavy-handed police efforts directed at the inner city benefit minority residents by making their neighborhoods safer places in which to grow up, work, and live.

4 The arguments fail. First, as an empirical matter it is far from clear that the minority community in Chicago supported the law or that minority communities generally favor "quality of life" policing efforts that send so many of their residents to jail. The majority of Chicago's African-American aldermen voted against the ordinance; one representative, predicting that the law would be targeted at young black men, compared it to South Africa's apartheid regime. And voter turnout rates are so low in the inner city that it is difficult to say whether any elected official speaks for that community. The notion that minorities no longer need the protection of constitutional law simply ignores the racial disparities evident at every stage of the criminal justice system.

5 It is also not clear that the antigang law actually benefited anyone, much less Chicago's minority communities. Chicago did experience a falling crime rate while the law was in effect, but so did the rest of the nation. And the crime rate continued to fall after the ordinance was invalidated. So it is

far from proven that arresting tens of thousands for standing in public had any positive effects.

Law Enforcement Must Build Trust

Most important, giving the police unfettered discretion to sweep the city 6
streets of "undesirable" youth probably undermines safety by incurring distrust among those community members whose trust the police need most. The law's most powerful tool is its legitimacy. The more people believe the law is legitimate, the more likely they are to internalize its mores, obey its strictures, and cooperate with police. When laws are enforced in discriminatory ways, they lose their legitimacy. Cynicism and alienation about the criminal law are nowhere higher than among minorities and the urban poor, and laws like Chicago's only feed the alienation by inviting selective enforcement.

Indeed, law enforcement authorities and experts have long understood 7
the importance of maintaining the community's faith and trust. Thirty years ago, the Kerner Commission reported that such support "will not be present when a substantial segment of the community feels threatened by the police and regards the police as an occupying force." The father of "quality of life" policing, George Kelling, has argued that street sweeps are antithetical to its goals precisely because they foster enmity, not community. And Attorney General Janet Reno has written that effective crime control requires "a greater sense of community and trust between law enforcement and the minority community." Yet her Justice Department, the City of Chicago, and the majority of our nation's state attorneys general fail to understand that you don't build trust by unleashing the police on minority communities with carte blanche to arrest anyone standing in public without an apparent purpose. Civil rights and civil liberties, far from impeding law enforcement, are critical to preserving its legitimacy.

Thinking Critically About Content

1. Make a list of the reasons, evidence, and statistics each writer uses to convince the reader of his position.
2. Explain how both writers use the anti-loitering laws in Chicago to argue different positions.
3. Which essay contains the most convincing evidence in your opinion? Why is it so convincing to you?

Thinking Critically About Essays

7. Willard believes that anti-loitering laws are effective and are needed to curb violence; Cole believes that anti-loitering laws are unconstitutional and unfairly target minority populations.
8. *Willard:*

   Introduction

   Background on high-crime communities

   Body paragraphs

   Evidence showing value of laws

   Statistics proving laws are effective

   Opposing viewpoint

   Response to opposing viewpoint

   Alternatives to loitering

   Conclusion

   Anti-loitering laws are the solution.

   Cole:

   Introduction

   Background showing issue of unconstitutionality

   Body paragraphs

   Opposing viewpoint

   Response to opposing viewpoint: facts, examples

   Evidence showing laws are ineffective

   Conclusion

   Anti-loitering laws violate civil rights.
9. Both writers agree that loitering is a

problem and that anti-loitering laws have cleaned the streets of many troublesome youths. However, Willard believes that these laws are effective in curbing violence and offer gang members a place to go, whereas Cole believes that the laws are targeting minorities who are not necessarily gang members, are infringing on civil rights, and are causing distrust for police officials.

10. Answers will vary.

TEACHING ON THE WEB

Links: Have students link to Web sites that argue a controversial issue. How do the Web sites try to persuade people to believe a certain way? Are the sites biased in any way?

Possible sites for the issue "Should food be genetically altered?":

Center for Food Safety polls page, www.centerforfoodsafety.org/facts&issues/polls.html

Genetic Engineering News, www.genengnews.com

International Forum for Genetic Engineering, www.ifgene.org/

TEACHING ON THE WEB

Research: Have students find a Web site

Thinking Critically About Purpose and Audience

4. What do you think the writers' purposes are in these essays?
5. What type of audience would be most interested in the subject of these two essays? Explain your answer.
6. If you changed your mind as a result of reading one of these essays, what in the essay caused the change?

Thinking Critically About Essays

7. State each writer's point of view in a single sentence.
8. How do both writers organize their essays? Make a rough outline of each essay to demonstrate your answer.
9. Which points do the two writers agree on? Which points do they disagree on? Explain your answer.
10. Write your own argument about the relationship between loitering and gang activity.

Writing Workshop

This final section gives you opportunities to apply what you have learned in this chapter to another writing assignment. This time, we provide very little prompting beyond a summary of the guidelines for writing an argument essay. This section will let you demonstrate that you can go through the entire writing process on your own with only occasional feedback from your peers. Loop back into the chapter as necessary when you have questions so that this process becomes as automatic to you as possible before you move on to new material. Then pause at the end of the chapter to reflect briefly on what you have learned.

Guidelines for Writing an Argument Essay

1. State your opinion on your topic in your thesis statement.
2. Find out as much as you can about your audience before you write.
3. Choose evidence that supports your thesis statement.
4. Anticipate opposing points of view.
5. Find some common ground.
6. Maintain a reasonable tone.
7. Organize your essay so that it presents your position as effectively as possible.

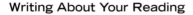

Writing About Your Reading

1. In "We Are Training Our Kids to Kill," Grossman tries to convince his readers that various forms of violence in the media teach our kids to kill. Argue for or against government control of violence on TV, in movies, and/or in video games.
2. These pro and con essays deal mainly with loitering as it relates to gang activity. Think of another strategy for fighting gang activity, and attempt to convince a group in authority to try your solution to the problem. Gather as much evidence as you can before you begin to write.
3. How can being able to develop good arguments and persuade people of your point of view help you in life? How might this ability give you the edge over other people on the job market?

Writing About Your World

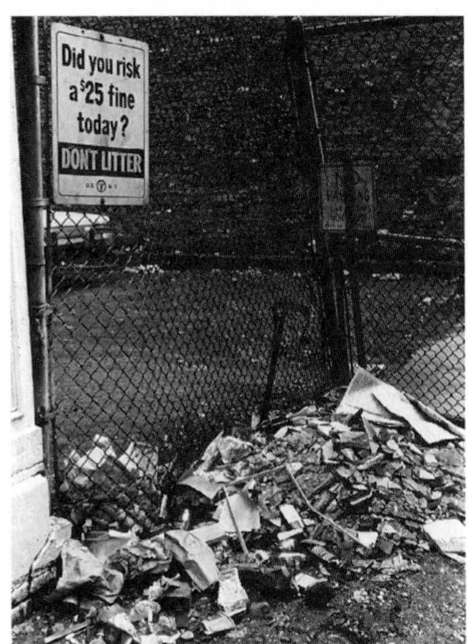

1. Explain what the photographer had in mind in creating this pictorial statement about littering. How does it appeal to its viewers? Write an essay explaining what the ad communicates.
2. Argue for or against a controversial political issue. Take a firm stand, and develop an essay supporting your position. You might want to look at the headlines in the newspaper to get some ideas for this assignment.

that tries to persuade people to do something. Have them examine the argument the Web site uses to determine if the argument is sound. Ask students to explain their answers.

TEACHING ON THE WEB

Discussion Topic: Divide students into groups of three or four, and ask them to discuss the different ways the Internet uses argument. When is the use of argument appropriate on the Internet? When is it not appropriate?

3. Write a letter to a potential employer for the job of your dreams, arguing that you are the best candidate for the job. Try to convince the employer not only that you are the perfect person for the job but also that you can take the position into new directions. Follow the format for a well-developed argument essay.
4. Create your own argument essay assignment (with the help of your instructor), and write a response to it.

Revising

Small Group Activity (5–10 minutes per writer) Working in groups of three or four, read your argument essays to each other. Those listening should record their reactions on a copy of the Peer Evaluation Form in Appendix 21. After your group goes through this process, give your evaluation forms to the appropriate writers so that each writer has two or three peer comment sheets for revising.

Paired Activity (5 minutes per writer) Using the completed Peer Evaluation Forms, work in pairs to decide what you should revise in your essay. If time allows, rewrite some of your sentences, and have your partner look at them.

Individual Activity Rewrite your paper, using the revising feedback you received from other students.

Editing

Paired Activity (5–10 minutes per writer) Swap papers with a classmate, and use the editing portion of your Peer Evaluation Form to identify as many grammar, punctuation, mechanics, and spelling errors as you can. If time allows, correct some of your errors, and have your partner look at them. Record your grammar, punctuation, and mechanics errors in the Error Log (Appendix 6) and your spelling errors in the Spelling Log (Appendix 7).

Individual Activity Rewrite your paper again, using the editing feedback you received from other students.

Reflecting on Your Writing When you have completed your own essay, answer these six questions.

1. What was most difficult about this assignment?
2. What was easiest?
3. What did you learn about arguing by completing this assignment?

4. What do you think are the strengths of your argument? Place a wavy line by the parts of your essay that you feel are very good.
5. What are the weaknesses, if any, of your paper? Place an X by the parts of your essay you would like help with. Write any questions you have in the margin.
6. What did you learn from this assignment about your own writing process—about preparing to write, about writing the first draft, about revising, and about editing?

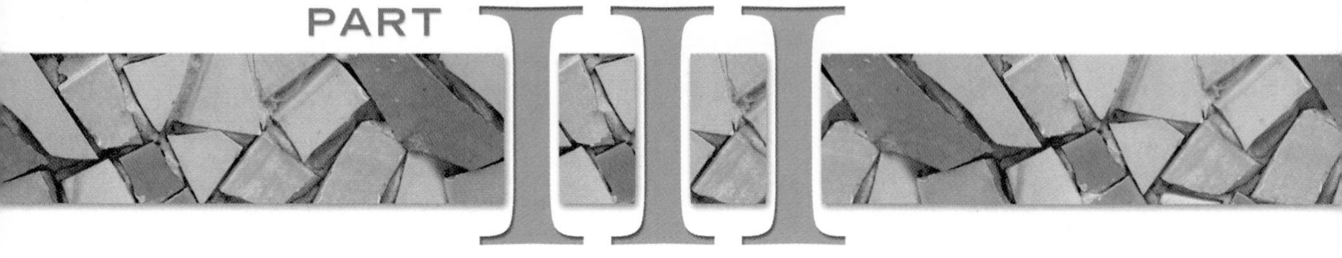

The Research Paper

"In order to understand complex issues and situations and events, we need to analyze them from multiple perspectives; every position or every viewpoint ought to have reasons to support it; and the quality of the conclusion is dependent on the quality of the reasoning that went before it."

—JOHN CHAFFEE

Part III discusses the research paper from assignment to final draft. It explains not only what this type of essay is but also how to write one, step by step. It provides you with a student model of a research paper and then guides you through the process of writing one on a topic of your own.

17 CHAPTER

Recognizing a Research Paper

TEACHING A RESEARCH PAPER
Have students bring in a research paper they have written in another class (or use the student essay in Chapter 22), and have them annotate their papers. Where do they use facts, statistics, and other supporting material or evidence? Is the evidence effective, and does it help them make their points? What transitions do they use? How can students learn to write more effective term papers by analyzing old ones?

TEACHING ON THE WEB
Research: Have students find Web sites that can help them understand better how to recognize or write a research paper. In what ways do these sites deal with these types of essays? How do students think the Web sites will help them write term papers in the future?

INSTRUCTOR'S RESOURCE MANUAL
For additional material about teaching recog-

The content of a research paper is based mainly on facts, statistics, and the opinions of others. The main difference between a research paper or term paper and other essays is that writers use information from outside reading material when writing a research paper. In other words, writers consult books, periodicals, and the Internet to find facts, statistics, and other material to support their main points.

Just as you develop the body of most essays with common knowledge or personal experience, you develop a research paper with trustworthy evidence from outside sources. To begin choosing appropriate sources, you must have a good sense of your thesis statement. Then, set out to find research that will back up your thesis statement. This support or evidence is the foundation of a research paper and should be carefully integrated with your original ideas.

In a research paper, the title gives the reader a clue about the subject of the essay. The introduction gives some background for understanding the topic and states the purpose of the paper in a thesis statement. Body paragraphs provide evidence to back up the thesis statement. And the conclusion wraps up the essay by restating the thesis statement and bringing the paper to a close.

The following essay by Mary Minor, a student, is a good example of a research paper. She solidly proves her thesis statement using books and articles from many different sources as evidence in her supporting paragraphs. As you read the first paragraph of this draft of her essay, notice her thesis statement. Then, in each supporting paragraph that follows the introductory paragraph, be aware of how this student develops her essay and supports her thesis statement with material from outside sources.

Children as Robots *Catchy title*

1 When children are infants, they are measured by certain "norms" to see if they are progressing through developmental stages at the rate of other infants their age. The norms are never clear-cut and leave room for

nizing a research paper, for journal entries, and for various tests, see the *Instructor's Resource Manual*, Section II, Part III.

Interesting comparison

individual differences. When a child hits the age of two or enters daycare, "norms" become all-important. More than in any other time in history, the 1990s brought about a change in norms that left parents confused. Now, in the twenty-first century, the "terrible twos" and "trying threes" no longer seem to be the best descriptions of toddlerhood. Today, children who are too terrible at the age of two or too trying at the age of three are diagnosed with either Attention Deficit Disorder (ADD) or Attention Deficit Hyperactivity Disorder (ADHD). "Both neurological conditions seem to [have been] the childhood plague of the '90s" (Higdon 84), and children continue to be diagnosed at an alarming rate. Children are often misdiagnosed with ADD or ADHD and suffer unnecessarily when medicated for a disorder they may not have.

In-text citation (MLA)

Direct quotation

Thesis statement

The American Psychological Association now 2
classifies this phenomenon as one disease with subcategories, yet the terms ADD and ADHD are often used interchangeably, even though individuals may have symptoms of inattention, hyperactivity, or both (American 87). The *Diagnostic and Statistical Manual of Medical Disorders* (DSM-IV) defines ADHD as a "persistent pattern of inattention and/or hyperactivity-impulsivity that is more frequently displayed and more severe than is typically observed in individuals at a comparable level of development" (American 85). What's more, the disease ADD has become the most common childhood mental heath disorder (Pelham, Fabiano, and Massetti 449) in the United States today, afflicting an "estimated . . . 3 to 12 percent of children" (Parker-Pope, par. 1). William Carey, a professor of pediatrics at the University of Pennsylvania, argues that drugs are too often used to solve conflicts with children: "the behaviors associated with the diagnosis reflect a continuum or spectrum of normal temperaments rather than a disorder." He declared that ADHD "appears to be a set of normal behavioral variations" that lead to "dissonant environmental interactions" (Breggin 13). Given the fact that children are identified as having this disease based on what a

Statistic

Quotation used to define problem

person may consider "normal" behavior, it is unfortunate for the children being diagnosed that nobody can agree on what "normal" means. As a result, specialists need to be careful when recommending treatments for what could be everyday behavior.

3 Many children today who do not fit the "norm" of adult expectations may be diagnosed with ADD. Labeling a child's behavior based on a set of norms is ludicrous since these qualities cannot accurately be measured, let alone defined. According to Thomas Armstrong, author of *The Myth of the ADD Child,* "Once the influential American Psychiatric Association declared ADD a disorder in 1980, the DSM defined it more and more broadly. . . . Increasing numbers of children are caught in the ever-widening definition net and are then labeled ADD" (914). Even though we have a definition of this disorder, nobody really knows for sure what causes it. Registered Nurse Marie Dunn feels that parents should be aware that "ADD-ADHD describes a child's behavior and does not explain the cause (which is unknown), predict the best treatment, or determine how the disorder will progress" (22). In an article in *The New England Journal of Medicine,* Dr. Marsha Rappley contends that the diagnosis is controversial because of the "subjective nature" of the test, leading many professionals to believe that ADD and ADHD is "overdiagnosed and overtreated" (171). If our leading professionals in the field can't decide on a reliable and accurate diagnostic test, we surely can't expect that they can identify a case of ADHD.

Author and book introduced before quotation

Only page number needed since author already introduced

Transition from definition to further problems

Transition sentence to new topic

4 Because there are no reliable tests for ADD, nobody is really able to tell if a child actually has this disorder. Even the American Psychiatric Association admits, "There are no laboratory tests, neurological assessments, or attentional assessments that have been established as a diagnostic in the clinical assessment of Attention-Deficit/Hyperactivity Disorder. . . . It is not yet known what fundamental cognitive deficits are responsible for [overactive behavior]" (American 88). Yet numerous children are diagnosed with this disease and are medicated because of it.

Transition sentence to next paragraph about Ritalin

5 There are as many speculations about the cause of ADD and ADHD as there are experts. Unfortunately, the ones lost in the confusion are the children, and this is due to the fact that Ritalin, the most widely used method of treatment for this disorder, works so well that few additional medical tests are done. Insurance companies and teachers often encourage parents to see drugs as the answer: "HMOs are encouraging quick diagnoses and the use of low-cost drugs, . . . [but] the 'quick fix' isn't always the best solution for the child" (Dunn 22). While Ritalin seems to work for many children, Dr. Rappley is concerned about its side effects. Studies show that short-term use of Ritalin can cause appetite suppression, stomachache, headache, deceleration of growth (Rappley 168, 179), hallucinations, depression, heart failure, and brain damage (Breggin 14). The long-term effects are not available yet because children have not been on Ritalin long enough to determine the repercussions of long-term use. It is irresponsible of doctors to prescribe children drugs that could cause serious complications later in life. We have no absolute information about ADD, only a set of symptoms, which include excessive talking, fidgeting, and similar behaviors that are normal for children. In other words, parents face the decision of whether or not to put their child on strong drugs when nobody has yet proved that a disorder exists.

Citation after paraphrase

6 Unfortunately, teachers are often the first to be involved in diagnosing a child, and they "sometimes urge parents to find a medical solution to behavioral problems" (Dunn 22). Ken Livingston explains that between the rising pressures of standardized tests and serious behavior problems, teachers are often faced with daunting challenges. The real problem, he insists, lies in our view of education:

Block indention for long quotations

> The real problem may be that the concept of compulsory, cookie-cutter education needs rethinking. In spite of the rhetoric in schools of education about the importance of taking into account the individual needs of children in a classroom, the current system of public education is designed to make that nearly impossible. . . . When it is

> difficult or inconvenient to change the environment, we don't think twice about changing the brain of the person who has to live in it. (qtd. in Breggin 257)

Parents are often pressured into placing their children on drugs with the hope that their children will receive better grades and play better with other children. However, this pressure may be unwarranted. Jane M. Healy, the author of *Endangered Minds,* argues that "students who take their medication do become more tractable, completing more repetitive 'work,' such as worksheets. . . . However, drugs per se do not make them score better on tests of academic achievement or of higher-level thinking and problem-solving" (qtd. in Breggin 82). Teachers may see a more compliant child, but Ritalin and other stimulants cannot make children more creative, better problem solvers, or faster learners.

7 Some children are so hard to control that mind-altering drugs such as Ritalin appear to be a blessing, but drugs, if used at all, should be used *only* for a short period of time—until the "real" cause of the problem behavior is found. Dr. Rappley argues that in some children, symptoms identified as the symptoms of ADHD may in fact be caused by "learning and language disorders, oppositional defiant disorder, conduct disorder, anxiety, depression, as well as bipolar, post-traumatic stress, tic, and adjustment disorders" (166). In a study on the effects of Ritalin, Mary Solano and Esther Wender praised the success of Ritalin to create perseverance in children. They claimed that perseverance "with its relative inflexibility of the mind, is precisely what makes the children more willing and able to focus on boring, repetitive, uninspiring classroom materials. It also makes them more able to sit for hours over their homework when they'd much rather be doing something else" (Breggin 89). One must wonder, however, whose suffering Ritalin is relieving—the teachers' and parents' or the children's. While Solano and Wender had good intentions, their study demonstrates why children should not be medicated for an ill-defined disease.

Credible opinion used to support argument

Opposite argument addressed

Despite major controversy in the medical field, however, there has been no proof that drugs are being overprescribed for American children. Some experts even feel that children may be under-treated (Breggin 11–20). While some studies have concluded that children are overmedicated, others insist the opposite, which again means that each child is treated according to the most popular opinion. Many fear that children are being overdiagnosed due to the subjectivity of the diagnostic test. In fact, Nicholas Cummings, author of "Expanding a Shrinking Economic Base," explains, "When the APA revised the criteria in the DSM-IV-R for diagnosing ADD/ADHD, the number of children who qualified literally quadrupled" (93). Unfortunately, some populations are diagnosed more frequently than others. Fifteen to twenty percent of school-age boys are medicated with a stimulant (Breggin 3). With a statistic as drastic as this, it is astonishing that experts disagree on this subject. 8

Opposite argument refuted with quotation

Even if drugs can be beneficial in some instances, long-term usage is potentially dangerous because stimulants like Ritalin, Dexedrine, and Adderall are presently classified by the DEA and the International Narcotics Control Board "together with amphetamines and methamphetamine ('speed'), as well as cocaine, for purposes of examining patterns of addiction, abuse, and toxicity" (Breggin 96). To give a prescription for such drugs to a child without comprehensive medical testing is inexcusable (Vatz and Weinberg, par. 22). Doctors need to agree that children are overmedicated for a disease that may not exist and find more acceptable ways to curb disruptive behavior. Many children exhibit the symptoms of ADHD due to family problems or other environmental factors. Diet may also play a major role in this scenario. The removal of certain foods, especially those that cause allergies or contain artificial food colorings, or the addition of dietary supplements (Breggin 211) may very well eliminate the symptoms. When doctors quote the Hippocratic Oath, they say, "I will apply dietetic measures for the benefit of the sick 9

Facts used to show other possible reasons for hyperactivity in children

according to my ability and judgment; I will keep them from harm and injustice" ("Hippocratic Oath"). Sworn to dietetically treat their patients, doctors should remember this oath before prescribing drugs for a disease that nobody can prove exists.

Conclusion

10 Perhaps these "diseases" are nothing more than a belief system in an ever-increasing conformist society. Every effort should be made to find the cause of the real medical problems underlying ADD and ADHD before we even think about giving our children drugs. A doctor who doesn't order medical tests for a child with symptoms of ADD is negligent, to say the least, and the failure of a doctor to discuss alternatives to drug therapy with parents when diagnosing ADHD is more than inexcusable; it is unforgivable. More patients would seek alternative treatments like behavior therapy if they knew their child was diagnosed on the basis of nothing more than a list of symptoms that cannot be defined or measured. After all, most parents do not want their child placed on long-term stimulant drugs. It is time to say good-bye to conformist American classrooms and diagnoses. Perhaps some people don't fit the norm because they have personalities.

Reference to thesis statement

Call to action

Concluding statement

Works Cited

Alphabetical order

Book

American Psychiatric Association. *The Diagnostic and Statistical Manual of Medical Disorders.* Arlington, VA: APA, 2000.

Armstrong, Thomas. *The Myth of the ADD Child: 50 Ways to Improve Your Child's Behavior and Attention Span without Drugs, Labels, or Coercion.* New York: Dutton, 1995.

Breggin, Peter. *Talking Back to Ritalin: What Doctors Aren't Telling You About Stimulants and ADHD.* Cambridge, MA: Perseus, 2001.

Cummings, Nicholas. "Expanding a Shrinking Economic Base: The Right Way, the Wrong Way, and the Mental Health Way." *Destructive Trends in Mental Health: The Well Intentioned Path to Harm.* Ed. Rogers

Double spaced with no extra spaces between entries

All lines after the first indented

Wright and Nicholas Cummings. New York: Routledge, 2005. 87–113.

Dunn, Marie. "Is Ritalin the Answer?" *American Journal of Nursing* 102.12 (2002): 22.

Journal article

General-circulation magazine

Higdon, Hal. "Getting Their Attention." *Runner's World* July 1999: 84–87.

"Hippocratic Oath." *World Book Encyclopedia.* Vol. 9. 2003 ed.

Encyclopedia

Parker-Pope, Tara. "Studies Linking Ritalin and Depression Highlight Risk of Overdiagnosing ADHD." *Wall Street Journal* 25 Jan. 2005. D1. Wilson Web. California State U Bakersfield Lib., Bakersfield, CA. 1 Feb. 2006 <http://vnweb.hwwilsonweb.com>.

Online source

Pelham, William E. Jr., Gregory A. Fabiano, and Greta M. Massetti. "Evidence-based Assessment of Attention Deficit Hyperactivity Disorder in Children and Adolescents." *Journal of Clinical Child and Adolescent Psychology* 34.3 (2005): 449–476.

Rappley, Marsha. "Attention deficit Hyperactivity Disorder." *The New England Journal of Medicine* 352.2 (2005): 165–173.

Vatz, Richard E., and Lee S. Weinberg. "Problems in Diagnosing and Treating ADD/ADHD." *USA Today* 129.2670 (Mar. 2001): 64–65. Wilson Web. California State U Bakersfield Lib., Bakersfield, CA. 5 Feb. 2006 <http://vnweb. hwwilsonweb.com>.

PRACTICE 1 Before continuing, choose one of the following topics for your own work in the rest of Part III:

Police brutality
Alzheimer's disease
Herbal medicine
Assisted suicide
Nursing homes
Censorship
Government spending
Steroids
Pollution
Drug treatment programs
Cloning
Date rape
Child abuse
Alcohol and crime
Bilingual education

CHAPTER 18

Avoiding Plagiarism

TEACHING AVOIDING PLAGIARISM
Have students submit an old essay to www.turnitin.com, an online service that checks student papers for instances of plagiarism. This site can help students identify plagiarism in their own writing when they write research papers. For fun, you might have students submit a highly plagiarized paper just to see how thorough the site really is.

TEACHING ON THE WEB
Research: As a class, research how the Internet sells papers or how students can copy from Web sites. Then discuss why these avenues are unethical and unfair to both the instructor and the student.

INSTRUCTOR'S RESOURCE MANUAL
For additional material about teaching students to avoid plagiarism, for journal entries, and for various tests, see the *Instructor's Resource*

Plagiarism is using someone else's words or ideas as if they were your own. Because it is dishonest, plagiarism is a serious offense in college and beyond. When you work with outside sources, you must give credit to the authors who wrote them. In other words, if you quote, paraphrase, or summarize from another source, you must provide your reader with information about that source, such as the author's name, the title of the book or essay, and the year it was written. Whenever you use other people's words or ideas without giving them credit, you are plagiarizing.

If you don't cite your sources properly, your readers will think certain words and ideas are yours when they actually came from someone else. When you steal material in this way in college, you can be dismissed from school. When you commit the same offense in the professional world, you can get fired or end up in court. So make sure you understand what plagiarism is as you move through this chapter.

COMMON KNOWLEDGE

If you are referring to information such as historical events, dates of presidents' terms, and known facts, like the effects of ultraviolet rays or smoking, you do not have to cite a source. This material is called *common knowledge* because it can be found in a number of different sources. You can use this information freely because you are not borrowing anyone's original words or ideas.

ORIGINAL IDEAS

If, however, you want to use someone's specific words or ideas, you must give that person credit by recording where you found this information. This process is called *citing* or *documenting* your sources, and it involves noting in your paper where you found the idea. Since research papers are developed around sources that support your position, citations are an essential ingredient in any term paper.

As you can see in Mary Minor's paper in Chapter 17, every source is acknowledged at least twice: (1) in the paper directly after a quotation or idea and (2) at the end of the paper in a list. The first type of citation is known as an in-text citation, and the second type is a list of sources cited in the paper. These two types of documentation work together for the readers. At the note-taking stage, you should make sure that you have all the information on your sources that you will need later to acknowledge them in proper form in your paper. Having to track down missing details when you prepare your lists of works cited is frustrating and time consuming.

Manual, Section II, Part III.

PRACTICE 1 Identify the following information as either common knowledge (CK) or original (O).

1. __O__ In a typical day, for human beings to drink the equivalent of what the glassy-winged sharpshooter insect drinks, humans would have to drink 4,000 gallons of liquid, half the amount in a standard swimming pool.

2. __CK__ William Shakespeare was born and died on the same day, April 23, 52 years apart.

3. __CK__ Abraham Lincoln was shot in Ford's Theater by John Wilkes Booth.

4. __CK__ A human being cannot survive more than three days without water.

5. __O__ The Paleozoic era produced the first shellfish and corals in the Cambrian period, the first fishes in the Ordovician period, and the first land plants in the Silurian period.

6. __CK__ Tom Hanks has won two Oscars, one for his role in *Philadelphia* and one for the title role in *Forrest Gump*.

7. __CK__ Aerobic respiration consists of oxygen plus organic matter that produces carbon dioxide, water, and energy.

8. __CK__ The success of *Survivor* caused many other reality shows to be produced.

9. __O__ The longest palindromic word in the English language is *saippuakivikauppias*.

10. __CK__ AIDS is a disease that can be caught by having unprotected sex.

USING AND SYNTHESIZING SOURCES

When writers use more than one source in an essay, they are *synthesizing* their sources. In other words, they are taking pieces of information from different sources and weaving them into their own argument. If you've written any type of paper using more than one outside source, you were synthesizing material.

As you write a research paper, your own argument establishes the order of your ideas. Then your sources provide evidence or proof for your argument.

Look at how Mary Minor uses sources. Here is a paragraph from her first draft:

> Many children today who do not fit the "norm" of adult expectations may be diagnosed with ADD. Labeling a child's behavior based on a set of "norms" is ludicrous since these qualities cannot accurately be measured, let alone defined. According to Thomas Armstrong, author of *The Myth of the ADD Child,* "Once the influential American Psychiatric Association declared ADD a disorder in 1980, the DSM defined it more and more broadly. . . . Increasing numbers of children are caught in the ever-widening definition net and are then labeled ADD" (914). In an article in *The New England Journal of Medicine,* Dr. Marsha Rappley contends that the diagnosis is controversial because of the "subjective nature" of the test, leading many professionals to believe that ADD and ADHD is "overdiagnosed and overtreated" (171).

As Mary was revising this paragraph, she realized she was forcing the reader to make connections between her sources and her argument because she was not providing explanations that made those connections. So she revised her paragraph, connecting her sources to her own ideas and making her argument clearer.

> (1) Many children today who do not fit the "norm" of adult expectations may be diagnosed with ADD. (2) Labeling a child's behavior based on a set of "norms" is ludicrous since these qualities cannot accurately be measured, let alone defined. (3) According to Thomas Armstrong, author of *The Myth of the ADD Child,* "Once

> the influential American Psychiatric Association declared ADD a disorder in 1980, the DSM defined it more and more broadly. . . . (4) Increasing numbers of children are caught in the ever-widening definition net and are then labeled ADD" (914). (5) Even though we have a definition of this disorder, nobody really knows for sure what causes it. (6) Registered Nurse Marie Dunn feels that parents should be aware that "ADD-ADHD describes a child's behavior and does not explain the cause (which is unknown), predict the best treatment, or determine how the disorder will progress" (22). (7) In an article in *The New England Journal of Medicine,* Dr. Marsha Rappley contends that the diagnosis is controversial because of the "subjective nature" of the test, leading many professionals to believe that ADD and ADHD is "overdiagnosed and overtreated" (171). (8) If our leading professionals in the field can't decide on a reliable and accurate diagnostic test, we surely can't expect that they can identify a case of ADHD.

By adding the fifth sentence, "Even though we have a definition of this disorder, nobody really knows for sure what causes it," Mary explains in her own voice the significance of the previous quotation and tells her readers what she wants them to be thinking about after they read it. Similarly, the sentence Mary adds to the end of this paragraph also furthers her argument by clarifying the quotation before it: "If our leading professionals in the field can't decide on a reliable and accurate diagnostic test, we surely can't expect that they can identify a case of ADHD." This sentence, which also acts as the paragraph's concluding sentence, shows readers that the professionals are arguing among themselves about the disease, so we should be suspicious of any diagnosis of it. Notice, also, how this last sentence provides a transition into Mary's discussion about the scarcity of reliable tests for ADHD.

To better understand how Mary's paragraph works as a combination of her ideas and her sources, look at the following breakdown of her paragraph:

(1) **Mary's** topic sentence

(2) **Mary's** explanation of her topic sentence, extending the idea of norms

(3–4) **Quotation** from Source A, Thomas Armstrong, who provides information about ADD (with Source A Works Cited information at end)

(5) **Mary's** statement about Source A, elaborating on the issue

(6) **Quotation** from Source B, Marie Dunn, who shows us we really don't know much about ADD (with Source B Works Cited information at end)

(7) **Paraphrase/quotation** from Source C, Marsha Rappley, who explains the controversy surrounding ADD (with Source C Works Cited information at end)

(8) **Mary's** statement that pulls sources together and shows a problem with definitions of ADHD.

This skeleton outline of Mary's paragraph should help you see how she balances her opinions/observations and her sources so they work as one unit that supports her main argument. If you get stuck writing your own paragraphs, referring back to this outline might help you see where you need to add information.

Before you get to this stage, however, you must think about what information you want to use from your sources and how you might present that information. Once you have a tentative thesis statement, you can start working directly with your evidence.

DIRECT QUOTATION, PARAPHRASE, AND SUMMARY

Now that you see how to incorporate sources into your argument, you need to decide whether you will quote, paraphrase, or summarize them. This section explains these three options to you. We will begin with an original source and show you how to take and acknowledge material from this source in different ways.

The following quotation is from "Shedding the Weight of My Dad's Obsession" by Linda Lee Andujar. It was published in *Newsweek* magazine on November 13, 2000, on page 17.

Original Source

> My slightly chubby figure had become a target for my physician father's frustration as he struggled to establish his medical practice. Dad told me constantly that if I was a pound overweight, I would be teased at

> school and nobody would like me. I stayed away from the other kids, fearing harsh words that never came. When I was 16, Daddy came up with the ultimate punishment: any day that I weighed more than 118 pounds (the weight my father had deemed ideal for my 5-foot, 4-inch frame), I'd have to pay him.

Direct Quotation

If you use a direct quotation from another source, you must put the exact material you want to use in quotation marks:

> Linda Lee Andujar, in her essay "Shedding the Weight of My Dad's Obsession," describes her father's unreasonable responses to her weight problem: "When I was 16, Daddy came up with the ultimate punishment: any day that I weighed more than 118 pounds (the weight my father had deemed ideal for my 5-foot, 4-inch frame), I'd have to pay him" (17).

Direct Quotation with Some Words Omitted

If you want to leave something out of the quotation, use three dots (with spaces before and after each dot). Omitting words like this is known as *ellipsis*.

> Linda Lee Andujar, in her essay "Shedding the Weight of My Dad's Obsession," reveals her father's response to her weight problem:, "Any day that I weighed more than 118 pounds . . . , I'd have to pay him" (17).

Paraphrase

When you paraphrase, you are restating the main ideas of a quotation **in your own words.** *Paraphrase* literally means "similar phrasing," so it is usually about the same length as the original. Paraphrasing is one of the most difficult skills to master in college, but one trick you can use is to read the material, put it aside, and write a sentence or two from memory. Then compare what you wrote with the original to make sure they are similar but not exactly the same. If you look at the source while you are trying to paraphrase it, you might inadvertently take a word or phrase from the original, which would make you guilty of plagiarism.

Even though this information is in your own words, you still need to let your readers know where you found it. A paraphrase of our original source might look like this:

> Linda Lee Andujar, in her essay "Shedding the Weight of My Dad's Obsession," explains that her father was ashamed of his daughter's weight when he was a young doctor. He believed that if she was overweight, she would "be teased" by her classmates, so she avoided other children. Her father ultimately set a weight limit on her and charged her for going over that limit (17).

Summary

To summarize, state the author's main idea in your own words. A summary is much briefer than the original or a paraphrase. As with a paraphrase, you need to furnish the details of your original source. Here is a summary of our original source:

> Linda Lee Andujar, in her essay "Shedding the Weight of my Dad's Obsession," explains that her father's "obsession" with her weight caused her to avoid other children and pay her dad if she went over the weight limit he set (17).

TAKING NOTES ON SOURCES

As you consider using your sources as direct quotations, paraphrases, and summaries, you will need to keep careful track of them. For the list of sources at the end of your paper, you should provide your reader with several items of information for each source you use. The best time to start keeping track of this information is when you are taking notes.

As you take notes, notecards are an excellent tool because you can move them around as your paper takes shape. Put only one idea on a notecard. Taking notes this way will save you a lot of time in the future because you won't be scrambling around looking for the information on the source you just quoted. Taking notes electronically is another option. Whatever your choice, if you cannot find the original source for information you used in your paper and therefore cannot tell your reader where you found the quotation, then you cannot use the material.

As you read your sources, you should consider whether you might want to directly quote, paraphrase, or summarize the material. A general rule to follow is that you never want to have more than 10 percent of directly quoted information in your paper, which means 90 percent of the outside information you use in your essay should be paraphrased or summarized. The best way to determine whether or not you should use a direct quotation is by asking yourself if this is the best possible way to relay this information.

If you can't phrase it any better than the original, then you should use a direct quotation. In most cases, however, you should try to put your research in your own words. Only occasionally should you use the author's exact words in your paper. When you are reading and taking notes on your sources, you should keep this in mind.

To avoid plagiarism when taking notes and writing your paper, write down all the information you will need later to cite that source.

For a book:

- Book title
- Author or authors
- Editor or editors (if applicable)
- City where published
- Publisher
- Year of publication

For an article:

- Article title
- Author or authors
- Title of the magazine or journal
- Date of issue (for a magazine)
- Year and volume number (for a journal)
- Pages on which the article appeared

If you put all this information on one card, you can record just the author's last name on all other cards from that same source. If you are using more than one book or article by the same author, add the source's date to the card. For both books and articles, you should also record the page where you found the information. That way you can easily find it again or cite it in your paper.

The format in which this information should be presented will depend on the field of study. A good handbook will help you with the formats of the various documentation styles, which include Modern Language Association (MLA) style for the humanities, American Psychological Association (APA) style for the social sciences, and *Chicago Manual* (CM) style for mathematics and science. Make sure you understand which documentation style your instructor wants you to use, because they are all slightly different from each other.

In this book, we are using the Modern Language Association style of citation. The Andujar essay in the MLA format would look like this:

> Andujar, Linda Lee. "Shedding the Weight of my Father's Obsession." *Newsweek* 13 Nov. 2000, 17.

PRACTICE 2 Quote from, paraphrase, and summarize the following original sources. Document the source correctly in each case by looking up the MLA documentation style in a handbook.

1. The following paragraph is from "We are Training Our Kids to Kill" by Dave Grossman, originally published in the *Saturday Evening Post* in July/August 1999 on pages 64–66, 68, 70, 72. The quoted paragraph appeared on page 65.

> This virus of violence is occurring worldwide. The explanation for it has to be some new factor that is occurring in all of these countries. There are many factors involved, and none should be discounted: for example, the prevalence of guns in our society. But violence is rising in many nations with Draconian gun laws. And though we should never downplay child abuse, poverty, or racism, there is only one new variable present in each of these countries that bears the exact same fruit: media violence presented as entertainment for children.

Quotation: *Answers will vary but must include the in-text citation Grossman 65.*

Paraphrase: *Answers will vary but must include the in-text citation Grossman 65.*

Summary: *Answers will vary but must include the in-text citation Grossman 65.*

Works Cited Citation: *Grossman, Dave. "We Are Training Our Kids to Kill," Saturday Evening Post July/Aug. 1999: 64–66+.*

2. The following paragraph is from "Writer's Retreat" by Stan Higgins. It was originally published in *The Writer* in November 1991, volume 104, issue 11, on pages 21–23. The quoted paragraph appeared on page 21.

> During the day I wash dishes, clean tables, and mop floors. They call it Vocational Training. And today, as every day at three p.m., I return to my cozy, bathroom-size suite and drag out my tiny portable. We've all night, just the two of us, my blue typewriter that has been my steady cell-mate for six years, through seven facilities across two states, and I. Today's goal is three pages. I blow dust from the cover and clean the keys. The Muse calls. *Tack-tack. Tack. Tack-tack-tack.* My typewriter sings its staccato song as I search for a fertile word or idea, some harmonious junction of thought and paper. Locked in solitary combat with my machine, nothing exists outside my cell, or so I pretend. I type a line. My door opens. Two blue-uniformed guards stand there grinning. "Guess what?" one says. "Your number came up."

Quotation: *Answers will vary but must include the in-text citation Higgins 21.*

Paraphrase: *Answers will vary but must include the in-text citation Higgins 21.*

Summary: *Answers will vary but must include the in-text citation Higgins 21.*

Works Cited Citation: *Higgins, Stan. "Writer's Retreat." The Writer 104.11 (1991): 21–23.*

3. The following paragraph is from "Don't Be Cruel" by Dr. Roger Flax. It was originally published in *TWA Ambassador* in March 1992, on pages 49–51. The quoted paragraph appeared on page 49.

> Picture this scenario: Seymour Axshun (we'll call him), a terrific manager who has been a loyal employee

> for several years, messes up on an assignment. He misses a deadline on a proposal, and that three-day delay costs the company $9,100. Seymour's boss, Sy Kottick, has a near coronary over the incident, lashes out at Seymour, and criticizes him mercilessly. In front of four of Seymour's co-workers, Kottick shouts, "Axshun, how many times do I have to tell you to be more efficient with your planning? You blew it, and your mistake will cost us almost $10,000. I don't know what it takes to drill into your head that you must meet deadlines. It's disgusting, and I'm fed up. If you treated the money as if it were your own, you wouldn't be so careless."

Quotation: *Answers will vary but must include the in-text citation Flax 49.*

____

Paraphrase: *Answers will vary but must include the in-text citation Flax 49.*

____

Summary: *Answers will vary but must include the in-text citation Flax 49.*

____

Works Cited Citation: *Flax, Roger. "Don't Be Cruel." TWA Ambassador Mar. 1992: 49–51.*

4. The following paragraph is from " "Dawn's Early Light" by Richard Rodriguez. It was found in *Online NewsHour* at http://www.pbs.org/newshour/essays/jan-june04/rodriguez_01-30.htm. There were 11 paragraphs in this essay; the following is paragraph 4.

> Now they come, children following the footsteps of parents and grandparents, often at the risk of death or injury. We say about them that they are disrespectful of American laws. But for every illegal worker employed today in America, there is an employer—one of us—equally disrespectful of American law. Mexicans reveal

our hypocrisy to ourselves. They, in their relentless movement back and forth, are forcing us to see America within the Americas.

Quotation: *Answers will vary but must include the in-text citation Rodriguez, par. 4.*

Paraphrase: *Answers will vary but must include the in-text citation Rodriguez, par. 4.*

Summary: *Answers will vary but must include the in-text citation Rodriguez, par. 4.*

Works Cited Citation: *Rodriguez, Richard. "Dawn's Early Light." Online NewsHour 13 Nov. 2004. 11 pars. <http://www.pbs.org/newshour/essays/jan-june04/rodriguez_01-30.htm>.*

5. The following paragraph is from the essay "What Are Friends For?" by Marion Winik. It was originally published on pages 85–89 in a book titled *Telling: Confessions, Concessions, and Other Flashes of Light*, which was published by Villard Books in New York City in 1994. The quoted paragraph appeared on page 89.

> At the other end of the spectrum are Hero Friends. These people are better than the rest of us; that's all there is to it. Their career is something you wanted to be when you grew up—painter, forest ranger, tireless doer of good. They have beautiful homes filled with special handmade things presented to them by villagers in the remote areas they have visited in their extensive travels. Yet they are modest. They never gossip. They are always helping others, especially those who have suffered a death in the family or an illness. You would think people like this would just make you sick, but somehow they don't.

Quotation: *Answers will vary but must include the in-text citation Winik 89.*

Paraphrase: *Answers will vary but must include the in-text citation Winik 89.*

Summary: *Answers will vary but must include the in-text citation Winik 89.*

Works Cited Citation: *Winik, Marion. "What Are Friends For?" Telling: Confessions, Concessions, and Other Flashes of Light. New York: Villard, 1994: 85–89.*

CHAPTER 19

Finding Sources

No matter what you are studying in college, you should know how to find outside sources using the library through a computer. You can access an enormous amount of information that will help you generate paper topics, teach you new information, challenge your thinking, support your opinions, and make you smile. In today's electronic world, learning how to use the resources available through the library's services is a basic survival skill.

TEACHING FINDING SOURCES

Invite a librarian to your class or plan a visit to the library to discuss the best ways of finding sources in the library. Ask the librarian to outline the design of your library and answer any questions the students may have. If time allows, have the librarian give your students a tour of your campus library.

CREDIBILITY OF SOURCES

When you are looking for information to use in your essays, you must be careful about what you choose. Your sources must be relevant, reliable, and recent. This "three *R*s" approach to finding sources will help you locate convincing evidence to support your arguments.

Since anyone can put material on the Internet, you need to make sure you are not using biased or unreliable information in your academic papers. To use Web sites intelligently, follow these four guidelines.

TEACHING ON THE WEB

Research: As a class, look at various types of Web sites, and discuss the issue of credibility of Web sources. Talk about how the extensions .com, .edu, .gov, and .org can help students make preliminary decisions about the Web sites they are finding. Also discuss how authorship of the text, ownership of the site, and other clues can help students evaluate the credibility of Internet sources.

1. **Check the end of a Web URL address.** It will be either *.com*, *.edu*, *.gov*, or *.org*. The last three are generally reputable resources, but you must be very careful of *.com* (which stands for "communication") sources, and anyone can purchase a *.com* site. For example, www.whitehouse.com is not a site for the President's home, as you might suspect. On the other hand, *.edu* stands for "education," *.gov* for "government," and *.org* for "organization." Any site, however, has the potential for bias, and you should consider the material carefully.
2. **Pay attention to the argument a site makes.** Who is the author and what is his or her purpose for entering information on the site? If you log onto a Martin Luther King Jr. site and are inundated with racial slurs, chances are you've found a site that was created by a faction of the Ku Klux Klan. If the information does not fit the site or if the author has an obvious agenda, avoid the site.

INSTRUCTOR'S RESOURCE MANUAL

For additional material about teaching students

to find sources, for journal entries, and for various tests, see the *Instructor's Resource Manual,* Section II, Part III.

3. **Make sure the site is providing fact and not opinion.** For academic purposes, facts and statistics are generally more useful than opinions. If you are looking for a site that deals with gun control, you'll want to avoid the site that tells you story after story about innocent children dying or praises American liberty but fails to give you any specific information. Instead, you'll want to find a site that gives you examples that can be verified and supported with statistics.
4. **Does the site provide information about the other side of the argument?** If a site provides you with details only about its own viewpoint, you should wonder why it is omitting information. If you find a site on prayer in school and only see opinions about the reasons prayer should not be allowed in schools, you should be curious about why the site doesn't present the argument on the other side. Will facts about the other side make you change your mind? The best sites provide both sides of an argument so the source can, in turn, show why one side is more valid than the other. If you find a Web site that does not offer balanced information, consider it biased, and avoid it.

These four guidelines will help you determine whether or not you should use information you find on the Web. But if you want to be certain the information you are using will be acceptable for your instructor, you should rely on academic sources. These sources are different from other sources because they have been "refereed" or "peer reviewed." This means the authors of the essays send them to the publication and the editors of the publication send the essays anonymously to readers for review. If the readers accept the pieces for publication, they consider the essays to be well researched and worth reading. If you can, you should use only these sources. You should note, however, that you still need to evaluate your peer-reviewed source to make sure the argument is sound. The best place to find these sources online is discussed in the following section.

CONSULTING ONLINE DATABASES, FULL-TEXT INDEXES, AND ELECTRONIC JOURNAL COLLECTIONS

The best places to begin searching for outside sources are online databases, full-text indexes, and electronic journal collections. You should have access to these services from home through your library's home page or from a computer in your library. We will discuss each one separately. You may need a reference librarian to help you find these for the first time.

Online Databases

Online databases can direct you to an incredible number of books and journals on a wide range of subjects. The following are some online indexes found in WilsonWeb database, which is an information retrieval system that contains indexes on many different subjects and is used by many libraries.

Index	**Primary Use**
Biological and Agriculture Index	Agriculture and Biology
Business Full Text	Business and Finance
Education Full Text	Education
General Science Full Text	Astronomy, Biology, Botany, Chemistry, Geology, Genetics, Mathematics, Medicine, Nutrition, Oceanography, Physics, Physiology, and Zoology
Humanities Full Text	Archeology, Art, Communications, Dance, Film, Folklore, Gender Studies, History, Journalism, Linguistics, Music, Performing Arts, Philosophy, Religion, and Theology
Library Literature & Information Science Full Text	Library and Information Sciences
OmniFile Full Text Mega	Multidisciplinary database that includes indexing, abstracts, and full text from the Wilson Education, General Science, Humanities, Readers' Guide, Social Sciences, and Business databases. It also includes the full-text articles from the Wilson Applied Science and Technology, Art, Biological and Agricultural, Legal, and Library Literature and Information Science databases.
Reader's Guide Full Text	Indexing and abstracting of the most popular general-interest periodicals published in the United States and Canada

Social Sciences Full Text	Addiction studies, Anthropology, Community Health, Criminal Justice, Economics, Environmental Studies, Ethics, Family Studies, Gender Studies, Geography, Gerontology, International Relations, Law, Minority Studies, Public Administration, Political Science, Psychiatry, Psychology, Public Welfare, Social Work, Sociology, and Urban Studies

- Indexing for Omni starts in 1982.
- Abstracting generally starts in 1984 (Omni), 1993, or 1994 depending on the database.
- Full text coverage generally starts in January 1994, 1995, or 1996 depending on the database.

Full-Text Indexes

The following indexes take you directly to complete journal articles online. In other words, you can print the journal articles you find right from your computer.

Index	**Primary Use**
ABI Inform	News and business
Dow Jones	News and business
EBSCOhost*	Many subject areas
Expanded Academic ASAP*	General information in several disciplines
HRAF	Ethnographies
Lexis-Nexis	News, business, and law
WilsonWeb*	Popular magazines and newspapers, social science, humanities, business, general science, and education journals

*Not all articles will be available in full text.

Electronic Journal Collections

Electronic journal collections are similar to online databases in that you can print complete journal articles directly from your computer. The following collections might help you find information about the topic you have chosen.

Collection	Primary Use
Academic Press's IDEAL	Articles published by academic publishers
American Chemical Society's Web Editions	American Chemical Society's 26 scientific journals
American Mathematical Journals	American Mathematical Society's proceedings and transactions
JSTOR	Back issues of core journals in the humanities, social sciences, and sciences
Project Muse	Humanities, social sciences, and math

Once you access an online database, index, or collection, you can easily find articles and books on your topic. You can do online searches by author, title, or subject, but, since you will most likely be looking for articles on a topic, you will use the subject function most often. When you are searching for a title by subject, you should be aware of *Boolean connectors or operators*, which are shortcuts to help you narrow a search field.

Using Boolean Connectors or Operators

The Boolean connectors or operators for requesting a search are *AND*, *OR*, and *NOT*. By using these words, you can limit the search and find information directly related to your topic. If you type "AND" between your key words (for example, *television programs AND violence*), you are asking the computer to combine the key words for the search. If you put "OR" between the key words (*television OR video games*), you are separating the words and asking the computer to find articles and books with either one of them. If you add "NOT" (*television NOT video games*), you limit the search by excluding certain terms from the search.

Accessing Sources

Once you type your topic into the search function of a database, index, or journal collection, the computer will display the number of articles and books it has found in a "results list." Following are some examples of articles found on the topic of *television programs AND violence* in an online database, a full-text index, and an electronic journal collection.

From an Online Database

9 of 409 in Academic Search Elite in EBSCOhost

Title: Age-Based Ratings, Content Designations, and ***Television*** Content: Is There a Problem? Authors: Signorielli, Nancy[1] *NancyS@udel.edu*

Source: *Mass Communication & Society;* Nov2005, Vol. 8 Issue 4, p277-298, 22p, 7 charts

Document Type: Article

Subject Terms:

*BROADCASTING

*SOCIAL problems

*TELEVISION broadcasting

*TELEVISION programs — Rating

*VIOLENCE

*TELEVISION programming

NAICS/Industry Codes:

334220 Radio and Television Broadcasting and Wireless Communications Equipment Manufacturing

515120 Television Broadcasting

541910 Marketing Research and Public Opinion Polling

Abstract: An analysis of 9 week-long samples of prime-time network programming broadcast between the fall of 1997 and the fall of 2003 found that more than 8 out of 10 ***programs*** were labeled with an age-based rating (TV-G, TV-PG, TV-14, or TV-MA), whereas fewer than 4 in 10 ***programs*** were also labeled with content-based ratings (V, S, L, or D). Although ***programs*** with age- and content-based ratings accurately reflected sexual and violent content, a sizable number of ***programs*** without content-based ratings also had sexual and violent content. Ratings provide parents with incomplete information on which to base viewing decisions. [*ABSTRACT FROM AUTHOR*]

Author Affiliations: [1]Department of Communication, University of Delaware

ISSN: 1520-5436

DOI: 10.1207/s15327825mcs0804_1

Accession Number: 18449412

Persistent link to the record:
http://voyager.lib.csubak.edu:2048/login?url=http://search.epnet.com/login.aspx?direct=true&db=afh&an=18449412&loginpage=login.asp&site=ehost

Database: Academic Search Elite

From a Full-Text Index
Entry 17 of 72 (from Omni Full Text Mega)

Title: "Are the Current Media Rating Systems Effective?"

Personal Author: Miller, Patti

Journal Name: *Congressional Digest*

Source: *Congressional Digest* v. 84 no. 2 (February 2005) p. 57,59

Publication Year: 2005

ISSN: 0010-5899

Language of Document: English

Abstract: Part of an issue on indecency in the media. In testimony delivered before the Senate Commerce Subcommittee on Science, Technology, and Space during the September 28, 2004, hearings on entertainment media rating systems, Patti Miller, director of Children Now's Children and the Media Program, argues against current ratings systems. She notes that a recent Harvard University School of Public Health study revealed that there has been a substantial increase in violence, sex, and profanity over the last decade, suggesting that the age-based movie ratings are increasingly lenient. She also outlines recommendations from Children Now that should be implemented in order to ensure that current ratings systems are effective in assisting parents.

Subject(s): Motion pictures/Rating; Television programs/Content ratings; Mass media/Content ratings; Video games/Rating of content; Children Now (Organization)

Documentation Type: Feature Article

Database: Readers' Guide (Current Events); Social Science

Accession Number: 200503203738018

From an Electronic Journal Collection
First hit from JSTOR

100% **Television Violence and Socialization Theory**

Patricia M. Edgar; Donald E. Edgar

The Public Opinion Quarterly > Vol. 35, No. 4 (Winter, 1971), pp. 608-612
Stable URL: http://links.jstor.org/sici?sici=0033-362X%28197124%2F197224%2935%3A4%3C608%3ATVAST%3E2.0.CO%3B2-9
Article Information | Page of First Match | Print | Download | Save Citation]

Notice that these examples contain all of the information you need for citing those works in the text and at the end of your paper. So make sure you keep lists like this when you print them so that you can cite your sources correctly.

PRACTICE 1 For each of the following topics, find a book from an online database, an article from a full-text journal, and an article from an electronic journal source. Record the title and the database, index, or source where you found it.

Example: Topic: television programs and violence
Database: EBSCOhost
Title: "Must-Bleed TV"
Index: Social Science Index in WilsonWeb
Title: "How the Media Compound Urban Problems"
Electronic Journal: Omni Full Text Mega
Title: "Cable Relents on Channels for the Family"

1. Topic: Drug testing in college sports

   Database: *Answers will vary.*

   Title: *Answers will vary.*

   Index: *Answers will vary.*

   Title: *Answers will vary.*

   Electronic Journal: *Answers will vary.*

   Title: *Answers will vary.*

2. Topic: Affirmative action and the workforce

   Database: *Answers will vary.*

   Title: *Answers will vary.*

   Index: *Answers will vary.*

   Title: *Answers will vary.*

   Electronic Journal: *Answers will vary.*

   Title: *Answers will vary.*

3. Topic: Prison pampering

   Database: *Answers will vary.*

   Title: *Answers will vary.*

   Index: *Answers will vary.*

   Title: *Answers will vary.*

   Electronic Journal: *Answers will vary.*

   Title: *Answers will vary.*

4. Topic: Women in combat

   Database: *Answers will vary.*

   Title: *Answers will vary.*

   Index: *Answers will vary.*

   Title: *Answers will vary.*

   Electronic Journal: *Answers will vary.*

   Title: *Answers will vary.*

5. Topic: Using animals for testing

   Database: *Answers will vary.*

   Title: *Answers will vary.*

   Index: *Answers will vary.*

   Title: *Answers will vary.*

   Electronic Journal: *Answers will vary.*

   Title: *Answers will vary.*

SEARCHING FOR WEB SITES

To find a Web site related to your topic, you should go to the Internet through whichever browser you have (Netscape Communicator or Navigator, Microsoft Internet Explorer, etc.). Your browser probably has a search engine of its own, which will let you search the Internet. Or you might want to use a search engine that automatically refers you to sites related to your topic: Both www.dogpile.com and www.google.com are examples of search engines that can save you a lot of time. For example, www.google.com searches nearly 1.5 million Web sites in mere seconds and is an excellent source for research.

Once you access a search engine, type in your topic as if you were searching a database. Most search engines will then begin helping you narrow your search and will provide a list of other possible topics. Here are some examples for the topic of Violence and Television.

Topic	**Other Possible Topics**
Violence and television	Television programs and violence
	On TV violence
	Television violence
	TV violence children
	Violence on television
	Causes of TV violence
	Media violence

When the search is complete, your search engine will list the different Web sites in the order it thinks they will be most helpful to you. It will also briefly describe each Web site. After the description, you will most often find the Web site address. The following are the first three "hits" or Web sites from www.dogpile.com for the topic *violence and television*.

1. National Coalition on TV Violence

   Learn about the effects of TV violence and facts about the V-Chip, and get ideas to help kids avoid violent entertainment.

   www.nctvv.org

2. American Psych. Association—Violence on Television

   Association investigates the effect of television violence on children and discusses ways parents can intervene to minimize its impact.

   www.apa.org

3. APA HelpCenter: Warning Signs of Teen Violence

   The American Psychological Association and MTV team up to get important information to the nation's youth about warning signs of violent behavior, including violence in schools. The Warning Signs site provides a violence prevention guide and resource.

   helping.apa.org

PRACTICE 2 For each of the following topics, find a different Web page through a different search engine, and list the Web page title, the explanation, and the Web address.

Example: Topic: television programs and violence

Search engine: google.com

Web page title: "Violence on TV: The Desensitizing of America"

Explanation: Extensive viewing of television violence by children causes greater aggressiveness. Sometimes, watching a single violent program can increase aggressiveness . . .

Web address: www.ridgenet.org/szaflik/tvrating.htm

1. Topic: Bilingual education in California

   Search engine: *Answers will vary.* ________________

   Web page title: *Answers will vary.* ________________

Explanation: *Answers will vary.* ____________________

____

Web address: *Answers will vary.* ____________________

2. Topic: Benefits of the U.S. space program

   Search engine: *Answers will vary.* ____________________

   Web page title: *Answers will vary.* ____________________

   Explanation: *Answers will vary.* ____________________

   ____

   Web address: *Answers will vary.* ____________________

3. Topic: Legalizing marijuana

   Search engine: *Answers will vary.* ____________________

   Web page title: *Answers will vary.* ____________________

   Explanation: *Answers will vary.* ____________________

   ____

   Web address: *Answers will vary.* ____________________

4. Topic: Homeopathic medicine

   Search engine: *Answers will vary.* ____________________

   Web page title: *Answers will vary.* ____________________

   Explanation: *Answers will vary.* ____________________

   ____

   Web address: *Answers will vary.* ____________________

5. Topic: Women's soccer

Search engine: *Answers will vary.*

Web page title: *Answers will vary.*

Explanation: *Answers will vary.*

Web address: *Answers will vary.*

USING THE LIBRARY

Once you have compiled a list of books and journals from databases and indexes or from Web sites, you should use your library to check out books or copy journal articles that were not available online. First, you need to access your library's online catalog to see if your library has the book. (If your library does not have computers, use the traditional card catalog.) Ask a librarian how to access your particular catalog through your school. You might also ask if this information is available online. You can search for authors and subjects through your library's catalog in much the same way that you would search online databases or program search engines. But since you have already done the preliminary research, all you have to do is search for the books and journals you need. Find the "title" section of the catalog, and type in the title of the book or journal you need in this section. For help finding books and journals in your college library, ask a librarian.

If you are searching for a chapter or an essay contained in a book, be sure to type in the main book title. For example, if you searched for "I Just Wanna Be Average" (by Mike Rose), your library computer will tell you that the library does not carry it. You must type in the title of the book it came from, *Lives on the Boundary*, to find the essay. Once you have located the titles of your books or journals in the library's catalog, you should write down the call numbers so you can find the sources in your library. Then it's just a matter of finding the book itself in the stacks.

PRACTICE 3 Find five books from research you have done or are currently doing, and, using the "title" portion of your library's catalog, locate the call numbers.

Example: **Title:** *Youth Culture: Identity in a Postmodern World*

Call number: HV 1431 Y684 1998

1. Title: Answers will vary.

   Call number: Answers will vary.

2. Title: Answers will vary.

   Call number: Answers will vary.

3. Title: Answers will vary.

   Call number: Answers will vary.

4. Title: Answers will vary.

   Call number: Answers will vary.

5. Title: Answers will vary.

   Call number: Answers will vary.

CHAPTER 20

Writing a Research Paper

A research paper is really just an essay with supporting material that comes from outside sources. This type of writing assignment has all the elements of a typical essay. The following chart compares a standard essay and a research paper.

Standard Essay		Research Paper
Introduction with thesis statement	⟷	Introduction with thesis statement
Body paragraphs with facts and personal experience to support thesis statement	⟷	Body paragraphs with documented evidence to support thesis statement
Concluding paragraph	⟷	Concluding paragraph

Keep this outline in mind as you read how to construct a good research paper. Laying out some clear guidelines is the best place to start.

1. **Choose a subject.** You might be choosing a subject from infinite possibilities or working with an assigned topic. Doing some general reading online or in the library is often necessary to get you started. As you consider various topics, you should ask one very important question before you begin planning your essay: Will you be able to find enough information to back up your thesis statement? To make sure you are able to find enough material to use as good evidence in the body paragraphs of your essay, you must do a good job of choosing a subject, narrowing that subject, and then writing a working thesis statement. You will prove this thesis statement with the information you find when you search for sources on your topic. If you were writing a research paper on pursuing a degree in college, for example, your initial prewriting for the thesis statement might look like this:

TEACHING WRITING A RESEARCH PAPER
Divide students into 11 groups, and have each group present one of the 11 guidelines from this chapter through pantomime or pictures. See if the other students can guess which guideline each group is representing.

TEACHING ON THE WEB
Research: Have students find other student essays with sources online. Have them evaluate the effectiveness of the papers using the guidelines from this chapter. Do certain Web sites provide better model essays than others? Why do students think this is the case?

INSTRUCTOR'S RESOURCE MANUAL
For additional material about teaching how to write a research paper, for journal entries, and for various tests, see the *Instructor's Resource Manual,* Section II, Part III.

General Subject: College and university degrees
More Specific: Bachelor's degree
More Specific: Bachelor's degree in English

This limited subject would be perfect for a research paper. You could search for books, catalogs, and periodicals on what it takes to earn a bachelor's degree in English from various colleges and universities. While you are looking, you could be thinking about how to narrow your subject even further.

Mary Minor (in Chapter 17) might have started with a general topic like "childhood disorders," limited it to "childhood behavioral disorders," and finally settled on "ADD and ADHD as childhood behavioral disorders."

PRACTICE 1 Choose a topic from the list on page 445. Why did you choose this topic?

PRACTICE 2 Limit this topic so that you can write a paper about five pages long.

2. **Write a good, clear thesis statement about your subject.** Just as a thesis statement is the controlling idea of an essay, a thesis statement also provides the controlling idea for your argument in a research paper. This statement will guide the writing of your entire paper. Your assignments throughout college will usually be broad topics. To compose a good research paper, you need to narrow a broad topic to an idea that you can prove within a limited number of pages. A working thesis statement will provide the direction for your essay, and the evidence you collect in your research is what proves the thesis statement.

   A good way to start your first draft is to read some general sources on your topic. This reading will help you discover the range of your subject and will guide you toward a thesis. Before you start writing the first draft of your paper, make sure you write a sentence that clearly states your topic and your position on that topic. This is your working thesis statement and will be the controlling idea for your entire paper. Your thesis may change several times before your essay is finished, but making this statement and taking a position is a necessary first step. It will help you move from the broad subject of your assignment to your own perspective on the topic. This will also help you focus your essay and save you time in your search for good resources to back up your thesis statement.

   Just as in a standard essay, the thesis statement in your research paper is a contract between you and your readers. The thesis statement tells your readers what the main idea of your essay will be and sets guidelines for the paragraphs in the body of your essay. If you don't deliver what your thesis statement promises, your readers will be disappointed. The thesis statement is usually the last sentence in the introduction. It outlines your purpose and position on the essay's general topic and gives your readers an idea of the type of resources you will use to develop your essay.

Mary Minor's controlling idea or thesis statement appears at the end of her first paragraph:

> Children are often misdiagnosed with ADD or ADHD and suffer unnecessarily when medicated for a disorder they may not have.

Her entire essay is about children who are too readily diagnosed with ADD or ADHD simply because they do not fall into society's "norm" for children's behavior. The paragraphs following this thesis statement supply evidence that proves her claim is true.

PRACTICE 3 List your thoughts and opinions on the topic you chose in Practice 1.

PRACTICE 4 Put your topic and your position on that topic into a working thesis statement.

3. **Find sources that are relevant, reliable, and recent to support your thesis statement.** The thesis statement of a research paper is really only the beginning of the process. To convince your readers that what you say in your essay is worth reading, you must support your thesis statement with evidence. The evidence of a term paper lies in the sources that you use to back up your thesis statement. The sources must be relevant, reliable, and recent. This "three *R*s" approach to supporting evidence in a research paper will help you write a solid essay with convincing evidence.

   Mary Minor's thesis statement suggests that young children are being too readily diagnosed with ADD and ADHD. To convince her readers that her thesis is correct, she uses a book, scientific journals, an encyclopedia, online journal articles, and general-circulation magazines as sources of evidence. Here is a breakdown of how she used her sources.

   - **Book:** *The Myth of the ADD Child*

     This source provides well-researched information from an expert's point of view. Mary uses this source early in her paper to help define the scope of her study.

- **Scientific journals:** *CQ Researcher, Science News, Qualitative Health Research, American Journal of Public Health*

  These sources supply the reader with specific evidence put forth by experts in the field of ADD and ADHD research and diagnosis. Mary uses this information to prove that her thesis statement is true.

- **Encyclopedia:** *World Book Encyclopedia*

  Mary uses this source to provide the reader with an understandable definition of the Hippocratic Oath. This definition plays an important role in Mary's stance on her topic.

- **Online journal articles:** *Clinical Reference Systems*

  The article from this source was printed from WilsonWeb. The information in this article defines hyperactivity in children for the general reader.

- **General-circulation magazines:** *U.S. News and World Report, Camping Magazine, Time, Runner's World, Maclean's*

  These sources supply information readily available at a newsstand, yet highly informative and applicable to Mary's topic. Information from articles in these magazines speaks to the average citizen. Even though these magazines are not scientific journals, the evidence in them is extremely useful because it was intended to make specialized information understandable to the general reader.

Mary Minor uses sources in her essay that do a thorough job of supporting her thesis statement. Information from articles in these books, journals, and magazines speaks to the average citizen. Even though they are not highly technical scientific sources, the evidence in them is relevant, reliable, and recent.

PRACTICE 5 Review Chapter 19 to make sure that you understand the options available to you for finding sources to use in your essay.

PRACTICE 6 Find five sources that give you information about the limited topic that you chose. Make sure they are relevant, reliable, and recent.

4. **Take notes to avoid plagiarism.** Now is the time to read your sources and take careful notes—putting the ideas in your own words or putting the writer's words in quotation marks if you record the exact words. You should also note the page numbers of all information you take down. If you don't take notes carefully, you will never be able to trace information that you want to use in your paper to its original source. Also, trying to put someone's ideas into your own words at the notetaking stage is a very good skill that will help you as you write.

Taking notes on notecards allows you to move your cards around and put ideas into different paragraphs. When you rearrange cards, you can work with them until you think the order will support what you are trying to prove. This notecard method actually saves time in the long run.

Mary Minor had to read and take notes on all the sources she found. She first made a set of bibliography cards with a notecard for every source she found. For the books, she put book title, author or editor, city where published, publisher, and year of publication on each card; for the articles, she recorded article title, author, title of the magazine or journal, date of issue or volume and issue numbers, and page numbers on each card. Then she began to read her sources. She wrote only one idea or quotation on a notecard, and she remembered to record on each notecard the author's name and the page number on which she found the information. She also made sure, as she took notes, to restate information in her own words or else put the author's exact words in quotation marks.

PRACTICE 7 Review Chapter 18 to make sure you understand what plagiarism is and how to avoid it.

PRACTICE 8 Read and take notes on your sources using notecards. Make sure each of your cards has a source and page number on it.

5. **Make a working outline of your paper.** To do this, you just need to start rearranging the notecards you have made. Start by putting all your notecards into small stacks of related ideas. Which ideas might work well together? Which should you put in the introduction? Which do you want to save for your conclusion? When you get all your notecards in stacks, label each group of cards according to its topic. These labels will then become the topics of your paper. You are now ready to start your working outline.

   A good way to begin an outline is to write your tentative thesis statement at the top of a page and then list under that thesis the topics you have developed. These topics should be arranged in some logical order that will help you prove your main point and is easy to follow. Each topic should also directly support your thesis statement. Leave room in your outline to add subtopics and details throughout the paper. This outline then becomes a guide for your writing. It will change and grow with every paragraph that you add to your paper.

   Mary started developing her paper by putting related notecards into stacks. Next, she labeled her stacks of notecards and then organized these topics in different ways until they started making sense to her. Her list of topics, with her thesis statement at the top, became her working outline. She eventually turned these topics into topic sentences for her body paragraphs. The stack of cards for each topic became the content of her body paragraphs.

PRACTICE 9 Divide your notecards into topics that logically support your thesis statement. Then label each stack of cards.

PRACTICE 10 Start a working outline of your paper by listing your thesis statement and your supporting topics.

6. **Construct an introduction that leads up to your thesis statement.** The introduction to a research paper is your chance to make a great first impression. Just like a firm handshake and a warm smile in a job interview, an essay's introduction should capture your readers' interest, set the tone for your essay, and state your specific purpose. Introductions often have a funnel effect. They typically begin with general information and then narrow the focus to your position on a particular issue. Regardless of your method, your introduction should "hook" your readers by grabbing their attention and letting them know what you are going to try to prove in your essay.

   To lead up to the thesis statement, your introductory paragraph should stimulate your readers' interest. Some effective ways of capturing your audience's attention and giving necessary background information are (1) to use a quotation; (2) to tell a story that relates to your topic; (3) to provide a revealing fact, statistic, or definition; (4) to offer an interesting comparison; or (5) to ask an intriguing question. Be sure your introduction gives readers all the information they will need to follow your logic through the rest of your paper.

   Mary's introduction starts out with a hypothetical situation that parents face as their children may or may not develop "normally." The paragraph then discusses parents' confusion with their children's behavior and introduces ADD and ADHD. The last sentence of the first paragraph contains Mary's thesis statement and ends the introduction.

PRACTICE 11 Make a rough outline of your ideas for a possible introduction to your research paper.

PRACTICE 12 Write a rough draft of your introduction, ending with your thesis statement.

7. **Develop as many supporting paragraphs or body paragraphs as you think are necessary to explain your thesis statement.** Following the introductory paragraph, a research paper includes several body paragraphs

that support and explain the essay's thesis statement. Each body paragraph covers a topic that is directly related to the thesis statement.

Supporting paragraphs, or body paragraphs, usually include a topic sentence, which is a general statement of the paragraph's contents, and examples or details that support the topic sentence. (See Chapter 6 for methods to use when you develop and organize paragraphs.)

To write your supporting paragraphs, you should first organize your notecards within each of your stacks. Next, add these details to your working outline. Then write your supporting paragraphs by following your working outline and your notecards. Make adjustments in your outline as you write so that you can keep track of your ideas and make sure you are developing them in a logical fashion. The body of the paper and your outline should change and develop together with each sentence that you write.

After you write your body paragraphs, look at your thesis statement again to make sure it introduces what you say in the rest of your paper. Your thesis statement should refer to all of your topics, even if only indirectly, in the order you discuss them. It should also prepare your readers for the conclusions you are going to draw.

Mary's paper contains eight body paragraphs, each making a separate point that is directly related to her thesis:

Paragraph	**Point**
2	ADD and ADHD are defined as "a short attention span" and are the most commonly diagnosed childhood diseases.
3	Diagnosing children who do not fit a "norm" is ludicrous, especially since there is no accurate definition or diagnosis of ADD or ADHD.
4	No physical exam can determine if a child has ADD or ADHD.
5	There are as many theories about the causes of ADD as there are experts, so we are only treating the symptoms of these disorders.
6	Teachers, parents, and students get caught up in the diagnosis.

7	Drugs should only be a short-term answer to the hyperactive child.
8	No proof is available that says we overprescribe drugs for American children.
9	Long-term use of drugs for ADD and ADHD is potentially dangerous.

Like the foundation of a solid building, these paragraphs provide support for the position Mary takes in her thesis statement. The stronger the supporting paragraphs are, the stronger the paper will be.

In addition to strong topic sentences, you should also use concluding sentences in your body paragraphs to help reinforce your thesis statement or build a transition to the next paragraph. Concluding sentences bring a paragraph to a close just like a conclusion brings an essay to a close, and well-crafted concluding sentences also focus your readers on the highlights of your argument.

PRACTICE 13 Organize the notecards within each of your stacks so that they make sense. Add these details to your working outline.

PRACTICE 14 Write a rough draft of your body paragraphs. Remember that you will be revising and editing this draft a little later, so just concentrate on getting your ideas written up in an organized way. Revise your thesis statement, if necessary, to introduce all your body paragraphs.

8. **Make sure you use your sources as evidence for your argument.** Although your argument will evolve as you read your sources, you should decide on your general position before you begin to take notes. Be sure to find appropriate sources that help you develop your argument. The best way to do this is to tell your reader the significance of the direct quotations, paraphrases, or summaries that you use. Look, for example, at one of the paragraphs in Mary's paper:

> Despite major controversy in the medical field, however, there has been no proof that drugs are being overprescribed for American children. Some experts even feel that children may be under-treated (Breggin 11–20). While some studies have concluded that children are overmedicated, others insist the opposite, which again means that each child is treated according to the most popular opinion. Many fear that children are being overdiagnosed due to the subjectivity of the

> diagnostic test. In fact, Nicholas Cummings, author of "Expanding a Shrinking Economic Base," explains, "When the APA revised the criteria in the DSM-IV-R for diagnosing ADD/ADHD, the number of children who qualified literally quadrupled" (93). Unfortunately, some populations are diagnosed more frequently than others. Fifteen to twenty percent of school-age boys are medicated with a stimulant (Breggin 3). With a statistic as drastic as this, it is astonishing that experts disagree on this subject.

Notice how Mary does not stop with her source's remarks. Instead, she includes a point about the significance of what each source says. She reminds her readers that she is arguing against drugging young children unnecessarily.

If you simply provide a series of quotations and let them argue for you, you are not demonstrating your understanding of the quotations or showing how they fit into your argument. Make sure to use the quotations as support for your argument and not let them serve as the argument itself.

PRACTICE 15 Consider the different ways your sources will support your own argument. Then organize them in a manner that best helps you prove your main point.

PRACTICE 16 Write your body paragraphs using your sources as evidence in your argument. Be careful not to choose sources haphazardly to include in your body paragraphs. You need to have a reason for using each of your sources.

9. **Write a concluding paragraph.** The concluding paragraph is the final paragraph of an essay. In its most basic form, it should summarize the main points of the essay and remind readers of the thesis statement.

   The best conclusions expand on these two basic requirements and bring the essay to a close with one of these creative strategies: (1) Ask a question that provokes thought on the part of the reader, (2) predict the future, (3) offer a solution to a problem, or (4) call the reader to action. Each of these options sends a specific message and creates a slightly different effect at the end of the paper. The most important responsibility of the last paragraph is to bring the essay to an effective close. It is the last information that readers see before they form their own opinions or take action.

Mary's conclusion offers a solution to the problem raised in the second sentence of the paragraph:

> Every effort should be made to find the cause of the real medical problems underlying ADD and ADHD before we even think about giving our children drugs.

Toward the end of her conclusion, she calls the reader to action:

> It is time to say good-bye to conformist American classrooms and diagnoses.

She ends by reflecting on her thesis in one last, short line:

> Perhaps some people don't fit the norm because they have personalities.

Her concluding paragraph refocuses the reader's attention on the problem, offers a solution, and then calls the reader to action.

PRACTICE 17 Make a rough outline of your ideas for a possible conclusion to your research paper. Choose a strategy that will effectively bring your paper to a close.

PRACTICE 18 Write a rough draft of your conclusion, reminding your readers of your thesis statement.

10. **Think of a catchy title.** Your title is what readers see first in any paper. A title is a phrase, usually no more than a few words, placed at the beginning of your essay that suggests or sums up the subject, purpose, or focus of the essay. Some titles are very imaginative, drawing on different sources for their meaning. Others are straightforward, like the title of this chapter—"Writing a Research Paper." Besides suggesting an essay's purpose, a good title catches an audience's attention.

    Mary Minor's title, "Children as Robots," will catch most readers' attention because referring to children as "robots" is intriguing, and readers will want to find out just how and why this might occur. That's exactly what a title should do—make your readers want to read your paper.

PRACTICE 19 Jot down some catchy titles for your paper.

PRACTICE 20 Choose a title for your paper.

11. **Check your sources and documentation format throughout your paper and at the end.** Finding and using good, solid sources for evidence in a research paper is essential, and equally important is the acknowledgment of those sources. If you use a source and do not cite it correctly

or forget to cite it, you are guilty of plagiarism, which can lead to a failing grade on the paper. So you need to learn when to cite a source (see Chapter 19), what documentation style to use (MLA, APA, or other appropriate format), and how to cite sources. You should check with your instructor to find out which format you should use in a particular course.

The two types of citations support each other: (a) The *in-text citation* indicates the source of a quotation or idea right after it appears in the essay; (b) then, at the end, a list of all the sources cited in the paper must appear on the *Works Cited* or *Reference* page. Many textbooks demonstrate the various forms of documentation, so you should look up the format that your instructor wants you to use. Then keep this text handy when you write papers with sources.

Mary uses the MLA format on her paper, which she wrote for an English class. Usually, English instructors ask their students to use MLA. Mary includes a variety of sources in her paper, which we can use to illustrate the two types of citations. Listed here are some sample in-text citations, with the corresponding entries at the end of Mary's paper.

Book—name of author, title of book, city of publication, publisher, date of publication

In-Text Citation: (914)
Works Cited: Armstrong, Thomas. *The Myth of the ADD Child: 50 Ways to Improve Your Child's Behavior and Attention Span Without Drugs, Labels, or Coercion*. New York: Dutton, 1995.

Note: Notice how Mary introduced Armstrong before providing readers with this page number so she doesn't have to repeat the author's name in the citation.

Journal—name of author, title of article, name of journal, volume number, year, page number

In-Text Citation: (166)
Works Cited: Rappley, Marsha. "Attention Deficit Hyperactivity Disorder." *The New England Journal of Medicine* 352.2 (2005): 165–173.

Encyclopedia—name of author, title of article, name of encyclopedia, volume number, year

In-Text Citation: ("Hippocratic Oath")
Works Cited: "Hippocratic Oath." *World Book Encyclopedia*. Vol. 9. 1999 ed.

Note: If the author is not given, begin with the title of the article.

Online Database—name of author, title of article, name of database, date of publication, date you accessed the material, URL in angle brackets

In-Text Citation: (Vatz and Weinberg, par. 22)
Works Cited: Vatz, Richard E., and Lee S. Weinberg. "Problems in Diagnosing and Treating ADD/ADHD." *USA Today* 129.2670 (Mar. 2001): 64–65. WilsonWeb. California State U Bakersfield Lib., Bakersfield, CA. 5 Feb. 2006 <http://vnweb. hwwilsonweb.com>.

Note: If some information required in the citation is missing, include whatever is available.

General-Circulation Magazine—name of author, title of article, name of magazine, date of publication, page numbers

In-Text Citation: (Higdon 84)
Works Cited: Higdon, Hal. "Getting Their Attention." *Runner's World* July 1999: 84–87.

Note: If the author is not given, begin with the title of the article.

These examples from Mary's essay are just a few of the various types of sources that you will probably use in your term papers. Every source is cited in a slightly different way, depending on the type of source and the documentation style. Not even the best writers know the correct format for every source they use. So when you have chosen your sources and determined that they are relevant, reliable, and recent (the three *R*s), your last step is to consult an appropriate, current manual or Web site to make sure you cite each source correctly.

PRACTICE 21 Make sure that the material from every source in your essay has an in-text citation. Then create a list of sources at the end of your paper in an approved documentation format (see Chapter 21).

PRACTICE 22 Check the format of your in-text citations and your list of works cited by consulting a current handbook.

CHAPTER 21

Documenting Sources

As you have already learned in this part of the text, you must document each source you use in your research paper with two types of citations that support each other: an in-text citation and an end-of-paper citation. Both kinds of citations are important, and both follow very strict guidelines based on the documentation style you use.

TEACHING DOCUMENTING SOURCES

Bring to class several types of sources, such as anthologies, newspapers, journal articles, translations, etc. In each of the sources, mark a passage for students to either directly quote or paraphrase. (Choose passage lengths depending on whether you will have students paraphrase or directly quote.) Provide students a handout that leads them through an exercise that has them find the source, present an introduction, and provide an in-text citation and an end-of-paper citation. For example, your handout may look like the following; sources are in brackets at the beginning of each entry:

For each of the items below, create an in-text citation (following the directions given) and an end-of-text citation (Works Cited [MLA], References [APA], or Bibliography [CM]).

INTRODUCING YOUR SOURCES

Once you evaluate your sources and figure out which ones will help you establish your argument, you then need to learn how to seamlessly integrate them into your paper. In other words, you need to introduce them effectively while showing readers they are credible and offer valuable evidence to back up your argument. Integrating your sources into your argument will help your readers understand the kind of information you are using. You also must show them you are using evidence based in fact and you are using credible sources.

When you use a source for the first time, always (1) introduce the author(s) using the full name(s), (2) give the title of the source (use quotes for works inside larger works and italics or underlining for books), and (3) quote or paraphrase the information you need to build your argument. Here are some examples of good introductions of Roger Flax's "Don't Be Cruel."

1. Dr. Roger Flax in "Don't Be Cruel" argues that positive criticism can motivate rather than humiliate.
2. Positive criticism, asserts Dr. Roger Flax in "Don't Be Cruel," can motivate rather than humiliate.
3. According to Dr. Roger Flax in "Don't Be Cruel," positive criticism can motivate rather than humiliate.
4. Positive criticism can motivate rather than humiliate, explains Dr. Roger Flax in "Don't Be Cruel."

1. [Article in a Monthly Journal] Find one of the sources published monthly. Go to the marked page, and quote the highlighted information using the name of the person who gave the quote. (*Hint:* A quote within a quote is called an indirect source.)

2. [Harry Potter book] Next, find a novel by one author. (*Hint:* Think Magic.) Again, find the marked page, and quote the highlighted material. (Remember to introduce all quotations.)

3. [Movie with Tom Hanks] Seek and you will find Tom's Soul (*Hint:* Think *Forrest Gump* and *Sleepless in Seattle*). Now suspend reality for a moment, and imagine that you want to include a quote from one of his movies in your paper. (You can make up this quote, based upon the information given to you about the movie.) You want to use this quote as a catchy way to interest your readers in your paper.

4. [Chart in a book] Your quest has now led you to search for a more visual source, like a chart in a book. Introduce the information designated by the highlight.

5. [Dante's *Inferno*] Behold the lyrical path through hell (*Hint:* This has nothing to do

5. In "Don't Be Cruel," Dr. Roger Flax points out that positive criticism can motivate rather than humiliate.
6. Dr. Roger Flax demonstrates in his essay "Don't Be Cruel" how positive criticism can motivate rather than humiliate.
7. Dr. Roger Flax strongly recommends in his essay "Don't Be Cruel" that we use positive criticism to motivate others rather than negative criticism, which only humiliates and degrades.

These model sentences are only a few options for introducing Flax's ideas; you can probably think of many more. Notice how all of these examples use the word *Dr.* so that readers understand he is an authority on his subject. Also, the main words in the titles are capitalized, and commas and end punctuation—when used with quotations—go inside the quotation marks. Next, the verbs in these examples are active choices that each express a slightly different meaning. Finally, you would refer to the author by last name only—"According to Flax"—the next time you use the source and mention the author.

DOCUMENTATION FORMAT

In many cases throughout your college career, the documentation style you use will be determined by your instructor. Documentation requirements vary according to your field of study. As mentioned previously, three of the major documentation styles are Modern Language Association (MLA), used in humanities courses; American Psychological Association (APA), used in social science courses; and *Chicago Manual* (CM), used in mathematics and science classes. Because you may have to write different papers using all of these documentation styles, you should have a basic understanding of their differences.

In-Text Citations

The major difference among in-text citations for MLA, APA, and CM is that MLA and APA use parenthetical references while CM uses a footnote/endnote system. Look at the differences in the following sentences:

MLA: According to James S. Travano, a noted child psychologist, "When middle school children are exposed to sex education in their health courses, the likelihood of them becoming sexually active before the age of 14 decreases by 12%" (27).

APA: According to J. S. Travano, a noted child psychologist, "When middle school children are exposed to sex education in their health courses, the likelihood of them becoming sexually active before the age of 14 decreases by 12%" (2006, p. 27).

CM: According to James S. Travano, a noted child psychologist, "When middle school children are exposed to sex education in their health courses, the likelihood of them becoming sexually active before the age of 14 decreases by 12%."[1]

Although the information is slightly varied, MLA and APA furnish the page number for the source (APA with a "p." and MLA without a "p"). APA also includes the year the article was written. For CM, a reader would find the publication information (including the page number of the source) in a footnote/endnote.

On the other hand, certain in-text features are similar in all three documentation styles:

- You should include citation information directly after every quotation.
- You should include citation information after you have finished paraphrasing a source. (This could extend to more than one sentence.)
- Punctuation follows the parenthetical citation, not the quotation.
- Longer quotes are indented in block form to one inch and do not require quotation marks.
- Blocked quotes are double spaced in the same size font as the paper.

End-of-Paper Citations

One of the most obvious differences among MLA, APA, and CM is how they list their sources at the end of the paper: MLA includes a "Works Cited" page; APA lists "References"; and CM has a "Bibliography." Some general differences exist among these three lists of sources. Works Cited and References pages list only those sources that you actually cite in your paper. These sources are listed alphabetically. Your in-text citations will work with your references page in that the in-text citations tell the readers the name and page number of the source you are using, and the Works Cited/References pages provide for readers the full bibliographic information.

A Bibliography lists every source you looked at while researching your paper. Documentation styles that include a Bibliography use a separate page for notes to show which of the sources in the Bibliography you actually cited in your paper. Pages for notes use a numbering system that corresponds to a number in the body of the paper.

Writers using a Bibliography have the advantage of showing their readers all the sources they read for the paper, even if they took no material directly from a source.

with an erupting volcano). Quote the highlighted passage in the form it would take on a page. This is a translation. (*Hint*: No free-standing quotes, and remember about block quotations.)

6. [City's newspaper] Forage through the forest of prose for the source that bears this city's namesake. Summarize the highlighted information as if you had previously introduced your source, relying solely on a parenthetical citation.

7. [*Time* or *Newsweek*] Finally, your journey is almost complete, but first, you must find a weekly source. Summarize the highlighted material as if this is the first time the source is used.

Bonus: Numerically identify the order in which these sources should appear on your Works Cited/References/Bibliograpy page. Remember, these pages should be arranged alphabetically.

TEACHING ON THE WEB

Research: Provide your students with a few sources, and have them learn to document sources using MLA, APA, and CMS online. Have them find in-text citation information as well as Works Cited, References, and

Endnotes/Bibliography citations.

MLA: www.mla.org

APA: www.apa.org

CMS: www.chicagomanualofstyle.org

INSTRUCTOR'S RESOURCE MANUAL
For additional material about documenting sources, for journal entries, and for various tests, see the *Instructor's Resource Manual*, Section II, Part III.

Regardless of which documentation style you use, the source lists at the end of the paper are all formatted the same:

- The title is centered, and the title is in regular font. In other words, the title is not bolded, underlined, put in quotation marks, or italicized (unless you include another title in your own title).
- The page numbers are continuous from the body of the paper.
- The entries are all double spaced.
- The entries all use a hanging indent (which can be accessed either through the "Paragraph" feature under "Format" or by manipulating the hour glass on the ruler). *Note:* Some documentation styles prefer paragraph indenting.
- The entries are all alphabetized. *Note:* You do not rearrange authors' names in a single entry so that they appear alphabetical. Leave the order as it appears on your source.

Regardless of the documentation style, the in-text citations, end-of-paper sources, and footnotes/endnotes (if applicable) all work together to help readers know all the bibliographic information about the source you are using.

MLA Versus APA

Because MLA and APA are the most popular documentation styles, you should know the major differences between the two. The logic behind both documentation styles is very similar, but subtle differences exist in form.

In-Text Citations

MLA	APA
• Author's full names are used.	• Author's last name and first initial are used.
• Dates don't necessarily have to be mentioned.	• Dates must follow either the author's name in the sentence or in the parentheses following the sentence.
• A parenthetical citation includes author's last name and a page number: (Turner 49).	• A parenthetical citation includes author's last name, date, and a page number: (Turner, 2005, p. 49).

Works Cited/References Page Notice the differences in the following citation. MLA and APA both require the same information, but just in a different order.

> **MLA:**
> Ames, Carole, and Jennifer Archer. "Achievement Goals in the Classroom: Students' Learning Strategies and Motivation Processes." *Journal of Educational Psychology* 80.3 (1988): 260–267.
>
> **APA:**
> Ames, C., & Archer, J. (1988). Achievement goals in the classroom: Students' learning strategies and motivation processes. *Journal of Educational Psychology*, 80 (3), 260–267.

For more on the differences between MLA and APA (as well as the other documentation styles), consult a research handbook.

USING A HANDBOOK

In order to learn how to cite sources properly, you need to know how to navigate a research handbook. Handbooks provide information on both in-text and end-of-paper citations. After writing a few research papers, you'll become quite adept at introducing your sources and using in-text citations, but you will never remember how to cite one kind of source from another. Therefore, knowing how to navigate a handbook is important to documenting your sources properly. Once you understand the logic of citing, you should be able to use the handbook quite easily.

Look at the following source for a Works Cited:

> Ames, Carole, and Jennifer Archer. "Achievement Goals in the Classroom: Students' Learning Strategies and Motivation Processes." *Journal of Educational Psychology* 80.3 (1988): 260–267.

In order to put this entry together, you need to look at two different source examples: (1) How to Cite Two or More Authors and (2) How to Cite an Article in a Journal. If this source were found online, you would also need to include the URL information and possibly the retrieval date you found the article. Sometimes, you'll need to look at three or four different source examples in order to piece together one entry on your Works Cited or other reference page. The point here is that you can't expect to find a listing for every single source you have. If you have a journal article with two authors, handbooks typically only list how to cite that information when they show how to cite a book with two authors. The handbook authors expect that you will figure out that citing a journal article with two authors is exactly the same as citing a book with two authors. So when you use a handbook and cannot figure out how to do something, chances are the answer is in there somewhere; you just have to find it and piece together a citation using the logic of other entries. Once you understand how to use the Documentation Styles sections of a handbook, you'll always be able to figure out how to properly cite sources.

If you have difficulty understanding the logic of your handbook or cannot figure out how to cite a specific source, you might want to consider a trip to your campus's tutoring center so they can show you how it works. And, of course, you can always ask your instructor.

SOME FINAL TIPS

et al.

If you use a source that has four or more authors (MLA) or three or more authors (APA), you are allowed to shorten the citation. Let's say you are using MLA and have a source with the following authors: Valerie Turner, Rebecca Hewett, Jan Titus, and Heather Morgan. The first time you mention these authors, you must provide all of their names, but instead of constantly saying throughout your paper, "Turner, Hewett, Titus, and Morgan assert that . . . ," you can shorten it by saying, "Turner et al. assert . . ." The "et al." means "and others." A trap many students fall into is thinking the "al." is singular, when it actually means "others," so be sure to treat this as a plural noun when you use it.

.pdf versus html

Given the opportunity, always download electronic research as a .pdf file. A .pdf file is like a snapshot of the original printed version, so it retains any formatting, including pictures. More importantly, though, a .pdf file retains original page numbers. If you have the original page numbers, you can cite your source using those page numbers. If you don't have page numbers, you have to use paragraph numbers in your citations.

CHAPTER 22

Revising and Editing a Research Paper

In this chapter, you will revise and edit a new student term paper and then revise and edit your own paper. The checklists for this process are provided within the chapter, which guides you through this process step by step.

REVISING AND EDITING A STUDENT'S RESEARCH PAPER

Here is the first draft of an essay written by Rick Schroeder, a student. It demonstrates the guidelines for writing a successful essay with sources that you have learned in Chapters 17 through 21.

Space Bucks

Every year an enormous amount of money is poured into NASA for space exploration. Does this research justify the expense? Many people would gratefully sacrifice the money just to prove that Americans can compete in the space arena. An overwhelming force drives us into the unknown realms of our universe in the same way that Christopher Columbus was adventurously driven to search for what was once called the New World. On the other hand, many tax-payers believe that more justification is needed for the large amount of money put into NASA research. But what these "non-supporters" tend to overlook is NASA's chance "to lead the exploration and development of the space frontier, advancing science, technology, enterprise, and building institutions and systems that make accessible vast new resources" (United States). NASA is a worthwhile organization that many people benefit from. 1

TEACHING HOW TO REVISE AND EDIT A RESEARCH PAPER

Divide students into groups of three or four. Using the guidelines from Chapter 20, have students evaluate Rick Schroeder's term paper. Does it follow every guideline? What places in the paper need work? Once students have evaluated the paper based on the guidelines, have them apply the revising and editing checklists to the paper while they keep their evaluations close at hand.

TEACHING ON THE WEB

Research: Have students go online to find credible sources on nuclear testing that might work well in Rick's paper. How difficult or easy is it to find sources for this topic? How difficult would it be to incorporate these new sources into the essay? What is the predominant belief about this issue, based on the evidence students find on the Web?

INSTRUCTOR'S RESOURCE MANUAL
For additional material about teaching students to revise and edit their research papers, for journal entries, and for various tests, see the *Instructor's Resource Manual,* Section II, Part III.

2 Most significantly, technology research that results from space exploration greatly benefit the field of medicine. The International Space Station (ISS), which was built by 16 different nations, is one of the biggest and most costly projects that NASA has constructed and is essential for research in space technology. Scientists aboard the ISS have the opportunity to test various theories and conduct experiments in several different fields of science using the microgravity on this station in space (NASA *Space Station*). Some of the most important research that will be done onboard the ISS involves searching for cures for both osteoporosis and cancer (Von Brook, Siegel, and Foster 67). Also, according to Von Brook, Siegel, and Foster, the authors of *Space Exploration: The Dream and the Reality,* some additional examples of "space-pioneer medical technology include a cardiac pacemaker that can be automatically recharged without surgery, a human tissue simulator that relieves chronic pain, anti-contamination hospital garments, x-rays that can penetrate bone and produce pictures of body tissues and organs," and several other advances in autism, diabetes, heart disease, and premature birth (69). These are just a few of the contributions from space exploration that help improve the quality of life for humanity on a day-to-day basis. Without NASA's research, scientists would never have discovered these contributions. Therefore, we must continue to fund NASA and all its programs.

3 The vast number of effective medicines, treatments, and machines used to test for and treat illnesses would be enough to warrant the space exploration funds if they were the only benefits to society from the NASA research. But another benefit of NASA's research is their ability to monitor the environment to ensure continued life on Earth. Since the ISS is a permanent structure that will observe the earth for the next 30 years, scientists will be able to monitor the earth and distinguish changes that have been made over time to its environment (Von Brook, Siegel, and Foster 67). These studies could lead to more breakthroughs and solutions for many environmental problems. For example, the balance between farming and water conservation will soon be made vastly more efficient due to advancements made by NASA using satellite imaging to dettermine watering priorities for irrigated farm lands (Rumsfeld 11). This information will help both the farmers and the general population—especially in a state like California where water rights are a volatile issue.

4 Not only can the space exploration program help solve environmental problems, but it can also identify those problems. In fact, the space program gave us "our first real perspective on global warming, ozone layer depletion, deforestation, and other environmental scourges" (Von Brook, Siegel, and

Foster 69). Yet not all environmental benefits are plans for the future. Von Brook, Siegel, and Foster state,

> we have already achieved very promising results with indoor air pollution and wastewater treatment using NASA technology. Today, NASA researchers are contributing steadily to our knowledge of landfill leachate treatment, hazardous waste disposal, tropical rainforest, and ground water pollution. (69)

Recently, astronauts aboard the space station spent ten days creating a topographic map of all locations on the world within 60 degrees of the equator. A topographic map of uniform scale circling the entire globe has never before been created, and NASA accomplished this feat in 10 days. This model of the earth can now be used to monitor changes on the earth's surface, providing a very useful tool humanity can use for many reasons, including fighting forest fires (Jet Propulsion Laboratory). The environment must be preserved, and since this task is made easier with the benefits of space exploration, we must continue to fund research for NASA.

5 Science, however, is not the only aspect of life that NASA affects, for it also greatly influences the economy. According to Von Brook, Siegel, and Foster, "Space exploration . . . is the best investment for our future because it sharpens the skills and harnesses the talents of all Americans involved" (70). Sharpening the talents of Americans is important, yet the real question at hand is the economics of space exploration. A single space shuttle costs, for example, from $10,000 to $20,000 per kilogram (Alpert 93). This is definitely a substantial amount of money to pay for a single launch. In 1975, NASA sponsored a study to design a space station it was never funded. A group of scientists created a plan for a circular station that would provide room for 10,000 colonists. The station would have cost $500 billion. However, the station would have paid for itself within 30 years because of enormous solar-power satellites that would be installed. A solar-energy-collection satellite would receive eight times as much energy as a collector on earth. The satellite would also produce five billion watts of electricity. Which is approximately five times that of an average power plant (Alpert 93–94). The economic benefits of this power are enormous considering the energy crises that tend to afflict parts of the United States.

6 Given the proper chance, much of space exploration could pay for itself. Von Brook, Siegel, and Foster claim that "the Apollo mission yielded a 7-to-1 return of every dollar invested" (70). This does not suggest enormous waste. As Rumsfeld speculates, "An international space industry has developed, with

revenues exceeding $80 billion in 2000. Industry forecasts project revenues will more than triple in the next decade" (11). Not only could a space project pay for itself, but the ISS will provide "50,000 jobs directly associated with spin-off technology," which "means greater national pride and fewer Americans that will require public support for basic needs like food and housing."

7 One major problem of NASA's budget, however, is the cuts it will cause for other programs. Unfortunately, NASA shares a budget with the Environmental Protection Agency (EPA), the Department of Housing and Urban Development (HUD), and the Veterans Administration (Von Brook, Siegel, and Foster 66). This means that budget cuts are mandatory for the other agencies if any one program requires more capital. Von Brook, Siegel, and Foster explain, "This puts some of the nation's most futuristic plans competing directly against some of America's most pressing social needs" (66). Nevertheless, Americans and humanity must look passed the present problems and see into the future for solutions. Social needs have plagued society for centuries. We have tried to throw money at these problems in the past, which has been ineffective, so new solutions must be sought. The answers can be found by looking beyond the problems that humanity faces today and into the future of space exploration.

8 NASA is an important and vital force in American society. As long as our desire to explore space continues to exist, advances and discoveries will follow. The benefits come not only in the form of space exploration, but also in medical, environmental, and economic advances that are necessary to the survival and progress of humanity. But NASA cannot continue to provide these major discoveries with a diminishing budget. In fact, NASA's 2002 budget allocation was less than the money it received in 1994 (NASA *FY 2003 Budget*). This budget desicion will affect all of American society for hundreds of years to come. An agency with the potential of NASA that has proven its usefulness time and time again should not be inadequately funded. It needs a generous budget that will let it continue to improve the quality of life for all Americans.

Works Cited

Alpert, Mark. "Making Money in Space." *The Future of Space Exploration.* 1 Jan. 1999: 92–95.

Jet Propulsion Laboratory. "Earth Has a New Look." *NASA News.* Jet Propulsion Laboratory, California Institute of Technology, Pasadena, California. News Release: 2003–116. August 22, 2003.

National Aeronautical and Space Agency (NASA). Chart: *FY 2003 Budget vs. History* and *Background Material NASA FY 2003 Budget Briefing.* 5 Sept. 2003 <http://www1.nasa.gov/audience/formedia features/MP_Budget_Previous.html>.

Space Station Benefits. 4 Oct. 2003 <http://spaceflight.nasa.gov/station/benefits/index.html>.

Rumsfeld, Donald H. (chairman). *Report of the Commission to Assess United States National Security Space Management and Organization.* Pursuant to Public Law 106–65. January 11, 2001. 28 Sept. 2003 <www.defenselink.mil/pubs/space20010111 .html>.

United States. The Report of the National Commission on Space. *Pioneering the Space Frontier.* Toronto: Bantam Books, 1986.

Von Brook, Patricia, Mark A. Siegel, and Carol D. Foster. *Space Exploration: The Dream and the Reality.* Eds. Patricia Von Brook, Mark A. Siegel, and Carol D. Foster. Wylie, Texas: Information Plus, 1990.

Rick's first draft now needs to be revised and edited. First, apply the following Revising Checklist to the content of Rick's draft. When you are satisfied that his ideas are fully developed and well organized, use the Editing Checklist on page 500 to correct his grammatical and mechanics errors. Do the tasks, and answer the questions after each checklist. Then write your suggested changes directly on Rick's draft.

REVISING CHECKLIST

THESIS STATEMENT

- ✔ Does the thesis statement contain the essay's controlling idea and an opinion about that idea?
- ✔ Does the thesis appear as the last sentence of the introduction?

BASIC ELEMENTS

- ✔ Does the title draw in the readers?
- ✔ Does the introduction capture the readers' attention and build up to the thesis statement effectively?
- ✔ Does each body paragraph deal with a single topic?
- ✔ Does the conclusion bring the essay to a close in an interesting way?

DEVELOPMENT

- ✔ Do the body paragraphs adequately support the thesis statement?
- ✔ Does each body paragraph have a focused topic sentence?
- ✔ Does each body paragraph contain *specific* details that support the topic sentence?
- ✔ Does each body paragraph include *enough* details to explain the topic sentence fully?
- ✔ Are the sources relevant, reliable, and recent?
- ✔ Are references given for original sources to avoid plagiarism?
- ✔ Is the documentation format correct—in the paper and at the end?

UNITY

- ✔ Do the essay's topic sentences relate directly to the thesis statement?
- ✔ Do the details in each body paragraph support its topic sentence?

ORGANIZATION

- ✔ Is the essay organized logically?
- ✔ Is each body paragraph organized logically?

COHERENCE

- ✔ Are transitions used effectively so that paragraphs move smoothly and logically from one to the next?
- ✔ Do the sentences move smoothly and logically from one to the next?

Revising

Thesis Statement

1. What is the main idea in Rick's research paper?

   NASA's space exploration budget is justified and should be funded.

2. Put brackets around Rick's thesis statement. Does it introduce his main point?

   No

3. Rewrite it to introduce all the topics in his essay.

   Here is one possibility: NASA's space exploration budget is justified; therefore, every effort should be made to fund NASA's programs.

Basic Elements

1. Give Rick's essay an alternate title.

   Answers will vary.

2. Rewrite Rick's introduction so that it captures the readers' attention in a different way and builds up to the thesis statement at the end of the paragraph.

   Answers will vary.

3. Does each of Rick's body paragraphs deal with only one topic?

   Yes

4. Rewrite Rick's conclusion with a twist of your own.

   Answers will vary.

Development

1. Do Rick's topic sentences support his thesis statement? Write out your revision of Rick's thesis statement, and list his six topic sentences.

   Thesis: *NASA's space exploration budget is justified; therefore, every effort should be made to fund NASA's programs.*

   Topics: *1. Most significantly, technology research that results from space exploration greatly benefits, the field of medicine.*

2. The vast number of effective medicines, treatments, and machines used to test for and treat illnesses would be enough to warrant the space exploration funds if they were the only benefits to society from the NASA research.

3. Not only can the space exploration program help solve environmental problems, but it can also identify those problems.

4. Science, however, is not the only aspect of life that NASA affects, for it also greatly influences the economy.

5. Given the proper chance, much of space exploration could pay for itself.

6. One major problem of NASA's budget, however, is the cuts it will cause for other programs.

2. Does your revised thesis statement accurately introduce Rick's topic sentences?

   Answers will vary.

3. Are Rick's examples specific?

   Yes

   Add an even more specific detail to one of his paragraphs.

4. Does he offer enough examples or details in each paragraph?

   Yes

For help, see Chapter 19.

5. Are Rick's sources relevant, reliable, and recent?

   Yes

For help, see Chapter 21.

6. Does he give references for all original sources in his paper?

   No

Find the one sentence in paragraph 6 that is plagiarized and needs the reference "(Von Brook, Sigel, and Foster 68)."

Sentence 6

7. Is the documentation format correct in his paper? For help, see Chapter 21.

Yes

8. Is the format on his Works Cited page correct? For help, see Chapter 21.

Yes

Unity

1. Read each of Rick's topic sentences with his thesis statement in mind. Do they go together?

Yes

2. Revise any topic sentences that are not directly related to his thesis. *Topic sentences are all related.*
3. Read each of Rick's paragraphs with its topic sentence in mind. Drop or rewrite any sentences that are not directly related to the paragraph's topic sentences. *All sentences are directly related to the paragraph's topic sentences.*

Organization

1. Review your list of Rick's topics in item 1 under "Development," and decide if they are organized logically. *They are logical.*
2. What is his method of organization?

From one extreme to another (most important to least important)

3. Read Rick's paper again to see if all his sentences are arranged logically.
4. Move any sentences that are out of order. *All sentences are in order.*

Coherence

1. Circle five transitions that Rick uses. For a list of transitions, see page 101.
2. Explain how three of these transitions make Rick's paper easier to read. *Answers will vary.*

Now rewrite Rick's paper with your revisions.

EDITING CHECKLIST

SENTENCES

- ✔ Does each sentence have a main subject and verb?
- ✔ Do all subjects and verbs agree?
- ✔ Do all pronouns agree with their nouns?
- ✔ Are modifiers as close as possible to the words they modify?

PUNCTUATION AND MECHANICS

- ✔ Are sentences punctuated correctly?
- ✔ Are words capitalized properly?

WORD CHOICE AND SPELLING

- ✔ Are words used correctly?
- ✔ Are words spelled correctly?

Editing

Sentences

Subjects and Verbs

For help with subjects and verbs, see Chapter 25.

1. Underline the subjects once and verbs twice in paragraph 5 of Rick's essay. Remember that sentences can have more than one subject-verb set.
2. Does each sentence have at least one subject and verb that can stand alone?

   No

For help with fragments, see Chapter 26.

For help with run-togethers, see Chapter 27.

3. Did you find and correct Rick's fragment in paragraph 5? If not, find and correct it now. *Sentence 12*
4. Did you find and correct Rick's run-together sentence in paragraph 5? If not, find and correct it now. *Sentence 6*

Subject-Verb Agreement

1. Read aloud the subjects and verbs in paragraph 2 of Rick's revised essay.
2. Correct any subjects and verbs that do not agree. *Sentence 1*

3. Now read aloud the subjects and verbs in the rest of his revised essay.
4. Correct any subjects and verbs that do not agree. *The rest of the subjects and verbs agree.*

For help with subject-verb agreement, see Chapter 30.

Pronoun Agreement

1. Find any pronouns in your revision of Rick's essay that do not agree with their nouns.
2. Correct any pronouns that do not agree with their nouns. *All pronouns agree with their nouns.*

For help with pronoun agreement, see Chapter 34.

Modifier Errors

1. Find any modifiers in your revision of Rick's essay that are not as close as possible to the words they modify. *There are no modifier errors.*
2. Rewrite sentences if necessary so that modifiers are as close as possible to the words they modify.

For help with modifier errors, see Chapter 37.

Punctuation and Mechanics

Punctuation

1. Read your revision of Rick's essay for any errors in punctuation.
2. Make sure any fragments and run-together sentences you revised are punctuated correctly. *There are no punctuation errors.*

For help with punctuation, see Chapters 38–42.

Mechanics

1. Read your revisions of Rick's essay for any errors in capitalization.
2. Be sure to check the capitalization in the fragments and run-together sentences you revised. *All capitals are correct.*

For help with capitalization, see Chapter 43.

Word Choice and Spelling

Confused Words

1. Find any words used incorrectly in your revision of Rick's essay.
2. Did you find and correct the confused word? *passed/past (para. 7)*

For help with confused words, see Chapter 49.

Spelling

1. Use spell-check and a dictionary to check the spelling in your revision of Rick's essay.
2. Did you find and correct his two misspelled words? *dettermine/determine (para. 3) and desicion/decision (para. 8)*

For help with spelling, see Chapter 50.

Now rewrite Rick's paper again with your editing corrections.

REVISING AND EDITING YOUR OWN RESEARCH PAPER

Now revise and edit the essay that you wrote in Chapter 20. The following questions will help you apply the Revising and Editing Checklists to your own writing.

Revising

Thesis Statement

1. What is the main idea of your research paper?

____

2. Put brackets around your thesis statement. Does it introduce your main idea?

____

3. How can you change it to introduce all the topics in your paper?

____

____

Basic Elements

1. Give your essay an alternative title.

____

2. Does your introduction capture the readers' attention and build up to the thesis statement at the end of the paragraph?

____

3. Does each of your body paragraphs deal with only one topic?

____

4. Does your conclusion bring the essay to a close in an interesting way?

____

TEACHING HOW TO REVISE AND EDIT YOUR OWN RESEARCH PAPER

Have students send an essay they wrote in your class to an online writing lab (OWL) for revising and editing feedback. Have students include a printout of the OWL's comments when they turn in their final draft of the essay, and have them reflect on the online tutorials by answering the following questions:

What was your most important learning experience from the OWL?

What was your least important learning experience from the OWL?

How can an OWL be beneficial with other papers you may be writing for other classes?

For a complete list of OWLs, go to iwca.syr.edu/iwca/iwcaowls.html. One of the best is owl.english.purdue.edu.

For further help with editing, consult www.prenhall.com/troyka

TEACHING ON THE WEB

Research: Have students find different ways the Internet can help them revise and edit their writing. Are certain Web sites more

Development

1. Do your topics support your thesis statement? List your revised thesis statement and your topics.

   Thesis: ______________________________

   Topics: ______________________________

   ____

   ____

2. Are your examples specific? Add another more specific detail to at least one of your paragraphs.
3. Do you furnish enough examples or details in each paragraph? Add at least one new example or detail to one of your paragraphs.
4. Check your sources to make sure they are relevant, reliable, and recent. Find new sources if necessary. For help, see Chapter 19.
5. Do you give references for all original sources in your paper to avoid plagiarism? For help, see Chapter 21.
6. Is the documentation format correct in your paper? For help, see Chapter 21.
7. Is the format on your Works Cited page correct? For help, see Chapter 21.

helpful than others? How are the sites different?

INSTRUCTOR'S RESOURCE MANUAL
For additional material about teaching revising and editing research papers, for journal entries, and for various tests, see the *Instructor's Resource Manual*, Section II, Part III.

Unity

1. Read each of your topic sentences with your thesis statement in mind. Do they go together?

   ____

2. Revise your topic sentences so that they are directly related.
3. Read each of your paragraphs with its topic sentence in mind.
4. Drop or rewrite any sentences in your body paragraphs not directly related to their topic sentences.

Organization

1. Review the list of your topics in item 1 under "Development," and decide if your topics are organized logically.

2. What is your method of organization?

____

3. Do you think your method of organization is the most effective one for your purpose? Explain your answer.

____

____

4. Read your essay again to see if all your sentences are arranged logically.
5. Move any sentences that are out of order.

Coherence

For a list of transitions, see page 101.

For a list of pronouns, see pages 7–8.

1. Circle five transitions, repetitions, synonyms, or pronouns you use.
2. Explain how two of these make your essay easier to read.

____

____

Now rewrite your paper with your revisions.

Editing

Sentences

Subjects and Verbs

For help with subjects and verbs, see Chapter 25.

1. In a paragraph of your choice, underline your subjects once and verbs twice. Remember that sentences can have more than one subject-verb set.
2. Does each sentence have at least one subject and verb that can stand alone?

____

For help with fragments, see Chapter 26.

For help with run-togethers, see Chapter 27.

3. Correct any fragments you have written.
4. Correct any run-together sentences you have written.

Subject-Verb Agreement

For help with subject-verb agreement, see Chapter 30.

1. Read aloud the subjects and verbs you underlined in your revised essay.
2. Correct any subjects and verbs that do not agree.

Pronoun Agreement

1. Find any pronouns in your revised essay that do not agree with their nouns.
2. Correct any pronouns that do not agree with their nouns.

For help with pronoun agreement, see Chapter 34.

Modifier Errors

1. Find any modifiers in your revised essay that are not as close as possible to the words they modify.
2. Rewrite sentences if necessary so that your modifiers are as close as possible to the words they modify.

For help with modifier errors, see Chapter 37.

Punctuation and Mechanics

Punctuation

1. Read your revised essay for any errors in punctuation.
2. Make sure any fragments and run-together sentences you revised are punctuated correctly.

For help with punctuation, see Chapters 38–42.

Mechanics

1. Read your revised essay for any errors in capitalization.
2. Be sure to check your capitalization if you revised any fragments or run-together sentences.

For help with capitalization, see Chapter 43.

Word Choice and Spelling

Confused Words

1. Find any words used incorrectly in your revised essay.
2. Correct any errors you find.

For help with confused words, see Chapter 49.

Spelling

1. Use spell-check and a dictionary to check your spelling.
2. Correct any misspelled words.

For help with spelling, see Chapter 50.

Now rewrite your paper again with your editing corrections.

CHAPTER 23

Writing Workshop

TEACHING IDEAS FOR WRITING

The following eight writing projects are based on Howard Gardner's multiple intelligences:

Theme: Media

Verbal/Linguistic

Research the changes in the alcohol ads over the past five years. How have they changed? Are they more or less effective now? Write an essay explaining these changes.

Musical/Rhythmic

Research a controversial fine arts issue of your choice. Use various forms of the media to help you get ideas for this assignment. Then take a firm stand on the issue, and develop an essay supporting your position.

Logical/Mathematical

Research a special activity in which you want to participate. Get all the facts, including costs, time, and supplies needed. Then write a letter to your parents or guardians

WRITING A RESEARCH PAPER

This chapter will serve as a review of Part III as it also gives you some guided practice in writing research papers. First, it provides a summary of the guidelines for writing a term paper and then furnishes you with some new research topics. The rest of the chapter is devoted to the processes of revising and editing.

Guidelines for Writing a Research Paper

1. Choose a subject.
2. Do some general reading, and write a good, clear thesis statement about your subject.
3. Find sources that are relevant, reliable, and recent to support your thesis statement.
4. Take notes to avoid plagiarism.
5. Make a working outline of your paper.
6. Construct an introduction that leads up to your thesis statement.
7. Develop as many supporting paragraphs or body paragraphs as you think are necessary to explain your thesis statement.
8. Make sure you use your sources as evidence for your argument.
9. Write a concluding paragraph.
10. Think of a catchy title.
11. Check your sources and documentation format throughout your paper and at the end.

1. Research the changes in the antidrug ads over the past five years. How have they changed? Are they more or less effective now? Write an essay explaining these changes.

2. Research a controversial political issue of your choice. Then take a firm stand on the issue, and develop an essay supporting your position. You might want to look at headlines in the newspaper to get some ideas for this assignment.
3. Research a special trip that you want to take. Get all the information you need. Then write a letter to a close friend, inviting him or her to join you.
4. Create your own assignment (with the help of your instructor), and write a response to it.

REVISING WORKSHOP

Small Group Activity (5–10 minutes per writer) In groups of three or four, read your research papers to each other. The listeners should record their reactions on a copy of the Peer Evaluation Form in Appendix 3A. After your group goes through this process, give your evaluation forms to the appropriate writers so that each writer has two or three peer comment sheets for revising.

Paired Activity (5 minutes per writer) Using the completed Peer Evaluation Forms, work in pairs to decide what you should revise in your essay. If time allows, rewrite some of your sentences, and have your partner check them.

Individual Activity Rewrite your paper, using the revising feedback you received from other students.

EDITING WORKSHOP

Paired Activity (5–10 minutes per writer) Swap papers with a classmate, and use the editing portion of your Peer Evaluation Forms to identify as many grammar, punctuation, mechanics, and spelling errors as you can. Mark the errors on the student paper with the correction symbols on the inside back cover. If time allows, correct some of your errors, and have your partner check them.

Individual Activity Rewrite your paper again, using the editing feedback you received from other students. Record your grammar errors in the Error Log (Appendix 6) and your spelling errors in the Spelling Log (Appendix 7).

asking them to pay for or support this activity in some way. Try to convince them to see the event from your perspective.

Visual/Spatial

Draw a picture of an issue you would like to research. Then list the types of sources you would consult. Write an essay explaining your research plan.

Bodily/Kinesthetic

Produce a short scene from a play, TV show, or movie. Use costumes, create a small set, and choose music and lighting. If possible, videotape the performance. How hard was it to put the production together? Write an essay about the process you went through to produce this show.

Intrapersonal

Go to a children's play in your city, and watch children discover different aspects of the theater. Write an essay describing your observations.

Interpersonal

Keep a journal about the different TV shows you watch, music you listen to, or movies you see. When do you watch or listen to certain shows or songs? Does the way you want to be entertained change with your moods? Write an essay based on your journal entries that explains your reaction to these different media.

Naturalist

Go to an outdoor production of a play or concert. How is a play that is performed outdoors different from a play that is presented indoors? What limitations, if any, do outdoor performers have to overcome? Write an essay discussing the benefits or disadvantages of going to an outdoor performance of a play.

REFLECTING ON YOUR WRITING

When you have completed your own essay, answer these six questions:

1. What was most difficult about this assignment?
2. What was easiest?
3. What did you learn about research papers by completing this assignment?
4. What do you think are the strengths of your paper? Place a wavy line in the margin by the parts of your essay that you feel are very good.
5. What are the weaknesses, if any, of your paper? Place an X in the margin by the parts of your essay you would like help with. Write any questions you have in the margin.
6. What did you learn from this assignment about your own writing process—about preparing to write, about writing the first draft, about revising, and about editing?

The Handbook

This part of *Mosaics* provides you with a complete handbook for editing your writing. You can use it as a reference tool as you write or as a source of instruction and practice in areas where you need work. This Handbook consists of an introduction and eight units:

INTRODUCTION
- Chapter 24: Parts of Speech, Phrases, Clauses

UNIT 1: SENTENCES
- Chapter 25: Subjects and Verbs
- Chapter 26: Fragments
- Chapter 27: Fused Sentences and Comma Splices

UNIT 2: VERBS
- Chapter 28: Regular and Irregular Verbs
- Chapter 29: Verb Tense
- Chapter 30: Subject-Verb Agreement
- Chapter 31: More on Verbs

UNIT 3: PRONOUNS
- Chapter 32: Pronoun Problems
- Chapter 33: Pronoun Reference and Point of View
- Chapter 34: Pronoun Agreement

UNIT 4: MODIFIERS
- Chapter 35: Adjectives
- Chapter 36: Adverbs
- Chapter 37: Modifier Errors

UNIT 5: PUNCTUATION
- Chapter 38: End Punctuation
- Chapter 39: Commas
- Chapter 40: Apostrophes
- Chapter 41: Quotation Marks
- Chapter 42: Other Punctuation Marks

UNIT 6: MECHANICS
- Chapter 43: Capitalization
- Chapter 44: Abbreviations and Numbers

UNIT 7: EFFECTIVE SENTENCES
- Chapter 45: Varying Sentence Structure
- Chapter 46: Parallelism
- Chapter 47: Combining Sentences

UNIT 8: CHOOSING THE RIGHT WORD
- Chapter 48: Standard and Nonstandard English
- Chapter 49: Easily Confused Words
- Chapter 50: Spelling

UNIT TESTS

The chapters in each unit start with a **self-test** to help you identify your strengths and weaknesses in that area. Then the chapters teach specific sentence skills and provide exercises so you can practice what you have learned. You will really know this material when you can use it in your own writing. So each chapter ends with an exercise that asks you to **write your own sentences** and then work with another student to **edit each other's writing.**

The **Editing Symbols** on the inside back cover will give you marks for highlighting errors in your papers. In addition, the Error Log (Appendix 6) and Spelling Log (Appendix 7) will help you tailor the instruction to your own needs and keep track of your progress.

At the end of the handbook are **Unit Tests** that you can take to see if you have mastered the combined skills in each unit. The first test helps you establish your EQ or Editing Quotient, showing you which errors you already recognize in the Handbook. Then two pretests for each unit are provided that ask you to apply what you have learned in that unit. The first test is made up of separate, numbered sentences so you can concentrate on individual skills; the second asks you to apply your knowledge to an entire paragraph as you would in your own writing and in peer evaluation exercises. Two similar posttests for each unit are furnished after the complete set of pretests.

CHAPTER 24

Introduction: Parts of Speech, Phrases, and Clauses

This handbook uses very little terminology. But sometimes talking about the language and the way it works is difficult without a shared understanding of certain basic grammar terms. For that reason, your instructor may ask you to study parts of this introduction to review basic grammar—parts of speech, phrases, and clauses. You might also use this introduction for reference. This section has three parts: Parts of Speech, Phrases, and Clauses.

PARTS OF SPEECH

TEST YOURSELF

In the following paragraph, label the parts of speech listed here:

4 verbs (v)	2 adverbs (adv)
4 nouns (n)	2 prepositions (prep)
2 pronouns (pro)	2 conjunctions (conj)
2 adjectives (adj)	2 interjections (int)

Professional basketball is definitely this nation's best spectator sport. The talented players move around the court so quickly that the audience never has a chance to become bored. Boy, I'll never forget that Saturday night last February when my favorite uncle took me to see the Spurs game against the Trailblazers. It was an important home game for San Antonio, so the arena was packed. The Spurs were behind throughout most of the game, but they pulled through and won with a three-pointer in the last few seconds. Wow! I have never seen so many people on their feet, screaming at the top of their lungs.

(Answers are in Appendix 4.)

TEACHING PARTS OF SPEECH

Play a game of Memory (Concentration) by creating two identical batches of words on index cards. For instance, have two cards for each of the following words: *walk, house, you, red, never, during, can't,* and *Hey!* Make sure you have many sets of words representing each part of speech. Shuffle the cards, and number the back of each card, starting with 1.

Line your wall with butcher paper, and attach a piece of removable tape to the front of each index card (so that each can be removed and placed back into position many times). Place the index cards, word side down, on the paper in the order of their number. For instance, 1–10 in the first row, 11–20 in the second row, and so on.

Have students form teams of three or four and try to find the matching words. When a team uncovers two words that match, it must identify the part of speech before getting credit for the match. Otherwise, the pair goes back onto the board for another team to uncover and label.

The team that accumulates the most cards wins.

INSTRUCTOR'S RESOURCE MANUAL

For more sample words, for more exercises, and for quizzes, see the *Instructor's Resource Manual,* Section II, Part IV.

Every sentence is made up of a variety of words that play different roles. Each word, like each part of a coordinated outfit, serves a distinct function. These functions fall into eight categories:

1. Verbs
2. Nouns
3. Pronouns
4. Adjectives
5. Adverbs
6. Prepositions
7. Conjunctions
8. Interjections

Some words, such as *is,* can function in only one way—in this case, as a verb. Other words, however, can serve as different parts of speech depending on how they are used in a sentence. For example, look at the different ways the word *show* can be used:

Verb: The artists **show** their work at a gallery.
(*Show* is a verb here, telling what the artists do.)

Noun: The **show** will start in 10 minutes.
(*Show* functions as a noun here, telling what will start in 10 minutes.)

Adjective: The little boy loves to sing **show** tunes.
(*Show* is an adjective here, modifying the noun *tunes.*)

Verbs

The **verb** is the most important word in a sentence because every other word depends on it in some way. Verbs tell what's going on in a sentence.

There are three types of verbs: action, linking, and helping. An **action verb** tells what someone or something is doing. A **linking verb** tells what someone or something is, feels, or looks like. Sometimes an action or linking verb has **helping verbs**—words that add information, such as when an action is taking place. A **complete verb** consists of an action or linking verb and all the helping verbs.

Action: The girl **wandered** too far from the campsite.

Action: Luca **ran** to the bus stop.

Linking: He **looks** very tired.

Linking: It **was** a real surprise to see you.

Helping: My aunt and uncle **will be** arriving tomorrow.

Helping: My grandmother **has** been very ill lately.

Complete Verb: My aunt and uncle **will be arriving** tomorrow.

Complete Verb: My grandmother **has been** very ill lately.

PRACTICE 1: Identifying In each of the following sentences, underline the complete verbs. Some sentences have more than one verb.

1. I read *Moby Dick* for my literature class.
2. The best place for inexpensive fast food is Taco Bell.
3. You seem tired.
4. I wonder if Chad was going to be attending.
5. The teenager climbed to the top of the mountain before he stopped for lunch.

PRACTICE 2: Completing Fill in each blank in the following paragraph with a verb. *Answers will vary.*

This year my sister (1) ______________ to get married. She and her fiancé (2) ______________ in Dallas, Texas, so I had to buy a plane ticket from Los Angeles. First, I tried the computer and (3) ______________ all of the Web sites that people talk about, but I couldn't find any good deals. Finally, I (4) ______________ a travel agent and asked her to tell me what my best options were. The best deal she (5) ______________ was $280 round-trip, so I charged it to a credit card. I guess my sister is worth it.

PRACTICE 3: Writing Your Own Write a sentence of your own for each of the following verbs. *Answers will vary.*

1. was sitting ____
2. handled ____
3. seems ____
4. had been taking ____
5. buy ____

Nouns

People often think of **nouns** as "naming words" because they identify—or name—people (*student*, *Susan*, *mom*, *server*), places (*city*, *ocean*, *Thomasville*), or things (*bush*, *airplane*, *chair*, *shirt*). Nouns also name ideas (*liberty*, *justice*), qualities (*bravery*, *patience*), emotions (*sadness*, *happiness*), and actions (*challenge*, *compromise*). A **common noun** names something general (*singer*, *hill*, *water*, *theater*). A **proper noun** names something specific (*Nicole Kidman*, *Angel Falls*, *Coke*, *McDonald's*).

Hint: To test whether a word is a noun, try putting *a*, *an*, or *the* in front of it:

Nouns:	a squirrel, an orange, the hope
NOT Nouns:	a funny, an over, the eat

This test does not work with proper nouns:

NOT	a Natalie, the New York

PRACTICE 4: Identifying Underline all the nouns in the following sentences.

1. The Golden Gate Bridge is a popular tourist attraction in San Francisco.
2. Collectors will spend much money on limited-edition coins.
3. My son is wearing my favorite shirt.
4. In October, we are planning a trip to Seattle.
5. *Emeril Live* was voted the most popular TV cooking show.

PRACTICE 5: Completing Fill in each blank in the following paragraph with a noun that will make each sentence complete. *Answers will vary.*

Last May, I joined a volunteer organization called (1) ______________. Within a month, the secretary left, and I was nominated to take his place. I had to put all of the (2) ______________ about the organization and its members into my computer and then create a mail merge. With this database, I was able to make labels and (3) ______________ very easily. My first assignment was to create a form letter and send it to all of the (4) ______________ who promised to send money to the group. I finally saw the (5) ______________ of all the grammar lessons I had in my English classes, and I learned that writing good letters is harder than I thought.

PRACTICE 6: Writing Your Own Write a sentence of your own for each of the following nouns. *Answers will vary.*

1. pastor ______________________________
2. Sea World ______________________________
3. strength ______________________________
4. audience ______________________________
5. actions ______________________________

Pronouns

Pronouns can do anything nouns can do. In fact, **pronouns** can take the place of nouns. Without pronouns, you would find yourself repeating nouns and producing boring sentences. Compare the following sentences, for example:

> **George** drove **George's** car very fast to **George's** house because **George** had to get home early.
>
> **George** drove **his** car very fast to **his** house because **he** had to get home early.

There are many different types of pronouns, but you only need to focus on the following four types for now.

Most Common Pronouns

Personal (refer to people or things)

Singular:	*First person:*	*I, me, my, mine*
	Second person:	*you, your, yours*
	Third person:	*he, she, it, him, her, hers, his, its*
Plural:	*First person:*	*we, us, our, ours*
	Second person:	*you, your, yours*
	Third person:	*they, them, their, theirs*

Demonstrative (point out someone or something)

Singular:	*this, that*
Plural:	*these, those*

Relative (introduce a dependent clause)

who, whom, whose, which, that

Indefinite (refer to someone or something general, not specific)

Singular:	*another, anybody, anyone, anything, each, either, everybody, everyone, everything, little, much, neither, nobody, none, no one, nothing, one, other, somebody, someone, something*
Plural:	*both, few, many, others, several*
Either Singular or Plural:	*all, any, more, most, some*

Hint: When any of these words are used with nouns, they are pronouns used as adjectives.

Adjective: He can have **some candy.**
Pronoun: He can have **some.**
Adjective: The baby wants **that toy.**
Pronoun: The baby wants **that.**

PRACTICE 7: Identifying Underline all the pronouns in the following sentences. Don't underline words that look like pronouns but are really adjectives.

1. Some of the wedding guests were vegetarians.
2. Those are the biggest shoes I have ever seen.
3. Somebody had better admit to this.
4. After his car was stolen, everything else seemed to go wrong for him too.
5. Does anyone else need anything while I'm up?

PRACTICE 8: Completing In the following paragraph, replace the nouns in parentheses with pronouns.

Mike first tried rollerblading when (1) ___he___ (Mike) was 19. It was pretty funny to watch (2) ___him___ (Mike) buy the shin guards and wrist guards, put (3) ___them___ (the shin guards and wrist guards) on, and then roll down the sidewalk out of control. (4) ___His___ (Mike's) two best friends, Carl and Luis, wanted to learn also, but when they saw the hard time Mike was having, (5) ___they___ (Carl and Luis) were too afraid.

PRACTICE 9: Writing Your Own Write a sentence of your own for each of the following pronouns. *Answers will vary.*

1. anyone ______________________________
2. these ______________________________
3. who ______________________________
4. many ______________________________
5. our ______________________________

Adjectives

Adjectives modify—or describe—nouns or pronouns. Adjectives generally make sentences clear and vivid.

> **Without Adjectives:** She brought an umbrella, a towel, and an iPod to the beach.
>
> **With Adjectives:** She brought a **bright orange** umbrella, a **striped blue** towel, and a **new** iPod to the beach.

PRACTICE 10: Identifying Underline all the adjectives in the following sentences.

1. His long black goatee was formed into two sharp points.
2. The talented musicians gave a two-hour concert for an excited audience.
3. Grisham's best-selling novel, *Runaway Jury*, is about a strange man and his intelligent girlfriend.
4. Getting a good parking place is sometimes impossible.
5. Matthew signed his name using a smooth ballpoint pen.

PRACTICE 11: Completing Fill in each blank in the following paragraph with an adjective. *Answers will vary.*

> My girlfriend and I went to a (1) ______________ baseball game at the Anaheim Stadium last weekend. The Angels were playing the Texas Rangers, and the Rangers were much more (2) ______________. This year, the Rangers have (3) ______________ infielders, and their batters are pretty (4) ______________ also. Overall, the teams were unequally matched, and it was (5) ______________ that one of them was going to lose pretty badly.

PRACTICE 12: Writing Your Own Write a sentence of your own for each of the following adjectives. *Answers will vary.*

1. gorgeous____
2. dark ____
3. tempting ____
4. thrifty ____
5. sixth ____

Adverbs

Adverbs modify—or describe—adjectives, verbs, and other adverbs. They do *not* modify nouns. Adverbs also answer the following questions:

How?	thoughtfully, kindly, briefly, quietly
When?	soon, tomorrow, late, now
Where?	inside, somewhere, everywhere, there
How often?	daily, always, annually, rarely
To what extent?	generally, specifically, exactly, very

Hint: Notice that adverbs often end in *-ly*. That might help you recognize them.

PRACTICE 13: Identifying Underline all the adverbs in the following sentences.

1. He almost passed Stephanie when he was running aimlessly down the hall.
2. That was the very last time George Clooney was on television.
3. It was quite disappointing to lose after nearly six months of training.
4. Are you absolutely sure that you remembered to set the alarm?
5. I try to buy groceries weekly so that we are never missing the basic necessities.

PRACTICE 14: Completing Fill in each blank in the following paragraph with an adverb. *Answers will vary.*

When Shanika (1) ______________ lost her job at the grocery store, she felt desperate. She (2) ______________ began calling her friends and relatives, asking if they knew of any job openings. (3) ______________ for Shanika, her Aunt Betsy owned a hair salon that needed a receptionist. Shanika didn't know anything about beauty parlors, but she (4) ______________ agreed to work there because she needed the money. After only three weeks, Shanika became very interested in the salon, and she (5) ______________ decided to take classes at a local beauty college and earn a license in cosmetology.

PRACTICE 15: Writing Your Own Write a sentence of your own for each of the following adverbs. *Answers will vary.*

1. sometimes ____
2. hardly ____
3. gently ____
4. too ____
5. tomorrow ____

Prepositions

Prepositions indicate relationships among the ideas in a sentence. Something is *at, in, by, next to, behind, around, near,* or *under* something else. A preposition is always followed by a noun or a pronoun called the **object of the preposition.** Together, they form a **prepositional phrase.**

Preposition	+	**Object**	=	**Prepositional Phrase**
near	+	the beach	=	near the beach
for	+	the party	=	for the party

Here is a list of some common prepositions.

Common Prepositions

about	*beside*	*into*	*since*
above	*between*	*like*	*through*
across	*beyond*	*near*	*throughout*
after	*by*	*next to*	*to*
against	*despite*	*of*	*toward*
among	*down*	*off*	*under*
around	*during*	*on*	*until*
as	*except*	*on top of*	*up*
at	*for*	*out*	*upon*
before	*from*	*out of*	*up to*
behind	*in*	*outside*	*with*
below	*in front of*	*over*	*within*
beneath	*inside*	*past*	*without*

Hint: *To* + a verb (as in *to go, to come, to feel*) is not a prepositional phrase. It is a verb phrase, which we will deal with later in this chapter.

PRACTICE 16: Identifying Underline all the prepositions in the following sentences.

1. When I stepped off the bus, I looked down the street and saw an old man in a white hat.
2. The cabin is over the big hill, past the creek, and down a winding dirt path.
3. If you go to Maui, stay in Kaanapali at a resort hotel beside the ocean.
4. The paper in my printer is jammed, so the light on the top won't stop blinking.
5. After the party, I found confetti in my hair, on the carpet, behind the sofa, and in all four corners of the room.

PRACTICE 17: Completing Fill in each blank in the following paragraph with a preposition. *Answers will vary.*

I was so surprised when I saw Carlos walking (1) ______________ campus toward me. The last time we talked was eight months ago, when he was still living (2) ______________ Kendra. He decided to take some time (3) ______________ work to finish his degree, and he was hoping to have it completed (4) ______________ the next year. I was very proud (5) ______________ him for setting these priorities.

PRACTICE 18: Writing Your Own Write a sentence of your own for each of the following prepositions. *Answers will vary.*

1. with ____
2. beside ____
3. on top of ____
4. until ____
5. against ____

Conjunctions

Conjunctions connect groups of words. Without conjunctions, most of our writing would be choppy and boring. The two types of conjunctions are easy to remember because their names state their purpose: *Coordinating conjunctions* link equal ideas, and *subordinating conjunctions* make one idea subordinate to—or dependent on—another.

Coordinating conjunctions connect parts of a sentence that are of equal importance or weight. These parts can be **independent clauses,** a group of words with a subject and verb that can stand alone as a sentence (see page 526). There are only seven coordinating conjunctions:

Coordinating Conjunctions

and, but, or, nor, for, so, yet

Coordinating:	*Johanna* ***and*** *Melvin arrived late.*
Coordinating:	*My sister wanted to go shopping* ***and*** *I jogging.*
Coordinating:	*The teacher was very demanding,* ***but*** *I learned a lot from him.*

Subordinating conjunctions join two ideas by making one dependent on the other. The idea introduced by the subordinating conjunction becomes a **dependent clause,** a group of words with a subject and a verb that cannot stand alone as a sentence (see page 526). The other part of the sentence is an independent clause.

Subordinating: I won't leave **until** he comes home. (Dependent Clause: until he comes home)

Subordinating: **Unless** you study more, you won't be accepted to college. (Dependent Clause: Unless you study more)

Common Subordinating Conjunctions

after	*because*	*since*	*until*
although	*before*	*so*	*when*
as	*even if*	*so that*	*whenever*
as if	*even though*	*than*	*where*
as long as	*how*	*that*	*wherever*
as soon as	*if*	*though*	*whether*
as though	*in order that*	*unless*	*while*

PRACTICE 19: Identifying Underline all the conjunctions in the following sentences.

1. My best personality trait is my sense of humor, but people also say that I'm a good listener.
2. The homecoming game was a lot of fun, yet I didn't see anyone I knew.
3. While the other people were touring the city, Thomas stayed in the hotel room and took a nap.
4. Carmen will be in our study group as long as we meet at her house.
5. Shane volunteered to take us to the airport even though his car seats only four people.

PRACTICE 20: Completing Fill in each blank in the following paragraph with a conjunction. *Answers will vary.*

Babysitting is definitely not an easy job, (1) ______________ it is a fast way to make money. One couple I babysit for has two children, and (2) ______________ one of them is a perfect angel, the other one is constantly getting into trouble. Michael is the troublemaker, (3) ______________ he is 6 years old. (4) ______________ I arrive at his house, he runs to his room and begins pulling everything off of his bookshelves. Of course, I clean everything up (5) ______________ his parents get home, so they never see how messy the house gets when they leave.

PRACTICE 21: Writing Your Own Write a sentence of your own for each of the following conjunctions. *Answers will vary.*

1. or ____
2. even if ____
3. whether ____
4. yet ____
5. since ____

Interjections

Interjections are words that express strong emotion, surprise, or disappointment. An interjection is usually followed by an exclamation point or a comma.

Interjection: **Whoa!** You're going too fast.

Interjection: **Ouch,** that hurt!

Other common interjections include *aha*, *alas*, *great*, *hallelujah*, *neat*, *oh*, *oops*, *ouch*, *well*, *whoa*, *yeah*, and *yippee*.

PRACTICE 22: Identifying Underline all the interjections in the following sentences.

1. My goodness! This wind is going to blow down my fence!
2. I just won the lottery! Hallelujah!

3. Boy, I'm beat. I can't walk another step.

4. We just got a new car! Cool!

5. Good grief! Am I the only one working today?

PRACTICE 23: Completing Fill in each blank in the following paragraph with an interjection. *Answers will vary.*

(1) ______________, I thought that was the easiest test this professor has ever given. (2) ______________! I was really worried about this test. (3) ______________, it's over! I spent two weeks solid studying for this test. For the last two nights, I've slept only four hours. (4) ______________, am I ever tired. But at least the test is behind me, (5) ______________!

PRACTICE 24: Writing Your Own Write a sentence of your own for each of the following interjections. *Answers will vary.*

1. help ______________________________
2. mercy ______________________________
3. wow ______________________________
4. yippee ______________________________
5. ouch ______________________________

TEACHING PHRASES Divide students into two groups, and provide them with a series of cards containing phrases that can be made into five different sentences. Here are some examples:

baking in the morning / is causing / long days

my best friend / has enjoyed / her new job / in my father's bakery

my father / has owned / a bakery / for many years

PHRASES

TEST YOURSELF

Underline the phrases in the following sentences.

- Using the computer, I got most of the research done for my report.
- To be totally confident, I checked for spelling and grammar errors twice.
- Susan lives in the gray house at the end of Maple Avenue behind the bank.
- Tess is going to be a professional dancer when she gets older.
- Do you want to join us for dinner this evening?

(Answers are in Appendix 4.)

A **phrase** is a group of words that function together as a unit. Phrases cannot stand alone, however, because they are missing a subject, a verb, or both.

Phrases: the silver moon, a boneless fish

Phrases: threw out the trash, navigated the river, floated to the top

Phrases: after piano lessons, in the crowded boat, by the beach

Phrases: jumping into the water, to be smart

Notice that all these groups of words are missing a subject, a verb, or both.

PRACTICE 25: Identifying Underline ten phrases in the following sentences.

1. Walking to the store, I did see two small boys riding bicycles.
2. My favorite hobbies have to be mountain biking and snow skiing.
3. If you want something for a snack, look in the cabinet above the refrigerator.
4. The grocery store clerk scanned the items and pointed to the total at the bottom of the register tape.
5. I was buying a few antiques at the little store in downtown McKinley.

PRACTICE 26: Completing Fill in each blank in the following paragraph with a phrase. *Answers will vary.*

Marci, my roommate, drove (1) ______________ this weekend because she wanted to visit her relatives there. She also mentioned that there is an outlet mall in the city, where she plans to (2) ______________ for some (3) ______________. She said the drive is only about two hours, and she listens to the radio (4) ______________. I think her relatives are in the food industry, so maybe she'll come home (5) ______________.

PRACTICE 27: Writing Your Own Write a sentence of your own for each of the following phrases. *Answers will vary.*

1. the brave contestant ______________________________
2. hoping to be chosen ______________________________
3. on the blackboard ______________________________
4. to make a point ______________________________
5. encouraged by the reward money ______________________________

running a bakery / has been / a challenge / for my father

my mother / has been trying / to get me / to become a baker too

The sentences should all focus on the same theme.

Give students the cards in random order, and have them try to create five sentences that all make sense. For instance, if they create the sentence *My best friend has enjoyed her new job baking in the morning* and if they get the last three sentences correct, they will be left with *in my father's bakery is causing long days*. Obviously, this does not make sense, so they will have to figure out how to make all the sentences work. The first group to get all five sentences in a logical order wins. Remember that the sentences can be rearranged and still be logical.

The major objective of this exercise is to show students how phrases work as a part of a larger whole—a sentence.

INSTRUCTOR'S RESOURCE MANUAL

For more sample phrases and sentences, for more exercises, and for quizzes, see the *Instructor's Resource Manual*, Section II, Part IV.

TEACHING CLAUSES

For about five minutes, have students write down as many song titles as they can think of—no made-up titles allowed. Be sure they write down the full titles. After they have completed their lists, have them cross out all song titles that are only phrases, leaving only titles that are clauses. The student with the most titles that are clauses wins.

INSTRUCTOR'S RESOURCE MANUAL

For more exercises and for quizzes, see the *Instructor's Resource Manual*, Section II, Part IV.

CLAUSES

TEST YOURSELF

Underline the clauses in the following sentences.

- Magdalena will be a great attorney because she argues so well.
- You don't understand the math concept, so I will keep going over it with you.
- If Shane is going to drive, he should have car insurance.
- After finishing the big test, we all went out for pizza.
- I enjoyed the vacation even though I had one really bad seafood dinner.

(Answers are in Appendix 4.)

Like phrases, **clauses** are groups of words. But unlike phrases, a clause always contains a subject and a verb. There are two types of clauses: *independent* and *dependent*.

An **independent clause** contains a subject and a verb and can stand alone and make sense by itself. Every complete sentence must have at least one independent clause.

Independent Clause: The doctor held the baby very gently.

Now look at the following group of words. It is a clause because it contains a subject and a verb. But it is a **dependent clause** because it is introduced by a word that makes it dependent, *because*.

Dependent Clause: **Because** the doctor held the baby very gently.

This clause cannot stand alone. It must be connected to an independent clause to make sense. Here is one way to complete the dependent clause and form a complete sentence.

Dependent / **Independent**

Because the doctor held the baby very gently, the baby stopped crying.

Hint: Subordinating conjunctions (such as *since*, *although*, *because*, *while*) and relative pronouns (*who*, *whom*, *whose*, *which*, *that*) make clauses dependent. (For more information on subordinating conjunctions, see page 522, and on relative pronouns, see page 515.)

PRACTICE 28: Identifying Each of the following sentences is made up of two clauses. Circle the coordinating or subordinating conjunctions and relative pronouns. Then label each clause either independent (Ind) or dependent (Dep).

1. (As soon as) Vanessa arrived, she began telling the others what to do. *Dep / Ind*
2. (When) the car approached, the driver turned off the headlights. *Dep / Ind*
3. We wanted to know (that) you arrived safely. *Ind / Dep*
4. Tomas can turn in his paper late, (but) he will not receive full credit. *Ind / Ind*
5. Mr. Johnson was the teacher (who) influenced my life the most. *Ind / Dep*

PRACTICE 29: Completing Add an independent or dependent clause that will complete each sentence and make sense. *Answers will vary.*

Steven, (1) who ______________, takes his textbooks to the beach to study. He says that (2) whenever ______________, the sound of the ocean relaxes him. Of course, he also enjoys the view. One night he stayed out (3) until ______________, and his parents were afraid that something awful had happened to him. I'm sure he just lost track of time, (4) unless ______________. He is definitely a "beach bum" (5) because ______________.

PRACTICE 30: Writing Your Own Write five independent clauses. Then add at least one dependent clause to each independent clause. *Answers will vary.*

CHAPTER REVIEW

You might want to reread the examples in this chapter before you do the following exercises.

REVIEW PRACTICE 1: Identifying Use the following abbreviations to label the underlined words in these sentences.

v	Verb	adv	Adverb
n	Noun	prep	Preposition
pro	Pronoun	conj	Conjunction
adj	Adjective	int	Interjection
ph	Phrase	cl	Clause

1. Wow, that man looks just like my uncle Bob. *int / n*
2. Tiffany is going shopping at the new mall on Harbor Boulevard tomorrow. *v / n / adv*

3. Frank is truly my best friend, but sometimes he can't keep a secret. *adv, conj, n*
4. Whenever Lindsay feels sad, she drives into the mountains and looks at the stars. *cl, v, ph*
5. The most popular music artist of the 1960s was definitely Elvis Presley. *n, prep, adv*
6. Gee, are you sure we had to read the entire novel before class today? *int, pro, adj, adv*
7. Ryan wants to take piano lessons, so he can compose music for the poetry he has written. *ph, v, pro*
8. Mikella took her dog to the vet and found out it has a lung infection. *conj, pro, adj*
9. Though I didn't want to accept the job, I felt pressured by my mother. *cl, prep*
10. This morning was dark and cloudy, so I stayed in bed until noon. *adj, conj, ph*

REVIEW PRACTICE 2: Completing Fill in each blank in the following paragraph with an appropriate word, phrase, or clause, as indicated. *Answers will vary.*

The most foolish purchase I ever made was a new (1) ____________ (noun) for my computer. When I went to the (2) ____________ (adjective) store, the salesman (3) ____________ (verb) that I needed this item. I asked him what the part would do (4) ____________ (preposition) my computer, and he promised it would make a big difference in the way the computer operated. (5) ____________ (interjection), did I believe him! I knew my computer was pretty old, (6) ____________ (conjunction) I really didn't want to spend a lot of money on it. Still, I (7) ____________ (adverb) bought the part and took (8) ____________ (pronoun) home to try it out. After (9) ____________ (clause), I turned on the computer, and it began to heat up. Suddenly, smoke began coming (10) ____________ (phrase), and I realized the computer had just crashed.

REVIEW PRACTICE 3: Writing Your Own Write your own paragraph about your favorite pet. What did you name it? What kind of animal was it? *Answers will vary.*

REVIEW PRACTICE 4: Editing Your Writing Exchange paragraphs from Review Practice 3 with a classmate, and do the following: *Answers will vary.*

1. Circle any words that are used incorrectly.
2. Underline any phrases that do not read smoothly.
3. Put an X in the margin where you find a dependent clause that is not connected to an independent clause.

Then return the paragraph to its writer, and use the information in the Introduction to edit your own paragraph. Record your errors on the Error Log in Appendix 6.

UNIT 1

Sentences

Writing complete, correct sentences is one of the most difficult tasks for college writers. It involves understanding the transition from oral to written English. As a student, you must make decisions about sentences that you don't have to deal with when you speak, such as what makes up a sentence and how to punctuate it. What is important, however, is that you address these issues. This unit will help you start making the transfer from oral to written English.

To help you start editing your writing, we will focus on the following sentence elements:

CHAPTER 25

Subjects and Verbs

CHECKLIST for Identifying Subjects and Verbs

✔ Does each of your sentences contain a subject?

✔ Does each of your sentences contain a verb?

TEST YOURSELF

Underline the subjects once and the verbs twice in the following sentences.

- You are my best friend.
- Hang up your clothes.
- They really wanted to be here tonight.
- He made a sandwich and put it in a brown paper bag.
- Susie and Tom went to the dance.

(Answers are in Appendix 4.)

UNIT PRETEST

To check your students' abilities with the collective skills in this unit, a Unit Pretest is available on pages 764–765.

TEACHING SUBJECTS AND VERBS

Cut words out of magazines until you have about 20 assorted parts of speech. Place these in an envelope. Create such an envelope for each of your students. Also, bring each student a glue stick and a blank piece of paper.

Have your students create a poem with the words they are given, gluing them in sequence on the paper. When the students have finished, have them underline their subjects once and their verbs twice.

Have the students read their poems aloud. Then have them vote for their favorite poem and perhaps even award prizes.

A sentence has a message to communicate, but for that message to be meaningful, the sentence must have a subject and a verb. The subject is the topic of the sentence, what the sentence is about. The verb is the sentence's motor. It moves the message forward to its destination. Without these two parts, the sentence is not complete.

SUBJECTS

To be complete, every sentence must have a subject. The **subject** tells who or what the sentence is about.

Subject ↓	
He	always came home on time.
Action **movies**	appeal to teenagers.

INSTRUCTOR'S RESOURCE MANUAL
For more exercises and for quizzes, see the *Instructor's Resource Manual,* Section II, Part IV.

UNIT POSTTEST
To check your students' mastery of the collective skills in this unit, a Unit Posttest is available on pages 776–777.

Compound Subjects

When two or more separate words tell what the sentence is about, the sentence has a **compound subject.**

Compound Subject: **Painting** and **sewing** are my hobbies.
Compound Subject: **My brother** and **I** live with my grandmother.

Hint: Note that *and* is not part of the compound subject.

Unstated Subjects

Sometimes a subject does not actually appear in a sentence but is understood. This occurs in commands and requests. The understood subject is always *you,* meaning either someone specific or anyone in general.

Command: Get up now or you'll be late.

s
Unstated Subject: **(You)** get up now or you'll be late.
Request: Write me an e-mail soon, please.

s
Unstated Subject: **(You)** write me an e-mail soon, please.

Subjects and Prepositional Phrases

The subject of a sentence cannot be part of a prepositional phrase. A **prepositional phrase** is a group of words that begins with a **preposition,** a word like *in, on, under, after,* or *from.* Here are some examples of prepositional phrases:

in the yard	**next to** it	**before** supper
on the plane	**behind** the chair	**instead of** me
under the rug	**around** the circle	**across** the road
after school	**into** the boat	**for** the family
from the White House	**during** the storm	**at** college

(See page 520 for a more complete list of prepositions.)

If you are looking for the subject of a sentence, first cross out all the prepositional phrases. Then figure out what the sentence is about.

s s
~~During the game~~, the coaches and the players had a fight ~~with the other team~~.

s
The new store ~~around the corner~~ sells designer jeans.

s
Some ~~of our luggage~~ was lost ~~on the trip~~.

PRACTICE 1: Identifying Cross out the prepositional phrases in each of the following sentences, and then underline the subjects.

1. The golfer stood quietly ~~in front of the ball~~.
2. Marty and Mike gave a presentation ~~at the big convention~~.
3. Two ~~of the graduates~~ had perfect grade point averages.
4. Before I go ~~to the store,~~ I need to balance my checkbook.
5. Get the mayonnaise ~~out of the refrigerator~~. *"You" implied*

PRACTICE 2: Completing Fill in each blank in the following sentences with a subject without using a person's name. *Answers will vary.*

1. ______________ was voted the best restaurant in this area.
2. Walking to class, ______________ thought seriously about changing his major.
3. Sometimes, ______________ is a great bargain.
4. ______________ and ______________ are two very positive personality traits.
5. ______________ was late to work again.

PRACTICE 3: Writing Your Own Write five sentences of your own, and underline the subjects. *Answers will vary.*

VERBS

To be complete, a sentence must have a verb as well as a subject. A **verb** tells what the subject is doing or what is happening.

	Verb ↓
He	always **came** home on time.
Action movies	**appeal** to teenagers.

Action Verbs

An **action verb** tells what a subject is doing. Some examples of action verbs are *skip*, *ski*, *stare*, *flip*, *breathe*, *remember*, *restate*, *sigh*, *cry*, *decrease*, *write*, and *pant*.

Action Verb: The children **laughed** at the clown.
Action Verb: The car **crashed** into the tree.

Linking Verbs

A **linking verb** connects the subject to other words in the sentence that say something about it. Linking verbs are also called **state-of-being verbs** because they do not show action. Rather, they say that something "is" a particular way. The most common linking verb is *be* (*am, are, is, was, were*).

Linking Verb: The horses **are** in the stable.
Linking Verb: I **am** unhappy with the results.

Other common linking verbs are *remain*, *act*, *look*, *grow*, and *seem*.

Linking Verb: Darnell **remains** enthusiastic about school.
Linking Verb: I **act** happy even when I'm not.
Linking Verb: The yard **looks** neglected.
Linking Verb: She **grew** fonder of her aunt.
Linking Verb: Lupe **seems** happy with her new house.

Some words, like *smell* and *taste*, can be either action verbs or linking verbs.

Action Verb: I **smell** smoke.
Linking Verb: This house **smells** like flowers.

Action Verb: She **tasted** the soup.
Linking Verb: It **tasted** too salty.

Compound Verbs

Just as a verb can have more than one subject, some subjects can have more than one verb. These are called **compound verbs.**

Compound Verb: She **cooks** and **cleans** every day.
Compound Verb: He **runs** and **swims** twice a week in the summer.

Hint: A sentence can have both a compound subject and a compound verb.

s s v v
Joe and **Mitchell jumped** into the boat and **started** the motor.

Helping Verbs

Often the **main verb** (the action verb or linking verb) in a sentence needs help to convey its meaning. **Helping verbs** add information, such as when an action took place. The **complete verb** consists of a main verb and all its helping verbs.

Complete Verb: The children **will return** tomorrow.
Complete Verb: It **might rain** this weekend.
Complete Verb: We **should have gone** to the concert.
Complete Verb: My uncle **has given** me money for Christmas.
Complete Verb: My sister **will be coming** for my wedding.
Complete Verb: You **should** not **go** home with him.

Hint: Note that *not* isn't part of the helping verb. Similarly, *never*, *always*, *only*, *just*, and *still* are never part of the verb.

Complete Verb: I **have** always **liked** history classes.

The most common helping verbs are

be, *am*, *is*, *are*, *was*, *were*
have, *has*, *had*
do, *did*

Other common helping verbs are

may, *might*
can, *could*
will, *would*
should, *used to*, *ought to*

PRACTICE 4: Identifying Underline the complete verbs in each of the following sentences.

1. The students seemed tired in class Monday morning.
2. One of my professors is a popular public speaker.
3. High school students must read *The Scarlet Letter*.
4. Timothy will go to the championships.
5. Get out of the rain.

PRACTICE 5: Completing Fill in each blank in the following sentences with a verb. Avoid using *is*, *are*, *was*, and *were* except as helping verbs. *Answers will vary.*

1. Chad ______________ extreme pain after falling from the ladder and landing on his back.
2. The specialist ______________ her client about the different options.

3. Both the parents and the teachers ______________ about the need for more meetings.

4. My ill child ______________ throughout the night.

5. Red stickers on the price tags ______________ the sale items.

PRACTICE 6: Writing Your Own Write five sentences of your own, and underline all the verbs in each. *Answers will vary.*

CHAPTER REVIEW

You might want to reread the examples in this chapter before you do the following exercises.

REVIEW PRACTICE 1: Identifying Underline the subjects once and the verbs twice in each of the following sentences. Cross out the prepositional phrases first.

1. The horses ~~in the corral~~ are being trained ~~for racing~~.
2. Matilda received a scholarship ~~for her biology research~~.
3. Salespeople can earn thousands ~~of dollars~~ ~~in commissions~~ every year.
4. Each month, my office pays us ~~for overtime~~.
5. The bikes and the helmets are ~~on sale~~ right now.
6. I am going ~~to the grocery store~~ ~~for dinner~~.
7. Tonya's computer crashed the other day, and she used mine ~~for her homework~~.
8. Grandma will not join us ~~for dinner~~.
9. Joe and Christine are building a new house.
10. The baby played ~~with the blocks~~ and stacked them ~~on top~~ ~~of each other~~.

REVIEW PRACTICE 2: Completing Fill in the missing subjects or verbs in each of the following sentences. *Answers will vary.*

1. Tonight's dinner ______________ like leftovers.

2. ______________ can't remember where we said we would meet.

3. Taking that midterm ______________ my hardest challenge last week.

4. The catcher and the pitcher ______________ with the referee.

5. If you want to go with us, you ______________ to come along.

6. When Tiffany left this morning, ______________ didn't know when she would be back.

7. ______________ wear lab coats to set them apart from students.

8. Yesterday I ______________ an old box of letters from my friends in high school.

9. (You) ______________ your room before we leave.

10. ______________ was the best entertainment of the evening.

REVIEW PRACTICE 3: Writing Your Own Write a paragraph about a major decision you made within the past three years. How has it affected your life? What did you learn from the process? *Answers will vary.*

REVIEW PRACTICE 4: Editing Your Writing Exchange paragraphs from Review Practice 3 with another student, and do the following: *Answers will vary.*

1. Underline the subjects once.

2. Underline the verbs twice.

Then return the paragraph to its writer, and edit any sentences in your own paragraph that do not have both a subject and a verb. Record your errors on the Error Log in Appendix 6.

CHAPTER 26

Fragments

CHECKLIST for Identifying and Correcting Fragments

✔ Does each sentence have a subject?

✔ Does each sentence have a verb?

UNIT PRETEST
To check your students' abilities with the collective skills in this unit, a Unit Pretest is available on pages 764–765.

TEACHING FRAGMENTS
Buy blank flash cards in an educational supply store, and on each card, put words and phrases that can be combined to form sentences: subordinating conjunctions, relative pronouns, phrases, subjects, verbs, and so on.

Give each student a certain number of flash cards with words on them. Then have the students create sentences out of their words and stand in front of the class in the order of their sentence. For instance, three stu-

TEST YOURSELF

Put an X by the sentences that are fragments.

- _____ I wanted to go to the gym yesterday.
- _____ Whose tie doesn't match his suit.
- _____ Giving up his seat for an elderly woman.
- _____ Paul asked for the most popular menu item.
- _____ While the captain was away from the cockpit.

(Answers are in Appendix 4.)

One of the most common errors in college writing is the fragment. A fragment is a piece of a sentence that is punctuated as a complete sentence. But it does not express a complete thought. Once you learn how to identify fragments, you can avoid them in your writing.

ABOUT FRAGMENTS

A complete sentence must have both a subject and a verb. If one or both are missing or if the subject and verb are introduced by a dependent word, you have only part of a sentence, a **fragment.** Even if it begins with a capital letter and ends with a period, it cannot stand alone and must be corrected in your writing. The five most common types of fragments are explained in this chapter.

Type 1: Afterthought Fragments
He goes to school during the day. **And works at night.**

Type 2: *-ing* Fragments
Finding no one at the house. Kenny walked back home.

Type 3: *to* Fragments
The school started a tutoring program. **To help improve SAT scores.**

Type 4: Dependent-Clause Fragments
Because I decided to go back to school. My boss fired me.

Type 5: Relative-Clause Fragments
Last summer I visited Rome. **Which is a beautiful city.**

dents might hold up the sentence *the car/was swerving/on the street.* Have another student add *because* to the beginning of the sentence to show how one word can create a fragment.

Have students make other sentences in the same way. Then add and subtract words from these sentences so that students can see the way fragments are both formed and fixed.

INSTRUCTOR'S RESOURCE MANUAL
For suggested words, phrases, and clauses, for more exercises, and for quizzes, see the *Instructor's Resource Manual*, Section II, Part IV.

UNIT POSTTEST
To check your students' mastery of the collective skills in this unit, a Unit Posttest is available on pages 776–777.

Ways to Correct Fragments

Once you have identified a fragment, you have two options for correcting it. You can connect the fragment to the sentence before or after it or make the fragment into an independent clause.

Correction 1: *Connect the fragment to the sentence before or after it.*
Correction 2: *Make the fragment into an independent clause:*
(a) either add the missing subject and/or verb, or
(b) drop the subordinating word before the fragment.

We will discuss these corrections for each type of fragment.

IDENTIFYING AND CORRECTING FRAGMENTS

The rest of this chapter discusses the five types of fragments and the corrections for each type.

Type 1: Afterthought Fragments

Afterthought fragments occur when you add an idea to a sentence but don't punctuate it correctly.

Fragment: He goes to school during the day. **And works at night.**

The phrase *And works at night* is punctuated and capitalized as a complete sentence. Because this group of words lacks a subject, however, it is a fragment.

Correction 1: *Connect the fragment to the sentence before or after it.*
Example: He goes to school during the day **and** works at night.

Correction 2: *Make the fragment into an independent clause.*
Example: He goes to school during the day**. He** works at night.

The first correction connects the fragment to the sentence before it. The second correction makes the fragment an independent clause with its own subject and verb.

PRACTICE 1A: Identifying Underline the afterthought fragments in each of the following sentences.

1. The men on the opposing team were very strong. Everyone was scared to play them. Especially me.
2. Mark peered into the window of his locked car and saw his keys. Stuck in the ignition.
3. I am thinking about buying a really special car next year. For example, a Chevy Tahoe.
4. Carlene turned in her paper on time and knew she would get a good grade. Because she really liked her topic.
5. "Keeping up with the Joneses" is an expression. That my mother uses a lot.

PRACTICE 1B: Correcting Correct the fragments in Practice 1A by rewriting each sentence. *Answers will vary.*

PRACTICE 2: Completing Correct the following afterthought fragments using both correction 1 and correction 2. Rewrite any corrected sentences that you think could be smoother. *Answers will vary.*

1. The child drew in a coloring book. With brand new crayons.
2. I am going to buy some new books to read. For example, the Harry Potter books.
3. Jennifer usually drives very fast. Sometimes running stop signs.
4. My friends are going to the beach. In Santa Barbara for the weekend.
5. He walked over to my desk very slowly. And smiled in a playful way.

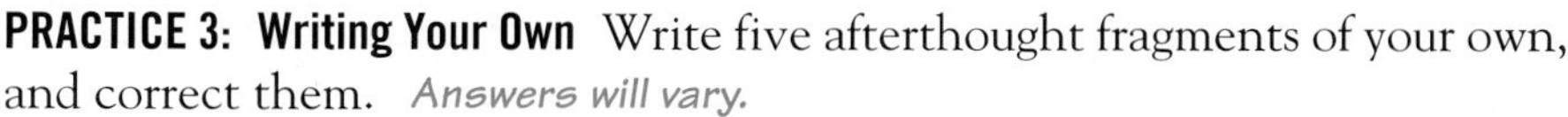

PRACTICE 3: Writing Your Own Write five afterthought fragments of your own, and correct them. *Answers will vary.*

Type 2: *-ing* Fragments

Words that end in *-ing* are forms of verbs that cannot be the main verbs in their sentences. For an *-ing* word to function as a verb, it must have a helping verb with it (*be*, *do*, or *have*; see pages 534–535).

Fragment: **Finding no one at the house.** Kenny walked back home.

Finding is not a verb in this sentence because it has no helping verb. Also, this group of words is a fragment because it has no subject.

Correction 1: *Connect the fragment to the sentence before or after it.*
Example: **Finding no one at the house,** Kenny walked home.

Correction 2: *Make the fragment into an independent clause.*
Example: **He found no one at the house.** Kenny walked home.

Hint: When you connect an *-ing* fragment to a sentence, insert a comma between the two sentence parts. You should insert the comma whether the *-ing* part comes at the beginning or the end of the sentence.

Kenny walked home**, finding no one at the house.**

Finding no one at the house, Kenny walked home.

PRACTICE 4A: Identifying Underline the *-ing* fragments in each of the following sentences.

1. Driving to the store. I thought about all of the things I needed to buy.
2. The baseball player dropped the ball. Tripping over his shoelace while running to make the catch.
3. Mr. Holland was the best music teacher I ever had. Treating everyone with respect.
4. I plan to read at least one book each month. Challenging my brother to do the same.
5. Wanting to leave her parents' house. Marissa got married when she was eighteen years old.

PRACTICE 4B: Correcting Correct the fragments in Practice 4A by rewriting each sentence. *Students will probably connect fragments to independent clauses with commas and change the capitalization after the commas.*

PRACTICE 5: Completing Correct each of the following *-ing* fragments using both methods. Remember to insert a comma when using correction 1. *Answers will vary.*

1. Making the best grade in the class. Carlos was excited to tell his parents about it.
2. I think I hurt my back. Trying to move the sofa.
3. Looking back at my senior year in high school. I can't believe I dated that guy.
4. Wondering whether he left his car windows down. Shawn saw the rain begin to fall.
5. Jamar was glad he survived the accident. Seeing the damage to his car.

PRACTICE 6: Writing Your Own Write five *-ing* fragments of your own, and correct them. *Answers will vary.*

Type 3: *to* Fragments

When *to* is added to a verb (*to see, to hop, to skip, to jump*), the combination cannot be a main verb in its sentence. As a result, this group of words is often involved in a fragment.

Fragment: The school started a tutoring program. **To improve SAT scores.**

Because *to* + a verb cannot function as the main verb of its sentence, *to improve SAT scores* is a fragment as it is punctuated here.

Correction 1: *Connect the fragment to the sentence before or after it.*
Example: The school started a tutoring program **to improve SAT scores.**

Correction 2: *Make the fragment into an independent clause.*
Example: The school started a tutoring program. **It wanted to improve SAT scores.**

Hint: A *to* fragment can also occur at the beginning of a sentence. In this case, insert a comma between the two sentence parts when correcting the fragment.

To improve SAT scores, the school started a tutoring program.

PRACTICE 7A: Identifying Underline the *to* fragments in each of the following sentences.

1. To make the crowd more excited. The rodeo clown came out and chased the bull around the arena.
2. To grow perfect roses. You should attend free classes at Home Depot.
3. The baby screamed loudly. To tell his parents he was hungry.
4. We stopped eating fried foods and sweets. To lose weight before summer.
5. To improve their chances of getting to the World Series. The St. Louis Cardinals moved Albert Pujols up in the batting order.

PRACTICE 7B: Correcting Correct the fragments in Practice 7A by rewriting each sentence. *Answers will vary.*

PRACTICE 8: Completing Correct the following *to* fragments using both correction 1 and correction 2. Try putting the fragment at the beginning of the sentence instead of always at the end. Remember to insert a comma when you add the *to* fragment to the beginning of a sentence. *Answers will vary.*

1. Avoid driving faster than the posted speed limit. To get the best gas mileage.
2. He wanted to buy a new suit. To impress his boss.
3. Suzanne told Warren that she had a boyfriend. To avoid hurting his feelings.
4. The bank is closed on Labor Day. To give the employees time with their families.
5. I put the names and addresses in a mail merge. To make it easier to print labels.

PRACTICE 9: Writing Your Own Write five *to* fragments of your own, and correct them. *Answers will vary.*

Type 4: Dependent-Clause Fragments

A group of words that begins with a **subordinating conjunction** (see the list that follows) is called a **dependent clause** and cannot stand alone. Even though it has a subject and a verb, it is a fragment because it depends on an independent clause to complete its meaning. An **independent clause** is a group of words with a subject and a verb that can stand alone. (See pages 526–527 for help with clauses.)

Here is a list of some commonly used subordinating conjunctions that create dependent clauses.

Subordinating Conjunctions

after	*because*	*since*	*until*
although	*before*	*so*	*when*
as	*even if*	*so that*	*whenever*
as if	*even though*	*than*	*where*
as long as	*how*	*that*	*wherever*
as soon as	*if*	*though*	*whether*
as though	*in order that*	*unless*	*while*

Fragment: **Because I decided to go back to school.** My boss fired me.

This sentence has a subject and a verb, but it is introduced by a subordinating conjunction, *because*. As a result, this sentence is a dependent clause and cannot stand alone.

Correction 1: *Connect the fragment to the sentence before or after it.*
Example: **Because I decided to go back to school,** my boss fired me.

Correction 2: *Make the fragment into an independent clause.*
Example: ~~Because~~ I decided to go back to school. My boss fired me.

Hint: If the dependent clause comes first, put a comma between the two parts of the sentence. If the dependent clause comes second, the comma is not necessary.

Because I decided to go back to school, my boss fired me.
My boss fired me **because I decided to go back to school.**

PRACTICE 10A: Identifying Underline the dependent-clause fragments in each of the following sentences.

1. I love to eat sushi. Although it's sometimes very expensive.
2. It is good to know some trivia. So that you can participate in lots of conversations.
3. After the child finished riding on it. The rocking horse stood in the corner.
4. I will have Thanksgiving dinner at my house again. As long as my parents get along with my in-laws.
5. Before she goes to work in the morning. Margaret takes her children to school.

PRACTICE 10B: Correcting Correct the fragments in Practice 10A by rewriting each sentence. *Answers will vary.*

PRACTICE 11: Completing Correct the following dependent-clause fragments using both correction 1 and correction 2. When you use correction 1, remember to add a comma if the dependent clause comes first. *Answers will vary.*

1. Manny takes his basketball with him. Wherever he goes.
2. While I'm out of town. My mother will take care of my house.
3. The power bill is higher this month. Though we didn't run the air conditioner very often.
4. When she got home from work. Jamie made green beans for dinner.
5. Russ always watches TV for an hour. After he finishes studying.

PRACTICE 12: Writing Your Own Write five dependent-clause fragments of your own, and correct them. *Answers will vary.*

Type 5: Relative-Clause Fragments

A **relative clause** is a dependent clause that begins with a relative pronoun: *who, whom, whose, which,* or *that.* When a relative clause is punctuated as a sentence, the result is a fragment.

Fragment: Last summer I visited Rome. **Which is a beautiful city.**

Which is a beautiful city is a clause fragment that begins with the relative pronoun *which*. This word automatically makes the words that follow it a dependent clause, so they cannot stand alone as a sentence.

Correction 1: *Connect the fragment to the sentence before or after it.*
Example: Last summer I visited Rome, **which is a beautiful city.**

Correction 2: *Make the fragment into an independent clause.*
Example: Last summer I visited Rome. **It is a beautiful city.**

PRACTICE 13A: Identifying Underline the relative-clause fragments in the following sentences.

1. I made an appointment with the doctor. Whom my cousin recommended.
2. The child ate the pills. That the father left on the bathroom counter.
3. The station got a new captain. Who transferred from another department.
4. At the car wash, I talked to the man. Whose nametag said "Sylvester."
5. Karen got a job at the bakery. Which makes fresh donuts every morning.

PRACTICE 13B: Correcting Correct the fragments in Practice 13A by rewriting each sentence. *Answers will vary.*

PRACTICE 14: Completing Correct the following relative-clause fragments using both correction 1 and correction 2. *Answers will vary.*

1. Paul studied for the midterm with Charlotte. Who scored the highest on the first exam.
2. My girlfriend works at the bank. That is located on the corner of F Street and Market Avenue.
3. I put more memory in my computer. Which cost me about $70.
4. My boss is the man with the goatee. Whose ties are usually very colorful.
5. Penny shops only at grocery stores. That offer double coupons.

PRACTICE 15: Writing Your Own Write five relative-clause fragments of your own, and correct them. *Answers will vary.*

CHAPTER REVIEW

You might want to reread the examples in this chapter before you do the following exercises.

REVIEW PRACTICE 1: Identifying Underline the fragments in the following paragraph.

> Buying an old home can be a good experience. If the house is inspected thoroughly before any papers are signed. Thinking we were getting an incredible deal. We rushed into buying a thirty-year-old house in an established neighborhood. The house had lots of personality and big living rooms. To make it perfect for entertaining. Unfortunately, there were several problems with the house that we didn't see right away. For example, plumbing problems. Faulty wiring. Not enough insulation. We put thousands of dollars into repairs. Before we could even invite our friends over for dinner. Even though the house wasn't expensive to buy. It became very expensive for us to maintain. Eventually, we had to sell it. To keep from losing more money. The man who bought it was a contractor. Who could do most of the repairs himself. Which is a big advantage that we didn't have.

REVIEW PRACTICE 2: Correcting Correct all the fragments you underlined in Review Practice 1 by rewriting the paragraph. *Answers will vary.*

REVIEW PRACTICE 3: Writing Your Own Write a paragraph about your dream vacation. Where would you go? How long would you stay? Who would go with you, or would you go alone? *Answers will vary.*

REVIEW PRACTICE 4: Editing Your Writing Exchange paragraphs from Review Practice 3 with another student, and do the following: *Answers will vary.*

1. Put brackets around any fragments that you find.
2. Identify the types of fragments that you find.

Then return the paper to its writer, and use the information in this chapter to correct any fragments in your own paragraph. Record your errors on the Error Log in Appendix 6.

27

CHAPTER

Fused Sentences and Comma Splices

CHECKLIST for Identifying and Correcting Fused Sentences and Comma Splices

✔ Do any sentences run together without punctuation?

✔ Are any sentences incorrectly joined with only a comma?

UNIT PRETEST

To check your students' abilities with the collective skills in this unit, a Unit Pretest is available on pages 764–765.

TEACHING FUSED SENTENCES AND COMMA SPLICES

One of the major misconceptions about run-together sentences is that long sentences are usually fused sentences and comma splices. After all, they run on and on and on. One way to dispel this myth is to write two sentences on the board (one very short and one very long) and ask students to identify the run-together sentence. For this to work, make sure the run-together is

TEST YOURSELF

Mark any incorrect sentences here with a slash between the independent clauses that are not joined properly.

- The rainstorm washed out my garden, I had just planted spring bulbs.
- When we cleaned the house, we found the TV remote control it was between the sofa cushions.
- People in authority are often criticized and seldom thanked.
- The kids didn't find all of the Easter eggs during the hunt, when we finally found them, they were rotten.
- You should ask Aubri to cut your hair she's been cutting mine for four years.

(Answers are in Appendix 4.)

When we cram two separate statements into a single sentence without correct punctuation, we create what are called *fused sentences* and *comma splices*. These run-together sentences generally distort our message and cause problems for our readers. In this chapter, you will learn how to identify and avoid these errors in your writing.

IDENTIFYING FUSED SENTENCES AND COMMA SPLICES

Whereas a fragment is a piece of a sentence, **fused sentences** and **comma splices** are made up of two sentences written as one. In both cases, the first sentence runs into the next without the proper punctuation between the two.

Fused Sentence: The bus stopped we got off.
Comma Splice: The bus stopped, we got off.

Both of these sentences incorrectly join two independent clauses. The difference between them is one comma.

A **fused sentence** is two sentences "fused" or jammed together without any punctuation. Look at these examples:

Fused Sentence: Rosa's favorite subject is math she always does very well on her math tests.

This example consists of two independent clauses with no punctuation between them:

1. Rosa's favorite subject is math.
2. She always does very well on her math tests.

Fused Sentence: My grandfather likes to cook his own meals he doesn't want anyone to do it for him.

This example also consists of two independent clauses with no punctuation between them:

1. My grandfather likes to cook his own meals.
2. He doesn't want anyone to do it for him.

Like a fused sentence, a **comma splice** incorrectly joins two independent clauses. However, a comma splice puts a comma between the two independent clauses. The only difference between a fused sentence and a comma splice is the comma. Look at the following examples:

Comma Splice: Rosa's favorite subject is math, she always does very well on her math tests.
Comma Splice: My grandfather likes to cook his own meals, he doesn't want anyone to do it for him.

Both of these sentences consist of two independent clauses. But a comma is not the proper punctuation to separate these two clauses.

the very short sentence. Here is an example:

Which of the following is the run-together sentence?

I love chocolate it tastes good.

I love chocolate, not only because it tastes good but also because it reminds me of all the fun times that my sister and I had when we were little kids and would buy all different types of candy that we would eat until we got sick.

Students will invariably choose the longer sentence as the run-together sentence because of its length. Showing students that even very short sentences can be run-togethers forces students to look at the grammar of the sentence and not the length.

INSTRUCTOR'S RESOURCE MANUAL

For more sample run-together sentences, for more exercises, and for quizzes, see the *Instructor's Resource Manual*, Section II, Part IV.

UNIT POSTTEST

To check your students' mastery of the collective skills in this unit, a Unit Posttest is available on pages 776–777.

PRACTICE 1: Identifying Put a slash between the independent clauses that are not joined correctly.

1. Paul plays hockey every Thursday/he usually gets home after dark.
2. My mom always tucked me into bed at night,/that's what I remember most about her.
3. Toni borrowed my pencil yesterday/then she lost it.
4. My boyfriend made my favorite cake for my birthday,/I had to eat the whole thing.
5. The child needed a bone marrow transplant,/we raised $10,000 last night for her cause.

PRACTICE 2: Identifying For each incorrect sentence in the following paragraph, put a slash between the independent clauses that are not joined properly.

The fitness craze is sweeping across America,/it seems like everyone has a gym membership. The best-selling food items have "light," "lite," or "fat free" on the packaging, and people are watching their cholesterol and counting calories. Only the thinnest models are shown in food advertisements/they symbolize good health, responsible eating habits, and overall physical attractiveness. Ironically, thin people are even used in ads for unhealthy food items, like candy and soft drinks,/this sends a very confusing message to the consumer. The stereotypes are not fair/not everyone can have the "perfect" body seen in the ads. Some people are just born with bigger body shapes, and there is nothing wrong or unattractive about that. These people should learn to eat healthy foods,/they should not try to be unnaturally thin.

PRACTICE 3: Writing Your Own Write five fused sentences. Then write the same sentences as comma splices. *Answers will vary.*

CORRECTING FUSED SENTENCES AND COMMA SPLICES

You have four different options for correcting your fused sentences and comma splices.

1. *Separate the two sentences with a period, and capitalize the next word.*
2. *Separate the two sentences with a comma, and add a coordinating conjunction* (and, but, for, nor, or, so, *or* yet).

3. *Change one of the sentences into a dependent clause with a subordinating conjunction (such as* if, because, since, after, *or* when*) or a relative pronoun* (who, whom, whose, which, *or* that*).*
4. *Separate the two sentences with a semicolon.*

Correction 1: Use a Period

Separate the two sentences with a period, and capitalize the next word.

Rosa's favorite subject is math**. She** always does very well on her math tests.

My grandfather likes to cook his own meals**. He** doesn't want anyone to do it for him.

PRACTICE 4: Correcting Correct all the sentences in Practice 1 using correction 1. *Students should insert a period where the slashes are and capitalize the next word.*

PRACTICE 5: Correcting Correct the paragraph in Practice 2 using correction 1. *Students should insert a period where the slashes are and capitalize the next word.*

PRACTICE 6: Writing Your Own Correct the sentences you wrote in Practice 3 using correction 1. *Answers will vary.*

Correction 2: Use a Coordinating Conjunction

Separate the two sentences with a comma, and add a coordinating conjunction (and, but, for, nor, or, so, *or* yet)*.*

Rosa's favorite subject is math**, so** she always does very well on her math tests.

My grandfather likes to cook his own meals**, and** he doesn't want anyone to do it for him.

PRACTICE 7: Correcting Correct all the sentences in Practice 1 using correction 2. *Students should insert a comma and a coordinating conjunction where the slashes are.*

PRACTICE 8: Correcting Correct the paragraph in Practice 2 using correction 2. *Students should insert a comma and a coordinating conjunction where the slashes are.*

PRACTICE 9: Writing Your Own Correct the sentences you wrote in Practice 3 using correction 2. *Answers will vary.*

Correction 3: Create a Dependent Clause

Change one of the sentences into a dependent clause with a subordinating conjunction (such as if, because, since, after, *or* when*) or a relative pronoun (*who, whom, whose, which, *or* that*).*

Rosa's favorite subject is math **because** she always does very well on her math tests.

Since my grandfather likes to cook his own meals, he doesn't want anyone to do it for him.

For a list of subordinating conjunctions, see page 522.

Hint: If you put the dependent clause at the beginning of the sentence, add a comma between the two sentence parts.

Because she always does very well on her math tests, Rosa's favorite subject is math.

PRACTICE 10: Correcting Correct all the sentences in Practice 1 using correction 3. *Students should change one of the sentences in each run-together into a dependent clause with a subordinating conjunction.*

PRACTICE 11: Correcting Correct the paragraph in Practice 2 using correction 3. *Students should change one of the sentences in each run-together into a dependent clause with a subordinating conjunction.*

PRACTICE 12: Writing Your Own Correct the sentences you wrote in Practice 3 using correction 3. *Answers will vary.*

Correction 4: Use a Semicolon

Separate the two sentences with a semicolon.

Rosa's favorite subject is math**;** she always does very well on her math tests.

My grandfather likes to cook his own meals**;** he doesn't want anyone to do it for him.

You can also use a **transition,** a word or an expression that indicates how the two parts of the sentence are related, with a semicolon. A transition often makes the sentence smoother. It is preceded by a semicolon and followed by a comma.

Rosa's favorite subject is math**; as a result,** she always does very well on her math tests.

My grandfather likes to cook his own meals**; therefore,** he doesn't want anyone to do it for him.

Here are some transitions commonly used with semicolons.

Transitions Used with a Semicolon Before and a Comma After

also	*however*	*furthermore*	*instead*
meanwhile	*consequently*	*for example*	*similarly*
in contrast	*therefore*	*for instance*	*otherwise*
of course	*finally*	*in fact*	*nevertheless*

PRACTICE 13: Correcting Correct all the sentences in Practice 1 using correction 4. *Students should put semicolons where the slashes are.*

PRACTICE 14: Correcting Correct the paragraph in Practice 2 using correction 4. *Students should put semicolons where the slashes are.*

PRACTICE 15: Writing Your Own Correct the sentences you wrote in Practice 3 using correction 4. *Answers will vary.*

CHAPTER REVIEW

You might want to reread the examples in this chapter before you do the following exercises.

REVIEW PRACTICE 1: Identifying Label each of the following sentences as fused (F), comma splice (CS), or correct (C).

1. _CS_ My sister woke up late this morning, she made us late for school.
2. _F_ River rafting can be dangerous you need an experienced guide.
3. _CS_ When I dyed my hair black, I didn't know it might turn my scalp black too, it did.
4. _C_ People who compete in triathlons are excellent athletes because the events are very difficult.
5. _F_ Mike made an ice sculpture in his art class it was a penguin with a fish in its mouth.
6. _CS_ Terry needed to mow his lawn, the grass was very high, and the neighbors were complaining.
7. _C_ I drove my car without engine oil, and the repairs were incredibly expensive.

8. ___F___ The big earthquake was on the front page of the newspaper many homes and businesses were destroyed.

9. ___F___ We had the perfect beach vacation planned, but then it rained the whole time we were so disappointed.

10. ___CS___ If you stay out in the sun very long, you should use sunblock, skin cancer is a horrible disease.

REVIEW PRACTICE 2: Completing Correct the fused sentences and comma splices in Review Practice 1. *Answers will vary.*

REVIEW PRACTICE 3: Writing Your Own Write a paragraph about your favorite season of the year. Why do you enjoy it? What do you do during this time of year? *Answers will vary.*

REVIEW PRACTICE 4: Editing Through Collaboration Exchange paragraphs from Review Practice 3 with another student, and do the following: *Answers will vary.*

1. Put brackets around any sentences that have more than one independent clause.

2. Circle the words that connect these clauses.

Then return the paper to its writer, and use the information in this chapter to correct any run-together sentences in your own paragraph. Record your errors on the Error Log in Appendix 6.

Verbs

Verbs can do just about anything we ask them to do. Because they have so many forms, they can play lots of different roles in a sentence: The bells *ring* on the hour; voices *rang* through the air; we could hear the clock *ringing* miles away. As you can see from these examples, even small changes, like a single letter, mean something; as a result, verbs make communication more interesting and accurate. But using verbs correctly takes concentration and effort on your part.

In this unit, we will discuss the following aspects of verbs and verb use:

CHAPTER 28

Regular and Irregular Verbs

CHECKLIST for Using Regular and Irregular Verbs

✔ Are regular verbs in their correct forms?

✔ Are irregular verbs in their correct forms?

UNIT PRETEST

To check your students' abilities with the collective skills in this unit, a Unit Pretest is available on pages 765–766.

TEACHING REGULAR AND IRREGULAR VERBS

Have students create mnemonic devices for the irregular verbs that give them the most trouble. For instance, a silly poem based on the game of Battleship might help students remember *sink, sank, sunk:*

If you *sink* my battle-ship,
then you *sank* it.
But I must say,
"You've *sunk* my battleship!"

TEST YOURSELF

Underline the complete verbs in each of the following sentences. Then mark an X if the form of any of the verbs is incorrect.

- _____ The pipe has bursted.
- _____ Sim reacted to the scene calmly.
- _____ I bought my car at an auction.
- _____ We had hid in the basement.
- _____ Sorry, I eated all the cookies.

(Answers are in Appendix 4.)

All verbs are either regular or irregular. *Regular verbs* form the past tense and past participle by adding *-d* or *-ed* to the present tense. If a verb does not form its past tense and past participle this way, it is called an *irregular verb*.

REGULAR VERBS

Here are the principal parts (present, past, and past participle forms) of some regular verbs. They are **regular verbs** because their past tense and past participle end in *-d* or *-ed*. The past participle is the verb form often used with helping verbs like *have*, *has*, or *had*.

Some Regular Verbs

PRESENT TENSE	PAST TENSE	PAST PARTICIPLE (USED WITH HELPING WORDS LIKE *HAVE, HAS, HAD*)
talk	*talked*	*talked*
sigh	*sighed*	*sighed*
drag	*dragged*	*dragged*
enter	*entered*	*entered*
consider	*considered*	*considered*

Have students create as many mnemonic devices as they can to help them remember irregular verbs. Then ask them to read their devices to the class.

INSTRUCTOR'S RESOURCE MANUAL
For more exercises and for quizzes, see the *Instructor's Resource Manual*, Section II, Part IV.

UNIT POSTTEST
To check your students' mastery of the collective skills in this unit, a Unit Posttest is available on pages 778–779.

The different forms of a verb tell when something happened—in the *present* (I *talk*) or in the *past* (I *talked*, I *have talked*, I *had talked*).

PRACTICE 1: Identifying Put an X to the left of the incorrect verb forms in the following chart.

	Present Tense	Past Tense	Past Participle
1.	_____ clap	_____ clapped	_____ clapped
2.	_____ help	__X__ helpt	_____ helped
3.	__X__ watched	_____ watched	_____ watched
4.	_____ gaze	_____ gazed	__X__ gazd
5.	__X__ reclined	_____ reclined	_____ reclined

PRACTICE 2: Completing Write the correct forms of the following regular verbs.

	Present Tense	Past Tense	Past Participle
1. smoke	smoke	smoked	smoked
2. create	create	created	created
3. paste	paste	pasted	pasted
4. buzz	buzz	buzzed	buzzed
5. pick	pick	picked	picked

PRACTICE 3: Writing Your Own Write five sentences using at least five of the verb forms from Practice 1. *Answers will vary.*

IRREGULAR VERBS

Irregular verbs do not form their past tense and past participle with *-d* or *-ed*. That is why they are irregular. Some follow certain patterns (*spring, sprang, sprung; ring, rang, rung; drink, drank, drunk; sink, sank, sunk*). But the only sure way to know the forms of an irregular verb is to spend time learning them. As you write, you can check a dictionary or the following list.

Irregular Verbs

PRESENT	PAST	PAST PARTICIPLE (USED WITH HELPING WORDS LIKE *HAVE, HAS, HAD*)
am	*was*	*been*
are	*were*	*been*
be	*was*	*been*
bear	*bore*	*borne, born*
beat	*beat*	*beaten*
begin	*began*	*begun*
bend	*bent*	*bent*
bid	*bid*	*bid*
bind	*bound*	*bound*
bite	*bit*	*bitten*
blow	*blew*	*blown*
break	*broke*	*broken*
bring	*brought (not brang)*	*brought (not brung)*
build	*built*	*built*
burst	*burst (not bursted)*	*burst*
buy	*bought*	*bought*
choose	*chose*	*chosen*
come	*came*	*come*
cost	*cost (not costed)*	*cost*

cut	*cut*	*cut*
deal	*dealt*	*dealt*
do	*did (not done)*	*done*
draw	*drew*	*drawn*
drink	*drank*	*drunk*
drive	*drove*	*driven*
eat	*ate*	*eaten*
fall	*fell*	*fallen*
feed	*fed*	*fed*
feel	*felt*	*felt*
fight	*fought*	*fought*
find	*found*	*found*
flee	*fled*	*fled*
fly	*flew*	*flown*
forget	*forgot*	*forgotten*
forgive	*forgave*	*forgiven*
freeze	*froze*	*frozen*
get	*got*	*got, gotten*
go	*went*	*gone*
grow	*grew*	*grown*
hang[1] *(a picture)*	*hung*	*hung*
has	*had*	*had*
have	*had*	*had*
hear	*heard*	*heard*
hide	*hid*	*hidden*
hurt	*hurt (not hurted)*	*hurt*
is	*was*	*been*
know	*knew*	*known*
lay	*laid*	*laid*
lead	*led*	*led*
leave	*left*	*left*
lend	*lent*	*lent*
lie[2]	*lay*	*lain*
lose	*lost*	*lost*

meet	*met*	*met*
pay	*paid*	*paid*
prove	*proved*	*proved, proven*
put	*put*	*put*
read [rēēd]	*read [rĕd]*	*read [rĕd]*
ride	*rode*	*ridden*
ring	*rang*	*rung*
rise	*rose*	*risen*
run	*ran*	*run*
say	*said*	*said*
see	*saw (not seen)*	*seen*
set	*set*	*set*
shake	*shook*	*shaken*
shine[3] *(a light)*	*shone*	*shone*
shrink	*shrank*	*shrunk*
sing	*sang*	*sung*
sink	*sank*	*sunk*
sit	*sat*	*sat*
sleep	*slept*	*slept*
speak	*spoke*	*spoken*
spend	*spent*	*spent*
spread	*spread*	*spread*
spring	*sprang (not sprung)*	*sprung*
stand	*stood*	*stood*
steal	*stole*	*stolen*
stick	*stuck*	*stuck*
stink	*stank (not stunk)*	*stunk*
strike	*struck*	*struck, stricken*
strive	*strove*	*striven, strived*
swear	*swore*	*sworn*
sweep	*swept*	*swept*
swell	*swelled*	*swelled, swollen*
swim	*swam*	*swum*
swing	*swung*	*swung*

take	*took*	*taken*
teach	*taught*	*taught*
tear	*tore*	*torn*
tell	*told*	*told*
think	*thought*	*thought*
throw	*threw*	*thrown*
understand	*understood*	*understood*
wake	*woke*	*woken*
wear	*wore*	*worn*
weave	*wove*	*woven*
win	*won*	*won*
wring	*wrung*	*wrung*
write	*wrote*	*written*

1. *Hang* meaning "execute by hanging" is regular: *hang, hanged, hanged.*
2. *Lie* meaning "tell a lie" is regular: *lie, lied, lied.*
3. *Shine* meaning "brighten by polishing" is regular: *shine, shined, shined.*

PRACTICE 4: Identifying Put an X to the left of the incorrect verb forms in the following chart.

Present Tense	Past Tense	Past Participle
1. _____ bear	_X_ beared	_____ borne
2. _____ shrink	_____ shrank	_X_ shrank
3. _____ swing	_____ swung	_X_ swang
4. _____ deal	_X_ dealed	_____ dealt
5. _X_ chose	_____ chose	_____ chosen

PRACTICE 5: Completing Write the correct forms of the following irregular verbs.

	Present Tense	Past Tense	Past Participle
1. am	am	was	been
2. write	write	wrote	written

3. sweep	*sweep*	*swept*	*swept*
4. fall	*fall*	*fell*	*fallen*
5. swell	*swell*	*swelled*	*swelled, swollen*

PRACTICE 6: Writing Your Own Write five sentences using at least five of the verb forms from the chart in Practice 5. *Answers will vary.*

USING *LIE/LAY* AND *SIT/SET* CORRECTLY

Two pairs of verbs are often used incorrectly—*lie/lay* and *sit/set*.

Lie/Lay

	Present Tense	Past Tense	Past Participle
lie (recline or lie down)	lie	lay	(have, has, had) lain
lay (put or place down)	lay	laid	(have, has, had) laid

The verb *lay* always takes an object. You must lay something down:

Lay down *what?*
Lay down *your books*.

Sit/Set

	Present Tense	Past Tense	Past Participle
sit (get into a seated position)	sit	sat	(have, has, had) sat
set (put or place down)	set	set	(have, has, had) set

Like the verb *lay*, the verb *set* must always have an object. You must set something down:

Set *what?*
Set *the presents* over here.

PRACTICE 7: Identifying Underline the correct verb in the following sentences.

1. After I (sat, set) down, I felt much better.
2. All day I have (lain, laid) in my room watching TV.

3. He has (lay, laid) the blanket down for our picnic.

4. We had to (sat, set) our watches to exactly the same time.

5. (Lie, Lay) the pieces of the puzzle out on the table, please.

PRACTICE 8: Completing Fill in each blank in the following sentences with the correct form of *lie/lay* or *sit/set*.

1. Suzy has ___lain___ in the bathtub for so long that her skin has wrinkled.
2. I could have ___lain/sat___ in the moonlight looking at the stars all night.
3. The cook ___laid/set___ out all the ingredients.
4. Please ___set___ those heavy boxes down before you strain your back.
5. I think I will go and ___lie/sit___ down for a while.

PRACTICE 9: Writing Your Own Write five sentences using variations of *lie/lay* or *sit/set*. *Answers will vary.*

CHAPTER REVIEW

You might want to reread the examples in this chapter before you do the following exercises.

REVIEW PRACTICE 1: Identifying Write out the past tense and past participle of each verb listed here and then identify the verb as either regular or irregular.

	Present Tense	Past Tense	Past Participle	Type of Verb
1.	brush	brushed	brushed	regular
2.	fix	fixed	fixed	regular
3.	wear	wore	worn	irregular
4.	buy	bought	bought	irregular
5.	suffer	suffered	suffered	regular
6.	have	had	had	irregular
7.	type	typed	typed	regular

8. feel	*felt*	*felt*	*irregular*
9. touch	*touched*	*touched*	*regular*
10. teach	*taught*	*taught*	*irregular*

REVIEW PRACTICE 2: Completing Fill in each blank in the following sentences with a regular or irregular verb that makes sense. *Answers may vary.*

1. Yesterday, I ___*sat*___ at my computer and tried to write my essay.
2. Tilda ___*came*___ over to my house last night.
3. I always smile and ___*wave*___ my hand to the people on the Mardi Gras floats.
4. Geraldo has ___*spilled*___ his drink all over the waitress.
5. Carlos and Tom have ___*missed*___ class again.
6. You should never ___*drop/shake*___ an infant; doing so can cause brain damage and death.
7. The groom smiled at his bride and ___*placed*___ the ring on her third finger.
8. The plumbing in the house has ___*sprung*___ a leak.
9. Mary Ann ___*hung*___ the picture in her bedroom.
10. All cozy in my bed, I ___*slept*___ right through the earthquake.

REVIEW PRACTICE 3: Writing Your Own Write a paragraph explaining the most important parts of your daily routine. Be sure to explain why each activity is important. *Answers will vary.*

REVIEW PRACTICE 4: Editing Your Writing Exchange paragraphs from Review Practice 3 with another student, and do the following: *Answers will vary.*

1. Circle any verb forms that are not correct.
2. Suggest a correction for these incorrect forms.

Then return the paper to its writer, and use the information in this chapter to correct the verb forms in your own paragraph. Record your errors on the Error Log in Appendix 6.

CHAPTER 29

Verb Tense

CHECKLIST for Correcting Tense Problems

- ✔ Are present-tense verbs in the correct form?
- ✔ Are past-tense verbs in the correct form?
- ✔ Are *-ing* verbs used with the correct helping verbs?
- ✔ Are the forms of *be*, *do*, and *have* used correctly

TEST YOURSELF

Underline the complete verbs in each sentence. Then mark an X if the form of any of the verbs is incorrect.

- _____ Jean always laugh when I tell that joke.
- _____ Mark jumped over the hurdle and crossed the finish line.
- _____ I had spoke to the sales clerk about a discount.
- _____ Students ain't allowed to bring food and drink into the computer lab.
- _____ My two cats be playing in the sunshine.

(Answers are in Appendix 4.)

When we hear the word *verb,* we often think of action. We also know that action occurs in time. We are naturally interested in whether something happened today or yesterday or if it will happen at some time in the future. The time of an action is indicated by the **tense** of a verb, specifically in the ending of a verb or in a helping word. This chapter discusses the most common errors in using verb tense.

UNIT PRETEST

To check your students' abilities with the collective skills in this unit, a Unit Pretest is available on pages 765–766.

TEACHING VERB TENSE

Put the following grids on the board:

Past:

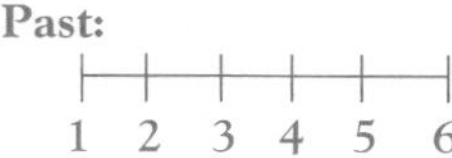

Present:

Future:

PRESENT TENSE

One of the most common errors in college writing is reversing the present-tense endings—adding an *-s* where none is needed and omitting the *-s* where it is required. This error causes problems in subject-verb agreement. Make sure you understand this mistake, and then proofread carefully to avoid it in your writing.

Present Tense

Singular		Plural	
INCORRECT	CORRECT	INCORRECT	CORRECT
NOT *I walks*	*I walk*	***NOT*** *we walks*	*we walk*
NOT *you walks*	*you walk*	***NOT*** *you walks*	*you walk*
NOT *he, she, it walk*	*he, she, it walks*	***NOT*** *they walks*	*they walk*

You also need to be able to spot these same errors in sentences.

Incorrect	Correct
That car run me off the road.	**That car ran** me off the road.
My mother hate my boyfriend.	**My mother hates** my boyfriend.
You speaks too fast.	**You speak** too fast.
They trims the trees once a year.	**They trim** the trees once a year.

PRACTICE 1A: Identifying Underline the present-tense errors in each of the following sentences.

1. I loves to sit in a cool theater on a hot summer day. *(love)*
2. You babbles too much. *(babble)*
3. My baby sister play well with her cousin. *(plays)*
4. We seems to be lost. *(seem)*
5. Next week, they plans on going to the party after the show. *(plan)*

PRACTICE 1B: Correcting Correct the present-tense errors in Practice 1A by rewriting each sentence. *See Practice 1A.*

Place a picture of a horse and buggy at the 1 on the "Past" line, a car at the 1 on the "Present" line, and a spaceship at the 1 on the "Future" line.

Divide your students into three teams, one for each tense. Provide students with sentences that are not in their team's tense. The first team to correctly change the sentence into its assigned tense moves one space forward on the grid. For instance, the following sentence might be given to the Past and Present teams: "We will search for the answer." If the Past team changes the sentence to "We searched for the answer," its horse and buggy moves forward one space; if the Present team changes it to "We search for the answer," its car moves forward; and so on.

The first vehicle to reach the end of the grid wins.

INSTRUCTOR'S RESOURCE MANUAL

For more sample sentences, for more exercises, and for quizzes, see the *Instructor's Resource Manual*, Section II, Part IV.

UNIT POSTTEST

To check your students' mastery of the collective skills in this unit, a Unit Posttest is available on pages 778–779.

PRACTICE 2: Completing Fill in each blank in the following paragraph with the correct present-tense verbs. *Answers may vary.*

My brother always (1) ___*asks*___ me to help him with his paper route. Usually I don't mind because he (2) ___*gives*___ me money and we (3) ___*get*___ to work together. It's strange, too, because I actually (4) ___*enjoy*___ rolling up the papers. But lately my brother has been sleeping late while I do all the work. So I told him I was going on strike until I got either more money or more help. Do you know what he did? He fired me! Can you (5) ___*believe*___ that?

PRACTICE 3: Writing Your Own Write a sentence of your own for each of the following present-tense verbs. *Answers will vary.*

1. relieve ____________________
2. feels ____________________
3. skates ____________________
4. asks ____________________
5. skip ____________________

PAST TENSE

Just as we know that a verb is in the present tense by its ending, we can tell that a verb is in the past tense by its ending. Regular verbs form the past tense by adding *-d* or *-ed*. But some writers forget the ending when they are writing the past tense. Understanding this problem and then proofreading carefully will help you catch this error.

Past Tense

Singular		Plural	
INCORRECT	CORRECT	INCORRECT	CORRECT
NOT *I walk*	*I walked*	***NOT*** *we walk*	*we walked*
NOT *you walk*	*you walked*	***NOT*** *you walk*	*you walked*
NOT *he, she, it walk*	*he, she, it walked*	***NOT*** *they walk*	*they walked*

You also need to be able to spot these same errors in sentences.

Incorrect	**Correct**
She run fast.	**She ran** fast.
He see the game.	**He saw** the game.
The girl study hard.	**The girl studied** hard.
Yes, **we learn** a lot.	Yes, **we learned** a lot.

PRACTICE 4A: Identifying Underline the past-tense errors in the following sentences.

1. When we were in high school, we talk on the phone for hours. *(talked)*
2. The radio station play the song over and over again. *(played)*
3. Yesterday you edit your work. *(edited)*
4. She close all the windows when she left. *(closed)*
5. I just realize that I have already done these exercises. *(realized)*

PRACTICE 4B: Correcting Correct the past-tense errors in Practice 4A by rewriting each sentence. *See Practice 4A.*

PRACTICE 5: Completing Fill in each blank in the following paragraph with the correct past-tense verb. *Answers will vary.*

Yesterday, it was so hot that several of my friends (1) ______________ to go to the beach. They (2) ______________ a lunch, put on their swimsuits, and (3) ______________ into the car. Sadly, I had a cold, so I (4) ______________ home. Boy, am I glad I did. My friends were stuck in traffic for two hours with no air conditioning. This is the one time I (5) ______________ my lucky stars for a cold.

PRACTICE 6: Writing Your Own Write a sentence of your own for each of the following past-tense verbs. *Answers will vary.*

1. rained ____
2. fixed ____
3. sipped ____
4. lifted ____
5. visited ____

USING HELPING WORDS WITH PAST PARTICIPLES

Helping words are used with the past participle form, *not* with the past-tense form. It is incorrect to use a helping verb (such as *is*, *was*, *were*, *have*, *has*, or *had*) with the past tense. Make sure you understand how to use helping words with past participles, and then proofread your written work to avoid making these errors.

Incorrect	Correct
They **have went.**	They **have gone.**
She **has decide** to get married.	She **has decided** to get married.
I **have ate** breakfast already.	I **have eaten** breakfast already.
We **had took** the test early.	We **had taken** the test early.

PRACTICE 7A: Identifying Underline the incorrect helping words and past participles in each of the following sentences.

1. I have sang that song in French. *(have sung)*
2. Kendra and Misty have hid all the Easter eggs. *(have hidden)*
3. The plane has flew over the ocean. *(has flown)*
4. We have did all the necessary repairs to the fence. *(have done)*
5. She has forget the phone number. *(has forgotten)*

PRACTICE 7B: Correcting Correct the helping verb and past participle errors in Practice 7A by rewriting each sentence. *See Practice 7A.*

PRACTICE 8: Completing Fill in each blank in the following paragraph with helping verbs and past participles that make sense. *Answers will vary.*

It all started in elementary school. I was a new student and didn't know a single person. For two weeks, I (1) ______________ my lunch alone. No one had even talked to me. Even though I didn't show it, my classmates' neglect (2) ______________ my feelings. My little heart (3) ______________. But one day, a wonderful boy named John happened to notice me. I (4) ______________ my lunch, so he decided to share his with me. From that day forward, we (5) ______________ the best of friends.

PRACTICE 9: Writing Your Own Write a sentence of your own for each of the following helping words and past participles. *Answers will vary.*

1. have drunk ______________________________
2. has seen ______________________________
3. had woven ______________________________
4. has risen ______________________________
5. have hidden ______________________________

USING *-ING* VERBS CORRECTLY

Verbs ending in *-ing* describe action that is going on or that was going on for a while. To be a complete verb, an *-ing* verb is always used with a helping verb. Two common errors occur with *-ing* verbs:

1. Using *be* or *been* instead of the correct helping verb
2. Using no helping verb at all

Learn the correct forms, and proofread carefully to catch these errors.

Incorrect	Correct
The car **be going** too fast.	The car **is going** too fast.
	The car **was going** too fast.
The car **been going** too fast.	The car **has been going** too fast.
	The car **had been going** too fast.
We **watching** a movie.	We **are watching** a movie.
	We **have been watching** a movie.
	We **were watching** a movie.
	We **had been watching** a movie.

PRACTICE 10A: Identifying Underline the incorrect helping verbs and *-ing* forms in each of the following sentences.

1. The cat be chasing the dog! *(is chasing)*
2. The patient been waiting for the doctor for over an hour. *(has been waiting)*
3. That building be leaning to the side for over twenty years. *(has been leaning)*
4. I feeling sick because I ate an entire pizza by myself. *(am feeling)*
5. We be driving down Sunset Boulevard. *(are driving)*

PRACTICE 10B: Correcting Correct the verb form errors in Practice 10A by rewriting each sentence. *See Practice 10A.*

PRACTICE 11: Completing Fill in each blank in the following paragraph with the correct helping verb and *-ing* form. *Answers will vary.*

I (1) ______________ one of the best days of my life. It started while I (2) ______________ my clothes and found $20 in my pocket. Then on my way to work, I was pulled over by a police officer. While he (3) ______________ out the ticket, I made him laugh so hard that he tore it up and let me go with a warning. But the best part of my day happened while I was at work. I (4) ______________ to the radio when I heard my name announced. I had just won a trip to Hawaii! I (5) ______________ up and down and screaming. My boss was so happy for me that he gave me the rest of the day off.

PRACTICE 12: Writing Your Own Write a sentence of your own for each of the following verbs. *Answers will vary.*

1. is wishing ____
2. has been writing ____________________________________
3. were laying ____
4. was driving ____
5. had been sailing ____________________________________

PROBLEMS WITH *BE*

The verb *be* can cause problems in both the present tense and the past tense. The following chart demonstrates these problems. Learn how to use these forms correctly, and then always proofread your written work carefully to avoid these errors.

The Verb *be*

Present Tense

Singular		Plural	
INCORRECT	CORRECT	INCORRECT	CORRECT
NOT *I* ***be/ain't***	*I* ***am/am not***	***NOT*** *we* ***be/ain't***	*we* ***are/are not***
NOT *you* ***be/ain't***	*you* ***are/are not***	***NOT*** *you* ***be/ain't***	*you* ***are/are not***
NOT *he, she, it* ***be/ain't***	*he, she, it* ***is/is not***	***NOT*** *they* ***be/ain't***	*they* ***are/are not***

Past Tense

Singular		Plural	
INCORRECT	CORRECT	INCORRECT	CORRECT
NOT** I **were	*I **was***	***NOT** we **was***	*we **were***
NOT** you **was	*you **were***	***NOT** you **was***	*you **were***
NOT** he, she, it **were	*he, she, it **was***	***NOT** they **was***	*they **were***

PRACTICE 13A: Identifying Underline the incorrect forms of *be* in each of the following sentences.

1. I ain't going to travel by plane. *(am not)*
2. You is going to have to study for this exam. *(are)*
3. He be the person you need to talk to about enrollment. *(is)*
4. You was supposed to take your clothes off before you ironed them. *(were)*
5. They was not having any fun. *(were)*

PRACTICE 13B: Correcting Correct the incorrect forms of *be* in Practice 13A by rewriting each sentence. *See Practice 13A.*

PRACTICE 14: Completing Fill in each blank in the following paragraph with the correct form of *be*.

Crystal (1) ____*is*____ an adventurous person. She (2) ____*is*____ willing to try just about anything, and she usually talks me into going along with her. We have jumped out of a plane, off a bridge, and off a mountain—with a parachute or a bungee cord, of course. But when she decided we should have our belly buttons pierced, I panicked. Now, I (3) ____*am*____ not a coward, but I knew this little adventure (4) ____*was*____ going to hurt. Danger I like, but pain—well, that's a different story. This (5) ____*was*____ one adventure I had to say no to.

PRACTICE 15: Writing Your Own Write a sentence of your own for each of the following verbs. *Answers will vary.*

1. am not ____________________
2. is ____________________

3. was ____

4. are ____

5. were ____

PROBLEMS WITH *DO*

Another verb that causes sentence problems in the present and past tenses is *do*. The following chart shows these problems. Learn the correct forms, and proofread to avoid errors.

The Verb *do*

Present Tense

Singular		Plural	
INCORRECT	CORRECT	INCORRECT	CORRECT
NOT *I* ***does***	*I* ***do***	***NOT*** *we* ***does***	*we* ***do***
NOT *you* ***does***	*you* ***do***	***NOT*** *you* ***does***	*you* ***do***
NOT *he, she, it* ***do***	*he, she, it* ***does***	***NOT*** *they* ***does***	*they* ***do***

Past Tense

Singular		Plural	
INCORRECT	CORRECT	INCORRECT	CORRECT
NOT *I* ***done***	*I* ***did***	***NOT*** *we* ***done***	*we* ***did***
NOT *you* ***done***	*you* ***did***	***NOT*** *you* ***done***	*you* ***did***
NOT *he, she, it* ***done***	*he, she, it* ***did***	***NOT*** *they* ***done***	*they* ***did***

PRACTICE 16A: Identifying Underline the incorrect forms of *do* in each of the following sentences.

1. We always does the prewriting exercises before organizing our essays. *(do)*
2. She done it again. *(did)*
3. You does a good job even when you don't have to. *(do)*
4. Yes, that computer certainly do need a new modem. *(does)*
5. Henry, you done let the cat out! *(remove done)*

PRACTICE 16B: Correcting Correct the incorrect forms of *do* in Practice 16A by rewriting each sentence. *See Practice 16A.*

PRACTICE 17: Completing Fill in each blank in the following paragraph with the correct form of *do*.

I (1) ___*do*___ believe it was love at first sight. She had the prettiest brown eyes and the silkiest blonde hair I had ever seen. My friends warned me that she wasn't right for me, but they (2) ___*did*___ n't understand—we were made for each other. Now, I admit that she (3) ___*did/does*___ slobber a bit and her hair (4) ___*did/does*___ shed in the summer, but she's always happy to see me and doesn't mind my stupid mistakes. Adopting Porsche, my golden retriever, was the best thing I ever (5) ___*did*___ .

PRACTICE 18: Writing Your Own Write a sentence of your own for each of the following verbs. *Answers will vary.*

1. do ________________________________
2. does ________________________________
3. did ________________________________
4. does ________________________________
5. do ________________________________

PROBLEMS WITH *HAVE*

Along with *be* and *do*, the verb *have* causes sentence problems in the present and past tenses. The following chart demonstrates these problems. Learn the correct forms, and proofread to avoid errors with *have*.

The Verb *have*

Present Tense

Singular		Plural	
INCORRECT	CORRECT	INCORRECT	CORRECT
NOT *I* ***has***	*I* ***have***	***NOT*** *we* ***has***	*we* ***have***
NOT *you* ***has***	*you* ***have***	***NOT*** *you* ***has***	*you* ***have***
NOT *he, she, it* ***have***	*he, she, it* ***has***	***NOT*** *they* ***has***	*they* ***have***

Past Tense

Singular		Plural	
INCORRECT	CORRECT	INCORRECT	CORRECT
NOT *I* ***has***	*I* ***had***	***NOT*** *we* ***has***	*we* ***had***
NOT *you* ***have***	*you* ***had***	***NOT*** *you* ***has***	*you* ***had***
NOT *he, she, it* ***have***	*he, she, it* ***had***	***NOT*** *they* ***has***	*they* ***had***

PRACTICE 19A: Identifying Underline the incorrect forms of *have* in each of the following sentences.

1. We has already taken up too much space. *(have)*
2. Yesterday, I has money in my account; today I has none. *(had, have)*
3. If George is late, then he have to come in through the back entrance. *(has)*
4. You has a great deal of courage when dealing with angry customers. *(have)*
5. Sabine and Jackie has taken the rest of the afternoon off. *(have)*

PRACTICE 19B: Correcting Correct the incorrect forms of *have* in Practice 19A by rewriting each sentence. *See Practice 19A.*

PRACTICE 20: Completing Fill in each blank in the following paragraph with the correct form of *have*.

"I (1) ___*have*___ a secret," said my little brother Bubba, "but you (2) ___*have*___ to promise not to tell." Now Bubba (3) ___*has*___ the most wonderful imagination, and I knew to expect the unexpected since we (4) ___*have*___ shared many secrets in the past. So I said, "OK, what is it?" He leaned closer, cupped his hand to my ear, and whispered, "Babies don't really come from the stork." "No!" I exclaimed, pretending to be shocked. "Where do they come from?" I asked. "Why, they come from eggs," he proudly said. I (5) ___*had*___ the hardest time keeping a straight face.

PRACTICE 21: Writing Your Own Write a sentence of your own for each of the following verbs. *Answers will vary.*

1. have ______________________________
2. has ______________________________

3. had ______________________________

4. has ______________________________

5. have ______________________________

CHAPTER REVIEW

You might want to reread the examples in this chapter before you do the following exercises.

REVIEW PRACTICE 1: Identifying Underline the incorrect verb forms in the following sentences. Check problem areas carefully: Is an *-s* needed, or is there an unnecessary *-s* ending? Do all past-tense regular verbs end in *-d* or *-ed?* Is the past participle used with helping words? Is the correct helping verb used with *-ing* verbs? Are the forms of *be*, *do*, and *have* correct?

1. Janet and Henry likes to go for long drives in the mountains. *(like)*
2. Our high school band has strove to be the best in the nation. *(has striven)*
3. I be sorry for your troubles. *(am)*
4. I enjoys a hot cup of coffee while I work. *(enjoy)*
5. You done a wise thing when you signed up for classes early. *(did)*
6. The birds be flying south for the winter. *(are flying)*
7. I have wove the tapestry threads back together. *(have woven)*
8. That fat cat been sleeping in the sun all day. *(has been sleeping)*
9. Those two girls think they has all the answers. *(have)*
10. Last Christmas, we bake most of our gifts. *(baked)*

REVIEW PRACTICE 2: Correcting Correct the errors in Review Practice 1 by rewriting each sentence. *See Review Practice 1.*

REVIEW PRACTICE 3: Writing Your Own Write a short paragraph describing your favorite pet. Be careful to use all verbs in the correct tense. Check in particular for errors with *be*, *do*, and *have*. *Answers will vary.*

REVIEW PRACTICE 4: Editing Through Collaboration Exchange paragraphs from Review Practice 3 with another student, and do the following: *Answers will vary.*

1. Underline any incorrect tenses.
2. Circle any incorrect verb forms.

Then return the paper to its writer, and use the information in this chapter to correct any verb errors in your own paragraph. Record your errors on the Error Log in Appendix 6.

30 CHAPTER

Subject-Verb Agreement

CHECKLIST for Correcting Subject-Verb Agreement Problems

✔ Do all subjects agree with their verbs?

UNIT PRETEST
To check your students' abilities with the collective skills in this unit, a Unit Pretest is available on pages 765–766.

TEACHING SUBJECT-VERB AGREEMENT
Create several sentences that demonstrate subject-verb agreement errors. (You could use the examples from the chapter as models.) Put words and phrases from these sentences on index cards. Then put three or four long strips of Velcro horizontally across a piece of poster board, and place squares of the other side of the Velcro on the backs of the index cards.

Now attach index cards to the poster

TEST YOURSELF

Underline the subjects once and the complete verbs twice in the following sentences. Put an X by the sentence if its subject and verb do not agree.

- _____ Neither the shorts nor the shirt fit me.
- _____ Chips and dip is my favorite snack.
- _____ There were a large storm last night.
- _____ Some of the soil along with the fertilizer are for the orchard.
- _____ Cotton and silk are more comfortable than wool.

(Answers are in Appendix 4.)

Almost every day, we come across situations that require us to reach an agreement with someone. For example, you and a friend might have to agree on which movie to see, or you and your manager might have to agree on how many hours you'll work in the coming week. Whatever the issue, agreement is essential in most aspects of life—including writing. In this chapter, you will learn how to resolve conflicts in your sentences by making sure your subjects and verbs agree.

SUBJECT-VERB AGREEMENT

Subject-verb agreement simply means that singular subjects must be paired with singular verbs and plural subjects with plural verbs. Look at this example:

Singular: **She works** in Baltimore.

The subject *she* is singular because it refers to only one person. The verb *works* is singular and matches the singular subject. Here is the same sentence in plural form:

Plural: **They work** in Baltimore.

The subject *they* is plural, referring to more than one person, and the verb *work* is also plural.

PRACTICE 1: Identifying Underline the verb that agrees with its subject in each of the following sentences.

1. In her free time, Cassie (be, is) a volunteer nurse.
2. The girls usually (store, stores) their gear in the lockers.
3. Rocky, my 80-pound dog, (eat, eats) more food in a day than I do.
4. I (do, does) all of my reading for my classes at least one week ahead of time.
5. You (has, have) something green in your hair.

PRACTICE 2: Completing Fill in each blank in the following sentences with a present-tense verb that agrees with its subject. *Answers will vary.*

1. Every evening, Michael ______________ by the fire.
2. They ______________ many questions.
3. Neil ______________ everything chocolate.
4. We rarely ______________ down that path, for it is always dark and eerie.
5. He ______________ to only classical music.

PRACTICE 3: Writing Your Own Write five sentences of your own, and underline the subjects and verbs. Make sure that your subjects and verbs agree. *Answers will vary.*

board so that you create a few simple sentences with no words separating the subjects and their verbs. Next, add phrase cards to the sentences, separating the subjects and verbs to show students that verbs do not change even though information may come between a subject and its verb.

Demonstrate some common agreement errors by placing incorrect verbs with subjects.

Once students understand how subjects and verbs agree, test your students by putting sentences with subject-verb agreement errors on the board and asking them to come to the board to find and correct the errors.

INSTRUCTOR'S RESOURCE MANUAL

For more sample sentences, for more exercises, and for quizzes, see the *Instructor's Resource Manual*, Section II, Part IV.

UNIT POSTTEST

To check your students' mastery of the collective skills in this unit, a Unit Posttest is available on pages 778–779.

WORDS SEPARATING SUBJECTS AND VERBS

With sentences that are as simple and direct as *She works in Baltimore*, checking that the subject and verb agree is easy. But problems can arise when words come between the subject and the verb. Often the words between the subject and verb are prepositional phrases. If you follow the advice given in Chapter 25, you will be able to find the subject and verb: *Cross out all the prepositional phrases in a sentence. The subject and verb will be among the words that are left.* Here are some examples:

s v

Prepositional Phrases: The **notebook** ~~for history class~~ **is** ~~in my backpack~~.

When you cross out the prepositional phrases, you can tell that the singular subject, *notebook*, and the singular verb, *is*, agree.

s v

Prepositional Phrases: The **roses** ~~in my garden~~ **bloom** ~~in April~~.

When you cross out the prepositional phrases, you can tell that the plural subject, *roses*, and the plural verb, *bloom*, agree.

PRACTICE 4: Identifying Underline the subject once and the verb twice in each of the following sentences. Cross out the prepositional phrases first. Put an X to the left of any sentence in which the subject and verb do not agree.

1. __X__ Cindy, ~~unlike many people today,~~ do so much ~~for others~~.
2. __X__ That man ~~in the red pants~~ think a lot ~~about his social life~~.
3. __X__ Frog legs, ~~in spite of popular opinion~~, tastes ~~like frog legs~~.
4. _____ The flowers ~~in the garden~~ smell nice.
5. __X__ The economy ~~in America~~ seem to be getting stronger.

PRACTICE 5: Completing Fill in each blank in the following sentences with a present-tense verb that agrees with its subject. *Answers will vary.*

1. My little brother, despite being told otherwise, still _______________ in Santa Claus.

2. The train for San Francisco ______________ in the station at 7:45 p.m.

3. MTV, unlike VH1, ______________ to air more music videos.

4. The boxes in the hallway ______________ in the moving van.

5. The wind during a thunderstorm always ______________ me.

PRACTICE 6: Writing Your Own Write five sentences of your own with at least one prepositional phrase in each, and underline the subjects and verbs. Make sure that your subjects and verbs agree. *Answers will vary.*

MORE THAN ONE SUBJECT

Sometimes a subject consists of more than one person, place, thing, or idea. These subjects are called **compound** (as discussed in Chapter 25). Follow these three rules when matching a verb to a compound subject:

1. When compound subjects are joined by *and*, use a plural verb.

   Plural: **Thursday and Friday were** hot days.

   The singular words *Thursday and Friday* together make a plural subject. Therefore, the plural verb *were* is needed.

2. When the subject appears to have more than one part but the parts refer to a single unit, use a singular verb.

   Singular: **Macaroni and cheese is** Eli's favorite food.

   Macaroni is one item and *cheese* is one item, but Eli does not eat one without the other, so they form a single unit. Because they are a single unit, they require a singular verb—*is*.

3. When compound subjects are joined by *or* or *nor*, make the verb agree with the subject closest to it.

   Singular: Neither hot dogs nor **chicken was** on the menu.

   The part of the compound subject closest to the verb is *chicken*, which is singular. Therefore, the verb must be singular—*was*.

   Plural: Neither chicken nor **hot dogs were** on the menu.

   This time, the part of the compound subject closest to the verb is *hot dogs*, which is plural. Therefore, the verb must be plural—*were*.

PRACTICE 7: Identifying Underline the verb that agrees with its subject in each of the following sentences. Cross out the prepositional phrases first.

1. You and I (was, were) going the wrong way ~~down a one-way street~~.
2. Chicken and dumplings (taste, tastes) better ~~with a little salt and pepper.~~
3. Either the mosquitoes or the wind (cause, causes) my skin problems.
4. Celery and peanut butter (is, are) my favorite snack.
5. Neither the professor nor the students (knows, know) the answer ~~to this question~~.

PRACTICE 8: Completing Fill in each blank in the following sentences with a present-tense verb that agrees with its subject. Avoid *is* and *are*. Cross out the prepositional phrases first. *Answers will vary.*

1. Either lilies or tulips ______________ well in the spring.
2. Pie and ice cream ______________ the best dessert.
3. The ants and flies in the house ______________ me.
4. The train and the passengers ______________ sometime this evening.
5. Neither the entrees nor the dessert ______________ appetizing tonight.

PRACTICE 9: Writing Your Own Write a sentence of your own for each of the following compound subjects. Make sure that your subjects and verbs agree. *Answers will vary.*

1. either the handouts or the manuscript ______________________________
2. brooms and brushes ______________________________
3. neither the nurses nor the doctor ______________________________
4. ham and cheese ______________________________
5. the horse and her foal ______________________________

VERBS BEFORE SUBJECTS

When the subject follows its verb, the subject may be hard to find, which makes the process of agreeing subjects and verbs difficult. Subjects come after verbs in two particular situations—when the sentence begins with *here* or *there* and when a question begins with *Who, What, Where, When, Why,* or *How.* Here are some examples:

Verb Before Subject: Here **are** the **decorations** ~~for the party~~.

Verb Before Subject: There **is iced tea** ~~in the refrigerator~~.

In sentences that begin with *here* or *there*, the verb always comes before the subject. Don't forget to cross out prepositional phrases to help you identify the subject. One of the words that's left will be the subject, and then you can check that the verb agrees with it.

Verb Before Subject: Who **is** (v) that attractive **man** (s) ~~in the blue suit~~?

Verb Before Subject: Where **are** (v) the valuable **paintings** (s) **kept?** (v)

Verb Before Subject: When **are** (v) **you** (s) **flying** (v) ~~to Rome~~?

In questions that begin with *Who, What, When, Where, Why,* and *How,* the verb comes before the subject or is split by the subject, as in the last two examples.

PRACTICE 10: Identifying Underline the subject once and the verb twice in each of the following sentences. Cross out the prepositional phrases first.

1. Here lies the cause ~~of the problem despite the evidence~~.
2. Who is the leader ~~of your group~~?
3. How do you feel ~~after your recent operation~~?
4. Where ~~in the world~~ are my keys?
5. There ~~on the table~~ are your books.

PRACTICE 11: Completing Fill in each blank in the following sentences with a verb that agrees with its subject. Cross out the prepositional phrases first.

Answers will vary.

1. Where ______________ the rest of the apricot pie?
2. Over the hill, there ______________ a great swimming hole.

3. Why ____________ their dirty clothes on the bathroom floor?

4. How many times ____________ your sister asked you to fix that hair dryer?

5. What ____________ this mess in the front yard?

PRACTICE 12: Writing Your Own Write a sentence of your own for each of the following words and phrases. Make sure that your subjects and verbs agree.
Answers will vary.

1. there may be ____

2. what has been ____

3. how did he ____

4. when is ____

5. here is ____

COLLECTIVE NOUNS

Collective nouns name a group of people or things. Examples include such nouns as *army*, *audience*, *band*, *class*, *committee*, *crew*, *crowd*, *family*, *flock*, *gang*, *jury*, *majority*, *minority*, *orchestra*, *senate*, *team*, and *troop*. Collective nouns can be singular or plural. They are singular when they refer to a group as a single unit. They are plural when they refer to the individual actions or feelings of the group members.

s v
Singular: The string **quartet performs** three times a year.

Quartet refers to the entire unit or group. Therefore, it requires the singular verb *performs*.

s v
Plural: The string **quartet get** their new instruments on Monday.

Here *quartet* refers to the individual members, who will each get a new instrument, so the plural verb *get* is used.

PRACTICE 13: Identifying Underline the correct verb in each of the following sentences. Cross out the prepositional phrases first.

1. The audience (listen, listens) intently ~~to the guest speaker~~.

2. The majority (have, has) voted ~~at different polling booths~~.

3. The orchestra (play, plays) different selections, depending ~~on the concert~~.

4. Our high school cheerleading squad (is, are) all going ~~to different colleges~~.

5. The litter ~~of puppies~~ (get, gets) a bath today.

PRACTICE 14: Completing Fill in each blank in the following sentences with a present-tense verb that agrees with its subject. Cross out the prepositional phrases first. *Answers will vary.*

1. A flock ~~of geese~~ always ______________ south ~~for the winter~~.

2. The crew ______________ trouble making sure everyone has a good time.

3. The school orchestra ______________ this competition every year.

4. The army ______________ students who have degrees ~~as officers~~.

5. The senate ______________ according ~~to individual beliefs~~.

PRACTICE 15: Writing Your Own Write a sentence of your own using each of the following words as a plural subject. Make sure that your subjects and verbs agree. *Answers will vary.*

1. committee ____

2. gang ____

3. class ____

4. minority ____

5. group ____

INDEFINITE PRONOUNS

Indefinite pronouns do not refer to anyone or anything specific. Some indefinite pronouns are always singular, and some are always plural. A few can be either singular or plural, depending on the other words in the sentence. When an indefinite pronoun is the subject of a sentence, the verb must agree with the pronoun. Here is a list of indefinite pronouns.

Indefinite Pronouns

ALWAYS SINGULAR		ALWAYS PLURAL	EITHER SINGULAR OR PLURAL
another	*neither*	*both*	*all*
anybody	*nobody*	*few*	*any*
anyone	*none*	*many*	*more*
anything	*no one*	*others*	*most*
each	*nothing*	*several*	*some*
either	*one*		
everybody	*other*		
everyone	*somebody*		
everything	*someone*		
little	*something*		
much			

s v
Singular: **No one** ever **changes** at work.

s v
Everybody refuses to work harder.

s v v
Plural: **Many take** long lunches and **go** home early.

s v v
Others stay late but **are** tired and unmotivated.

The pronouns that can be either singular or plural are singular when they refer to singular words and plural when they refer to plural words.

s v
Singular: **Some** of Abby's *day* **was** hectic.

Some is singular because it refers to *day*, which is singular. The singular verb *was* agrees with the singular subject *some*.

s v
Plural: **Some** of Abby's *co-workers* **were** late.

Some is plural because it refers to *co-workers*, which is plural. The plural verb *were* agrees with the plural subject *some*.

PRACTICE 16: Identifying Underline the verb that agrees with its subject in each of the following sentences. Cross out the prepositional phrases first.

1. All ~~of my money~~ (is, are) gone.
2. Both ~~of the pools~~ (was, were) treated ~~with chlorine~~.
3. No one (do, does) more work than she.
4. Something (fly, flies) ~~into my window~~ every night and (buzz, buzzes) ~~around my head~~.
5. Most ~~of Omar's friends~~ (seem, seems) friendly.

PRACTICE 17: Completing Fill in each blank in the following sentences with a present-tense verb that agrees with its subject. Cross out the prepositional phrases first. *Answers will vary.*

1. Most ~~of the people~~ ______________ ~~to work in the mornings~~.
2. No one really ______________ if he will accept the job.
3. Both ______________ the consequences ~~of their actions~~.
4. None ~~of the fake contestants~~ ______________ it was a joke.
5. Somebody ______________ moving my things ~~off my desk~~.

PRACTICE 18: Writing Your Own Write a sentence of your own using each of the following words as a subject, combined with one of the following verbs: *is*, *are*, *was*, *were*. Make sure that your subjects and verbs agree. *Answers will vary.*

1. anything ____
2. others ____
3. some ____
4. any ____
5. several ____

CHAPTER REVIEW

You might want to reread the examples in this chapter before you do the following exercises.

REVIEW PRACTICE 1: Identifying Underline the subject once and the verb twice in each of the following sentences. Cross out the prepositional phrases first. Then put an X to the left of each sentence in which the subject and verb do not agree. Correct the subjects and verbs that don't agree by rewriting the incorrect sentences.

1. __X__ There sit the man who will be the next president of the United States. *(sits)*
2. __X__ The moon and the stars in the evening sky shines brightly. *(shine)*
3. __X__ The team usually practice off the track every Tuesday. *(practices)*
4. _____ Some of the fish in that tank appear to be sick.
5. _____ Doctor, how is the patient in room 204?
6. __X__ Something very sharp keep punching me in the back. *(keeps)*
7. __X__ Sour cream and onion are my favorite type of dip. *(is)*
8. __X__ Here are the recipe from my grandmother. *(is)*
9. __X__ Neither the chairs nor the table match the décor in this room. *(matches)*
10. _____ My gang of artistic friends finds the new trends exciting.

REVIEW PRACTICE 2: Completing Fill in each blank in the following sentences with a present-tense verb that agrees with its subject. *Answers will vary.*

1. My gang ______________ late for the show.
2. Neither wind nor rain nor snow ______________ us from going outside.
3. Here ______________ where Eugene's great-grandmother built her first house.
4. Several of the guests ______________ the secret code to the room back stage.
5. None of the water ______________ safe for drinking.

6. Where ______________ the tourists go for information about hotels?

7. Nothing ______________ to be wrong with the car.

8. The track team ______________ 5 miles every day, regardless of the weather.

9. Steven's mother and father ______________ planning a vacation to Paris.

10. There in that apartment building ______________ my former high school principal.

REVIEW PRACTICE 3: Writing Your Own Write a paragraph explaining why you did or did not join a committee, team, or other group. Make sure that your subjects and verbs agree. *Answers will vary.*

REVIEW PRACTICE 4: Editing Through Collaboration Exchange paragraphs from Review Practice 3 with another student, and do the following: *Answers will vary.*

1. Underline the subject once in each sentence.

2. Underline the verbs twice.

3. Put an X by any verbs that do not agree with their subjects.

Then return the paper to its writer, and use the information in this chapter to correct any subject-verb agreement errors in your own paragraph. Record your errors on the Error Log in Appendix 6.

31 CHAPTER

More on Verbs

CHECKLIST for Correcting Tense and Voice Problems

✔ Are verb tenses consistent?

✔ Are sentences written in the active voice?

UNIT PRETEST

To check your students' abilities with the collective skills in this unit, a Unit Pretest is available on pages 765–766.

TEACHING MORE ON VERBS

Create a short paragraph with inconsistent tenses. You might use words like *today* and *yesterday* to help create confusion. For example, "I am studying today for the hardest final I have ever taken. I had been studying for over two weeks, and I still will not feel like I'm prepared. The test was given tomorrow."

Have students rewrite the paragraph three times, once for each tense: past, present, and future. Make sure they adjust all words to indicate the

TEST YOURSELF

Label each sentence I if the verb tenses are inconsistent or P if it uses the passive voice.

- _____ George raced across the field and catches the ball.
- _____ The old record was broken by Justin.
- _____ That painting was done by a famous artist.
- _____ In the future, we may live on Mars, and we have produced our food in greenhouses.
- _____ First, the baker prepares the dough, and then she will cut out the cookies.

(Answers are in Appendix 4.)

Verbs communicate the action and time of each sentence. So it is important that you use verb tense consistently. Also, you should strive to write in the active, not the passive, voice. This chapter provides help with both of these sentence skills.

CONSISTENT VERB TENSE

Verb tense refers to the time an action takes place—in the present, the past, or the future. The verb tenses in a sentence should be consistent. That is, if you start out using one tense, you should not switch tenses unless absolutely necessary. Switching tenses can be confusing. Here are some examples:

Not: When the sun **sinks** (Present) into the bay and the moon **rises** (Present) from behind the trees, the pelicans **flew** (Past) away to the south.

Correct: When the sun **sinks** (Present) into the bay and the moon **rises** (Present) from behind the trees, the pelicans **fly** (Present) away to the south.

Not: They **skidded** (Past) off the road yesterday when the rain **is** (Present) heavy.

Correct: They **skidded** (Past) off the road yesterday when the rain **was** (Past) heavy.

Not: My brother **will receive** (Future) his degree in June, and then he **moves** (Present) to Boston.

Correct: My brother **will receive** (Future) his degree in June, and then he **will move** (Future) to Boston.

PRACTICE 1A: Identifying In the following sentences, write C if the verb tense is consistent or I if it is inconsistent.

1. __I__ Scott walked to the store and buy some milk.
2. __I__ Last evening, Charles waited at the park for his friends, but they never make it.

correct time (for example, use *today* with the present and *yesterday* with the past).

INSTRUCTOR'S RESOURCE MANUAL
For more sample paragraphs, for more exercises, and for quizzes, see the *Instructor's Resource Manual*, Section II, Part IV.

UNIT POSTTEST
To check your students' mastery of the collective skills in this unit, a Unit Posttest is available on pages 778–779.

3. ___I___ According to the instructor, we will need to bring a change of clothes, and we have to get all of our medical records updated.

4. ___I___ They grilled fresh fish over the fire and sleep under the stars.

5. ___C___ The salesclerk was rude to me, yet I thanked her anyway.

PRACTICE 1B: Correcting Correct the verb tense errors in Practice 1A by rewriting the inconsistent sentences. *Answers will vary.*

PRACTICE 2: Completing Fill in each blank in the following sentences with consistent verbs. *Answers will vary.*

1. During Kendra's vacation, she ______________ along the beach and ______________ souvenirs for her friends and family.
2. Out of the box ______________ the cat, and then he ______________ under the table.
3. Oh, no, I ______________ to bring the decorations for the prom, and I ______________ the invitations sitting on my kitchen counter.
4. Actors and singers generally ______________ a lot of media coverage and ______________ featured on many special television shows.
5. Madonna's music and videos ______________ many people, but her loyal fans ______________ her.

PRACTICE 3: Writing Your Own Write five sentences of your own with at least two verbs in each. Make sure your tenses are consistent. *Answers will vary.*

USING THE ACTIVE VOICE

In the **active voice,** the subject performs the action. In the **passive voice,** the subject receives the action. Compare the following two examples:

Passive Voice: The mayor **was accused** of stealing **by the police.**
Active Voice: **The police accused** the mayor of stealing.

The active voice adds energy to your writing. Here is another example. Notice the difference between active and passive.

Passive Voice: **A cake was baked** for Tim's birthday **by my grandmother.**
Active Voice: **My grandmother baked a cake** for Tim's birthday.

PRACTICE 4A: Identifying Write A if the sentence is in the active voice and P if it is in the passive voice.

1. __A__ The astronauts landed on the moon and planted a flag.
2. __P__ Flowers are being sent to the funeral home.
3. __A__ Jordan hit the ball over the fence into the neighbor's yard.
4. __P__ The experimental medicines were shipped to the laboratory for further testing.
5. __P__ People who heckle the politicians will be escorted from the building.

PRACTICE 4B: Correcting Rewrite the passive sentences in Practice 4A in the active voice. *Answers will vary.*

PRACTICE 5: Completing Complete the following sentences in the active voice. *Answers will vary.*

1. Many boxes of clothes ______________________________
2. A can of hairspray ______________________________
3. A plate of food ______________________________
4. The boy's hat ______________________________
5. The trip ______________________________

PRACTICE 6: Writing Your Own Write five sentences in the passive voice. Then rewrite them in the active voice. *Answers will vary.*

CHAPTER REVIEW

You might want to reread the examples in this chapter before you do the following exercises.

REVIEW PRACTICE 1: Identifying Label each sentence I if the verb tenses are inconsistent, P if it is in the passive voice, or C if it is correct. Then correct the inconsistent and passive sentences by rewriting them. *Answers will vary.*

1. __C__ You should pick up the trash in the yard.
2. __I__ The yacht keeps listing to the left and will need to be fixed before anyone can board her.

3. __P__ The ornaments sitting above the fireplace were given to my grandmother by famous people and were some of her favorite belongings.

4. __I__ Tomorrow, you and I will go to the lake and fished for trout.

5. __I__ I drank the Sprite and eat all the cookies.

6. __I__ Ken wished he had remembered his girlfriend's birthday and prays that she will forgive him.

7. __P__ The wad of gum was placed under the desk by a naughty boy.

8. __P__ The piano is played by Jeannie, and the songs are sung by Mark.

9. __P__ Your purchases will be sent to you later this week.

10. __C__ Caring individuals think of others before themselves and perform unselfish acts.

REVIEW PRACTICE 2: Completing Fill in each blank with consistent, active verbs. *Answers will vary.*

1. Mike ____________ the house on time but ____________ stuck in traffic.
2. I ____________ the hot coffee too quickly and ____________ my tongue.
3. The pebble in my shoe ____________ my foot, so I ____________ down.
4. The bird ____________ out the window and ____________ south.
5. Clare still ____________ in the Easter Bunny, but then she ____________ only 3 years old.

REVIEW PRACTICE 3: Writing Your Own Write a paragraph about a recent, difficult decision you have made. Be sure to give the reasons for your decision. Keep your tenses consistent, and use the active voice. *Answers will vary.*

REVIEW PRACTICE 4: Editing Through Collaboration Exchange paragraphs from Review Practice 3 with another student, and do the following: *Answers will vary.*

1. Circle all verbs that are not consistent in tense.
2. Underline any verbs in the passive voice.

Then return the paper to its writer, and use the information in this chapter to correct any verb consistency or voice errors in your own paragraph. Record your errors on the Error Log in Appendix 6.

Pronouns

Pronouns generally go almost unnoticed in writing and speaking, even though these words can do anything nouns can do. In fact, much like your inborn sense of balance, pronouns work in sentences to make your writing precise and coherent. Without pronouns, writers and speakers would find themselves repeating nouns over and over, producing sentences that are unnatural and boring. For example, notice how awkward the following paragraph would be without pronouns:

> Robert wrote a rough draft of Robert's essay last night. Then Robert asked Robert's girlfriend to read over Robert's essay with Robert. After Robert's girlfriend helped Robert find errors, Robert made corrections. Then Robert set aside the essay for a day before Robert took the essay out and began revising again.

When we let pronouns take over and do their jobs, we produce a much more fluent paragraph:

> Robert wrote a rough draft of his essay last night. Then he asked his girlfriend to read over his essay with him. After she helped Robert find errors, he made corrections. Then he set aside the essay for a day before he took it out and began revising again.

Problems with pronouns occur when the words pronouns refer to aren't clear or when pronouns and their antecedents—the words they refer to—are too far apart. In this unit, we will deal with the following aspects of pronouns:

32 CHAPTER

Pronoun Problems

CHECKLIST for Using Pronouns

✔ Are all subject pronouns used correctly?

✔ Are all object pronouns used correctly?

✔ Are all possessive pronouns used correctly?

✔ Are pronouns used in *than* or *as* comparisons in the correct form?

✔ Are the pronouns *this*, *that*, *these*, and *those* used correctly?

UNIT PRETEST

To check your students' abilities with the collective skills in this unit, a Unit Pretest is available on pages 766–768.

TEACHING PRONOUN PROBLEMS

Divide students into groups of three or four, and provide them with a paragraph that has several pronoun errors. Here is an example:

Mine brother can be so selfish. He has difficulty sharing. He believes that these here

TEST YOURSELF

Correct the pronoun errors in the following sentences.

- The ball was their's to begin with.
- Tom told Valerie and I the most exciting story.
- James can type a lot faster than me.
- Those there running shoes are Kim's.
- Me and Julio are going to the movies tonight.

(Answers are in Appendix 4.)

Pronouns are words that take the place of nouns. They help us avoid repeating nouns. In this chapter, we'll discuss five types of pronoun problems: (1) using the wrong pronoun as a subject, (2) using the wrong pronoun as an object, (3) using an apostrophe with a possessive pronoun, (4) misusing pronouns in comparisons, and (5) misusing demonstrative pronouns.

PRONOUNS AS SUBJECTS

Single pronouns as subjects usually don't cause problems.

Subject Pronoun: **I** attended the opera with my aunt and uncle.
Subject Pronoun: **They** relocated to New York.

You wouldn't say "*Me* attended the game" or "*Them* went to Los Angeles." But an error often occurs when a sentence has a compound subject and one or more of the subjects is a pronoun.

NOT **The boys and us** competed all the time.
Correct: **The boys and we** competed all the time.

NOT **Her and me** decided to go to Paris.
Correct: **She and I** decided to go to Paris.

To test whether you have used the correct form of the pronoun in a compound subject, try each subject alone.

Subject Pronoun? **The boys and us** competed for the trophy.
Test: **The boys** competed for the trophy. **YES**
Test: **Us** competed for the trophy. **NO**
Test: **We** competed for the trophy. **YES**
Correction: **The boys and we** competed for the trophy.

Here is a list of subject pronouns.

Subject Pronouns

SINGULAR	PLURAL
I	*we*
you	*you*
he, she, it	*they*

PRACTICE 1: Identifying Underline the pronouns used as subjects in each of the following sentences.

1. Diane and he will be gone for at least a week.
2. He is going to have to work faster if he wants to meet the deadline.
3. "I really don't want to go," he said.

books are only to be read by he or that them there clothes are only for he to wear. He was always more selfish than me. I always loved to share my stuff with others. You would not even believe he had the same parents as me because him is so selfish. I hope someday someone teaches him about the art of sharing.

Ask students to correct all the pronoun errors in the paragraph.

The first group to correct all the pronoun errors wins.

INSTRUCTOR'S RESOURCE MANUAL

For more sample paragraphs, for more exercises, and for quizzes, see the *Instructor's Resource Manual,* Section II, Part IV.

UNIT POSTTEST

To check your students' mastery of the collective skills in this unit, a Unit Posttest is available on pages 779–781.

4. We cannot use the elevator because it is not working.

5. She and I have been best friends since I can remember.

PRACTICE 2: Completing Fill in each blank in the following paragraph with a subject pronoun.

At first, my friends had me convinced that (1)___*I*___ should go on the annual deep-sea fishing trip. (2)___*They*___ spoke on and on about how much fun the last trip was. But before long, Brian admitted that (3)___*he*___ got sick once the boat was out at sea. Then Misty explained how the captain of the boat cut off the heads of the fish and gutted them. (4)___*She*___ found the whole process exciting. (5)___*You*___ can just imagine my reaction! I don't think I'll be joining my friends on their fishing trip.

PRACTICE 3: Writing Your Own Write a sentence of your own for each of the following subject pronouns. *Answers will vary.*

1. they ______________________________

2. you ______________________________

3. he ______________________________

4. it ______________________________

5. I ______________________________

PRONOUNS AS OBJECTS

One of the most frequent pronoun errors is using a subject pronoun when the sentence calls for an object pronoun. The sentence may require an object after a verb, showing that someone or something receives the action of the verb. Or it may be an object of a preposition that is required (see page 520 for a list of prepositions).

NOT	She gave **Kenisha and I** some money.
Correct:	She gave **Kenisha and me** some money.
NOT	The secret is between **you and I.**
Correct:	The secret is between **you and me.**

Like the subject pronoun error, the object pronoun error usually occurs with compound objects. Also like the subject pronoun error, you can test whether you are using the correct pronoun by using each object separately.

Object Pronoun?	She gave **Kenisha and I** some money.
Test:	She gave **Kenisha** some money. **YES**
Test:	She gave **I** some money. **NO**
Test:	She gave **me** some money. **YES**
Correction:	She gave **Kenisha and me** some money.

Here is a list of object pronouns:

Object Pronouns

SINGULAR	PLURAL
me	*us*
you	*you*
him, her, it	*them*

PRACTICE 4: Identifying Underline the correct object pronoun in each of the following sentences.

1. Natalie's grandmother raised (her, she) since she was 5.
2. The wonderful neighbors welcomed (we, us) to the community with a cake.
3. Corrina accidentally sprayed my sister and (I, me) with the hose.
4. All are going on the trip except for you and (him, he).
5. For (her, she), I will sit through this awful movie.

PRACTICE 5: Completing Fill in each blank in the following sentences with an object pronoun. *Answers will vary.*

1. Between the two of __________, we should be able to fix the problem.
2. He asked you and __________ to the same dance.
3. Unlike __________, I am going to take emergency gear on this hiking trip.
4. According to you and __________, the test will take one hour.
5. The priest took __________ on a tour of the temple.

PRACTICE 6: Writing Your Own Write a sentence of your own for each of the following object pronouns. *Answers will vary.*

1. us ______________________________
2. him ______________________________
3. me ______________________________
4. them ______________________________
5. her ______________________________

POSSESSIVE PRONOUNS

Possessive pronouns show ownership (***my*** *house*, ***her*** *baseball*, ***our*** *family*). (See pages 515–517 for a list of pronouns.) An apostrophe is used with nouns to show ownership (***Jack's*** *dog, the* ***farmer's*** *tractor, the* ***people's*** *opinions*). But an apostrophe is never used with possessive pronouns.

Possessive Pronouns

SINGULAR	PLURAL
my, mine	*our, ours*
your, yours	*you, yours*
his, her, hers	*their, theirs*

NOT	That house is **their's.**
Correct:	That house is **theirs.**
NOT	The book on the table is **your's.**
Correct:	The book on the table is **yours.**
NOT	The dog chased **it's** tail.
Correct:	The dog chased **its** tail.

PRACTICE 7: Identifying Underline the correct possessive pronoun in each of the following sentences.

1. The computer needs its monitor fixed.
2. Both of my aunts live in New Mexico.

3. That piece of cake on the counter is hers.

4. The children left their toys in the driveway.

5. Hey! That was his.

PRACTICE 8: Completing Fill in each blank in the following sentences with a possessive pronoun. *Answers will vary.*

1. These books aren't __________, so they must be __________.

2. __________ dogs bothered the neighbors so much that we had to move.

3. The filming crew left __________ equipment on the set.

4. Look at John's dog carrying __________ bowl in his mouth.

5. The copy machine won't work because __________ ink cartridge is empty.

PRACTICE 9: Writing Your Own Write a sentence of your own for each of the following possessive pronouns. *Answers will vary.*

1. mine ______________________________

2. theirs ______________________________

3. his ______________________________

4. its ______________________________

5. our ______________________________

PRONOUNS IN COMPARISONS

Sometimes pronoun problems occur in comparisons with *than* or *as*. An object pronoun may be mistakenly used instead of a subject pronoun. To find out if you are using the right pronoun, you should finish the sentence as shown here.

NOT	She can analyze poems better than **me.**
Correct:	She can analyze poems better than **I** [can analyze poems].
NOT	Lilly is not as good a piano player as **him.**
Correct:	Lilly is not as good a piano player as **he** [is].

Hint: Sometimes an object pronoun is required in a *than* or *as* comparison. But errors rarely occur in this case because the subject pronoun sounds so unnatural.

NOT Kay dislikes him more than she dislikes **I.**

Correct: Kay dislikes him more than she dislikes **me.**

PRACTICE 10: Identifying Underline the correct pronoun in each of the following comparisons.

1. Mark is much neater than (I, me).
2. Cindy, the head majorette at our high school, can twirl a baton as well as (we, us).
3. Simone is not as talented an artist as (him, he).
4. Those other puppies are much fatter than (they, them).
5. Carlos is just as happy as (she, her).

PRACTICE 11: Completing Fill in each blank in the following sentences with an appropriate pronoun for comparison. *Answers will vary.*

1. After he appeared in *Star Wars*, Harrison Ford became a bigger star than ___________.
2. Joey can throw a ball as far as ___________.
3. My friends managed to stay longer in the haunted house than ___________ did.
4. He makes you just as mad as he makes ___________.
5. Julia, whose parents are well-known artists, is a more talented painter than ___________.

PRACTICE 12: Writing Your Own Write a sentence of your own using each of the following pronouns in *than* or *as* comparisons. *Answers will vary.*

1. I ____
2. she ____
3. they ____

4. we ____

5. he ____

DEMONSTRATIVE PRONOUNS

There are four demonstrative pronouns: *this*, *that*, *these*, and *those*. **Demonstrative pronouns** point to specific people or objects. Use *this* and *these* to refer to items that are near and *that* and *those* to refer to items farther away. Look at the following examples.

Demonstrative (near): **This** is my room.
Demonstrative (near): **These** are yesterday's notes.
Demonstrative (farther): **That** is the town hall.
Demonstrative (farther): **Those** are the cheerleaders for the other team.

Sometimes demonstrative pronouns are not used correctly.

NOT	Correct
this here, that there	this, that
these here, these ones	these
them, those there, those ones	those

NOT **Them** are the clothes she bought.
Correct: **Those** are the clothes she bought.

NOT I'd like to have **these here** books.
Correct: I'd like to have **these** books.

NOT I found **those ones** in the attic.
Correct: I found **those** in the attic.

NOT **Those there** are the ones I like.
Correct: **Those** are the ones I like.

When demonstrative pronouns are used with nouns, they become adjectives.

Pronoun: **That** is mine.
Adjective: **That computer** is mine.

Pronoun: **Those** are actions you may regret.
Adjective: You may regret **those actions.**

The problems that occur with demonstrative pronouns can also occur when these pronouns act as adjectives.

NOT Please give me **that there** paper.
Correct: Please give me **that** paper.

PRACTICE 13A: Identifying Underline the demonstrative pronoun errors in each of the following sentences.

1. The babies usually play with those there toys. *(those)*
2. This here test is just too difficult. *(This)*
3. I believe that there pair of shoes will do nicely for this outfit. *(that)*
4. These ones should be brought in out of the rain. *(These)*
5. I can carry this here if you'll take that there. *(this, that)*

PRACTICE 13B: Correcting Correct the demonstrative pronoun errors in Practice 13A by rewriting the incorrect sentences. *See Practice 13A.*

PRACTICE 14: Completing Fill in each blank in the following sentences with a logical demonstrative pronoun. *Answers will vary.*

1. ___________ are the skates he wanted.
2. Would you like ___________ curtains for your house?
3. ___________ Corvette belongs to my uncle.
4. She baked ___________ cookies herself.
5. I want ___________ for my bathroom.

PRACTICE 15: Writing Your Own Write four sentences of your own, one using each demonstrative pronoun. Be sure you don't use these pronouns as adjectives in your sentences. *Answers will vary.*

CHAPTER REVIEW

You might want to reread the examples in this chapter before you do the following exercises.

REVIEW PRACTICE 1: Identifying Underline the pronoun errors in each of the following sentences.

1. The football team and us went out for pizza after the game. *(we)*
2. I think the fish is trying to tell you its' tank needs to be cleaned. *(its)*
3. That secret was supposed to remain between you and I. *(me)*
4. My brother at age four was as big as him at age six. *(he)*
5. These here tarts are the best I've ever tasted. *(These)*
6. Due to the power outage, him and me had dinner by candlelight. *(he and I)*
7. I do believe you are stronger than him. *(he)*
8. Hers' money is already spent even though she started out with $100. *(Her)*
9. One of my high school teachers taught she and me how to fly a plane. *(her)*
10. I know that those there CDs belong to me. *(those)*

REVIEW PRACTICE 2: Completing Correct the pronoun errors in Review Practice 1 by rewriting the incorrect sentences. *See Review Practice 1.*

REVIEW PRACTICE 3: Writing Your Own Write a short paragraph about your most treasured object. Why is it one of your favorite possessions? *Answers will vary.*

REVIEW PRACTICE 4: Editing Through Collaboration Exchange paragraphs from Review Practice 3 with another student, and do the following: *Answers will vary.*

1. Circle all pronouns.
2. Check that all the subject and object pronouns are used correctly. Also check that possessive pronouns, pronouns used in comparisons, and demonstrative pronouns are used correctly. Put an X through any that are not in the correct form.

Then return the paper to its writer, and use the information in this chapter to correct the pronoun errors in your own paragraph. Record your errors on the Error Log in Appendix 6.

33 CHAPTER

Pronoun Reference and Point of View

CHECKLIST for Correcting Problems with Pronoun Reference and Point of View

✔ Does every pronoun have a clear antecedent?

✔ Are pronouns as close as possible to the words they refer to?

✔ Do you maintain a single point of view?

UNIT PRETEST

To check your students' abilities with the collective skills in this unit, a Unit Pretest is available on pages 766–768.

TEACHING PRONOUN REFERENCE AND POINT OF VIEW

Provide students with a series of pictures that have a unique point of view. Ask them to study each picture to guess who they think might have taken the picture and from what point of view (for example, a young woman, trying to show the beauty of a father and child).

After the students have analyzed a few

TEST YOURSELF

Underline the pronouns in these sentences. Then put an X over any pronouns that are confusing or unclear.

- It says to schedule your own appointments.
- Millie and Tanya were planning to go to Las Vegas, but her car broke.
- I created a backup plan because you should always be prepared for the unexpected.
- You know they are covering up evidence of alien beings.
- Jimmy forgot the answer to questions 1 and 10, but he remembered it the next day.

(Answers are in Appendix 4.)

Anytime you use a pronoun, it must clearly refer to a specific word. The word it refers to is called its **antecedent.** Two kinds of problems occur with pronoun references: The antecedent may be unclear, or the antecedent may be missing. You should also be careful to stick to the same point of view in your writing. If, for example, you start out talking about "I," you should not shift to "you" in the middle of the sentence.

PRONOUN REFERENCE

Sometimes a sentence is confusing because the reader can't tell what a pronoun is referring to. The confusion may occur because the pronoun's antecedent is unclear or is completely missing.

Unclear Antecedents

In the following examples, the word each pronoun is referring to is unclear.

Unclear: A bucket and an oar lay in the boat. As Rachel reached for **it,** the boat moved.
(Was Rachel reaching for *the bucket* or *the oar?* Only Rachel knows for sure.)

Clear: A bucket and an oar lay in the boat. As Rachel reached for **the bucket,** the boat moved.

Clear: A bucket and an oar lay in the boat. As Rachel reached for **the oar,** the boat moved.

Unclear: Michael told Oliver that **he** should change jobs.
(Does *he* refer to *Michael* or *Oliver?* Only the writer knows.)

Clear: Michael told Oliver that **Oliver** should change jobs.

Clear: Talking with Oliver, **Michael** said that **Michael himself** should change jobs.

How can you be sure that every pronoun you use has a clear antecedent? First, you can proofread carefully. Probably an even better test, though, is to ask a friend to read what you have written and tell you if your meaning is clear or not.

Missing Antecedents

Every pronoun should have a clear antecedent, the word it refers to. But what happens when there is no antecedent at all? The writer's message is not communicated. Two words in particular should alert you to the possibility of missing antecedents: *it* and *they.*

The following sentences have missing antecedents:

Missing Antecedent: In a recent political poll, **it** shows that most people consider their votes unimportant.
(What does *it* refer to? It has no antecedent.)

pictures, have them change their positions about who they think took the picture and what his or her point of view might be. Shifting their opinions will probably be difficult.

Point out to students that this kind of difficulty occurs when students shift point of view in their sentences or don't provide a reference for readers when using pronouns. Readers will experience the same type of confusion when pronoun reference and point of view shift unnecessarily or are unclear.

INSTRUCTOR'S RESOURCE MANUAL

For more exercises and for quizzes, see the *Instructor's Resource Manual,* Section II, Part IV.

UNIT POSTTEST

To check your students' mastery of the collective skills in this unit, a Unit Posttest is available on pages 779–781.

Clear:	A **recent political poll** shows that most people consider their votes unimportant.
Missing Antecedent:	**They** say that a fool and his money are soon parted. (Who is *they?*)
Clear:	**An old saying** states that a fool and his money are soon parted.

PRACTICE 1A: Identifying Underline the pronouns in each of the following sentences. Then put an X next to any sentences with missing or unclear antecedents.

1. __X__ According to recent surveys, it says that more people are getting a college education.
2. __X__ My red pen should be in my purse, but I can't find it.
3. _____ The sitting room must have its baseboards cleaned.
4. __X__ Talking with Kesha and Mindy, I learned that she is moving to Texas!
5. __X__ They say you can catch more flies with honey than with vinegar.

PRACTICE 1B: Correcting Correct the sentences with pronoun errors in Practice 1A by rewriting them. *Answers will vary.*

PRACTICE 2: Completing Correct the unclear or missing pronoun references in the following sentences by rewriting them. Pronouns that should be corrected are underlined. *Answers will vary.*

1. It says that we are all required to be at the meeting.
2. They always told me to treat people the way I want to be treated.
3. According to Sue and Hanna, she has been accepted into Yale.
4. We have chocolate and vanilla ice cream, but it tastes better.
5. It indicates that we should have turned left at the first light.

PRACTICE 3: Writing Your Own Write five sentences of your own using pronouns with clear antecedents. *Answers will vary.*

SHIFTING POINT OF VIEW

Point of view refers to whether a statement is made in the first person, the second person, or the third person. Each person—or point of view—requires different pronouns. The following chart lists the pronouns for each point of view.

Point of View

First Person:	*I, we*
Second Person:	*you, you*
Third Person:	*he, she, it, they*

If you begin writing from one point of view, you should stay in that point of view. Do not shift to another point of view. For example, if you start out writing "I," you should continue with "I" and not shift to "you." Shifting point of view is a very common error in college writing.

Shift: If **a person** doesn't study, **you** will not do well in school.
Correct: If **a person** doesn't study, **he or she** will not do well in school.

Shift: **I** changed jobs because **you** have more opportunities here.
Correct: **I** changed jobs because **I** have more opportunities here.

PRACTICE 4A: Identifying Underline the pronouns that shift in point of view in the following sentences.

1. If you don't eat a good diet, they may find their health suffering. *(you, your)*
2. One can always find unique merchandise at the more exclusive stores, but you have to be willing to pay the price. *(one has)*
3. I hinted that I didn't want to take part in the play, but you never know if you've gotten the message across. *(I, I've)*
4. I see a couple of concerts a year because everyone needs a little culture in his or her life. *(I need, my)*
5. I've already started writing my research paper because you should never wait until the last minute. *(I)*

PRACTICE 4B: Correcting Correct the point-of-view errors in Practice 4A by rewriting the incorrect sentences. *See Practice 4A. Answers may vary.*

PRACTICE 5: Completing Complete the following sentences with pronouns that stay in the same point of view.

1. I decided to pack lightly and carry my luggage on board the airplane, so ___*I*___ know my luggage will arrive when I do.
2. I should taste these dishes since ___*I*___ never know if I'm going to like them until I try them.
3. A person is expected to follow the rules of the road; otherwise, ___*he or she*___ may cause an accident.
4. I always wear a smile on my face since ___*I*___ never know who might be around.
5. One should pay attention; then ___*one*___ might not feel so confused.

PRACTICE 6: Writing Your Own Write a sentence of your own for each of the following pronouns. Be sure the pronouns have clear antecedents and do not shift point of view. *Answers will vary.*

1. they ______________________________
2. you ______________________________
3. I ______________________________
4. it ______________________________
5. we ______________________________

CHAPTER REVIEW

You might want to reread the examples in this chapter before you do the following exercises.

REVIEW PRACTICE 1: Identifying Label the following sentences U if the antecedent is unclear, M if the antecedent is missing, or S if the sentence shifts point of view. Then correct the pronoun errors by rewriting the incorrect sentences.

1. __S__ If one forgets the answer, then you should look it up.

2. __M__ They say you should never accept rides from strangers.

3. __U__ Janie bought milk, bread, cheese, and lettuce at the grocery store, but she left it in the car.

4. __S__ A person should always look both ways before crossing the street; otherwise, you might get hit by a car.

5. __U__ Stacy and Myra have already left for the show, but she forgot her wallet.

6. __M__ It explains that the majority of the citizens are in favor of the proposed freeway.

7. __S__ I asked my friends about my decision because you always value your friends' advice.

8. __M__ It pointed out that "every cloud has a silver lining."

9. __U__ Steven told Jason that he was going to be late.

10. __U__ I ordered two pairs of jeans, a pair of shorts, and a pair of shoes from a catalog. I received it one week later.

REVIEW PRACTICE 2: Completing Correct the pronoun errors in the following sentences by rewriting each incorrect sentence. *Answers will vary.*

1. I am going to purchase the most expensive champagne I can find, for you know that will impress the guests.

2. According to this announcement, it says we need to arrive no later than 2:00 p.m.

3. Jake and Dean will probably get into good colleges, even though he has a higher GPA.

4. A person should manage time wisely since you only have 24 hours in a day.

5. They are always carrying on about how bad the humidity is in the South.

6. Before Carla and Trisha left town, she bought a new swimsuit.

7. We were gossiping about Jarrett and Jeremy when he walked right by us.

8. One should study for the test if you want to pass it.

9. I had my hands full with a squirming puppy and a hissing cat until I decided to set him down.

10. You know what they say: "Never go to bed with a wet head."

REVIEW PRACTICE 3: Writing Your Own Write a paragraph about a new experience you have had. Include at least six different pronouns. *Answers will vary.*

REVIEW PRACTICE 4: Editing Through Collaboration Exchange paragraphs from Review Practice 3 with another student, and do the following: *Answers will vary.*

1. Underline all pronouns.

2. Draw arrows to the words they modify.

3. Put an X through any pronouns that do not refer to a clear antecedent or that shift point of view.

Then return the paper to its writer, and use the information in this chapter to correct any pronoun reference and point-of-view errors in your own paragraph. Record your errors on the Error Log in Appendix 6.

CHAPTER 34

Pronoun Agreement

CHECKLIST for Correcting Pronoun Agreement Problems

✔ Do all pronouns and their antecedents agree in number (singular or plural)?

✔ Do any pronouns that refer to indefinite pronouns agree in number?

✔ Are any pronouns used in a sexist way?

TEST YOURSELF

Underline the pronouns in each sentence, and draw an arrow to their antecedents. Put an X over any pronouns that do not agree with their antecedents.

- Somebody left his lights on in his car.
- A judge must put aside her bias.
- Each of the children needs their permission slip signed.
- None of the fans could keep their voices quiet.
- A motorcyclist must take care of her gear.

(Answers are in Appendix 4.)

As you learned in Chapter 25, subjects and verbs must agree for clear communication. If the subject is singular, the verb must be singular; if the subject is plural, the verb must be plural. The same holds true for pronouns and the words they refer to—their *antecedents*. They must agree in number—both singular or both plural. Usually, pronoun agreement is not a problem, as these sentences show:

UNIT PRETEST
To check your students' abilities with the collective skills in this unit, a Unit Pretest is available on pages 766–768.

TEACHING PRONOUN AGREEMENT
Create two sets of index cards: one of musical performers (made from pictures cut out of magazines) and another of personal pronouns. The performer cards should have pictures of both single performers and groups. Divide the students into small groups, and divide the performer cards evenly among the groups.

Provide sentences on the board, and ask teams to identify pronoun antecedent errors in the sentences. When a team gets an answer correct, give it a random pronoun card.

The team should then match the pronoun card with a performer card (for example, a "her" card could go with Faith Hill or Madonna, a "their" card with Aerosmith or Supernova).

The first team to correctly match all its performer cards with pronoun cards wins.

INSTRUCTOR'S RESOURCE MANUAL
For sample sentences, for more exercises and for quizzes, see the *Instructor's Resource Manual*, Section II, Part IV.

UNIT POSTTEST
To check your students' mastery of the collective skills in this unit, a Unit Posttest is available on pages 779–781.

Singular: **Dr. Gomez** told **his** patient to stop smoking.
Plural: **Carlos** and **Gina** took **their** children to Disney World.

INDEFINITE PRONOUNS

Pronoun agreement may become a problem with indefinite pronouns. Indefinite pronouns that are always singular give writers the most trouble.

NOT **One** of the students finished **their** test early.
(How many students finished early? Only one, so use a singular pronoun.)
Correct: **One** of the students finished **her** test early.
Correct: **One** of the students finished **his** test early.

NOT **Somebody** just drove **their** new car into a ditch.
(How many people just drove a car into a ditch? One person, so use a singular pronoun.)
Correct: **Somebody** just drove **her** new car into a ditch.
Correct: **Somebody** just drove **his** new car into a ditch.

Here is a list of indefinite pronouns that are always singular.

Singular Indefinite Pronouns

another	*everybody*	*neither*	*one*
anybody	*everyone*	*nobody*	*other*
anyone	*everything*	*none*	*somebody*
anything	*little*	*no one*	*someone*
each	*much*	*nothing*	*something*
either			

Hint: A few indefinite pronouns can be either singular or plural, depending on their meaning in the sentence. These pronouns are *any*, *all*, *more*, *most*, and *some*.

Singular: **Some** of the money was left over, so we gave **it** to charity.
Plural: **Some** of the donations were left over, so we gave **them** to charity.

In the first sentence, *money* is singular, so the singular pronoun *it* is used. In the second sentence, *donations* is plural, so the plural pronoun *them* is used.

PRACTICE 1: Identifying Underline the correct pronoun from the choices in parentheses, and be prepared to explain your choices.

1. All of the infants had (his or her, <u>their</u>) footprints and handprints recorded at the hospital.
2. None of the cars needs (<u>its</u>, their) tires changed.
3. Anyone can get (<u>his or her</u>, their) high school diploma.
4. Before anybody can join the club, (<u>he or she</u>, they) must fill out an enrollment form.
5. The farmers and the farmworkers need (his or her, <u>their</u>) work hours shortened.

PRACTICE 2: Completing Fill in each blank in the following sentences with a pronoun that agrees with its antecedent.

1. Fabiola and Fabian asked ___*their*___ questions at the same time.
2. Everyone should listen more closely to ___*his or her*___ teacher.
3. Matt lost ___*his*___ backpack at the park.
4. Someone who could do a thing like that should have ___*his or her*___ head examined.
5. Something in the car leaked all ___*its*___ fluids onto the driveway.

PRACTICE 3: Writing Your Own Write a sentence of your own for each of the following pronouns. *Answers will vary.*

1. none ______________________________
2. other ______________________________
3. no one ______________________________
4. everything ______________________________
5. someone ______________________________

AVOIDING SEXISM

In the first section of this chapter, you learned that you should use singular pronouns to refer to singular indefinite pronouns. For example, the indefinite pronoun *someone* requires a singular pronoun, *his* or *her* (not the plural *their*). But what if you don't know whether the person referred to is male or female? Then you have a choice: (1) You can say "he or she" or "his or her"; (2) you can make the sentence plural; or (3) you can rewrite the sentence to avoid the problem. What you should not do is ignore half the population by referring to all humans as a single gender.

NOT If **anyone** wants to go, **he** is welcome to do so.
Correct: If **anyone** wants to go, **he or she** is welcome to do so.
Correct: **People** who want to go are welcome to do so.

NOT **Everyone** remembered to bring **his** lunch.
Correct: **Everyone** remembered to bring **his or her** lunch.
Correct: **All** the students remembered to bring **their** lunch.

Sexism in writing can also occur in ways other than with indefinite pronouns. We often assume that doctors, lawyers, and bank presidents are men and that nurses, schoolteachers, and secretaries are women. But that is not very accurate.

NOT Ask a **fireman** if **he** thinks the wiring is safe.
(Why automatically assume that the person fighting fires is a male instead of a female?)
Correct: Ask a **firefighter** if **he or she** thinks the wiring is safe.

NOT The **mailman** delivered my neighbor's mail to my house by mistake.
(Since both men and women deliver mail, the more correct term is *mail carrier*.)
Correct: The **mail carrier** delivered my neighbor's mail to my house by mistake.

NOT An **assistant** cannot reveal **her** boss's confidential business.
(Why leave the men who are assistants out of this sentence?)
Correct: An **assistant** cannot reveal **his or her** boss's confidential business.

Correct: **Assistants** cannot reveal **their** boss's confidential business.

PRACTICE 4A: Identifying Underline the sexist references in the following sentences.

1. The chairperson should keep his board informed of new developments. *(his or her)*
2. A nurse gives her time and patience freely. *(his or her)*
3. Each person is responsible for makeup work if he misses an assignment. *(he or she)*
4. Everybody must cook food if she plans to eat. *(he or she)*
5. A good sailor knows his knots. *(his or her)*

PRACTICE 4B: Correcting Correct the sexist pronouns in Practice 4A by rewriting the incorrect sentences. *See Practice 4A.*

PRACTICE 5: Completing Fill in each blank in the following sentences with an appropriate pronoun.

1. A technician might become frustrated with ___*his or her*___ job.
2. A hairdresser who attracts celebrity customers can name ___*his or her*___ price.
3. An accountant needs help with ___*his or her*___ accounts.
4. Somebody wrote ___*his or her*___ phone number on the bathroom wall.
5. Sometimes a child forgets ___*his or her*___ lunch.

PRACTICE 6: Writing Your Own Write a sentence of your own for each of the following antecedents. Include at least one pronoun in each sentence. *Answers will vary.*

1. doctor ______________________________
2. politician ______________________________
3. police officer ______________________________
4. spokesperson ______________________________
5. FBI agent ______________________________

CHAPTER REVIEW

You might want to reread the examples in this chapter before you do the following exercises.

REVIEW PRACTICE 1: Identifying Underline and correct the pronoun errors in the following sentences.

1. Anyone who wants their book signed should stand in this line. *(his or her)*
2. A good assistant keeps her dictionary within easy reach. *(his or her)*
3. A surfer can lose his wave. *(his or her)*
4. Only one of the contestants turned in their enrollment form on time. *(his or her)*
5. The politician who cares about his people will win the election. *(his or her)*
6. Each of the photographers has their own camera. *(his or her)*
7. Everyone needs their funny bone tickled every now and then. *(his or her)*
8. A tattoo artist should always clean her equipment before each new client. *(his or her)*
9. A teacher should always ask her students if they understand the assignment. *(his or her)*
10. Someone that messy should clean their room more often. *(his or her)*

REVIEW PRACTICE 2: Completing Fill in each blank in the following sentences with an appropriate pronoun.

1. Neither of the criminals wanted ___*his or her*___ picture taken.
2. A racecar driver depends on ___*his or her*___ car and skill to win the race.
3. A housecleaner brings ___*his or her*___ own supplies.
4. Each of the boys can do ___*his*___ own work.
5. None of the students wanted to disappoint ___*his or her*___ teacher.
6. At the reunion, everyone talked to ___*his or her*___ friends.

7. Another person left ___*his or her*___ homework behind.

8. Somebody needs to water ___*his or her*___ lawn.

9. Everyone should be nice to ___*his or her*___ neighbors.

10. Nobody should park ___*his or her*___ car in a no-parking zone.

REVIEW PRACTICE 3: Writing Your Own Write a paragraph describing your favorite type of music. Why is it your favorite? *Answers will vary.*

REVIEW PRACTICE 4: Editing Through Collaboration Exchange paragraphs from Review Practice 3 with another student, and do the following: *Answers will vary.*

1. Underline any pronouns.

2. Circle any pronouns that do not agree with the words they refer to.

Then return the paper to its writer, and use the information in this chapter to correct any pronoun agreement errors in your own paragraph. Record your errors on the Error Log in Appendix 6.

Modifiers

Words that modify—usually called adjectives and adverbs—add details to sentences, either describing, limiting, or identifying so that sentences become more vivid and interesting. They work like accessories in our everyday lives. Without jewelry, scarves, ties, and cuff links, we are still dressed. But accessories give a little extra flair to our wardrobe. Without modifiers, our writing would be bland, boring, and lifeless. However, to use adjectives and adverbs correctly, you need to learn about their different forms and functions.

In the chapters in this unit, you will learn about adjectives, adverbs, and various problems with the placement of these words in sentences:

Chapter 35: Adjectives
Chapter 36: Adverbs
Chapter 37: Modifier Errors
Unit 4 Pretests: pp. 768–769
Unit 4 Posttests: pp. 781–782

CHAPTER 35

Adjectives

CHECKLIST for Using Adjectives Correctly

✔ Are all adjectives that show comparison used correctly?

✔ Are the forms of *good* and *bad* used correctly?

TEST YOURSELF

Underline the adjectives in the following sentences. Then put an X over the adjectives that are used incorrectly.

- The kites were very colorful.
- She has the worstest hair color that I have ever seen.
- We were more busier this week than last week.
- He is the oldest of the two brothers.
- The Ford Mustang is more better than the Nissan Sentra.

(Answers are in Appendix 4.)

Adjectives are modifiers. They help us communicate more clearly (I have a *green* car; I want a *red* one) and vividly (the movie was *funny* and *romantic*). Without adjectives, our language would be drab and boring.

USING ADJECTIVES

Adjectives are words that modify—or describe—nouns or pronouns. Adjectives often tell how something or someone looks: *dark, light, tall, short, large, small.* Most adjectives come before the words they modify, but with linking verbs (such as *is, are, look, become,* and *feel*), adjectives follow the words they modify.

UNIT PRETEST

To check your students' abilities with the collective skills in this unit, a Unit Pretest is available on pages 768–769.

TEACHING ADJECTIVES

Provide students with a sentence that contains no adjectives, and have the students draw a picture that represents the sentence (for example, "the house on the street").

Restate the sentence, but this time add a couple of adjectives ("the two-story house on the narrow street"), and have students redraw the sentence on a new sheet of paper.

Continue this procedure a few more times until the students are drawing an elaborate picture ("the two-story, red brick house with a white, three-foot-tall picket fence on the narrow, shaded, deserted street").

Have students compare their first and last drawings to see the detail they added when a few adjectives were inserted into the description.

INSTRUCTOR'S RESOURCE MANUAL

For more sample sentences, for more exercises, and for quizzes, see the *Instructor's Resource Manual*, Section II, Part IV.

UNIT POSTTEST

To check your students' mastery of the collective skills in this unit, a Unit Posttest is available on pages 781–782.

Adjectives Before a Noun: We felt the **cold, icy** snow.
Adjectives After a Linking Verb: The snow was **cold** and **icy.**

PRACTICE 1: Identifying In the following sentences, underline the adjectives, and circle the words they modify.

1. Michael left a shiny red apple on the wooden desk on Monday morning.
2. Mrs. Johnson gave the two-year-old boy a piece of hard candy.
3. Our family doctor wants us to come in for our annual checkups.
4. I read a great book by John Grisham last week.
5. Grandma's beautiful garden is a quiet place for me to read, draw, or take a quick nap.

PRACTICE 2: Completing Fill in each blank in the following sentences with logical adjectives. *Answers will vary.*

During my (1) _____________ year of high school, I asked the head cheerleader to go to the prom with me. I was (2) _____________ when she agreed to be my date, and I really wanted to impress her. I rented an expensive tuxedo, bought a (3) _____________ corsage for her to wear on her wrist, and made sure to pick her up on time. The (4) _____________ price was worth it because when we arrived at the dance, all of my buddies patted me on the back and said, "You two look (5) _____________ together!"

PRACTICE 3: Writing Your Own Write a sentence of your own for each of the following adjectives. *Answers will vary.*

1. curious ____
2. durable ____
3. thirteen ____
4. helpful ____
5. short-tempered ____

COMPARING WITH ADJECTIVES

Most adjectives have three forms: a **basic** form, a **comparative** form (used to compare two items or indicate a greater degree), and a **superlative** form (used to compare three or more items or indicate the greatest degree).

For positive comparisons, adjectives form the comparative and superlative in two different ways.

1. For one-syllable adjectives and some two-syllable adjectives, use *-er* to compare two items and *-est* to compare three or more items.

Basic	Comparative (used to compare two items)	Superlative (used to compare three or more items)
bold	bolder	boldest
warm	warmer	warmest
numb	number	numbest
wise	wiser	wisest

2. For some two-syllable adjectives and all longer adjectives, use *more* to compare two items and *most* to compare three or more items.

Basic	Comparative (used to compare two items)	Superlative (used to compare three or more items)
friendly	more friendly	most friendly
peaceful	more peaceful	most peaceful
wonderful	more wonderful	most wonderful
appropriate	more appropriate	most appropriate

For negative comparisons, use *less* to compare two items and *least* to compare three or more items.

Basic	Comparative (used to compare two items)	Superlative (used to compare three or more items)
loud	less loud	least loud
funny	less funny	least funny
popular	less popular	least popular

Hint: Some adjectives are not usually compared. For example, one person cannot be "more dead" than another. Here are some more examples.

broken	final	square
empty	impossible	supreme
equal	singular	unanimous

PRACTICE 4: Identifying Underline the adjectives, and note whether they are basic (B), comparative (C), or superlative (S).

1. S The most logical decision would be to appoint Sam to the position.
2. B Today the students showed how dedicated they can be.
3. C Mita was happier about the engagement than her father was.
4. S The strongest students always score the highest on the exam.
5. C The food Nora and Richard ate on vacation was less healthy than what they eat at home.

PRACTICE 5: Completing Fill in each blank in the following paragraph with the correct comparative or superlative form of the adjective in parentheses.

One summer afternoon, I was hiking high in the mountains when the sky above me grew suddenly (1) darker (dark) than I have ever seen it. It looked like rain was going to fall soon, and I happened to be in an (2) unsheltered (unsheltered) place on the mountain. I looked around to find the (3) most suitable (suitable) tree to sit under, but there weren't any that would protect me. Even the (4) thickest (thick) tree was very puny and wouldn't keep the rain off of my head. Quickly, I realized I had no option but to run (5) faster (fast) than the rain to find shelter farther down the hill.

PRACTICE 6: Writing Your Own Write a sentence of your own for each of the following adjectives.

1. a superlative form of *pretty* prettiest/least pretty
2. the basic form of *sensible* sensible
3. a comparative form of *talented* more/less talented
4. a superlative form of *disgusting* most/least disgusting
5. a comparative form of *tall* taller/less tall

COMMON ADJECTIVE ERRORS

Two types of problems occur with adjectives used in comparisons.

1. Instead of using one method for forming the comparative or superlative, both are used. That is, both *-er* and *more* or *less* are used to compare two items or both *-est* and *most* or *least* are used to compare three or more items.

    NOT My youngest son is **more taller** than his brothers.
    Correct: My youngest son is **taller** than his brothers.

    NOT This is the **most happiest** day of my life.
    Correct: This is the **happiest** day of my life.

2. The second type of error occurs when the comparative or superlative is used with the wrong number of items. The comparative form should be used for two items and the superlative for three or more items.

    NOT Marina is the **smartest** of the two sisters.
    Correct: Marina is the **smarter** of the two sisters.

    NOT History is the **harder** of my three classes this semester.
    Correct: History is the **hardest** of my three classes this semester.

PRACTICE 7A: Identifying Underline the adjectives in the following sentences that are used incorrectly in comparisons. Mark sentences that are correct C.

1. _____ The most rudest customers are usually the ones who are trying to get something for free. *rudest*
2. _____ Bob and Chad are both good-looking, but Bob is smartest. *smarter*
3. __C__ This class would be more fun if we could meet outside sometimes.
4. _____ The most rainiest day of the year was April 15. *rainiest*
5. _____ The bigger house in town is at 1859 Pine Street. *biggest*

PRACTICE 7B: Correcting Correct the adjective errors in Practice 7A by rewriting the incorrect sentences. *See Practice 7A.*

PRACTICE 8: Completing Choose the correct adjective forms in the following paragraph to complete the sentences.

Giving the dog a bath is the (1) *most difficult* (more difficult, most difficult) chore in our house, and somehow it always seems to be my job. My sister Stephanie and I share most of the chores, but I am definitely (2) *more responsible* (more responsible, most responsible) than she is. Usually, I do my chores without complaining, but bathing the dog is just unfair. We have an Australian sheepdog, and he is the (3) *clumsiest* (clumsiest, most clumsiest) thing alive. He seems to find every puddle of mud and sticky stuff to step in, and it quickly gets all over his fur. Unfortunately, though, he has a great dislike for baths, so the struggle to wash him is (4) *trickier* (trickiest, trickier) than it should be. And Stephanie is no help at all. While I'm fighting to hose him down, she just stands back and laughs at me, which makes me even (5) *madder* (madder, more madder).

PRACTICE 9: Writing Your Own Write a sentence of your own for each of the following adjectives. *Answers will vary*

1. strongest ______________________________
2. more truthful ______________________________
3. most gracious ______________________________
4. larger ______________________________
5. most frightening ______________________________

USING *GOOD* AND *BAD* CORRECTLY

The adjectives *good* and *bad* are irregular. They do not form the comparative and superlative like most other adjectives. Here are the correct forms for these two irregular adjectives:

Basic	**Comparative (used to compare two items)**	**Superlative (used to compare three or more items)**
good	better	best
bad	worse	worst

Problems occur with *good* and *bad* when writers don't know how to form their comparative and superlative forms.

NOT more better, more worse, worser, most best, most worst, bestest, worstest

Correct: better, worse, best, worst

These errors appear in sentences in the following ways:

NOT That is the **worstest** food I've ever tasted.

Correct: That is the **worst** food I've ever tasted.

NOT Air pollution is getting **more worse** every year.

Correct: Air pollution is getting **worse** every year.

PRACTICE 10A: Identifying In the following sentences, underline the forms of *good* and *bad* used correctly, and circle the forms of *good* and *bad* used incorrectly.

1. Both options are good, but getting a raise is more better (*better*) than getting time off from work.
2. Giving that presentation in my psychology class was the worstest (*worst*) experience of my college career.
3. Giving your time to a charity is more good (*better*) than just giving your money.
4. Sean wanted to go to Princeton, but his grades were worse than he thought.
5. Doing the laundry is more worse (*worse*) than getting a root canal.

PRACTICE 10B: Correcting Correct the errors with *good* and *bad* in Practice 10A by rewriting the incorrect sentences. *See Practice 10A.*

PRACTICE 11: Completing Using the correct forms of *good* or *bad*, complete the following paragraph.

The (1) ___*worst*___ day of my life was July 8, 2001. I remember it (2) ___*better*___ than any other. I had just bought a brand new convertible and was taking it to the beach for a couple of days of fun in the sun. Fortunately, my (3) ___*best*___ friend, Tara, was with me, because just 20 miles outside town, the engine of my dream car overheated! What was (4) ___*worse*___ was neither of us had a cell phone, and the closest pay phone was more than a mile away.

We finally found a phone and called another friend, and then we waited and waited for a tow truck. After spending more than $3,000 in repairs, I found that my dream car had become my (5) ___worst___ nightmare.

PRACTICE 12: Writing Your Own Write a sentence of your own for each of the following forms of *good* and *bad*. *Answers will vary.*

1. best ______________________________
2. bad ______________________________
3. worse ______________________________
4. better ______________________________
5. worst ______________________________

CHAPTER REVIEW

You might want to reread the examples in this chapter before you do the following exercises.

REVIEW PRACTICE 1: Identifying Label the following adjectives basic (B), comparative (C), superlative (S), or not able to be compared (X).

1. ___C___ sillier
2. ___S___ most ridiculous
3. ___X___ dead
4. ___B___ tempting
5. ___C___ more stubborn
6. ___S___ meatiest
7. ___S___ most appealing
8. ___X___ broken
9. ___B___ tired
10. ___C___ lovelier

REVIEW PRACTICE 2: Completing Supply the comparative and superlative forms (both positive and negative) for each of the following adjectives.

	Basic	Comparative	Superlative
1.	welcome	*more/less welcome*	*most/least welcome*
2.	justifiable	*more/less justifiable*	*most/least justifiable*
3.	scary	*scarier, less scary*	*scariest, least scary*
4.	kind	*kinder, less kind*	*kindest, least kind*
5.	mystical	*more/less mystical*	*most/least mystical*
6.	strong	*stronger, less strong*	*strongest, least strong*
7.	foolish	*more/less foolish*	*most/least foolish*
8.	confusing	*more/less confusing*	*most/least confusing*
9.	extraordinary	*more/less extraordinary*	*most/least extraordinary*
10.	loving	*more/less loving*	*most/least loving*

REVIEW PRACTICE 3: Writing Your Own Write a paragraph describing the first pet you ever owned. What kind of animal was it? What did it look like? How did it act? What did you name it, and why did you choose that name? *Answers will vary.*

REVIEW PRACTICE 4: Editing Through Collaboration Exchange paragraphs from Review Practice 3 with another student, and do the following: *Answers will vary.*

1. Underline all the adjectives.
2. Circle those that are not in the correct form.

Then return the paper to its writer, and use the information in this chapter to correct any adjective errors in your own paragraph. Record your errors on the Error Log in Appendix 6.

36 CHAPTER

Adverbs

CHECKLIST for Using Adverbs

✔ Are all adverbs that show comparison used correctly?

✔ Are *good/well* and *bad/badly* used correctly?

UNIT PRETEST

To check your students' abilities with the collective skills in this unit, a Unit Pretest is available on pages 768–769.

TEACHING ADVERBS

Choose a student, and give him or her oral directions, like "walk to the other side of the room." The student should follow the directions.

Next, add an adverb to the sentence, and have the student again follow directions ("walk *slowly* to the other side of the room").

Continue changing or adding more adverbs to the directions so that students can see how adverbs affect the

TEST YOURSELF

Underline the adverbs in the following sentences. Then put an X over the adverbs that are used incorrectly.

- The pants fit me too loose, so I returned them to the store.
- Tori wasn't never so happy as after she won the lottery.
- When Madeline returned from Paris, she said she had a real good time.
- We happily made more ice cream when our first supply ran out.
- I wanted so bad to win the race, but I couldn't catch up.

(Answers are in Appendix 4.)

Like adjectives, adverbs help us communicate more clearly (she talked *slowly*) and more vividly (he sang *beautifully*). They make their sentences more interesting.

USING ADVERBS

Adverbs modify verbs, adjectives, and other adverbs. They answer the questions *how? when? where? how often?* and *to what extent?* Look at the following examples.

How:	My grandfather walked **slowly** up the stairs.
When:	Classes **always** begin after Labor Day.
Where:	Music lessons are held **here.**
How often:	I shop at K-Mart **regularly.**
To what extent:	The airport is **extremely** busy during the holidays.

Some words are always adverbs, including *here*, *there*, *not*, *never*, *now*, *again*, *almost*, *often*, and *well*.

Other adverbs are formed by adding *-ly* to an adjective:

Adjective	Adverb
dim	dimly
soft	softly
careless	carelessly

Hint: Not all words that end in *-ly* are adverbs. Some, such as *friendly*, *early*, *lonely*, *chilly*, and *lively*, are adjectives.

PRACTICE 1: Identifying In the following sentences, underline the adverbs, and circle the words they modify.

1. We (drove) quickly to Los Angeles so that we wouldn't miss the concert.
2. I never (saw) that girl again.
3. Dirk suddenly (changed) his mind and agreed to host the party.
4. Stephen successfully (completed) the nursing program.
5. When the children became impatient during the drive, we continuously (told) them, "We're almost (there)."

PRACTICE 2: Completing Fill in each blank in the following sentences with an adverb that makes sense. *Answers will vary.*

Sam's mom (1) _______________ drove him to the airport, where he caught a plane to Houston, Texas. He was going to visit his grandparents (2) _______________. Sam was only 10 years old, but he had (3) _______________ flown alone before. When the plane landed in Houston, Sam (4) _______________ grabbed his carry-on luggage and (5) _______________ ran to meet "Papa" and "Nonny."

meaning of a sentence. Don't forget to add negative as well as positive words to remind students of the full range of adverbs ("do *not* walk to the other side of the room").

INSTRUCTOR'S RESOURCE MANUAL

For more sample sentences, for more exercises, and for quizzes, see the *Instructor's Resource Manual,* Section II, Part IV.

UNIT POSTTEST

To check your students' mastery of the collective skills in this unit, a Unit Posttest is available on pages 781–782.

PRACTICE 3: Writing Your Own Write a sentence of your own for each of the following adverbs. *Answers will vary.*

1. now ______________________________
2. briskly ______________________________
3. innocently ______________________________
4. lazily ______________________________
5. often ______________________________

COMPARING WITH ADVERBS

Like adjectives, most adverbs have three forms: a **basic** form, a **comparative** form (used to compare two items), and a **superlative** form (used to compare three or more items).

For positive comparisons, adverbs form the comparative and superlative forms in two different ways:

1. For one-syllable adverbs, use *-er* to compare two items and *-est* to compare three or more items.

Basic	Comparative (used to compare two items)	Superlative (used to compare three or more items)
soon	sooner	soonest
fast	faster	fastest

2. For adverbs of two or more syllables, use *more* to compare two items and *most* to compare three or more items.

Basic	Comparative (used to compare two items)	Superlative (used to compare three or more items)
strangely	more strangely	most strangely
carefully	more carefully	most carefully
happily	more happily	most happily

For negative comparisons, adverbs, like adjectives, use *less* to compare two items and *least* to compare three or more items.

Basic	**Comparative (used to compare two items)**	**Superlative (used to compare three or more items)**
close	less close	least close
quickly	less quickly	least quickly
creatively	less creatively	least creatively

Hint: Like adjectives, certain adverbs are not usually compared. Something cannot last "more eternally" or work "more invisibly." The following adverbs cannot logically be compared.

endlessly	eternally	infinitely
equally	impossibly	invisibly

PRACTICE 4: Identifying Underline the adverbs, and note whether they are basic (B), comparative (C), or superlative (S).

1. C When Jack joined the gym, he began to lose weight more quickly.
2. C The sun shone more brightly after the rain stopped.
3. S Valencia is the most rapidly growing city in southern California.
4. C People enroll less often in the morning classes than the afternoon classes.
5. B Priscilla rudely interrupted her mother and walked out of the room.

PRACTICE 5: Completing Fill in each blank in the following paragraph with the correct comparative or superlative form of the adverb in parentheses.

At one time, *Highlights* was the (1) most widely (widely) read children's magazine. It had (2) more simply (simply) written stories for the younger readers and (3) more intellectually (intellectually) challenging games for the older kids than any other magazine. Because of the wide variety of material in each issue, *Highlights* was the (4) most highly (highly) acclaimed publication for American youth. Now, though, *Highlights* has lots of competition, and big publishers are creating magazines for young readers (5) ___more often___ (often) than they used to.

PRACTICE 6: Writing Your Own Write a sentence of your own for each of the following adverbs. *Answers will vary.*

1. a superlative form of *readily* ______________________
2. a comparative form of *eagerly* ______________________
3. the basic form of *unhappily* ______________________
4. a superlative form of *angrily* ______________________
5. a comparative form of *honestly* ______________________

ADJECTIVE OR ADVERB?

One of the most common errors with modifiers is using an adjective when an adverb is called for. Keep in mind that adjectives modify nouns and pronouns, whereas adverbs modify verbs, adjectives, and other adverbs. Adverbs *do not* modify nouns or pronouns. Here are some examples.

NOT She spoke too **slow.** [adjective]
Correct: She spoke too **slowly.** [adverb]

NOT We were **real** sorry about the accident. [adjective]
Correct: We were **really** sorry about the accident. [adverb]

PRACTICE 7A: Identifying Underline the adverbs in the following sentences. Write C next to the sentences that are correct.

1. _____ Adam Sandler's character snored loud in *Little Nicky*. *(loudly)*
2. ___C___ I rocked the baby gently to put her to sleep.
3. _____ Mr. Simpson talked too quick, and I didn't understand the assignment. *(quickly)*
4. _____ Before we left the zoo, we checked the map careful to make sure we'd seen everything. *(carefully)*
5. _____ Cook the beans slow so they don't burn. *(slowly)*

PRACTICE 7B: Correcting Correct the adverb errors in Practice 7A by rewriting the incorrect sentences. *See Practice 7A.*

PRACTICE 8: Completing Choose the correct adverb to complete the sentences in the following paragraph.

Zack and I went to Six Flags Magic Mountain last weekend and had a (1)___*really*___ (real, really) good time. When we pulled into the parking lot, we could hear the roller coasters zooming (2)___*loudly*___ (loudly, loud) overhead, and we could smell the yummy junk food. After we got through the gates, we ran (3)___*quickly*___ (quick, quickly) to the line for the ride Shockwave. The line moved along (4)___*smoothly*___ (smoothly, smooth), and we were on the ride within 20 minutes. When Shockwave was over, we (5)___*gladly*___ (glad, gladly) got in line to ride it again.

PRACTICE 9: Writing Your Own Write a sentence of your own for each of the following adverbs. *Answers will vary.*

1. specifically ____________________
2. tightly ____________________
3. greatly ____________________
4. sadly ____________________
5. coldly ____________________

DOUBLE NEGATIVES

Another problem that involves adverbs is the **double negative**—using two negative words in one clause. Examples of negative words include *no, not, never, none, nothing, neither, nowhere, nobody, barely,* and *hardly*. A double negative creates the opposite meaning of what is intended.

Double Negative: She **never** had **no** time to rest.

The actual meaning of these double negatives is "She did have time to rest."

Correction: She had **no** time to rest.

Double Negative: My brother does **not** give me **nothing.**

The actual meaning of these double negatives is "My brother does give me something."

Correction: My brother does **not** give me **anything.**

Double negatives often occur with contractions.

Double Negative: There **aren't hardly** any apples left.

The actual meaning of these double negatives is "There are plenty of apples left."

Correction: There are **hardly** any apples left.

Using two negatives is confusing and grammatically wrong. Be on the lookout for negative words, and use only one per clause.

PRACTICE 10A: Identifying Mark each of the following sentences either correct (C) or incorrect (X).

1. _X_ He didn't never study, but he always passed the tests. *(~~didn't~~ never did study)*
2. _X_ Tabitha wasn't hardly four years old when her mother passed away. *(~~wasn't~~ hardly)*
3. _X_ Nobody showed up for none of the practices last week. *(~~none~~ any)*
4. _C_ Hawkins doesn't really know what he wants to do.
5. _X_ I wouldn't go nowhere with him. *(~~nowhere~~ anywhere)*

PRACTICE 10B: Correcting Correct the double negatives in Practice 10A by rewriting the incorrect sentences. *See Practice 10A.*

PRACTICE 11: Completing Choose the correct negative modifiers to complete the following paragraph.

Last summer, I went to the beach and (1) _was hardly_ (was hardly, wasn't hardly) prepared for the sunshiny weather. I didn't buy (2) _any_ (any, no) sunscreen before I left because I had a decent tan already. To my surprise, I started to burn after only three hours on the beach, and there (3) _wasn't anything_ (wasn't nothing, wasn't anything) I could do about it. I thought the burning feeling wouldn't (4) _ever_ (ever, never) go away. And no matter what lotions and ointments I put on, I couldn't get (5) _any_ (no, any) relief. Next time, I'll remember to bring some sunscreen.

PRACTICE 12: Writing Your Own Write a sentence of your own for each of the following negative words. *Answers will vary.*

1. never ______________________________
2. not ______________________________

3. barely ______________________________

4. nobody ______________________________

5. nowhere ______________________________

USING *GOOD/WELL* AND *BAD/BADLY* CORRECTLY

The pairs *good/well* and *bad/badly* are so frequently misused that they deserve special attention.

Good is an adjective; *well* is an adverb or adjective.
Use *good* with a noun (n) or after a linking verb (lv).

Adjective: Juan is a **good** boy. (n: boy)

Adjective: She looks **good.** (lv: looks)

Use *well* for someone's health or after an action verb (av).

Adjective: He is **well** again. [health] (lv: is)

Adverb: The baby sleeps **well** at night. (av: sleeps)

Bad is an adjective; *badly* is an adverb.

Use *bad* with a noun (n) or after a linking verb (lv). Always use *bad* after *feel* if you're talking about emotions.

Adjective: He seems like a **bad** person. (n: person)

Adjective: I feel **bad** that I got a ticket. (lv: feel)

Use *badly* with an adjective (adj) or after an action verb (av).

Adverb: The house was **badly** burned. (adj: burned)

Adverb: He swims **badly.** (av: swims)

PRACTICE 13A: Identifying Label each of the following sentences either correct (C) or incorrect (X).

1. ___*X*___ I want to do good in this job so my boss will like me. *(~~good~~, well)*
2. ___*X*___ My favorite team is playing bad this week. *(~~bad~~, badly)*
3. ___*C*___ Vilma sings well and is pursuing a career in opera.
4. ___*C*___ Rachel said she felt bad about Mr. Brown's accident.
5. ___*X*___ I wanted so bad to go diving, but I couldn't. *(~~bad~~, badly)*

PRACTICE 13B: Correcting Correct the adverb errors in Practice 13A by rewriting the incorrect sentences. *See Practice 13A.*

PRACTICE 14: Completing Choose the correct modifiers to complete the following paragraph.

When Scott was in high school, there was only one thing he could do really (1) ___*well*___ (good, well). He struggled with academics, he played most sports very (2) ___*badly*___ (bad, badly), and he was never popular with the girls. But his one strength was music. From the moment he picked up his first guitar, he was always (3) ___*good*___ (good, well) at creating songs. Fortunately, his natural talent earned him several (4) ___*good*___ (good, well) scholarship offers from big-name universities. Unfortunately, his (5) ___*bad*___ (bad, badly) study habits in high school made college more difficult for him, but he survived.

PRACTICE 15: Writing Your Own Write a sentence of your own for each of the following modifiers. *Answers will vary.*

1. well ______________________
2. badly ______________________
3. good ______________________
4. bad ______________________
5. well ______________________

CHAPTER REVIEW

You might want to reread the examples in this chapter before you do the following exercises.

REVIEW PRACTICE 1: Identifying Underline the correct word in each of the following sentences.

1. Tia and Sue Ann studied together for the midterm, but Tia took notes (more, most) thoroughly.
2. We don't have (no, any) money for rent this month.
3. His speech seemed to go on (endlessly, more endlessly, most endlessly).
4. Of all the teachers at this school, Mrs. Thompson speaks the (more clearly, most clearly).
5. Jose drives (more fast, faster) than I do.
6. During the baseball game, I struck out (less, least) often than Jack did.
7. She plays the flute very (good, well) and is in the orchestra.
8. My senior year in high school, I was voted (less, least) likely to drop out of college.
9. He hurt his knee so (bad, badly) it required medical attention.
10. The children were (real, really) tired after spending the day at the lake.

REVIEW PRACTICE 2: Completing Fill in each blank in the following paragraph with an adverb that makes sense. Try not to use any adverb more than once.
Answers will vary.

Working as a food server can be very challenging. I take my job (1) ______________ than the other servers, so I can (2) ______________ count on coming home with better tips. But sometimes there are customers I just can't please, no matter how (3) ______________ I want to. Also, there are the minor problems that happen (4) ______________, like the kitchen running out of chicken or the bartender forgetting to make the drinks for my table. Because I'm determined to do my job (5) ______________, though, my customers like me and keep coming back.

REVIEW PRACTICE 3: Writing Your Own If you could prepare anything you wanted for dinner tonight, what would you make? Write a paragraph about this meal. How would you prepare it? How would you serve it? How many courses would it consist of? *Answers will vary.*

REVIEW PRACTICE 4: Editing Through Collaboration Exchange paragraphs from Review Practice 3 with another student, and do the following: *Answers will vary.*

1. Underline all the adverbs.
2. Circle those that are not in the correct form.
3. Put an X above any double negatives.

Then return the paper to its writer, and use the information in this chapter to correct any adverb errors in your own paragraph. Record your errors on the Error Log in Appendix 6.

CHAPTER 37

Modifier Errors

CHECKLIST for Identifying and Correcting Modifier Problems

✔ Are modifiers as close as possible to the words they modify?

✔ Are any sentences confusing because the words that the modifiers refer to are missing?

TEST YOURSELF

Underline the modifier problem in each sentence.

- After studying together, his grades really improved.
- Before doing the laundry, the car needed to be washed.
- To get a good job, the interview must go well.
- The professor told the class he was retiring before he dismissed them.
- I wrote a letter to the newspaper that complained about rising power bills.

(Answers are in Appendix 4.)

UNIT PRETEST

To check your students' abilities with the collective skills in this unit, a Unit Pretest is available on pages 768–769.

TEACHING MODIFIER ERRORS

Have students get out a piece of paper and draw pictures representing the following sentences: "Picking flowers, my nose became red and itchy," and "I chased the dog wearing my underwear." Collect the pictures, and point out to the students that most of them drew the pictures incorrectly (most of them will—especially for the first example).

Explain that literally, the first sentence says the nose was

As you know, a modifier describes another word or group of words. Sometimes, however, a modifier is too far from the words it refers to (*misplaced modifier*), or the word it refers to is missing altogether (*dangling modifier*). As a result, the sentence is confusing.

MISPLACED MODIFIERS

A modifier should be placed as close as possible to the word or words it modifies, but this does not always happen. A **misplaced modifier** is too far from the word or words it refers to, making the meaning of the sentence unclear. Look at these examples.

picking the flowers and the second says the dog was wearing the underwear.

Showing students how misplaced modifiers change the meaning of sentences can help them identify their own modifier errors.

INSTRUCTOR'S RESOURCE MANUAL

For more sample sentences, for more exercises, and for quizzes, see the *Instructor's Resource Manual*, Section II, Part IV.

UNIT POSTTEST

To check your students' mastery of the collective skills in this unit, a Unit Posttest is available on pages 781–782.

Misplaced: The instructor explained why plagiarism is wrong **on Friday.**

(Is plagiarism wrong only on Friday? Probably not. So the modifier *on Friday* needs to be moved closer to the word it actually modifies.)

Correct: The instructor explained **on Friday** why plagiarism is wrong.

Misplaced: In most states, it is illegal to carry liquor in a car **that has been opened.**

(It is the liquor, not the car, that must not have been opened. So the modifier *that has been opened* needs to be moved closer to the word it modifies.)

Correct: In most states, it is illegal to carry liquor **that has been opened** in a car.

Certain modifiers that limit meaning are often misplaced, causing problems. Look at how meaning changes by moving the limiting word *only* in the following sentences:

Only Aunt Emily says that Lilly was a bad cook.
(Aunt Emily says this, but no one else does.)

Aunt Emily **only** says that Lilly was a bad cook.
(Aunt Emily says this, but she doesn't really mean it.)

Aunt Emily says **only** that Lilly was a bad cook.
(Aunt Emily says this but nothing more.)

Aunt Emily says that **only** Lilly was a bad cook.
(Lilly—and no one else—was a bad cook.)

Aunt Emily says that Lilly **only** was a bad cook.
(Aunt Emily says that there were some who were good cooks and Lilly was the only bad one.)

Aunt Emily says that Lilly was **only** a bad cook.
(Lilly was a bad cook, but she wasn't bad at other things.)

Aunt Emily says that Lilly was a bad cook **only.**
(Lilly was a bad cook, but she wasn't bad at other things.)

Here is a list of common limiting words.

almost	hardly	merely	only
even	just	nearly	scarcely

PRACTICE 1A: Identifying Underline the misplaced modifiers in the following sentences.

1. Tina told Tom that to win the lottery she had a great chance.
2. The car leaked all its oil by the time I called a mechanic in the driveway.
3. Brittany went to the mall with Jim wearing her favorite hat.
4. I sold Luigi my old watch after I bought an expensive new one for $10.
5. We made a pie in the kitchen with lots of blueberries.

PRACTICE 1B: Correcting Correct the misplaced modifiers in Practice 1A by rewriting the incorrect sentences. *Answers will vary.*

PRACTICE 2: Completing Fill in each blank in the following paragraph with a modifier that makes sense. Include at least two phrases. *Answers will vary.*

Several years ago, Rodger owned a (1) ______________ farm in Kentucky where he grew corn and wheat. He also had (2) ______________ orchards of apples that he (3) ______________ harvested every September. His children had (4) ______________ the farm. Shortly before Rodger died, he trained his children (5) ______________ the family business.

PRACTICE 3: Writing Your Own Write a sentence of your own for each of the following modifiers. *Answers will vary.*

1. before summer ____
2. since the company hired him ________________________________
3. while driving to the store __________________________________
4. after she bought the car ___________________________________
5. though no one was there ___________________________________

DANGLING MODIFIERS

Modifiers are "dangling" when they have nothing to refer to in a sentence. **Dangling modifiers** (starting with an *-ing* word or with *to*) often appear at the beginning of a sentence. Here is an example.

Dangling: **Reaching the top of the hill,** the view was beautiful.

A modifier usually modifies the words closest to it. So the phrase *Reaching the top of the hill* modifies *view*. But it's not the view that reaches the top of the hill. In fact, there is no logical word in the sentence that the phrase modifies. It is left dangling. You can correct a dangling modifier in one of two ways—by inserting the missing word that is being referred to or by rewriting the sentence.

Correct: **Reaching the top of the hill,** we saw a beautiful view.
Correct: **When we reached the top of the hill,** the view we saw was beautiful.

Dangling: **To get into the movie,** an ID must be presented.
Correct: **To get into the movie,** you must present an ID.
Correct: You must present an ID **to get into the movie.**

Dangling: The garage was empty **after moving the tools.**
Correct: **After moving the tools,** we had an empty garage.
Correct: The garage was empty **after we moved the tools.**

PRACTICE 4A: Identifying Underline the dangling modifiers in the following sentences.

1. To get a good deal, time must be spent comparing prices.
2. Screaming for help, the chair fell over with the little boy in it.
3. As an only daughter with four brothers, there was never enough food in the house.
4. To get a driver's license, two tests must be passed.
5. Giving the dog a bath, the bathroom floor became flooded.

PRACTICE 4B: Correcting Correct the dangling modifiers in Practice 4A by rewriting the incorrect sentences. *Answers will vary.*

PRACTICE 5: Completing Fill in each blank in the following paragraph with a modifier that makes sense. Include at least two phrases. *Answers will vary.*

(1) _______________ professional baseball teams begin spring training. The coaches plan on (2) _______________ weight lifting and lots of running. Hundreds of (3) _______________ athletes begin training each season, but within days, many get cut from the major league teams. These men usually get placed on (4) _______________ teams. These men hope to play well throughout the season and (5) _______________ move up.

PRACTICE 6: Writing Your Own Write a sentence of your own for each of the following phrases. *Answers will vary.*

1. warm and bright ______________________________
2. shaking my hand ______________________________
3. to understand the opposite sex ______________________________
4. getting a chance to see the ocean ______________________________
5. to win an argument ______________________________

CHAPTER REVIEW

You might want to reread the examples in this chapter before you do the following exercises.

REVIEW PRACTICE 1: Identifying Underline the modifier errors in the following sentences.

1. Turning in my essay late, my computer crashed.
2. I am flying to Atlanta on Friday and returning Monday to attend a wedding.
3. To make a perfect chocolate dessert, the oven temperature must be carefully watched.
4. I put away my clothes and then called some friends in the closet.
5. Throwing the ball across the room, the lamp fell over and broke.
6. Jennifer complained that she forgot to send out invitations in an angry voice.
7. I found a pressed flower in my Shakespeare textbook from my wedding.
8. Driving to the movie theater, teenagers kept stepping out into the street in front of us.
9. Maria has a picture of her cousins at the beach in her locker.
10. To please your parents, good grades should be earned on every report card.

REVIEW PRACTICE 2: Completing Rewrite the sentences in Review Practice 1 so that the phrases you underlined are as close as possible to the words they modify. *Answers will vary.*

REVIEW PRACTICE 3: Writing Your Own Write a paragraph about your greatest accomplishment. What did you do? How hard did you work for it? What was your reward? *Answers will vary.*

REVIEW PRACTICE 4: Editing Through Collaboration Exchange paragraphs from Review Practice 3 with another student, and do the following: *Answers will vary.*

1. Underline any misplaced modifiers.
2. Put brackets around any dangling modifiers.

Then return the paper to its writer, and use the information in this chapter to correct any modifier problems in your own paragraph. Record your errors on the Error Log in Appendix 6.

Punctuation

Can you imagine streets and highways without stoplights or traffic signs? Driving would become a life-or-death adventure as motorists made risky trips with no signals to guide or protect them. Good writers, like conscientious drivers, prefer to leave little to chance. They observe the rules of punctuation to ensure that their readers arrive at their intended meaning. Without punctuation, sentences would run together, ideas would be unclear, and words would be misread. Writers need to use markers, like periods, commas, and dashes, to help them communicate as efficiently and effectively as possible.

Look at the difference punctuation makes in the meaning of the following letter.

Dear John:

I want a man who knows what love is all about. You are generous, kind, thoughtful. People who are not like you admit to being useless and inferior. You have ruined me for other men. I yearn for you. I have no feelings whatsoever when we're apart. I can be forever happy—will you let me be yours? Susan

Dear John,

I want a man who knows what love is. All about you are generous, kind, thoughtful people, who are not like you. Admit to being useless and inferior. You have ruined me. For other men, I yearn. For you, I have no feelings whatsoever. When we're apart, I can be forever happy. Will you let me be? Yours, Susan

This unit will help you write the love letter you actually want to write—with the punctuation that gets your message across. It will also provide you with guidelines for using the following punctuation:

38 CHAPTER

End Punctuation

CHECKLIST for Using End Punctuation

✔ Does each sentence end with a period, a question mark, or an exclamation point?

✔ Are question marks used when asking questions?

✔ Do sentences that exclaim end with exclamation points?

UNIT PRETEST
To check your students' abilities with the collective skills in this unit, a Unit Pretest is available on pages 769–771.

TEACHING END PUNCTUATION
Distribute a lively, animated paragraph with the end punctuation taken out. Read the paragraph aloud to the class to show how dull the paragraph is without the punctuation.

Then hand out the paragraph with the punctuation inserted, and ask three or four students to read the paragraph aloud with a lot of enthusiasm. This

TEST YOURSELF

Add the appropriate end punctuation to the following sentences.

- How are we going to get there
- That's amazing
- Get me a Pepsi, please
- This will never happen to me
- Can you make your own dinner tonight

(Answers are in Appendix 4.)

End punctuation signals the end of a sentence in three ways: The **period** ends a statement, the **question mark** signals a question, and the **exclamation point** marks an exclamation.

PERIOD

1. A period is used with statements, mild commands, and indirect questions.

   Statement: The boy rode to school on the bus.

Command: Ride the bus to school today.
Indirect Question: I asked him why he rode the bus to school today.

2. A period is also used with abbreviations and numbers.

Abbreviations: Mr. Johnson lives at 9 Kings Rd., next door to Dr. Tina Lopez.
Numbers: $16.95 4.5 $876.98 0.066

PRACTICE 1: Identifying In the following sentences, circle the periods used incorrectly, and add those that are missing.

1. Walt is buying the house on the corner of Sonora Ave. and Eureka St.
2. I bought a new computer monitor for $210.0.0
3. Mr. Bernard just married Ms. Walters.
4. Tara's dentist is named Dr. Jones, and his office is on 4th. St.
5. Bring your child to the library on the corner of Jackson Drive. and Lovejoy Pl..

PRACTICE 2: Completing Add periods to the following paragraph where they are needed.

Jane Seymour is a very talented actress who stars in a TV series called *Dr. Quinn, Medicine Woman*. Ms. Seymour also has twin boys who are in grade school, and she wrote a book about her experience mothering twins. Her husband is very supportive of her acting and writing activities. He helps with the children and even offered quotes for her book. The book sells for about $20.50 and is published by St. Martin's Press.

PRACTICE 3: Writing Your Own Write a sentence of your own for each of the following descriptions. *Answers will vary.*

1. a statement about cooking
2. a statement including a dollar amount
3. a statement including an address with an abbreviated street name

shows students how end punctuation defines parameters, but it also demonstrates the variety with which people express punctuation marks.

INSTRUCTOR'S RESOURCE MANUAL

For sample paragraphs, for more exercises, and for quizzes, see the *Instructor's Resource Manual,* Section II, Part IV.

UNIT POSTTEST

To check your students' mastery of the collective skills in this unit, a Unit Posttest is available on pages 782–784.

4. an indirect question about a psychology midterm

5. a command to do a household chore

QUESTION MARK

The question mark is used after a direct question.

Question Mark: Do you have homework to do**?**
Question Mark: "Can you get your homework done on time**?**" her mother asked.

PRACTICE 4: Identifying In the following sentences, circle the question marks used incorrectly, and add those that are needed.

1. Did you buy that jacket only last week.?
2. I wonder when the party starts?
3. Stephanie said, "Are you wearing my watch?" *no changes*
4. Tina asked Whit how he was feeling?
5. This is my biggest concern: How are we going to protect the rain forests.?

PRACTICE 5: Completing Add question marks to the following paragraph where they are needed.

What are the three most important things to remember about writing.? First, choose topics that you are interested in. Why should you write about something that bores you.? Second, remember that writing is a process. Should you ever turn in your first draft.? No way. Writing gets better and better the more drafts you write. Third, give yourself plenty of time for editing and revision. Don't you think it's better that you catch the errors before your instructor does.? Writing will be less of a chore if you remember these things and apply them to each assignment.

PRACTICE 6: Writing Your Own Write a sentence of your own for each of the following descriptions. *Answers will vary.*

1. a direct question about driving ______________________________
2. an indirect question about your favorite sport ____________________
3. a direct question about a family member ________________________

4. an indirect question about the next major holiday ____________________

5. a direct question about lunch ______________________________________

EXCLAMATION POINT

The exclamation point indicates strong feeling.

If it is used too often, it is not as effective as it could be. You shouldn't use more than one exclamation point at a time.

Exclamation Point: Never!

Exclamation Point: You don't mean it!

Exclamation Point: Give me my homework or I'll scream!

Exclamation Point: "You scared me to death!" she said.

PRACTICE 7: Identifying Circle the punctuation used incorrectly, and add those that are needed.

1. That's outrageous(.)!

2. I can't believe it(.)!

3. He said(!) "Great job, Julian!"

4. You can't mean that(?)!

5. "Don't hurt my baby(,)!" yelled the mother.

PRACTICE 8: Completing Add exclamation points to the following paragraph where they are appropriate.

Paintball is my favorite pastime, and I play every weekend. It's so much fun.! Last Saturday, Steve and Jay were on one team, and Tim and I were on another. Within an hour, Tim and I cornered Jay and took him out. "Pop.! Pop.!" But suddenly, Steve came around a tree and pointed his paintball gun right at Tim.

"Duck,!" I yelled.

Tim quickly hit the ground, but it was too late. "Pop.! Pop.!"

"Yeah,!" Steve yelled as he hit Tim right in the chest with paintballs.

But I was even quicker. "Pop.!" One shot and Steve had red paint right in the middle of his stomach.

"Last remaining survivor again,!" I screamed in delight.

PRACTICE 9: Writing Your Own Write five sentences of your own using exclamation points correctly. *Answers will vary.*

CHAPTER REVIEW

You might want to reread the examples in this chapter before you do the following exercises.

REVIEW PRACTICE 1: Identifying For each sentence, add the correct end punctuation.

1. Do you have any tattoos*?*
2. Stop lying to me*.*
3. Are you sure you can help me*?*
4. No! Not yet*!*
5. Is there a problem with this software*?*
6. Sometimes I think I'll never graduate*.*
7. My cousin wants to know if we're going to leave soon*.*
8. Take the keys to my car*.*
9. That's impossible*!*
10. You should study tomorrow while you're off work*.*

REVIEW PRACTICE 2: Completing Turn sentences 1–5 into questions and sentences 6–10 into exclamations.

1. The plumber came today. *Did the plumber come today?*
2. The Jets are going to win the Super Bowl. *Are the Jets going to win the Super Bowl?*
3. Delores made the afghan. *Did Delores make the afghan?*
4. You are going to be my date. *Are you going to be my date?*
5. The baby hasn't been fed yet. *Has the baby been fed yet?*
6. Don't forget to do the dishes. *!*
7. We have ten minutes to get on the plane. *!*

8. Are you serious? *You're serious!*

9. I don't want to tell you. *!*

10. This is a great day. *!*

REVIEW PRACTICE 3: Writing Your Own Write a paragraph about an emotional experience or event in your life. Was it exciting, happy, sad, disappointing, frustrating, or challenging? What happened? Who was involved? Include all three types of end punctuation—period, question mark, and exclamation point. *Answers will vary.*

REVIEW PRACTICE 4: Editing Through Collaboration Exchange paragraphs from Review Practice 3 with another student, and do the following: *Answers will vary.*

1. Circle any errors in end punctuation.

2. Suggest the correct punctuation above your circle.

Then return the paragraph to its writer, and use the information in this chapter to correct any end punctuation errors in your own paragraph. Record your errors on the Error Log in Appendix 6.

39 CHAPTER

Commas

CHECKLIST for Using Commas

- ✔ Are commas used to separate items in a series?
- ✔ Are commas used to set off introductory material?
- ✔ Is there a comma before *and, but, for, nor, or, so,* and *yet* when they are followed by an independent clause?
- ✔ Are commas used to set off interrupting material in a sentence?
- ✔ Are commas used to set off direct quotations?
- ✔ Are commas used correctly in numbers, dates, addresses, and letters?

UNIT PRETEST

To check your students' abilities with the collective skills in this unit, a Unit Pretest is available on pages 769–771.

TEACHING COMMAS

Write 10 sentences that contain comma errors. Put each sentence on a small poster board so that you have 10 poster boards. Then create a duplicate set of poster boards. Divide the class into two teams. Place a set of 10 poster boards in front of each team

TEST YOURSELF

Add commas to the following sentences.

- We drove to the beach and we had a picnic.
- Before I eat breakfast I take a multivitamin.
- "This is my favorite restaurant" said Matt.
- E-mail though makes corresponding easy and fast.
- They were married on February 14 2004 in Las Vegas Nevada.

(Answers are in Appendix 4.)

The **comma** is the most frequently used punctuation mark, but it is also the most often misused. Commas make sentences easier to read by separating the parts of sentences. Following the rules in this chapter will help you write clear sentences that are easy to read.

COMMAS WITH ITEMS IN A SERIES

Use commas to separate items in a series.

This means that you should put a comma between all items in a series.

Series: The house had three bedrooms**,** two baths**,** and a pool.

Series: She caught the fish**,** cleaned it**,** and then cooked it.

Series: William can have a new car if his grades improve**,** if he gets a job**,** and if he does his chores at home.

Sometimes this rule applies to a series of adjectives in front of a noun, but sometimes it does not. Look at these two examples.

Adjectives with Commas: The **foggy, cold** weather is finally over.

Adjectives Without Commas: The **loose bottom** knob fell off my TV.

Both of these examples are correct. So how do you know whether or not to use commas? You can use one of two tests. One test is to insert the word *and* between the adjectives. If the sentence makes sense, use a comma. Another test is to switch the order of the adjectives. If the sentence still reads clearly, use a comma between the two words.

Test 1: The **foggy and cold** weather is finally over. **OK, so use a comma**

Test 2: The **cold, foggy** weather is finally over. **OK, so use a comma**

Test 1: The **loose and bottom** knob fell off my TV. **Not OK, so no comma**

Test 2: The **bottom loose** knob fell off my TV. **Not OK, so no comma**

PRACTICE 1: Identifying In the following sentences, circle the commas that are used incorrectly, and add any commas that are missing.

1. In my free time, I like to read, sew, and make jelly.
2. My girlfriend is very good, at tennis, volleyball, and golf.
3. The best things, about gardening are the relaxation, the sense of accomplishment, and the feeling of being one with nature.
4. To play professional basketball, one must practice regularly, play competitively, and get a big break.
5. The sofa, the ottoman, and the computer desk are going to be donated to Goodwill.

with the sentences facing down.

Begin a tag team relay in which each team uses a marker to fix or supply the commas. When the first person finishes the first sentence, he or she hands the marker to the next person, who moves to the next sentence. The second person places commas in the second sentence and then hands the marker to the next person, and so on. Time the teams.

When the students have completed all the sentences, check to make sure that all the commas are correctly placed. Add five seconds to the team's time for each incorrect or missed comma. The team to finish with the lowest time wins.

INSTRUCTOR'S RESOURCE MANUAL

For sample sentences, for more exercises, and for quizzes, see the *Instructor's Resource Manual*, Section II, Part IV.

UNIT POSTTEST

To check your students' mastery of the collective skills in this unit, a Unit Posttest is available on pages 782–784.

PRACTICE 2: Completing Add the missing commas to the following paragraph.

We are flying to Dallas this weekend to attend a friend's wedding. Before we leave, I need to do the laundry, pay the bills, and arrange for a house sitter. My husband's childhood friend is the one getting married, so he also hopes to see some of his other friends there—especially Gene, Brad, and Dwayne. During the past two months, we bought airline tickets, arranged for a rental car, and reserved a hotel room. Now all we have to do is make it to the airport on time! I'm also trying to decide whether to wear navy, pink, or gray, and my husband is getting his best suit altered. Though it has required lots of time, energy, and money, we are really looking forward to this trip.

PRACTICE 3: Writing Your Own Write a sentence of your own for each of the following sets of items. *Answers will vary.*

1. three things to do at the mall ______________________
2. three sports you like to play ______________________
3. three items on a to-do list ______________________
4. three popular magazines ______________________
5. three of your favorite snack foods ______________________

COMMAS WITH INTRODUCTORY WORDS

Use a comma to set off an introductory word, phrase, or clause from the rest of its sentence.

If you are unsure whether to add a comma, try reading the sentence with your reader in mind. If you want your reader to pause after the introductory word or phrase, you should insert a comma.

Introductory Word: **No,** it didn't rain.

Introductory Word: **Really,** the weather wasn't as bad as we thought it would be.

Introductory Phrase: **On the whole,** this is a great town to live in.

Introductory Phrase: **To prove this to my relatives,** I took them for a tour of the town.

Introductory Clause: **As the doors opened,** the light poured in.

Introductory Clause: **When the movie was over,** everyone was silent.

PRACTICE 4: Identifying In the following sentences, circle the commas that are used incorrectly, and add any commas that are missing.

1. Three years, ago, we lived in Boise.
2. As the fire continued, to burn, the firefighters feared it would get out of control.
3. Sure, I can take you to the store.
4. After spilling the water, the little boy began to cry.
5. The next time you go, to Macy's, can you pick up a gift certificate for me?

PRACTICE 5: Completing Add the missing commas to the following paragraph.

When Terina was seven years old, we took her to Disneyland. Since she was tall enough to ride all of the rides, she really enjoyed herself. First, we had to take pictures with Mickey and Minnie. Of course, we couldn't miss them! Next, we got in line for Space Mountain, which turned out to be Terina's favorite ride. By the end of the day, we had ridden Space Mountain five times.

PRACTICE 6: Writing Your Own Write a sentence of your own for each of the following introductory words, phrases, or clauses. *Answers will vary.*

1. well ______________________________
2. when we thought it was almost over ______________________________
3. yes ______________________________
4. as the mail carrier arrived ______________________________
5. wanting to win the lottery ______________________________

COMMAS WITH INDEPENDENT CLAUSES

Use a comma before *and*, *but*, *for*, *nor*, *or*, *so*, and *yet* when they join two independent clauses. (Remember that an independent clause must have both a subject and a verb.)

Independent Clauses: The boy flew to London**, and** he took a boat to France.

Independent Clauses: He enjoyed the flight**, but** he liked the boat ride more.

Hint: Do not use a comma when a single subject has two verbs.

s v no comma v
The **boy flew** to London and **left** for France the next day.

Adding a comma when none is needed is one of the most common errors in college writing assignments. Only if the second verb has its own subject should you add a comma.

s v comma s v
The **boy flew** to London**,** and **he left** for France the next day.

PRACTICE 7: Identifying In the following sentences, underline the subjects once and the coordinating conjunctions twice. Then circle any commas that are used incorrectly, and add any commas that are missing.

1. My computer crashed, so I lost my whole research paper.
2. The car looks great, and drives even better.
3. Going to the mountains was a good idea, and we had a very nice time.
4. The cat will curl up on the sofa, or the rug by the fireplace.
5. My cousin wants to get married, but I think she's too young.

PRACTICE 8: Completing Add the missing commas to the following paragraph.

For my last birthday, my grandmother gave me $100, so I wanted to spend it on clothes. I went to the mall, and I found three outfits that were perfect. I couldn't decide on just one, but I didn't have enough money for them all. I needed the dressy outfit more, yet the casual outfit was a great bargain. Finally, I settled on one suit, but I'm saving money to go back and get the others. I'll go back within a month, or maybe I'll just wait until after my next holiday gift.

PRACTICE 9: Writing Your Own Write a sentence of your own using each of the following coordinating conjunctions to separate two independent clauses.
Answers will vary.

1. or ______________________________
2. and ______________________________

3. so ______________________________

4. but ______________________________

5. yet ______________________________

COMMAS WITH INTERRUPTERS

Use a comma before and after a word or phrase that interrupts the flow of a sentence.

Most words that interrupt a sentence are not necessary for understanding the main point of a sentence. Setting them off makes it easier to recognize the main point.

Word: My next-door neighbor**, Carlos,** is from Portugal.
Word: I didn't hear the phone ring**, however,** because I was in the shower.
Phrase: My textbook**, *Ancient Rome*,** is on the desk.
Phrase: One of the most popular vacation spots**, according to recent surveys,** is Disneyland.
Phrase: Mr. Colby**, president of the school board,** has been elected mayor.

A very common type of interrupter is a clause that begins with *who*, *whose*, *which*, *when*, or *where* and is not necessary for understanding the main point of the sentence:

Clause: The new mall**, which is downtown,** has three restaurants.

Because the information "which is downtown" is not necessary for understanding the main idea of the sentence, it is set off with commas.

Clause: Carol Roth**, who has a Ph.D. in history,** is my new neighbor.

The main point here is that Carol Roth is my new neighbor. Since the other information isn't necessary for understanding the sentence, it can be set off with commas.

Hint: Do not use commas with *who*, *whose*, *which*, *when*, or *where* if the information is necessary for understanding the main point of the sentence.

My friend **who is a circus clown** just arrived in town.

Because the information in the *who* clause is necessary to understand which friend just arrived in town, you should not set it off with commas.

Hint: Do not use commas to set off clauses beginning with *that*.

The mall **that is downtown** has three restaurants.

PRACTICE 10: Identifying Label each sentence C if commas are used correctly with the underlined words and phrases or X if they are not.

1. _C_ Jacquelyn Smith, who used to be a model, has a line of clothing at Kmart.
2. _X_ My girlfriend Cheri, is almost 23 years old.
3. _C_ The AMC theater, my favorite hangout, is located on Main Street.
4. _X_ Joe's leather jacket, which he's had only four months has a broken zipper.
5. _X_ *Air Force One*, the airplane, used by the United States president, is the most secure aircraft in the world.

PRACTICE 11: Completing Insert commas around the interrupting words and phrases in the following paragraph.

My favorite grandmother,Gram,turned 80 this year. My grandfather died last August, and we didn't want Gram living alone. She was able to take care of herself,however,and didn't want to go to a retirement home. Recently, we visited Rosewood,which is a very popular retirement community,and she was impressed with the facilities. There are group homes,of course,with "around the clock" care, but there are also condominiums where residents can live alone or with roommates. The entire neighborhood is monitored by security guards,which is reassuring,and the medical staff is always available. Gram's been there for three weeks now and said,when we asked,that she's never been happier.

PRACTICE 12: Writing Your Own Write a sentence of your own for each of the following phrases. *Answers will vary.*

1. who is very brave ______________________________
2. which costs over $100 ______________________________

3. however ______________________________

4. the mayor's wife ______________________________

5. taking the keys ______________________________

COMMAS WITH DIRECT QUOTATIONS

Use commas to mark direct quotations.

A direct quotation records a person's exact words. Commas set off the exact words from the rest of the sentence, making it easier to understand who said what.

Direct Quotation: My friends often say**, "You are so lucky."**
Direct Quotation: **"You are so lucky,"** my friends often say.
Direct Quotation: **"You are so lucky,"** says my grandmother**, "to have good friends."**

Hint: If a quotation ends with a question mark or an exclamation point, do not use a comma. Only one punctuation mark is needed.

NOT **"What did he want?,"** she asked.

Correct: **"What did he want?"** she asked.

PRACTICE 13: Identifying In the following sentences, circle the commas that are used incorrectly, and add any commas that are missing.

1. Tonya noted,"I want the Kings to win tonight."
2. "If you go now," he said,"don't come back."
3. "Are you absolutely sure?," David asked.
4. "That cat," Christine said,"sets off my allergies."
5. Mr. Avery remarked,"The paper will not be accepted late."

PRACTICE 14: Completing Add the missing commas to the following passage.

"Are you going to the game tonight?" Dirk asked Lonnie.
"Of course," she replied,"I wouldn't miss it."
"But the Mets will probably be slaughtered," Dirk said.
"What difference does that make?" she questioned.
Dirk answered,"I just don't want to pay money to watch them lose."
"Well, I'm a real loyal fan!" Lonnie emphasized as she walked away.

PRACTICE 15: Writing Your Own Write five sentences of your own using commas to set off direct quotations. *Answers will vary.*

OTHER USES OF COMMAS

Use commas in the following ways.

Numbers: What is **2,502,500** divided by **10,522?**

A comma is optional in numbers of four digits: **4000** or **4,000**.

Dates: My great grandfather was born in December 1888 in London and died on **July 23, 1972,** in Denver.

Notice that there is a comma both before and after the year.

Addresses: Ashley moved from **Chicago, Illinois,** to **15305 Jefferson Ave., Boston, MA 09643.**

Notice that there is no comma between the state and zip code.

Letters: **Dear Alisha,**
Yours truly,

PRACTICE 16: Identifying In the following sentences, circle the commas that are used incorrectly, and add any commas that are missing.

1. The new Honda Accord costs more than $23,000.
2. Michael Finley plays basketball with the Mavericks and lives in Dallas, Texas.
3. My five-year anniversary is June, 16, 2005.
4. Jamie lives in Los Altos, California, with her two kids.
5. Yours truly, Deena

PRACTICE 17: Completing Add the missing commas to the following paragraph.

Norma graduated from Texas State University in San Marcos, Texas, on June 5, 2004. There were more than 3,000 people in the audience, including Norma's friends and family. Her parents drove all the way from Tulsa, Oklahoma, and they stayed in Texas all weekend. After the graduation ceremonies, Norma and her loved ones spent the weekend visiting the Austin area and other parts of Texas that Norma didn't get to see while attending school.

PRACTICE 18: Writing Your Own Write a sentence of your own for each of the following items. *Answers will vary.*

1. your date of birth

    ____

2. the city and state where you were born

    ____

3. your full address, including the ZIP code

    ____

4. the estimated number of people who attend your school

    ____

5. the amount of money you would like to make per year after college graduation

    ____

CHAPTER REVIEW

You might want to reread the examples in this chapter before you do the following exercises.

REVIEW PRACTICE 1: Identifying Add the missing commas to the following sentences.

1. When I was 12 years old, my father took me to Honolulu,Hawaii.
2. Seth wanted more dessert,but he was on a diet.
3. Although James read that book before,he couldn't remember how it ended.
4. The Prelude is,of course,the best Honda vehicle.
5. I proudly cheered as Nick,my best friend,scored a touchdown.

6. "We will begin discussing genetics next Tuesday," said the professor.

7. Azaleas, carnations, and roses are my favorite flowers.

8. The beautiful, tall, brown-haired model walked down the catwalk.

9. There are 300,400 people in this county.

10. Craig and I started dating on August 7, 2001.

REVIEW PRACTICE 2: Completing Add the missing commas to the following paragraph.

My only cat, Mango, is Siamese. I still remember when she was born; it was February 14, 1997, Valentine's Day. There are more than 1,000 different breeds of cats, but the Siamese are the most strikingly beautiful. Mango is a friendly cat, however, unlike most Siamese. When I first brought her home, my friends said, "She'll be a spoiled brat," but I have come to love her.

REVIEW PRACTICE 3: Writing Your Own Write a paragraph about the importance of computer knowledge. What are the benefits of computer technology? Why should we be familiar with it? *Answers will vary.*

REVIEW PRACTICE 4: Editing Through Collaboration Exchange paragraphs from Review Practice 3 with another student, and do the following: *Answers will vary.*

1. Circle any misplaced commas.

2. Suggest corrections for the incorrect commas.

Then return the paper to its writer, and use the information in this chapter to correct any comma errors in your own paragraph. Record your errors on the Error Log in Appendix 6.

CHAPTER 40

Apostrophes

CHECKLIST for Using Apostrophes

✔ Are apostrophes used correctly in contractions?

✔ Are apostrophes used correctly to show possession?

TEST YOURSELF

Add an apostrophe or an apostrophe and *-s* to the following sentences.

- The flight crew was surprised by the pilots rudeness when he boarded the plane.
- Its important that the car has its engine checked every 3,000 miles.
- Whats going to happen after Dominics gone?
- The mens bathroom is located on the third floor.
- James house is the third one on the left.

(Answers are in Appendix 4.)

The **apostrophe** looks like a single quotation mark. Its two main purposes are to indicate where letters have been left out and to show ownership.

MARKING CONTRACTIONS

Use an apostrophe to show that letters have been omitted to form a contraction.

UNIT PRETEST

To check your students' abilities with the collective skills in this unit, a Unit Pretest is available on pages 769–771.

TEACHING APOSTROPHES

Create a game of *Jeopardy!* with the following categories: "Understanding Contractions," "Forming Contractions," "Identifying Correct and Incorrect Possessives," and "Forming Possessives." Write questions like the following to fit each category.

Understanding Contractions:

Answer: The word that *can't* stands for
Question: What is *cannot?*

Forming Contractions:

Answer: The contraction made from the words *should have*
Question: What is *should've?*

Identifying Correct and Incorrect Possessives:

Answer: Of *hers, his,* and *it's*, the word that is an incorrect possessive pronoun
Question: What is *it's?*

Forming Possessives

Answer: Another way to write "the house of the family named Jones"
Question: What is "the Joneses' house"?

Divide the class into teams to play the game. The team to get the most correct answers wins.

INSTRUCTOR'S RESOURCE MANUAL
For directions on how to play the game and a complete set of questions and answers, for more exercises, and for quizzes, see the *Instructor's Resource Manual*, Section II, Part IV.

A **contraction** is the shortening of one or more words. Our everyday speech is filled with contractions.

I have	=	I've (*h* and *a* have been omitted)
you are	=	you're (*a* has been omitted)
let us	=	let's (*u* has been omitted)

Here is a list of commonly used contractions.

Some Common Contractions

I am	=	*I'm*	*we have*	=	*we've*
I would	=	*I'd*	*we will*	=	*we'll*
I will	=	*I'll*	*they are*	=	*they're*
you have	=	*you've*	*they have*	=	*they've*
you will	=	*you'll*	*do not*	=	*don't*
he is	=	*he's*	*did not*	=	*didn't*
she will	=	*she'll*	*have not*	=	*haven't*
it is	=	*it's*	*could not*	=	*couldn't*

Hint: Two words that are frequently misused are *it's* and *its*.

it's = contraction: it is (*or* it has)	**It's** too late to go to the movie.
its = pronoun: belonging to it	**Its** eyes are really large.

To see if you are using the correct word, say the sentence with the words *it is*. If that is what you want to say, add an apostrophe to the word.

? I think **its** burning.
Test: I think **it is** burning. **YES, add an apostrophe**

This sentence makes sense with *it is*, so you should write *it's*.

Correct: I think **it's** burning.

? The dog wagged **its** tail.
Test: The dog wagged **it is** tail. **NO, so no apostrophe**

This sentence does not make sense with *it is*, so you should not use the apostrophe in *its*.

Correct: The dog wagged **its** tail.

PRACTICE 1: Identifying In the following sentences, circle the apostrophes that are used incorrectly, and add any apostrophes that are missing.

1. I've got to find a better job.
2. The attorney said she's working overtime on this case.
3. They'll be glad to see you at the party.
4. It's a good thing they didn't bring their baby to the wedding.
5. Cameron doesn't get paid until Friday.

PRACTICE 2: Completing Write contractions for the following words.

1. she + would = *she'd*
2. did + not = *didn't*
3. will + not = *won't*
4. they + will = *they'll*
5. should + have = *should've*

PRACTICE 3: Writing Your Own Write a sentence of your own for each of the contractions you wrote in Practice 2. *Answers will vary.*

UNIT POSTTEST
To check your students' mastery of the collective skills in this unit, a Unit Posttest is available on pages 782–784.

SHOWING POSSESSION

Use an apostrophe to show possession.

1. For a singular word, use *'s* to indicate possession or ownership. You can always replace a possessive with *of* plus the noun or pronoun.

the soldier**'s** rifle	=	the rifle **of the soldier**
someone**'s** house	=	the house **of someone**
doctor**'s** office	=	the office **of the doctor**
yesterday**'s** paper	=	the paper **of yesterday**

2. For plural nouns ending in *-s*, use only an apostrophe.

the soldiers**'** rifles	=	the rifles **of the soldiers**
the doctors**'** office	=	the office **of the doctors**
the painters**'** studio	=	the studio **of the painters**
the students**'** grades	=	the grades **of the students**
the brothers**'** boat	=	the boat **of the brothers**

3. For plural nouns that do not end in *-s*, add *'s*.

the men**'s** pants	=	the pants **of the men**
the deer**'s** antlers	=	the antlers **of the deer**
the criteria**'s** importance	=	the importance **of the criteria**

PRACTICE 4: Identifying In the following sentences, circle the apostrophes that are used incorrectly, and add any apostrophes that are missing.

1. The boy's bicycle had a flat tire.
2. The disaster was Jennifer's fault.
3. Our two cats' water bowl was empty.
4. We knew the airline's food would be tasty.
5. Today's temperature reached 83 degrees.

PRACTICE 5: Completing Write a possessive for each of the following phrases.

1. the feet of Charles *Charles's feet*
2. the guests of Dr. Blakeney *Dr. Blakeney's guests*
3. the tide of the ocean *the ocean's tide*
4. the shirts of the men *the men's shirts*
5. the assignment of the students *the students' assignment*

PRACTICE 6: Writing Your Own Write a sentence of your own for each of the possessives you wrote in Practice 5. *Answers will vary.*

COMMON APOSTROPHE ERRORS

Two common errors occur with apostrophes. The following guidelines will help you avoid these errors.

No Apostrophe with Possessive Pronouns

Do not use an apostrophe with a possessive pronoun.

Possessive pronouns already show ownership, so they do not need an apostrophe.

Error	Correct
his'	his
her's *or* hers'	hers
it's *or* its'	its
your's *or* yours'	yours
our's *or* ours'	ours
their's *or* theirs'	theirs

No Apostrophe to Form the Plural

Do not use an apostrophe to form a plural word.

This error occurs most often with plural words ending in *-s*. An apostrophe indicates possession or contraction; it does *not* indicate the plural. Therefore, a plural word never takes an apostrophe unless it is possessive.

NOT The **clothes'** are in the dryer.
Correct: The **clothes** are in the dryer.

NOT She bought a case of **soda's** last week.
Correct: She bought a case of **sodas** last week.

NOT Get your coffee and **donut's** here.
Correct: Get your coffee and **donuts** here.

PRACTICE 7: Identifying In the following sentences, circle the apostrophes that are used incorrectly, and add any apostrophes that are missing.

1. I've been to that store five time's, and I've never seen shoes like yours'.
2. My brother's are working for my father's company.
3. Sam left his' car's window's down, and it is starting to rain.
4. The soccer player's are meeting at noon.
5. The big story in the newspaper's is yesterday's flood.

PRACTICE 8: Completing Write a possessive for each of the following phrases.

1. the house belonging to them *their house*
2. the pants she owns *her pants*
3. the soda you are holding *your soda*

4. the price of it *its price*

5. the feet of him *his feet*

PRACTICE 9: Writing Your Own Write a sentence of your own for each of the possessives you wrote in Practice 8. *Answers will vary.*

CHAPTER REVIEW

You might want to reread the examples in this chapter before you do the following exercises.

REVIEW PRACTICE 1: Identifying In the following sentences, circle the apostrophes that are used incorrectly, and add any apostrophes that are missing.

1. Mr. Thompson's diner serves many pasta entrée's.
2. Two plumber's came to fix the leaks.
3. I thought I picked up my purse, but it was really her's.
4. Naomi was'nt pleased with the restaurant's service.
5. The rose's in my front yard haven't bloomed yet.
6. It's amazing that Tricia cut her hair as short as yours.
7. His' new house is in Highland Park.
8. You've got to see Ming's new jet ski's.
9. Our high school's head cheerleader is getting a full athletic scholarship to college.
10. Mary's parent's ordered four pizza's for her party.

REVIEW PRACTICE 2: Completing Add the missing apostrophes to the following sentences.

1. The truck's brakes went out while it was coming over the hill.
2. We haven't heard from Ben since he left his father's ranch and headed for ours.
3. My next-door neighbor's uncle is a big Hollywood actor.

4. Sarah's diet consisted of hot dogs and sodas.

5. The freeways are crowded because yesterday's fire still hasn't been contained.

6. I think it's time for us to go to our house and for you to go to yours.

7. Devon's kids were playing dominoes.

8. Maurice can't ever beat me at backgammon.

9. Stella's going to the game with us.

10. Both cars' gas tanks are empty.

REVIEW PRACTICE 3: Writing Your Own Write a paragraph about your favorite teacher. What was his or her name? What was special about this person?
Answers will vary.

REVIEW PRACTICE 4: Editing Through Collaboration Exchange paragraphs from Review Practice 3 with another student, and do the following: *Answers will vary.*

1. Circle any misplaced or missing apostrophes.

2. Indicate whether they mark possession (P) or contraction (C).

Then return the paper to its writer, and use the information in this chapter to correct any apostrophe errors in your own paragraph. Record your errors on the Error Log in Appendix 6.

41 CHAPTER

Quotation Marks

CHECKLIST for Using Quotation Marks

✔ Are quotation marks used to indicate someone's exact words?

✔ Are all periods and commas inside quotation marks?

✔ Are words capitalized correctly in quotations?

✔ Are quotation marks used to indicate the title of a short work, such as a short story or a poem?

UNIT PRETEST

To check your students' abilities with the collective skills in this unit, a Unit Pretest is available on pages 769–771.

TEACHING QUOTATION MARKS

Present the class with an excerpt from a play (one with numerous stage directions and comments) written as one long paragraph with no quotation marks to distinguish the spoken language from the stage directions. Have a student read the excerpt from the play. Students will

TEST YOURSELF

Add quotation marks where needed in the following sentences.

- Can we go out to dinner tonight? she asked.
- Jeri screamed, Don't go in there!
- If you can't find my house, Tom said, call me on your cell phone.
- My favorite poem is The Red Wheelbarrow by William Carlos Williams.
- David said, I'll fix your car this weekend.

(Answers are in Appendix 4.)

Quotation marks are punctuation marks that work together in pairs. Their most common use is to indicate someone's exact words. They are also used to mark the title of a short piece of writing, such as a short story or a poem.

DIRECT QUOTATIONS

Use quotation marks to indicate a **direct quotation**—someone's exact words.

Here are some examples that show the three basic forms of a direct quotation.

Direct Quotation: "I will not lend you the money," said the banker.

In this first example, the quoted words come first.

Direct Quotation: The banker said, "I will not lend you the money."

Here the quoted words come after the speaker is named.

Direct Quotation: "I will not," the banker said, "lend you the money."

In this example, the quoted words are interrupted, and the speaker is named in the middle. This form emphasizes the first few words.

INDIRECT QUOTATIONS

If you just talk about someone's words, you do not need quotation marks. Indirect quotations usually include the word *that,* as in *said that.* In questions, the wording is often *asked if.* Look at these examples of **indirect quotations.**

Direct Quotation: "I lost my job at the supermarket," said Bob.

These are Bob's exact words, so you must use quotation marks.

Indirect Quotation: Bob **said that** he lost his job at the supermarket.

This sentence explains what Bob said but does not use Bob's exact words. So quotation marks should not be used.

Direct Quotation: "The train trip took eight hours," said Kira.
Indirect Quotation: Kira **said that** the train trip took eight hours.

Direct Quotation: "Did you get the car fixed?" Mom asked.
Indirect Quotation: Mom **asked if** I had gotten the car fixed.

see how difficult distinguishing the stage remarks from the words is and will then understand the value of marking direct quotations.

Then have students work in groups of three or four to punctuate the paragraph correctly by adding quotation marks and proper spacing.

INSTRUCTOR'S RESOURCE MANUAL

For sample paragraphs, for more exercises and for quizzes, see the *Instructor's Resource Manual,* Section II, Part IV.

UNIT POSTTEST

To check your students' mastery of the collective skills in this unit, a Unit Posttest is available on pages 782–784.

PRACTICE 1: Identifying In the following sentences, circle the quotation marks used incorrectly, and add any quotation marks that are missing.

1. "Help me!" yelled the drowning woman."
2. "If you can't take the heat," my mom used to say, "stay out of the kitchen."
3. Martina asked, "Have you found my jacket?" *Correct*
4. Steffan said, "My goal is to "get into the Olympics."
5. Chonda said that "she enjoyed the movie last night."

PRACTICE 2: Completing Add the missing quotation marks to the following paragraph.

When I went into the salon, my hairdresser asked, "How do you want your hair cut today?" "I don't really know," I replied, "but I brought in a couple of pictures of haircuts I like." "Those are cute," she said. "Do you think my hair would look good like that?" I asked. "Absolutely!" she exclaimed. Then she set to work with the scissors. When she was finished, I looked in the mirror in horror. "That's not what I had in mind," I told her. "But it looks just like the pictures," she said. "How can you say that?" I exclaimed. "The haircuts I showed you are shoulder-length, and mine is now above my ears!" "Well," she said, "it will always grow back."

PRACTICE 3: Writing Your Own Write a sentence of your own for each of the following expressions. *Answers will vary.*

1. a question asked by Claudia ______________________________
2. a statement spoken by the manager ______________________________
3. an exclamation spoken by Becky ______________________________
4. an indirect question that Jared asked ______________________________
5. a statement spoken by the electrician ______________________________

CAPITALIZING AND USING OTHER PUNCTUATION MARKS WITH QUOTATION MARKS

When you are quoting someone's complete sentences, begin with a capital letter, and use appropriate end punctuation—a period, a question mark,

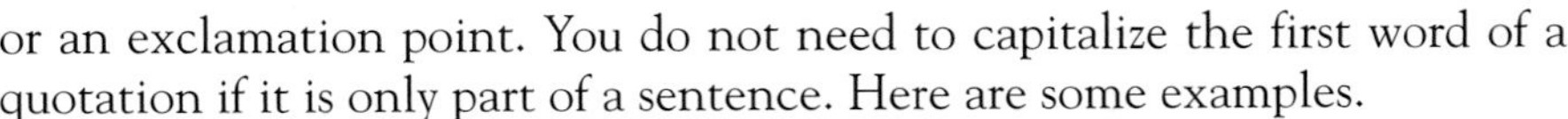

or an exclamation point. You do not need to capitalize the first word of a quotation if it is only part of a sentence. Here are some examples.

Capitalize the first letter of the first word being quoted, and put a period at the end of the sentence if it is a statement. Separate the spoken words from the rest of the sentence with a comma.

> **“H**e doesn’t seem very nice**,”** she said.
>
> He said**, “T**urn off the music**.”**

If the quotation ends with a question mark or an exclamation point, use that punctuation instead of a comma or a period.

> **“W**hy do you want to know**?”** she asked.
>
> **H**e yelled**, “T**urn off that music**!”**

In a quotation that is interrupted, capitalize the first word being quoted, but do not capitalize words in the middle of the sentence. Use a comma both before and after the interruption. End with a period if it is a statement.

> **“Y**es**,”** said the bus driver**, “**this bus goes downtown**.”**

You do not need to capitalize the first word of a quotation that is only part of a sentence.

> I don’t think that he will ever **“f**ind himself**.”**

Hint: Look at the examples again. Notice that periods and commas always go inside the quotation marks.

NOT	“Yes”**,** he said, “we’re ready to leave”**.**
Correct:	“Yes**,”** he said, “we’re ready to leave**.”**

PRACTICE 4: Identifying In the following sentences, circle the quotation marks, capital letters, and other punctuation marks that are used incorrectly, and add any missing quotation marks and punctuation.

1. “Is there a doctor in the house”?”the man screamed.
2. “I can’t believe,” she said, “That you’ve never seen the ocean.”
3. Margarita asked, “Are you ever going to meet me for coffee”?
4. “This is the last time” he promised, “that I come home late”
5. Garrett said, “I want to take the trolley to the restaurant on the corner.”

PRACTICE 5: Completing Add the missing quotation marks and punctuation to the following paragraph.

I was having car problems, so I drove to the auto shop on the corner."What do you think is wrong with my car?"I asked the mechanic."I can't tell you,"he said,"until I take a look at it myself."I replied,"I'll leave it with you this afternoon, and you can tell me later today what you find out."" That would be great," he said. Finally, around 4:00 p.m., he called me on the phone."Your car needs a new clutch,"he said."No way!"I exclaimed."Sorry, mister,"he calmly replied, "but that's all I found to be wrong with it."I explained,"But I just replaced the clutch four months ago."" Well," he said,"I hope you saved your receipt and warranty paperwork."

PRACTICE 6: Writing Your Own Write a sentence of your own for each of the following direct quotations, punctuated correctly. *Answers will vary.*

1. "No, I won't" ______________________________
2. "How are we going to do that" ______________________________
3. "This is the most important priority" ______________________________
4. "Yes" "you can come to the party" ______________________________
5. "Don't worry" "you didn't miss anything" ______________________________

QUOTATION MARKS AROUND TITLES

Put quotation marks around the titles of short works that are parts of larger works. The titles of longer works are put in italics (or underlined).

Quotation Marks	**Italics/Underlining**
"The Yellow Wallpaper" (short story)	*American Short Stories* (book)
"Song of Myself" (poem)	*Leaves of Grass* (book)
"My Girl" (song)	*The Temptations' Greatest Hits* (CD)
"Explore New Orleans" (magazine article)	*New Orleans Monthly* (magazine)
"Convicts Escape" (newspaper article)	*New York Times* (newspaper)
"The Wedding" (episode on TV series)	*Friends* (TV series)

PRACTICE 7: Identifying Put an X in front of each sentence with errors in quotation marks or italics/underlining. Add any missing quotation marks and italics or underlining.

1. __X__ My favorite song by the Beatles is *Yellow Submarine*. *("Yellow Submarine")*
2. __X__ When Juliet was in high school, she read Shirley Jackson's famous short story The Lottery. *("The Lottery")*
3. _____ Getting through *Moby Dick* by Herman Melville took me three weeks.
4. __X__ My first boyfriend recited William Blake's poem *The Garden of Love* to me on my front porch. *("The Garden of Love")*
5. __X__ The "New York Times" ran a long article called *Japan's Princess Gives Birth* about Crown Princess Masako. *(New York Times, "Japan's Princess Gives Birth")*

PRACTICE 8: Completing Place quotation marks around the titles of short works, and underline the titles of long works in the following paragraph.

> Mark got a great job with the <u>Chicago Tribune</u> last summer. He is now working as the editor of the entertainment section, and he writes a column called"Making a Mark." In his column, he reviews celebrity events and activities, such as concerts, hit movies, and best-selling books. For one article, he interviewed several people from <u>Survivor</u>, the popular reality TV show. He also attended a John Mayer concert and quoted lines from the song"Waiting on the World to Change"on his CD <u>Continuum</u>. Another article featured Nikki Giovanni, who read her poem"Dream"during their interview. Mark has become friends with some very interesting and well-known people, and he is now looking forward to speaking with Steven Spielberg on the set of the latest sequel to <u>Jurassic Park</u>.

PRACTICE 9: Writing Your Own Write a sentence of your own for each of the following items. Make up a title if you can't think of one. *Answers will vary.*

1. a short story ________________________________
2. a song ________________________________
3. a TV show ________________________________
4. a CD ________________________________
5. a magazine article ________________________________

CHAPTER REVIEW

You might want to reread the examples in this chapter before you do the following exercises.

REVIEW PRACTICE 1: Identifying Add the missing quotation marks and punctuation to the following sentences.

1. Patty sang Fergie's "London Bridge" at the karaoke party.
2. Our next writing assignment is a critical review of Robert Browning's poem "My Last Duchess."
3. "You don't have to go to work today," I told Gerard.
4. Marjorie won the short story contest with a tale she wrote about her grandmother called "It's a Happy Day."
5. Devonne asked, "Where does Jack live?"
6. When Princess Diana died, the Boston Globe ran an article called "Too Soon."
7. The scores came in, and our coach yelled, "Great job, team!"
8. "I can't make it to the meeting," she said, "but I'll call you tonight to find out what I missed."
9. "What do you want to eat for breakfast?" Charise asked.
10. I submitted an article to Golf Magazine called "How to Swing like Tiger Woods."

REVIEW PRACTICE 2: Completing Add the missing quotation marks, commas, and underlining for italics to the following dialogue.

"Hurry up," I said, "or we're going to be late for the Beastie Boys Concert."

"I'm coming," John replied. "Just hold your horses!"

"The write-up in USA Today said this was going to be their biggest concert ever," I told him. I asked John if he too had read that article, but he said that he hadn't.

"I didn't have time to read today," he explained, "because I was busy buying a CD of their greatest hits. Now," John said, "I'm really excited about the concert tonight!"

REVIEW PRACTICE 3: Writing Your Own In paragraph form, record a conversation you had this week. Who were you talking to? What did you talk about? What were your exact words? *Answers will vary.*

REVIEW PRACTICE 4: Editing Through Collaboration Exchange paragraphs from Review Practice 3 with another student, and do the following: *Answers will vary.*

1. Circle any incorrect or missing quotation marks.
2. Underline any faulty punctuation.
3. Put an X over any incorrect use of italics/underlining.

Then return the paper to its writer, and use the information in this chapter to correct any errors with quotation marks and italics/underlining in your own paragraph. Record your errors on the Error Log in Appendix 6.

42 CHAPTER

Other Punctuation Marks

CHECKLIST for Using Semicolons, Colons, Dashes, and Parentheses

✔ Are semicolons used to join two closely related complete sentences?

✔ Are long items in a series that already contain commas separated by semicolons?

✔ Are colons used correctly to introduce a list?

✔ Are dashes used to emphasize or further explain a point?

✔ Are parentheses used to include additional, but not necessary, information?

UNIT PRETEST

To check your students' abilities with the collective skills in this unit, a Unit Pretest is available on pages 769–771.

TEACHING OTHER PUNCTUATION MARKS

Before class, put a series of sentence parts and punctuation marks on small pieces of cardboard. The sentence parts should include clauses, phrases, and single parts of speech.

TEST YOURSELF

Add semicolons, colons, dashes, or parentheses to the following sentences.

- Kris left for the dance Sean decided to stay home.
- We wanted to win therefore we practiced every day.
- The computer's advertised price didn't include several important parts a monitor, a printer, and speakers.
- Ramon asked the best question during the interview "Why should we vote for you?"
- Bring the jelly to a "rolling boil" a boil that cannot be stirred down.

(Answers are in Appendix 4.)

This chapter explains the uses of the **semicolon, colon, dash,** and **parentheses.** We'll look at these punctuation marks one by one.

SEMICOLONS

Semicolons are used to separate equal parts of a sentence. They are also used to avoid confusion when listing items in a series.

1. Use a semicolon to separate two closely related independent clauses.

   An independent clause is a group of words with a subject and a verb that can stand alone as a sentence. You might use a semicolon instead of a coordinating conjunction (*and, but, for, nor, or, so, yet*) or a period. Any one of the three options would be correct.

	Independent Independent
Semicolon:	Sam never drove to school**; he** always rode his bike.
Conjunction:	Sam never drove to school**, for** he always rode his bike.
Period:	Sam never drove to school**. He** always rode his bike.

2. Use a semicolon to join two independent clauses that are connected by such words as *however, therefore, furthermore, moreover, for example*, or *consequently*. Put a comma after the connecting word.

	Independent Independent
Semicolon:	Traveling can be expensive**; nevertheless,** it's always enjoyable.
Semicolon:	Brad is very smart**; furthermore,** he was offered seven scholarships.
Semicolon:	He has trouble in math**; therefore,** he hired a tutor.

3. Use a semicolon to separate items in a series when any of the items contain commas.

NOT	On the flight to New York, Mei Lin read a popular new thriller with a surprise ending**,** took a long**,** relaxing nap**,** and watched an incredibly dull movie about a rock star.
Correct:	On the flight to New York, Mei Lin read a popular new thriller with a surprise ending**;** took a long**,** relaxing nap**;** and watched an incredibly dull movie about a rock star.

PRACTICE 1: Identifying In the following sentences, circle the semicolons that are used incorrectly, and add any commas and semicolons that are missing.

Assign several pieces of cardboard to each student, and have the students begin by wearing one card. Then have students who are sentence parts stand in front of the class to form a sentence. For example, seven students might make the following sentence:

I went grocery shopping (clause)

after school (prep. phrase)

because (subordinating conj.)

I needed food (clause)

fruit/milk/bread (3 words)

Then have the people who are punctuation marks go to the correct places in the sentence (for example, a colon after *food* and commas after *fruit* and *milk*). By moving students around, show them how punctuation changes when certain words, phrases, and clauses are rearranged, added, or inserted.

INSTRUCTOR'S RESOURCE MANUAL

For more words, phrases, and clauses, for more exercises, and for quizzes, see the *Instructor's Resource Manual*, Section II, Part IV.

UNIT POSTTEST
To check your students' mastery of the collective skills in this unit, a Unit Posttest is available on pages 782–784.

1. The car needed new front tires; the old ones were quite bald.
2. Lisa's 10-month-old son didn't take a nap today; however(;), he was very pleasant.
3. I must have lost my keys; I can't(;) find them anywhere.
4. Our team is the strongest(;), and we are prepared to win.
5. Mr. Banderas teaches Spanish; writes novels(;), books(;), and short stories; and reviews movies in his spare time.

PRACTICE 2: Completing Add semicolons to the following paragraph.

When I was in junior high, my school had a big dance; I dreaded it from the day it was announced. I didn't have a boyfriend; I didn't have the right clothes, shoes, or hairstyle; and I didn't have any money saved up for things like that. Even worse, I knew my parents felt I was too young to go; nonetheless, I knew my friends would keep asking me if I was going. Finally, I thought of a good excuse: I told my friends my grandmother was having major surgery. My friends probably knew I was lying; however, nobody said anything more to me about it.

PRACTICE 3: Writing Your Own Write five sentences of your own using semicolons correctly. *Answers will vary.*

COLONS

1. The main use of the colon is to introduce a list or thought. Here are some examples:

   Colon: Buy the following items for the trip**:** toothpaste, toothbrush, razor, soap, and makeup.
   Colon: The fair had some new attractions**:** a double ferris wheel, a roller coaster, and an antique merry-go-round.
   Colon: The choice was simple**:** return the merchandise.

   The most common error with colons is using one where it isn't needed.

2. Do not use a colon after the words *such as* or *including*. A complete sentence must come before a colon.

NOT Cook only fresh vegetables, **such as:** green beans, broccoli, and spinach.

Correct: Cook only fresh vegetables, **such as** green beans, broccoli, and spinach.

NOT We went to many countries in Europe, **including:** Spain and Portugal.

Correct: We went to many countries in Europe, **including** Spain and Portugal.

3. In addition, you should not use a colon after a verb or after a preposition. Remember that a complete sentence must come before a colon.

NOT The movies to be reviewed **are:** *Pirates of the Caribbean* and *Superman*.

Correct: The movies to be reviewed **are** *Pirates of the Caribbean* and *Superman*.

NOT The box was full **of:** books, old dolls, and scrapbooks.

Correct: The box was full **of** books, old dolls, and scrapbooks.

PRACTICE 4: Identifying In the following sentences, circle the colons that are used incorrectly, and add any colons that are missing.

1. The best things about summer are: swimming, biking, and picnics.
2. The man asked me for the following items: my driver's license, my Social Security number, and my credit cards.
3. We accidentally left many things at home, such as: my toothbrush, our hair dryer, and the baby's bottle.
4. I was most impressed by: the atmosphere, the prices, and the service.
5. The most expensive parts to repair were: the carburetor, the ignition system, and the fuel injector.

PRACTICE 5: Completing Add colons to the following paragraph.

Reading is an excellent way to spend free time. A good book can do many things: take you to a faraway place, introduce you to different people, and expose you to extraordinary experiences. I especially like two kinds of books:science fiction and romance novels. These genres are totally opposite, I know, but they have just what I like: action, strange characters, and suspension of disbelief. When I am reading, I am in a world of my own. I escape all of my everyday problems: my difficult job, my nagging mother, and sometimes even my homework.

PRACTICE 6: Writing Your Own Write five sentences of your own using colons correctly. *Answers will vary.*

DASHES AND PARENTHESES

Both **dashes** and **parentheses** mark breaks in the flow of a sentence. A dash suggests an abrupt pause in a statement, while parentheses surround words that could actually be taken out of a sentence grammatically.

Dashes

1. Use dashes to emphasize or draw attention to a point.

   Dash: I know what I want to be—a doctor.

   In this example, the beginning of the sentence introduces an idea, and the dash then sets off the answer.

   Dash: Money and time—these are what I need.

   In this example, the key words are set off at the beginning, and the explanation follows. Beginning this way adds some suspense to the sentence.

   Dashes: I know what I want in a husband—a sense of humor—and I plan to get it.

   The dashes divide this sentence into three distinct parts, which makes the reader pause and think about each part.

Parentheses

Whereas dashes set off material that the writer wants to emphasize, parentheses do just the opposite. They are always used in pairs.

2. Use parentheses to set off information that is interesting or helpful but not necessary for understanding the sentence.

   Parentheses: When in Rome **(as the saying goes),** do as the Romans do.

Parentheses: The senator's position on the proposal **(Senate Bill 193)** has changed several times.

3. Parentheses are also used to mark a person's life span and to number items in a sentence.

Parentheses: Herman Melville **(1819–1891)** wrote the classic *Moby Dick*.

Parentheses: My boss gave me three things to do today: **(1)** answer the mail, **(2)** file receipts, and **(3)** send out bills.

PRACTICE 7: Identifying Use dashes or parentheses with the underlined words in the following sentences.

1. One powerful tool for student research is becoming more popular than the library—the Internet.
2. My brother—the police chief—keeps his phone number unlisted.
3. Nick (head of the math department) hires the new teachers. *(or dashes)*
4. I signaled the oncoming car (by flashing my lights,) but it still didn't turn its headlights on.
5. Cheryl got her passport so she can (1) visit other countries, (2) go diving in all of the seven seas, and (3) photograph royalty.

PRACTICE 8: Completing Add dashes and parentheses to the following paragraph.

In high school, I volunteered to work on the yearbook. Mrs. Brady was our instructor—a round lady with bright red cheeks and a strange laugh. She immediately set us to work on several things (mostly after school), as we accumulated photos and news about the school's major events. I remember one lesson I learned in that class—never procrastinate. If I failed to finish an assignment (something that rarely happened), someone else would do it instead, and that person's work would be published instead of mine. I'll never forget my year with Mrs. Brady.

PRACTICE 9: Writing Your Own Write three sentences of your own using dashes and two using parentheses. *Answers will vary.*

CHAPTER REVIEW

You might want to reread the examples in this chapter before you do the following exercises.

REVIEW PRACTICE 1: Identifying Add semicolons, colons, dashes, and parentheses to the following sentences.

1. We are going to the grocery store; we have nothing in the pantry.
2. There are only three people I trust: Krista, Tanya, and Lucy.
3. He is always home; however, he doesn't ever help out around the house.
4. I bought the car in my favorite color—neon yellow. *(or colon)*
5. Put the flowers on the table outside (the one by the wall,) and the presents can go there too. *(or dashes)*
6. My favorite book was made into a movie—*Beloved*.
7. There are many things to do today: pick up the dry cleaning, vacuum the carpets, and wash the dishes.
8. The chicken coop needs to be cleaned out; it is full of leaves and tree branches.
9. We will pick up Derek, Jenny, and Carmen; load up with sunscreen; and go to the beach.
10. I got your favorite ice cream for your birthday—fudge ripple. *(or colon)*

REVIEW PRACTICE 2: Completing Add semicolons, colons, dashes, and parentheses to the following paragraph.

Today was an extremely windy day, so we decided to fly kites. We drove to Kite Hill (a place where I went as a kid), and we climbed to the very top. We took out the kites and other necessary things: masking tape, string, and ribbons. This way we were prepared to repair our kites, if necessary. The wind was perfect; we couldn't have asked for better weather. There was only one thing we forgot—the picnic lunch! Fortunately, Lamar remembered to pack the cooler with sodas—mostly

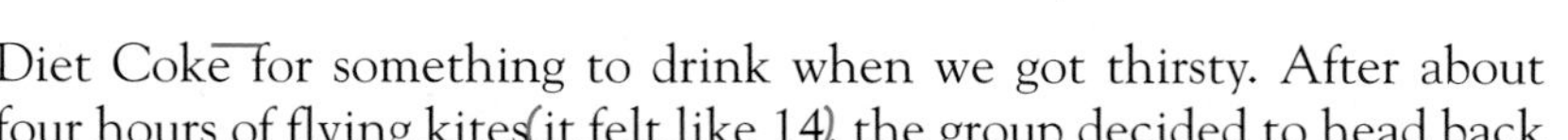

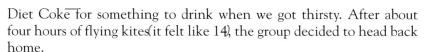

Diet Coke—for something to drink when we got thirsty. After about four hours of flying kites (it felt like 14), the group decided to head back home.

REVIEW PRACTICE 3: Writing Your Own Write a paragraph explaining some of your five-year goals. What do you plan to be doing in five years? What do you want to have accomplished? *Answers will vary.*

REVIEW PRACTICE 4: Editing Through Collaboration Exchange paragraphs from Review Practice 3 with another student, and do the following: *Answers will vary.*

1. Circle any incorrect or missing semicolons.
2. Circle any incorrect or missing colons.
3. Circle any incorrect or missing dashes.
4. Circle any incorrect or missing parentheses.

Then return the paper to its writer, and use the information in this chapter to correct any punctuation errors in your own paragraph. Record your errors on the Error Log in Appendix 6.

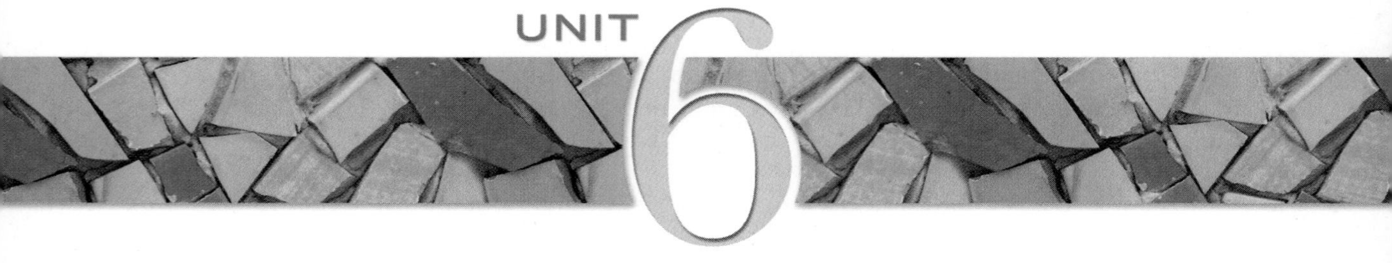

Mechanics

The mechanical aspects of a sentence are much like the mechanical features of a car, an appliance, or a clock. They are some of the smallest—yet most important—details in a sentence. In writing, the term *mechanics* refers to capitalization, abbreviations, and numbers. We usually take these items for granted, but when they are used incorrectly, a sentence, just like a mechanical appliance with a weak spring, starts to break down.

Following a few simple guidelines will help you keep your sentences running smoothly and efficiently. These guidelines are explained in two chapters:

Chapter 43: Capitalization
Chapter 44: Abbreviations and Numbers
Unit 6 Pretests: pp. 771–772
Unit 6 Posttests: pp. 784–786

CHAPTER 43

Capitalization

CHECKLIST for Editing Capitalization

✔ Are all proper nouns capitalized?

✔ Are all words in titles capitalized correctly?

✔ Have you followed the other rules for capitalizing correctly?

TEST YOURSELF

Correct the capitalization errors in the following sentences.

- According to uncle Bob, mother makes the best texas sheet cake.
- Antonio is a native american.
- "the shortest path," he said, "Is down baker street."
- issa loves to go to walt disney world.
- Last year, I saw the red hot chili peppers in concert.

(Answers are in Appendix 4.)

Because every sentence begins with a capital letter, **capitalization** is the best place to start discussing the mechanics of good writing. Capital letters signal where sentences begin. They also call attention to certain kinds of words, making sentences easier to read and understand.

Correct capitalization coupled with correct punctuation adds up to good, clear writing. Here are some guidelines to help you capitalize correctly.

1. Capitalize the first word of every sentence, including the first word of a quotation that forms a sentence.

   My favorite city is Rome.

   "**R**ome is my favorite city," he said.

   He said, "**M**y favorite city is Rome."

UNIT PRETEST

To check your students' abilities with the collective skills in this unit, a Unit Pretest is available on pages 771–772.

TEACHING CAPITALIZATION

Show students copies of real e-mails that contain no capitalization whatsoever. At the same time, show students copies of chat room conversations where people who type in all caps are told to "stop yelling."

Have students rewrite the e-mails with correct capitalization.

After the exercise, talk to students about how capitalization marks sentence boundaries.

INSTRUCTOR'S RESOURCE MANUAL
For sample sentences, for more exercises, and for quizzes, see the *Instructor's Resource Manual*, Section II, Part IV.

UNIT POSTTEST
To check your students' mastery of the collective skills in this unit, a Unit Posttest is available on pages 784–786.

Do not capitalize the second part of a quotation that is split.

"My favorite city," he said, "is Rome."

2. Capitalize all proper nouns. Do not capitalize common nouns.

Common Nouns	**Proper Nouns**
person	Eleanor Roosevelt
state	Minnesota
building	Empire State Building
river	Mississippi River
airplane	*Air Force One*

Here are some examples of proper nouns.

People:	Sarah, Julia Roberts, Tiger Woods
Groups:	Australians, Apaches, Europeans, British, Latino
Languages:	Russian, Italian, French
Religions, Religious Books, Holy Days:	Catholicism, Buddhism, Koran, Bible, Yom Kippur, Kwanzaa, Easter
Organizations:	Boston Red Sox, Democratic Party, American Civil Liberties Union, Kiwanis Club, Alpha Gamma Delta
Places:	Smoky Mountains National Park, Antarctica, Louisville, Jefferson County, Madison Avenue, Highway 101, Golden Gate Bridge, John F. Kennedy International Airport
Institutions, Agencies, Businesses:	Washington High School, Baltimore Public Library, United Way, Grady Memorial Hospital, Time Warner
Brand Names, Ships, Aircraft:	Mustang, Wisk, Pepsi, U.S.S. *Alabama*, *Challenger*

3. Capitalize titles used with people's names or in place of their names.

Mr. Ralph W. Gerber, Ms. Rachel Lorca, Dr. Leticia Johnson, Aunt Jane, Grandpa Bob, Cousin Maria, Sis, Nana

Do not capitalize words that identify family relationships.

NOT I saw my Grandfather yesterday.

Correct:	I saw my grandfather yesterday.
Correct:	I saw Grandfather yesterday.

4. Capitalize the titles of creative works.

Books:	*The Catcher in the Rye*
Short Stories:	"Sonny's Blues"
Plays:	*The Glass Menagerie*
Poems:	"My Last Duchess"
Articles:	"Two New Inns Now Open for Business"
Magazines:	*Newsweek*
Songs:	"Cheeseburger in Paradise"
Albums or CDs:	*Jimmy Buffet's Greatest Hits*
Films:	*Lady and the Tramp*
TV Series:	*The West Wing*
Works of Art:	*The Bedroom at Arles*
Computer Programs:	Apple Works

Do not capitalize *a, an, the,* or short prepositions unless they are the first or last word in a title.

5. Capitalize days of the week, months, holidays, and special events.

Monday, July, Presidents' Day, Thanksgiving, Cinco de Mayo, Mardi Gras

Do not capitalize the names of seasons: *summer, fall, winter, spring.*

6. Capitalize the names of historical events, periods, and documents:

the French Revolution, the Jurassic Period, World War II, the Sixties, the Battle of Bunker Hill, the Magna Carta

7. Capitalize specific course titles and the names of language courses.

Economics 201, Philosophy 101, Spanish 200, Civilizations of the Ancient World

Do not capitalize a course or subject you are referring to in a general way unless the course is a language.

my economics course, my philosophy course, my Spanish course, my history course

8. Capitalize references to regions of the country but not words that merely indicate direction.

If you travel **n**orth from Houston, you will end up in the **M**idwest, probably in Kansas or Nebraska.

9. Capitalize the opening of a letter and the first word of the closing.

Dear **D**r. **H**amlin, **D**ear **S**ir,
Best wishes, **S**incerely,

Notice that a comma comes after the opening and closing.

PRACTICE 1: Identifying Underline and correct the capitalization errors in the following sentences.

1. The irs is auditing aunt Joan. *(IRS, Aunt)*
2. Debbie and Sue bought their mother a bottle of chanel's coco perfume for mother's Day. *(Chanel's, Coco, Mother's)*
3. In our History class, we are studying the great wall of china. *(history, Great Wall, China)*
4. This Winter, emilio will visit uncle Luis, who lives somewhere in the south. *(winter, Emilio, Uncle, South)*
5. David Bowie's song "changes" is a classic from the seventies. *(Changes, Seventies)*

PRACTICE 2: Completing Fill in each blank with words that complete the sentence. Be sure to capitalize words correctly. (You can make up titles if necessary.) *Answers will vary.*

1. In my ______________ class, we had to read ______________.
2. Blanca bought a new truck, a ______________.
3. ______________ should be in charge of the charity drive.
4. I wish I could get tickets to see ______________ in concert.
5. We are going to ______________ for our vacation.

PRACTICE 3: Writing Your Own Write five sentences of your own that cover at least five of the capitalization rules. *Answers will vary.*

CHAPTER REVIEW

You might want to reread the examples in this chapter before you do the following exercises.

REVIEW PRACTICE 1: Identifying Underline and correct the capitalization errors in the following sentences.

1. In April's edition of *people* magazine, LeAnn rimes talks about her love of Country music. *(People, Rimes, country)*
2. We decided to get married even though he's a member of the democratic party and I am a member of the republican party. *(Democratic Party, Republican Party)*
3. Raphael was born on October 31, 1972—he was a halloween baby. *(Halloween)*
4. Many Fathers, Sons, and Brothers fought against each other in the american civil war. *(fathers, sons, brothers, American Civil War)*
5. Ernesto's uncle has a beautiful statue of the buddha in his garden. *(Buddha)*
6. I watch *late night with David Letterman* for entertainment. *(Late Night)*
7. Christy can speak both english and spanish. *(English, Spanish)*
8. We celebrate both christmas and kwanzaa. *(Christmas, Kwanzaa)*
9. My Father used to drive me around town in his 1968 convertible ford mustang. *(father, Ford Mustang)*
10. The spider said to the fly, "welcome to my home." *(Welcome)*

REVIEW PRACTICE 2: Completing Fill in each blank with words that complete the sentence. Be sure to capitalize words correctly. *Answers will vary.*

1. Over the weekend, I watched my favorite movie, ______________.
2. In history, we are studying the ______________.
3. I was born on ______________.
4. Ashley wears nothing but ______________ clothes.
5. Fred and ______________ both plan to major in ______________.

6. He has an unusual accent because he's from ______________.

7. If you travel ______________ on Highway 101, you will eventually reach Santa Cruz.

8. My favorite relative, ______________, will visit soon.

9. Every summer, we go to ______________ to fish.

10. Even though she's a ______________ and I'm a ______________, we are still the best of friends.

REVIEW PRACTICE 3: Writing Your Own Write a paragraph about the most unusual person you've met or the most unusual place you've visited. What made this person or place unique? *Answers will vary.*

REVIEW PRACTICE 4: Editing Through Collaboration Exchange paragraphs from Review Practice 3 with another student, and do the following tasks: *Answers will vary.*

1. Circle any capital letters that don't follow the capitalization rules.

2. Write the rule number next to the error for the writer to refer to.

Then return the paper to its writer, and use the information in this chapter to correct any capitalization errors in your own paragraph. Record your errors on the Error Log in Appendix 6.

CHAPTER 44

Abbreviations and Numbers

CHECKLIST for Using Abbreviations and Numbers

✔ Are titles before and after proper names abbreviated correctly?
✔ Are government agencies and other organizations abbreviated correctly?
✔ Are numbers *zero* through *nine* spelled out?
✔ Are numbers 10 and over written as figures (10, 25, 1–20, 324)?

TEST YOURSELF

Underline and correct the abbreviation and number errors in these sentences.

- He earned two million three hundred thousand dollars last year.
- My cat had 5 kittens.
- Sherril moved from England to the U.S.
- Mister Johnson always drinks hot chocolate in the mornings.
- I work for the Internal Revenue Service.

(Answers are in Appendix 4.)

UNIT PRETEST
To check your students' abilities with the collective skills in this unit, a Unit Pretest is available on pages 771–772.

TEACHING ABBREVIATIONS AND NUMBERS
Have students work in groups of three or four to write a paragraph that is filled with abbreviation and number errors. Have them be as inventive as possible

Like capitalization, **abbreviations** and **numbers** are also mechanical features of writing that help us communicate what we want to say. Following the rules that govern their use will make your writing as precise as possible.

yet still make the paragraph coherent.

Have the groups exchange paragraphs and try to decipher the paragraphs they now have. Point out how distracting abbreviations and numbers can be when they are not used correctly.

INSTRUCTOR'S RESOURCE MANUAL

For a sample paragraph, for more exercises, and for quizzes, see the *Instructor's Resource Manual*, Section II, Part IV.

UNIT POSTTEST

To check your students' mastery of the collective skills in this unit, a Unit Posttest is available on pages 784–786.

ABBREVIATIONS

Abbreviations help make communication precise and accurate. Here are a few rules to guide you.

1. Abbreviate titles before proper names.

   Mr. Michael Charles, **Mrs.** Marschel, **Ms.** Susan Deffaa, **Dr.** Frank Hilbig, **Rev.** Billy Graham, **Sen.** Diane Feinstein, **Sgt.** Arturo Lopez

   Abbreviate religious, governmental, and military titles when used with an entire name. Do not abbreviate them when used only with a last name.

   NOT We thought that **Gov.** Peterson would be reelected.
   Correct: We thought that **Governor** Peterson would be reelected.
   Correct: We thought **Gov.** Richard Peterson would be reelected.

   Professor is not usually abbreviated: **Professor** Mya Belle is teaching this class.

2. Abbreviate academic degrees.

   B.S. (Bachelor of Science)
   R.N. (Registered Nurse)

3. Use the following abbreviations with numbers.

   a.m. or **A.M.** **p.m.** or **P.M.** **B.C.** and **A.D.** or **B.C.E.** and **C.E.**

4. Abbreviate *United States* only when it is used as an adjective.

   NOT The **U.S.** is in North America.
   Correct: The **United States** is in North America.
   Correct: The **U.S.** Senate will consider this bill today.

5. Abbreviate only the names of well-known government agencies, businesses, and educational institutions by using their initials without periods.

   FBI (Federal Bureau of Investigation)
   NBC (National Broadcasting Corporation)
   USC (University of Southern California)
   ACLU (American Civil Liberties Union)

6. Abbreviate state names when addressing mail or writing out the postal address. Otherwise, spell out the names of states.

   Maria's new address is 7124 Funston Street, San Francisco, **CA** 90555.

   Maria has moved to San Francisco, **California.**

PRACTICE 1: Identifying Correct the underlined words in each of the following sentences.

1. Prof. Smith said that I was a wonderful writer. *(Professor)*
2. The United States economy has many markets. *(U.S.)*
3. When I can't sleep, I watch Music Television. *(MTV)*
4. Last night, sergeant David Montgomery devised the winning strategy. *(Sgt.)*
5. Candice moved to 237 Bella Avenue, Houma, Louisiana 79337. *(LA)*

PRACTICE 2: Completing In each sentence, write either an abbreviation or the complete word, whichever is correct.

1. We were caught speeding at 10 *p.m.* (p.m., post meridian).
2. Alisha will be attending *California State University* (CSU, California State University) and will get her *B.A.* (B.A., bachelor of arts) degree in English.
3. Darryl and Pat are visiting relatives in Orlando, *Florida* (FL, Florida).
4. We moved to the *United States* (U.S., United States) when I was four years old.
5. (Sen., Senator) *Senator* Matthews always has a kind word.

PRACTICE 3: Writing Your Own Write a sentence of your own for each of the following abbreviations. *Answers will vary.*

1. Mr. ______________________________
2. a.m. ______________________________

3. ABC ____________________

4. A.A. ____________________

5. U.S. ____________________

NUMBERS

Most writers ask the same question about using numbers: When should a number be spelled out, and when is it all right to use numerals? The following simple rules will help you make this decision.

1. Spell out numbers from *zero* to *nine*. Use figures for numbers 10 and higher.

   I have **three** dogs.
   My mother-in-law has **19** grandchildren and **11** great-grandchildren.

   Do not mix spelled-out numbers and figures in a sentence if they refer to the same types of items. Use numerals for all numbers in that case.

   NOT I have **three** dogs, **18** goldfish, and **two** canaries.
   Correct: I have **3** dogs, **18** goldfish, and **2** canaries.

2. For very large numbers, use a combination of figures and words.

   The state's new budget is approximately **$32 million.**
   Computer sales for the company reached **2.1 million** units.

3. Always spell out a number that begins a sentence. If this becomes awkward, reword the sentence.

   Thirty-five people died in the crash.
   Approximately **260,000** people live in Mobile, Alabama.

4. Use figures for dates, addresses, zip codes, telephone numbers, identification numbers, and time.

   On August **1, 1965,** my parents moved to **215** Circle Drive, Santa Fe, NM **71730.**
   My new telephone number is **(555) 877-1420.**
   My Social Security number is **123-45-6789.**
   My alarm went off at **5:00** a.m.

5. Use figures for fractions, decimals, and percentages.

   To make the dessert, you need ½ cup of butter and **16** ounces of chocolate.

His blood-alcohol level was **0.09.**

Over **5 percent** of Californians are of Hispanic background.

Notice that *percent* is written out and is all one word.

6. Use figures for exact measurements, including amounts of money. Use a dollar sign for amounts over $1.

   The room measures **9** feet by **12** feet.

   She bought gas for **$2.79** a gallon today—**25** cents more than yesterday.

7. Use figures for the parts of a book.

   Chapter **10** page **120** Exercise **8** questions **1** and **7**

   Notice that *Chapter* and *Exercise* are capitalized.

PRACTICE 4: Identifying Underline and correct any errors with numbers in each of the following sentences.

1. On August third, 2001, sixteen dogs escaped from the pound. *(3, 16)*
2. The park, which measures approximately two thousand square feet, will cost five thousand dollars to landscape. *(2,000, $5,000)*
3. Mr. Thompson's old telephone number was three, nine, nine, four, two, zero, nine. *(399-4209)*
4. Almost twenty-five percent of my income comes from sales. *(25)*
5. The earthquake that hit at six forty-five last night measured 6.0 on the Richter scale. *(6:45)*

PRACTICE 5: Completing Fill in each blank in the following sentences with numbers in the proper form. *Answers will vary.*

1. Please read Chapter ______________ and answer questions ______________ through ______________.
2. I have ______________ pencils, ______________ bluebooks, and ______________ note cards; I am ready for this test.
3. ______________ percent of my time is spent doing homework.
4. Christmas is on ______________ every year.
5. He made $ ______________ million last year.

PRACTICE 6: Write Your Own Write a sentence demonstrating each of the following rules for numbers. *Answers will vary.*

1. Spell out numbers *zero* through *nine*. Use figures for numbers 10 and higher.
2. For very large numbers, use a combination of figures and words.
3. Always spell out a number that begins a sentence.
4. Use figures for dates, addresses, zip codes, telephone numbers, identification numbers, and time.
5. Use figures for fractions, decimals, and percentages.

CHAPTER REVIEW

You might want to reread the examples in this chapter before you do the following exercises.

REVIEW PRACTICE 1: Identifying Circle the abbreviation errors, and underline the number errors in each of the following sentences. Some sentences contain more than one error.

1. According to Prof. Gleason, there is a process to writing. *(Professor)*
2. At exactly 7:00 post meridiem, everyone will jump out of his or her hiding place and yell, "Surprise!" *(p.m. or P.M.)*
3. The crew will need explosives to blast the twenty-nine-ton boulder. *(29-ton)*
4. Gen. Brevington's retirement banquet will be held on January twenty-nine, 2007. *(General, 29)*
5. Only 2 of the 8 children remembered their permission slips. *(two, eight)*
6. Of all the people polled, only ten percent were in favor of the new law. *(10)*
7. 9 days from now, Columbia Broadcasting System is airing a special on former United States President Bill Clinton. *(Nine, CBS, U.S.)*
8. You can receive an associate of arts degree from your local community college. *(A.A.)*

9. The answers to questions four and five are in Chapter 21. *(4, 5)*

10. After winning the lottery for two million five hundred thousand dollars, Janene moved to Beverly Hills, CA. *($2.5 million, California)*

REVIEW PRACTICE 2: Completing Correct the errors in Review Practice 1 by rewriting the sentences. *See Review Practice 1.*

REVIEW PRACTICE 3: Writing Your Own Write a paragraph explaining the quickest route from your house to your school. Use numbers and abbreviations in your paragraph. *Answers will vary.*

REVIEW PRACTICE 4: Editing Through Collaboration Exchange paragraphs from Review Practice 3 with another student, and do the following: *Answers will vary.*

1. Underline all abbreviations, numbers, and figures.

2. Circle any abbreviations, numbers, or figures that are not in their correct form.

Then return the paper to its writer, and use the information in this chapter to correct any abbreviation and number errors in your own paragraph. Record your errors on the Error Log in Appendix 6.

Effective Sentences

At one time or another, you have probably been a member of a team. You may have actively participated in sports somewhere or been a part of a close-knit employee group. Or maybe you have taken part in classroom discussion groups or special projects that required your cooperation with your peers. Whatever the situation, teamwork is important in many everyday situations. To be a good team member, you must perform your individual duties with others in mind.

Sentences, too, require good teamwork to be successful. Each individual word, phrase, or clause has to express its own meaning but must also work together with other words, phrases, and clauses toward the common goal of communicating a clear message. In this unit, three chapters will help you write successful sentences that work in harmony with each other to say exactly what you want to say in the best way possible:

CHAPTER 45

Varying Sentence Structure

CHECKLIST for Varying Sentence Structure

✔ Do you add introductory material to vary your sentence structure?

✔ Do you occasionally reverse the order of some subjects and verbs?

✔ Do you move sentence parts to add variety to your sentences?

✔ Do you sometimes use questions and exclamations to vary your sentence structure?

TEST YOURSELF

Turn each of the following pairs of sentences into one sentence that is more interesting.

- I work too much. I am tired.
- My cat is very lazy. She sleeps more than 14 hours a day.
- He enjoys reading. He likes mysteries.
- I live in an old house. My family has lived here for generations.
- My brother loves to eat. He will eat anything.

(Answers are in Appendix 4.)

UNIT PRETEST

To check your students' abilities with the collective skills in this unit, a Unit Pretest is available on pages 772–774.

TEACHING VARYING SENTENCE STRUCTURE

Put students into groups of three or four, and provide them with a paragraph made up of simple sentences. All groups should receive the same paragraph.

Have each group make its paragraph more lively by using the guidelines in this chapter to vary sentence structure.

Then have the groups read their

Reading the same pattern sentence after sentence can become very monotonous for your readers. This chapter will help you solve this problem in your writing. Look at the following example.

> I have always loved animals. I am about to get my own dog for the first time. I am ready to be responsible enough to take care of it. I am excited about this new phase in my life. I got a part-time job. I can't wait to get my own dog.

paragraphs to the rest of the class, and let the students decide which paragraph is most exciting. Why did they choose the paragraph they did?

INSTRUCTOR'S RESOURCE MANUAL
For sample paragraphs, for more exercises, and for quizzes, see the *Instructor's Resource Manual*, Section II, Part IV.

UNIT POSTTEST
To check your students' mastery of the collective skills in this unit, a Unit Posttest is available on pages 786–788.

This paragraph has some terrific ideas, but they are expressed in such a monotonous way that the readers might doze off. What this paragraph needs is variety in its sentence structure. Here are some ideas for keeping your readers awake and ready to hear your good thoughts.

ADD INTRODUCTORY WORDS

Add some introductory words to your sentences so that they don't all start the same way.

> **For as long as I can remember,** I have always loved animals. **Now** I am about to get my own dog for the first time. I am ready to be responsible enough to take care of it. I am excited about this new phase in my life. **To pay for my new friend,** I got a part-time job. I can't wait to get my own dog.

PRACTICE 1: Identifying Underline the sentence in each pair that could be turned into an introductory word, phrase, or clause.

1. Misty had a terrible stomachache. It was late last night. *(Late last night,)*
2. We went to the river. We skipped over the rocks. *(When we went to the river,)*
3. We went to McDonald's for breakfast. We saw our friends. *(When we went to McDonald's for breakfast,)*
4. The sunsets are beautiful. It was spring. *(In the spring,)*
5. He is afraid of dogs. He was bitten by a dog once. *(Because he was bitten by a dog once,)*

PRACTICE 2: Completing Rewrite the sentences in Practice 1 by turning each sentence you underlined into an introductory word, phrase, or clause. *See Practice 1.*

PRACTICE 3: Writing Your Own Write five sentences of your own with introductory elements. *Answers will vary.*

REVERSE WORDS

Reverse the order of some subjects and verbs. For example, instead of *I am so excited*, try *Am I ever excited*. You can also add or drop words and change punctuation to make the sentence read smoothly.

> For as long as I can remember, I have always loved animals. Now I am about to get my own dog for the first time. I am ready to be responsible enough to take care of it. **Am I ever excited** about this new

phase in my life. To pay for my new friend, I got a part-time job. I can't wait to get my own dog.

PRACTICE 4: Identifying Underline the words or phrases you could reverse in each of the following sentences.

1. I am happy to know you. *(Am I happy to know you!)*

2. All the ingredients went into the pot. *(Into the pot went all the ingredients.)*

3. The cat jumped out of the hat. *(Out of the hat jumped the cat.)*

4. The children were happy. *(Were the children happy!)*

5. The strange creature appeared out of nowhere. *(Out of nowhere appeared the strange creature.)*

PRACTICE 5: Completing Rewrite the sentences in Practice 4 by reversing the words you underlined. *See Practice 4.*

PRACTICE 6: Writing Your Own Write five sentences of your own with subjects and verbs reversed. *Answers will vary.*

MOVE SENTENCE PARTS

Move around some parts of the sentence. Experiment to see which order works best.

For as long as I can remember, I have always loved animals. Now I am about to get my own dog for the first time. I am ready to be responsible enough to take care of it. Am I ever excited about this new phase in my life. **My part-time job can help me pay for my new friend.** I can't wait to get my own dog.

PRACTICE 7: Identifying Underline any parts of the following sentences that can be moved around.

1. To bake these cookies, you will need 2 cups of flour. *(Move to beginning of sentence.)*
2. Finally, I knew the truth. *(Move to end.)*
3. I was very full after lunch. *(Move to beginning.)*
4. You will find your shoes underneath your bed. *(Move to beginning.)*
5. If you enjoyed the film, you will probably like the book. *(Move to end.)*

PRACTICE 8: Completing Rewrite the sentences in Practice 7, moving the words you underlined. *See Practice 7.*

PRACTICE 9: Writing Your Own Write two sentences of your own. Then rewrite each sentence two different ways. *Answers will vary.*

VARY SENTENCE TYPE

Use a question, a command, or an exclamation occasionally.

For as long as I can remember, I have always loved animals. **Have you?** Now I am about to get my own dog for the first time. I am ready to be responsible enough to take care of it. **Am I ever excited about this new phase in my life!** My part-time job can help me pay for my new friend. I can't wait to get my own dog.

PRACTICE 10: Identifying Identify each of the following sentences as a statement (S), a question (Q), a command (C), or an exclamation (E).

1. __*Q*__ When is the meal being served
2. __*Q*__ Did you see that object flying in the sky
3. __*C*__ Bring me a glass of iced tea and a bowl of grapes
4. __*C*__ First do the prewriting exercises
5. __*S, E*__ I just hate it when that happens

PRACTICE 11: Completing Complete the following sentences, making them into questions, commands, or exclamations. Then supply the correct punctuation. *Answers will vary.*

1. Wow, I can't believe ______________________________
2. At the first intersection ______________________________
3. Why is ______________________________
4. Hand me ______________________________
5. Did you hear ______________________________

PRACTICE 12: Writing Your Own Write two statements, two questions, two commands, and two exclamations of your own. *Answers will vary.*

CHAPTER REVIEW

You might want to reread the examples in this chapter before you do the following exercises.

REVIEW PRACTICE 1: Identifying Underline the words or groups of words that have been added or moved in each revised sentence. Then use the following key to tell which rule was applied to the sentence:

1. Add introductory words.
2. Reverse the order of subject and verb.
3. Move around parts of the sentence.
4. Use a question, a command, or an exclamation occasionally.

1. Eat your peas. You aren't finished with dinner yet.

   __3__ You aren't finished with dinner until you eat your peas.

2. He did what?

   __2__ What did he do?

3. You went to the store around the corner. You bought some milk and bread.

   __1 or 4__ At the store around the corner, please buy some milk and bread.

4. To the park went he.

   __2__ To the park he went.

5. The fireflies flew. They flew all around us.

   __1 or 3__ All around us, the fireflies flew.

6. I believe that was mine.

   __4__ Hey, that was mine!

7. How many times a day do you brush your teeth?

   __3__ You brush your teeth how many times a day?

8. You are amazing!

 2 Are you amazing or what?

9. Out of the darkness came a terrible noise.

 2 Out of the darkness, a terrible noise came.

10. Carl does enjoy a good hamburger every now and then.

 3 Every now and then, Carl does enjoy a good hamburger.

REVIEW PRACTICE 2: Completing Vary the structure of the following sentences with at least three of the four ideas you just learned. *Answers will vary.*

A good teacher should be encouraging toward students. He or she should understand when a student is having problems and spend some one-on-one time together. The teacher should then help the student identify problems and give helpful instruction to solve the problem. A good teacher never makes fun of a student.

REVIEW PRACTICE 3: Writing Your Own Write a paragraph about a good deed you have performed. What made you decide to do what you did? Try to use each of the four ways you have learned to make sentences interesting. *Answers will vary.*

REVIEW PRACTICE 4: Editing Through Collaboration Exchange paragraphs from Review Practice 3 with another student, and do the following: *Answers will vary.*

1. Put brackets around any sentences that sound monotonous.

2. Suggest a way to vary each of these sentences.

Then return the paper to its writer, and use the information in this chapter to vary the sentence structure in your own paragraph. Record your errors on the Error Log in Appendix 6.

CHAPTER 46

Parallelism

CHECKLIST for Using Parallelism

✔ Can you use parallelism to add coherence to your sentences and paragraphs?

✔ Are all items in a series grammatically balanced?

TEST YOURSELF

Underline the parts in each of the following sentences that seem awkward or unbalanced.

- Tony enjoys hockey, football, and runs.
- My mom and dad give money to help the homeless and for building new homes.
- I finished high school, started college, and I am beginning a new job.
- I love the mountains because they're cool, clean, and feel refreshing.
- Listening to music, watching television, or to read a book are good ways to relax.

(Answers are in Appendix 4.)

When sentences are **parallel,** they are balanced. That is, words, phrases, or clauses in a series start with the same grammatical form. Parallel structures make your sentences interesting and clear.

Following is a paragraph that could be greatly improved with parallel structures.

UNIT PRETEST

To check your students' abilities with the collective skills in this unit, a Unit Pretest is available on pages 772–774.

TEACHING PARALLELISM

Draw a picture of two sets of train tracks that run parallel to each other. Draw a second picture of two sets of train tracks that eventually cross each other. Ask students the following question: If both tracks have trains heading toward each other and you were on one of the trains, which set of tracks would you prefer your train to be on? Of course, students will choose the parallel tracks. Ask them to discuss their choice.

Now explain to students that when sentences are not parallel, they are often like two trains heading for each other and about to collide. Then discuss how faulty parallelism can "wreck" an idea just as trains not on parallel tracks can collide.

Show them how parallelism is important to move ideas along smoothly. Use the examples in the text to prove your point.

INSTRUCTOR'S RESOURCE MANUAL

For more exercises and for quizzes, see the *Instructor's Resource Manual,* Section II, Part IV.

UNIT POSTTEST

To check your students' mastery of the collective skills in this unit, a Unit Posttest is available on pages 786–788.

My brother Ricardo was not excited when he was called in to work at the hospital today. He had been looking forward to this day off—his first in three weeks. He was planning to work out in the morning, swimming in the afternoon, and going to a movie in the evening. Instead he will be helping the patients, assisting the nurses, and will aid the doctors.

Words and phrases in a series should be parallel, which means they should start with the same type of word. Parallelism makes your sentence structure smoother and more interesting. Look at this sentence, for example.

NOT He had planned to **work out** in the morning,
swimming in the afternoon, and
going to a movie in the evening.

Parallel: He had planned to **work out** in the morning,
swim in the afternoon, and
go to the movies in the evening.

Parallel: He had planned on **working out** in the morning,
swimming in the afternoon, and
going to the movies in the evening.

Here is another sentence that would read better if the parts were parallel:

NOT Instead he will be **helping** the patients,
assisting the nurses, and
will aid the doctors.

Parallel: Instead he will be **helping** the patients,
assisting the nurses, and
aiding the doctors.

Parallel: Instead he will be helping **the patients,**
the nurses, and
the doctors.

Now read the paragraph with these two sentences made parallel or balanced.

My brother Ricardo was not excited when he was called in to work at the hospital today. He had been looking forward to this day off—his first in three weeks. He had planned to work out in the morning, swim in the afternoon, and go to a movie in the evening. Instead he will be helping the patients, the nurses, and the doctors.

PRACTICE 1: Identifying Underline the parallel structures in each of the following sentences.

1. Scott plans to hide in his cabin, do some fishing, and work on his novel.
2. The car needs new windows, tires, and paint.
3. Georgia believes that she is the most wonderful person in the world and that she deserves everyone's love and attention.
4. They camped under the stars, swam in the cool lakes, and enjoyed the fresh air.
5. Because of the pouring rain, extreme cold, and bitter wind, we decided to stay inside.

PRACTICE 2: Completing Make the underlined elements parallel in each of the following sentences. *Answers will vary.*

1. He will wear only clothes that have designer labels and they are expensive.

   ____

2. Regular exercise, drinking plenty of water, and eating lots of good food will help keep you healthy.

   ____

3. Dierdra went to the mall to get a bite to eat, to do some shopping, and will visit friends.

   ____

4. Please do not tap pens, talk to others, or eating food during the exam.

   ____

5. On his trip, he took pictures of mountains, fed animals, and some enjoyable people.

   ____

PRACTICE 3: Writing Your Own Write five sentences of your own using parallel structures in each. *Answers will vary.*

CHAPTER REVIEW

You might want to reread the examples in this chapter before you do the following exercises.

REVIEW PRACTICE 1: Identifying Underline the parallel structures in each of the following sentences.

1. Football, basketball, and hockey are all competitive sports.
2. Because of the terrible weather, the horrible traffic, and the missed bus, we didn't make our flight.
3. When I'm in love, the sun always shines, the stars always sparkle, and the moon always glows.
4. Marilyn went to the city's annual air show because she wanted to see the jet planes and because she wanted to try the interesting foods.
5. The biting mosquitoes, barking dogs, and burning sun made me miserable.
6. Please feed, bathe, and change the baby before I get home.
7. If Harvey cleans the house, does his homework, and begs for forgiveness, he may get out of his punishment.
8. I believe that people should be treated fairly and that everyone should get a second chance.
9. He was suspended because he fought, cheated, and disrespected others.
10. Today Mother paid the bills, balanced the checkbook, and washed the car.

REVIEW PRACTICE 2: Completing Complete each of the following sentences with parallel structures. *Answers will vary.*

1. I enjoy ______________, ______________, and ______________ in the summer.
2. Because of ______________ and because of ______________, Miriam didn't go to the movies.
3. You can be successful in college if you ______________, ______________, and ______________.

4. Even though Jeremy ______________, ______________, and ______________, he still can't find the problem.

5. ______________, ______________, and ______________ are essential items when hiking.

6. She cooks foods that ______________ and ______________.

7. My favorite foods are ______________, ______________, and ______________.

8. If I have to hear her ______________, ______________, and ______________ one more time, I'm going to scream.

9. The instructor has already explained ______________, ______________, and ______________.

10. If you ______________, ______________, and ______________, you just might survive boot camp.

REVIEW PRACTICE 3: Writing Your Own Write a paragraph about the best holiday you've ever had. What was the holiday? Why was it the best? Use two examples of parallelism in your paragraph. *Answers will vary.*

REVIEW PRACTICE 4: Editing Through Collaboration Exchange paragraphs from Review Practice 3 with another student, and do the following: *Answers will vary.*

1. Underline any items in a series.
2. Put brackets around any of these items that are not grammatically parallel.

Then return the paper to its writer, and use the information in this chapter to correct any parallelism errors in your own paragraph. Record your errors on the Error Log in Appendix 6.

47 CHAPTER

Combining Sentences

CHECKLIST for Combining Sentences

- ✔ Do you combine sentences to avoid too many short, choppy sentences in a row?
- ✔ Do you use different types of sentences?

UNIT PRETEST
To check your students' abilities with the collective skills in this unit, a Unit Pretest is available on pages 772–774.

TEACHING COMBINING SENTENCES
Have each student write a list of 10 simple sentences on a common subject (such as education, war, politics, ecology, animal rights, or final exams). Then have students work in pairs to create the following sentence patterns from the simple sentences:

TEST YOURSELF

Combine each set of sentences into one sentence.

- My brother is taking tennis lessons. He takes his lessons from a professional player.
- The baby is crying. She's hungry.
- It's too hot outside. Let's go for a swim.
- We moved overseas when I was 11 years old. I learned much about different cultures.
- I like to travel. Africa has many interesting animals and plants. I want to go to Africa.

(Answers are in Appendix 4.)

Still another way to add variety to your writing is to combine short, choppy sentences into longer sentences. You can combine simple sentences to make compound or complex sentences. You can also combine compound and complex sentences.

SIMPLE SENTENCES

A **simple sentence** consists of one independent clause. Remember that a clause has a subject and a main verb.

In the following examples, notice that a simple sentence can have more than one subject and more than one verb. (For more on compound subjects and compound verbs, see Chapter 25.)

s v
I have several very good friends.

s v v
I have good friends and enjoy being with them.

s s v
Martin and Louis are good friends.

s s v v
Martin and I do interesting things and go to interesting places.

PRACTICE 1: Identifying Underline the subjects once and the verbs twice in each of the following sentences. Then label the simple sentences SS.

1. _____ Most cats don't like the water, but most dogs do.
2. _SS_ Tommy and I like listening to the same types of music and watching the same types of shows.
3. _____ I feel that our luck is about to change.
4. _SS_ We left quickly because of the smell.
5. _SS_ We have pictures of the family throughout the house.

PRACTICE 2: Completing Make simple sentences out of the sentences in Practice 1 that are not simple. *Answers will vary.*

PRACTICE 3: Writing Your Own Write a simple sentence of your own for each of the following subjects and verbs. *Answers will vary.*

1. Jessy and Miguel ______________________________
2. we're eating and drinking ______________________________

Three compound sentences
Three complex sentences
Three compound-complex sentences

Have the class discuss the different effects of these sentence types.

INSTRUCTOR'S RESOURCE MANUAL
For more exercises and for quizzes, see the *Instructor's Resource Manual*, Section II, Part IV.

UNIT POSTTEST
To check your students' mastery of the collective skills in this unit, a Unit Posttest is available on pages 786–788.

3. the playful kittens ______________________________

4. looking and listening ______________________________

5. the hot pan ______________________________

COMPOUND SENTENCES

A **compound sentence** consists of two or more independent clauses joined by a coordinating conjunction (*and, but, for, nor, or, so,* or *yet*). In other words, you can create a compound sentence from two (or more) simple sentences.

Simple:	I can swim fast.
Simple:	I am a good long-distance swimmer.
Compound:	I can swim fast**, and** I am a good long-distance swimmer. (s: I, v: can swim; s: I, v: am)
Simple:	She has a very stressful job.
Simple:	She works out at the gym three times a week.
Compound:	She has a very stressful job**, so** she works out at the gym three times a week. (s: She, v: has; s: she, v: works)
Simple:	My parents are leaving for Hawaii on Tuesday.
Simple:	They won't be here for my birthday party.
Compound:	My parents are leaving for Hawaii on Tuesday**, so** they won't be here for my birthday party. (s: parents, v: are leaving; s: they, v: won't be)

Hint: As the examples show, a comma comes before the coordinating conjunction in a compound sentence.

PRACTICE 4: Identifying Underline the independent clauses in the following sentences, and circle the coordinating conjunctions.

1. I am not sick, and I feel fine.

2. You cannot bring food or drink in this building, but you can eat in the cafeteria.

3. We try not to gossip, for we know the damage loose lips can cause.

4. I do not like raspberries, (yet) I do like raspberry pie.

5. Christy likes fast cars, (so) she is going to buy a sports car.

PRACTICE 5: Completing Combine each pair of simple sentences into a compound sentence. *Answers will vary.*

1. I am leaving. I am late for an appointment.
2. Quickly, move out of the way. The angry elephant is going to charge us.
3. We usually take a month-long vacation. We are always happy to return home.
4. This food has been sitting out all day in the hot sun. It smells awful.
5. I have a lot of cousins. I haven't met them all.

PRACTICE 6: Writing Your Own Write five compound sentences of your own. *Answers will vary.*

COMPLEX SENTENCES

A **complex sentence** is composed of one independent clause and at least one dependent clause. A **dependent clause** begins with either a subordinating conjunction or a relative pronoun.

Subordinating Conjunctions

after	*because*	*since*	*until*
although	*before*	*so*	*when*
as	*even if*	*so that*	*whenever*
as if	*even though*	*than*	*where*
as long as	*how*	*that*	*wherever*
as soon as	*if*	*though*	*whether*
as though	*in order that*	*unless*	*while*

Relative Pronouns

who	*whom*	*whose*	*which*	*that*

You can use subordinating conjunctions and relative pronouns to make a simple sentence (an independent clause) into a dependent clause. Then you can add the new dependent clause to an independent clause to produce a complex sentence that adds interest and variety to your writing.

How do you know which simple sentence should be independent and which should be dependent? The idea that you think is more important should be the independent clause. The less important idea will then be the dependent clause.

Following are some examples of how to combine simple sentences to make a complex sentence.

Simple: Myra has a large collection of DVDs.
Simple: Myra watches the same few films over and over.

Dep
Complex: **Even though** Myra has a large collection of DVDs, she
Ind
watches the same few films over and over.

This complex sentence stresses that Myra watches the same films over and over. The size of her collection is of secondary importance.

Ind
Complex: She has a big collection of DVDs, though she watches
Dep
the same few films over and over.

In the previous complex sentence, the size of the collection is most important, so it is the independent clause.

Simple: The winner of the lottery was Laura.
Simple: Laura is my cousin.

Ind Dep
Complex: The winner of the lottery was Laura**, who** is my cousin.

This complex sentence answers the question "Who won the lottery?" The information about Laura being the cousin is of secondary importance.

Ind Dep
Complex: My cousin is Laura**, who** won the lottery.

This complex sentence answers the question "Who is your cousin?" The information that she won the lottery is secondary.

PRACTICE 7: Identifying Label the underlined part of each sentence as either an independent (Ind) or a dependent (Dep) clause.

1. _Dep_ Although I was tired, I still went to school.

2. _Dep_ Here is the furniture that you ordered.

3. _Ind_ Trish moved to the coast because she likes the beach.

4. _Dep_ My doctor is Janet Woo, who is also my mom.

5. _Ind_ If we cannot study at your house, then let's study at the library.

PRACTICE 8: Completing Finish each sentence, and label the new clause either dependent (Dep) or independent (Ind). *Answers will vary.*

1. _Ind_ Whenever John's face turns red, ______________________________.

2. _Ind_ ______________________________ because he forgot to call home.

3. _Dep_ Maya's mother, who ______________________________, is a great cook.

4. _Dep_ I like the blue one, ______________________________.

5. _Dep_ He climbed the mountain ______________________________.

PRACTICE 9: Writing Your Own Write five complex sentences, making sure you have one independent clause and at least one dependent clause in each. *Answers will vary.*

COMPOUND-COMPLEX SENTENCES

If you combine a compound sentence with a complex sentence, you produce a **compound-complex sentence.** That means your sentence has at least two independent clauses (to make it compound) and at least one dependent clause (to make it complex). Here are some examples.

Simple: My cousin likes scuba diving.
Simple: He is planning a trip to Hawaii.
Simple: He is excited about diving in Hawaii.

Compound-Complex: My cousin likes scuba diving [**Ind**]**, so** he is planning a trip to Hawaii [**Ind**]**, which** he is very excited about [**Dep**].

Simple: She bought a new house.
Simple: It has a pool and a spa.

Simple: The house was very expensive.

Compound-Complex: She bought a new house (Ind)**, which** has a pool and a spa (Dep)**, but** it was very expensive (Ind).

Simple: Today's weather is very bad.
Simple: The rain could make it difficult to drive.
Simple: This could delay your departure for home.

Compound-Complex: Today's weather is very bad (Ind)**, and** the rain could make it difficult to drive (Ind)**, which** could delay your departure for home (Dep).

Hint: Notice that we occasionally have to change words in combined sentences so that the sentences make sense.

PRACTICE 10: Identifying Underline the clauses in each of the following compound-complex sentences. Then identify each clause as either independent (Ind) or dependent (Dep).

1. Whenever I travel (*Dep*), I set an alarm clock (*Ind*), and I arrange for a wake-up call (*Ind*).
2. Sandy likes Anthony (*Ind*) because he is nice (*Dep*), but she also likes Mark (*Ind*).
3. After they fought (*Dep*), they decided to make up (*Ind*), and now they are inseparable (*Ind*).
4. The traffic (*Ind*), which is usually bad around noon (*Dep*), is very heavy today (*Ind*), so you'd better leave soon (*Ind*).
5. We went to the Virgin Islands (*Ind*) because we love the sun (*Dep*), yet it rained the whole time (*Ind*).

PRACTICE 11: Completing Expand each sentence into a compound-complex sentence. *Answers will vary.*

1. The boy likes oranges and pears.

   ____

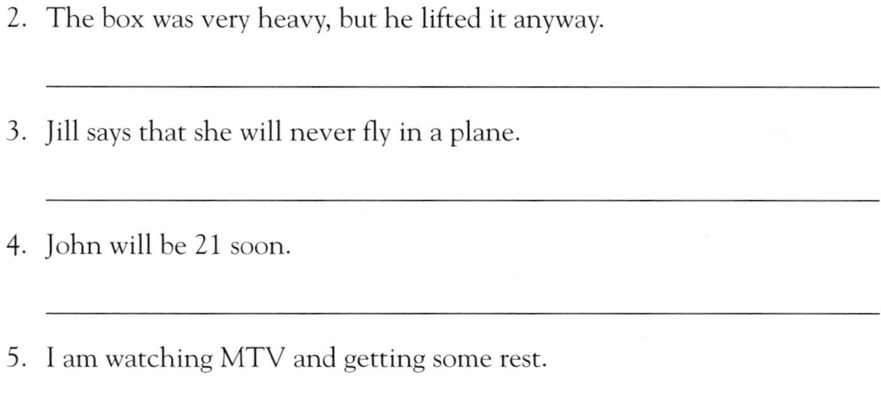

2. The box was very heavy, but he lifted it anyway.

____

3. Jill says that she will never fly in a plane.

____

4. John will be 21 soon.

____

5. I am watching MTV and getting some rest.

____

PRACTICE 12: Writing Your Own Write five compound-complex sentences of your own. *Answers will vary.*

CHAPTER REVIEW

You might want to reread the examples in this chapter before you do the following exercises.

REVIEW PRACTICE 1: Identifying Underline the independent clauses in each sentence. Then label the sentence simple (SS), compound (C), complex (CX), or compound-complex (CCX). The following definitions might help you.

Simple (SS)	=	one independent clause
Compound (C)	=	two or more independent clauses joined by *and, but, for, nor, or, so,* or *yet*
Complex (CX)	=	one independent clause and at least one dependent clause
Compound-complex (CCX)	=	at least two independent clauses and one or more dependent clauses

1. ___*SS*___ Casey and Floyd have left the building.
2. ___*CX*___ Even though he is quiet, he is very friendly.
3. ___*C*___ Marcy and David are boyfriend and girlfriend, and they are going to the prom together.

4. __SS__ The dog and cat ate my dinner last night.

5. __C__ Mrs. Glancy is my close friend, and she visits me often.

6. __CCX__ Marc is happy because Sheila is here, and he wants to ask her on a date.

7. __SS__ The folders are in the desk drawer.

8. __C__ The dog needs to be fed, and he needs a bath.

9. __CCX__ The gifts, which you bought yesterday, have been wrapped, and they are ready to be delivered.

10. __CX__ Because her alarm didn't go off, she was late for work.

REVIEW PRACTICE 2: Completing Combine each set of sentences to make the sentence pattern indicated in parentheses. You may need to change some wording in the sentences so they make sense. The list of sentence types in Review Practice 1 may help you with this exercise. *Answers will vary.*

1. Antoine bikes in the morning. He wants to stay in shape. He goes to the gym every weekend. (compound-complex)
2. I like to play in the mud. I always get dirty. (compound)
3. You should leave now. You should be at your appointment 15 minutes early to fill out paperwork. (complex)
4. Penny brought a stray dog home. Penny loves animals. Her mother wouldn't let her keep it. (compound-complex)
5. I slammed the car door on my thumb. I broke it. (complex)
6. I love to chew gum and pop bubbles. I can't chew gum in class. (complex)
7. The little girl lost her doll. She has looked everywhere for it. She is crying. (compound-complex)
8. The sun is shining. The birds are singing. (compound)
9. The reports are missing. I need them now. (compound)
10. It is October. The leaves are turning brown and falling from the tree. (complex)

REVIEW PRACTICE 3: Writing Your Own Write a paragraph about your fondest wish. What is it, and why do you wish for it? *Answers will vary.*

REVIEW PRACTICE 4: Editing Through Collaboration Exchange paragraphs from Review Practice 3 with another student, and do the following: *Answers will vary.*

1. Put brackets around any sentences that you think should be combined.

2. Underline sentences that are incorrectly combined (for example, ones that have a weak connecting word or no connecting word).

Then return the paper to its writer, and use the information in this chapter to combine sentences in your own paragraph. Record your errors on the Error Log in Appendix 6.

Choosing the Right Word

Choosing the right word is like choosing the right snack to satisfy your appetite. If you don't select the food you are craving, your hunger does not go away. In like manner, if you do not choose the right words to say what is on your mind, your readers will not be satisfied and will not understand your message.

Choosing the right word depends on your message, your purpose, and your audience. It also involves recognizing misused, nonstandard, and misspelled words. We deal with the following topics in Unit 8:

CHAPTER 48

Standard and Nonstandard English

CHECKLIST for Standard and Nonstandard English

✔ Do you consistently use standard English in your paper?

✔ Is your paper free of nonstandard, ungrammatical words?

✔ Have you changed any slang to standard English?

TEST YOURSELF

Label the following sentences as correct, incorrect, or slang.

- You shoulda seen Claudia's new hairstyle. ____________
- Where are my friends at? ____________
- Your new bike is really hot. ____________
- Randy was enthused about his date. ____________
- Christina Aguilera's new video rocks. ____________

(Answers are in Appendix 4.)

Choosing the right words for what you want to say is an important part of effective communication. This chapter will help you find the right words and phrases for the audience you are trying to reach.

Look, for example, at the following sentences. They all have a similar message, expressed in different words.

I want to do good in college, being as I can get a good job.

I be studying hard in college, so I can get a good job.

I'm going to hit the books so I can rake in the bucks.

I want to do well in college so I can get a good job.

Which of these sentences would you probably say to a friend or to someone in your family? Which would you most likely say in a job interview? Which would be good for a college paper?

UNIT PRETEST

To check your students' abilities with the collective skills in this unit, a Unit Pretest is available on pages 774–775.

TEACHING STANDARD AND NONSTANDARD ENGLISH

Give students a short scene (such as a portion of the balcony scene in *Romeo and Juliet*), and have them rewrite it using modern-day slang.

After students have finished this exercise, talk to them about the importance of knowing audience and purpose as a writer.

INSTRUCTOR'S RESOURCE MANUAL

For more exercises and for quizzes, see the

Instructor's Resource Manual, Section II, Part IV.

UNIT POSTTEST
To check your students' mastery of the collective skills in this unit, a Unit Posttest is available on pages 788–789.

The first three sentences are nonstandard English. They might be said or written to a friend or family member, but they would not be appropriate in an academic setting or in a job situation. Only the fourth sentence would be appropriate in an academic paper or in a job interview.

STANDARD AND NONSTANDARD ENGLISH

Most of the English language falls into one of two categories—either *standard* or *nonstandard*. **Standard English** is the language of college, business, and the media. It is used by reporters on television, by newspapers, in most magazines, and on Web sites created by schools, government agencies, businesses, and organizations. Standard English is always grammatically correct and free of slang.

Nonstandard English does not follow all the rules of grammar and often includes slang. Nonstandard English is not necessarily wrong, but it is more appropriate in some settings (with friends and family) than others. It is not appropriate in college or business writing. To understand the difference between standard and nonstandard English, compare the following paragraphs.

Nonstandard English

I was stoked to find out I would be getting a $300 refund on my taxes. My first thought was to blow it on a trip, maybe somewheres like Las Vegas. But none of my friends was enthused by that. Then I thought being as I watch television alot, I would buy a new TV with a built-in DVD player. My brother got hisself one last year. Then it hit me, hey, I'm gonna need some money to buy new duds for my job. Alright, I decided, I gotta buy clothes with the dough, irregardless of what I'd like to do with it.

Standard English

I was thrilled when I found out I would be getting a $300 refund on my taxes. My first thought was to spend it on a trip, maybe somewhere like Las Vegas. But none of my friends was enthusiastic about that. Then I thought that since I watch television a lot, I would buy a new TV with a built-in DVD player. My brother got himself one last year. Then I realized that I am going to need some money to buy new clothes for my job. All right, I decided, I have to buy clothes with the money, regardless of what I'd like to do with it.

In the rest of this chapter, you will learn how to recognize and correct ungrammatical English and how to avoid slang in your writing.

NONSTANDARD ENGLISH

Nonstandard English is ungrammatical. It does not follow the rules of standard English that are required in college writing. The academic and business worlds expect you to be able to recognize and avoid nonstandard English. This is not always easy because some nonstandard terms are used so often in speech that many people think they are acceptable in writing. The following list might help you choose the correct words in your own writing.

ain't

NOT My economics professor **ain't** giving us the test today.

CORRECT My economics professor **isn't** giving us the test today.

anywheres

NOT Lashawn buys her clothes **anywheres** she can find them.

CORRECT Lashawn buys her clothes **anywhere** she can find them.

be

NOT I **be** so happy.

CORRECT I **am** so happy.

(For additional help with *be*, see Chapter 29, "Verb Tense.")

being as, being that

NOT Emilio will not get to go home over the weekend, **being as** he has to work.

CORRECT Emilio will not get to go home over the weekend **because** he has to work.

coulda/could of, shoulda/should of

NOT He **could of** earned a better grade on the test if he'd studied.

CORRECT He **could have** (or **could've**) earned a better grade on the test if he'd studied.

different than

NOT She is **different than** us.

CORRECT She is **different from** us.

drug

NOT She **drug** the mattress across the room.

CORRECT She **dragged** the mattress across the room.

enthused

NOT Mary was **enthused** about the wedding.

CORRECT Mary was **enthusiastic** about the wedding.

everywheres

NOT My dog follows me **everywheres** I go.

CORRECT My dog follows me **everywhere** I go.

goes

NOT Then Lorie **goes,** "I'm leaving without you."

CORRECT Then Lorie **said,** "I'm leaving without you."

CORRECT Then Lorie **said** that she was leaving without me.

hisself

NOT Jackson made **hisself** a cheeseburger.

CORRECT Jackson made **himself** a cheeseburger.

in regards to

NOT We received a letter **in regards to** your complaint.

CORRECT We received a letter **in regard to** your complaint.

irregardless

NOT **Irregardless** of how long you study French, you'll never speak it like a native.

CORRECT **Regardless** of how long you study French, you'll never speak it like a native.

kinda/kind of, sorta/sort of

NOT The room smells **kinda** sweet, **sorta** like vanilla.

CORRECT The room smells **rather** sweet, **much like** vanilla.

most

NOT **Most** everyone accepted the invitation.

CORRECT **Almost** everyone accepted the invitation.

must of

NOT I **must of** lost my purse at the party.

CORRECT I **must have** lost my purse at the party.

off of

NOT Billy jumped **off of** the back of the truck.

CORRECT Billy jumped **off** the back of the truck.

oughta

NOT Sometimes I think I **oughta** watch less television.

CORRECT Sometimes I think I **ought to** watch less television.

real

NOT My boyfriend was **real** mad when I left him.

CORRECT My boyfriend was **really** mad when I left him.

somewheres

NOT Your jeans are **somewheres** in that pile of clothes.

CORRECT Your jeans are **somewhere** in that pile of clothes.

suppose to

NOT You were **suppose to** turn that paper in yesterday.

CORRECT You were **supposed to** turn that paper in yesterday.

theirselves

NOT They helped **theirselves** to the food in the buffet line.

CORRECT They helped **themselves** to the food in the buffet line.

use to

NOT I **use to** have a truck.

CORRECT I **used to** have a truck.

ways

NOT Curt's car broke down a long **ways** from home.

CORRECT Curt's car broke down a long **way** from home.

where . . . at

NOT **Where** is the nearest bakery **at?**

CORRECT **Where** is the nearest bakery?

PRACTICE 1A: Identifying Underline the ungrammatical words or phrases in each of the following sentences.

1. Do you know where the children are at? *(drop "at")*
2. Then John goes, "There is no way I'm going to touch that." *(says)*
3. Our production of *Romeo and Juliet* is kinda like the original, but sorta modern. *(much, rather)*

4. I coulda stayed at home instead of sitting here listening to this boring lecture. *(could have or could've)*

5. Justin was suppose to mail the invitations. *(supposed to)*

PRACTICE 1B: Correcting Correct the ungrammatical words and expressions in Practice 1A by rewriting the incorrect sentences. *See Practice 1A.*

PRACTICE 2: Completing Underline the ungrammatical word or words in each phrase, and change them to standard English.

1. Anywheres I go ___*Anywhere*___
2. She drug it ___*dragged*___
3. We are a long ways ___*way*___
4. He made hisself ___*himself*___
5. Being that Susan ___*Because*___

PRACTICE 3: Writing Your Own Write five sentences of your own using the grammatical words and phrases you chose in Practice 2. *Answers will vary.*

SLANG

Another example of nonstandard English is **slang,** popular words and expressions that come and go, much like the latest fashions. For example, in the 1950s, someone might call his or her special someone *dreamy*. In the 1960s, you might hear a boyfriend or girlfriend described as *groovy*, and in the 1990s, *sweet* was the popular slang term. Today your significant other might be *hot* or *dope*.

These expressions are slang because they are part of the spoken language that changes from generation to generation and from place to place. As you might suspect, slang communicates to a limited audience who share common interests and experiences. Some slang words, such as *cool* and *neat*, have become part of our language, but most slang is temporary. What's in today may be out tomorrow, so the best advice is to avoid slang in your writing.

PRACTICE 4: Identifying Underline the slang words and expressions in each of the following sentences.

1. *Return of the Mummy* rocks!

2. "Wassup?" I yelled to my homies.

3. This party is da bomb.

4. My mom tripped out when I got my tattoo.

5. Stewart is zoning on the video game.

PRACTICE 5: Completing Translate the following slang expressions into standard English.

1. Talk to the hand *Don't talk to me; I'm not listening to you.*

2. hella good *really good*

3. flyboy *popular guy; friend*

4. right back atcha *I could say the same thing to you.*

5. a wanna-be *someone who wants to be someone or something he or she is not*

PRACTICE 6: Writing Your Own List five slang words or expressions, and use them in sentences of your own. Then rewrite each sentence using standard English to replace the slang expressions. *Answers will vary.*

CHAPTER REVIEW

You might want to reread the examples in this chapter before you do the following exercises.

REVIEW PRACTICE 1: Identifying Underline the ungrammatical or slang words in the following sentences.

1. You really need to chill out.

2. He ain't going to know what's going on.

3. I was so enthused when I won the contest.

4. He's really jammin' to the music.

5. Hey, stop buggin' me.

6. Oops, I fell off of the ski lift.

7. He's no different than you or me.

8. She thinks she's all that.

9. You oughta take art lessons.

10. Sandra is really phat.

REVIEW PRACTICE 2: Completing Correct any nonstandard English in each of the following sentences by rewriting the sentences. *Answers may vary*

1. I be wide awake and can't sleep. *(am)*

2. Irregardless of them, Rufus is talking to hisself. *(Regardless, himself)*

3. Tony's making big money at his new job. *(a good salary)*

4. Those singers are bad. *(really good)*

5. My girlfriend was real mad when I forgot Valentine's Day. *(really)*

6. In regards to your question, I don't have an answer. *(In regard to)*

7. Watcha doin'? *(What are you doing?)*

8. Who's the real slim shady? *(person who is genuine)*

9. Jane could of found extra blankets if you were cold. *(could've)*

10. You are solid, man. *(honest)*

REVIEW PRACTICE 3: Writing Your Own Write a paragraph on how you spend your free time. Do you spend it with your friends or alone? What do you do and why? *Answers will vary.*

REVIEW PRACTICE 4: Editing Through Collaboration Exchange paragraphs from Review Practice 3 with another student, and do the following: *Answers will vary.*

1. Underline any ungrammatical language.

2. Circle any slang.

Then return the paper to its writer, and use the information in this chapter to correct any nonstandard or slang expressions in your own paragraph. Record your errors on the Error Log in Appendix 6.

CHAPTER 49

Easily Confused Words

CHECKLIST for Easily Confused Words

✔ Is the correct word chosen from the easily confused words?

✔ Are the following words used correctly: *its/it's, their/there/they're, to/too/two, who's/whose, your/you're?*

TEST YOURSELF

Choose the correct word in parentheses.

- Miranda couldn't (choose, chose) a college.
- (It's, Its) time to leave for the show.
- I can't (hear, here) with all this noise.
- (Weather, Whether) you go or not, I still want to attend.
- (Who's, Whose) responsible for this mess?

(Answers are in Appendix 4.)

UNIT PRETEST

To check your students' abilities with the collective skills in this unit, a Unit Pretest is available on pages 774–775.

TEACHING EASILY CONFUSED WORDS

Provide students with the following poem (author unknown), and ask them to rewrite it correctly.

ODE TO THE SPELL-CHECKER

Eye halve a spelling chequer,
It came with my pea sea.
It plainly marques for my revue
Miss steaks eye kin knot sea.
Eye strike a key and type a word

Some words are easily confused. They may look alike, sound alike, or have similar meanings, but they all play different roles in the English language. This chapter will help you choose the right words for your sentences.

EASILY CONFUSED WORDS, PART I

a/an: Use *a* before words that begin with a consonant. Use *an* before words that begin with a vowel (*a, e, i, o, u*).

a bill, **a** cat, **a** zebra

an artichoke, **an** Indian, **an** occasion

And weight four it two say
Weather eye am wrong oar write
It shows me straight a weigh.
As soon as a mist ache is maid
It nose bee fore two long,
And eye can put the error rite
Its rare lea ever wrong.
Eye have run this poem threw it;
I am shore your pleased two no.
Its letter perfect awl the weigh;
My chequer told me sew!

INSTRUCTOR'S RESOURCE MANUAL

For more exercises and for quizzes, see the *Instructor's Resource Manual*, Section II, Part IV.

UNIT POSTTEST

To check your students' mastery of the collective skills in this unit, a Unit Posttest is available on pages 788–789.

accept/except: *Accept* means "receive." *Except* means "other than."

Mary will not **accept** the gift.
Everyone went **except** Harry.

advice/advise: *Advice* means "helpful information." *Advise* means "give advice or help."

My mother usually gives me very good **advice.**
My parents **advise** me when I'm trying to make an important decision.

affect/effect: *Affect* (verb) means "influence." *Effect* means "bring about" (verb) or "a result" (noun).

She hopes speaking out won't **affect** her chance at promotion.
I believe that changes in the law will **effect** positive changes in society.
The weather had a bad **effect** on his health.

already/all ready: *Already* means "in the past." *All ready* means "completely prepared."

I have **already** taken that class.
We had packed the car and were **all ready** to go.

among/between: Use *among* when referring to three or more people or things. Use *between* when referring to only two people or things.

The students discussed the issues **among** themselves.
I can't decide **between** the two dresses.

bad/badly: *Bad* means "not good." *Badly* means "not well."

That meat is **bad,** so don't eat it.
He felt **bad** about the accident.
He was hurt **badly** in the accident.

beside/besides: *Beside* means "next to." *Besides* means "in addition (to)."

She sat **beside** him at lunch.
Besides sleeping, I can think of nothing else I want to do.

brake/break: *Brake* means "stop" or "the part that stops a moving vehicle." *Break* means "shatter, come apart" or "a rest between work periods."

She didn't **brake** soon enough to avoid the other car.

The **brakes** on my car are not dependable.
I watched the limb **break** off the tree.
Can we take a **break?**

breath/breathe: *Breath* means "air." *Breathe* means "taking in air."

Take a long, slow **breath.**
The air we have to **breathe** is unhealthy.

choose/chose: *Choose* means "select." *Chose* is the past tense of *choose*.

Please **choose** an answer.
He **chose** the wrong answer.

PRACTICE 1: Identifying Underline the correct word in each of the following sentences.

1. I can (advice, advise) you on what courses to take.
2. The little boy behaved (bad, badly) when his father left.
3. We were (already, all ready) to leave the house when she realized she didn't have her purse.
4. (Among, Between) the three of us, we should have enough money to buy lunch.
5. The cold water took my (breath, breathe) away.

PRACTICE 2: Completing Complete the following sentences with a correct word from Part I of this list.

1. I ____*chose*____ you to be on my team last year.
2. ____*Except*____ for the humidity, we had a wonderful trip.
3. We have to keep the secret ____*between*____ you and me.
4. Corkey was a ____*bad*____ dog; he chewed up my shoes.
5. Take my ____*advice*____ and bring a jacket.

PRACTICE 3: Writing Your Own Use each pair of words correctly in a sentence of your own. *Answers will vary.*

1. a/an ____

2. breath/breathe ______________________________________

3. affect/effect ____

4. already/all ready ____________________________________

5. beside/besides _______________________________________

EASILY CONFUSED WORDS, PART II

coarse/course: *Coarse* refers to something that is rough. *Course* refers to a class, a path, or a part of a meal.

> This pavement is **coarse.**
> My **course** in math is very interesting.
> The **course** they chose was difficult.
> I will prepare a four-**course** meal.

desert/dessert: *Desert* refers to dry, sandy land or means "abandon." *Dessert* refers to the last course of a meal.

> It is difficult to live in the **desert.**
> He **deserted** his family.
> We had strawberry shortcake for **dessert.**

Hint: You can remember that ***dessert*** has two *s*'s if you think of *strawberry shortcake*.

does/dose: *Does* means "performs." *Dose* refers to a specific portion of medicine.

> My sister **does** whatever she wants.
> Children should have only a small **dose** of the medicine.

fewer/less: *Fewer* refers to things that can be counted. *Less* refers to things that cannot be counted.

> There are **fewer** cotton fields than there used to be.
> She has much **less** time now that she has a new job.

good/well: *Good* modifies nouns. *Well* modifies verbs, adjectives, and adverbs. *Well* also refers to a state of health.

Bill looks **good** in his new suit.
I'm afraid I didn't do **well** on the test.
Kate isn't feeling **well** today.

hear/here: *Hear* refers to the act of listening. *Here* means "in this place."

My father can't **hear** as well as he used to.
Here is the book you asked for.

it's/its: *It's* is the contraction for *it is* or *it has*. *Its* is a possessive pronoun.

The teacher said **it's** important to answer all the questions.
The dog chased **its** tail.

knew/new: *Knew* is the past tense of *know*. *New* means "recent."

I thought everyone **knew** I had a **new** boyfriend.

know/no: *Know* means "understand." *No* means "not any" or is the opposite of *yes*.

We all **know** that we have **no** hope of defeating the other team.
No, I didn't realize that.

lay/lie: *Lay* means "set down." (Its principal parts are *lay, laid, laid*.) *Lie* means "recline." (Its principal parts are *lie, lay, lain*.)

He **lays** brick for a living.
He **laid** down the heavy sack.
She **lies** down at 2 p.m. every day for a nap.
I **lay** in the grass.

(For additional help with *lie* and *lay*, see Chapter 28, "Regular and Irregular Verbs.")

loose/lose: *Loose* means "free" or "unattached." *Lose* means "misplace" or "not win."

Hal's pants are too **loose.**
If I **lose** another $10, I'm going to quit gambling.

passed/past: *Passed* is the past tense of pass. *Past* refers to an earlier time or means "beyond."

John **passed** by his old house on the way to school.
It is interesting to study the **past.**
The dog ran **past** me and into the street.

PRACTICE 4: Identifying Underline the correct word in each of the following sentences.

1. We (passed, past) Edward on the freeway.
2. I think you have made a (good, well) choice.
3. With her second job, Marsha has (fewer, less) time to spend with her friends.
4. (It's, Its) going to be a beautiful day.
5. I cannot (loose, lose) this ring; it was given to me by my grandmother.

PRACTICE 5: Completing Complete the following sentences with a correct word from Part II of this list.

1. The restaurant served peach cobbler for ___*dessert*___.
2. How do you like my ___*new*___ car?
3. Mike ___*does*___ not want to go to the concert with us.
4. This business ___*course*___ will benefit me on the job.
5. I am not feeling ___*well*___ today.

PRACTICE 6: Writing Your Own Use each pair of words correctly in a sentence of your own. *Answers will vary.*

1. fewer/less ______________________________
2. knew/new ______________________________
3. hear/here ______________________________
4. it's/its ______________________________
5. lay/lie ______________________________

EASILY CONFUSED WORDS, PART III

principal/principle: *Principal* means "main, most important," "a school official," or "a sum of money." A *principle* is a rule. (Think of *principle* and *rule*—both end in *-le*.)

My **principal** reason for moving is to be closer to my family.
Mr. Kobler is the **principal** at Westside Elementary School.
My **principal** and interest payments vary each month.
He lives by one main **principle**—honesty.

quiet/quite: *Quiet* means "without noise." *Quite* means "very."

The house was **quiet.**
I am **quite** happy with my new car.

raise/rise: *Raise* means "increase" or "lift up." *Rise* means "get up from a sitting or reclining position."

The state is going to **raise** the tax on cigarettes.
Jane can **rise** slowly from her wheelchair.

set/sit: *Set* means "put down." *Sit* means "take a seated position."

Set the vase on the table.
I don't like to **sit** at a desk for long periods of time.

(For additional help with *sit* and *set*, see Chapter 28, "Regular and Irregular Verbs.")

than/then: *Than* is used in making comparisons. *Then* means "next."

My mother is younger **than** my father.
I took piano lessons; **then** I took guitar lessons.

their/there/they're: *Their* is possessive. *There* indicates location. *They're* is the contraction of *they are*.

Their house burned down last year.
Too many people are living **there.**
They're all going to London.

threw/through: *Threw*, the past tense of throw, means "tossed." *Through* means "finished" or "passing from one point to another."

The pitcher **threw** the ball.
I am **through** with dinner.
My brother and I rode **through** the forest on our bikes.

to/too/two: *To* means "toward" or is used with a verb. *Too* means "also" or "very." *Two* is a number.

I went **to** the store **to** buy some bread.
I bought some artichokes **too,** even though they were **too** expensive.
My mother has **two** sisters.

wear/were/where: *Wear* means "have on one's body." *Were* is the past tense of *be*. *Where* refers to a place.

Can you **wear** shorts to school?
Where were you yesterday?

weather/whether: *Weather* refers to outdoor conditions. *Whether* expresses possibility.

No one knows **whether** the **weather** will get better or worse.

who's/whose: *Who's* is a contraction of *who is* or *who has*. *Whose* is a possessive pronoun.

Who's going to decide **whose** car to take?

your/you're: *Your* means "belonging to you." *You're* is the contraction of *you are*.

Your attention to details proves **you're** a good worker.

PRACTICE 7: Identifying Underline the correct word in each of the following sentences.

1. Janene was (quiet, quite) pleased with your work.
2. (Your, You're) the best choice for this task.
3. Please (set, sit) here and wait for the doctor.
4. (Who's, Whose) planning on going to tonight's game?
5. Our (principal, principle) is retiring at the end of the year.

PRACTICE 8: Completing Complete the following sentences with a correct word from Part III of this list.

1. After the performance, the audience ___*threw*___ flowers at the performer's feet.
2. Beatrice's ___*principal*___ reason for quitting her job was the pay.

3. Finish your homework, and ___then___ you can watch television.

4. ___Where___ are you going dressed like that?

5. Why did you ___wear___ shorts in the winter?

PRACTICE 9: Writing Your Own Use each set of words correctly in a sentence of your own. *Answers will vary.*

1. raise/rise ______________________________

2. their/there/they're ______________________________

3. your/you're ______________________________

4. set/sit ______________________________

5. who's/whose ______________________________

CHAPTER REVIEW

You might want to reread the examples in this chapter before you do the following exercises.

REVIEW PRACTICE 1: Identifying Underline the correct word in each of the following sentences.

1. Your influence is having a positive (affect, effect) on people's lives.
2. (Who's, Whose) that girl with Paul?
3. Jade needs to stand (hear, here) when her name is announced.
4. (Your, You're) the one for me.
5. There are many different plants that grow in the (desert, dessert).
6. Sydney (choose, chose) the smallest puppy of the litter.
7. The picture has come (loose, lose) from its frame.
8. Please sit (beside, besides) me during the ceremony.
9. Your counselor gave you good (advice, advise), and you should take it.
10. Over (their, there, they're) is the house where I grew up.

REVIEW PRACTICE 2: Completing Complete the following sentences with a correct word from all three parts of the list. *Answers may vary.*

1. We *knew* each other when we were children.
2. Contestants should send in *new, their, two, loose* photographs of themselves.
3. The *weather* outside was so nice that we decided to walk.
4. If you leave now, you will *break* up our happy home.
5. The crowd was so *quiet* that you could hear people breathing.
6. Quantitative analysis is the most challenging *course* I have ever taken.
7. Jeffrey did not *hear* the phone ringing.
8. I laughed so hard that I couldn't catch my *breath*.
9. Because of our uninvited houseguests, we have *less, no* food in the house.
10. Faith has *already* donated to the cause.

REVIEW PRACTICE 3: Writing Your Own Write a paragraph explaining the qualities of a good friend. What are the qualities, and why do you think they are important? Try to use some of the easily confused words from this chapter. *Answers will vary.*

REVIEW PRACTICE 4: Editing Through Collaboration Exchange paragraphs from Review Practice 3 with another student, and do the following: *Answers will vary.*

1. Circle any words used incorrectly.
2. Write the correct form of the word above the error.

Then return the paper to its writer, and use the information in this chapter to correct any confused words in your own paragraph. Record your errors on the Error Log in Appendix 6.

CHAPTER 50

Spelling

CHECKLIST for Identifying Misspelled Words

✔ Do you follow the basic spelling rules?

✔ Are all words spelled correctly?

TEST YOURSELF

Underline and correct the misspelled words in the following sentences.

- What is your new addres?
- Turn left on the third avenu.
- I was using the wrong calender when I made out the scheduel.
- The dealer delt me a good hand.
- Please get all the items on the grocry list.

(Answers are in Appendix 4.)

If you think back over your education, you will realize that teachers believe spelling is important. There is a good reason they feel this way: Spelling errors send negative messages. Misspellings seem to leap out at readers, creating serious doubts about the writer's abilities in general. Because you will not always have access to spell-checkers—and because spell-checkers do not catch all spelling errors—improving your spelling skills is important.

SPELLING HINTS

The spelling rules in this chapter will help you become a better speller. But first, here are some practical hints that will also help you improve your spelling.

UNIT PRETEST

To check your students' abilities with the collective skills in this unit, a Unit Pretest is available on pages 774–775.

TEACHING SPELLING

Create a word search game (single letters in columns and rows of approximately 20 letters each), and provide students with a list of misspelled words. Tell students that the correctly spelled words are the words they are searching for inside the word search game. The first student to uncover all the correctly spelled words wins.

INSTRUCTOR'S RESOURCE MANUAL

For sample word search games, for more

exercises, and for quizzes, see the *Instructor's Resource Manual*, Section II, Part IV.

UNIT POSTTEST
To check your students' mastery of the collective skills in this unit, a Unit Posttest is available on pages 788–789.

1. Start a personal spelling list of your own. Use the list of commonly misspelled words on pages 747–751 as your starting point.
2. Study the lists of easily confused words in Chapter 49.
3. Avoid all nonstandard expressions (see Chapter 48).
4. Use a dictionary when you run across words you don't know.
5. Run the spell-check program if you are writing on a computer. Keep in mind, however, that spell-check cannot tell if you have incorrectly used one word in place of another (such as *to*, *too*, or *two*).

PRACTICE 1A: Identifying Underline the misspelled words in each of the following sentences. Refer to the list of easily confused words in Chapter 49 and to the list of most commonly misspelled words in this chapter as necessary.

1. "We want to go <u>to</u>," cried the children. *(too)*
2. The <u>baloon</u> floated away in the breeze. *(balloon)*
3. With John's promotion came a better <u>salry</u>. *(salary)*
4. This vacation has had a relaxing <u>affect</u> on my attitude. *(effect)*
5. It was an <u>akward</u> situation when the bride wouldn't say, "I do." *(awkward)*

PRACTICE 1B: Correcting Correct the spelling errors in Practice 1A by rewriting the incorrect sentences. *See Practice 1A.*

PRACTICE 2: Completing Fill in each blank in the following sentences with hints that help with spelling.

1. Use a ___*dictionary*___ to look up words you don't know.
2. You can always use the ___*spell-check program*___ on your computer, but you should remember that it cannot catch confused words, only misspelled words.
3. Start a ___*personal spelling list*___ to help you remember words you commonly misspell.
4. Study the list of ___*confused words*___ in Chapter ___*49*___.
5. Try to avoid all ___*nonstandard*___ English.

PRACTICE 3: Writing Your Own Choose the correctly spelled word in each pair, and write a sentence using it. Refer to the spelling list on pages 747–751 if necessary.
Sentences will vary.

1. concieve/conceive ______________________________
2. absence/absense ______________________________
3. vaccum/vacuum ______________________________
4. library/libary ______________________________
5. delt/dealt ______________________________

SPELLING RULES

Four basic spelling rules can help you avoid many misspellings. It pays to spend a little time learning them now.

1. **Words that end in *-e*:** When adding a suffix beginning with a vowel (*a*, *e*, *i*, *o*, *u*), drop the final *-e*.

achieve + -ing	=	achieving
include + -ed	=	included
value + -able	=	valuable

When adding a suffix beginning with a consonant, keep the final *-e*.

aware + -ness	=	awareness
improve + -ment	=	improvement
leisure + -ly	=	leisurely

2. **Words with *ie* and *ei*:** Put *i* before *e* except after *c* or when sounded like *ay* as in *neighbor* and *weigh*.

c + ei	**(no c) + ie**	**Exceptions**
receive	grieve	leisure
conceive	niece	foreign
deceive	friend	height
neighbor	relief	science

3. **Words that end in *-y*:** When adding a suffix to a word that ends in a consonant plus *-y*, change the *y* to *i*.

happy + -er	=	happier
dry + -ed	=	dried
easy + -est	=	easiest

4. **Words that double the final consonant:** When adding a suffix starting with a vowel to a one-syllable word, double the final consonant.

big + -est	=	biggest
quit + -er	=	quitter
bet + -ing	=	betting

With words of more than one syllable, double the final consonant if (1) the final syllable is stressed and (2) the word ends in a single vowel plus a single consonant.

begin + -ing	=	beginning
transmit + -ing	=	transmitting
excel + -ed	=	excelled

The word *travel* has more than one syllable. Should you double the final consonant? No, you should not, because the stress is on the *first* syllable (***tra'*** *vel*). The word ends in a vowel and a consonant, but that is not enough. Both parts of the rule must be met.

PRACTICE 4A: Identifying Underline the spelling errors in each of the following sentences.

1. It's not like we're <u>commiting</u> a crime. *(committing)*
2. The <u>boundarys</u> have been clearly marked. *(boundaries)*
3. You are so <u>wierd</u>. *(weird)*
4. Our <u>bagage</u> was lost somewhere in New York. *(baggage)*
5. The <u>facilitys</u> are near one another. *(facilities)*

PRACTICE 4B: Correcting Correct the spelling errors in Practice 4A by rewriting the incorrect sentences. *See Practice 4A.*

PRACTICE 5: Completing Complete the following spelling rules.

1. When adding a suffix beginning with a vowel to a word that ends in *-e*, ___*drop the final -e*___.
2. With words of more than one syllable, ___*double*___ the final consonant if (1) the final syllable is ___*stressed*___ and (2) the word ends in a single ___*vowel*___ plus a single ___*consonant*___.

3. Put *i* before *e* except after *c* or when sounded like *"ay"* as in *neighbor and weigh*.

4. When adding a suffix starting with a *vowel* to a one-syllable word, *double* the final consonant.

5. When adding a suffix to a word that ends in a consonant plus -y, change the *y* to *i*.

PRACTICE 6: Writing Your Own Make a list of words you commonly misspell. Then choose five of the words, and use each correctly in a sentence.
Answers will vary.

MOST COMMONLY MISSPELLED WORDS

Use the following list of commonly misspelled words to check your spelling when you write.

abbreviate
absence
accelerate
accessible
accidentally
accommodate
accompany
accomplish
accumulate
accurate
ache
achievement
acknowledgment
acre
actual
address
adequate
advertisement
afraid
aggravate
aisle
although

aluminum
amateur
ambulance
ancient
anonymous
anxiety
anxious
appreciate
appropriate
approximate
architect
arithmetic
artificial
assassin
athletic
attach
audience
authority
autumn
auxiliary
avenue
awkward

baggage
balloon
banana
bankrupt
banquet
beautiful
beggar
beginning
behavior
benefited
bicycle
biscuit
bought
boundary
brilliant
brought
buoyant
bureau
burglar
business
cabbage
cafeteria

calendar
campaign
canoe
canyon
captain
career
carriage
cashier
catastrophe
caterpillar
ceiling
cemetery
census
certain
certificate
challenge
champion
character
chief
children
chimney
coffee
collar
college
column
commit
committee
communicate
community
comparison
competent
competition
complexion
conceive
concession
concrete
condemn
conference
congratulate
conscience
consensus
continuous
convenience
cooperate
corporation
correspond
cough
counterfeit
courageous
courteous
cozy
criticize
curiosity
curious
curriculum
cylinder
dairy
dangerous
dealt
deceive
decision
definition
delicious
descend
describe
description
deteriorate
determine
development
dictionary
difficulty
diploma
disappear
disastrous
discipline
disease
dissatisfied
divisional
dormitory
economy
efficiency
eighth
elaborate
electricity
eligible
embarrass
emphasize
employee
encourage
enormous
enough
enthusiastic
envelope
environment
equipment
equivalent
especially
essential
establish
exaggerate
excellent
exceptionally
excessive
exhaust
exhilarating
existence
explanation
extinct

extraordinary
familiar
famous
fascinate
fashion
fatigue
faucet
February
fiery
financial
foreign
forfeit
fortunate
forty
freight
friend
fundamental
gauge
genius
genuine
geography
gnaw
government
graduation
grammar
grief
grocery
gruesome
guarantee
guess
guidance
handkerchief
handsome
haphazard
happiness
harass
height
hesitate
hoping
humorous
hygiene
hymn
icicle
illustrate
imaginary
immediately
immortal
impossible
incidentally
incredible
independence
indispensable
individual
inferior
infinite
influential
initial
initiation
innocence
installation
intelligence
interfere
interrupt
invitation
irrelevant
irrigate
issue
jealous
jewelry
journalism
judgment
kindergarten
knife
knowledge
knuckles
laboratory
laborious
language
laugh
laundry
league
legible
legislature
leisure
length
library
license
lieutenant
lightning
likable
liquid
listen
literature
machinery
magazine
magnificent
majority
manufacture
marriage
material
mathematics
maximum
mayor
meant
medicine
message
mileage
miniature

minimum
minute
mirror
miscellaneous
mischievous
miserable
misspell
monotonous
mortgage
mysterious
necessary
neighborhood
niece
nineteen
ninety
noticeable
nuisance
obedience
obstacle
occasion
occurred
official
omission
omitted
opponent
opportunity
opposite
original
outrageous
pamphlet
paragraph
parallel
parentheses
partial
particular
pastime
patience
peculiar
permanent
persistent
personnel
persuade
physician
pitcher
pneumonia
politician
possess
prairie
precede
precious
preferred
prejudice
previous
privilege
procedure
proceed
pronounce
psychology
publicly
questionnaire
quotient
realize
receipt
recipe
recommend
reign
religious
representative
reservoir
responsibility
restaurant
rhyme
rhythm
salary
satisfactory
scarcity
scenery
schedule
science
scissors
secretary
seize
separate
significant
similar
skiing
soldier
souvenir
sovereign
spaghetti
squirrel
statue
stomach
strength
subtle
succeed
success
sufficient
surprise
syllable
symptom
technique
temperature
temporary
terrible
theater
thief
thorough

tobacco	vacuum	weird
tomorrow	valuable	whose
tongue	various	width
tournament	vegetable	worst
tragedy	vehicle	wreckage
truly	vicinity	writing
unanimous	villain	yacht
undoubtedly	visible	yearn
unique	volunteer	yield
university	weather	zealous
usable	Wednesday	zoology
usually	weigh	

PRACTICE 7A: Identifying Underline any words that are misspelled in the following sentences.

1. This steak and lobster dinner is incredable. *(incredible)*
2. You shouldn't condem others for doing what you do. *(condemn)*
3. Valentine's Day is in Febuary. *(February)*
4. How long have you been writting that novel? *(writing)*
5. I know you will suceed in college. *(succeed)*

PRACTICE 7B: Correcting Correct any spelling errors that you identified in Practice 7A by rewriting the incorrect sentences. *See Practice 7A.*

PRACTICE 8: Completing Correct the spelling errors in the following paragraph.

I was eating a plate of spagetti *(spaghetti)* when the phone rang. It was my nieghbor *(neighbor)*. He said, "The big fight is begining *(beginning)* in 15 minutes, and my television screen just went out." He then beged *(begged)* me to let him come over and watch it at my house. So I told him that was fine. He neglected to tell me, however, that he wouldn't be alone. He and seven of his rowdy freinds *(friends)* invaded my house, ate my spagetti *(spaghetti)* and drank my soda, and left a catastrophy *(catastrophe)* behind. I think the next time I have a party, I'll have it at his house.

PRACTICE 9: Writing Your Own Write a complete sentence for each word listed here. *Answers will vary.*

1. appreciate ______________________________
2. laundry ______________________________
3. marriage ______________________________
4. excellent ______________________________
5. opposite ______________________________

CHAPTER REVIEW

You might want to reread the examples in this chapter before you do the following exercises.

REVIEW PRACTICE 1: Identifying Underline the misspelled words in each of the following sentences.

1. I'm trying to catch the rythm of this music. *(rhythm)*
2. You ate my desert. *(dessert)*
3. This essay shows improvment. *(improvement)*
4. Ramona is a genuis with figures. *(genius)*
5. The firy-hot peppers made my eyes water. *(fiery)*
6. Most teenagers want their independance. *(independence)*
7. If we stick to the scedule, we should make it home before tomorow. *(schedule, tomorrow)*
8. Breath deeply, and put your head between your legs. *(Breathe)*
9. My family lives in seperate states. *(separate)*
10. Dr. Murphy rides his bycicle to work every day. *(bicycle)*

REVIEW PRACTICE 2: Completing Correct the spelling errors in Review Practice 1 by rewriting the incorrect sentences. *See Review Practice 1.*

REVIEW PRACTICE 3: Writing Your Own Write a paragraph explaining how to become a better speller. Are there any hints that may help? *Answers will vary.*

REVIEW PRACTICE 4: Editing Through Collaboration Exchange paragraphs from Review Practice 3 with another student, and do the following: *Answers will vary.*

1. Underline any words that are used incorrectly.

2. Circle any misspelled words.

Then return the paper to its writer, and use the information in this chapter to correct any spelling errors in your own paragraph. Record your errors on the Spelling Log in Appendix 7.

UNIT TESTS

YOUR EQ (EDITING QUOTIENT)

A good way to approach editing is by finding your EQ (Editing Quotient). Knowing your EQ will help you look for specific errors in your writing and make your editing more efficient.

EQ Test In each of the following paragraphs, underline the errors you find, and label them a, b, c, and so on. Then list them on the lines below the paragraph. The number of lines corresponds to the number of errors in each paragraph. *EQ Answers start on page 758.*

The possible errors are listed here:

apostrophe	end punctuation	pronoun agreement
capitalization	fragment	spelling
comma	fused sentence	subject-verb agreement
comma splice	modifier	verb form
confused word	pronoun	

1. Many people seem to have a telephone permanently attached to one ear people have several phone lines going into their homes. And cell phones hanging off of their belts. People are talking on their cell phones in restaurants, in cars, and even in public bathrooms. When they go home, they go online to check e-mail. While the second line is ringing off the hook. Why would someone want to be available every second of the day? This rushed society will eventually have to slow down, people can't live at this pace for long.

    a. ______________________________

    b. ______________________________

    c. ______________________________

    d. ______________________________

2. Recently, a major computer software company was accused of being a monopoly. That is, it seemed to be trying to control the whole software industry. The company, reality software, sells many different types of software at reasonable prices. Which results in the company selling more products than its competitors. Reality Software also signed contracts with Computer Manufacturers that allow the manufacturers to install Reality programs on computers before they are sold. The courts, which guard against monopolies, say this is unfair to consumers, buyers should be able to choose their software. It is also unfair to other software companies. Because they are not given a fair chance to sell their products.

   a. ______________________________
   b. ______________________________
   c. ______________________________
   d. ______________________________
   e. ______________________________

3. Public speaking is a valuable tool no matter what career path a person take. At some point in every career, if a person is going to advance, they will have to speak to a group. In fact, the higher up the career ladder a person climb, the more public speaking will be required. It is good preparation, therefore, to take a public speaking course in college, a public speaking course not only teaches the skills involved in making a presentation but also builds a person's confidence.

   a. ______________________________
   b. ______________________________
   c. ______________________________
   d. ______________________________

4. Anyone who thinks a surprise birthday party takes a lot of time and work should try planning a wedding. Until a person plans his or her own wedding, they can't fully understand all the details that must be considered. Too my way of thinking, long engagements aren't to find out how compatible the couple is. There to allow enough time to find a place to hold the reception. On the date you want. Plus a good caterer

and music. Even the smallest detail must be considered, such as whether guests should throw rice birdseed or confetti at the happy couple after the ceremony.

a. ____________________

b. ____________________

c. ____________________

d. ____________________

e. ____________________

f. ____________________

g. ____________________

5. A famous author once said that his messy handwriting, almost kept him from becoming a writer. Struggling to be legible, the pages were impossible to read. No matter how hard he tried, his handwriting would become rushed and scribbled. He would write wonderful novels that only he could read, for his twenty-third birthday, his wife bought him a typewriter. He then began to write books. That people all over the world have read. If he were alive today, he could write on a computer.

   a. ____________________

   b. ____________________

   c. ____________________

   d. ____________________

6. Everyone has heard the term "best freind." What is a best friend? Some people beleive that their oldest friend is they're best friend. Yet a best friend can be someone from college or even someone who is family. Such as a brother or sister. No matter who qualifies as a best friend, two facts is true: A best freind is someone special and trustworthy. People may wonder how they could get along without their best friend? Most people couldn't.

   a. ____________________

   b. ____________________

   c. ____________________

   d. ____________________

e. ______________________________

f. ______________________________

g. ______________________________

7. If I had my way, I would require every college student to take a course in geography. It is embarassing how little the average American knows about his own country, to say nothing of other countries. For instance, do you know the capital of virginia? Could you name all the Great Lakes? On which continent is greece? If you can answer these questions you are one of very few people. People think geography is boring but it isn't. Its fascinating to learn about the world we live in.

   a. ______________________________

   b. ______________________________

   c. ______________________________

   d. ______________________________

   e. ______________________________

   f. ______________________________

   g. ______________________________

8. I believe that fast-food restaurants should change there names to "fast food sometimes, but at least faster than a sit-down restaurant." When I go through the drive-up window at a fast-food restaraunt, it is because I am in a hurry and want to get something to eat quickly, however, sometimes it would be quicker for me to go home and cook a three-course meal. I do not understand what could take so long. I pull up to the intercom, order my food, procede to the window, and wait. If fast food always lived up to its name I would be able to get food fast.

   a. ______________________________

   b. ______________________________

   c. ______________________________

   d. ______________________________

   e. ______________________________

9. Doing the family laundry used to be a chore for me but now I am a pro. First, I sort the clothes according to colors or whites. Before I learned

this basic rule, my poor brother had to wear pink underwear from time to time. Next, I put the clothes in the washing machine, and add detergent. If I'm doing whites I also add bleach. I close the lid, turn the dial to hot wash and cold rinse, and push the "start" button. I allow the washing machine to do it's work while I read a magazine. When it's time to put the clothes in the dryer, I pay attention to the drying instructions on the tags. Once I neglected this step, and my favorite pants shrinked. When the dryer has done its work, I remove the clothes immediately so they do not become rinkled.

a. ______________________________

b. ______________________________

c. ______________________________

d. ______________________________

e. ______________________________

f. ______________________________

10. It's fun to watch a person with their animals. For instance, the lady down the street takes her dog for a walk every morning. The dog is a tiny rat terrier, it is really cute. The lady puts a little leash on the dog. To keep him from running away. Even though the dogs legs are short, he can run real fast. The dog seems so happy during his walks. He jumps and yips. The lady and her dog are a good pair they enjoy walking with each other and keeping each other company.

a. ______________________________

b. ______________________________

c. ______________________________

d. ______________________________

e. ______________________________

f. ______________________________

EQ Answers Use the answers below to score your EQ. Mark the errors that you missed.

1. Many people seem to have a telephone permanently attached to one ear [a] people have several phone lines going into their homes. [b] And cell

phones hanging off of their belts. People are talking on their cell phones in restaurants, in cars, and even in public bathrooms. When they go home, they go online to check e-mail. [c]While the second line is ringing off the hook. Why would someone want to be available every second of the day? This rushed society will eventually have to slow down, [d] people can't live at this pace for long.

a. *fused sentence or end punctuation*

b. *fragment*

c. *fragment*

d. *comma splice or end punctuation*

2. Recently, a major computer software company was accused of being a monopoly. That is, it seemed to be trying to control the whole software industry. The company, [a]reality software, sells many different types of software at reasonable prices. [b]Which results in the company selling more products than its competitors. Reality Software also signed contracts with [c]Computer Manufacturers that allow the manufacturers to install Reality programs on computers before they are sold. The courts, which guard against monopolies, say this is unfair to consumers,[d]buyers should be able to choose their software. It is also unfair to other software companies. [e]Because they are not given a fair chance to sell their products.

   a. *capitalization*

   b. *fragment*

   c. *capitalization*

   d. *comma splice or end punctuation*

   e. *fragment*

3. Public speaking is a valuable tool no matter what career path a [a]person take. At some point in every career, if a person is going to advance, [b]they will have to speak to a group. In fact, the higher up the career ladder a [c]person climb, the more public speaking will be required. It is good preparation, therefore, to take a public speaking course in college,[d] a public speaking course not only teaches the skills involved in making a presentation but also builds a person's confidence.

   a. *subject-verb agreement*

   b. *pronoun agreement*

c. *subject-verb agreement*

d. *comma splice or end punctuation*

4. Anyone who thinks a surprise birthday party takes a lot of time and work should try planning a wedding. Until a person plans his or her own wedding, [a]they can't fully understand all the details that must be considered. [b]Too my way of thinking, long engagements aren't to find out how compatible the couple is. [c]There to allow enough time to find a place to hold the reception. [d]On the date you want. [e]Plus a good caterer and music. Even the smallest detail must be considered, such as whether guests should throw rice [f] birdseed [g] or confetti at the happy couple after the ceremony.

   a. *pronoun agreement*

   b. *confused word*

   c. *confused word*

   d. *fragment*

   e. *fragment*

   f. *comma*

   g. *comma*

5. A famous author once said that his messy handwriting,[a] almost kept him from becoming a writer. [b]Struggling to be legible, the pages were impossible to read. No matter how hard he tried, his handwriting would become rushed and scribbled. He would write wonderful novels that only he could read, [c] for his twenty-third birthday his wife bought him a typewriter. He then began to write books. [d]That people all over the world have read. If he were alive today, he could write on a computer.

   a. *comma*

   b. *modifier*

   c. *comma splice or end punctuation*

   d. *fragment*

6. Everyone has heard the term "best [a]freind." What is a best friend? Some people [b]beleive that their oldest friend is [c]they're best friend. Yet a best

friend can be someone from college or even someone who is family. [d]Such as a brother or sister. No matter who qualifies as a best friend, two [e]facts is true: A best [f]freind is someone special and trustworthy. People may wonder how they could get along without their best friend?[g] Most people couldn't.

a. *spelling*

b. *spelling*

c. *confused word*

d. *fragment*

e. *subject-verb agreement*

f. *spelling*

g. *end punctuation*

7. If I had my way, I would require every college student to take a course in geography. It is [a]embarassing how little the average American knows about [b]his own country, to say nothing of other countries. For instance, do you know the capital of [c]virginia? Can you name all the Great Lakes? On which continent is [d]greece? If you can answer these questions[e] you are one of very few people. People think geography is boring[f] but it isn't. [g]Its fascinating to learn about the world we live in.

a. *spelling*

b. *pronoun*

c. *capitalization*

d. *capitalization*

e. *comma*

f. *comma*

g. *confused word or apostrophe*

8. I believe that fast-food restaurants should change [a]there names to "fast food sometimes, but at least faster than a sit-down restaurant." When I go through the drive-up window at a fast-food [b]restaraunt, it is because I am in a hurry and want to get something to eat quickly, [c] however, sometimes it would be quicker for me to go home and cook a three-course meal. I do not understand what could take so long. I pull up to

the intercom, order my food, [d]procede to the window, and wait. If fast food always lived up to its name[e] I would be able to get food fast.

a. *confused word*

b. *spelling*

c. *comma splice or end punctuation*

d. *spelling*

e. *comma*

9. Doing the family laundry used to be a chore for me[a] but now I am a pro. First, I sort the clothes according to colors or whites. Before I learned this basic rule, my poor brother had to wear pink underwear from time to time. Next, I put the clothes in the washing machine,[b] and add detergent. If I'm doing whites[c] I also add bleach. I close the lid, turn the dial to hot wash and cold rinse, and push the "start" button. I allow the washing machine to do [d]it's work while I read a magazine. When it's time to put the clothes in the dryer, I pay attention to the drying instructions on the tags. Once I neglected this step, and my favorite pants [e]shrinked. When the dryer has done its work, I remove the clothes immediately so they do not become [f]rinkled.

   a. *comma*

   b. *comma*

   c. *comma*

   d. *confused word or apostrophe*

   e. *verb form*

   f. *spelling*

10. It's fun to watch a person with [a]their animals. For instance, the lady down the street takes her dog for a walk every morning. The dog is a tiny rat terrier, [b] it is really cute. The lady puts a little leash on the dog. [c]To keep him from running away. Even though the [d]dogs legs are short, he can run [e]real fast. The dog seems so happy during his walks. He jumps and yips. The lady and her dog are a good pair [f] they enjoy walking with each other and keeping each other company.

a. *pronoun agreement*

b. *comma splice or end punctuation*

c. *fragment*

d. *apostrophe*

e. *modifier*

f. *fused sentence or end punctuation*

Finding Your EQ Turn to Appendix 5, and chart the errors you didn't find in the EQ Test. Then plot your errors on the second EQ chart in Appendix 5, and see what pattern they form. *Answers will vary.*

UNIT PRETESTS

UNIT 1: SENTENCES

Here are some exercises that test your understanding of all the material in this unit: subjects and verbs, fragments, and fused sentences and comma splices.

Pretest I

A. Underline the subjects once and the verbs twice in the following sentences. Cross out the prepositional phrases first. Then put the fragments in brackets ([ ]), and put a slash (/) between the run-together sentences.

1. My cat was ~~in the tree~~ ~~for a half-hour~~ last night.
2. I love Christmas. [The beautiful lights.] [The carols.]
3. My dad's birthday is ~~in August~~ / we always have a party ~~for him~~.
4. I accidentally left my jacket. [~~In the library~~.]
5. Sandra has been reading more. [To improve her vocabulary.]
6. Henry was hungry because he skipped breakfast.
7. [Walking ~~to school~~.] We saw a squirrel.
8. Tonight, CSI is ~~on TV~~. [Which is my favorite show.]
9. Rosalie loves chocolate / it is her favorite dessert.
10. Cats are picky eaters. [For example, leaving their dinner.]
11. I am writing my paper so I can pass my class, / then I'll be able to graduate.
12. Brenda got ~~to school~~, and then she realized that she had left her book ~~at home~~.
13. Roger and Amy bought lunch ~~for all~~ ~~of their friends~~.
14. Alicia brought cookies ~~for the class~~.
15. I don't have my phone / I must have forgotten it.
16. Marlene finished the project tonight. [Which was a good idea.]
17. Unfortunately, Lena was called ~~to jury duty~~ tomorrow.
18. Lois missed the party ~~at Joe's house~~. [Since she had so much homework.]
19. We had dinner ~~at my favorite restaurant~~ / we go there once a month.
20. [To get an A ~~in the class~~.] Students must complete all assignments.

B. Correct the fragments and run-together sentences in Pretest IA by rewriting each incorrect sentence. *Answers will vary.*

Pretest II

A. Underline the subjects once and the verbs twice in the following paragraph. Cross out the prepositional phrases first. Then put the fragments in brackets ([ ]) and put a slash (/) between the run-together sentences.

> I will always remember my first job. I worked ~~at a movie theater~~. [~~During high school~~.] I mostly worked ~~behind the counter~~, / I made and sold the snacks. I also cleaned ~~behind the counter~~ and sometimes took tickets. [Which was easier.] The work was physically draining, and I was always tired. [When I got home.] When I graduated ~~from high school~~ and went ~~to college~~, I had to quit my job. [To have more time to study.] I will always remember that first job / I would never want to go back ~~to it~~ now.

B. Correct the fragments and run-together sentences in Pretest IIA by rewriting the paragraph. *Answers will vary.*

UNIT 2: VERBS

Here are some exercises that test your understanding of all the material in this unit: regular and irregular verbs, verb tense, subject-verb agreement, and more on verbs (consistent/inconsistent and active/passive).

Pretest I

A. Underline all the verb errors in the following sentences.

1. Larry have sit down his books on the table. *(has set)*
2. Jessica's cat like to lay in the sun. *(likes, lie)*
3. Students finds it hard to study for all their classes. *(find)*
4. Since Mr. Holmes retired, the school need a new professor. *(needs)*
5. On our last vacation, my parents almost sunk our boat. *(sank)*
6. They told Jenny that she had to spoke to the admissions office. *(speak)*
7. Although the book was wrote many years ago, it is still good. *(written)*
8. Yesterday, we watch the season finale of *Lost*. *(watched)*
9. Neither Jack nor David need my help with the homework assignment. *(needs)*

10. My sister grow three inches last year. *(grew)*
11. It was so warm that I had to lay down after school today. *(lie)*
12. They be working so hard on the assignment that they doesn't notice the time. *(were working, didn't)*
13. Since the dinner was burned, we has to go out to eat. *(had)*
14. The dog was fed by Jimmy last night. *(Jimmy fed the dog last night.)*
15. She have all of Green Day's CDs. *(has)*
16. They is going to Europe this summer. *(are)*
17. There go my favorite kind of car! *(goes)*
18. My study group meet every Tuesday afternoon. *(meets)*
19. Denise go swimming on Saturday mornings. *(goes)*
20. Our dog escaped from our backyard and runs down the street. *(ran)*

B. Correct the verb errors in Pretest IA by rewriting each incorrect sentence. *See Pretest IA.*

Pretest II

A. Underline the verb errors in the following paragraph.

Parents should *give* gave their children allowances because allowances help children *learn* learns how to manage money, which *gives* give them a sense of responsibility. Having their own money can allow children to make decisions about how they *want* wants to spend it. Making decisions *does* do help kids develop a feeling of responsibility because they are in control of what they buy and what they *have* has. *Kids have opportunities* Opportunities are given to kids when they are in control of their own money.

B. Correct the verb errors in Pretest IIA by rewriting the paragraph.
See Pretest IIA.

UNIT 3: PRONOUNS

Here are some exercises that test your understanding of all the material in this unit: pronoun problems, pronoun reference and point of view, and pronoun agreement.

Pretest I

A. Underline the pronoun errors in the following sentences.

1. This weekend is our fundraiser, and next weekend is theirs'. *(theirs)*
2. I'm not taking as many classes as her. *(she)*
3. Each student needs to buy their books by the first day of classes. *(his or her)*
4. Do you think I should get my hair cut like you'res? *(yours)*
5. A teacher should always treat her students fairly. *(his or her)*
6. Everyone must wipe their feet before coming in. *(his or her)*
7. I've lived in this here house for five years. *(this)*
8. Lana has more books than me. *(I)*
9. Jack and Justin went to the Janet Jackson concert, and he brought me back a t-shirt. *(Answers will vary.)*
10. We're not as good at bowling as them. *(they)*
11. Although Vanessa and Penelope left at 3:00 p.m., she did not arrive until 4:30 p.m. *(Answers will vary.)*
12. I always keep a flashlight in my car because you never know when you'll need one. *(I, I'll)*
13. A person must build up exercise slowly or you'll injure something. *(he or she will)*
14. You should probably plan out your classes before one registers. *(you register)*
15. Either one of the tutors should be able to help their students. *(his or her)*
16. He is better at drawing than her. *(she)*
17. Babies should sleep in its cribs. *(their)*
18. This here book is really good. *(this)*
19. Someone called my cell phone, but his number was blocked. *(his or her)*
20. When an engineer breaks his clipboard, he has to get a new one. *(his or her, he or she)*

B. Correct the pronoun errors in Pretest IA by rewriting each incorrect sentence. *See Pretest IA.*

Pretest II

A. Underline the pronoun errors in the following paragraph.

Exercising is important in maintaining good health. People should exercise at least three times per week to maintain his or her *(their)*

good health. Both aerobic and anaerobic exercise are beneficial to
he or she increases
overall health. When a person exercises aerobically, they increase
his or her *promotes*
their lung capacity and promote cardiovascular health. When a per-
he or she builds *burns*
son exercises anaerobically, they build muscle, burn excess fat, and
helps
help prevent osteoporosis. A combination of the two types of exercise is in the best interest of people who want to live longer lives and
their *lives*
enjoy his or her life to the fullest.

B. Correct the pronoun errors in Pretest IIA by rewriting the paragraph.
See Pretest IIA.

UNIT 4: MODIFIERS

Here are some exercises that test your understanding of all the material in this unit: adjectives, adverbs, and modifier errors.

Pretest I

A. Underline the modifier errors in the following sentences.

1. When you're in the library, you need to talk soft. *(softly)*
2. While watching TV, the commercials were too loud. *(While watching TV, I thought the commercials were too loud)*
3. She had a stomach ache after eating too quick. *(quickly)*
4. Luckily, the birds are more faster than the cats. *(faster)*
5. I can't think of nothing to write my paper on. *(can't think of anything)*
6. Tracy had to clean up the spill quiet so her roommate wouldn't hear. *(quietly)*
7. She went to the doctor, but he told her there wasn't nothing wrong with her. *(wasn't anything)*
8. Throw your trash away at the end of the show in the trash can. *(Throw your trash away in the trash can at the end of the show.)*
9. I don't look well today. *(good)*
10. You should drive more slow when the weather is bad. *(more slowly)*
11. Olive Garden has the most best garlic bread. *(best)*
12. Nate grateful accepted his award. *(gratefully)*
13. She speaks too soft on the phone; I can barely hear her. *(softly)*

14. To keep up with classmates, reading should always be done by them. *(To keep up with classmates, they should always read)*
15. Margie called Christa and Rebecca to ask her about the assignment last night. *(Answers will vary.)*
16. My stay in the hospital was my most worst experience. *(worst)*
17. I can't hardly bear to tell her the news. *(can hardly)*
18. People should wrap up their bread tight to prevent it from becoming stale. *(tightly)*
19. Since she lost weight, Beth's clothes fit her loose. *(loosely)*
20. The most enjoyable of the two classes was biology. *(more enjoyable)*

B. Correct the modifier errors in Pretest IA by rewriting each incorrect sentence. *See Pretest IA.*

Pretest II

A. Underline the modifier errors in the following paragraph.

Welfare reform is a very controversial issue. Many people think that welfare recipients are more lazy *(lazier)* than other people and that they don't deserve help. However, some welfare recipients are good people who have fallen on harder times *(hard times)*. Having medical problems, jobs are often not found *(People who have medical problems often can't find jobs.)*. Similarly, the job market is quick *(quickly)* becoming competitiver *(more competitive)*, and it is harder and harder to find a good job. Sometimes people who apply for welfare do have jobs but are having a hard time making ends meet. Although the welfare system could be more better *(better)*, we shouldn't complete *(completely)* abandon it.

B. Correct the modifier errors in Pretest IIA by rewriting the paragraph. *See Pretest IIA.*

UNIT 5: PUNCTUATION

Here are some exercises that test your understanding of all the material in this unit: end punctuation, commas, apostrophes, quotation marks, semicolons, colons, dashes, and parentheses.

Pretest I

A. Underline the punctuation errors in the following sentences.

1. I am 99.9% sure that it was Maggie on the bus.
2. I still need to get my chemistry, French, and math books.
3. You have to mop the kitchen, and do the laundry.
4. Do you know Jimmy.?
5. Our cat, Oreo, is black and white.
6. I have to get out of here!
7. Deborah's birthday is coming up next week.
8. She lives on 29 Palm St., Bakersfield, CA, 93311.
9. "I tried," she said, "but I just couldn't finish."
10. He can't understand why it's so hard for me to remember my assignments.
11. I love to go shopping for shoes, purses, and belts.
12. Wanting to get a new car, Julianne saved all her money.
13. I hadn't finished all of my homework, but I decided to go to the concert anyway.
14. We should do three things this weekend: clean out the garage, weed the flower beds, and mow the lawn.
15. I don't drink that much soda; I prefer coffee.
16. She loves to read mysteries, biographies, and romance novels.
17. "I can't believe he said that!" shouted Jamie.
18. My three brothers' cabin is in Tehachapi.
19. Lenore told me, that she had to call me back.
20. Edgar Allan Poe's best known short story, "The Tell-Tale Heart," is better than some of his other stories.

B. Correct the punctuation errors in Pretest IA by rewriting each incorrect sentence. *See Pretest IA.*

Pretest II

A. Underline the punctuation errors in the following paragraph.

I'm exhausted. I just got done planning my friend's baby shower. First I had to make a grocery list., then I had to figure out games to play. I had to purchase all of the prizes for the game winners, and prepare the food. The dinner, which consists of three courses, was difficult to plan, but I've done as much preparatory work as possible. Looking back, I wonder how I did it all?. Even though it was hard work, I'm glad to be able to do it for my friend. Besides, she had the baby—a lot more work than planning a baby shower. *!*

B. Correct the punctuation errors in Pretest IIA by rewriting the paragraph.
See Pretest IIA.

UNIT 6: MECHANICS

Here are some exercises that test your understanding of all the material in this unit: capitalization, abbreviations, and numbers.

Pretest I

A. Underline the errors in capitalization, abbreviations, and numbers in the following sentences.

1. I earned my bachelor of arts degree last June. *(B.A.)*
2. His house payment is more than one thousand dollars a month. *($1,000)*
3. The recipe calls for 3 and a quarter cups of flour. *3¼*
4. I think we should go to the hometown buffet on white lane. *(Hometown Buffet, White Lane)*
5. The necklace that the actress wore to the Academy Awards is worth two million dollars. *($2 million)*
6. We still need to find homes for 3 of the kittens. *(three)*
7. There's no need to leave the country to go sightseeing—there are plenty of things to see in the U.S. *(United States)*
8. "She left about an hour ago," Bernice told me. "but she'll be back at 2:00 p.m." *(But)*
9. All of my favorite shows are on the same station—American Broadcasting Company. *(ABC)*
10. Ella stayed in the U.S. for two months before going back to Germany. *(United States)*
11. Our new roof cost ten thousand dollars. *($10,000)*

12. Have you decided whether to take english 200 or anthropology 102 next quarter? *(English, Anthropology)*
13. I always go to Doctor Michaels when I am sick. *(Dr.)*
14. Misses Andrews has taught summer school for the past three years. *(Mrs.)*
15. I still need to read chapters five and six and answer questions one through 3 for tomorrow. *(5, 6, 1)*
16. We should use the modern language association's style of citation. *(MLA)*
17. I feed my canary every night at 7:30 post meridiem. *(p.m.)*
18. The movie was exciting; it was about people who work for the cia. *(CIA)*
19. Lindsey asked me to pick up the latest harry potter book. *(Harry Potter)*
20. The first sentence in the book is, "it was the best of times, it was the worst of times." *(It)*

B. Correct the errors in capitalization, abbreviations, and numbers in Pretest IA by rewriting each incorrect sentence. *See Pretest IA.*

Pretest II

A. Underline the errors in capitalization, abbreviations, and numbers in the following paragraph.

For spring break this year, my family and I are going to go to italy *(Italy)*. We will stay from monday, march second, to saturday, march seventh *(Monday March 2 Saturday March 7)*. I am really excited since I have never been to Italy. I am looking forward to meeting new Friends *(friends)* in italy *(Italy)*. We still have to finalize our hotel reservations. We are staying at 5597 carlson Ave *(Carlson Avenue)*, at a beautiful hotel. Even though we had to save up over one thousand dollars *($1000)* to be able to go on this trip, it is worth it to stay in such a beautiful place.

B. Correct the errors in capitalization, abbreviations, and numbers in Pretest IIA by rewriting the paragraph. *See Pretest IIA.*

UNIT 7: EFFECTIVE SENTENCES

Here are some exercises that test your understanding of all the material in this unit: varying sentence structure, parallelism, and combining sentences.

Pretest I

A. Label the errors in each of the following sentences in variety, parallelism, and sentence combining.

1. Monica has two pets. She has a cat and a dog. She wants to get a bird. *(variety, sentence combining)*
2. You should study before your test. You will pass. *(sentence combining)*
3. I got home late last night. I was late the night before that. I will probably be late tonight. *(variety, sentence combining)*
4. Our club meets every two weeks. We meet on Tuesdays. We meet in the Classroom Building. *(variety, sentence combining)*
5. I'd like to go to New York. I've never been out of California. *(sentence combining)*
6. Tonight, she is going to finish the report, eating dinner, and watched TV. *(parallelism)*
7. Shania told us about her date. They went to dinner. Then they went to the movies. *(variety, sentence combining)*
8. Chantel is a nurse. She works long hours. *(sentence combining)*
9. They had a sleepover. They stayed up all night. They watched movies. *(variety, sentence combining)*
10. The book was good. It was different from the movie. *(sentence combining)*
11. George takes English classes. He is an English major. *(sentence combining)*
12. Dinner will be provided. Sandwiches will be for dinner. *(sentence combining)*
13. I need to talk with Andrea. I have already tried to call her twice. She did not answer her phone. *(variety, sentence combining)*
14. Sometimes, I just feel like skipping class and stayed home. *(parallelism)*
15. We got the pictures developed. The pictures turned out well. You did a good job taking the pictures. *(variety, sentence combining)*
16. Tigers are beautiful. They have stripes. *(sentence combining)*
17. Lance should eat more vegetables. They are good for him. *(sentence combining)*
18. If you are ever on fire, you should stop, dropping, and rolled. *(parallelism)*
19. I'm having car trouble. My car won't start. It needs to be towed. *(variety, sentence combining)*
20. Marcus got pulled over. He was speeding. He got a ticket. *(variety, sentence combining)*

B. Correct the errors you identified in Pretest IA by rewriting each incorrect sentence. *Answers will vary.*

Pretest II

A. Label the errors in the following paragraph in variety, parallelism, and sentence combining.

(1) Playing the piano is fun. (2) Playing the piano is also a lot of work. (3) People who want to learn to play the piano have to practice every day. (4) Also, they have to learn to read music and taking lessons. (5) Playing the piano is not that hard. (6) Once people learn how, they can play in recitals, for family members, or just playing alone. (7) Playing the piano can even be relaxing for those who know how to do it well. (8) Knowing how to play the piano is a valuable skill.

1–2 variety, sentence combining; 4 parallelism; 6 parallelism; 7–8 variety, sentence combining

B. Correct the errors you identified in Pretest IIA by rewriting the paragraph. *Answers will vary.*

UNIT 8: CHOOSING THE RIGHT WORD

Here are some exercises that test your understanding of all the material in this unit: standard and nonstandard English, easily confused words, and spelling.

Pretest I

A. Underline the word choice and spelling errors in the following sentences.

1. We use to be best friends, but I hardly even see him anymore. *(used)*
2. When you're sick, you should lay down and rest. *(lie)*
3. After class, we went to Brandon's house and made bannana splits. *(banana)*
4. Anthony is lactose intolerant: He can't eat any diary products. *(dairy)*
5. I have something I need too give too you. *(to, to)*
6. They said that they are going to rise the price of gas again. *(raise)*
7. Good study habits are esential for students who want to succeed. *(essential)*

8. Our group discussion got <u>quiet</u> heated today. *(quite)*
9. My dad <u>flipped out</u> when he saw the dent in the car. *(was upset)*
10. I don't feel like reading, and, <u>beside</u>, I left my book at home. *(besides)*
11. I think that is <u>they're</u> dog. *(their)*
12. Didn't you say we'd meet <u>hear</u>? *(here)*
13. First, we'll pick up Lisa; <u>than</u>, we'll get Jordan. *(then)*
14. We think there might be a <u>bergler</u> in the neighborhood. *(burglar)*
15. <u>Who's</u> decision was it? *(Whose)*
16. I <u>would of</u> called you last night, but I thought you were <u>suppose</u> to get home late. *(would have or would've, supposed)*
17. She did well in all of her classes <u>accept</u> one. *(except)*
18. That movie <u>totally freaked me out</u>! *(really frightened me)*
19. His speech really <u>effected</u> me. *(affected)*
20. I hope our team doesn't <u>loose</u> again this year. *(lose)*

B. Combine the errors in Pretest IA by rewriting each incorrect sentence. *See Pretest IA.*

Pretest II

A. Underline the word choice and spelling errors in the following paragraph.

February *used* *discriminate*
<u>Febuary</u> is Black History Month. White people <u>use</u> to <u>descriminate</u> against black people. Now, Black History Month allows all people to *acknowledge*
<u>acnowledge</u> the contributions made by black people. One example is *refusal*
Rosa Parks; her <u>refusul</u> to sit at the back of the bus helped propel the Civil Rights Movement. Black people everywhere began fighting for *their* *Then*
<u>they're</u> rights. <u>Than</u>, segregation ended and society slowly began to integrate itself. Now, all *our*
<u>are</u> children can live together in harmony knowing that all people are created equal.

B. Correct the word choice and spelling errors in Pretest IIA by rewriting the paragraph. *See Pretest IIA.*

UNIT POSTTESTS

UNIT 1: SENTENCES

Here are some exercises that test your understanding of all the material in this unit: subjects and verbs, fragments, and fused sentences and comma splices.

Posttest I

A. Underline the subjects once and the verbs twice in the following sentences. Cross out the prepositional phrases first. Then put the fragments in brackets ([ ]), and put a slash (/) between the run-together sentences.

1. The cars and buses were stuck in traffic for two hours.
2. Spring is my favorite time of year for many reasons.[For example, flowers and trees blooming.][Lovers holding hands in the park.][New parents pushing babies in strollers.]
3. I got tickets to *Les Misérables* in Los Angeles/I haven't seen that play for years.
4. We're going to watch the Emmy Awards tonight.[Unless the Lakers game is on TV at the same time.]
5. Come with me to the mall.[To pick out a new dress for the dance.] *("You" implied)*
6. He feels like a failure because he did not pass the midterm.
7. [Listening to Tamara's problems.]Jeff wondered if he really wanted to date her anymore.
8. The patient talked to the police detectives.[Who came to investigate his accident.]
9. Stacy went off her diet this afternoon/she ate fast food.
10. Her parents made her feel important and special in many ways.[For example, attending every one of her soccer games.]
11. Lend me two dollars, so I can get a cup of coffee,/then I'll be able to wake up. *("You" implied)*
12. Dora and Robert bought souvenirs for all their relatives.

13. A free lunch was served.[To those who attended the seminar.]
14. The scoreboard shows two outs/that must be a mistake.
15. Marek sealed the envelope and put it in the mail,/then he realized that he had forgotten to enclose the check.
16. Sergei told me the good news.[Which made me very happy.]
17. Fortunately, Stan didn't have the car for the day.
18. Cheyenne went to the circus with her son.[Since she had the day off work.]
19. Kari Kruise has a morning show on my favorite radio station,/I listen to her religiously.
20. [To be selected for the scholarship.]An applicant must be interviewed by the scholarship committee.

B. Correct the fragments and run-together sentences in Posttest IA by rewriting each incorrect sentence. *Answers will vary.*

Posttest II

A. Underline the subjects once and the verbs twice in the following paragraph. Cross out the prepositional phrases first. Then put the fragments in brackets ([ ]), and put a slash (/) between the run-together sentences.

I began snow boarding when I was two years old,/I have always loved the cold weather and the thrill of racing down the hill. [The wind stinging my cheeks.] I began racing with a snow-boarding team. [When I was five years old.]We traveled to different resorts on the weekends. I did dry-land training every day during the week. Being on the team was fun because most of my friends were on the team. When I got to high school. I was able to teach snow boarding at our local ski area. Now I'm on my own, /I still love to be in the cold.[And to snow board with my family when I can.]

B. Correct the fragments and run-together sentences in Posttest IIA by rewriting the paragraph. *Answers will vary.*

UNIT 2: VERBS

Here are some exercises that test your understanding of all the material in this unit: regular and irregular verbs, verb tense, subject-verb agreement, and more on verbs (consistent/inconsistent and active/passive).

Posttest I

A. Underline all the verb errors in the following sentences.

1. Dennis has set in that chair for so long that his legs has gone numb. *(sat, have)*
2. My grandparents in New England likes to sit on the front porch in the summer time. *(like)*
3. Parents with small children finds it hard to spend quiet time together. *(find)*
4. The car is broken; it need a new starter. *(needs)*
5. You have sank the golf ball. *(sunk)*
6. Mr. and Mrs. Titus have spoke to the person in charge. *(spoken)*
7. I type that report a couple of weeks ago and hope my employer liked it. *(typed, hoped)*
8. Last year, we watch the Fourth of July fireworks from our house. *(watched)*
9. Neither the steak nor the hamburgers needs seasoning on the grill. *(need)*
10. She grow tulips every spring. *(grows)*
11. I love to lay in the sun while listening to music. *(lie)*
12. We be having so much fun that we doesn't want to go home. *(are, don't)*
13. Since there are no vacancies at the hotel, we has nowhere to go. *(have)*
14. The water was spilled on the floor by you. *(You spilled water on the floor.)*
15. Mrs. Turner always smile whenever she sees me. *(smiles)*
16. Your tuition and parking fees is due at the beginning of school. *(are)*
17. There go my dog down the street again. *(goes)*
18. The police crew routinely stop drivers on the road to test for drunk driving. *(stops)*
19. Everything always go wrong on Friday the thirteenth. *(goes)*
20. When the surf breaks through the reef, it gushes into our backyard and flooded the deck. *(floods)*

B. Correct the verb errors in Posttest IA by rewriting each incorrect sentence. *See Posttest IA.*

Posttest II

A. Underline the verb errors in the following paragraph.

Every child want *wants* a hobby growing up. Not every child be *is* interested in playing sports or singing, but most children likes *like* activities that interested *interest* them. Children should not just set *sit* around after school. Kids are allowed by hobbies *Hobbies allow kids* to express themselves freely. This help *helps* them develop social skills, and it do *does* a lot for their self-confidence. Hobbies kept *keep* them occupied with productive activities. Hobbies have also connect *connected* many kids with caring adults, who then encourage them at their hobbies. Adults also has *have* kids set fun goals for themselves. Kids are kept *Hobbies keep kids* occupied and out of trouble by hobbies.

B. Correct the verb errors in Posttest IIA by rewriting the paragraph.
See Posttest IIA.

UNIT 3: PRONOUNS

Here are some exercises that test your understanding of all the material in this unit: pronoun problems, pronoun reference and point of view, and pronoun agreement.

Posttest I

A. Underline the pronoun errors in the following sentences.

1. Of all the science entries, we thought ours' was the best. *(ours)*
2. I do not talk as much as him. *(he)*
3. Each of the girls needs to have their hair cut. *(her)*
4. These clothes are too outrageous to be mine; they must be yours'. *(yours)*
5. A parent needs to pick up her child from school. *(his or her)*
6. No one should harm their body. *(his or her)*

7. During the earthquake, those there shelves shook loose. *(those)*
8. Brenda can sew better than me. *(I)*
9. Emma and Candace have gone to the beach for the weekend, but she is going to have to return home sooner than expected. *(Answers will vary.)*
10. With a bit more practice, you will be just as good at these video games as them. *(they)*
11. Between Olga and Valerie, she should be able to finish the work on time. *(Answers will vary.)*
12. You try to be nice to strangers because we never know when we might need help. *(We)*
13. A body can only take on so much before you suffer from stress. *(it suffers)*
14. You can always seek help from the counselors if someone has questions. *(you have)*
15. Neither of the doctors could diagnose their patient's illness. *(his or her)*
16. I realize that she sings better than him. *(he)*
17. Most of the stories need its titles rewritten. *(their)*
18. These here mosquitoes are about to drive me crazy. *(These)*
19. Another person must have left his books in class. *(his or her)*
20. At least one nurse forgot her uniform. *(his or her)*

B. Correct the pronoun errors in Posttest IA by rewriting each incorrect sentence. *See Posttest IA.*

Posttest II

A. Underline the pronoun errors in the following paragraph.

Many scientists say that soft music helps calm people's nerves. Some school officials are beginning to play soft music for his or her *their* students at the beginning of the day and after lunch to calm them down. The scientists' studies show that if a person sits down and listens to soft, relaxing music for at least five minutes every day, they *he or she* can reduce your *his or her* heart rate and lower your *his or her* blood pressure. For a person who has heart problems, this here *this* is a good way to supplement their *his or her* medical care. Scientists have studied it *this problem* for a long time, so people should be as wise as them *(they)* and follow his or her *(their)* advice. This *(This idea)* will benefit them *(people)* greatly.

B. Correct the pronoun errors in Posttest IIA by rewriting the paragraph.
See Posttest IIA.

UNIT 4: MODIFIERS

Here are some exercises that test your understanding of all the material in this unit: adjectives, adverbs, and modifier errors.

Posttest I

A. Underline the modifier errors in the following sentences.

1. During the test, Professor Gupta said we could talk quiet with our lab partners. *(quietly)*
2. While weeding my flower beds, the snails were all over. *(While weeding my flower beds, I saw that)*
3. He swam badly during the meet after staying up too late the night before. *(After staying up too late the night before, he)*
4. Tell your boss that you are more better at your job than he realizes. *(better)*
5. Pauly didn't get his mother nothing for her birthday. *(anything)*
6. Curtis got distracted, and his car drifted more sudden than he expected to the center divider. *(drifted to the center divider more suddenly than he expected)*
7. The pilot flew the jet as if there wasn't nothing to fear. *(anything)*
8. Turn your paper in at the end of class to your teacher. *(Turn your paper in to your teacher)*
9. If you do good on the midterm, you don't have to take the final exam. *(well)*
10. Handle the antiques more gentle than you did this morning because they are fragile. *(gently)*
11. I heard the most worst pickup line on TV the other day. *(worst)*
12. Nadia walked proud across the stage at her graduation. *(proudly)*
13. Anabel tiptoed quiet through the bedroom so she wouldn't wake the baby. *(quietly)*
14. To avoid writing bad checks, your account balance should be checked often. *(To avoid writing bad checks, you should check your account balance often.)*
15. Zena went to Alicia's house to get a cookie recipe next door. *(Zena went next door to Alicia's house)*

16. Dr. Romano told the most funniest jokes while he was examining my broken arm. *(funniest)*
17. Grandpa can't barely hear anymore. *(can barely)*
18. Women wore girdles laced up tight to look like they had very small waists. *(tightly; To look like they had very small waists, women)*
19. When Beth changed the oil in her car, she put the oil cap on too loose, and it fell off. *(loosely)*
20. The most prepared of the two athletes was Kareem. *(more prepared)*

B. Correct the modifier errors in Posttest IA by rewriting each incorrect sentence. *See Posttest IA.*

Posttest II

A. Underline the modifier errors in the following paragraph.

Health care in America is getting expensiver *(more expensive)* every year. Compared to other employers, my employer is more realistic *(most realistic)* about coverage. *(To save money)* Some companies are not hardly *(hardly)* taking care of their employees to save money; many no longer offer a complete benefits package to full- or part-time employees. Many people *(who work hard)* cannot afford no individual insurance plans on top of their monthly bills who work hard. Having to pay for insurance, eye and dental exams are often not purchased *(people are not purchasing eye and dental exams)*. People are quick *(quickly)* running out of options for affordable health care. If employers can't afford to offer their employees insurance plans, maybe in the future companies can find a more better *(better)* way to accommodate those who work for them.

B. Correct the modifier errors in Posttest IIA by rewriting the paragraph. *See Posttest IIA.*

UNIT 5: PUNCTUATION

Here are some exercises that test your understanding of all the material in this unit: end punctuation, commas, apostrophes, quotation marks, semicolons, colons, dashes, and parentheses.

Posttest I

A. Underline the punctuation errors in the following sentences.

1. The normal human body temperature is 98,6°.
2. We are having grilled chicken, asparagus, and French bread for dinner tonight.
3. The car looks great, and drives even better.
4. Is your mother paying your tuition.?
5. We were late to school, as usual, because we had to stop for gas.
6. You make me so angry!
7. Emily's car is newer than ours.
8. My mother still lives at 4901 El Sendero Ave., San Antonio, TX 78233.
9. "Without question," Cameron said, "that is the best option we have."
10. People shouldn't start smoking because it's a hard habit to break.
11. My favorite animals at the zoo were the monkeys, the hippos, and the zebras.
12. Wanting to get better grades, Mary, studied all weekend.
13. My computer crashed, so I lost my whole research paper.
14. The conference will cover three important issues: race relations, the economy, and global warming.
15. My sister joined the Army last June; she committed, to four years.
16. My favorite movies are romances, dramas, and horror films.
17. "Don't even think about it!" Janelle exclaimed.
18. His two uncles' briefcases are both leather.
19. Martina asked, if I had found her jacket.
20. Brad Pitt's worst movie ever, *Fight Club*, was still better than the best Mike Myers movie, *Austin Powers*.

B. Correct the punctuation errors in Posttest IA by rewriting each incorrect sentence. *See Posttest IA.*

Posttest II

A. Underline the punctuation errors in the following paragraph.

Waiting on tables, is a lot harder than most people think!Its a job that involves people skills organization and quick thinking. While servers are responsible for four tables in most restaurants some smaller restaurants give their servers' up to ten tables. A restaurant's staff(made up of hosts, hostesses, cooks, and servers) must remember two very important points about service:promptness, and pleasantness. It is not always easy to be prompt and pleasant,. Many customers wonder how servers carry large heavy tray's? Waiting tables can be hard: but it can be rewarding a good way to earn some money on a fairly flexible schedule.

B. Correct the punctuation errors in Posttest IIA by rewriting the paragraph. *See Posttest IIA.*

UNIT 6: MECHANICS

Here are some exercises that test your understanding of all the material in this unit: capitalization, abbreviations, and numbers.

Posttest I

A. Underline the errors in capitalization, abbreviations, and numbers in the following sentences.

1. My brother plans to earn his bachelor of science in physics. *(B.S.)*
2. She invested one thousand four hundred dollars last year. *($1,400)*
3. In a pinch, you can substitute one-half cup of shortening for one-half cup of butter. *(½, ½)*
4. After lunch at the hard rock café, let's shop on Rodeo drive. *(Hard Rock Café, Drive)*

5. The owners of the company expect profits of six million five hundred thousand dollars this year. *($6.5 million)*
6. My dog had 4 puppies. *(four)*
7. Of all the countries my aunt has visited, the U.S. is her favorite. *(United States)*
8. "That looks great," said the hairdresser, "But we need to take a little more off the top." *(but)*
9. The police officer clocked me driving too fast in front of the Columbia Broadcasting System building. *(CBS)*
10. Marcus visited Australia and then returned to the U.S. *(United States)*
11. The fence will cost five hundred dollars to fix. *($500)*
12. This semester, I plan on taking psychology 101 and sociology 200. *(Psychology, Sociology)*
13. Bro. Thomas visited me in the hospital. *(Brother)*
14. Mister Matthews takes a walk every night before he goes to bed. *(Mr.)*
15. Before taking the exam, review questions 5 through twenty in Exercise twenty-nine. *(20, 29)*
16. Charlton Heston is a vocal member of the national rifle association (NRA). *(National Rifle Association)*
17. I wake up at exactly 5:30 ante meridiem every day. *(a.m.)*
18. I work for the fbi, not the cia. *(FBI, CIA)*
19. Monique purchased three bags of balloons, 10 rolls of streamers, two banners, and one piñata for the party. *(3, 2, 1)*
20. The letter opened with these words: "my dearest Ralph." *(My Dearest)*

B. Correct the errors in capitalization, abbreviations, and numbers in Posttest IA by rewriting each incorrect sentence. *See Posttest IA.*

Posttest II

A. Underline the errors in capitalization, abbreviations, and numbers in the following paragraph.

Last spring *(Spring)*, my family and I went to Alaska on vacation. We went for eleven *(11)* days; we stayed from monday *(Monday)*, June third *(3)* through thursday *(Thursday)*, June fourteenth *(14)*. Some of my extended family, including grandpa *(Grandpa)* Joe and auntie *(Auntie)* Jane, came with us. While we were there, we ate at Fish and chips *[Chips]*, which is a small diner on the coast. I found so many cute souvenirs for my Friends *[friends]*; I even found a postcard to mail to my elderly friend, Misses *[Mrs.]* Calen. However, I couldn't remember if her address was 6260 Minden Dr *[Drive]*, Carlsbad, New Mexico *[NM]* 88220 or 6220 Minden Ave *[Avenue]*, Carlsbad, New Mexico *[NM]* 88260, so I had to give the postcard to her when I got home. Even with all of the souvenirs I bought, the trip cost me only nine-hundred dollars *[$900]*, which is only thirty *[30]* percent of what our last family trip cost me.

B. Correct the errors in capitalization, abbreviations, and numbers in Posttest IIA by rewriting the paragraph. *See Posttest IIA.*

UNIT 7: EFFECTIVE SENTENCES

Here are some exercises that test your understanding of all the material in this unit: varying sentence structure, parallelism, and combining sentences.

Posttest I

A. Label the errors in each of the following sentences in variety, parallelism, and sentence combining.

1. We went on a trip to Canada. We visited many relatives. We had never even met these relatives before. *(variety, sentence combining)*
2. Myra should not eat before swimming. She will get sick. *(sentence combining)*
3. She's been in trouble before. She usually gets out of it. She knows how. *(variety, sentence combining)*
4. I worked late last night. I had a deadline to meet. The deadline was on my project. *(variety, sentence combining)*
5. I like the water. I don't know how to swim. *(sentence combining)*
6. We decided we would do nothing but relax, read, and swimming this weekend. *(parallelism)*
7. Salsa dancing is hard. You can do it if you practice. Practice takes time. *(variety, sentence combining)*
8. Hanna loves working with small children. She's a babysitter. *(sentence combining)*
9. The two boys dared each other. They jumped into the cold pool. It was 3 a.m. *(variety, sentence combining)*

10. The neighbors are complaining. The neighbors didn't like the loud noises. *(sentence combining)*
11. Becky likes math. Math is her major. *(sentence combining)*
12. You will have to buy lunch. You can bring your own. *(sentence combining)*
13. Take this letter to the post office for me. It is important. It will need postage. *(variety, sentence combining)*
14. He was racing across the field, was jumping over the hedges, and fell into the pond. *(parallelism)*
15. You are smart. You will understand this problem. This problem is complex. *(variety, sentence combining)*
16. The monkeys are jumping from tree to tree. They are lively. *(sentence combining)*
17. Leo shouldn't watch so much television. He should not stay up so late at night. *(sentence combining)*
18. My nieces are sleeping in my bed, wearing my clothes, and will drive me crazy. *(parallelism)*
19. He isn't going to work today because he feels ill. He has plenty of sick leave left. *(sentence combining)*
20. Our car broke down. Juanita and I decided to fly to Las Vegas. *(sentence combining)*

B. Correct the errors you identified in Posttest IA by rewriting each incorrect sentence. *Answers will vary.*

Posttest II

A. Label the errors in the following paragraph in variety, parallelism, and sentence combining.

(1) Learning to write is like learning to ride a bike. *(2)* Learning to write is fun once people learn how. *(3)* Learning to write involves learning several of the components of writing. *(4)* Some of the components of writing are grammar, audience, and to organize. *(5)* People are sometimes nervous about writing. *(6)* They don't know how to approach an assignment. *(7)* Once people master each component of writing, they usually enjoy journals, writing creative fiction, and even to write research papers. *(8)* Writing can become easy and fun. *(9)* People need to give

writing a chance. (10) People just need to practice. (11) They would see their writing improve.

1–3 variety, sentence combining; 4 parallelism; 5–6 sentence combining; 7 parallelism; 8–9 sentence combining; 10–11 sentence combining

B. Correct the errors you identified in Posttest IIA by rewriting the paragraph. *Answers will vary.*

UNIT 8: CHOOSING THE RIGHT WORD

Here are some exercises that test your understanding of all the material in this unit: standard and nonstandard English, easily confused words, and spelling.

Posttest I

A. Underline the word choice and spelling errors in the following sentences.

1. I use to walk to work, but now I have a car. *(used to)*
2. I plan to lay in my bed all day reading a good book. *(lie)*
3. When she realized her zipper was open, she was very embarassed. *(embarrassed)*
4. I cannot decieve you; I ate the last cookie. *(deceive)*
5. Jefferson lost his surfboard to. *(too)*
6. If the students work hard, they can rise enough money for their trip. *(raise)*
7. If our star player doesn't get here soon, we will have to forfiet the game. *(forfeit)*
8. Please be quite while in the libary. *(quiet, library)*
9. My best friend got busted for staying out to late. *(caught, too)*
10. Beside giving me a mother's unconditional love, my mom is also my best friend. *(Besides)*
11. Their already on the plane. *(They're)*
12. Speak louder—I can't here you. *(hear)*
13. Cassie is better with computers then he is. *(than)*
14. The theif stole Rhonda's stereo. *(thief)*
15. Leanne choose to volunteer at the homeless shelter. *(chose)*

16. Sam must <u>of</u> forgotten that we were <u>suppose</u> to have lunch today. *(must've or must have, supposed)*
17. Please <u>except</u> my congratulations on your promotion. *(accept)*
18. He's definitely <u>weirded out</u>. *(lost control)*
19. The <u>affect</u> was devastating on my ego. *(effect)*
20. The <u>course</u> material scratched the baby's skin. *(coarse)*

B. Correct the errors in Posttest IA by rewriting each incorrect sentence. *See Posttest IA.*

Posttest II

A. Underline the word choice and spelling errors in the following paragraph.

Protecting the <u>enviurnment</u> *(environment)* is important <u>everywheres</u> *(everywhere)*. People <u>use to</u> *(used to)* think less about <u>ecolegy</u> *(ecology)* <u>then</u> *(than)* they do today. They couldn't <u>concieve</u> *(conceive)* of the fact that a problem was being created by <u>exaust</u> *(exhaust)* and other toxins. Now <u>their</u> *(there)* are organizations dedicated to protecting us from <u>excesive polution</u> *(excessive pollution)*. These organizations help the <u>goverment</u> *(government)* make laws that protect the <u>enviurnment</u> *(environment)*. <u>Than</u> *(Then)*, stricter laws help the <u>goverment</u> *(government)* keep track of <u>whose</u> *(who's)* causing pollution problems in the United States. People must begin to take <u>responsability</u> *(responsibility)* for doing <u>there</u> *(their)* part to help protect <u>are</u> *(our)* air, land, and water; this is the only way <u>are</u> *(our)* children will have a clean place to live in the future.

B. Correct the word choice and spelling errors in Posttest IIA by rewriting the paragraph. *See Posttest IIA.*

APPENDIX 1 Critical Thinking Log

Circle the critical thinking questions that you missed after each essay you read. Have your instructor explain the pattern of errors.

Reading	Content	Purpose and Audience	Essays	Number Correct
Describing				
Mario Suarez	1 2 3	4 5 6	7 8 9 10	
Linda Hogan	1 2 3	4 5 6	7 8 9 10	
Narrating				
Lynda Barry	1 2 3	4 5 6	7 8 9 10	
Stan Higgins	1 2 3	4 5 6	7 8 9 10	
Illustrating				
Richard Rodriguez	1 2 3	4 5 6	7 8 9 10	
France Borel	1 2 3	4 5 6	7 8 9 10	
Analyzing a Process				
Roger Flax	1 2 3	4 5 6	7 8 9 10	
David Levy	1 2 3	4 5 6	7 8 9 10	
Comparing/Contrasting				
Yi-Fu Tuan	1 2 3	4 5 6	7 8 9 10	
Tony Cohan	1 2 3	4 5 6	7 8 9 10	
Dividing/Classifying				
Bernice Reagon	1 2 3	4 5 6	7 8 9 10	
Marion Winik	1 2 3	4 5 6	7 8 9 10	
Defining				
Isaac Asimov	1 2 3	4 5 6	7 8 9 10	
Janice Castro	1 2 3	4 5 6	7 8 9 10	
Analyzing Causes/Effects				
Linda Lee Andujar	1 2 3	4 5 6	7 8 9 10	
Stacey Colino	1 2 3	4 5 6	7 8 9 10	
Arguing				
Dave Grossman	1 2 3	4 5 6	7 8 9 10	
Willard and Cole	1 2 3	4 5 6	7 8 9 10	

The legend on the next page will help you identify your strengths and weaknesses in critical thinking.

Legend for Critical Thinking Log

Questions	Skill
1–2	Literal and interpretive understanding
3–6	Critical thinking and analysis
7–9	Analyzing sentences
10	Writing essays

APPENDIX 2A Revising

Description Peer Evaluation Form

Use the following questions to evaluate your partner's essay. Direct your comments to your partner. Explain your answers as thoroughly as possible to help your partner revise.

WRITER: ____________________ **PEER:** ____________________

Describing

1. Is the dominant impression clearly communicated?
2. Does the essay use objective and subjective descriptions when needed?
3. Does the essay draw on all five senses?
4. Does the essay show rather than tell?

Thesis Statement

5. Does the thesis statement contain the essay's controlling idea and an opinion about that idea?
6. Does the thesis appear as the last sentence of the introduction?

Basic Elements

7. Does the essay have all the basic elements? Is each one effective?

Development

8. Does each paragraph support the thesis statement?
9. Does each paragraph contain enough specific details to develop its topic sentence?

Unity

10. Do all the essay's topic sentences relate directly to the thesis statement?
11. Do the details in each paragraph support its topic sentence?

Organization

12. Is the essay organized logically?
13. Is each body paragraph organized logically?

Coherence

14. Are transitions used effectively so that paragraphs move smoothly and logically from one to the next?
15. Do the sentences move smoothly and logically from one to the next?

APPENDIX 2A Editing

Description Peer Evaluation Form

Use the following questions to help you find editing errors in your partner's essay. Mark the errors directly on your partner's paper using the editing symbols on the inside back cover.

WRITER: ______________________ **PEER:** ______________________

Sentences

1. Does each sentence have a subject and verb?
   Mark any fragments you find with **frag.**
   Put a slash (/) between any fused sentences and comma splices.
2. Do all subjects and verbs agree?
   Mark any subject-verb agreement errors you find with **sv.**
3. Do all pronouns agree with their nouns?
   Mark any pronoun errors you find with **pro agr.**
4. Are all modifiers as close as possible to the words they modify?
   Mark any modifier errors you find with **ad** (adjective or adverb problem), **mm** (misplaced modifier), or **dm** (dangling modifier).

Punctuation and Mechanics

5. Are sentences punctuated correctly?
   Mark any punctuation errors you find with the appropriate symbol under Unit 5 of the editing symbols (inside back cover).
6. Are words capitalized properly?
   Mark any capitalization errors you find with **lc** (lowercase) or **cap** (capital).

Word Choice and Spelling

7. Are words used correctly?
   Mark any words that are used incorrectly with **wc** (word choice) or **ww** (wrong word).
8. Are words spelled correctly?
   Mark any misspelled words you find with **sp.**

Narration Peer Evaluation Form

Use the following questions to evaluate your partner's essay. Direct your comments to your partner. Explain your answers as thoroughly as possible to help your partner revise.

WRITER: ____________________ PEER: ____________________

Narrating

1. What is the essay's main point? If you're not sure, show the writer how he or she can make the main point clearer.
2. Does the writer use the five W's and one H to construct the essay? Where does the essay need more information?
3. Does the writer develop the essay with vivid details? Where can more details be added?
4. Does the writer build excitement with careful pacing?

Thesis Statement

5. Does the thesis statement contain the essay's controlling idea and an opinion about that idea?
6. Does the thesis appear as the last sentence of the introduction?

Basic Elements

7. Does the essay have all the basic elements? Is each one effective?

Development

8. Does each paragraph support the thesis statement?
9. Does each paragraph contain enough specific details to develop its topic sentence?

Unity

10. Do all the essay's topic sentences relate directly to the thesis statement?
11. Do the details in each paragraph support its topic sentence?

Organization

12. Is the essay organized logically?
13. Is each body paragraph organized logically?

Coherence

14. Are transitions used effectively so that paragraphs move smoothly and logically from one to the next?
15. Do the sentences move smoothly and logically from one to the next?

APPENDIX 2B Editing

Narration Peer Evaluation Form

Use the following questions to help you find editing errors in your partner's essay. Mark the errors directly on your partner's paper using the editing symbols on the inside back cover.

WRITER: ______________________ PEER: ______________________

Sentences

1. Does each sentence have a subject and verb?
   Mark any fragments you find with **frag.**
   Put a slash (/) between any fused sentences and comma splices.
2. Do all subjects and verbs agree?
   Mark any subject-verb agreement errors you find with **sv.**
3. Do all pronouns agree with their nouns?
   Mark any pronoun errors you find with **pro agr.**
4. Are all modifiers as close as possible to the words they modify?
   Mark any modifier errors you find with **ad** (adjective or adverb problem), **mm** (misplaced modifier), or **dm** (dangling modifier).

Punctuation and Mechanics

5. Are sentences punctuated correctly?
   Mark any punctuation errors you find with the appropriate symbol under Unit 5 of the editing symbols (inside back cover).
6. Are words capitalized properly?
   Mark any capitalization errors you find with **lc** (lowercase) or **cap** (capital).

Word Choice and Spelling

7. Are words used correctly?
   Mark any words that are used incorrectly with **wc** (word choice) or **ww** (wrong word).
8. Are words spelled correctly?
   Mark any misspelled words you find with **sp.**

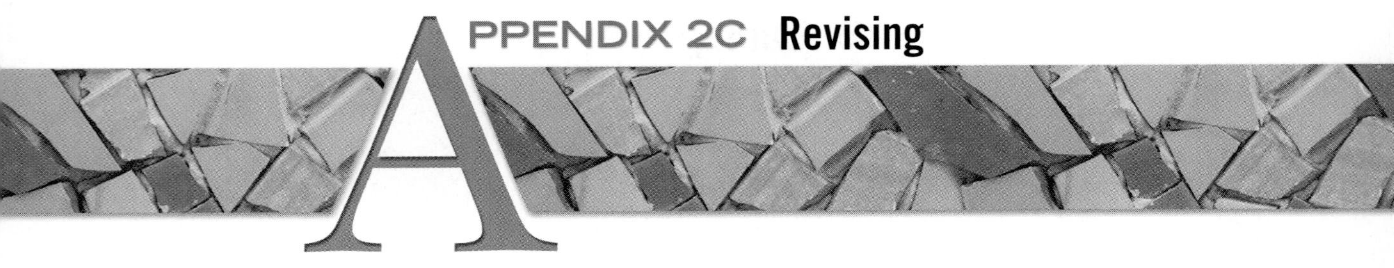

APPENDIX 2C Revising

Illustration Peer Evaluation Form

Use the following questions to evaluate your partner's essay. Direct your comments to your partner. Explain your answers as thoroughly as possible to help your partner revise.

WRITER: ______________________ PEER: ______________________

Illustrating

1. What is the essay's main point? If you're not sure, show the writer how he or she can make the main point clearer.
2. Did the writer choose examples that are relevant to the main point? If not, which examples need to be changed?
3. Does the writer choose examples that the reader can identify with? If not, which examples need to be changed?
4. Does the writer use a sufficient number of examples to make his or her point? Where can more examples be added?

Thesis Statement

5. Does the thesis statement contain the essay's controlling idea and an opinion about that idea?
6. Does the thesis appear as the last sentence of the introduction?

Basic Elements

7. Does the essay have all the basic elements? Is each one effective?

Development

8. Does each paragraph support the thesis statement?
9. Does each paragraph contain enough specific details to develop its topic sentence?

Unity

10. Do all the essay's topic sentences relate directly to the thesis statement?
11. Do the details in each paragraph support its topic sentence?

Organization

12. Is the essay organized logically?
13. Is each body paragraph organized logically?

Coherence

14. Are transitions used effectively so that paragraphs move smoothly and logically from one to the next?
15. Do the sentences move smoothly and logically from one to the next?

APPENDIX 2C Editing

Illustration Peer Evaluation Form

Use the following questions to help you find editing errors in your partner's essay. Mark the errors directly on your partner's paper using the editing symbols on the inside back cover.

WRITER: ______________________ **PEER:** ______________________

Sentences

1. Does each sentence have a subject and verb?

   Mark any fragments you find with **frag.**

   Put a slash (/) between any fused sentences and comma splices.
2. Do all subjects and verbs agree?

   Mark any subject-verb agreement errors you find with **sv.**
3. Do all pronouns agree with their nouns?

   Mark any pronoun errors you find with **pro agr.**
4. Are all modifiers as close as possible to the words they modify?

   Mark any modifier errors you find with **ad** (adjective or adverb problem), **mm** (misplaced modifier), or **dm** (dangling modifier).

Punctuation and Mechanics

5. Are sentences punctuated correctly?

   Mark any punctuation errors you find with the appropriate symbol under Unit 5 of the editing symbols (inside back cover).
6. Are words capitalized properly?

   Mark any capitalization errors you find with **lc** (lowercase) or **cap** (capital).

Word Choice and Spelling

7. Are words used correctly?

   Mark any words that are used incorrectly with **wc** (word choice) or **ww** (wrong word).
8. Are words spelled correctly?

   Mark any misspelled words you find with **sp.**

APPENDIX 2D Revising

Process Analysis Peer Evaluation Form

Use the following questions to evaluate your partner's essay. Direct your comments to your partner. Explain your answers as thoroughly as possible to help your partner revise.

WRITER: ______________________ PEER: ______________________

Analyzing a Process

1. Does the writer state in the thesis statement what the reader should be able to do or understand by the end of the essay? If not, what information does the thesis statement need to be clearer?
2. Does the writer know his or her audience?
3. Does the remainder of the essay explain the rest of the process? If not, what seems to be missing?
4. Does the writer end the process essay by considering the process as a whole?

Thesis Statement

5. Does the thesis statement contain the essay's controlling idea and an opinion about that idea?
6. Does the thesis appear as the last sentence of the introduction?

Basic Elements

7. Does the essay have all the basic elements? Is each one effective?

Development

8. Does each paragraph support the thesis statement?
9. Does each paragraph contain enough specific details to develop its topic sentence?

Unity

10. Do all the essay's topic sentences relate directly to the thesis statement?
11. Do the details in each paragraph support its topic sentence?

Organization

12. Is the essay organized logically?
13. Is each body paragraph organized logically?

Coherence

14. Are transitions used effectively so that paragraphs move smoothly and logically from one to the next?
15. Do the sentences move smoothly and logically from one to the next?

APPENDIX 2D Editing

Process Analysis Peer Evaluation Form

Use the following questions to help you find editing errors in your partner's essay. Mark the errors directly on your partner's paper using the editing symbols on the inside back cover.

WRITER: ______________________ **PEER:** ______________________

Sentences

1. Does each sentence have a subject and verb?
   Mark any fragments you find with **frag.**
   Put a slash (/) between any fused sentences and comma splices.
2. Do all subjects and verbs agree?
   Mark any subject-verb agreement errors you find with **sv.**
3. Do all pronouns agree with their nouns?
   Mark any pronoun errors you find with **pro agr.**
4. Are all modifiers as close as possible to the words they modify?
   Mark any modifier errors you find with **ad** (adjective or adverb problem), **mm** (misplaced modifier), or **dm** (dangling modifier).

Punctuation and Mechanics

5. Are sentences punctuated correctly?
   Mark any punctuation errors you find with the appropriate symbol under Unit 5 of the editing symbols (inside back cover).
6. Are words capitalized properly?
   Mark any capitalization errors you find with **lc** (lowercase) or **cap** (capital).

Word Choice and Spelling

7. Are words used correctly?
   Mark any words that are used incorrectly with **wc** (word choice) or **ww** (wrong word).
8. Are words spelled correctly?
   Mark any misspelled words you find with **sp.**

APPENDIX 2E Revising

Comparison/Contrast Peer Evaluation Form

Use the following questions to evaluate your partner's essay. Direct your comments to your partner. Explain your answers as thoroughly as possible to help your partner revise.

WRITER: ________________________ PEER: ________________________

Comparing and Contrasting

1. Does the writer state the point he or she is trying to make in the thesis statement?
2. Does the writer choose items to compare and contrast that will make his or her point most effectively? What details need to be added to make the comparison more effective?
3. Does the writer use as many specific details and examples as possible to expand the comparison?
4. Is the comparison developed in a balanced way?

Thesis Statement

5. Does the thesis statement contain the essay's controlling idea and an opinion about that idea?
6. Does the thesis appear as the last sentence of the introduction?

Basic Elements

7. Does the essay have all the basic elements? Is each one effective?

Development

8. Does each paragraph support the thesis statement?
9. Does each paragraph contain enough specific details to develop its topic sentence?

Unity

10. Do all the essay's topic sentences relate directly to the thesis statement?
11. Do the details in each paragraph support its topic sentence?

Organization

12. Is the essay organized logically?
13. Is each body paragraph organized logically?

Coherence

14. Are transitions used effectively so that paragraphs move smoothly and logically from one to the next?
15. Do the sentences move smoothly and logically from one to the next?

APPENDIX 2E Editing

Comparison/Contrast Peer Evaluation Form

Use the following questions to help you find editing errors in your partner's essay. Mark the errors directly on your partner's paper using the editing symbols on the inside back cover.

WRITER: ________________________ **PEER:** ________________________

Sentences

1. Does each sentence have a subject and verb?
   Mark any fragments you find with **frag.**
   Put a slash (/) between any fused sentences and comma splices.
2. Do all subjects and verbs agree?
   Mark any subject-verb agreement errors you find with **sv.**
3. Do all pronouns agree with their nouns?
   Mark any pronoun errors you find with **pro agr.**
4. Are all modifiers as close as possible to the words they modify?
   Mark any modifier errors you find with **ad** (adjective or adverb problem), **mm** (misplaced modifier), or **dm** (dangling modifier).

Punctuation and Mechanics

5. Are sentences punctuated correctly?
   Mark any punctuation errors you find with the appropriate symbol under Unit 5 of the editing symbols (inside back cover).
6. Are words capitalized properly?
   Mark any capitalization errors you find with **lc** (lowercase) or **cap** (capital).

Word Choice and Spelling

7. Are words used correctly?
   Mark any words that are used incorrectly with **wc** (word choice) or **ww** (wrong word).
8. Are words spelled correctly?
   Mark any misspelled words you find with **sp.**

APPENDIX 2F Revising

Division/Classification Peer Evaluation Form

Use the following questions to evaluate your partner's essay. Direct your comments to your partner. Explain your answers as thoroughly as possible to help your partner revise.

WRITER: ______________________ PEER: ______________________

Dividing and Classifying

1. What is the overall purpose for the essay, and is it stated in the thesis statement? If not, where does the essay need clarification?
2. Did the writer divide the general topic into categories that don't overlap?
3. Did the writer clearly explain each category?
4. Does each topic fit into a category?

Thesis Statement

5. Does the thesis statement contain the essay's controlling idea and an opinion about that idea?
6. Does the thesis appear as the last sentence of the introduction?

Basic Elements

7. Does the essay have all the basic elements? Is each one effective?

Development

8. Does each paragraph support the thesis statement?
9. Does each paragraph contain enough specific details to develop its topic sentence?

Unity

10. Do all the essay's topic sentences relate directly to the thesis statement?
11. Do the details in each paragraph support its topic sentence?

Organization

12. Is the essay organized logically?
13. Is each body paragraph organized logically?

Coherence

14. Are transitions used effectively so that paragraphs move smoothly and logically from one to the next?
15. Do the sentences move smoothly and logically from one to the next?

APPENDIX 2F Editing

Division/Classification Peer Evaluation Form

Use the following questions to help you find editing errors in your partner's essay. Mark the errors directly on your partner's paper using the editing symbols on the inside back cover.

WRITER: ______________________ **PEER:** ______________________

Sentences

1. Does each sentence have a subject and verb?
   Mark any fragments you find with **frag.**
   Put a slash (/) between any fused sentences and comma splices.
2. Do all subjects and verbs agree?
   Mark any subject-verb agreement errors you find with **sv.**
3. Do all pronouns agree with their nouns?
   Mark any pronoun errors you find with **pro agr.**
4. Are all modifiers as close as possible to the words they modify?
   Mark any modifier errors you find with **ad** (adjective or adverb problem), **mm** (misplaced modifier), or **dm** (dangling modifier).

Punctuation and Mechanics

5. Are sentences punctuated correctly?
   Mark any punctuation errors you find with the appropriate symbol under Unit 5 of the editing symbols (inside back cover).
6. Are words capitalized properly?
   Mark any capitalization errors you find with **lc** (lowercase) or **cap** (capital).

Word Choice and Spelling

7. Are words used correctly?
   Mark any words that are used incorrectly with **wc** (word choice) or **ww** (wrong word).
8. Are words spelled correctly?
   Mark any misspelled words you find with **sp.**

Definition Peer Evaluation Form

Use the following questions to evaluate your partner's paragraph. Direct your comments to your partner. Explain your answers as thoroughly as possible to help your partner revise.

WRITER: ________________________ PEER: ________________________

Defining

1. Did the writer choose a word or idea carefully and give readers a working definition of it in the thesis statement?
2. Does the writer define his or her term or idea by synonym, category, or negation? Is this approach effective? Why or why not?
3. Does the writer use examples to expand on his or her definition of the term or idea? Where does the definition need more information?
4. Does the writer use other rhetorical strategies, such as description, comparison, or process analysis, to support the definition?

Thesis Statement

5. Does the thesis statement contain the essay's controlling idea and an opinion about that idea?
6. Does the thesis appear as the last sentence of the introduction?

Basic Elements

7. Does the essay have all the basic elements? Is each one effective?

Development

8. Does each paragraph support the thesis statement?
9. Does each paragraph contain enough specific details to develop its topic sentence?

Unity

10. Do all the essay's topic sentences relate directly to the thesis statement?
11. Do the details in each paragraph support its topic sentence?

Organization

12. Is the essay organized logically?
13. Is each body paragraph organized logically?

Coherence

14. Are transitions used effectively so that paragraphs move smoothly and logically from one to the next?
15. Do the sentences move smoothly and logically from one to the next?

Definition Peer Evaluation Form

Use the following questions to help you find editing errors in your partner's essay. Mark the errors directly on your partner's paper using the editing symbols on the inside back cover.

WRITER: ______________________ **PEER:** ______________________

Sentences

1. Does each sentence have a subject and verb?
   Mark any fragments you find with **frag.**
   Put a slash (/) between any fused sentences and comma splices.
2. Do all subjects and verbs agree?
   Mark any subject-verb agreement errors you find with **sv.**
3. Do all pronouns agree with their nouns?
   Mark any pronoun errors you find with **pro agr.**
4. Are all modifiers as close as possible to the words they modify?
   Mark any modifier errors you find with **ad** (adjective or adverb problem), **mm** (misplaced modifier), or **dm** (dangling modifier).

Punctuation and Mechanics

5. Are sentences punctuated correctly?
   Mark any punctuation errors you find with the appropriate symbol under Unit 5 of the editing symbols (inside back cover).
6. Are words capitalized properly?
   Mark any capitalization errors you find with **lc** (lowercase) or **cap** (capital).

Word Choice and Spelling

7. Are words used correctly?
   Mark any words that are used incorrectly with **wc** (word choice) or **ww** (wrong word).
8. Are words spelled correctly?
   Mark any misspelled words you find with **sp.**

APPENDIX 2H Revising

Cause/Effect Peer Evaluation Form

Use the following questions to evaluate your partner's essay. Direct your comments to your partner. Explain your answers as thoroughly as possible to help your partner revise.

WRITER: ______________________ PEER: ______________________

Analyzing Causes and Effects

1. Does the thesis statement make a clear statement about what is being analyzed? If not, what information does it need to be clearer?
2. Did the writer choose facts and details to support the topic sentence? What details need to be added?
3. Does the writer confuse coincidence with causes or effects?
4. Does the writer include the real causes and effects for his or her topic? What details are unnecessary?

Thesis Statement

5. Does the thesis statement contain the essay's controlling idea and an opinion about that idea?
6. Does the thesis appear as the last sentence of the introduction?

Basic Elements

7. Does the essay have all the basic elements? Is each one effective?

Development

8. Does each paragraph support the thesis statement?
9. Does each paragraph contain enough specific details to develop its topic sentence?

Unity

10. Do all the essay's topic sentences relate directly to the thesis statement?
11. Do the details in each paragraph support its topic sentence?

Organization

12. Is the essay organized logically?
13. Is each body paragraph organized logically?

Coherence

14. Are transitions used effectively so that paragraphs move smoothly and logically from one to the next?
15. Do the sentences move smoothly and logically from one to the next?

APPENDIX 2H Editing

Cause/Effect Peer Evaluation Form

Use the following questions to help you find editing errors in your partner's essay. Mark the errors directly on your partner's paper using the editing symbols on the inside back cover.

WRITER: _________________________ **PEER:** _________________________

Sentences

1. Does each sentence have a subject and verb?
   Mark any fragments you find with **frag.**
   Put a slash (/) between any fused sentences and comma splices.
2. Do all subjects and verbs agree?
   Mark any subject-verb agreement errors you find with **sv.**
3. Do all pronouns agree with their nouns?
   Mark any pronoun errors you find with **pro agr.**
4. Are all modifiers as close as possible to the words they modify?
   Mark any modifier errors you find with **ad** (adjective or adverb problem), **mm** (misplaced modifier), or **dm** (dangling modifier).

Punctuation and Mechanics

5. Are sentences punctuated correctly?
   Mark any punctuation errors you find with the appropriate symbol under Unit 5 of the editing symbols (inside back cover).
6. Are words capitalized properly?
   Mark any capitalization errors you find with **lc** (lowercase) or **cap** (capital).

Word Choice and Spelling

7. Are words used correctly?
   Mark any words that are used incorrectly with **wc** (word choice) or **ww** (wrong word).
8. Are words spelled correctly?
   Mark any misspelled words you find with **sp.**

Argument Peer Evaluation Form

Use the following questions to evaluate your partner's essay. Direct your comments to your partner. Explain your answers as thoroughly as possible to help your partner revise.

WRITER: ______________________ PEER: ______________________

Arguing

1. Does the writer state his or her opinion on the subject matter in the thesis statement? What information is missing?
2. Who is the intended audience for this essay? Does the writer adequately persuade this audience? Why or why not?
3. Does the writer choose appropriate evidence to support the thesis statement? What evidence is needed? What evidence is unnecessary?
4. Does the writer anticipate the opposing points of view?
5. Does the writer find some common ground?
6. Does the writer maintain a reasonable tone?

Thesis Statement

7. Does the thesis statement contain the essay's controlling idea and an opinion about that idea?
8. Does the thesis appear as the last sentence of the introduction?

Basic Elements

9. Does the essay have all the basic elements? Is each one effective?

Development

10. Does each paragraph support the thesis statement?
11. Does each paragraph contain enough specific details to develop its topic sentence?

Unity

12. Do all the essay's topic sentences relate directly to the thesis statement?
13. Do the details in each paragraph support its topic sentence?

Organization

14. Is the essay organized logically?
15. Is each body paragraph organized logically?

Coherence

16. Are transitions used effectively so that paragraphs move smoothly and logically from one to the next?
17. Do the sentences move smoothly and logically from one to the next?

APPENDIX 21 Editing

Argument Peer Evaluation Form

Use the following questions to help you find editing errors in your partner's essay. Mark the errors directly on your partner's paper using the editing symbols on the inside back cover.

WRITER: ______________________ PEER: ______________________

Sentences

1. Does each sentence have a subject and verb?
   Mark any fragments you find with **frag.**
   Put a slash (/) between any fused sentences and comma splices.
2. Do all subjects and verbs agree?
   Mark any subject-verb agreement errors you find with **sv.**
3. Do all pronouns agree with their nouns?
   Mark any pronoun errors you find with **pro agr.**
4. Are all modifiers as close as possible to the words they modify?
   Mark any modifier errors you find with **ad** (adjective or adverb problem), **mm** (misplaced modifier), or **dm** (dangling modifier).

Punctuation and Mechanics

5. Are sentences punctuated correctly?
   Mark any punctuation errors you find with the appropriate symbol under Unit 5 of the editing symbols (inside back cover).
6. Are words capitalized properly?
   Mark any capitalization errors you find with **lc** (lowercase) or **cap** (capital).

Word Choice and Spelling

7. Are words used correctly?
   Mark any words that are used incorrectly with **wc** (word choice) or **ww** (wrong word).
8. Are words spelled correctly?
   Mark any misspelled words you find with **sp.**

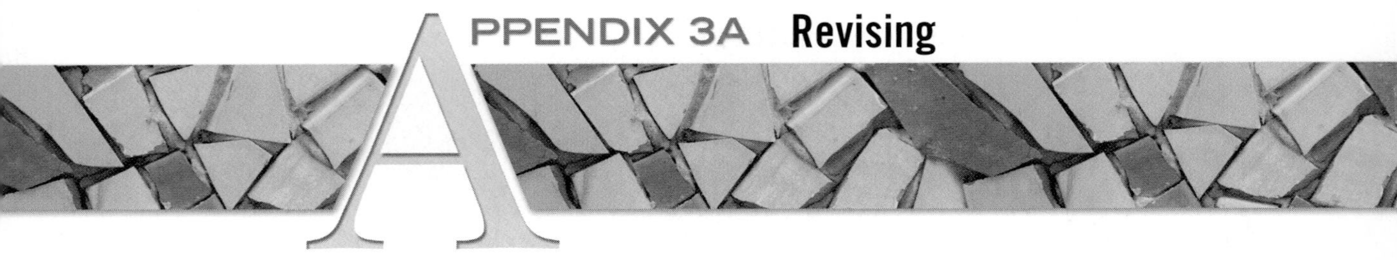

APPENDIX 3A Revising

Research Paper Peer Evaluation Form

Use the following questions to evaluate your partner's paper. Direct your comments to your partner. Explain your answers as thoroughly as possible to help your partner revise.

WRITER: ______________________ PEER: ______________________

Writing an Essay with Sources

1. Did the writer choose a subject that is neither too broad nor too narrow?
2. Did the writer find sources that are relevant, reliable, and recent to support the thesis?
3. Do you see any problems with plagiarism in the writer's paper?
4. Does the writer incorporate sources and document properly? Check the writer's sources and documentation format—in the paper and at the end.

Thesis Statement

5. Does the thesis statement contain the essay's controlling idea and an opinion about that idea?
6. Does the thesis appear as the last sentence of the introduction?

Basic Elements

7. Does the essay have all the basic elements? Is each one effective?

Development

8. Does each paragraph support the thesis statement?
9. Does each paragraph contain enough specific details to develop its topic sentence?

Unity

10. Do all the essay's topic sentences relate directly to the thesis statement?
11. Do the details in each paragraph support its topic sentence?

Organization

12. Is the essay organized logically?
13. Is each body paragraph organized logically?

Coherence

14. Are transitions used effectively so that paragraphs move smoothly and logically from one to the next?
15. Do the sentences move smoothly and logically from one to the next?

APPENDIX 3B Editing

Research Paper Peer Evaluation Form

Use the following questions to help you find editing errors in your partner's essay. Mark the errors directly on your partner's paper using the editing symbols on the inside back cover.

WRITER: ______________________ **PEER:** ______________________

Sentences

1. Does each sentence have a subject and verb?

   Mark any fragments you find with **frag.**

   Put a slash (/) between any fused sentences and comma splices.

2. Do all subjects and verbs agree?

   Mark any subject-verb agreement errors you find with **sv.**

3. Do all pronouns agree with their nouns?

   Mark any pronoun errors you find with **pro agr.**

4. Are all modifiers as close as possible to the words they modify?

   Mark any modifier errors you find with **ad** (adjective or adverb problem), **mm** (misplaced modifier), or **dm** (dangling modifier).

Punctuation and Mechanics

5. Are sentences punctuated correctly?

   Mark any punctuation errors you find with the appropriate symbol under Unit 5 of the editing symbols (inside back cover).

6. Are words capitalized properly?

   Mark any capitalization errors you find with **lc** (lowercase) or **cap** (capital).

Word Choice and Spelling

7. Are words used correctly?

   Mark any words that are used incorrectly with **wc** (word choice) or **ww** (wrong word).

8. Are words spelled correctly?

   Mark any misspelled words you find with **sp.**

APPENDIX 4 Test Yourself Answers

Here are the answers to the Test Yourself questions from the beginning of each chapter in the Handbook (Part IV). Where are your strengths? Where are your weaknesses?

Introduction: Chapter 24 Parts of Speech (p. 511)

adj n v adv adj n adj adj n adj
Professional basketball is definitely this nation's best spectator sport. The talented
n v prep n adv adv pro n adv v n
players move around the court so quickly that the audience never has a chance
prep v adj int pro/v adv v adj adj n adj n
to become bored. Boy, I'll never forget that Saturday night last February
conj pro adj n v pro prep v adj n prep n
when my favorite uncle took me to see the Spurs game against the Trailblazers.
pro v adj adj n prep n conj n v adj
It was an important home game for San Antonio, so the arena was packed. The
n v adv prep pro prep n conj pro v prep conj
Spurs were behind throughout most of the game, but they pulled through and
v prep adj n prep adj adj n int pro v adv v adv
won with a three- pointer in the last few seconds. Wow! I have never seen so
adj n prep pro n conj v prep n prep pro n
many people on their feet and screaming at the top of their lungs.

Introduction: Chapter 24 Phrases (p. 524)

Using the computer, I got most of the research done for my report.

To be totally confident, I checked for spelling and grammar errors twice.

Susan lives in the gray house at the end of Maple Avenue behind the bank.

Tess is going to be a professional dancer when she gets older.

Do you want to join us for dinner this evening?

Introduction: Chapter 24 Clauses (p. 526)

Magdalena will be a great attorney because she argues so well.

You don't understand the math concept, so I will keep going over it with you.

If Shane is going to drive, he should have car insurance.

After finishing the big test, we all went out for pizza.

I enjoyed the vacation even though I had one really bad seafood dinner.

Chapter 25: Subjects and Verbs (p. 531)

You are my best friend.

Hang up your clothes. (You)

They really wanted to be here tonight.

He made a sandwich and put it in a brown paper bag.

Susie and Tom went to the dance.

Chapter 26: Fragments (p. 538)

_____ I wanted to go to the gym yesterday.

__X__ Whose tie doesn't match his suit.

__X__ Giving up his seat for an elderly woman.

_____ Paul asked for the most popular menu item.

__X__ While the captain was away from the cockpit.

Chapter 27: Fused Sentences and Comma Splices (p. 548)

The rainstorm washed out my garden,/I had just planted spring bulbs.

When we cleaned the house, we found the TV remote control/it was between the sofa cushions.

People in authority are often criticized and seldom thanked.

The kids didn't find all of the Easter eggs during the hunt, /when we finally found them, they were rotten.

You should ask Aubri to cut your hair /she's been cutting mine for four years.

Chapter 28: Regular and Irregular Verbs (p. 556)

_X_ The pipe has bursted.

_____ Sim reacted to the scene calmly.

_____ I bought my car at an auction.

_X_ We had hid in the basement.

_X_ Sorry, I eated all the cookies.

Chapter 29: Verb Tense (p. 565)

_X_ Jean always laugh when I tell that joke.

_____ Mark jumped over the hurdle and crossed the finish line.

_X_ I had spoke to the sales clerk about a discount.

_X_ Students ain't allowed to bring food and drink into the computer lab.

_X_ My two cats be playing in the sunshine.

Chapter 30: Subject-Verb Agreement (p. 578)

_X_ Neither the shorts nor the shirt fit me.

_____ Chips and dip is my favorite snack.

_X_ There were a large storm last night.

_X_ Some of the soil along with the fertilizer are for the orchard.

_____ Cotton and silk are more comfortable than wool.

Chapter 31: More on Verbs (p. 590)

_I_ George raced across the field and catches the ball.

_P_ The old record was broken by Justin.

_P_ That painting was done by a famous artist.

___I___In the future, we may live on Mars, and we have produced our food in greenhouses.

___I___First, the baker prepares the dough, and then she will cut out the cookies.

Chapter 32: Pronoun Problems (p. 596)

The ball was ~~their's~~ to begin with. *(theirs)*

Tom told Valerie and ~~I~~ the most exciting story. *(me)*

James can type a lot faster than ~~me~~. *(I)*

Those ~~there~~ running shoes are Kim's. *(those)*

~~Me and~~ Julio are going to the movies tonight. *(Julio and I)*

Chapter 33: Pronoun Reference and Point of View (p. 606)

X
It says to schedule your own appointments.

X
Millie and Tanya were planning to go to Las Vegas, but her car broke.

X
I created a backup plan because you should always be prepared for the unexpected.

X X
You know they are covering up evidence of alien beings.

X
Jimmy forgot the answers to questions 1 and 10, but he remembered it the next day.

Chapter 34: Pronoun Agreement (p. 613)

X X
Somebody left his lights on in his car.

X
A judge must put aside her bias.

X
Each of the children needs their permission slip signed.

X
None of the fans could keep their voices quiet.

X
A motorcyclist must take care of her gear.

Chapter 35: Adjectives (p. 621)

The kites were very colorful.

X
She has the worstest hair color that I have ever seen.

X
We were more busier this week than last week.

X
He is the oldest of the two brothers.

X
The Ford Mustang is more better than the Nissan Sentra.

Chapter 36: Adverbs (p. 630)

X
The pants fit me too loose, so I returned them to the store.

X
Tori wasn't never so happy as after she won the lottery.

X
When Madeline returned from Paris, she said she had a real good time.

We happily made more ice cream when our first supply ran out.

X
I wanted so bad to win the race, but I couldn't catch up.

Chapter 37: Modifier Errors (p. 641)

After studying together, his grades really improved.

Before doing the laundry, the car needed to be washed.

To get a good job, the interview must go well.

The professor told the class he was retiring before he dismissed them.

I wrote a letter to the newspaper that complained about rising power bills.

Chapter 38: End Punctuation (p. 648)

How are we going to get there?

That's amazing!

Get me a Pepsi, please.

This will never happen to me!

Can you make your own dinner tonight?

Chapter 39: Commas (p. 654)

We drove to the beach, and we had a picnic.

Before I eat breakfast, I take a multivitamin.

"This is my favorite restaurant," said Matt.

E-mail, though, makes corresponding easy and fast.

They were married on February 14, 2004, in Las Vegas, Nevada.

Chapter 40: Apostrophes (p. 665)

The flight crew was surprised by the pilot's rudeness when he boarded the plane.

It's important that the car has its engine checked every 3,000 miles.

What's going to happen after Dominic's gone?

The men's bathroom is located on the third floor.

James's house is the third one on the left.

Chapter 41: Quotation Marks (p. 672)

"Can we go out to dinner tonight?" she asked.

Jeri screamed, "Don't go in there!"

"If you can't find my house," Tom said, "call me on your cell phone."

My favorite poem is "The Red Wheelbarrow" by William Carlos Williams.

David said, "I'll fix your car this weekend."

Chapter 42: Other Punctuation Marks (p. 680)

Kris left for the dance; Sean decided to stay home.

We wanted to win; therefore, we practiced every day.

The computer's advertised price didn't include several important parts: a monitor, a printer, and speakers. *(or —)*

Ramon asked the best question during the interview "Why should we vote for you?" *(or :)*

Bring the jelly to a "rolling boil"(a boil that cannot be stirred down)

Chapter 43: Capitalization (p. 689)

According to uncle Bob, mother makes the best texas sheet cake. *(Uncle, Mother, Texas)*

Antonio is a native american. *(Native American)*

"the shortest path," he said, "Is down baker street." *(The, is, Baker Street)*

issa loves to go to walt disney world. *(Issa, Walt Disney World)*

Last year, I saw the red hot chili peppers in concert. *(Red Hot Chili Peppers)*

Chapter 44: Abbreviations and Numbers (p. 695)

He earned two million three hundred thousand dollars last year. *($2,300,000)*

My cat had 5 kittens. *(five)*

Sherril moved from England to the U.S. *(United States)*

Mister Johnson always drinks hot chocolate in the mornings. *(Mr.)*

I work for the Internal Revenue Service. *(IRS)*

Chapter 45: Varying Sentence Structure (p. 703)

Answers will vary.

Chapter 46: Parallelism (p. 709)

Tony enjoys hockey, football, and runs.

My mom and dad give money to help the homeless and for building new homes.

I finished high school, started college, and I am beginning a new job.

I love the mountains because they're cool, clean, and feel refreshing.

Listening to music, watching television, or to read a book are good ways to relax.

Chapter 47: Combining Sentences (p. 714)

Answers will vary.

Chapter 48: Standard and Nonstandard English (p. 725)

You shoulda seen Claudia's new hairstyle. *(Incorrect)*

Where are my friends at? *(Incorrect)*

Your new bike is really hot. *(Slang)*

Randy was enthused about his date. *(Slang)*

Christina Aguilera's new video rocks. *(Slang)*

Chapter 49: Easily Confused Words (p. 733)

Miranda couldn't (choose, chose) a college.

(It's, Its) time to leave for the show.

I can't (hear, here) with all this noise.

(Weather, Whether) you go or not, I still want to attend.

(Who's, Whose) responsible for this mess?

Chapter 50: Spelling (p. 743)

What is your new adress? *(address)*

Turn left on the third avenu. *(avenue)*

I was using the wrong calender when I made out the scheduel. *(calendar, schedule)*

The dealer delt me a good hand. *(dealt)*

Please get all the items on the grocry list. *(grocery)*

APPENDIX 5 Editing Quotient Error Chart

Put an X in the square that corresponds to each error that you made. Then record your errors in the categories below to find out where you might need help.

	a	b	c	d	e	f	g
1							
2							
3							
4							
5							
6							
7							
8							
9							
10							

Fragments	1b ______ 1c ______ 2b ______ 2e ______ 4d ______ 4e ______ 5d ______ 6d ______ 10c ______
Fused sentences and comma splices	1a ______ 1d ______ 2d ______ 3d ______ 5c ______ 8c ______ 10b ______ 10f ______
Subject-verb agreement	3a ______ 3c ______ 6e ______
Verb forms	9e ______
Pronoun errors	7b ______
Pronoun agreement	3b ______ 4a ______ 10a ______
Modifiers	5b ______ 10e ______
End punctuation	1a ______ 1d ______ 2d ______ 3d ______ 5c ______ 6g ______ 8c ______ 10b ______ 10f ______

Commas	4f ______ 4g ______ 5a ______ 7e ______ 7f ______ 8e ______
	9a ______ 9b ______ 9c ______
Apostrophes	7g ______ 9d ______ 10d ______
Capitalization	2a ______ 2c ______ 7c ______ 7d ______
Confused words	4b ______ 4c ______ 6c ______ 7g ______ 8a ______ 9d ______
Spelling	6a ______ 6b ______ 6f ______ 7a ______ 8b ______ 8d ______
	9f ______

APPENDIX 6 Error Log

List any grammar, punctuation, and mechanics errors you make in your writing on the following chart. Then, to the right of this label, record (1) the actual error from your writing, (2) the rule for correcting this error, and (3) your correction.

Error	
Comma	**Example** I went to the new seafood restaurant and I ordered the shrimp.
	Rule Use a comma before *and, but, for, nor, or, so,* and *yet* when they join two independent clauses.
	Correction I went to the new seafood restaurant, and I ordered the shrimp.
Error	**Example**
	Rule
	Correction
Error	**Example**
	Rule
	Correction
Error	**Example**
	Rule
	Correction
Error	**Example**
	Rule
	Correction
Error	**Example**
	Rule
	Correction
Error	**Example**
	Rule
	Correction
Error	**Example**
	Rule
	Correction

Error	Example
	Rule
	Correction
Error	Example
	Rule
	Correction
Error	Example
	Rule
	Correction
Error	Example
	Rule
	Correction
Error	Example
	Rule
	Correction
Error	Example
	Rule
	Correction
Error	Example
	Rule
	Correction
Error	Example
	Rule
	Correction
Error	Example
	Rule
	Correction
Error	Example
	Rule
	Correction

APPENDIX 7 Spelling Log

On this chart, record any words you misspell, and write the correct spelling in the space next to the misspelled word. In the right column, write a note to yourself to help you remember the correct spelling. (See the first line for an example.) Refer to this chart as often as necessary to avoid misspelling the same words again.

Misspelled Word	Correct Spelling	Definition/Notes
there	their	there = place; their = pronoun; they're = "they are"

CREDITS

CHAPTER 8

"Dust Changes Everything," Margaret Bourke White, *The Nation*, 5/22/35. Reprinted with permission from May 22, 1935 issue of *The Nation*. For subscription information, call 1-800-333-8536. Portions of each week's Nation Magazine can be accessed at http://www.thenation.com.

"El Hoyo," Mario Suarez, *Short Takes*, Elizabeth Penfield, Longman, 1988 (Originally appeared in the *Arizona Quarterly*, Summer 1947). Reprinted by permission of The Arizona Board of Regents.

"Dwellings," by Linda Hogan, from *Dwellings: A Spiritual History of the Living World* by Linda Hogan. Copyright © 1995 by Linda Hogan. Used by permission of W.W. Norton & Company, Inc.

Photo: Jim Mone/AP Wide World Photos.

CHAPTER 9

"Girl," by Jane Maher. Reprinted by permission of Jane Maher.

"The Sanctuary of School," by Lynda Barry, *The New York Times*, *Educational Supplement*, Jan. 1992. Copyright © 1999 by The New York Times Co. Reprinted with permission.

"Writer's Retreat," by Stan Higgins, *The Writer* © 1991.

Photo: Kim Mould/Omni-Photo Communications, Inc.

CHAPTER 10

"Hold the Mayonnaise," by Julia Alvarez. Copyright © 1992 by Julia Alvarez. First published in The New York Times Magazine January 12, 1992. Reprinted by permission of Susan Bergholz Literary Services, New York. All rights reserved.

"Dawn's Early Light" by Richard Rodriguez. Copyright © 1994 by Richard Rodriguez. Originally aired on the MacNeil-Lehrer (PBS) on January 30th, 1994. Reprinted by permission of Georges Borchardt, Inc., on behalf of the author.

"The Decorated Body," by France Borel. "Le Vetement incarne: Les Metamorphoses du Corps" by France Borel © Editions Calmann-Levy, 1992.

Photo: White/Packert/Getty Images Inc.—Image Bank.

CHAPTER 11

"Dare to Change Your Job and Your Life in 7 Steps," by Carole Kancher, *Psychology Today*, March 2000. Reprinted by permission of Carole Kanchier, PhD.

"Don't Be Cruel," by Roger Flax, *TWA Ambassador*, March 1992. Used with permission of Horizon Productions Enterprise, LLC.

"Why We Have A Moon," by David Levy, *Parade Magazine*, Nov. 5, 2002, pp. 12–15. © 2002 David Levy. All rights reserved.

Photo: David Buffington/Getty Images, Inc.—Photodisc.

CHAPTER 12

"Thrills & Chills," by Eric Minton, *Psychology Today,* May 1999. Reprinted by permission of Eric Minton.

"American Space, Chinese Place," by Yi-Fu Tuan. geography.wisc.edu/~yifutuan/index.htm. Reprinted by permission of Yi-Fu Tuan Ph.D.

"Between Worlds," by Tony Cohan. From *On Mexican Time* by Tony Cohan, copyright © 2000 by Tony Cohan. Used by permission of Broadway Books, a division of Random House.

Photo: Massimo Mastrorillo/Corbis/Stock Market.

CHAPTER 13

"The Sound of Music: Enough Already," by Fran Lebowitz, *Metropolitan Life,* Dutton. Penguin Putnam, 1978. Reprinted by permission of International Creative Management, Inc. Copyright © 1978 by Fran Lebowitz.

"Black Music in Our Hands," by Bernice Reagon. Reprinted by permission of Bernice Johnson Reagon.

"What Are Friends For?," by Marion Winik. From *Telling Confessions, Concessions and Other Flashes of Light* by Marion Winik, copyright © by Marion Winik. Used by permission of Random House, Inc.

Photo: Marc P. Anderson/Pearson Education/PH College.

CHAPTER 14

"Dumpster Diving," by Lars Eighner. From *Travels with Lizbeth* by Lars Eigner. Copyright © 1993 by the author and reprinted with permission of St. Martin's Press, LLC.

"What Is Intelligence, Anyway?," by Isaac Asimov. Published by permission of The Estate of Isaac Aimov c/o Ralph M. Vicinana, Ltd.

"Spanglish Spoken Here," by Janice Castro. © 1998 Time Inc. Reprinted by permission.

Photo: Laimute E Druskis/Pearson Education/PH College.

CHAPTER 15

"Why Do Schools Flunk Biology?," by Lynell Hancock. From *Newsweek,* Nov 13, 2000 © 2000 Newsweek, Inc. All rights reserved. Reprinted by permission.

"Shedding the Weight of My Dad's Obsession," by Linda Lee Andujarm. From *Newsweek,* Feb. 19, 1996 © 1996 Newsweek, Inc. All rights reserved. Reprinted by permission.

"Happiness is Catching: Why Emotions are Contagious," by Stacey Colino, *Family Circle,* 3/12/96. Reprinted by permission of Stacey Colino.

Photo: Tony Freeman/PhotoEdit Inc.

CHAPTER 16

"Racial Profiling Is Unjust," by Bob Herbert. Copyright © 1999 by The New York Times Co. Reprinted with permission.

"We Are Training Our Kids To Kill," by Dave Grossman. Reprinted by permission of David Grossman, author of 'Stop Teaching Our Kids to Kill," "On Combat," and "On Killing." www.killology.com.

"Anti-Loitering Laws Can Reduce Gang Violence," by Richard Willard. Reprinted by permission of the Congressional Digest Corporation.

INDEX

D

E